'This is much more than a paeon of praise to Keating. There is wit and remarkable candour which puts it streets ahead of most political biographies . . . a penetrating insight into a Labor prime minister. Despite the millions of words already written about Keating, it adds much.'

Mike Steketee, *Weekend Australian*

'Watson's book is neither biography nor history nor Watson's personal journey nor a string of anecdotes, but a compound of all these things. It is the story of four tumultuous years told by an intelligent and curious insider, and no insider has ever done it better.'

Les Carlyon, *Bulletin*

'. . . a subtle and sympathetic analysis of the many facets of the twenty-fourth prime minister; a narrative of high and low politics in the Keating years; and a compendium of the wit and wisdom of Don Watson . . . in future, when I am asked, "What was Paul Keating really like?" the answer must be, "Go read Don Watson."'

Neal Blewett, *Australian Book Review*

'This big book has reset the benchmark for political writing in this country, with its ability to entertain and appal at the same time . . .'

Courier-Mail

'. . . always absorbing, usually illuminating, frequently disturbing, often stimulating . . . remarkably frank . . . Every page is enlightened by Watson's erudition.'

John Nethercote, *Canberra Times*

'. . . an intriguing account of a time and a place and a man – from a vantage point that is so unusual, so close and by such an intelligent and partisan witness, as to make it unrivalled in the annals of Australian political writing.'

Ramona Koval

'. . . no-one has better described the contradiction between mug lair and aesthete, guttersnipe and visionary . . . Watson has written a classic: an insider's account of the working of the political process, with its paranoia, its envies, its fevered inconsequentiality, its joys, crammed with wisdom and a lovely detachment.'

Evan Williams, *Sydney Morning Herald*

'. . . a beautifully told story that is sure to become an instant classic of political history.'

José Borghino, *Marie Claire*

'. . . it is the portrait of Keating that . . . is surely the book's triumph . . . it is impossible to leave *Recollections of a Bleeding Heart* without more affection for a politician and man who fought his own bouts of apathy and had a crack at dragging Australia out of its crippling slumber.'

Peter Lalor, *Daily Telegraph*

'This is truly one of the great works of Australian political writing.'

Troy Bramston, *Australian Journal of Politics and History*

'. . . a sheer delight to read . . . written by a man who would have difficulty putting together a dull sentence . . .'

Diana Simmonds, *Sun Herald*

'. . . enormously readable . . . a fascinating examination of the political process and, more particularly, a clear-eyed look at the epicentre of power . . . elegant, witty and humane'

Good Reading

'. . . a reflective book, full of questions, full of pondering. It is the book of an observer, a thinker . . . future historians will mine Watson's insights – and that alone makes his contribution valuable.'

Ken Spillman, *West Australian*

'Reading Don Watson's account of those turbulent years is a little like being the Prime Minister's Office resident mouse, privy to all the meetings, the rhetoric and the invective. A remarkable, honest, frank and at times humorous account of a turbulent time in our political history.'

Illawarra Mercury

'. . . a revealing and engrossing portrait of a brilliant, if perplexing man [and] a unique reflection on modern politics, government and Australia from a man who can write and who has a sense of proportion and humour.'

Brisbane News

'. . . a great human political biography of the life and times of a complex prime minister. In years to come, it will be ranked with some of the great political biographies of the past 100 years . . . a great work of political anthropology . . . a wonderfully entertaining memoir of an historian who is activist, participant and observer . . .'

Noel Turnbull, *Courier-Mail*

DON WATSON

Recollections of a Bleeding Heart

A PORTRAIT OF PAUL KEATING PM

VINTAGE

Every effort has been made to acknowledge and contact the owners of copyright for permission to reproduce material which falls under the 1968 Copyright Act. Any copyright holders who have inadvertently been omitted from acknowledgements and credits should contact the publisher and omissions will be rectified in subsequent editions.

A Vintage Book
Published by Random House Australia Pty Ltd
20 Alfred Street, Milsons Point, NSW 2061
http://www.randomhouse.com.au

Sydney   New York   Toronto
London   Auckland   Johannesburg

First published in Australia by Knopf in 2002
This Vintage edition first published 2003

Copyright © Don Watson, 2002

National Library of Australia
Cataloguing-in-Publication Entry

Watson, Don, 1949– .
Recollections of a bleeding heart : Portrait of Paul Keating PM.

Includes index.
ISBN 1 74051 214 6.

1. Keating, Paul, 1944– . 2. Australian Labor Party –
History – 20th century. 3. Premiers – Australia –
Biography. 4. Politicians – Australia – Biography. 5.
Australia – Politics and government – 1976–1990. 6.
Australia – Politics and government – 1990–2001. I. Title

994.065092

Front cover image of Paul Keating: Peter Morris, Sydney Morning Herald
Cover design by Mary Callahan and Darian Causby/Highway 51
Typeset in 12pt Bembo by Midland Typesetters, Maryborough, Victoria
Printed and bound by Griffin Press, Netley, South Australia

10 9 8 7 6 5 4 3 2 1

Terry Counihan, Dinny O'Hearn, Peter Kerr
In Memoriam

Man is the only animal that laughs and weeps; for he is the only animal that is struck with the difference between what things are and what they might have been.

WILLIAM HAZLITT

NOTE

IN NEW YEAR 1992 I accepted an invitation to be Paul Keating's speechwriter. I decided at the same time to record the experience in a diary. 'An exact diary is a window on to the heart that maketh it,' Lord Braybrook said about Samuel Pepys. But I did not keep an exact diary and sought a window not on to my heart but on to an intriguing politician in a critical year of politics—a year because that was all anyone expected the Keating Government to last. In the event he lasted as long, give or take a few months, as Curtin and Chifley. And so did the diary. From the inexact diary I have constructed an inexact history; and one with an inexact title because I am not exactly a 'bleeding heart'. The term appears to have been invented in the 1930s by Americans who hoped it would demoralise or incapacitate liberals, socialists or anyone else who opposed them. Counterattacking, the bleeding hearts invented 'redneck' and 'fascist' and, more recently, 'pointy head', 'econocrat' and 'suit'. Such terms are the missiles and tear-gas of politics which, in the end, is a war fought with words. And like other wars the truth about it generally has less to do with exactness than where one happens to be standing at the time.

I told Paul Keating early on that I was keeping a diary and intended to write a book about all he did, and I reminded him whenever I thought it might have slipped his mind. 'Are you, mate?' he would say and deploy one of his vague looks. Paul Keating inclined to the view that political autobiographies are invariably written by the self-serving and weak-minded, and he vowed he would no more write his own than take up bowls. I respect his judgment while maintaining a view that this book will have done some good if it causes him to change his mind. It will be almost as satisfying if competent and imaginative general historians are prompted by what they read here, or by what they find missing, to write the story of the Keating Government from a greater distance and at a more objective angle. Not that I think they will come much closer to exactness, but until they try, many people who served valiantly or in various ways influenced the course of events will be entitled to suspect there is no justice in history unless you write it yourself.

This book essentially records events as I saw and reacted to them from within the Prime Minister's Office. The view from ten thousand other places would no doubt be different. I cannot say that the diary was kept meticulously and with perfect regularity. Sometimes many days passed without an entry. But most of the threads were kept intact and the lost ones could usually be picked up again in the press clippings, media summaries, press releases, notes, memorandums, correspondence and much else that every day in politics leaves behind and I took home with me.

I also called on the generosity of Paul Keating who availed me of both his records and his time. The judgments are nonetheless my own, and he and others I refer to will agree with only some of them. Much was at stake in those four years and it is difficult to imagine this window opening on to general agreement about everything that happened.

That these recollections describe more chaos and tumult than the symptoms of an exact science leaves me confident that they are at least in the same large paddock as the truth. Persuading people that the leader controls events is one of the arts of politics, but if it was good enough for Abraham Lincoln to confess that events more often controlled him it should be good enough for the rest of us. That said, the book concerns a political leader who more than any other in the last quarter century *was* determined to be master of his environment rather than the opportunist waiting for the times to suit him. We can look to his family and mentors for the sources of this determination. We will find clues in his psychology. But it would be the gravest mistake to search these places and neglect the more obvious motive: call it vision, altruism, conviction or obsession, Paul Keating was governed by an idea for Australia, or rather by many ideas which over time cohered as one expanding vision. He practised politics precisely for the purpose of mastering events because politics was the only means by which he could turn this thing of his imagination into something real. Politics was power, it was the hunt, the game, a way to the unrivalled pleasure of destroying his enemies—but it was, as well, always an act of creation.

ABBREVIATIONS

ABA	Australian Broadcasting Authority
ABC	Australian Broadcasting Corporation
ACF	Australian Conservation Foundation
ACOSS	Australian Council of Social Services
ACTU	Australian Council of Trade Unions
AIRC	Australian Industrial Relations Commission
ANTA	Australian National Training Authority
APEC	Asia-Pacific Economic Cooperation forum
ASEAN	Association of South-East Asian Nations
ATSIC	Aboriginal and Torres Strait Islander Commission
CCF	Constitutional Centenary Foundation
CEDA	Committee for the Economic Development of Australia
CFMEU	Construction, Forestry, Mining and Energy Union
CHOGM	Commonwealth Heads of Government Meeting
COAG	Council of Australian Governments
CRA	Conzinc Riotinto of Australia Limited
DFAT	Department of Foreign Affairs and Trade
DIST	Department of Industry, Science and Technology
EPAC	Economic Planning Advisory Committee
ERC	Expenditure Review Committee
FAS	Family Allowance Supplement
FIRB	Foreign Investment Review Board
GATT	General Agreement on Tariffs and Trade
HECS	Higher Education Contribution Scheme
MUA	Maritime Union of Australia
NAFTA	North American Free Trade Agreement
NFF	National Farmers Federation
NMLS	National Media Liaison Service
OSW	Office for the Status of Women
PMC	(Department of the) Prime Minister and Cabinet
PMO	Prime Minister's Office
REDO	Regional Economic Development Organisation

CHAPTER 1

Nothing except a battle lost can be half so melancholy as a battle won.

WELLINGTON, DISPATCH FROM WATERLOO

I N THE LONG boom of the fifties and sixties when there were signs of progress everywhere, Paul Keating's father, Matt, talked fondly of the days before the war. As well as the Great Depression and its hardships he remembered a more easeful time when space abounded and more of Sydney's beauty remained on show. It was a softer Sydney, the patterns of life more leisurely. There were also the comforts of religion and tradition: and if one of the traditions was sectarian, who knows if that was not another source of certainty.

After the war it all changed. Out on the western frontier, Bankstown, where the Keatings lived, suddenly became a suburb. Just as quickly other suburbs joined it. Where there had been paddocks there were now subdivisions, streets and bungalows. Where there had been only Australians of Irish and English descent, there were 'New Australians': Greeks, Poles, Lithuanians and Latvians. Ten thousand new people a year came to Banks-town. The place boomed. Matt's family prospered. With two friends he escaped wage slavery and went into the business of transit cement mixers. For Matt and his wife, Min, it was all progress and all for the good. But he still talked about pre-war

Sydney as if they were golden years. You should have seen it then, he would say. And we had it all to ourselves.

Paul had something of the same. Change excited him. In what others saw as comfortable and familiar, he saw decay and lost opportunity. More than most politicians, he was fed by his imagination. His convictions often traced to a radical awareness of possibility. He liked movement, progress, crashing through, over-turning, shedding, giving the slip to history and his enemies in a single bound. Yet the thought seemed never to leave him that there had been once a more spacious, more perfect age. But the time had passed, eluding him; leaving him with this melancholy and this desire to fill his senses with such examples of its perfection as he could find. Because it would not be back: not this side of death at least, and about the other side no-one could say anything with certainty.

Matt Keating was dead. One Saturday afternoon in 1978 he set off from home for the shops at the top of the hill. He walked past the house where Paul and his wife Annita lived, and said hello to Paul who was washing his car in the front drive. Matt was just sixty. His hair was still black. But he had heart problems and the doctor had recently adjusted his medication, the anticoagulant Warfarin. Undeterred, he and Min were about to go on their first trip abroad. They had their bags packed for England. A few minutes after Matt passed by, a pedestrian told Paul that a man had collapsed on the footpath a little way up the hill. Paul Keating told the story many times, rather like a passion play. Matt was a good man, everyone said, including Annita who saw a lot of him in the first years of their marriage when she was in Bankstown with their baby Patrick, and Paul was so often in Canberra.

It might be thought from talking to Min Keating about her son, Paul, that her influence went no further than providing him with an environment in which his personality and ambition might thrive. As a child he enjoyed her unqualified love and approval. As a teenager he was provided with a room on the lower level of the house in Condell Park. He kept lovebirds there. He liked photography so it became a darkroom. When his interest in music developed it was soundproofed, and he listened to records on the hi-fi his mother had given him when he was ten. Then it was fitted with a telephone so he could pursue his interests in the wide world. Outside was the suburban frontier, incessant progress in lock step with the relentless advance of conformity. Down in his room he could invent himself, but in his parents' image, like an embryo in an egg. It was the beginning of what he came to call 'the refuge of the inner life'. At Berkelouws he bought second-hand copies of *Connoisseur* and 1930s *Strand* magazines. Rock and roll, Chopin and Beethoven found their way to his hi-fi. He managed a band called the Ramrods and when he set up a record-ing deal with EMI for them, he was led to the EMI library where he found recordings by Elisabeth Schwarzkopf and Maria Callas, Otto Klemperer and the Philharmonia Orchestra, Nathan Milstein and Dietrich Fischer-Dieskau. He developed a taste for the classical, for things of quality, provenance and class. By then Min's kitchen had become a place for Paul to meet with like-minded members of the Labor Party—young turks like Laurie Brereton, and older mentors like Ron Dyer and Doug McNally.

In two hours of conversation in 1996 Min Keating could not think of a single thing that her boy had ever done wrong. It is true, she said, that one day he snatched a hat from a Protestant boy's head and threw it into a tree, but that was all and it was soon forgiven. His grandmother, who lived with them until he was twelve or so, was even less inclined to think Paul capable of error or weakness: if a sharp word was addressed to him at the dinner table she refused to eat. It might sound like a mother talking, Min Keating says, but he *was* always wellbehaved and considerate and loved by his three younger siblings. He was attentive and sensitive to his mother. To his father, Matt, he was respectful and admiring, and Matt never raised his voice to his eldest son—which is some-thing that many people with fathers might find hard to believe. Paul was a marvellous boy and, in both his mother's judgment and his own, he bathed in unconditional love. 'I have found that those persons who consider themselves preferred by or favoured by their mothers,' wrote Sigmund Freud, 'manifest in life that confidence in themselves, and that unshakeable optimism, which often seem heroic, and not infrequently compel actual success.'

There was no apparent Oedipal rebellion. He took both his politics and his religion from his parents. Matt and Min were devout Catholics. He was an altar boy and in his mid-thirties in the national parliament clearly retained more than a shy hope that what he had been told as a child was true. Speaking on a condolence motion for an old friend and colleague Frank Stewart he said: 'He died after Easter Sunday and those of us who shared some of his view like to think that he died in a state of grace and will live an eternal life with Christ. Our most fervent wish is that his family will join him in a life with Christ after death.' Min bought tailor's offcuts to make Paul's clothes. He went to his first day at work in good cloth, a shining suit of armour as it were and better than anything the Establishment wore, and thereafter never went in anything else. When he got his first pay packet he brought home a little bust of Beethoven and gave it to his mother, she says, with the words, 'Here Mum, put some class in your life.' It still sat on her mantelpiece in 1996.

Condell Park adjoined Bankstown, the famous western Sydney suburb that had once been called Irish Town. Bankstown retained some of the communal strength of the country town it had once been, and whatever failings it might have had in this regard the Catholic Church made good. The community, the church, the Labor Party were all tough, tribal—like the family in whose soft bosom he grew. It was true that in the family voices were not raised and conflict was rare. But collectively they knew about conflict and raised voices and had no fear of them. The Keatings had been Langites, followers of John Thomas (Jack) Lang, the maverick one-time premier of New South Wales who had split from the Labor Party in 1940 and was expelled in 1943. Then there was the split in the Labor Party in the 1950s. They had inherited an awareness of Irish Catholic persecution, and knew a little about sectarianism in their own lifetimes. Keating often recalled how on his first day at his first job the manager, a Freemason also named Keating, said to him, you must be one of the

Keatings that was dragged up by the Catholics. He believed sectarianism still pervaded Australian society and the ALP at least into the 1970s. He told Craig McGregor in 1977, 'I resent it. You wouldn't have these doors closed against you if you weren't a tyke.' As a child an interior world pervaded with unqualified parental love had been given him, and as a young man he was granted dispensation to go to fight the enemies abroad. What becomes of such a special boy? He might easily become rather like Paul Keating.

Paul Keating, Prime Minister, told me the story more than once: how in his boyhood he went with his father to buy a newspaper at the local shop. At the shop the newspaper told a familiar story. A federal election had just been held and the front page announced, 'Menzies Back!' Not that the Keatings hadn't heard, or hadn't expected it, but seeing the news in black and white deepened Matt's gloom. To make the day more miserable still, as they crossed a vacant lot on the way home they were attacked by a pair of nesting magpies. Matt Keating rolled up the newspaper with the depressing headline and swatted at the birds and cursed Bob Menzies. 'Menzies bloody back!' Paul says that as he watched his father battle the birds, he knew that one day he would do something to make life miserable for the Liberal Party.

He would have to be patient. It must have been the election of November 1958 when those birds bombed—all the other elections during Paul Keating's adolescence were held in December, by which time fledglings have left the nest and parent birds are peaceful again. It was Menzies' fifth consecutive victory and he would have two more before he retired, and his successors would have another two. It would be twenty-three years before Labor got back on the Treasury benches, but when they did Paul Keating was there.

In our youth Bob Menzies was invincible. He rode gracefully on a long wave of economic prosperity, basked in the charismatic glow of a young Queen on the throne of England, watched as Bert Evatt, Labor's leader, first lost a good part of the ALP and then a good part of his mind. Politics became a sport for Menzies' personal indulgence, and it always had the same result: he won and his opponents looked like nincompoops. In 1941 he had been written off as a creature of the Establishment whose race was run. But Chifley let him in again, and then Evatt locked himself out. By the late fifties Menzies ran the country as if it were his own creation: blimpish and Anglophile, yet also contriving to look like the bell-wether of the nation's progress. He was master of all the mediums—parliament, town halls, radio and, when it arrived in 1956, television. Australia was his personal pond and he sailed on it like a superior rubber duck.

My family voted for Bob Menzies without fail: in every one of his seven successive election victories, and for the Liberal Party in the two that followed his retirement. Indeed, it is almost certain that no member of our family—no member known to us, at least—had voted Labor since Federation. To me, born in the year he was elected, Menzies was the known world. Labor was a mystery as dark as Satan and I scarcely knew how anyone with a soul to be saved could vote for them. We were dairy farmers. On all sides our antecedents were rural—small farms, reliable rainfall, steep hills, hard work. On all sides they were Protestant. Presbyterian mainly. Their roots were deep in the districts they helped to pioneer, and deep in Australia itself: the most recent branch has been here for at least five generations and the oldest came with the Second Fleet. There is a short streak of temperance on one side, and a very long streak of social and political conservatism on both. No Irish. A handful of children in the green uniforms of St Joseph's convent sat at the back of our school bus, but we hardly knew what a Catholic was. Our elders may have considered them an affront to reason and enlightenment, people without minds of their own because they were instructed from Rome, but we children didn't because we rarely spoke to them and when we did, it was derisively. They might as well have been Aborigines.

Our origins and sympathies were, like Menzies' own, Scots and English. The country from which for piddling crimes our convict ancestors were dispatched in 1789 was almost beyond criticism in our 1950s childhoods. British snobbery and class divisions were despised, the fall of Singapore in the Second World War was considered a betrayal and Earl Haig in the first one was a fool, and we subscribed to the national suspicion that the Poms had used Australians as cannon fodder in both. However, these were little more than blemishes on a relationship whose blessings were almost without measure. Britain was the fount of culture, character and tradition—and the market for our butter. We were not so graceless as to forget that the Americans had saved us from Japanese tyranny, but nor did we forget that they were late into both wars. We thought Americans lacked both humility and a genuine sense of humour. They were full of themselves. We voted Liberal and we honoured the Queen, and we went on doing it even after Britain joined the European Common Market in 1963 and abandoned her loyal Australian butter producers.

We were also Victorian. No other state had played any part in our history since my father's family left South Australia in 1900. When in 1969 I drove up to see the hippie musical, *Hair*, I became the first member of my family to visit Sydney. We might have described ourselves as 'provincial' were it not that we felt a certain worldliness conferred on us by membership of the British race and Commonwealth. And if the word 'provincial' suggests a regressive or inert mental state, it did not properly describe us: conservative yes, and forever expecting another Depression or an invasion from the north, but we had no doubt that the country was making progress and our family with it.

With the wars and Depression, it had been a long slog. When my father was twelve or so he and his younger brother (born a few months after Anzac and given the names Ian Hamilton after the British commander at Gallipoli) walked seven miles from their farm to the nearest town to see Cecil B. De Mille's *The Ten Commandments*. They walked home in the dark. The farm was a soldier settlement block, a reward for three years on the French battlefields. People like this were not inclined to believe in the perfectibility of man or society, or the capacity of governments to dispense justice. Justice in the main was dispensed as the Commandments had been, as the weather was. Just as the worst kind of church was that which put hierarchy and elaborate ritual between man and God, the worst kind of government was that which also put itself between man and his Maker, as if it could remodel His universe including the inequalities within it. Labor governments, in other words: socialists who fancied it was just to distribute the nation's wealth as if all were equally deserving; those who served and those who had not, those who led moral lives and those who didn't, and those who worked as hard as they could and those who did as little work as possible. Such views were in manifest defiance of commonsense and the laws of God and nature. Therefore Labor was an anathema. Labor was unions and men who hid in the crowd instead of pitting themselves against nature and the marketplace. Labor was centralised power. Labor was Bolshevism. Labor was Godless—and when not Godless, usually Catholic. And Irish. Labor insulted what they had done in the war and the memory of their fallen comrades. Nothing Labor did could dispel the suspicion that they held Britain and, by implication, the sacrifices we and others like us had made for it, in contempt.

The figure most loathed, when you got down to it, was Jack Lang. Lang was the great troublemaker. In the worst of the Depression when 30 per cent of the workforce was unemployed, Lang reneged on payment of his State's debts to Britain. Jack Lang, we gathered, had been the devil himself. Still, it might have been different after World War II had the Cold War not broken out, had the miners not gone on strike, had the communists pulled their heads in, had Chifley not tried to nationalise the banks. But it wasn't different—the pattern continued as before. Labor kept its socialisation objective: the 'socialisation of production, distribution and exchange'—we knew that plank in their platform by heart. It was all we knew of Labor and all we needed to know. When Menzies said that there was 'no substitute for hard work' and it was 'the first duty of every man to stand on his own two feet', and that Labor's socialism created instead 'flaccid dependence', it didn't matter that they were platitudes, they described precisely the principles of our moral economy. And when he said that communists were traitors and trade unionists were trouble-makers, he echoed the sentiments my father brought back from a stint in the Melbourne railway workshops where he had gone to work after rheumatic fever caused his discharge from the army in 1940.

Television came and we did not buy a set. After visits to Melbourne on the train my elders said what a shame it was to see so many aerials on the poor houses of Richmond. It was proof that the working classes lacked thrift and were too often their own worst enemies. We were close to poor ourselves, but being farmers we reckoned we worked harder, deferred gratification more conscientiously, earned more for the country than city people did, and never went on strike.

And this seemed to be our era at last—as if Menzies' good luck might yet rub off on us. Progress was slow, but our horizons widened. On the road on which we lived, a dozen farmers milking just forty or fifty cows raised and educated their families, delivering them with the aid of rural subsidies and scholarships into lives of reasonable comfort and opportunity. Until the 1950s no-one in our family had gone to school past the age of fourteen. But three out of four of us matriculated. Two of us went to university. In another unprecedented development we all kept our teeth. In 1967, La Trobe University opened in the working-class northern suburbs of Melbourne and I went in with a couple of hundred others from similar economic and educational back-grounds. Timing is everything. Had I been born five years earlier, in Paul Keating's year, I might not have gone to university. I would also have missed Bob Menzies' conscription ballot. As it turned out I went to university and was balloted out of the draft. In the process I took a turning which was another first for the family: I took a left turning. They should never have sent that boy to university, I could hear them say from miles away. But the Liberal Government had gone on too long. It had no meaning left in it—none at least that was not provided by the Cold War and the US alliance; no energy or direction; it was all drift and the Prime Minister, Bill McMahon, was egregious proof of its decline. I did not join the Labor Party, but my first vote was for Labor and every one since. Nonetheless I never found it hard to understand why many industrious Australians of a certain ancient Protestant cast of mind find Labor principles repellent to good sense and the national interest.

Almost everything in Paul Keating's youth was different from my own. The difference reflects the great divide in culture and experience that ran through the old, pre-multicultural Australia. All the familiar elements—ancestry, religion, politics, class, culture—were the opposite of mine. When those magpies bombed him he was fourteen and a student with the Brothers at De La Salle, Bankstown, where the things he was taught about 'the primary matters in life' stuck with him. At fifteen, in keeping with the habit of most boys of his class and generation, he left school. He took a job as a clerk with the Sydney County Council. And he joined the Labor Party and set about the essential task of reuniting disaffected local Catholics with it. At that age I would not have known *how* to join a party or where to find one. The fifteen-year-old Paul Keating was secure in both his religious and political attachments: ideologically, institutionally and socially they overlapped and reinforced each other. At school, at home and in the church, his education confirmed the certainties of childhood and left him, one presumes, with a sense of completeness and certainty that few fifteen-year-olds enjoy. When he was fifteen and wholly integrated, I was ten and attending a country con-solidated school, grinding towards the normal discomposure of adolescence.

Min, Annita and Paul Keating are united in their estimation of Matt Keating. He was a kind man; not weak by any means, Min says, but soft, a 'gentle soul'. Min met him at the Palais Royale in 1938 and admired his dancing. They married four years later. Matt supported Jack Lang and his splinter group of the war years, the Australian Labor Party (Anti-Communist) as it was known. For reasons indecipherable to anyone not expert in the cimmerian labyrinth of the human soul and the New South Wales Labor Party, Lang made himself an enemy of John Curtin and his federal

Labor Government. After the war, like other Langites, Matt melded readily with the Catholic-inspired, anti-communist Industrial Groups, though not with the man who increasingly drove them, the Victorian B.A. Santamaria. Matt was a boiler-maker employed at the State railway workshops. Possibly the noise of that place gave him tinnitus—a condition that causes bouts of incessant ringing in the ears. Paul had developed tinnitus by the time he became prime minister. In that long period of economic growth and suburban sprawl Matt's company flourished. By the late fifties Marlak Engineering was employing fifty people. In the late sixties, had their bank been prepared to advance the funds, they might have secured a substantial contract with the Malaysian Government. But the bank did not advance the funds. Matt and his friends sold the company for about a million dollars. Matt remained a Labor man of the old school who believed the ALP must have a radio station and a daily newspaper to succeed. In the 1940s he might have had an ambition to enter State parliament with the group led by Lang.

For the last twelve years of Lang's life Paul Keating saw him regularly, and for six of those years he saw him for an hour every Monday and Thursday. Lang was as old at the federation of the Commonwealth as Keating was when he entered parliament. He was Henry Lawson's brother-in-law. The old man impressed Keating with the power of his personality and the breadth of his history, the way he 'distinguished all the subtleties and felt all the pulses of the Labor movement'. Lang, Keating said, thought in black and white. There were no shades of grey. He was hated by the media and he hated them. In Keating's view, no politician had 'suffered the hate that Lang suffered'. But he loved the working class and believed that the articulate among them had a 'God-given duty' to serve their people: 'If God has given you the capacity to handle and grapple with politics and to be articulate you have a duty to serve your own class.' Keating declared 'a very great affection for him'. Lang died in September 1975 and Keating said these things in the House of Representatives to honour him. He also said that just as Lang's enemies had used the

NSW governor through the British Colonial Office to 'strike down' Lang's Depression Government, just then the present Opposition in the federal parliament was trying to use the Senate to strike down the Labor Government. Six weeks later they used the governor-general.

For all this, Paul Keating insists Jack Lang had no influence on his political thinking or his judgment of other political figures like Curtin. Lang was one of the three Labor politicians he most admired. The federal treasurer in the Depression, E.G. ('Ted') Theodore, was another. Theodore offended orthodoxy, and anticipated Keynes, by advocating re-inflation of the economy. His career was destroyed by a scandal over a business interest and he walked out of politics to go gold-mining with Frank Packer in Fiji. Theodore was a great rival of Lang's. The third Labor leader Keating admired was also a Lang opponent, John Curtin. The three of them were 'gallant people' who 'charged into the party, did things, took unusual attitudes, took risks—they were achievers'. He might have added a fourth, though he never led the party; the man he liked and listened to the most in the Whitlam Government: Rex Connor, the minister for minerals and energy, who wanted to build a mighty government-owned pipeline connecting Australian cities to the oil and gas reserves of the North West Shelf, the man who wanted to 'buy back the farm'. When the government fell, Keating succeeded Connor in the portfolio in the shadow ministry and deftly moved Connor's national policy ambitions from the state to the market. That would be the hallmark of Keating's career—not to change the objectives of the Labor Party, but to change the means.

Lang told him that some politicians were people of weight and substance and some were skyrockets who issued a great shower of sparks but 'a dead stick always fell to earth'. And it was Lang who advised that it was important 'to own things'. Paul Keating never told me of any other wisdom Lang imparted, but nor did he disguise his fondness for him. It was Keating who successfully moved the old man's reinstatement to the party early in the 1970s. His mother insists that Lang had little influence compared to Matt. She says Matt was by far the greatest influence on her son. It remains, however, that in 1969, when Matt advised Paul to wait another term before he made his run for parliament, Min said 'do it now' and Paul did it.

Paul Keating has another memory of an event just a couple of years after that 1958 election. On the way home to Bankstown his train made an unscheduled stop under a bridge and he sat reading about John F. Kennedy's victory in the United States presidential election. It might not have been the first time this thought had ever crossed his sixteen-year-old mind, but this was the time he always recalled. The thought was: if one Catholic can get to the White House another one can get to the prime minister's Lodge. In our house Kennedy's election prompted no such thoughts. In our family we did not aim in political directions, or to points so elevated. As children we were not in any danger of having our heads turned by hearing parents say that one day we would be prime minister. Paul Keating, on the other hand, pursued his political ambition as naturally as we went round the cows, and he went with an ambition to overthrow the very people and the very things which my family believed in as a matter of faith.

To the Keatings, the Menzies ascendancy was an affront to nature. Labor was the natural party of government in Australia. Labor was born to rule. What had Menzies done to earn his success, except stay upright while the Establishment and a torrent of good luck bore him along? An economic boom, a Cold War to suit his conservative creed, an incompetent opponent, a divided Labor Party and the dividends of Labor's postwar nation-building and welfare state—all these spoils were his to enjoy. It was not that Menzies stood for capital and the Keatings for labour. Matt Keating's transition from the workshop to a successful engineering business worked as leavening on his son's thinking. He would always take the view that it was one of the proper goals of Labor to create an economy in which more people could escape the factory floor and succeed in business as Matt had. Paul Keating never had an argument with capital, only with its distribution and availability.

By the time Paul Keating became Labor's leader the party had never subscribed so unequivocally to the doctrine of the free market: yet, despite some recent fraying, its relationship with the unions remained the defining one. That was the miracle of the Accord, and the legacy of a ruling group from both the political and industrial sides who believed that the world would be saved by intelligence rather than by ideology or morality. All Labor leaders have had to reconcile the seductions of glorious self-interest and Marx's view of capital as 'dead labour that, vampire-like, lives only by sucking labour, and lives the more, the more labour it sucks'. Populists, demagogues, pragmatists, Olympians and people of plain commonsense have led the Labor Party. None of those categories, singly or combined, defines Keating's response. He tended to believe in both sides equally and defended them with equal passion. None of his predecessors was more passionately pro-capital, but when roused to fight for labour, he also sounded more like Marx than any of them had.

Far more than any Australian, it was Winston Churchill who inspired him from his early teens. Churchill was not like other leaders: other leaders were pusillanimous, pedantic and safe. Churchill was none of these things. Churchill was lion-hearted, big-brained, in all things his own man. Churchill saw through the posturing and hokum. He recognised deceit, including self-deceit. In a favourite Keating phrase, he knew 'where the weight was'. When he was about twelve, Keating says, he read Hugh Trevor-Roper's *The Last Days of Hitler.* More than anything learned from his Catholic schooling, World War II made him conscious of evil, he says. It governed in the world wherever people had made faint-hearted, weak and wrong decisions. It was the mark of all great leaders that they understood this: they saw further, sought the truth stripped of piety and legalism, had the courage to go straight for it. Because his father's brother, Uncle Billy, had been captured there and later killed in Borneo by the Japanese, the young Keating was also conscious of the Singapore disaster. He read it as most historians did—as Britain abandoning Australia; sometimes he might say betraying it. But the Singapore business never dimmed his admiration for Churchill. Unlike those who led Britain and Australia in the 1930s—unlike Menzies—Churchill knew where the weight with Hitler was, and what would be the consequences of appeasement. He might say that Churchill had betrayed Australia at Singapore, but he had acted in what he took to be Britain's interests and the interests of beating Hitler. Keating's argument was less with the British leader than with Australians who could not draw the obvious lessons from it. His argument was therefore particularly with Menzies and his acolytes.

Bad as he was in Keating eyes, Menzies was no more the villain than those on the Labor side who made his success possible. Bert Evatt, Labor's federal leader, was a villain because he was inept—perhaps also because he was a rationalist, a middle-class lawyer and over many years an opponent of J.T. Lang. Worse, he had turned on the Catholic anti-communist forces in the party while giving comfort to their enemies the reds. In 1951, as leader of the Opposition he had defended the communists when Menzies tried to proscribe them. He had gone to bat for them again at the Petrov Commission in 1954 and after that partly self-made disaster the party had fallen apart. Evatt did not believe in communism, but he believed in civil liberties. The Keatings believed in Labor. When Evatt played into Menzies' hands and Labor split, it seemed to them the direst stupidity. Some on the Labor side said Evatt had stood for principle and saved the honour of the party, but in the Keatings' world people were inclined to say he was a bigger fool than the communists.

A day or two after New Year 1992, Mark Ryan phoned to ask if I'd like to write speeches for the new prime minister. Ryan had run Victorian premier John Cain's media office during the 1988 election campaign. In those days I was writing speeches for Cain. Soon after the election Ryan left Cain to join Keating's office and he thrived there. When Keating went to the back benches, Ryan was parked in Ros Kelly's office. Kelly was the Minister for the Environment, but Ryan's main occupation was rounding up the numbers to roll Hawke. Now he was running the Prime Minister's media office at the age of twenty-eight. Growing up on the edge of the desert in Quorn, South Australia, failed to starve him of personal confidence and self-possession. He had found his way to the Prime Minister's side not by riding on the party, by studying economics or even by apparent effort, but rather by exercising a kind of fearless natural gumption and one of those minds, ideal for politics, which when it runs up against a problem does not stick to it or get entangled, but bounces off in the direction of salvation. He would have done well in espionage, and he had something of that look as well.

I told him 'No'. I had family responsibilities. Children completing their final years at school. I wanted to get back to serious writing. I was sick of politics. The occasional speech perhaps, as I had done for Ros Kelly, but full-time was out of the question. Ryan typically did not press the case.

The speeches for Cain had supplemented my income, much of which came from writing Max Gillies' parodies of Bob Hawke. Speechwriting had its moments, but to do it properly and to make the drudgery and compromise bearable you need to feel some passion for the cause, the politician or the party. I lost half of that when Cain went, and by the time Keating got the job in Canberra I had lost it all. So long as one felt sorry about Cain one felt dark on the federal government which had made life hard for him. Cain resented Keating for starving Victoria of funds, and positively loathed him for unleashing economic rationalism and all its attendant villains on the country. I did not subscribe entirely to this view, but to enough of it to think he had a point. When my wife and her partner lost the business they had built over fifteen years, interest rates were as high as 20 per cent. Later, when I was in the job, I could never repress a snarl whenever Keating said that those interest rates had 'de-spivved Australia'. It was true up to a point. Entrepreneurs who had been held up to us by both sides of politics as models of the new economy in the eighties were now either going broke or going to gaol. The question was, who created the spivs? And who created the economics commentators, the secular priests of our time, who for a decade had told us how to think and what to expect? They were *not* broke because they had never risked a dollar of their own, or backed an idea of their own and, sadly, I sometimes thought, they couldn't be sent to gaol.

I spent three months in Tokyo in 1991 and when I came back Melbourne felt stunned and deserted. Empty shops and lease signs everywhere, quiet streets, not a crane in sight. There was a kind of sullen silence in the air. Of all recessions in my lifetime it was the only one to make you think the Depression must have been a bit like this. My complaint, however, was less the economic policy than the lack of direction and ideas. The Hawke Government had lost more than its economic credibility. It was spiritless, as if the leader's narcissism had leached the life from it. Max Gillies' early takes on Hawke had been gentle and moderately fond, but in later years the subject so consistently surpassed the satire it was difficult to find in the imagination anything to match it. It was a good time for disappointed radicals, I suppose, but it felt as if the entire national project might turn to dust. Manning Clark captured the mood on a postcard he sent not long before he died. 'I hope Australia does not peter out,' he wrote. It was the recession, but it was also the lack of anything to grip the mind. In two years or so it seemed only the war against Iraq seemed to light up Hawke. Everything in Australia seemed to drift.

Yet, from outside, it was often difficult to see the Keating alternative as anything but another species of hubris coupled to the same economics. As a backbencher in mid-1991, he had attacked Hawke's new federalism, setting himself up as the traditional Labor guardian of Commonwealth powers. In October 1991 he made a good speech on the subject at the National Press Club, by way of throwing down the gauntlet. But in a recession, who cared about the relative powers of the Commonwealth and the States? The people wanted to know if they had a future, or if the country did. In exile Keating proposed another traditional Labor measure, active government intervention in the economy to revive growth and boost employment. Because it was in contradiction of his earlier position on the recession, his enemies said it was a cynical tactic to buy more caucus votes. Perhaps it was, but it was also the result of his deciding that the recession was deeper than he had first thought, and he was amazed when Hawke did not read it the same way and change tack.

The electorate was scarcely more engaged by the argument over the economy than by the argument about new federalism. They were not interested in what either of them had to say. They hated the spectacle of Keating and Hawke fighting for supremacy. They hated the revelation of the Kirribilli agreement by which Keating was promised smooth succession to the leadership. Who was witness to this deal? Who voted for it? Not the people, but a millionaire and a trade unionist. The miracle was that the government was still in office; that in 1990 they had won an election with interest rates at 17 per cent or more and unemployment climbing towards the dreaded double digit. It must have encouraged some of them to think that if they could win that they could do anything.

So far had my own faith fallen, when John Hewson announced his radical right manifesto, Fightback, I found myself admiring it. Parts of it—the energy in it, the conviction. So did others who had never voted anything but Labor. A former stalwart of the Cain Government told me he would vote for it. One could hate its imitations of Thatcherism and the crassness of the philosophy, but at least there was a core of belief. Labor by contrast was doing a fair imitation of the Liberals at the end of their long era, and whoever led them risked comparisons with Sir William McMahon. In high-blown despair at all this, I vowed on New Year's Day 1992 to give up all political interests, including satire, speechwriting and reading the newspapers, and, even if it meant poverty, return to scholarship and creativity. I had a contract to co-write a history of Australia since the war with the historian Stuart Macintyre. I told the publisher to expect it that year. It was a few hours after this that Ryan phoned. When I told my wife and friends that I had turned the offer down they said I was mad. Do it, they said. It will be a fabulous experience and there's an election due—it will be all over in a year.

--

I met Paul Keating in the doorway of his office on 9 January. He was wearing one of those famous suits and patent leather shoes. Before I went in someone from the media office told me how inspiring it was to work for him; but he didn't look capable of inspiring anyone. He stood front-on and gave me his little short-arm handshake, and a look with his famous brown eyes. The first impression was tiredness, languor, withdrawal. By the time I left half an hour or so later it was sadness, melancholy. It would remain the dominant impression. It's why I liked him and knew at once that I wanted the job.

Hawke had been gone three weeks but you could sense his presence in the room. The new prime minister said he could still smell his cigars and the Lodge reeked of them. 'Old Silver' he called him, and every time he mentioned the name he flicked his eyes towards the big desk at the other end of the room as if Old Silver were in it or under it. I couldn't smell his cigars, but I wasn't the usurper. Hawke had been the only prime minister to sit at that desk, the only one to occupy this office. Keating was not as hostile to Hawke as I thought he might be, but he was frank. I said I wondered if there were any lengths to which Hawke would not go to have revenge. Keating said he was a bitter bastard and might make a bad enemy.

It seemed a reasonable question because of an interview Hawke had given the TV journalist Mike Willesee three days before. Hawke told Willesee that he thought the new prime minister might see the world through the 'prism' of his old mentor, that icon of bitterness and division, Jack Lang. Hawke had been the great consensus prime minister, the great healer of the wounds of 1975. Lang was the great splitter. Hawke put the Labor Party and the country together. Lang split the Labor Party in the thirties and spent much of the long time left to him (he was ninety-nine when he died and looked like Methuselah) heaping vituperation on his former colleagues, including another great healer (and reformed drinker) the wartime Labor prime minister, John Curtin. Lang was one of the least liked people in Australian political history and just then Paul Keating's polls suggested he would have run him close for that honour. John Curtin was one of the best loved people in Australian political history, and in his heyday nearly 80 per cent of the electorate approved of Hawke. As a young man Paul Keating sat at the feet of Jack Lang. Just now Bob Hawke chose to sit at John Curtin's.

Hawke told Mike Willesee that he didn't go in for heroes—he wasn't that sort of person—but if he had gone in for them John Curtin would be the one to get the nod. Curtin had been a brave and astute wartime leader. He stood up to the British, forged a new alliance with the Americans, and created the blueprint for a postwar new order based on Keynesian principles he had grasped even before the General Theory was published. He died in office and before his time, succumbing finally to the work and worry, plagued to the end by self-serving malcontents and ideologues of the Jack Lang variety. He was a martyr for his country, the Labor Party and intelligent commonsense. In Bob Hawke's view, and in many others', Curtin was not only Australia's greatest prime minister, but a great leader by any standards—world class might be the contemporary measurement—and no-one of goodwill who knew the facts could question his stature.

Paul Keating had questioned it, however. He had done it a year before in a speech which marked the beginning of his campaign to wrest the leadership from Hawke. This was the 'Placido Domingo' speech, delivered on the evening of 7 December 1990 at the National Press Club, Canberra. A mere kilometre from the Lodge, Keating told the assembled journalists that Australia had never had the great leaders it needed and deserved. The United States had had them. At crucial times in American history Washington, Lincoln and Roosevelt had taken their country and transformed it. But Australia had not been so fortunate. Our wartime leader and 'trier' that he was, John Curtin was not in that league. 'We've never had one such person, not one.' It was a frank, passionate speech—the more so because speeches at the Press Club dinner were supposed to be off the record. And the day before, one of Keating's closest friends, a key member of his fighting unit, the secretary of the Treasury, Chris

Higgins, had died of a heart attack at the age of forty-seven. Keating had begun his speech by talking about Higgins and what happens when someone who was making 'a serious contribution' and not getting much credit for it suddenly dies. He had a meeting with him at seven that evening and at nine he was dead. And when it happens 'you feel as if something is happening to you, something moving, the earth is moving on you'.

He went on to talk about Australia. Politics was about leadership, and countries needed leadership. People thought politicians were shits, but 'politicians change the world'. And the trouble with Australia was the country had never had a politician like that. Australia needed 'a national will and national leadership'. 'Leadership,' he said, 'is not about being popular. It's about being right and about being strong,' he said. 'And it's not whether you go through some shopping centre, tripping over TV crews' cords. It's about doing what you think the nation requires, making profound judgments about profound issues.' As the most popular prime minister on record, and grand master of the mall crawl, Bob Hawke was not likely to be in much doubt about his treasurer's meaning.

Mark Ryan recorded it, which was wise because well before it was over the journalists had decided what it meant, and within hours Keating's off-the-record address was news. The recording is a benefit to posterity because what he said and what has been made of it are very different things. As an impromptu political address it has few equals in Australian history, not only for what it precipitated—the demise of Hawke and the rise of Keating—but for the pungency of its messages about Australia. People wanting to discover what the Keating Government was about will find the gist of it in this speech. Australians apologise for themselves by saying that they do not have the 230 million people that the US has, he said; but 'they weren't 230 million when Thomas Jefferson was sitting in a house he had designed for himself in a paddock in the back end of Virginia writing the words, "Life, Liberty and the Pursuit of Human Happiness"'.

In his interview with Mike Willesee it was not the implied

slur on his own leadership that Hawke recalled, but the slur on Curtin. Against himself it was mere treachery, but to call Curtin a 'trier' was heresy. Hawke did not mention those with whom Keating had compared him. He told Willesee that he had urged Keating to study Curtin's achievements, but he had always resisted him. It was ignorant as well as mean of Keating to belittle such a man. Then again, said the wily Hawke, that was what Lang had done. And Keating had learned from Lang, of course. When Bob Hawke said that Paul Keating saw the world through the prism of Jack Lang he meant he saw it with the same twisted psycho-pathology which made Lang so hateful. It is reasonably safe to presume that he also meant that Keating's slighting reference to Curtin slighted R.J. Hawke. Hawke embraced Curtin's 'greatness' as if it were his own. Hadn't they both pulled the country together when it was most necessary? Hadn't they both given up drinking to serve Australia? Hadn't they both had to suffer fools and the envy and malice of colleagues? It was uncanny. They might have been father and son. So the deposed prime minister put aside the injury to himself and manfully defended his spiritual father instead. But if the Australian people were half as shrewd as Bob Hawke liked to say they were, very likely many viewers decided he was really putting his own case and appropriating Curtin's mantle as he did it.

The morning after the Placido Domingo speech Keating said he had not intended to wound or challenge Hawke, and thirteen months after it he said the same thing to me. Perhaps he was right. Perhaps only the subconscious could have been so ruthless. He had not been in a challenging frame of mind that night, he said. The speech was intended as a tribute to Chris Higgins, who had so devotedly served the economic revolution. To Keating, Higgins had been a 'star'. That night at the Press Club he had reflected on how few had been the 'stars' in Australia. He recalled what the English author, Bernard Levin, had once told him after a Placido Domingo recital—that Domingo was some-times brilliant, sometimes not, but he was always good, and this set him apart from his rivals. Keating told the Press Club, who after all loved to hear him boast, that he was the Placido Domingo of Australian politics. He meant that he would always give quality performances, because that's what the job demanded—and his performances would always be better than his opponents, better by far than John Hewson, the new, young leader of the Opposition with a doctorate in economics and a career in banking behind him. He had Hewson's measure, he told them: 'You know an opponent, you get to know them, you get the psychological grip, the feel, and I have him.' The press could write Paul Keating down, he said, but they'd never be able to deny him. It had been a speech to remind the press about the integrity of economic policy, finding where the 'value' was among all the 'fairy floss', the importance of spinning the tale, streaming the economics and the politics, selling the story of the great adventure in reform. The journalists were not entirely wrong to read it as they did, but in doing that they missed the philosophy underlying it.

That day in the office thirteen months after the Press Club speech, Keating told me that he admired Curtin but to rank him with Lincoln was like comparing 'Leonard Bernstein to Mahler'. Mahler was a 'star' and when you have heard or seen a 'star'—like Klemperer conducting Richard Strauss, or Kreisler or Heifetz playing the Bruch Violin Concerto—you don't want to hear the others. Music inspired Keating: he would take you to the Lodge on an afternoon and plant you dead centre between the giant speakers of his sound system and pump you full of these great performances. At two o'clock on a weekday afternoon I have seen a tear run down his face as Schwarzkopf sang that aria Brahms added to the *German Requiem*. Perhaps it put him in touch with the immortals as music can for some people, or with feelings he could not otherwise divine, but at our first meeting he said he listened because it humbled him. 'Before a big thing,' he said, 'I fill the room with music. It reminds me that what I have to do is just a speck of sand.'

I told him that I was not an economist. He said not to worry, he would teach me. There was less to it than a lot of people thought. I said to him that I thought Australia needed someone to lead it and ideas to govern it, and I wondered if he might be the person. I had not read the transcript of the speech then. Had I, his reply might have disappointed me. He said, 'I'm no leader, but I know what has to be done.' That's what he would always say. It could encourage you to think he was speaking candidly when he said that the speech was never meant to suggest he was the leader Australia needed.

Even if it had not precipitated the challenge to Hawke's leadership, the Placido speech might still be justly famous. Not only for the ideas about Australia it contained, but for the language. Long after his political career was over Keating told . me that he wished he had studied Marx and Weber, for the pleasure it would have given him to grapple with their ideas. But his loss was politics' gain. It left his language blessedly free of the social sciences, and being also free of the law, it was almost completely unconstrained. In its natural environment it served as the raw instrument of his intelligence, a shillelagh or a paint brush as circumstances demanded. With it he could sell an idea better than anybody else in the government. He painted word pictures, created images and moods at a stroke. He could turn ideas into icons, make phrases that stuck. He could cut through to the meaning and, as Gough Whitlam said, restate it in a useful form faster than any politician of his generation. The way people spoke reflected the way they thought and the way they acted. If they talked in circles they walked in circles. If they talked in legalese they legislated their way round problems instead of cutting through them. If they qualified everything they said, everything they did would be qualified. Politics was full of them: people, he said, with brains like sparrows' nests—all shit and sticks.

Sometimes Keating murdered the language (and sometimes it deserved to be murdered), but when he was on a roll with it he could remind you of what language can be and what it can do— of what it was, perhaps, before the academy got hold of it. At these times he also reminded speechwriters that they are never more than a step removed from being supernumeraries.

There was an extraordinary intimacy about the man. He talked as if we had known each other for years. He wanted the job badly three years ago, he said, but now he was tired. He had used up most of his 'horsepower'. You 'use up a lot of horsepower in these jobs', he said. But the truth was most of the work had already been done. Most of the big changes had been made. The rest was mainly management and fine tuning and not letting it slip. Some micro reform, but there really wasn't a lot more that needed doing.

He took the leadership from Hawke because it was owed him and it had been promised him. All through the eighties he had done more of the work than anybody else and come up with more of the ideas. He had helped make Hawke prime minister. He had defended him when he was in trouble. In 1987, in Paul Keating's view at least, it was he who had blown a hole in John Howard's tax proposals and that was crucial to winning the election. Hawke could not talk about winning four elections without acknowledging the crucial role Keating had played in at least the last two of them. In 1988 he had delivered the budget which 'brought home the bacon': the one with the $5.5 billion surplus, the public sector borrowing requirement at zero, 'the best set of government accounts Australia has had in its history', he said. He had delivered Australia from the shadow of the banana republic. Andrew Peacock said he was 'wallowing in shattered aspiration' for the leadership. But Keating, looking like a cat with a mouthful of canary, said he still got a kick out of being the treasurer; it was the 'high side of the street'. But no sooner had he said it than Hawke went on television and said Paul Keating was not irreplaceable—and Keating seethed.

Still, he put it behind him and laboured on. In 1989 at the Menzies Hotel in Sydney he made the speech which pulled the government back to economic fundamentals and preserved its credibility with the markets and the press. He had stiffened Hawke's spine when it seemed to turn to jelly, then tramped the country in the campaign of the following year. He had been the principal force in parliament, in the cabinet, in the caucus, in the party. It was Keating more than anyone else who had made the Labor Party relatively 'phobia free'. He'd got the party thinking internationally and that had got the country thinking internationally. When the government was judged, his stamp would be indelible. There was no show without Keating, and when after his first challenge failed he went to the back benches for six months, the point was proved. Within weeks the new treasurer John Kerin had been humiliated. The government's response to the Opposition's new free-market vision was feeble. Hewson had bolted in the polls and for the first time in a decade the Liberals now occupied the high ground of policy. There was no denying that Hawke had given Labor leadership, or that the success of Labor's model owed a great deal to his unique combination of intellect, salesmanship and charisma. His style had more in common with modern American fundamentalist preaching than anything picked up from John Curtin, but it worked. That charisma made all around him braver. It helped Paul Keating to have him there, a political buffer for the saturnine architect of unpopular reform. If Keating sometimes protected his leader in the parliament, Hawke's favours came in the form of that aura of conviction—half chapel, half floor show—he cast over the electorate in a period of great change. The two of them made a formidable double act. Together they personified the policy model. But by the end of the decade Keating reckoned Hawke was no longer offering leadership. By 1991 he was speaking of three wasted years—for the government, for the country and for Paul Keating. Keating had put the country's interests before his own—the government's interests, the party's interests, everything before his own. When Keating realised that Hawke would not keep his promise he marched in on him, here in this office where we sat. He fronted him over there at the desk and Hawke had said no, he was not going to give it to him; he took the Placido Domingo speech to be a personal attack which voided the agreement. Besides, he was enjoying the job too much, he said, and he intended to be still in it when he went to London later in the year, because he had been promised the keys to the city.

He might not have killed the father in the Freudian sense, but when he overthrew Hawke, Keating did 'kill' a brother and an elder of the tribe. That did not mean he had done anything that required an apology, or a demonstration of remorse. There is no clear reason why he should have felt any guilt at all. It had happened in the natural element of both men and according to the customs of the tribe, not to say of all politics and war. Keating had done no more than Hawke had when on the eve of the 1983 election he snatched the leadership and the prime ministership from Bill Hayden. Hawke never seemed consumed by remorse, although giving Hayden the governor-general's job might be interpreted as an act of reparation. Nevertheless, it was not the way Keating wanted to get the job. It sounds trite, but there was no happiness in the memory, just another pain to add to the melancholy.

Keating's relationship to Hawke was not like Hawke's to Hayden. It was more brotherly. The bitter three-year struggle for the leadership masks a legacy of shared adventure and achievement. Together they had transformed the party, the electorate and the economy. There had been something great about the partnership, and not the least part of the pleasure for Keating might have been the sublimation of his ambition in those years. So long as he knew his time was coming, he could enjoy the role of indispensable lieutenant; he could play hard man, maverick, power behind the throne; he could be whatever it suited him to be, including both the antithesis of Hawke and his most loyal and able ally. And with every step make himself the intriguing—for some, irresistible—shape of the future. The press gallery fell in love with him and, when the final struggle began, supported him openly. Being treasurer always has its drawbacks, but Keating overcame them with shows of fearlessness, colour and elan which lent the job a certain nobility and made his claim on the prime ministership morally indisputable. When Hawke hung on past the appointed time Keating's feelings of betrayal went beyond frustration. It was much more than having his political ambitions thwarted: this was a violation of the natural order, a defiance of the Gods. The two of them had, in Keating's argot, put together a nice little story, with all the threads joining nicely, with a nice little ending—and Hawke had sabotaged it. There was something shocking about it. Keating always denied that the execution of Hawke caused him any grief. That of course does not rule out the possibility that it depressed him. And even if the overthrow of Hawke did not disturb his mind, the possibility remains that he was deeply troubled by the circumstances which made the execution necessary. His father's death apart, had anything else in his life given him more reason to mourn?

Media support for Keating grew in inverse proportion to public sympathy. By the time of the first ballot most newspaper editors seemed convinced that he would make the better prime minister and when he lost it—by 22 votes—they were not dissuaded. The press gallery, by their own admission, were 'enthralled', 'seduced'. They liked what they called his 'word magic'. They looked forward to the 'touch of excitement' he had promised them he would bring. After that first ballot he told them with a wry beguiling grin: 'I want to thank you, because I like you. I don't know why I do, but I do. I don't like all of you, but I like most of you.' It was the Bankstown lover at work, the laconic Lothario. 'Yes, he seduces us from time to time,' said Alan Ramsey, the *Sydney Morning Herald*'s commentator. Ramsey was arguably the pre-eminent print journalist in the gallery. 'He seduces the government, the cabinet and the caucus. He's been the dominant figure in the past two years. He also behaves like a thug from time to time,' he said. The Hawke camp had been angry enough with the press bias before the ballot; they were understandably livid when support for Keating blatantly continued after his defeat. In the years to come it was tempting to think that a lot of the goodwill he needed from the gallery as prime minister had been burnt up in the struggle to get the job. Before the victory over Hawke the media owed Keating for providing much of the substance and theatre of politics; it is just possible that after the victory some of them had it in their minds that Keating was in their inexhaustible debt.

The new Prime Minister Keating had no trouble making a case for himself, but his legitimacy depended on more than the logic or the justice of his position. He was going to have to earn that, and the task would be more difficult because he came without a story to tell. He had had *such* a story not long ago and he had been such a master at telling it. He had pulled off an economic revolution that every preceding generation of Australians would have found odious and unthinkable. Story-telling had been the key. He had achieved something a Marxist might call praxis—he managed to raise the theoretical conscious-ness of the people consistent with the revolutionary changes he was making to the real world. But the story unravelled with the recession, and calling it 'the recession we had to have', having also said that he controlled those who controlled monetary policy, seemed only to confirm that he was the author of a failure.

Not without reason, Hawke and others had wondered if Keating was 'wide' enough to be prime minister. His greatest supporters thought he might have spent too long in the treasurer's office. As prime minister he needed to prove himself all over again, if not to reinvent himself, then to at least renew the govern-ment. It would require fresh thinking and energy. But at that meeting in January 1992, neither was evident. The absence was partly due to his conviction that most of the work had been done. The big changes had been made. What remained might be signif-icant but it was significant tinkering. He was emphatic about that. Another thought was enervating him: the timing was all wrong. In 1988 he was at his peak, there was still some time in the economic cycle and the tide was not so far out politically. He had wanted the job badly then: the job he had first imagined might be his late in 1960 when a tyke like himself became president of the United States.

And thirty years later, here he was in the office he had coveted. But he didn't feel triumphant at all. The government's cycle had well and truly finished and it trailed miserably in the polls, and his own excitement and energy had ebbed. It was bizarre that at forty-six he could think it had come to him too late in life. Yet fundamentally that was what he told me three weeks after he won the job. It was not just the political mess, or the let-down anyone is prone to feel when a long-held ambition is finally realised. There was always the other, singular, private Keating drama that you couldn't get at, and that he struggled to control. It is hard for someone who is not a psychologist to describe this state of mind. It is a bit like depression, and I think that often he was depressed. A less clinical but perhaps more suggestive description is the 'bewildered solitude' of Robert Musil's *The Man Without Qualities*: 'whereas all other lives exist a hundredfold, being seen in the same way by those who lead them as by all the others who confirm them, his true life existed only for himself'. One way or another he was always somewhere else. Even when you had his most earnest attention, or some policy issue did, when he was in full political flight, he was never more than a moment removed from his personal drama.

He told me he would give the electorate 'quality'. You could sell 'quality'. You couldn't sell 'crap'. 'What we'll give them will be 24 carat,' he said. He did not believe Labor could win the next election, which had to be held within the next fifteen months. But he would have a go. I said, more or less, that if he would have a go I would. He more or less welcomed me aboard, and in doing so said, 'No-one who ever took this job was less exhilarated about it than I am.'

But as I reached the door he said, 'It's got to be fun.' He showed me out and passed me on to his principal adviser, the alarmingly tall and bald Don Russell in his dark Boss suit with his big gold ring, who sat in the room opposite his master's door like a firedog missing its pair. And with what turned out to be an almost permanent expression of slightly puzzled, slightly smug nonchalance, Dr Russell signed me up. My first speech would be the Prime Minister's Australia Day address.

A former Treasury official and then an adviser to Keating when he was treasurer, Russell had been honeymooning in France when news came that Keating had won. (It was a measure of how far they thought the job had drifted from their grasp—Ryan was holidaying in Germany.) People said Russell was very skilled at fusing the economic with the political, that he could make political and economic desiderata seem to be one and the same. He had enemies who said that he was a bloodless economic rationalist, notorious for remarking that from the treasurer's office he had heard the economy snap—like a neck—under the weight of official interest rates, that he had given the country a recession and taken off for Paris. Mark Ryan and Simon Balderstone, who were both his colleagues and friends, called him the Chief Pointy Head, or the Tall Bald Pointy Head, 'pointy head' meaning economist, economic rationalist or econocrat. With his fellow economic advisers he believed the economy was the main game, by which he meant the only one to really matter. Everything else was 'flim flam' or 'fairy floss' and deserving mockery and condescension. But Russell defied categorisation: on one reading he was a solipsist who handled people and affairs with that mixture of cold calculation and serene ineptness which to many outsiders—and some insiders—came to embody the house style of the Keating office. He was insouciant, insensitive and calculating. While the rest of us endured political life with egos uncertain and fragile from disappointment and exposure, his seemed as limitless as the unweaned child's. Yet like the child, he was also soft and open to persuasion; it was just as true to say that he was in the game for the excitement of nation-building and the addiction of politics. He liked the idea of a 'virtuous circle' of sound policy, good works and astute politics. That was the creative impulse in him: he was an optimist who, whatever else he lacked in comparison to J. M. Keynes, shared his cheerfulness about the prospects for good in economic theory intelligently and intuitively applied, and believed good should be its aim. What was more, he was probably the only person alive with the capacity to think along the singular and formidably effective lines that Keating did. He also had the virtue of utter loyalty to his prime minister, and even at the worst of times I liked him.

I returned to the Victorian beach where I had been holidaying and wrote the Australia Day speech. I did an interview with Michelle Grattan from a phone booth. I told an ABC reporter that I thought the Prime Minister was misunderstood. John Cain phoned to say congratulations, but Keating didn't deserve me. I flew back to Canberra in a new suit from Henry Bucks, in business class with all the other suits. I applied for a Diner's Club card. In the space of a week I drifted a thousand miles from ordinary life. I took a room on a weekly basis at the Telopea Park Motel, and paid in cash from my travel allowance. I began to make the daily fifteen-minute walks to and from the parliament. The Prime Minister read the Australia Day speech in his office and said to me, nodding, 'Good words'.

Chapter 2

. . . no-one seems able to think in turns of phrase that are not hackneyed: prose consists less and less of words chosen for the sake of their meaning, and more and more of phrases tacked together like the sections of a prefabricated henhouse.

George Orwell, 'Politics and the English Language'

Australia's national parliament is interred in a vast lawn beneath a giant rattling aluminium Hills Hoist of a flagpole on a hill, an elephantine expression of the suburban dream, yet wanting only a few sheep and a Southern Cross windmill on it to also represent the rural rump. Little tractors with flashing lights incessantly mow and fertilise the grass. The gardeners wear neat brown uniforms and broad hats suggesting a sanitised link with the frontier or our Olympic team. There are always magpies on the lawns, an occasional one dead from weedkiller, and high in the eaves currawongs watch with evil yellow eyes. The north entrance is principally for visitors and tourists. Staff come in the other end—the 'executive' or 'ministerial' entrance. The building is so big, its interior so vast and confusing, that when I was first required to go from one entrance to the other I could only manage it by going outside and walking over the hill. It's easier to get your bearings outside: there's the water spout on Lake Burley Griffin, the Presbyterian church by Canberra Avenue, the Brindabella ranges, and the old Parliament House—and at night one can navigate by familiar constellations in the blanket of stars.

Inside it wants for nothing except reality. It smells of nothing, tastes of nothing, and is the colour of nothing. Having no past or provenance it evokes nothing, unless it is the end of history. When it's empty of people it sounds of nothing, except, if you stop and listen for a while, the call of a currawong or the squeak of car tyres on the tiles somewhere outside, the hum of computers and the rattling of the flagpole. Members of the League of Rights, whose right-wing ideas have a degree of currency in some parts of rural Australia, including the parts I come from, say the flagpole disguises electronic equipment for monitoring the lives of law-abiding Australians. They believe the whole building is designed in the interests of the Fabian conspirators who run the country. They say it contains a bomb shelter for the exclusive use of Australia's political leaders, but from what I could see the cavernous underground was a garage for those little tractors. One night Mark Ryan and I got lost in the underground corridors for what seemed a long time, and came up in a gloomy void which turned out to be the kitchen of the cafeteria. In fairness to the League of Rights, it is true that the House was not built with much sensitivity to the feelings of 'remote' Australians. And who in Australia is not remote from Canberra? And vice versa? To stand in one of the courtyards at three on a frosty morning is to know just how remote Canberra is.

The fluorescent light and vast spaces of Australia's parliament seem to leach the senses. The place lacks red blood cells. Beyond the chambers there is no sign of the great contest of ideas for which a national parliament exists. Unlike the old Parliament House where opponents bumped past each other in the corridors, met each other's eyes, exchanged brutalities in the bar, stood side by side at urinals, in the new building the Opposition is separated from the government by a divide as great as any which separates all of them from their constituents. As with dogs which meet only through a fence and cannot sniff each other's backsides, it deepens the everyday animus. The only place of communion is a coffee shop which in our days was run by a convivial Italian called Aussie whose day-long brio, like a wattle bird, only served to highlight the empty pall of the building. One day when lost upstairs I stumbled upon some kind of meditation room. I peered in but no-one was meditating at the time. Later when I mentioned it to colleagues they gave me the impression that only the Greens and Democrats used to go there and that it was not a place for people who valued their credibility.

One walked from the Prime Minister's Office to the coffee shop across vast parquetry floors in canyons of space, past a pool with signs beside it begging the hourly lines of tourists not to throw coins, cold sculpture, minimalist paintings, straight plastered lines, pale-faced advisers in dark suits—a row of portraits in oils of past Speakers of the House the only human-looking things. In courtyards behind glass there are patches of real air, real light and real bird noise. Secretaries huddle in the doorways and under the birches, smoking; gardeners in their seasonal uniforms, sunglasses and government-issue wading boots stand knee-deep in ponds and scoop leaves from the water with nets. Even as you stride across this great space in your suit with your white face and what you imagine to be fateful information swimming in your head, it can cross your mind that you are dreaming or extinct.

Malcolm Fraser was prime minister when plans for the new parliament were drawn up, and the location and design of the prime minister's suite of offices—the PMO—is believed to show his influence. It was constructed on the lines of a rabbit burrow. A long, bending corridor connected the media office at one end with the prime minister's suite almost at the other—beyond were a sitting room and a dining room and rooms for the Federal Police, led by Bob Heggie whose young face can be seen in the photograph taken on the steps of the old parliament on the day that Kerr dismissed Gough Whitlam and in many subsequent photos of Labor prime ministers. Deborah Hope, who was Annita Keating's adviser, Nicola Head, who managed correspondence, and Guy Nelligan, the PM's 'manager of hospitality and catering' and effectively his butler, were down that end. There were also security men in blue uniforms. In Hawke's day, I was told, the legendary Labor speechwriter Graham Freudenberg secreted himself in a den at that end of the tunnel where he could smoke cigarettes in peace. People say that the office's design reflects the mistrustful, or even the guilty, side of Fraser's nature after the Dismissal and betokens an era when political demonstrations were common. It may also be related to the explosion at the Sydney Hilton in 1978. Foregoing the pastoralist's traditional attachments to blue horizons and broad verandahs, Mr Fraser, we were told, insisted that the office be on the ground floor and obscured from the general view. So, while upstairs backbenchers bathed in Arcadian light and gazed at the beautiful Brindabellas, down below the prime minister of Australia stared at the walls of his bunker and so did all who served him. The prime minister does have a courtyard—an austere, tiled, wisteria-lined quadrangle into which the PM is brought and taken away by car, door to door. Sometimes the press were summoned to this compound for doorstop interviews. We could watch the news being made through the diaphanous curtains of his window, willing him to wind it up quickly before he got some curly or irritating question and said something that set a hare running or made the *wrong* news, wishing we had an invisible wire attached to the seat of his pants with which we could winch him back in.

If you live in a burrow long enough you become a bit like other things that live in burrows; it narrows your vision but it may also heighten your instincts. In the white light and the white noise we were like white rabbits. Counting the police and security people permanently stationed with us, there were about fifty of us in the PMO and its attached media office. A dozen or so were policy and media senior advisers, and there were other advisers and a raft of executive and personal assistants, and Guy the butler and Jimmy the driver. For four years and three months, all day and often all night, people walked and ran up and down the burrow. So constant was the activity, six years later I can still see the faces and the way they walked, the colour and shape of the files which in that environment defined them. The men who came from the old treasurer's office, Don Russell, Mark Ryan and Stephen Smith, had a distinctive gait in which the upper body stayed very still—it might have been unconsciously modelled on Keating's suave amble. There was a slow swaggering version, and an urgent higher gear which put the whole office on alert. They would shoot up the corridor like buck rabbits sensing danger abroad, and everyone else would try to control the beating of their hearts.

Among all those called senior advisers in 1992 there were three economists: Russell, Ric Simes, who had come to Keating's office from the Treasury, and John Edwards, who had been a Fairfax journalist before completing an economics doctorate in Washington in the 1980s. They all had PhDs, and all were devout free-marketeers, and all were lean and looked hungry. Perhaps because he was the most recent convert to the economic religion and came from a Labor Party background, Edwards seemed to have the edge in zealotry. Perhaps he had this edge because he also had an edge in articulateness. Simes was the driest, but he also seemed to be the most reliable, the one whose figures could generally be trusted. Edwards had been given responsibility for industrial relations, and a roving brief across several portfolios including trade, and he usually wrote the early drafts of speeches about the economy. Ashton Calvert, a dapper Japanese-speaking Tasmanian from the Department of Foreign Affairs and Trade, was Keating's foreign affairs adviser. Anne de Salis, a super-efficient career bureaucrat who acted as a kind of chief of staff and took responsibility for advice on multiculturalism and women's matters, was the only woman with senior adviser status in the first six months. The one senior adviser to continue from the Hawke office was Simon Balderstone, a former *Age* journalist with an unparalleled and endearing grasp of the Australian vernacular, and on one hand a misshapen little finger that had been frost-bitten on Mount Everest. He had worked for Graham Richardson when the senator had been minister for the environment and was one of those who liked the man. In Keating's office Balderstone's portfolios were environment, Aborigines and sport. Stephen Smith was a young West Australian Labor operator in the Bob Hogg mould, but brisker. In fact I have no memory of him seated or standing still. He had been ALP State secretary in WA, and while in this role saw to the removal of the Labor Premier, Peter Dowding. With Ryan he had done much of the legwork rounding up the numbers for Keating. It seemed remarkable that with those two scalps in his belt he was not more fearsome or perfidious-looking. He was designated senior adviser (politics).

There was someone to manage every kind of business in the place, and it took me at least a year to work out who managed what. Scott Wheeler and, when he went to London, Claire Nairn, both of whom seemed to be always smiling gently and carrying quantities of folders and binders up the corridor, managed cabinet business. Maree Keft, who managed the office, seemed always to be carrying folders in the other direction. The Prime Minister had also brought with him a tax economist from the Treasury, Peter Robinson, who was called senior political adviser under which title went the worst of all jobs, making (and breaking) his appointments. Linda Craige was his young, matter-of-fact personal secretary, and among other flawlessly efficient PAs there was the dauntless, unflappable Nina England. For a couple of years the four PAs one greeted on entering the office were, in order of seating, Deana, Nina and Gina . . . and Anna who often spoke in Portuguese. The Prime Minister also brought his driver Jimmy Warner with him. Jimmy was always somewhere about, chatting to the women, smoking by his car in the courtyard, reminding you just by his presence that a real world existed outside. If he was going to the TAB he'd tell you and he'd put a bet on if you asked him. Jimmy and the coppers were essential leavening in the mix. It would have been unbearable without them. As Keating said, it was more like a family than an office, and it could be as fractious and dysfunctional as a family too. One could marvel at our capacity for high speed organisation and productivity, and despair utterly at our frequent mismanagement. Yet the place was nearly always civil and warm and, rail about it as one often did, some sense of duty and devotion held things together.

The battle lines were not always distinct, and the opposing forces were less than uniform in composition, but the Prime Minister's Office was nonetheless an ideological battlefield. In a place where pragmatism and compromise are the prerequisites of life for everyone, the term 'ideological' might seem misplaced. But no other word will do. Whatever name it goes by, supply-side economics, neoclassical economics or economic rationalism, it is no less an ideology for being expressed in the language of economics. Those who professed it were attached not just to the idea of the free market—all of us were attached to that—but to a whole worldview, a web of meaning and belief by which all events were interpreted and all potential actions measured. That was what they meant by the 'main game'. They believed, furthermore, that they were on the side of history; their ideas were irrefutably the right ones, that what they did was the best hope for the nation and its people—the last best hope, indeed, of mankind. Their responses tended to be reflexive, as ideological responses are; and, like ideologues, they sometimes marginalised those who did not respond in the same way. They were believers, a little company with special knowledge, they knew what the game was. They shared a belief in a new order, and that they were the ones who would lead us to it. There was an element of cleansing about it—cleanse the economy of government where prudent, cleanse companies of inefficiencies including people, cleanse people of outmoded thought, of false consciousness.

On the opposing side there was less clarity and certainty. At such times as we bleeding hearts were united it was more by opposition to the economists than by any other common ground. And yet we professed no radically different species of economics: a little more sympathy for what we understood of Keynes, a little more traditional Laborism, a little more Christian or any other kind of charity. A bit more industry policy here, a bit more protection there. It was essentially an argument about what constituted commonsense. No-one was proposing anything as radical as *Australia Reconstructed*—the big document of the 1980s labour movement whose influences could be traced to, among other things, Scandinavian social democracy and even 1970s Eurocommunism. What we did propose was broadening the battlefront—fighting sometimes on a symbolic level, including in the mainstream of policy debate, uttering thoughts about history and identity, the arts, regional differences and regional development. If one pretended to imitate the simple lines of the neoclassical, the other resembled the chaos and relativism of the postmodern mixed with some ancient humanism. The arguments, by and large, concerned the dimensions of the game: one side said that the economic agenda defined it all but absolutely and nearly everything else was decoration. The other side said that both as a worldview and as politics this was absurdly and fatally narrow. One side said that markets always 'clear' and government intervention is futile and counterproductive; the other side, those without training in economics, could not see how, politically or morally, governments could govern on this basis. This side also believed reality did not admit sufficiently of knowable truth and predictable behaviour to justify such a fundamentalist faith. The pendulum might swing and the markets might clear, but what government on three-year terms can wait to find out? And, some of us thought, who cares? If perfect equilibrium can be reached at all it could only be in perfect circumstances, and as the circumstances of human society can never be more perfect than the human personality, what was the point? It was as rational to apply to political economy the principles of rocket science or poultry management. Only occasionally in the office, but often in one's head, the argument bounced off the extremes of the two positions: for the most part it was conducted in a narrower corridor with a fair degree of give and take. Essentially the end result was a form of new Keynesianism—an imperfect but pragmatic mix of market forces and government intervention. What else? That was the other characteristic of the argument—it frequently seemed pointless.

Neither view did for the changes that were unfolding all around. History and economics alike informed us that recovery would bring with it a rise in inflation and a fall in unemployment—it brought neither. There could be no doubt that as the recovery continued, general happiness would increase and the government would be rewarded with the gratitude of the people—it didn't and it wasn't. Both sides assumed that the people would be impressed by low inflation—they were not. Neither side saw the full implications of globalisation or the technological revolution, or the consequences for social policy of productivity improvements known otherwise as 'downsizing' or 'job shedding'. As truth became undeniable they responded, but they never saw it coming.

We bleeding hearts brought our own ideological baggage and were seen by the pointy heads to have a tendency to populism which, though it might be dressed as Realpolitik, was too much like a longing for approval and a debilitating fear of the people's judgment. In exaggeratedly categorical terms, the pointy heads' faith was in the market; the bleeding heart invested the populace with God-like virtue, which led on to pollsters being priests and their polls the Word, or at least the signs which must be read. In the name of the people, the bleeding hearts were likely to sacrifice policy purity; in the name of policy purity, the pointy heads would sacrifice the people. Bleeding hearts were said to be disposed to panic; among pointy heads, paralysis was common. The problem for the pointy heads was to maintain the coherence of a belief system in the face of political and economic realities which sometimes confounded it. The problem for the bleeding hearts was to arrive at some coherent analysis—or story—from the mess of moral certainties and political cynicism which informed their thinking.

The office family was visited on most days by people who were in the nature of cousins: the department secretary, Mike Keating and his troops, including Sandy Hollway who had been Hawke's chief of staff. David Epstein and later Terry Counihan from the National Media Liaison Service (NMLS, known as Animals). There were accepted friends from among the caucus—Warren Snowdon, George Gear, Chris Schacht and Brian Courtice, for instance. I never worked out why they came so regularly and others said they couldn't get in. Or why Gareth Evans regularly rolled down the corridor and most times stuck his head round the door with a word, and Ralph Willis and Brian Howe and Simon Crean were hardly ever seen. Gordon Bilney, who was not interested in influencing us beyond his portfolio interest, dropped in at will; and, for instance, Robert Ray, who *was* interested, complained that the place was sealed off. Bob Hogg, the party's national secretary, and his deputies, Ian Henderson and Gary Gray in his tracksuit trousers and massive runners, came and went as they liked and usually to tell us that Labor's research showed that things were worse than we thought. Of course some of us knew that they were worse than we thought, but it was not possible to say that. You never knew who might turn up in the PMO. There was nothing to stop anyone coming in and I never heard of anyone being asked to leave. You would glance through your window and there might be a rock singer with a shaved head strolling down the corridor, or a delegation of red-faced grain growers, an advertising whiz, the Prime Minister of New Zealand or the Dalai Lama; the member for Capricornia or somewhere would suddenly pop his head in and tell you to tell the PM to remember the words of William Tecumseh Sherman before the battle of whatever. I looked up from my desk one night and Courtney Walsh, the formidable West Indian fast bowler, was standing in my doorway. He said something like, 'Where do I find de tall blond girl, man?' 'Down the other end,' I said, 'but she's gone home.'

A political adviser is a kind of funnel and should be wide at one end and narrow at the other. The wide end is to take in information from every imaginable source, the narrow end to fit snugly in the prime minister's ear. The wide end is permanently open to the media, the public service, the polls, other ministers and their staff, the caucus, the party secretariat and the rank and file, wives and friends, eccentrics, critics, lobbies, political geniuses and idiots alike. The narrow end discharges the decoction when it is all boiled down—one droplet at a time for preference, so he can quietly absorb it. It is a sure sign of the novice that he sprays his advice all over the place. Inside the funnel, of course, there must be a filter.

Presumably no two prime ministers' offices are the same, but vary according to the personalities which inhabit them, particularly the personality of the prime minister. Ours always had a large if not defining element of chaos about it: 'organised chaos' or 'creative chaos', Don Russell used to call it, but often it was just chaos or even 'hopeless chaos'. I imagine offices also vary according to the nature and the state of the government. Paul Keating's government was almost always under siege or on the verge of it; and for better or worse, Paul Keating defined how the government travelled. From where I sat he *was* the government—or sometimes *we* were. It was not that anyone thought the PMO had an absolute monopoly on wisdom. In fact much that was attempted or done was driven by or drawn down from the perceptions and advice of people outside. But it remains true that the leader has to lead and can't if he listens to every voice he hears. It is also true that those who complained most loudly that Keating and his office did not listen to outsiders were least often seen and never heard and their complaints came second-hand.

We were cut off, without question. It was like a clam opening and closing according to some unseen stimulus—aggression, fear, the need to breathe. Working in a burrow made tunnel vision almost a condition of the job. It did not mean, necessarily, that you did not hear or see what was going on outside; rather that your focus had to be intense. It was less than an ideal state for everyone, inside or outside. When it was over I wondered if it had been a form of madness. But I don't know if there was any choice. Whatever we imagine ourselves to be, advisers—and this I became—are effectively in service, like footmen, bodyguards, astrologers and jesters, and they can serve no-one else or any other cause or interest. It simply will not work any other way.

After a while you didn't have to look to know what was going on. You could sense urgency, panic, elation without turning your head or moving from your chair. Your brain became connected to that corridor and the corridor was connected to other brains and the sounds of voices, doors opening and closing, padding feet and other intangible signals told you the temper of the place without interruption to your work. Silence was welcome, though there never was true silence. The computers buzzed, the phones rang incessantly and a clutch of personal assistants answered them. The PAs were assembled at a point where the burrow opened out, before turning past pigeonholes and on into the media office. Day and night, amid myriad other essential tasks, they typed away and took phone calls from everyone in the country who had a whinge. It was a clearing house for the culture of complaint. Some of the callers were cranks and some were visionaries and many of them were regulars. The Hewett brothers, Hal and Don, who had grapes and avocados in Sunraysia, were visionaries but rang so regularly they were sometimes mistaken for cranks. The most persistent or annoying of these callers the PAs put on 'hands free' and continued typing while offering a polite word every now and then, and you could hear the voices of the lonely, the furious and the inspired rattling away when you passed.

After a year or so I settled in a room adjacent to the big bend in the burrow where it swept around towards the PM's front doors. This billabong-like position combined a small disadvantage with a large advantage. The disadvantage was that people often gathered noisily outside, as flotsam does in river bends. It was, however, the only office which allowed me to keep a watch on the PM's doors and an ear on the principal adviser's. It was the place nearest to the pulse. Not that I needed to know everything, but something about the job made *wanting* to know inescapable. It was important to know roughly his whereabouts, his company and his mood. I knew either by their voices or by the sound of the door being closed so their voices could not be heard. I knew who the principal adviser was talking to and when the PM had entered by the new door which connected their offices. I knew by the movement of Mark Ryan and Greg Turnbull when something was breaking or threatening with the media. After a while I didn't have to listen to hear it, any more than I had to listen for the sound of the shredder through the wall after Question Time. You would hear him on the TV monitor moving that further questions be put on the notice paper, and five minutes later the thing would whirr away as he shredded his notes. I can still hear it now.

Time was punctuated by TV stings and reality defined by what the news said reality had been in the preceding hour, or day or week, and what, as a consequence of this, it was likely to be in the foreseeable future. Between real and recorded time there was never more than a thin transparent membrane. It might feel like an illusion one moment, the next like hyper-reality—and why wouldn't it feel like that in a place where truth was processed? We waded through information: none of it, excepting that in our collective memory, with a provenance of more than a week. It came as newspapers, whole or in clippings from all over the country; from the NMLS daily media summaries of what the shock-jocks, talkback callers and political gurus were saying. It came from people who never stopped phoning or faxing. It came from the press gallery which our media advisers regularly roved to see what the journalists thought the story was, and if it was the wrong story they pointed them towards the right one and hoped it made a difference to the news. Every day began and ended with the news, and weeks ended with the Saturday columns, especially Ramsey's in the *Sydney Morning Herald*. Many half days were ruled at either end by news, many hours began one way and ended another with the news. Time existed for the news. The news decided the shape of your day—what you would think, how you would feel, what you would do. It was addictive and exhausting: addictive because it was the fastest gratification to be had—what you say at 10.45 is news at 11; or even better it obliges your enemies at 11.15 to say something other than what they intended to say, perhaps something you didn't want said. It was exhausting because you lost as often as you won and the gratification of success was about as sustaining as a jelly bean. And yet this was LIFE.

Daily life in the PMO was a truth contest. All day long truth was asserted, denied, demolished, reasserted. And there wasn't a book in the place.

There was a mass of more substantial information, of

course—huge deposits of it in the departments down the hill and in the minds of their very capable senior officials. The Department of Prime Minister and Cabinet was the great resource, including the corporate memory. If Paul Keating had had his way the office would have moved out of the parliament building and into the department's premises—he meant away from the press gallery and towards where the weight and value were. It was to the department that the PMO went for all information and advice of substance—for policy, for anything requiring a sophisticated argument or documentation and for drafts or notes for speeches. The department is the great privilege of office. Who knows what you could do with it if half your life was not consumed by politics? Yet it was never the unmixed blessing it should have been.

In August 1992 a schoolgirl was murdered near her home at Bargo, south of Sydney. It was one of those murders which for a while haunts everyone who reads about it. When it happened I wrote in my diary that it felt as if the Prime Minister should write to the girl's parents. It was the kind of event which some political leaders in some political cultures would feel impelled to speak about for everyone's outraged feelings. However, Australia is not one of those political cultures, and the people are particularly sensitive to any indication that a politician is seeking political advantage from someone else's misfortune. Mass murder demands a response, but a single murder demands that politicians keep their distance. How does one choose between murders, and if murders, why not car accidents, why not all other tragedies which befall citizens?

The town where the girl was murdered lies beneath the flight path between Canberra and Sydney. Once or twice Paul Keating looked out the window of the plane and remarked that down there was where the girl had been murdered. As millions of other Australians must have when the murder occurred, we talked about how shocking it was and how the parents of the girl must feel.

Three years after the murder I was shown a letter to the girl's parents that had been written in the Department of Prime

Minister and Cabinet on behalf of the Prime Minister. It responded to a letter from friends of the family telling the Prime Minister that since the death of their daughter the parents had created an organisation to assist other victims of violent crimes, and asking him if he would be kind enough to write them a few lines of appreciation.

The Prime Minister had not seen the letter from the parents' friends or the one which had been drafted in reply. The reply was to be sent on his behalf, as so much correspondence inevitably is. I saw the letter because a PA in our office, Cheryl Griffiths, showed it to me. It was grotesque: it resembled a pro forma, opening with the usual formalities and maintaining an oppressive bureaucratic tone to the end. I wrote a new draft, gave it to the Prime Minister who added some thoughts of his own and signed it personally. Appalling as it was to think that the original letter might have reached the parents with the Prime Minister's signature stamped on it, even worse was the thought that nowhere in the Department of Prime Minister and Cabinet was there someone capable of responding adequately to a letter whose subjects were grief and courage. The department might reply that they are civil servants, not priests or counsellors, but this would only prove that between governments and ordinary human responses there is a gaping chasm, not that the chasm is unbridgeable or necessary.

Even in the darkest corners of his mind, George Orwell probably did not imagine prose like this: 'Given the within year and budget time flexibility accorded to the science agencies in the determination of resource allocation from within their global budget, a multi-parameter approach to maintaining the agencies budgets in real terms is not appropriate.' Singling out this 1995 sentence from the Department of Finance is not entirely fair to its anonymous author, because this is no more than a *specimen* of the standard language. Admittedly, it is drawn from the extreme end where economics overrides all other civilised rules and accomplishments, but it is an extreme example of a generally debased currency. In that forbidding building on the hill and others surrounding, people tacked verbal henhouses together all day long, and communicated with each other and the public as if they had trained at the school where policemen are taught how to speak to the media and give evidence in court.

Orwell insisted that the point about language was not 'frivolous': language that inhibits clear thinking was damaging because 'to think clearly is a necessary first step toward political regeneration'. To this we can add the regeneration of trust and understanding between the people and their governments, along with more and better ideas, extra efficiency, more sympathy, and more happiness. But not so long as we describe them as productivity improvements and other enhanced outcomes in real terms. Bureaucratic language tends naturally towards the bloodless, but that is not the same as dead or useless. Dead was how it came. Almost every draft speech and document from the departments arrived verbless, grey and hackneyed. In Orwell's words, it 'anaesthetises a portion of one's brain'. Often it felt like much more than a portion. The essential function of words in government is to keep intact the threads of common sensibility which join the people to their representatives and institutions. It is one of the failures of modern government, and one of its mysteries, that words so rarely do this. It is just as puzzling that governments seem unconcerned about it. That was another point that Orwell made: the process was 'easily reversible' if we would take the necessary trouble.

Modern democratic politicians use words for two main purposes—to simplify and to mystify. They simplify because they cannot describe matters in even half their complexity and expect to be understood or listened to. They use messages: simple one or two-line messages which they hope will work like semaphores as they beat their way through the tangle of political life. These messages take on a meaning independent of the complex reality, they become the currency of the debate, the story, in the end they become the reality itself; at least that is the aim. The terms 'setting the agenda', 'agenda setting' or 'seizing the agenda' in part describe this process. The other side of politics, of course, attempts to establish its own agenda. The government's message is: Take heart! We are nearly through! The Opposition counters: Despair! We are lost! Politicians are always trying to find the words which will stick. 'A nickname is the heaviest stone the devil can throw at a man,' said William Hazlitt, and described precisely what is meant when words are used to 'nail' a rival politician—'nail it to his forehead', as Paul Keating used to say. It is done in the hope that one's enemy thereafter will be branded and the public will interpret his every word and action in this light: he cannot be trusted, he is weak, he is a loser, and so on. The same effort is made to destroy his policies and his beliefs. It is a form of caricature or satire. This means it can be the distilled truth or an outrageous lie. It doesn't matter so long as the public believe it. Very often it is a matter of finding the words which describe otherwise inarticulate public sentiment. Then they can be very powerful, as the words 'five minutes of economic sunshine' were for John Howard when higher interest rates threatened early in 1995.

The art of obfuscation is no less important. Rival politicians are always demanding of each other that they say 'yes or no'. Journalists are always declaring that it is simple, surely: will you or won't you, did you or did you not, is it or isn't it? Sometimes politicians do not know the answer. Sometimes they do, but also know that uttering it is tantamount to sticking themselves with a knife there and then, or setting themselves up for a more horrible demise in a fortnight, or contradicting policy, the opinion polls or something a colleague said. However slippery you look, it is generally better to dodge, not least because the media will make you pay horribly if you choose any of the alternatives.

Inevitably, successful politicians develop forms of words which, combined with certain defiant inflections and gestures, enable them to retreat safely to the tangle without appearing to take a backward step. Truly skilled practitioners take the audience with them. Terms like 'At the end of the day', 'Look, Kerry, what it comes down to is . . .', 'Yes, but in terms of . . .', 'What you are saying is . . .', 'There are no quick fixes here . . .', 'I think the Australian people understand that . . .' have evolved to accommodate the near impossibility of answering half the questions they are asked. These of course are not really words at all: like the bureaucratic letter to the parents of the murdered child, they are substitutes for words, words without meaning. But they are the verbal currency of modern politics.

Like politicians at all times and in all places, modern politicians use symbols and slogans: a flag, a head on a stake, a battle cry from which the word 'slogan' comes—the Scots Gaelic *sluagh* for spirit or multitude, and *ganuin* for shout or cry. A slogan is a cry from the dead. At the end of every democratic term the competing parties distil all their belief and ambition to one slogan, and hope their policies will coalesce in some potent way around it. Yet the pressure of modern politics forces politicians to use verbal devices which are the equivalent of slogans every working day. The paradox is obvious: the more 'open' the democracy the more closed the language will become. The more extensive the media 'scrutiny' the more essential for politicians to find ways of hiding. The more the people seek an open dialogue the more essential it is for politicians to create a set of standardised responses: not to lie, but to keep an intractable truth at bay. Can anyone be expected to explain the details of every policy, the complexities of parliamentary procedure, or to explain the provenance of every unfolding story in a few seconds on talkback radio? The people want a satisfactory answer, and the media will murder you for not giving one. Politicians know they cannot throw their hands in the air and say: 'I haven't a clue. It surpasseth all understanding.' Instead they become adept at answers which sound satisfactory. They say: 'Well in respect of your first question, these things take time and they take commitment, time and commitment, but that doesn't mean we can afford to be complacent because we can't, but the government is committed to this and we're no less committed because these things take time.' More than any other word, 'commitment' defines the travesty of modern political language. It is used in corporate mission statements, official government publications and correspondence, political speeches and policy documents to suggest a solemn promise that something will be done. It is in fact a standard means of saying nothing. In his interview with Willesee, Bob Hawke said he was 'committed' to John Curtin. When they say they are committed to something it means neither that they believe it (if they do, why not say so?) nor that they will do it (if they will, why not do so?). It became a minor mission or obsession to root out 'commitment' from every speech, press release and policy document that came my way. I tried to do the same with the word 'enhance'. Did I dream or really see a document called 'Enhancing Australia'?

The fish stinks from the head down, Paul Keating was fond of saying; the so-called dumbing down of society probably begins where political power starts. Entire intellectual debates about the direction of society rage unnoticed. Scholarly treatises and essays are written on politicians and the political system. They may as well have been written about grasshoppers for all their influence on those who practise politics. Parliamentary debates rarely show much sign of the history and culture that once informed them—and, presumably, in some remote way still do. It is principally because of the media. The media determine the form and, very often, the subject of debate. It is because of the media—particularly because of the televising of parliament—that Question Time in the House is now seen as a window onto a despised breed. Televising them made politicians performers, as televising court cases does to judges and lawyers. That is why one of parliament's most celebrated performers, Paul Keating, was opposed to televising proceedings, why later he so often fulminated against Bob Hawke for allowing it. He knew it would reduce the parliamentary procedure to its essence, but only at the expense of other subtle and important functions. Given that so much of the political debate is about 'winning' the daily or weekly news, parliament needed shoring up against the tyranny of this populism, against the inevitable ignorance of nightly viewers and daily talkback hosts and audiences. Viewers do not understand the nature of the combat; they see it as real when it is theatre, and theatre when it is real. Reality itself they have no hope of seeing in short, carefully edited grabs; and with less and less understanding of the purpose and traditions of the place.

Paul Keating never read Elias Canetti but he knew his meaning when he said a modern parliament 'is all that is left of the original lethal clash'. It is the continuation of the civil war, but in a form of warfare which has renounced killing: '. . . it is played out in many forms, with threats, abuse and physical provocation which may lead to blows or missiles. But the counting of the vote ends the battle. It is assumed that 360 men would have defeated 240 . . .'

> Now no-one has ever really believed that the majority decision is necessarily the wiser one because it has received the greater number of votes. It is will against will as in war. Each is convinced that right and reason are on his side. Conviction comes easily and the purpose of a party is, precisely, to keep this will and conviction alive.

This very nearly precise description of Keating's view of parliamentary politics explains why he thought civilians should be kept at a safe distance. He would phone the responsible officials and complain about the creative camerawork. They were there to record the national parliament, not play at being Steven Spielberg. That was the nub of it. The more politics and the media merged, the more people competing in the arena, the less meaning the show would have. Politicians used to pour their more sophisticated ideas into second reading speeches and, if they were good, the media used to report them. Not any more. There was no drama in them. They could not pull focus. The media would make a great display of sharing the public's loathing of loud, vituperative Question Times; but you could not win in Question Time by being quiet and accommodating—and you couldn't win in the media. Indeed, whenever Keating drew back from the conflict and tried to maintain a statesmanlike posture for more than a couple of days the media would ask if he was not looking like a loser. Those who lamented the decline in standards, the contempt for tradition, the passing of the old Latin phrases and Burkean wisdom have only themselves to blame. They cannot expect the House to retain its dignity and traditions when those who have no understanding of either swarm all over the place like tourists at a foreign shrine. You can't have Latin and wit and mass media democracy.

In such a landscape a speechwriter might easily be a hedgehog—rarely seen and never heard, snuffling about like some relic of times when people spoke in complete sentences and philosophy and rhetoric mattered. If politics depended entirely on short grabs and appropriate gestures for the cameras, press releases, leaks, backgrounding and disingenuous conversations with the public, speechwriters would be well on the way to extinction. Speeches are neither economical nor reflexive: the meaning must be searched for, there is little chance of spontaneity or drama. And yet the speech retains its ritual function. It remains the principal means of flesh-to-flesh contact between the politician and the people; it is the best means of framing the philosophical dimensions of a policy and often it provides an opportunity to set a new direction, create a new story, nail an opponent or massage one's way out of a predicament.

A speech is a gesture towards order and respectability in a world which prizes spontaneity and tends towards chaos. In making speeches politicians are required to transform themselves from the political incarnates of ordinary people to performers. Performance does not come easily to everyone. Performance is also antithetical to that seductive element of the democratic culture which enjoins us to never get above the mass. Before they can teach, embolden or lead, politicians must in some degree pass up this democratic temptation to take refuge in the ordinary, including their own ordinary, albeit often constructed, selves. Speechmaking makes it harder to slum it. It demands that they take their vocation seriously; that they give up the laconic for the rhetorical, which is much riskier, and become defenders of the faith, harbingers of the new, the embodiment not of the ordinary but of the possible. Few politicians will do this wholeheartedly. By nature they are averse to risk and reading a speech risks their most precious possession—their credibility. Performance defies reality and reality is the thing politicians must have to trade. Their grasp of the reality of ordinary lives is their gravitas, their base lode. The very act of speechmaking threatens this grasp.

As a result, very often politicians shun the script and extemporise. Some even wait until they are on the podium to do it, believing that being seen to put the thing aside will show the audience that they reject artifice and are real like them. The same kind of thinking is at work when political leaders combine a prepared text with ad lib observations, jokes, asides and other spontaneous departures to prove they can think for themselves and on their feet. Even when it adds little or nothing to the meaning and coherence of the words, this spontaneity can create rapport between audience and speaker and greatly enliven an occasion. It is less successful when meaning and coherence are largely or completely destroyed. Sometimes it is better to give up trying to entertain the audience and just read the speech for the record. The record is the other essential function of the speech. Almost everything a prime minister says is recorded now. Doorstops, press conferences, media interviews, talkback radio, parliament—they are all taped and transcribed and released to the press. But these are fragments: a speech—even an unreported speech—is a whole thing, it is an artefact, a kind of proof that we have not submitted to modernity or barbarism.

Regardless of its content, the speech is of itself a civilised gesture. By simply turning up with the thing the political leader is showing respect—to a business group, a trade union, a welfare lobby, a gathering of old-age pensioners. Only rarely is the speech as important as the fact of his turning up to give it. That is another reason why there is no replacing speeches. Further proof of this ritual quality is contained in the reception of the words. The most eloquent rhetoric rarely draws more applause than the usual niceties, because these niceties are what people expect. That may be why we always put the clichés at the beginning: once the organisers and the audience have been thanked and praised, they can relax and stop listening, at least until the end when they will be thanked and praised again. And they go home happy, muttering to each other that he said all the right things. As for the speech's middle, a writer might spend several days and nights putting a complex argument in plain and arresting language and see the words no better received than the impenetrable sludge he has laboured to abolish. Only occasionally will an original form of words be noticed over a platitude. It ought to be one of the more valuable tasks a speechwriter can perform to force economic jargon into words laypeople might understand, to make the language lively and direct, but in truth it makes little difference. Certain classes of people will always complain about prolixity, jargon and buzz words. The press hardly ever do: perhaps they understand that it is the ritual that matters and not the confetti. They pay attention to the words or judge the quality of a speech only when the speech is the issue—an address to a foreign parliament, for instance, or a campaign launch. For the most part they listen for the key phrases and ritual obeisance and tick the boxes. We all learn to say 'Lest We Forget', but who remembers what we are in danger of forgetting? Who ever really knew?

Vaclav Havel, the Czech president and writer, describes how political leaders habitually employ comforting 'standardised' words that fail to describe actual experience. Havel comes from a very different political culture, but his observation applies equally to the modern Australian democracy. Much more than they did a generation ago, politicians (and bureaucrats and company executives) use words and phrases that not only leave truth untouched, but actually keep it at bay. Words are door sausages, stuffed into cracks to keep reality outside. In societies with much to live down 'standardised words' are an essential element in the social glue; with them myths are constructed, truth forgotten, traduced or consigned to a 'no go' area. In this country, terms like 'black armband history' achieve this sort of purpose; so do remarks like 'I don't think the Australian people want to sit around navel gazing about the past.' Both techniques—the nickname or slur, and the enlistment of popular prejudice, real or presumed—are available to politicians and their speechwriters every day. They are taken up in the interests of major historical denial relatively rarely, but on the newswaves every hour we hear the business of politics conducted in language just as slovenly and deceitful and with the same kind of result—namely the more we hear of it the less we remember what it once purported to describe. 'In terms of', 'This is a great country', 'This is a young country', 'The fair go', 'We have a commitment to the fair go', 'We are committed to enhancing the fair go in terms of social justice for everyone regardless of their social background'. These words work like a narcotic on the brain, like those kinds of dementia which empty the brain of memory and judgment. But they are the terms of intellectual exchange in politics and policy-making.

In a modern democracy, speechwriters can therefore make themselves useful by subverting this hideous language. It might be the best thing they can do. They do not need to be great or particularly expert writers, just conscientious.

While everything in a speech goes on the record, only a small part of it will ever become news. A good speech makes it easy for the press to decide which part that will be. Insofar as a speech is a vehicle for the preferred political story, the most quotable grabs must concern that story. They must sit prominently and discretely in the text and thus be easily grabbed. In extreme cases the media adviser may think it desirable to physically point them out to journalists. In a speech of more than twenty minutes it is often difficult to avoid related or topical issues that have the potential to complicate the message or compete with the preferred story. But avoid them one must. If the story is bacon you don't want people talking about eggs. They may seem inseparable from the argument, you might have a very good line about them, but it soon becomes clear that the more reasons you have for including them the more obviously they must be shunted off or buried.

At the core a speech is an embrace. A bad speech is a failed attempt at comfort, friendship or seduction and the speechmaker suffers an identical indignity. A good speech is a lover's embrace, or a brother's, father's, friend's or mother's depending on the circumstances. You want to sit on the metaphorical mountain and with an arm sneaking round their shoulder speak of things you have in common—your love of trees or cows, the sacrifice of soldiers, your loathing of tariffs or welfare. Test the water with a swipe at the supporting mother's benefit. If it proves impossible to match their dreams and dreads with yours, talk about the weather, the sky under which we all stand, the universal mystery of existence. And once we've found what grabs them, move on. To say it's an act of seduction suggests something more cynical than we intend—but it *is* very like it. We search for anything that suggests we are conjoined, that we're all in it together at some essential level, even if we have to go all the way back to the very *first* embrace where we all started. In fact if you can get back to that you can generally put it down as a successful excursion.

Speechwriters write speeches but politicians own them. If a speech sinks, the politician sinks with it. If it bores people, fails to inspire, if the jokes don't work, if it misjudges the audience, if the figures or anything else is wrong in fact, the politician suffers the consequences. A political leader *chooses* from the words the speechwriter has chosen: if he chooses all or half of them, it doesn't matter, the speech is his and never the writer's. This is as it should be. In any event, most speeches owe something—often a lot—to other minds.

When Paul Keating agreed to make a speech, a draft was generally requested from the relevant department. If not a draft, extensive notes. The next stage frequently involved the staff of the relevant minister, and the appropriate adviser in the Prime Minister's Office. The draft I wrote was usually very different from any draft sent me, partly because discussions with Russell, Ryan and sometimes the Prime Minister determined the politics of the speech, and partly because no-one can write a good speech without having the right to think independently. Many good ideas are only created out of the process of writing, and a good polemic requires the same freedom. It has to roll from the writer's head before it can roll from the speaker's mouth. It *is* a spoken art, ultimately, and most speeches I wrote began as sentences spoken aloud to myself.

Once I had a draft it was circulated among other advisers for the purpose of checking facts, the policy direction and the political focus. Would it give us the story we wanted? Was the message present in convenient, unmistakable, easily quoted form? Were there hidden clangers, rods with which to beat us, lines that might be misinterpreted because the phrasing was ambiguous or left itself open to a mischievous reading? The point at which Paul Keating was shown a draft depended on the importance of the occasion. He might see the first draft of a big policy speech. Some speeches he would read in the car on the way to deliver them. One line in a speech could determine for better or worse the political debate for a month or more. For this and other reasons, including the habits of the Prime Minister, big speeches were often corrected and reprinted and matched against the copy that was 'boxed' in the press gallery, even as the Prime Minister was putting on his coat and the plane was waiting half-loaded with staff on the tarmac at Fairbairn. It was also for this reason of course that the actual constituents in the audience were often a relatively minor consideration.

Of all our political expectations none is more remarkable or unfair than our insistence that our prime minister govern for all of us. We expect him to know what we, in all our myriad manifestations as citizens, are feeling—even when our feelings are at odds with what an equal number of our fellow citizens are feeling, or are inflamed beyond reason by false and misleading information, or the lack of information, or the comforts and irritations we receive from talkback radio hosts. We expect him to find wisdom in our perceptions, however false and ill-informed our perceptions may be. We expect him to know what we are needing; what we are going through; what we are hoping for; what we are uncertain about and sensitive to. We expect him to share and give voice to our aspirations. We demand that he barrack for us and our children and against our enemies, though they may be more necessitous than ourselves. We expect him to listen to us and yet to lead us; to obey our will and yet be leader enough to have a will of his own; to reflect our view and yet project his vision. It's a tall order, but one a prime minister had better be seen to obey. If he doesn't, they'll say he's out of touch—and to be told you're out of touch in the modern political environment is like being told that the sentence is death.

The language of national leadership, like the concept of the nation itself, asks us to make a huge empirical leap. It asks us to set aside everything we have learned from birth, including every prejudice; everything we know to be true about human nature and the nature of societies; all that is obvious about social and political boundaries; and speak as if words can defy history, culture and reason and persuade us that we are—to coin a phrase—one nation. That is the essential project for a prime minister's speech-writer.

John Maynard Keynes said that he took up economics because it suited a man who had an artist's temperament but not his facility. It is difficult not to liken this to Keating, whose temperament was similar and who, more than Keynes, treated economics as an art form. Let us say that Paul Keating was temperamentally an artist, and the artist is the archetype of every individual's struggle to protect the 'true self' against the world. Therein perhaps lies the key to Keating's puzzle (and the dilemma of everyone who worked with him)—what the psychologist, D.W. Winnicott, identified as 'the co-existence of two trends, the urgent need to communicate and the still more urgent need not to be found'. Nothing could quickly dislodge him from the refuge once he was in it, nothing could persuade him that he ought to reduce the amount of time he spent there. It was a need as basic as eating, a right as inviolable as religion. It had been those old English maga-zines and Chopin and Beethoven in the lead-lined room at Condell Park. At the Lodge it was Christie's catalogues, Mahler, Copland, Richard Strauss. And his other remarkable, beautiful objects. And his wife and his family.

Paul Keating's happiness was built around his wife, Annita.

It is not true to say he put her on a pedestal—to say that he put her on a column of ivory with a frieze of diamond-crusted acanthus leaves is nearer the mark. She was his treasure, his prize, his fortune. He had charmed her in flight, pursued her around the world, won her and taken her back to his castle and his clan. He would never talk about Annita as he talked about the antiques which he also brought back, but sometimes when he talked about antiques he might have been talking about something more animate than a clock. 'Most people catch antiques in the zoo, but I like to catch them in the wild,' he once said.

His marriage was a love affair from beginning to end. It had not a trace of convenience, compromise or doubt. Those things that plague the modern marriage—which have always plagued marriage—were unknown to him. She was his golden-haired exotic beauty. He called her Dutchy, because she was Dutch. They had four children who she raised in the old-fashioned way, sharing his belief that they must all have a 'real' childhood beyond the reach of his public life and the world of adults. She was a traditional mother. He was a traditional—antediluvian by some lights—father: soft, caring and, although he told journalists that he used to buy the birdseed for the family, completely immune to the domestic duty of modern men. He was frequently away. He brought work and colleagues home. He spent weekends on the telephone, and reading and clipping the week's newspapers. And when he was not doing that he was listening to his records, or hunting for antiques or browsing in his Christie's catalogue. And Annita was always there for him. With Annita he lived as he had as a child and adolescent, assured of unqualified love and approval.

Those like Mark Ryan, who helped in the overthrow of Hawke, say that Paul Keating frequently seemed more concerned with renovating his house in Elizabeth Bay, or leaving politics and making a fortune from the piggery in which he had bought a half share, or refashioning the career of Geoffrey Tozer, the concert pianist. They felt sometimes that they were more interested in getting him into the job than he was. It might have been because he felt the world had been corrupted by Hawke's breach of faith, and that he would be a metaphorical prince on a dunghill. He almost certainly wondered if it was wise or worth his time to pursue a job that he was likely to lose within a year. Yet as prime minister, with Hawke no longer an issue, he sent the same conflicting signals. In conversation he would sulkily retreat from goals he most desired, or values he professed most avidly and which he knew his advisers shared. In total contradiction of everything he professed in the Placido Domingo speech, he would rail against the whole idea of leadership, usually when leadership was demanded of him. He would play the delinquent stricken with ennui; he would slide low in his chair like James Dean in *East of Eden* and say the leadership thing wasn't worth a crumpet. He would stare at an antique chair in a Christie's catalogue and tell you that nothing had excited him as much in the previous month as the austere beauty of that object. To the whole most sought after thing he would affect *belle indifférence*. To his father figures he was invariably the good son, the avenging warrior and hero. But what we saw sometimes was the antihero, the rebel without a cause, the son looking for somewhere to hide. It was alternately very funny and very trying. Throughout the first year in the Lodge his attitude and behaviour provoked sporadic outbursts of anger and amazement. A week from the 1993 election the former Hawke adviser, Peter Barron, snarled down the phone to me that when it was over Labor people would come after him asking why he had taken the leadership from the most popular prime minister in the country's history if he didn't want it. At the time it seemed a reasonably good question.

Paul Keating was always paradoxical. He was gentle in one environment, savage in another; energetic and focused one day, the next inert and remote; contrary when agreement was an easier and more sensible course, reasonable and conciliatory when he might easily have been provoked. There was also something compulsive about his behaviour. He would behave destructively for no apparent reason, other than that no-one was looking, or too many people were demanding that he behave well. There was at once an obsession with order and perfection and a desire to create chaos. He would do things which were bound to hurt himself and frequently others. He would be late for no good reason. He would make a metaphorical mess and expect others to clean it up for him. And he would also go to inordinate lengths to save someone from hurt, apply uncanny commonsense to the most vexing problems, act with prodigious efficiency and dispatch, be a joy to be around. Paul Keating is a kind, charming and very intelligent man who would risk his own life to save yours or to get an unwanted crease out of his trousers.

Sometimes he seemed like a man who believed the world was disintegrating and it was his lonely desperate task to try to hold it together. And there were times when he seemed to say: this has all become too predictable, unleash the dogs, let all hell break loose. He sat behind a desk elbow-deep in a confusion of newspapers, documents, press releases, things that had been put there five minutes ago and things from months before—and he would be splendidly, meticulously dressed. And he would take out his big Mont Blanc fountain pen, and screw off its lid, and screw the cap off the ink and fill the pen carefully, and wipe the nib with blotting paper, and screw the cap back on the pen, and the lid back on the ink, and he'd read the letter again, and then he would sign P.J. Keating in copperplate so large and elaborate that, unravelled, it must have stretched for half a metre. And he would apply the blotting paper.

Something in Paul Keating's life had created these contradictory impulses. The paradox might have been nothing more than a reflection of what he grew up with—the paradox of a 'soft' father and a 'hard' mother, or at least one who was always ambitious for her son. All that love may have been more conditional than it seemed—being, paradoxically, love and ambition at the same time. Perhaps he had once hoped the prime ministership would resolve these things and could not always hide the despair he felt when it did not. A psychologist might say the unstinting approval of his mother and family kept alive in him the competing senses of omnipotence and threatening annihilation that the child experiences. So Keating would periodically annihilate his environment in a pre-emptive strike against the threat it posed, return to the warm centre and contemplate, say, the comfortingly pure lines of a Second Empire clock or a Palladian building. The quiet of the neoclassical follows the clamour of the revolution. Yet this interpretation suggests an absence of calculation or consciousness, when to be around Keating was to have the opposite sense. His moods shifted, logic might desert him, but one always sensed his mind working.

Paul Keating often seemed melancholy. Melancholy is grief and longing associated with loss of some kind, but the melancholic is unaware of what the loss has been. Melancholy attacks the ego, empties it, crushes it, leaving the sufferer feeling worthless and abandoned. It may be that Keating only seemed melancholic. It may be that he was mourning. Where melancholy empties the person experiencing it, mourning empties the mourner's world, leaving it like an abandoned house. Very often that was how Paul Keating seemed to feel, without knowing why or even knowing that he was feeling it. They are very common sensations and not usually impossible obstacles to normal life. But the condition empties one of energy and purpose. It is like struggling through a thick fog in lead boots. It was frequently the way with Paul Keating and sometimes it became like this for those who served him. Depression or exhaustion, melancholy or mourning; whatever it was, it seemed to come and go and come again. It goes without saying that the Australian public saw the symptoms but were as oblivious to their cause as very often he seemed to be.

Paul Keating gave his first nationally televised address as prime minister at a breakfast on Australia Day 1992. He read my speech in a marquee just across the fence from his new Sydney residence in Kirribilli. Admiralty House, the governor-general's Sydney home, has Australia's best front garden with a sparkling view across the water to Circular Quay, the Opera House and the Harbour Bridge. Yachts and windsurfers race here and there, ferries chug up and down, tugboats, barges, colossal tankers—all in sight of the spot where European settlement began and no scene in Australia speaks more eloquently of the bounty.

The guests sluiced down their cantaloupes and eggs with champagne and orange juice, waiters rattled the crockery, wind creaked in the canvas. 'Few eras have been so uncertain—or so promising,' the Prime Minister said. Australia must be strong enough and independent enough to prosper in the age unfolding and play a useful part in it. 'In one sense we have never been so alone,' he said, 'in another we have never been so much a part of the world.' If they had not occurred at the astonishing speed of the recent global upheaval, the changes in Australia had 'been just as profound'. Deregulation of the economy, the new attitude to Asia and the development of a multicultural society were creating a new, more vigorous Australia in a fluid international environment. Change was essential, and by changing, Australians had proved their capacity to flourish in the new order. The Prime Minister, the architect of so much change, spared a moment to reflect on the unchanging things in the nation's life and the people who believed in them and in their characters personified them. He wondered if many 'older' Australians did not fear for the traditions of their country and the values for which they had worked and fought. He meant his father's generation, the Australians of his childhood who were now not so enthusiastic about cultural diversity and globalisation; who didn't quite see the link between their values and current ones despite what politicians liked to say, who felt that they experienced reality at a great remove from that which politicians and the media described, who saw in contemporary Australia few signs of the country they had imagined in their youth. The lines were directed at the disenchanted on both sides of politics. They might have been spoken to Paul Keating's parents or to his speech-writer's, none of whom were familiar with the view from Admiralty House. 'I suspect there are many Australians who are wondering if *their* Australia will survive the changes—if there will be a place for the "old Australia" in the new,' he said. He could only answer the question by saying that there was no other way to preserve Australia's character and best traditions than to remake the nation. Much of the 'old Australia' had been born in that 'great flowering of the Australian spirit', the last decade of the last century; the new Australia could be born in this one, he firmly believed. But old and new had to find common ground and common purpose.

Like life and death, no-one can say why some words take root and some blow away in the wind, but it depends a lot on the media. The speech disappeared with the breakfast plates and was never heard of again. It was far from a manifesto, but the 1992 Australia Day address in the governor-general's front garden on the shores of the harbour in the city of the elites stands as both a useful summary of the Keating Government's philosophy and ambitions and a prologue which, we can see now, half anticipates its own doom.

CHAPTER 3

'The horror of the moment,' the King went on, 'I shall never forget.'

'You will, though,' the Queen said, 'if you don't make a memorandum of it.'

LEWIS CARROLL, THROUGH THE LOOKING GLASS

NO SOONER HAD Paul Keating been sworn in than George Bush turned up in Sydney. When he agreed to be the first US president in twenty-five years to visit his country's faithful ally, Bush thought his friend Bob Hawke would greet him at the airport. Hawke no doubt thought so too and, having provided enthusiastic Australian assistance in the recent war against Iraq, he surely expected it to be an occasion of some warmth. Hawke might have been conscious of a certain gratifying historical symmetry: he would be confirming the renewal of an alliance forged in World War II by his spiritual father, John Curtin. In everything but the domestic arena the times were perfect for Hawke: a world in transition but seeming to move in the direction he preferred, away from ideology and towards consensus. He was ripe for the role of elder statesman. He and George might have played a round of golf together, and generally conducted affairs in what Keating called in his speech of welcome to the President, 'the warm fog of sentimentality that swirls around the [Australia–US] relationship on these occasions'.

It must have been galling for Hawke to see Keating waiting to welcome Bush and take him to Kirribilli House where, the policemen told us, brown patches at the top of the lawn were scars from eight years of a relentlessly practised golf swing. It was impossible not to imagine him glistening brown, bare-legged and bare-chested, frolicking on the green sward that runs down to the harbour, waving to the tourist ferries that sailed by hoping for a glimpse. The new incumbent, in dark suit or reefer jacket, liked to stay in the shadows of the verandah.

It is easy to forget, but 1991 was a stupendous year. It began with Desert Storm and ended with the establishment of the Commonwealth of Independent States (CIS) where the old Soviet Union had been. People spoke of a 'new world order', but apart from being very different from the old one, no-one knew what it was. The coalition of nations which Bush had put together for the Gulf War seemed to be one manifestation of it, along with a United Nations of renewed purpose, a new spirit of cooperation among the well-behaved nations. The division of the Cold War would be replaced by cooperation, hostility by mutual goodwill, ideology by general agreement on free-market economics and its natural political bedfellow, liberal democracy. Of the many hopes abounding at the time, nuclear disarmament seemed a possibility, along with international efforts to arrest the spread of environmental pollution, and perhaps there would be a cultural dividend: the collapse or weakening of nation states might liberate the cultures they had overwhelmed, recreating pre-industrial, even ancient patterns of self-governance and expression.

The annihilation of Iraq's army notwithstanding, by the end of 1991 no-one confused Operation Desert Storm with the New World Order. Indeed, by then people were speaking of a retreat to tribalism and savagery as nations broke up and old boundaries fell away. The distinctly medieval figure of Boris Yeltsin standing on a tank outside the Russian parliament to defend the future against the past had been a portent of the confusion. New rogues emerged from the rubble. Yugoslavia broke up. Chechnya would soon be a bloodbath. Somalia. Rwanda. Whatever the new order turned out to be, peace and harmony would not be the hallmark, no matter how much cooperation the US could extract from like-minded countries. Nor was the combination of firepower and virtue always going to triumph. Saddam's army was obliterated with high technology, but Saddam remained in his castle.

Less startling, but no less definitive, the information revolution accelerated at a rate invisible to the public eye. The World Wide Web was created in 1991. Sometime in 1992 a delegation came to the Prime Minister's Office to demonstrate its marvels. Outside the cabinet room, preliminary to a lecture on the potential of IT and the imperatives it set for government, a young man offered a teaser. He showed how in a matter of seconds he could call up documents from the innards of the Library of Congress in Washington. We watched only half-believing as a letter appeared on the screen. It was a letter from the Soviet Archives, from Lenin to some Civil War Bolshevik commander coolly authorising the execution of several kulaks. We were as Lorenzo de Medici might have been when Leonardo brought him a design for a helicopter. The information revolution did not stop to make such historical comparisons, and just as well perhaps. 'I don't know much about this Lenin character,' said the young man, 'but he didn't like those kulaks.'

Globalisation was an older phenomenon and better known and understood, though no-one could say where it was taking us. Economic reform in the 1980s went hand in hand with the emerging global economy. In 1991 there were plenty on both sides of politics who loathed what had been done in globalisation's name. With financial deregulation, lowered tariff walls and a free-floating dollar there was a widespread sense that the country had lost control of its destiny. This was a tolerable notion only so long as the economy boomed. When they applied the monetary brakes to haul the current account deficit into line and threw the country into deep recession, the old line about opening the country up to the world and its new opportunities did not meet with much enthusiasm. No line did really.

For the Keating Government the reforms were inescapable—as inescapable as the reality of globalisation. Between 1985 and 1994 the share of world trade in the international economy rose three times faster than between 1975 and 1985, a third of it *within* transnational companies. The bulk of this trade comprised parts and components moving across national borders for assembly into end products. In roughly the same period direct investment abroad trebled. In the face of this it is hard to see how Australia's Labor Government could have kept the financial parapets up, or why it would want to. At the same time the economies of East Asia, growing at 8 per cent or more each year, were bringing their barriers down and becoming significant players in global trade. In 1991 these economies were in the midst of a miracle, growing at twice the global average, doubling per capita income every ten years—a feat which took fifty years in Britain and the United States during their industrial revolutions. It was widely believed that the next century would be an Asian century. When people talked about how to do business in 1991 they talked about the way the Japanese did it. Some said they did it unfairly or corruptly, but no-one then was saying that they did it ineffectively; no-one was predicting that the Japanese economy would stall for a decade. Rather more people were predicting the decline of the United States, already outgunned by Japan and destined, they reckoned, to be overwhelmed by China as well.

While Asia rattled along at this phenomenal rate, most of the developed world was either mired in recession or precariously balanced on the edge of it. Accompanied by a group of American businesspeople, along with the 475 officials and more than 400 media who had followed him to Australia, George Bush went on to Japan. He went echoing the anti-Japanese sentiments of the American people, growling about the trade balance, closed Japanese beef and rice markets and what the Americans saw as a miserly Japanese response to the Gulf War. He came away amid images of the President of the United States gagging into a table-cloth at an official dinner while his Japanese hosts watched in polite bemusement. It was easy to see the awful incident as a symbol of America's fall. With hindsight, however, it might have been a portent of what the US would soon do to its rivals. The

Americans would run away with the information revolution and with the global economy and ride them into the next millennium more powerful than any country has ever been.

In the end it would be America's decade, but the fact remained, as Paul Keating never tired of saying, two-thirds of Australia's exports went to Asia. Australian coal and iron ore had been to the industrialisation of Japan and Korea what Australian wool had been to British textile mills. The preferred term is 'complementarity of interests'—our minerals and agriculture for their development needs. And as they reached new stages of development we had to discover new 'complementarities'.

Commodities remained a staple of the trade with Asia, but over the previous ten years the growth was twice as fast in exports of manufactures and services. Keating would tell the story again and again. And, a further symbol of Australia's break with its commodity-dependent past and the evolution of a sophisticated economy, ETMs—elaborately transformed manufactures—made up an increasing portion of the trade. 'You used to think of us as suppliers of wool, wheat, meat, metals and ores, but now we're selling you bionic ears and systems of traffic management,' he would tell politely listening businessmen at lunches in Tokyo and Seoul and Singapore. We weren't selling all that *many* bionic ears or traffic management systems, but the point was worth making, and not just in Asia.

Australia's future *was* tied up in the region. Australians had known this, after a fashion, for a long while. It had been a mantra of one kind or another since World War II. The economic dimension of the relationship had been well understood since the trade treaty with Japan stirred up so much acrimony in the early fifties. Then we began selling wool to China, the country we feared and loathed and whose government we refused to recognise. Our future in the region loomed largest in our minds when the economic met the geopolitical or xenophobic, when it met in the realms of paradox and irony. In the eighties we welcomed Japanese tourists in precisely that spirit. What Australians had not done was embrace the fact that their country's relationships with the Asian economies would crucially and inescapably determine its future, and that no-one but Australians could determine the nature of those relationships. These things were understood, but not as matters of urgency, not as issues immediately requiring policy and resolution. In December 1991, Keating himself had not entirely apprehended the dimensions of the challenge. It was not yet part of the economic story he had dedicated himself to writing. It became so very quickly and the meetings with George Bush were the catalyst for change.

When Paul Keating sat down with George Bush at Kirribilli House he had been briefed by officials of the Department of Foreign Affairs and Trade and by Ashton Calvert. Two or three years earlier, when Keating was positioning himself for the leadership, Bob Hawke had advised him to 'broaden' himself. Foreign Affairs had been a ministerial option for him. He refused, he said later, because he wanted to keep his hands on the economic levers, and in any event Gareth Evans had proven himself an exceptional minister. Keating had only ever been treasurer, and Calvert had reason to think he would need intensive coaching in a game which was not, by Treasury lights, the main one. Calvert, an astute, punctilious professional of undisguised ambition and a streak of zeal, might have had more reason for concern after Keating made an uncertain speech of welcome to Bush in Canberra. I did not see it, but my father did and said he wished he hadn't. The words he used were 'pathetic' and 'embarrassing'. It was not what Paul Keating had said, but the uncertain manner in which he said it that led Mark Ryan to persuade the new PM and his advisers to employ a speechwriter.

If the performance was not his finest, there were, nonetheless, some clues to Keating's thinking in that speech, and a couple of themes which would soon become familiar. He made the point that Australians and Americans had both inherited continents, the 'gift outright' as the American poet Robert Frost called it. '[A]t first we were still England's colonials. In time we gave ourselves to our new countries and the people and the land became one,' Frost wrote. There was in there an echo of Henry Lawson declaring that

Australians must choose 'between the old dead tree and the young tree green'. Lawson's line was a favourite of Manning Clark's, and its inclusion in the speech may owe something to the days when Keating was prime minister in waiting and occasionally visited the Clarks at their home in Canberra's Tasmania Circle to talk and listen to music. When many liberal intellectuals in the eighties held Keating in suspicion or loathing, Manning Clark found him intriguing. He told me that Keating was a man with a soul.

Those quotations in his welcome speech to Bush were not declared by journalists to be republican in sympathy or a politically contrived diversion from the main game. It is likely the media thought they were just the sort of words that political leaders were prone to use when welcoming other political leaders—words as tribute or exchange, when the language of the 'main game' was not appropriate. Civilised words. Though not the central theme of the speech, they were more than idle thoughts. For the same sentiments reappeared not only in debates he later sparked about the republic and the flag and Australian history and the wars, but also in social policy, in his efforts for the arts, in trying to remake relations with Aboriginal Australia, in the embrace of new technology, and indeed in foreign and economic policy. It was all there in that hesitant first speech, delivered several weeks before his office was infiltrated by flaky social policy advisers and a bolshie speechwriter without a degree in economics who were blamed for later doctrinal lapses.

The substance of Keating's speech was trade. He raised the matter of the US Export Enhancement Programs (EEPs) which so irritated Australian farmers, and he arranged for the farmers to meet the President. He stressed the importance of the General Agreement on Tariffs and Trade (GATT) in this new world after the Cold War. The GATT was the main hope for providing the framework the world needed: 'a framework for . . . countries re-entering the world economy for the first time in either half a century or most of a century'. He had in mind 'an institutional framework of a Bretton Woods style but in trade'. The GATT demanded leadership of the Bretton Woods kind, but as Keating said in an interview in 1992, the world was lacking leadership. The world needed leaders 'big enough to match the moment', but instead it was drifting back to the world of 1914.

The Uruguay Round of the GATT had gone on and on, and it would continue for another three years. Some of us imagined the delegates sweating it out in Uruguay, but the meeting was held in Geneva. Every time the Prime Minister addressed a foreign audience he was obliged to express his hope that the 'Uruguay Round of the GATT will reach a successful resolution'. It was like a prayer. There was good reason to pray: the negotiations of the Uruguay Round were aimed at adding agriculture to the liberalised GATT regime for manufactured exports. The developing countries had a profound interest in the outcome. Someone made the point by calculating that the annual subsidy of a French cow was a little more than the annual wage of a worker in a developing country. Australia had an equally profound interest because, despite the trend towards manufactures and services, it resembled a developing country in its reliance on commodities as a component of its exports. Highly efficient Australian farmers, and less efficient Indonesian or Malaysian farmers, had in common the need to reform a market for agricultural produce corrupted by massive European subsidies, retaliatory American EEPs, and Japanese whose embargoes on imported rice matched the French in defining the point at which the liberal 'new world order' transgressed the sovereign assumptions of the old nation state. With some justification, the French wanted to keep their traditional peasantry alive, and off the streets of Paris. Quite understandably, the Japanese wanted to keep traditional Japanese rice growers on their tiny plots of land to preserve the national culture, the strain and purity of their rice, the country's food staple, and their traditional vote for the ruling LDP.

The Uruguay Round *was* big picture; it was a central issue in the evolution of the new world order. It was also the main conduit by which Australia found a role for itself in making this new order. The GATT focused Australian minds on the potential of multilateralism: on combining with like interests, however culturally or historically diverse, to gain benefits which could never be achieved by Australia acting alone. It was at the instigation of the Australian Government in 1986 that the Cairns Group was formed. Countries from Asia, South America and Eastern Europe formed a coalition within the GATT to lobby for a new deal in agriculture. When, in December 1993, the GATT delivered, the deal for Australia was worth about $5 billion in exports. For world trade the OECD estimated the increase in activity would exceed $400 billion.

The Cairns Group yielded more than dollars. It proved the benefits of multilateralism, and the potential for a small country like Australia to have some say in the shape of the New World Order. At the same time it proved Australia's capacity to tread creatively with the Asian countries on common ground. It demonstrated the benefits of an approach to Asia that was new in conception and unprecedented in intensity. The same motivation led Paul Keating to vigorously pursue the Asia–Pacific Economic Cooperation forum (APEC) and much else in the name of the Keating doctrine that Australia should seek its future security '*in* Asia, not *from* Asia'.

The new prime minister was very keen on foreign policy—keener indeed than on some other things his advisers would have liked him to be keen on. Many prime ministers are attracted to foreign policy but not all of them are as good at it as Keating was. It was not that he liked the travel. He was forever trying to shorten trips and limit the number of countries he visited. But he brought a talent to it which immediately impressed Calvert, and went on impressing those who watched him work over the next four years. When the Prime Minister had finished laying out his views to Bush and Brent Scowcroft at Kirribilli, Scowcroft said he had never heard an American describe American interests so well. Keating thrived in the foreign policy environment and seemed happier there than in any domestic role. Characteristically, he saw it as an extension of his work as treasurer and as an opportunity to extend the reach of those achievements. Australia's economic fortunes would be determined by events in the wider world. The relationships Australia established with the world were therefore crucial. Most crucial of all was the relationship with the booming Asian economies. And with the end of the Cold War, the *opportunity* was there. It had all the elements needed to excite his imagination, test his mettle, bring out the best in him.

Keating liked the clash of armies: he was a politician of the older kind, not embarrassed or frightened by power any more than a financier is embarrassed or frightened by money or a dentist by teeth. Power is the currency of politics, the reason for it, the stock in trade. Power was his creative medium. He was never more at home than in its company. His knowledge of history, including Australian history, was not particularly wide or great. He did not share the curious fascination of many of his Labor colleagues with the American Civil War. But history was a serious interest which could always be aroused and he had a powerful sense of its machinery and direction—the energy in it. The key to his curiosity was his awareness of the calamitous price of failure in policy and leadership. He liked the twentieth century: Barbara Tuchman on the outbreak of war in 1914; William Manchester's biography of Churchill.

Unlike some of his colleagues, Paul Keating was not prone to recite the names and dates of battles. He seemed less intrigued by what happened in the two World Wars than by what was not done to prevent them and subsequent wars occurring. He admired Churchill for trying to wake up Britain and the British Conservative Party to the menace of Hitler. Joseph Chamberlain, the earlier Chamberlain, who said that 'commerce is the greatest of all political interests', he admired for his understanding of power and the clarity of his vision. Joseph Chamberlain was a 'star', but as usual there were not enough like him.

Deep in Keating's mind resided a belief that the worst things happen not because of what the villains do, but what the non-villains fail to do to stop them. The villains, after all, are a given, like snakes and wolves and stinging nettles. They lurk in nature. That is one reason why idealists, moralists and liberals so often found Keating distasteful: he was not disposed to see such a very great distinction between evil-doers and do-gooders. It is probably the Catholic in him. Keating's ancestry bypasses the debate about man's perfectibility, liberalism and most everything else that came out of the Enlightenment. He came to the Labor Party not through Karl Marx or Tom Mann or even Jack Lang, but through the Catholic Church. As he told Bob Geldof in an interview in 1992, and again in 1994 at a huge gathering in a hall on the west coast of Ireland from whence came his ancestors: 'Catholicism gives you the view that we were born equally and we die equally and that no one of us is intrinsically worth more than the other.' Keating does not go back to Rousseau but to Richelieu; not to Cook but to de Quiros; not to Drake but to the Spaniards of the Armada. When Arthur Phillip was planting the Union Jack at Circular Quay, Keating had at least one foot on the deck of La Pérouse's ship anchored outside the Sydney heads. He is a pre-Vatican II Bankstown tyke. Wholly secure in faith and family, he was made for fearless adventure. A parallel may be seen in his scheme for Australia: secure and strong in its domestic life, the cords of affection all wrapped around, the nation could boldly go abroad. Like Vasco da Gama. The notion of 'openness' as the guiding principle of Australian economic and foreign policy was by no means an exclusively Keating idea, but psychologically no-one was better suited to pursue it. The phrase 'phobia free' is typical in mixing far-sighted policy with a bit of derring-do.

There had always been a sense of threat in Australian attitudes to Asia: a race threat, a communist threat, more recently an economic threat. Threat was one of the progenitors of the Commonwealth. It showed in the offspring: the Federation comprised both notions of the nation state—the political and the 'ethnic'. The first, deriving from the Enlightenment, gave us the national parliament, the constitution and the laws. The second, derived from a collective racial and cultural identity coupled with an understandable sense of isolation and peril, gave us (in whole or part) the White Australia policy, the navy, the continuing

emotional and institutional attachment to Britain and the dis-
enfranchisement of Aborigines. Public enthusiasm for the visiting
American Fleet—the Great White Fleet—in 1908 was another
measure of the new nation's state of mind. Throughout the
century Australia sought the protection of great powers, and went
to war in large part to earn that protection. Ever since the men
and women of the First Fleet had huddled in Sydney Cove
awaiting the arrival of supplies, European Australians lived in
dread of abandonment, the day when there could be no denying
that they were on their own. Now that day had come, and Paul
Keating thought it was a *great* day. The possibility of engineering
a new set of relationships for Australia, new institutions and structures and a whole new regional environment for the twenty-first
century constituted an irresistible challenge. It promised adventure of a kind that he could no longer find in domestic politics.

Keating's thinking about these issues would travel a long way
in the next twelve months, but with Bush he proposed some of the
bases. He stressed Australia's interest in multilateral institutional
structures in the Asia-Pacific, as opposed to Bush's expressed preference for a security framework in which Washington was the 'hub'
and the 'spokes' were a series of bilateral treaties with its friends in
the region. Keating wanted to keep the US in the neighbourhood,
but he did not want Australia to be either a spoke of American
policy or a cheerleader. He wanted collective dialogue in the region,
and he wanted Australia involved in it. He expressed the view that
the US should not fear 'negotiations between countries in the Asia-
Pacific which were not conducted through Washington', which was
to say, not along the lines of the 'hub and spokes' model. He said they
should take a more 'relaxed' and favourable view of the multilateral
dialogues emerging in the region, whether ASEAN or APEC.
Australia's trade and Australia's security—Australia's future, in other
words—lay with Asia. Australia's interests therefore lay in developing
economic and strategic partnerships with the region. US interests lay
not in suspicion or retreat to any form of isolationism, but in
engagement. This was the logic of the post-Cold War world in the
Asia-Pacific.

The idea of regular heads of government meetings in the Asia-Pacific had come from Allan Gyngell. A reserved, ironic, astute professional of wider interests and a loathing of sport and jingoism, Gyngell was then head of the International Division of DFAT. He had been provoked by two weeks in Zimbabwe at a Commonwealth Heads of Government Meeting (CHOGM) with Bob Hawke. Gyngell thought it absurd that so much of an Australian prime minister's time and attention went into CHOGM and the South Pacific Forum while the heads of government of the countries of Asia and the Pacific had no institutionalised means of meeting. He thought it 'distorted' Australian foreign policy. APEC he considered a possible vehicle for the meetings, but he believed the 'Three Chinas' might present too great an obstacle. Keating seized on his idea, and on APEC as the vehicle. APEC was built on the concept of the Asia-Pacific, on the notion that the United States would and should always be a major player. Keating believed in this emphatically. Better to bring the US in from the start and embed it in whatever structures and institutions evolved. Thus he suggested to Bush that the United States might consider an APEC heads of government meeting. It would signal a new era in the Asia-Pacific, an entirely new approach to the conundrums of its future. It was a very bold suggestion, and if Bush said he'd take it on board it is possible he didn't mean to.

The old order was dead, the new was waiting to be born. In the interregnum, as Antonio Gramsci said in a different context, all sorts of curious aberrations appear. Not that these things are much noticed at the time. On the first day of 1992 the new prime minister might have explained it to the people: the Cold War was over, and history possibly at an end. The international situation was, as DFAT liked to say, 'very fluid'. A technological revolution was about to overthrow our way of life and replace it with something we could not yet discern. Our future depended on how we coped with this, and with the challenge of a global economy emerging with unstoppable force. It depended on how well we remade ourselves in the region, and how well the region could be made. These were the goals, and of course a satisfactory conclusion to the Uruguay Round of the GATT. Had he said this, a dozen and a half DFAT officials and a couple of the better informed journalists might have clapped. And when they stopped, the silence would have resumed with still greater menace. There was a recession. That was all that mattered.

Nine hundred thousand people who wanted work could not get work. Countless people had lost their businesses and their savings and the product of half a lifetime's work. They had invested in their own future, believing that theirs and the country's were as one; believing, essentially, what the government and all the other agents of influence had told them they should believe. Go for it! Use your initiative! And what had the government done? They put interest rates up to 17 per cent or more. They tightened monetary policy so hard they heard it 'snap' in the treasurer's office. Asset prices had been absurdly inflated, but when they fell just about everything else fell with them. The new Prime Minister was prone to say that at least the spivs had been cleaned out and the 'inflation stick' was broken, as if the medicine was appropriate to the disease. For twelve months, government, Treasury and the Reserve Bank kept the noose tight to prevent the outbreak of an inflationary boom. And when they loosened it ever so slightly, they still recoiled from the idea of fiscal stimulus, in case it caused 'overheating'. Sometimes it was as if they were the only ones in the whole country who did not know that the economy remained cold, insensible and almost beyond the reach of monetary, fiscal or any other ministration. The spivs and speculators might have been cleaned out, but so were a lot of other people. And with them went much goodwill towards the government.

Not without reason. Having steered the country away from recession or worse after the 1987 stock market crash, the Hawke Government found itself with an economy roaring out of control. Imports flooded in, the current account deficit ballooned. There was talk of a wage break-out. The pressure mounted to hike interest rates and in 1989 that was what happened. Just who was doing it and who decided to keep them hiked—the Treasurer,

Treasury or the Reserve Bank—is not as clear as one might expect, given the decisions were in the hands of the same trusted circle Keating had always worked with. Don Russell said Treasury were the most inclined to keep rates up. In Treasury Chris Higgins, David Morgan and Ted Evans were monetary hawks; at the Reserve Bank, Bernie Fraser, and before him Bob Johnston, were doves but under hawkish pressure. Paul Keating and Don Russell were trying to stop the political and economic cycles from getting out of kilter, the left from going wobbly, and the right— principally in the shape of the Minister for Finance, Peter Walsh— from quitting in disgust. They were therefore required to be dovish and hawkish at the same time. What is certain is that between the 1987 crash and the 1990 election none of them— Hawke or Keating, Reserve Bank or Treasury—picked the direction of the economy. First they failed to pick the post-crash boom, and then they didn't see the bust in time. Equally, no-one had foreseen quite what deregulation meant; how in the scramble for a share of the market the banks would lend recklessly, asset prices would inflate, the crooks would multiply—and the day of reckoning would come. Strangely, it was not so difficult for economic illiterates on the ground to sense something was wrong. Never had such bank managers been encountered. One knew entrepreneurs who themselves marvelled at how slack lending practices had become. It was impossible to foresee how the banks behaved, Peter Walsh said. This was not entirely true. Max Gillies and John Clarke predicted it in a satirical sketch on the ABC's *The Gillies Report* in 1985. The bankers they portrayed were wearing party hats, drinking bubbly and blowing whistles and everything they said indicated that they would be taking their responsibilities very seriously indeed. It was a rare period, and living through it felt rare. Everyone knew it had to end, but not what form the end would take—not until the *new* bank manager showed up.

Through all the tumult, Keating was the main player. One minute he was fighting off critics who said it was irresponsible to pay the big tax cuts he delivered in 1989 to keep the Accord alive and wages under control; the next minute he was straightening up his prime minister, the caucus and any other waverers in the labour movement who wanted to abandon fiscal and monetary discipline and go in for 'economic ratbaggery'; and all the while, against the growing doubts in good ministers like Walsh, Button and Dawkins, he was proclaiming that the government's strategy had been right, that it would work. He maintained an air of supreme confidence in the soundness of the 1988 Budget (of whose surplus he was so proud), in the correctness of his policy settings, the proof of government success in sustained growth and investment, in the million and a half new jobs created since the first Accord, and in his ability to engineer a soft landing for the economy. There would be no recession. But everywhere there were signs to contradict him.

At the same time as he wrestled with these contrarieties, he fought the potentially even more destructive monster of his thwarted leadership ambitions. In 1988 when Hawke made it clear that he wanted to stay on as prime minister past the next election, and within hours of the 1988 Budget told the media that his treasurer was not indispensable, Keating was driven to fury. He forced Hawke to the 'Kirribilli agreement' about succession in the government's next term. He persuaded the party that they could maintain economic discipline and fight the 1990 election with the same murderous interest rate regime, albeit with the monetary arrows, as if literally to feather the landing, now pointing down. Labor won. But Keating's ambition and anger continued to bubble and seethe. In pursuit of the micro-economic reforms that some critics demanded and others abhorred he fought and lost a battle on telecommunications reform with Kim Beazley. Beazley was for just one competitor with Telecom, Keating for an open market. John Button's faith in Labor's model wavered as the current account deficit refused to respond. Keating publicly savaged him. John Dawkins was coming to the belief that Australia might need an arm of industry policy like MITI in Japan. Who could blame Keating if he showed signs of crankiness? The recession was a personal blow which only his instinctive resort to hubris could disguise. Colleagues who saw no problems he did not see and whose exhaustion was no greater than his had lost faith and imagination for the fight. Having experienced the same difficulties of making the economic imperatives match political imperatives, Peter Walsh disencumbered himself of the latter and became a journalist and thorn in Keating's side. Keating went on with the struggle, streaming the two strands of political and economic policy. Yet as each month passed it became clearer that Hawke intended denying him the leadership.

In mid-1989 the academic economist John Pitchford wrote that the government should not be fixated with the current account, and warned that if monetary policy continued in the same vein the country would suffer the worst downturn since the 1930s. On 21 June in the same year, the economist Bruce Chapman, like Pitchford from the Australian National University, and a consultant to the Education Minister, John Dawkins, wrote to Dawkins saying that tightening monetary policy to correct the current account was misguided and, furthermore, '[a]t the current rate of real interest (11–12 per cent) there could be considerable and potentially very adverse effects on investment showing up in the next 12–18 months'. He warned there was a significant risk of recession. The minister did not reply. Interest rates were lifted higher. Within twelve months of Chapman's letter, unemployment had risen to more than 9 per cent; a year later it went through 11 per cent, which was half a per cent higher than Chapman's 1989 research had indicated. On 29 November 1990, in contradiction of his claims that there would be no recession, Paul Keating told a press conference that Australia was in a recession 'we had to have'. The political misjudgment of the statement aside, he might have been right. Britain, America and Europe had followed the same course, and Japan was also headed that way. Keating could also say in melioration of his error that in the end he stood against the most zealous of the monetary hawks and turned the rates down at the beginning of 1990. For all that, even if a recession was certain, it seems just as certain that it need not have been as severe or as long-lasting.

'It always remains true,' George Eliot said in *Middlemarch*, 'that if we had been greater, circumstances would have been less strong against us.' It was the kind of lesson Paul Keating might read to someone else, but not one in which he himself habitually took comfort. There was comfort to be had in it, nonetheless. For all his extraordinary efforts, the circumstances—the needs of the economy he had created and the needs of the electorate he must satisfy—were in the end greater than he was. They were greater because contradictions would grow deeper and the extremes drift further apart until it was beyond the ability of any politician to pull them back together.

When Keating took office the public at large did not want to know about regional relationships, or the relationship with Asia or the Prime Minister's thoughts on the international strategic environment. It was not a time for foreign policy. On 26 December he sent a message on behalf of the Australian people to Moscow, congratulating Gorbachev for his part in ending the Cold War, constructing the CIS out of the ruins of the USSR, and for his efforts to reduce the number of nuclear weapons in the world which had put back 'the hands of the doomsday clock'. These were truly momentous times. Two generations of a world divided, each side bristling with weapons of mass destruction, millions denied freedom—the only world anyone under fifty had known was now ended. Francis Fukayama wrote that we were on the threshold of 'a world where struggle over all the large issues has been largely settled'. Ideology was dead (again). Economics had replaced it; along with technology and consumerism, as if the only thing left to argue about would be whether to buy an Apple, an IBM or a Toshiba, which among the educated classes might lead on to a rousing exchange about the overvalued yen. Socialism was dead. Nationalism was dead. Cold War bipolarism was dead. Post-Cold War multilateralism was alive. All that the world lacked was a name by which to call it: The post-Cold War world? The post-industrial world? The postmodern world? It was not unlike the world according to Paul Keating. Of course Keating was essentially *pre-modern*—but wasn't it this which made him postmodern? Either way, it mattered not at all in a recession. They danced in the street when the World Wars ended. But not this time.

Politics and history are alike and inseparable in that the craft of both is storytelling. Masters of both juggle past and present to create coherent narratives, the historian to make the past knowable, the politician to do this with the present. They are similar, if not sometimes identical, in both substance and methodology. The unceasing conflict at the centre of politics is essentially epistemological: What happened? What is happening? What is likely to happen? And how do we know? How much can be learned from observation, what is *a priori*, what axiomatic and what mythical? What is the status of imagination and intuition? At the core of every conversation in a political office, including the conversations politicians have with themselves, are the questions: What will happen? and Why should I believe you? Politics is the art of the knowable. The protagonists usually divide between the empirical and statistical and the psychological and anthropological. There is the science of polling, the wisdom of experience and the hunch or instinct. There is the ideological and the imagined, the empathetic. There is the world of Treasury and Finance and there is Giambattista Vico's conception of historical knowledge, his 'fantasia' which is not like 'knowledge of how to ride a bicycle or engage in statistical research or win a battle . . . [but] more like knowing what it is to be poor, to belong to a nation, to be converted to a religion, to fall in love, to be seized by nameless terror, to be delighted by a work of art'.

Great musicians seem to draw music from their instruments as if their genius is to discover what has always been there. The cello and the cellist become as one. Politics knows no such perfection and political systems which attempt it are invariably grotesque. Treasury officials have no business imagining other people's worlds and couldn't if they tried. Yet, while generally they know that the perfect blend of invisible technique and spiritual empathy is beyond their powers, political leaders are nevertheless impelled towards it. De Tocqueville's imperative still points the way: 'If you do not connect the notion of right with private interest, which is the only immutable point in the human heart, what means will you have of governing the world except by fear?' When in policy and rhetoric governments and their leaders do connect what is right and good with what is wanted, they achieve something like a state of grace. It is like the blessing of providence: one good work seems to lead to another; everything connects, including the press. Government has a glow about it. As the cellist finds the music in the cello, when the political leader finds harmony in the chaos we might be tempted to believe that a genius has tapped something in the natural order. It never lasts, of course, and no-one expects it to. But consciously or not, advisers to governments and leaders are always looking for the harmony. Speechwriters have no other purpose.

There were times in the 1980s when Paul Keating had something of this blessed state about him. The 1988 Budget, heroic performances in Question Time, consummate Press Club appearances, the final pursuit of Hawke. Each epiphany was short-lived, and in every case it was not the people but the press gallery who sang the descant to Keating's policy and personality. Yet over the whole course of that decade no other politician was so drawn to a political state of grace or seemed as likely to achieve it. Sometimes he described himself as being like Zeus hurling down the lightning; sometimes he was the rod that draws the bolts and earths them and thereby creates peace out of the chaos. States of grace are not easily reached. That was the problem for Paul Keating: he became prime minister not because virtue is its own reward—Hawke had denied him that—but because he had fought and taken it. He was left exhausted; and worse, he had to live with thanklessness and loathing. Whatever it was in the wider world, the main game of Keating's advisers was to tap what energy remained and keep at bay the sense of grievance and frustration which often threatened to overturn his political judgment and sometimes did.

Nothing so surely betrayed the fatigue in Keating's first government as his remark that most of the work had been done.

He said it in our first interview. He said it again half a dozen times. After the second or third time it had become apparent that, far from lightening the burden of office, the work already done had made it heavier. The effort of the previous nine years had taken a physical toll, depleting the cabinet, advisers and the public service. Many of the best had left and others were making plans to go. Some of those who stayed had already run their race. They looked tired and they acted like it. There was the suspicion of an idea that the good old days had gone: not just the great days of reform, but the days when the treasurer's office had been, to use the words Keating used when he farewelled Tom Mockridge, one of his most loved advisers, a 'family', a 'nice little crew'. It was not an employer/employee sort of place, everyone was an adviser of some sort, and no-one was called 'comrade'. It was an environment, he said, for breeding generals not corporals—which sounds rather like the one he grew up in, or at the very least like the idealised Bankstown he sometimes described where Labor reckoned it was born to rule. However, in 1992 people who would not have been considered fit a few years earlier were finding their way into influential positions. The draining of the talent pool meant that the increasingly heavy baggage had to be carried by fewer and fewer people.

It seemed to Keating and some of those close to him that most of the work had been done because so much *had* been done. The revolution was all but complete. They would concede that more work was required in the micro-economic area, particularly on the waterfront, and in the labour market generally where progress towards enterprise bargaining needed a push of one kind or another. It was not that the game was over, or that inaction was the most appropriate strategy, but because they could never quite get it out of their heads that market forces were bound to haul the economy up. There were times when they spoke as if the day was just around the corner when the bell would ring and everyone could go home. And therefore one should not overdo things.

George Eliot reckoned all sensible people 'early discern that the mysterious complexity of our life is not to be embraced by maxims'. Among political operators and economists this is not as well known as commonsense would suggest. Eliot said it was absurd to think that people could arrive at a decent concept of justice without having lived 'a life vivid and intense enough to have created a wide fellow feeling with all that is human'. The wide fellow feeling was also missing from much of our office. It is difficult to say whether the maxims followed from the lack of it, or the lack of it from the maxims, but politically speaking it did not matter.

They believed implicitly in their own virtue. They had pursued economic reform in the national interest. Their courage and zeal had saved the country and given it a future as surely as the soldiers who drove back the Japanese. It had been good policy and good leadership. The recession notwithstanding, in 1992 far from failure or disappointment, a sense of accomplishment prevailed among the architects of these reforms. They were like an old guard of revolutionaries. They had laboured all the nights long, they had fought the battles, taken the risks and won. They had remade Australia. The faith wavered more in some than others, but all believed when they got their courage up that the recession had not only been necessary and inevitable, but would actually profit the nation. Religious and revolutionary zealots also talk about cleansing and renewal (was this the real meaning of 'de-spivving'?), but the pointy heads called it productivity improvement. They said the recession had forced changes in Australian business and industry on which real competitiveness and, therefore, prosperity depended. They are still inclined to say it, and point to the last decade of low inflation growth as proof.

It was easy to sympathise with this assessment, and with the notion that economics was the main game of government. But an irresistible sense of their own virtue and their own historic role had endowed them with some of the characteristics of the puritan. There was but one truth and it had been given to them, and all the rest was just a sideshow. The sideshow starred Plato, Aristotle, Jesus, Mohammed, Leonardo, Shakespeare, Machiavelli, Montaigne, Mozart, Mill, Marx, Keynes and countless others of some calibre, and it contained divertissements like history, philosophy, psychology, religion, art, literature, physics, sociology, sport, sex, aviation and evolution. The sideshow was everything *else* extracted from our frontal lobes. But it was a mere preliminary to the main game which was economics after AD 1975 or so, and starred a few politicians, bureaucrats and media writers. Like other puritans, they were quite unaware of the irony of their position. Worldly in all things to do with markets and expert in their own history, they appeared to know nothing and cared less about virtually everything else. They were like some new chapter of the Amish or the Emperer of Lilliput commanding that all eggs must be broken at the smaller end. At one extreme it was an almost touching naivete; at the other it had moderately chilling echoes of Year One—as if all human history had been folly until they took over. It was often impossible to escape the conclusion that the pointy heads were in gross denial.

For all that, they were only part-time ideologues. They were not Thatcherites, or Friedmanites or Reaganites. It was their primary belief that markets were self-correcting and tended towards equilibrium and full employment, and that state intervention in the economy was counterproductive. In this they represented a species of monetarism, but it is unlikely that any of them, and certainly not Keating, would have called themselves monetarists, and none of them dared renounce a significant role for government. They were essentially economic liberals, but none of them, publicly at least, ever advocated a basic tenet of the creed, a wholly deregulated labour market. They were eclectic. In fact they prided themselves on being different. They had defied the neo-liberal dogma that the state must leave *everything* to the market. After all, they had rebuilt a system of national health care; created a sophisticated social safety net out of family allowance supplements (FAS), unemployment benefits, pharmaceutical benefits, benefits for the aged; through HECs enabled all young people to get the higher education and training they needed; and through Accords with the trade union movement traded all these arrangements in the interests of social justice for wage restraint. In

1992 social justice was a continuing priority and its best representations, like Medicare and the FAS, were as proud a part of the
record and as much articles of faith as deregulated financial
markets and a floating dollar. For all the deregulation, more of the
social edifice erected by Labor governments and shored up by
conservative ones was still standing in Australia. Where governments in Great Britain and New Zealand had taken to the labour
market with a neo-liberal axe, the Australian Labor Government
had preserved minimum wages, industry awards and centralised
wage fixing. Conservatives pointed to these other countries as
salutary examples of the government's failings. The government
pointed to them as proof of their Labor credentials, of what
Australian workers and Australian society had been spared.
Conservatives tended to think that the process should have *begun*
with the labour market. The government maintained that by less
ruthless means it had achieved as much.

They were Labor pragmatists. In proportion to the degree
Labor had taken on free-market doctrine the Coalition had been
driven to try to outflank them on the right; and in the same
proportion Labor had offered Australians a safety net, to temper
the wind to the shorn lamb as the saying used to go, and to leave
the Coalition in the wilderness and looking like a wolf. They had
liberated capitalism in a radically *un*-Labor way, while civilising it
as the Labor tradition demanded.

Pragmatic though it was and had to be, the governing ethos
of Labor, and particularly of those around Keating, was policy
integrity. True, some saw integrity and doctrinal purity as the
same thing, and some may have inclined to the view that pure
politics was always the best policy. But no-one saw slumming it
as an option. In what Don Russell liked to call the 'virtuous
circle', to advocate measures which satisfied immediate political
or psychological needs but squandered public money and long-
term opportunities for improvement was to forfeit credibility. To
advocate measures which were at once economically sound and
politically clever—to be a liberaliser and a civiliser, for instance—
was to be virtuous, and only the virtuous were credible. People

like Russell were devoted to Keating because he was policy-driven. Like Keating himself, they were prepared to be unpopular; and like him also, they were capable of recognising political necessity when they saw it.

John Hewson and Fightback were the measure of the distance Labor would not travel with free-market doctrine. That they had not gone the whole way was plain from Hewson's boundless capacity to hector Keating for what he believed was a job half done. It should not have been difficult, then, for Keating to find room to counter-punch. In Hewson he had an opponent who just three or four years earlier had said that men like Christopher Skase and Alan Bond were the new breed and the future of Australian business. But Labor had created the conditions in which such people had flourished, and Labor had been too friendly with them to upbraid Hewson for his misjudgment. In addition there was plenty on Keating's record suggesting he was not as unsympathetic to Fightback-like solutions as he pretended; and, of course, in 1986 he had tried to persuade the Labor Government to adopt Fightback's most contentious plank—a goods and services tax.

It was clear from the start that Keating must lure John Hewson on to unfamiliar ground. Very soon after it became safe to say that all ground was available except the patches known to a minor merchant banker with a Baptist background and an economics degree from Johns Hopkins. Yet what should have been an easy manoeuvre for the Prime Minister and his office often proved unwieldy and fraught. This was partly because in recent years they had traversed very similar ground themselves and could not be seen in obvious contradiction of their own policies and beliefs. It was also because Keating and his economic advisers, not to say the departments of Treasury, Finance and Prime Minister and Cabinet *were* in their bones free-market economists; not so stuck on the doctrine as Hewson, but it was never less than a challenge to lever them off.

The most immediate irksome consequence of this adhesion was their unwillingness to conscientiously address the social consequences of a recession which fell most heavily on those Labor was sworn to protect. The monetarist element in the creed inclined the wetter of them to think fiscal policy was all but impotent as an agent of growth and employment, the drier to sound sometimes as if they thought it downright dangerous and immoral.

Such nice considerations were lost on nine-tenths of the outside world, of course. From outside it felt as if the government had not only lost the sympathy of its traditional constituencies, it had lost sympathy *for* them: indeed, it seemed insensible to national sentiment regardless of class or voting habits. Inside, this was quickly confirmed. What was more, not everyone seemed convinced that a problem existed. For years Keating had talked about pulling the levers of economic policy, as if by this process one could play the main game with something like scientific certainty of success. In 1991 and 1992, and in fact beyond, the levers refused to work, not in time with the political cycle at least. It has been said that everything ordinary people want, economic rationalism opposes: they want jobs and secure employment, they want good wages and conditions, they want wealth to be distributed fairly, they want influence in their own lives, their communities' and their country's. They want recognition, which some people say is a primary human need, but economic rationalism recognises the bottom line instead. It is a reasonable supposition that they want history, at least insofar as they want to belong to a story, but economic rationalism is an ideology to accompany the *end* of history. Labor had not gone all the way down the economic rationalist road, but far enough to break the cords which bind a government to the social reality and the people's mood. They did not seem to understand how depressed the public was, nor how badly the government was thought of. Naturally, when at last they began to pull these other levers, which no popularly elected government can ever do without, they found them rusted up or connected only to a void.

Keating called this view of the world through the lens of the economy the 'big picture'. It was a stimulating metaphor which implied, if not quite omniscience, the ability of an enterprising and well-led government to see, and therefore to shape, the country's destiny. There was more than hubris in this. The big picture was to be read as the antithesis of myopic, timid, opportunistic and populist government. It was a grand notion. The big picture of its nature valued work, ideas, imagination, loyalty and the discipline to judge what belonged in the picture and what did not. If you couldn't see the big picture, you didn't belong. It was the day to day struggle for advisers in the Prime Minister's Office to persuade the PM that their portfolios belonged in it. Native Title, constitutional reform, social policy, the environment, regional development, the arts: not all of them made it all of the time, and none made it without having to regularly restate its case. Still, the big picture kept expanding, and the Prime Minister began to use different phrases to describe it: enlargers and straiteners (from the historian Manning Clark); lovers and others (from the painter John Olsen); even the true believers were related to people who saw the big picture.

The big picture was usually criticised because it too readily disregarded the—often human—details. It was a concept of government which surpassed local interest and much which modern political sensibility takes to be a right among constituents. Unlikely as the combination sounds, Paul Keating was with Edmund Burke who told voters in Bristol in 1774 that the parliament to which they elected him was an 'assembly of *one* nation, with *one* interest, that of the whole; where, not local purposes, not local prejudices ought to guide, but the general good'. Keating would have been happy to instruct John Laws's listeners in the same principle: he was grateful but he should not be expected to say it all the time, not when he had the national interest to serve. His picture was bigger than theirs. The big picture generated its own rhetorical style, its own imagery, and too often for comfort, its own imperatives. In a pragmatic democracy, never much given to grand ideas and suspicious of those who had them, the big picture was always prone to excite antipathy among voters who sensed they were not a part of it. In the recession many people probably thought it was an insufferable conceit. Paul Keating might have moved on but they were still mired in frustration and despair.

A more profound criticism might be that the big picture could never be big enough. Much that happened to Australia happened beyond its horizons. The first year of the Keating Government was one of the more fierce in Australia's political history, and as the parties jockeyed for every jot of advantage they covered vast amounts of policy ground. If this wasn't the big picture nothing was. Yet as globalisation gathered momentum and the new technology expanded at a blinding rate, while the world rearranged itself, there was a sense in which Australian politics was merely the equivalent of a magic lantern show. All those debates had to be had; all of them, to varying degrees, would determine Australia's future. But the great debate was never had: this debate concerned the options available to Australia in the midst of a technological revolution and a globalising world economy and culture. That debate would have made it clear that while Labor's efforts to reposition Australia in the eighties had been valiant and good, the big picture had outgrown them. It is true that much of what Keating attempted as prime minister was a response to this revolution: engagement in Asia, the continuing stress on free trade and multilateralism, the reforms to communications, the attempt to introduce a new regime in education and training, even the effort to define a cultural policy or create a republic were efforts to position Australia in this emerging new world. By the 1996 election he was explaining it in great sweeps and details, but often to uncomprehending or uninterested audiences who felt that the economic revolution in Asia was either remote or threatening, the technological revolution of no benefit to those it did not reach. They listened in silence as he painted his big picture and, as it were, walked out of the frame. It was as if they were telling him that he had pursued the national interest for too long—the electors of Australia would assert the *provincial* interest and vote for the small picture over the big one. So deep did the resentment run, and so passionately was the regional interest asserted, it has always been tempting to think that the democratic revolution which swept Eastern Europe with the collapse of the Soviet Union somehow found its way to the Australian provinces.

Perhaps it was, as many people said, that Keating had lost touch with too many of them. The perception of arrogance which always hung about him had become too general. He wasn't arrogant; he classified people not according to their stations but to their thoughts and sentiments, and thought himself superior only to his political opponents. Boredom was the feeling he could not conceal, but people could hardly be blamed for thinking it was arrogance. He had grown tired of politics' magic lantern show years before, but in the course of his prime ministership almost everything at some stage or other drifted towards the same kind of passing ritual. Budget deficits and surpluses came and went, foreign debt remained, and always would. It was a fact of life like the chronic current account, equally immune to remedies and despair. Unemployment would eventually come down and truly there was not a lot a government could do to hasten it. But there would always be bleeding hearts who talked as if he was insensible to the 'human cost', and cynics and attention-seekers who said the same thing for different reasons; and people who believed that the show was everything in life and governments should never lift their gaze beyond the average punter in the front rows; and the usual quotient of mugs and pedants and bottom feeders, and very few stars. He had done his best and it was better than most other people's best, but his enemies would go on belting him and he would have to reach again into his reserves of energy and loathing and belt them back, harder. The Australian political show would go on. It was like war, except no-one gets killed, just ground down, and in the end we are all dead.

CHAPTER 4

It has been proved over and over again that a straight out defensive will always be defeated by a bold offensive and the best and only defence is attack.

H. GORDON BENNETT, WHY SINGAPORE FELL

D EMOCRATIC POLITICS BEING what it is—an amusement with serious consequences like the Roman colosseum— it was necessary for the new prime minister to diligently pursue policy solutions to the nation's almost-crisis without for a moment sacrificing the requirements of television. The media had been very helpful in his quest for the job and he was not averse to them per se, but he did not concede them a right to expect interviews with his wife or children or be allowed inside his house for the asking. The names of his wife and children were not on the ballot paper, he said. The media could always say that his family were a potential political asset and they only wanted to do him a favour. His media advisers inclined to the same view. So Channel 9's *60 Minutes* team was allowed in to film the Keatings at home and give Australians a look at their new leader with his family, which is to say as a real person like themselves and in an environment essentially like their own.

Into this soft overlay Jana Wendt inserted a hard interview, albeit one in which the Prime Minister wore casual clothes and sat on the couch in the 'brown room' of the Lodge. Like his office, the book-lined brown room with a big Rupert Bunny pastoral nude on the wall still smelt of Bob's cigars. The room was home to the stereo system with the mighty speakers and it would be a surprise if Wendt left without being given something to listen to. Her famous wide-apart eyes sparkled for the camera. His eyes sparkled back. If nothing else, he was probably the only politician in the land who could match her irises. She smiled a sexy, wily smile. He smiled one back. She asked him about leadership and he said that he and Hawke had different ideas about it. Bob was a good leader whose idea of leadership was to let others lead. He, Keating, reckoned leaders had to do it themselves. They had to 'strike out' and set directions. So why did Hawke's leadership work, she asked. Because he had talented and dedicated people to call on, said Keating. It wouldn't have worked for a moment had they been less so. He did not seem to have himself in mind, but it could not have escaped some viewers that there was no more persuasive evidence for his argument.

Wendt asked him what it felt like to be so unpopular, and he said popularity was not everything, but more people would like him when they saw his works. She asked if it wasn't a fact that Australians could see a phoney coming from a mile off, and he replied to the effect that four miles was more like it and in a fog. This being agreed, Wendt put it to the Prime Minister that he was at the mercy of an impossible contradiction: to wit, he could not become more popular without being phoney and he could not be phoney without becoming less popular. The Prime Minister said something to the effect that people would have to wait and see.

There was a time when Australian prime ministers thrilled to the thought of a royal visit. In the presence of his monarch (or a reasonably close relation), even a mug politician might contrive to resemble a person of substance; a smart one like Bob Menzies could look positively august. Any doubt that this time was past should have been dispelled by the visit of Queen Elizabeth in February 1992. Still feeling his way round the job, the recession hanging round his neck, looking a forlorn hope in the polls, if ever a prime minister was in need of an electoral leg-up it was Paul Keating just then. But the country's affections had shifted long ago and the government saw not the slightest potential for political advantage in her visit. No-one in the PM's office, including the Prime Minister, seemed to give it a moment's thought until the day she arrived. Flying up to Sydney that afternoon, the Prime Minister perused the newspapers; Annita, her protocol. It is not necessary to curtsy, she reported. The Prime Minister, as he so often did, shrugged and turned his dreaming gaze out the window.

Bill Hayden, the Governor-General, stepped from a car into the late afternoon sun, his face glowing like Grange Hermitage. The hired Qantas jumbo rolled roaring and fuming to a halt in a corner of Sydney airport where a couple of hundred people with bouquets and little flags waited behind a low fence. The Prime Minister and Mrs Keating joined the Governor-General and his wife in a line of dignitaries along a red carpet rolled out at the bottom of the stairs. The grin on the GG's face was surely ironic: he was, after all, the man who might have been prime minister, but in 1983, just when the prize seemed his, Keating had plumped for Hawke and helped to turf Hayden out. Now Keating had turfed out Hawke and there he was, Mr Innocent, with his Italian trouser cuffs billowing in the soft summer breeze. But Bill Hayden *was* governor-general, and he *was* about to show the Queen around. It was like Alice in Wonderland. Why wouldn't a man grin?

The door opened and out she stepped, in a red hat and a red dress, the Queen of Australia. All the way from London. The Prince followed. Just the two of them. Like a pair of migratory birds in a confused magnetic field. If she had taken a look and turned and gone back inside, and the door had slammed shut, and the jumbo had reversed and flown away—what a moment that would have been, and what years of folly and humbug she would have saved us.

The crowd gave a shrill cheer as she descended the steps. The Governor-General stepped forward and greeted Her Majesty. Mrs Hayden bobbed. The Governor-General introduced her to the Prime Minister. Mrs Keating did not bob. Mrs Greiner, the

Premier's wife, bobbed. They all faced a brick wall and a band played 'God Save the Queen'. Then it played 'Advance Australia Fair'. The first shot of a twenty-one gun salute caused the Queen to start.

The Queen and the Prince walked over to the crowd to chat and accept flowers. If anyone noticed that Annita Keating had failed to curtsy they didn't complain. Indeed some of the people seemed to be as interested in Mrs Keating as they were in the Queen. She did look rather princess-like: as they ambled elegantly across the bitumen, just for a moment it was possible to think that Paul and Annita Keating were the future of Australia. Her Majesty and the Prince drove out the gate in the Bentley. The domestic staff who, unnoticed, had filed out the back of the plane, followed in two minibuses marked Household 1 and Household 2.

Constitutional monarchies have much to recommend them, and in some parts of the postmodern world they might work better than they have ever worked before. They are uncannily suited to the media culture, outlast the soap operas which they frequently resemble, and are ultimately immune to satire for the same reason that stranded whales are. Royals are just the rest of us with feathers on, yet they also offer something bigger than ourselves. That's why they can hold societies together, and in a way that threatens scarcely anything. As children in 1954, we stood in blazing heat for hours to watch the Queen make one circuit of the Warragul trotting track, and we went home feeling blessed. It worked in those days, for better or worse.

But it wasn't working in 1992. There was no magic and very little devotion. Because it so clearly reflected the pragmatism of a republic more than the magic of monarchy, the perfunctory ceremony at Mascot might have been taken as a moment which signalled the way ahead. Everyone there, including quite possibly Her Majesty and her supporters, must have sensed that they were going through motions prescribed by an era that was all but past. The Prime Minister and those associated with him felt it more acutely because just then so much, including their survival, was hanging in the balance.

The royal visit coincided with the preparation of a major economic statement on which the government's future depended. Over the next couple of weeks, while the Queen drifted in and out of the nation's life and the media, here and in London, made as much as they could for as long as they could of Mrs Keating's missing curtsy, the government sought the means by which the nation's economy might be jolted back to life. In doing that it naturally hoped to revive its own fortunes which in February 1992 were beginning to provoke comparisons with McMahon and Whitlam in their dying days. One heard the same expressions of contempt and anger, and it was all but axiomatic that Labor's time was up.

Not that the people had yet bought the alternative, the new economic bible, Fightback, and its apostle, John Hewson. The Australian people are among those who are suspicious of anyone going among them like a missionary, possibly because they're sensitive to the implication that they might be savages. And they were not insensible to some of the blessings Labor had brought them—Medicare, family allowances, Accords, rescued rainforests. Had they been asked whether they wanted, via Fightback, more rather than less of Labor's deregulatory, low-tariff economics they almost certainly would have answered 'less'. They shunned the notion of the level playing field; reckoned their country was being sold to foreign interests; shuddered when they thought about the national debt; fumed when they saw Argentinian tinned tomatoes dumped in their stores at half the price of the local product. The general disgruntlement was all in the research, for those who needed the research. It was also on the airwaves, ad nauseam. It was in the atmosphere, at least for the vast majority who were breathing it. But the alternative to Labor was a policy promising more of the same, but meaner, and with a 15 per cent GST on everything including food.

Labor had a chance of winning the arguments if only it could have them. But while it fought on the enemy's ground, with every visible sign suggesting it had failed and had no answers and no vision and no moral or intellectual authority—of which the recession offered a million (unemployed) proofs—it was not in the contest. Keating became prime minister of a government under siege, in full psychological retreat but with nowhere to run. You could sense the depression and fear on the fringes of the camp, and you knew that if he failed to quickly stage a counter-attack, a gruesome rout was inevitable. He told his staff that winning an election might not be within reach, but in the meantime he intended to make Hewson's life a misery. Yet he knew as well as anybody else that lacerating Hewson was not going to mean salvation: if the people wanted to see anyone bleed it was Keating. Most of all, however, they wanted to see their leaders attend to their problems. All that year Keating struggled with this conundrum: every time he inflicted damage on his enemies he turned to the people covered in blood and gore, which only his admirers interpreted as heroism while all the rest grew angrier at what they saw as self-indulgence. And his opponents came to realise that his savage instinct to destroy them could be turned against him. They baited him in the parliament, turned their backs on him, brayed so loudly that he had to shout, knowing that every now and then he was bound to go too far and the grab on the evening news would confirm the public's view that he was not fit for the job. The only required reading for this dilemma was the story about the tar baby. Yet when Keating went quiet for a day or two, invariably the media reported that the fight had gone out of him, and you knew from the look on the Opposition's faces that on such days they felt they had him beaten.

The problem of finding language appropriate to the times went further than the parliament. Reciting the government's achievements in the eighties was not a useful tactic in a recession. Labor had become adept at telling the story of the country's progress through those reforms, a remarkably effective means of keeping the people engaged and believing, particularly when the storyteller was the engaging Paul Keating. But the recession brought the story undone. The remedies for recessions are economic, of course, but recessions change more than the economy. The willingness of people to trust and believe is also changed. The government could continue to concentrate on the economic 'main game', and adopt whatever economic strategies it fancied, but it could not go on telling passengers why the plane was falling when what they craved was a reason to believe that the thing wasn't going to crash. And if it *was* going to crash, they wanted someone to blame.

But Keating loved the language of economics as much as he loved the discipline itself, at least in the neoclassical form in which he learned it. He loved its clean lines in the way he loved neoclassical architecture and design, or a Japanese beam, the exquisite moment when form and function coincide. He talked economics in the way men talk about machinery: he had invested the dismal science with images of belts and pulleys and the delight of pulling levers which made inanimate objects obey you. But what was beautiful to Paul Keating now made his audience's eyes glaze with fatigue and irritation. You could see it in a room. It didn't work any more because they could no longer suspend their disbelief. They thought the whole decade-long experiment had failed.

Keating knew, and he was regularly told, that it was folly for a prime minister to talk like a treasurer, the more so when he needed to engage on ground where his opponent was least comfortable. The lesson about language should have been plain enough from the doozey uttered at the onset of recession. 'This is the recession we had to have' was a monster not because it was untrue, but because it gave so little hope and bore so little trace of regret. Its unpleasantness and its inexhaustible utility to political opponents derived from the sense it gave that Paul Keating, who had installed the new economic order, was now sanctioning penalties in the name of its new economic laws. In fact he wasn't: rather, he was trying to say plainly that the recession was a nasty but necessary section on the journey. But the line sounded less like the voice of a man with the good of society in view than some Leninist reciting the laws of history over another wagonload of kulaks. It was politics conducted from the heights of certainty; and as Kenneth Arrow, the father of the theory of general equilibrium, one of the laws of free-market economics, once said, 'Vast ills follow a belief in certainty.'

Keating's ability to make a potent formula from the combination of policy imperatives and political ones had not only been the principal engine of economic reform in the preceding decade, it had been the bane of his opponents, forcing them into a cycle of more and more extreme positions followed by embarrassing retreats. But just now Keating had lost the recipe. He needed a proof of the government's—and his own—renewal. Once he had this, so long as it was as credible as Fightback, he could begin to exploit his greatest advantage—the office of prime minister. *His* policies would be implemented; *they* would have a visible reality. Thereafter, Hewson's attacks could be painted as spoiling—as the sort of thing he would say, being the sort of man who could not resist the lure of personal advantage in talking the country down! And while Keating was getting on with the job, this yuppie was going around with this Fightback, this academic abstraction, this snake oil, this magic pudding, this diabolical manifesto. If only he could get into the arena he'd be able to throw a few bombs of his own.

Strictly speaking, Australia was not in recession. Strictly speaking, it was in recovery. The last two quarters had recorded economic growth. But so long as there was nothing visible to indicate a recovery and much to indicate a recession, the population were not comforted. A pall still hung over the cities and towns; in window after window, the signs said 'For Lease'. In political terms, the growth figures were a well-baited trap: there would have to be many more tangible signs of recovery, and more quarters of growth, before it was safe to say publicly that the recession was over. The Prime Minister, who had been treasurer when the recession began and who through one famously ill-judged remark had made it all his own, was also under pressure to show signs of contrition. They were times to test him. It was all the harder to make good policy because public opinion had run amok: everyone had a solution, and when they didn't have a solution they most certainly had a problem. But the trouble was the government wouldn't listen. If only they'd listen. Everyone said that.

Listening was not Keating's most comfortable posture. Not that he wasn't good at it: no-one could pick up the thread of an argument more quickly, and as often as not he would reach the conclusion and judge the implications long before the person he was listening to did. But he was averse to listening for the sake of being seen to. He hated meaningful eye contact and double-fisted handshakes and heartfelt confessions of failure. He believed emphatically that, whatever the polls might indicate or the media demand, no good could come of demeaning himself or his office, or that weighing heavy on the government's shortcomings would earn him more respect. He knew that the most effective and responsible economic measures were not necessarily the most politically attractive; the most popular remedies for unemployment and ailing businesses were not always the most likely to work; and the most thoroughgoing mea culpa was unlikely to be more than a transparently disingenuous exercise which would benefit no-one but his political opponents. So they wanted him to apologise for the recession—should he also apologise for the million and a half jobs Labor's renovated economy had created? For the boom in manufactured exports? For the improved terms of trade? For rescuing the country's economy from the wrecker's yard? Should he apologise for the recession in the United States and Britain and Europe as well? Should he apologise for 'breaking the back of inflation'? Every time the word 'apologise' was mentioned, he seethed. Did John Howard apologise for the 1982 recession, for doing nothing in seven years to arrest the country's decline? The talk-show kings and the people who listened to them could say what they like. The Opposition could bleat. Jana Wendt could conduct a television show trial, put him in the dock for the recession. The party could point to any amount of research indicating that an apology would help. Staffers could say, 'but once you've done it, mate, it clears the decks'. Keating would not do it.

But he would listen. He spent February travelling the country, consulting with business groups and governments about the design of a big economic statement, a blueprint for economic recovery and national development over the next decade. The recovery was weaker than everyone had hoped, expected and believed. The task was to boost confidence, encourage investment and provide the certainty business needed to plan. With his Treasurer, John Dawkins, Finance Minister, Ralph Willis and Minister for Industry, John Button, he roved from one capital to another meeting managing directors, CEOs, industry groups and premiers. In a letter to the *Australian Financial Review,* one business organisation said it was pleasing to have the PM's ear, and they hoped he got the right message, namely: a lower Australian dollar was essential, but any price effects of a lower dollar should not flow into wage increases; micro-economic reform must at least keep pace with tariff reductions; and taxes on business inputs ought to be reduced, particularly wholesale sales tax, payroll tax, petroleum excise and other imposts which curiously the Coalition was promising to abolish. Within cabinet, debate concerned the degree to which government should compensate industry for tariff reductions. Most emphatically on the side of this kind of industry policy stood Simon Crean. Keating stood emphatically against. In the end there was a good deal of Crean in the statement.

On 2 February the Prime Minister announced that the consultations were at an end and the statement would be delivered in the parliament on 26 February. He wanted a big hit, and he wanted it in the first week of the sitting to quickly assert himself over Hewson in the nation's 'pre-eminent forum' and his natural environment. Labor had been effectively out of the contest for more than twelve months, the caucus had lost heart. With the big statement Keating hoped to get back in the ring and create some enthusiasm for the fight. In the meantime he made a small statement with bigger implications for the shape of his philosophy than any commentator discerned. Early in February he abolished a $2.50 Medicare co-payment introduced late in Hawke's term, and restored the rebate from the 1991 Budget. It meant persuading the minister, Brian Howe, and the cabinet back to a position from which Keating would not be moved: that the co-payment compromised the integrity of Medicare and would lead to its unravelling as a truly universal health-care system.

All these deliberations were punctuated by the execution of his formal duties to the Queen. It is instructive that at none of these functions, including the most intimate dinners, did the Queen of Australia ask her Prime Minister about the state of Australia's economy, the country's prospects, the condition of the Australian people. It's more instructive than blameworthy, because almost certainly she felt that it was not her business to ask. Had she done so, she might have received instruction along the following lines. 'The recession is bad, ma'am, but bad as it is, it is not as bad as my opponents in their tawdry way are making out; and the economy will be the better for it in the long run—or will be at least if we don't bend to the bleeding hearts on our side or give it back to the other mob. We're going to come out with a low inflation recovery—a quality recovery. We're de-spivving the place. Getting rid of the spivs, ma'am. There'll be a lot more quality about the place—that's what we're about, quality. It's tough on the unemployed and we're going to do something for them. But remember this, nothing beats growth. You can have all the job creation programs in the world, but if you haven't got growth you won't have employment. You'll have a lot of kids planting trees and sitting under the stars smoking weed but you won't make a mark on unemployment. Whitlam tried all that and not only did it fail, it became a hallmark of his failure. So we've got this big statement and I'm going round the country listening to all these characters, but quite frankly, Your Majesty, there's not much they can tell me that I don't know already. But you know what these jobs are like—you have to do a lot of things when you'd be better off spending the time with your kids.' He said as much at doorstop interviews; but, he said, sometimes 'there's the odd little jewel that falls out' of these discussions and he would be listening for it. 'I've always been a good listener,' he said. 'In public life you have to be.'

Despite his intention to create it in others, and indeed in the nation, it was the first week of February before the Prime Minister managed to work up enthusiasm. Until then, the big economic statement had been a long list of recommendations to give the economy a modest stimulus, make life easier for the private sector, the climate more conducive to investment, the labour market a little freer. Most of the ideas were worthwhile, a few of them clever and original, but weeks went by and no-one could say convincingly what the statement was about. No-one said what was really at the heart of it because the heart of it was that the markets, in which all faith had been invested, had failed, and the government—the wasteful, inefficient, despised public sector—was obliged to do the mopping up. At the heart of the 1992 statement was a question about capitalism and the role of government. Would Australia go further towards a definition of government as that vehicle which comes along behind the market system managing its by-products and shoring up its future; or would Labor reassert the public sector, in Robert Heilbroner's (following Adam Smith's) terms, 'as an indispensable source of strength for a private economy, not as a wasteful drag on it'? Of course the question was never asked because the answer had long since been agreed upon. A certain amount of denial was necessary to maintain this position, in particular the act of self-effacement at the centre of the proceedings: after all, the government was consulting the private sector on what public sector solutions it wanted for its failure. Furthermore, all blame for this failure was to be accepted by the government and the solutions were to be couched in terms which stressed the virtues of the private sector over the public.

Then in twenty minutes on a Friday evening Keating explained it to me on scraps of paper with the aid of certain props, like his telephone and its cord to represent the way a national power grid would work, and a rail line round the continent, the way we would get competition and productivity into the Commonwealth, the way the Commonwealth would take over tertiary and further education and pour $700 million into it and make the 'weak reed in education a reed of equal strength'. The statement would 'bind' the strength into the country. 'Strength' became a key word. Rex Connor would have loved it. So did I. It was the moment when I saw what people meant about Keating's power to inspire.

It had been a painful process until then. I had not been able to see any sign of a philosophy or logic to the statement, and had my first altercation with John Edwards about it. If anyone truly fitted the description 'economic rationalist' it was probably Edwards, although it might have been just something he liked to affect from time to time. Like Russell (and everyone who ever wanted to work effectively in politics) he had something of the Machiavellian about him, and he was blessed with the same high intelligence and cool reserve, but he was not a bureaucrat like Russell so he was an operator of a different kind, and the two of them did not much like each other. Edwards ran his own race in the office—he was the only one who maintained a fitness regime, the only one it seemed sometimes to maintain a life beyond politics. On this occasion he attempted a frontal mugging. At a meeting of advisers he said the speech I had so far prepared lacked an intellectual framework and depth, a central idea. At that stage the speech was no more than ten pages long. I said I had received nothing from those devising the statement about what the central idea was. I did not know what was in the statement or why we were delivering one. It was true. That was why later that afternoon the Prime Minister had me in his office, half an hour before the last plane left for Melbourne. He was telling me that the objective of the exercise was to stage a recovery that would not be wasted in a speculative, inflationary boom. Australia had to come out of the recession leaner and more efficient and with growth that could be sustained. That is what this statement would do: kick-start the economy and judiciously invest in measures of permanent national benefit. It would clear the nation's arteries so this time there would be no boom followed by a heart attack or stroke.

As the speech and the document grew, certain words and phrases hatched like moths from invisible cocoons: 'closing gaps', 'building partnerships', 'overcoming distances', finding 'common goals' and a sense of 'national purpose', making the country 'stronger' and more cohesive and more 'civilised', giving a greater meaning to the 'idea of Australia'. It was 'binding' rhetoric. The not very attractive word 'inclusive' crept in, and became a mantra of sorts.

In announcing such goals the government was not to be seen as changing course, or admitting deficiencies in the reform process so far; rather, the government was writing a new chapter of the same story, taking it into areas where for various historical reasons the wheels had not been greased since World War II or even Federation. Selling Keating's economic initiatives always depended on the assumption that there was only one story and only one person who could tell it. He would now explain to the country how a lot of our productive capacity was tied up in utilities owned and run by the States with no competition to drive their efficiency and no rationale to make them serve the nation's industry. Electricity, for instance: a national electricity grid would be created and we would separate generation from distribution, which was the key to getting competition into it. And rail: the government would fulfil the national dream of a single-gauge rail system from Brisbane to Perth. We would build new roads and bridges. And aviation: Labor would get Qantas flying domestic routes. And, because no country could hope to prosper without skills and skills were the best thing you could give the unemployed if you couldn't give them jobs, the Commonwealth would establish a national training authority. There would be much more, including new depreciation regimes to encourage business investment in buildings, plant and equipment, export incentives, investment incentives, private sector involvement in major infrastructure projects and incentives for private companies to invest in research and development because, like training, it was imperative for every nation in the modern age. And at an overall cost of $600 million or $300 million—the judgement excited great passion—a one-off payment of $125–250 would be made to every Australian family in receipt of the Family Allowance.

Although some of us couldn't entirely see the point, the statement would promise tax cuts. The cuts were designed on the assumptions of rising inflation, lower unemployment and economic growth and the greater revenue the government could expect. They were called tax cuts, although a cynic might have said this was only because the public was not yet ready to hear their prime minister say, 'we will return to middle income earners all future bracket creep'. A cynic might also have said that they were promised less for their value to middle income earners than for their value as a political counterweight to Hewson's program. The Prime Minister could now say that whereas Hewson gave tax cuts with one hand and with the other took them away through a consumption tax, with Labor you could have tax cuts and no GST. I asked Keating to tell me again why these tax cuts were good for us when he drove me to the airport one night soon after the statement. He said it was because they made it much easier to win the argument with Hewson; and, besides, the people chosen to get them deserved them, because they had got little or nothing out of the Accord. Other arguments surfaced at other times— the boost they would give the recovery, for instance. Outside the airport that night the PM said John Edwards had come up with the idea and if he got nothing else from him between then and the election he had already paid his way.

It is certain that not everyone in cabinet and the bureau-cracy found the idea as compelling as the Prime Minister did. The left thought tax cuts were inconsistent with the need to reduce unemployment, despite the claims about getting 'productivity and incentive effects' from them, and how they would only be paid as the economy improved. Ultimately the economic assumptions on which they rested proved unsound, and even had they been sound, the political premise was unconvincing. In a whole year I never heard any member of the public say that they needed tax cuts, or that in a recession tax cuts were what the country needed. In fact it seemed distinctly possible that the people judged them to be an extravagant bribe, if indeed they noticed them at all. And the longer growth and employment stayed away and all the signs of recession remained, the more irrelevant they seemed to be, both to their problems and the country's. It is true that the tax cuts gave a certain structure to the government's rhetoric, a certain wholeness to the non-Fightback vision; but it might have done just as well to concentrate on the Coalition's proposals and argue that the last thing the country needed in a recession was a demand-dampening GST and tax cuts for those in comfortable employment. However, nobody wanted to believe that the recession was so tenacious and pervasive and nobody did believe that growth and employment would be so long in coming. In any case, the consequences would not be felt by this government, which was the one that needed saving.

John Button reckoned it had been like extracting teeth, and saw a certain irony in responding to the recommendations of business which he had passed on to Keating two years earlier and been biffed for his trouble. It was often the way: you could not impose an idea on Keating, even if it seemed manifestly for his own good. Often it was because his brain was sharper and his vision longer. If politicians didn't learn to distrust everything bowled up to them and keep reasonably independent minds we would have mayhem. Keating got more things done because he didn't waste a lot of time chasing turkeys. Winning him over was hard work, it could take months, even years. A good argument was a minimum requirement, but often it required as well the patient application of psychology which would allow him to own the idea. More than any measure it contained, the 1992 statement needed Keating to own it.

When Keating owned something he invested it with an almost religious force. It needed a core of creativity, pure lines arcing out from it, each connected to the other. The thing had to have a meaning at the centre, it had to be of a whole, it had to offer the promise of perfection. He had to be able to draw it on a piece of paper, like a mandala, and demonstrate how one thing was connected to all the others. When he found he could do it with this statement, he also found it was of a kind with everything he had done since 1983. Whatever other people may have meant, this was what Keating meant when he spoke of the big picture. This would be no volte-face forced on him by failure, as the critics hoped and expected. It would not dwell mawkishly on the recession, or pander to the emotional need of others for revenge. This would overleap them all. Keating overleaping was a joy to behold. Had she given him an opening, he could have persuaded the Queen.

There comes a time in the preparation of most budgets and other big statements when the government's most crucial task is managing the media anticipation. Leaks real and imaginary wash around, lobbies raise the height of the bar, in every media outlet the government is second-guessed. Oppositions do all these things and more and hope the thing will be stillborn or deformed. A point is reached where the real statement can at best do no more than dampen these concocted fears, or at worst confirm them. In these voids between conception and delivery the best thing a government can have is a natural disaster with significant but not overwhelming loss of life. Failing that, diversions sometimes have to be created.

Thus it was that Mark Ryan said on a flight to Perth for business consultations that it would be no bad thing to suggest to an ABC radio interviewer that he raise the matter of the Australian flag. In the hotel foyer on the way to the interview the PM walked directly past the Australian cricket captain, Allan Border, and several other members of the team who that morning were commencing a Test match against the West Indies. 'That was the Australian cricket team,' we said as he reached the exit. 'Where was that, mate?' he asked and walked through the doors. Outside, a woman sat in a wheelchair waiting for his autograph. The PM walked straight past her to the car. When we told him he must go back and speak to her, he hesitated. Did she really want to see *him*? Didn't it look crook? It was the sort of thing Hawkey would do. He went back with his pen unsheathed, and charmed her.

The interview went roughly according to plan. 'I don't think the Australian flag should have the flag of another country in the corner of it,' he said. 'It sends an ambiguous signal to the world. It suggests that we're still in some kind of colonial rela-tionship with Britain.' On the way to the airport he stopped off to see Kim Beazley and Susie Annus and their new baby. In the eastern States the flag story was up and running in the media and the expected fulminations were flowing from the Coalition. As the PM boarded the plane, Michelle Grattan was on the phone from Canberra telling Mark Ryan that she thought it was all a blatant diversion from unemployment and the economy. Ryan said he was shocked she should think us so calculating. The PM shrugged when told of the disquiet and asked the RAAF what music they had on board. The saltpans round Esperance glistened in the sunset as Grieg's Piano Concerto played in the little jet. The PM had had a meeting with the Aboriginal leader, Charles Perkins. Now something in the desert landscape below prompted him to say out of the blue: 'We'll never be any good, never feel at home until we set things right with them.'

The flag thing was a deliberate diversion from the main game, but it sprang principally from the manifest silliness, at least it seemed to everyone on the plane that day, of having a Union Jack on the Australian flag. The mood of the country also formed part of the motive. It could not readily be gleaned from the media commentators or from the debate between the parties, but well before 1992 it was possible to see that the country was sunk in more than an economic mire. Depression is the best word for it; it was a state of mind, one characterised by an absence of energy, belief and hope. Matters were made worse by the people having been educated so thoroughly in the economic main game by their government and especially by Paul Keating. Every talk-show host and every caller knew the imperatives, and when they were not adequately dealt with they took it personally. Should someone on the radio say that the foreign debt meant that every Australian man, woman and child owed the rest of the world $871.50 the people were half-disposed to budget for it. No doubt there were Australians who, like me, agonised in the supermarket between tomatoes tinned in Victoria after some industry policy saved the company, and tastier and cheaper Italian tinned tomatoes. In the great scheme of life it seemed mad that the current account deficit should cause such disquiet in the soul, but it did. That's what happens when you pursue the main game. The decade of economic reform had been tiring, the recession exhausting. And one agonised over tomatoes.

The extraordinary thing was not that the country was tired and angry: it was that some people could not see that any recovery worthy of the name had to address this emotional deficit. Had they despised history (or psychology, anthropology and theology) just a little less it might not have been so difficult to understand that economics was not the source of all life's nourishment. The evidence is boundless and compelling, but the most instructive example for the government's purposes was the example of a century before: in the 1890s the people had laboured under a much greater economic calamity, and yet by the end of that decade the idea of Australia had been sufficiently charged with meaning for the Commonwealth to be created, along with a labour movement, a coherent species of liberalism and a national school of writers and painters imaginatively in touch with the land. The legend of the nineties, the so-called first blooming of a national consciousness, was born amid economic gloom. It was not to revive the wattle and bottle tradition or to get people singing patriotic songs and marching in the streets that the government raised the question of the national flag and the prospect of an Australian republic, but to re-weight the equation between economics and society. Nor was it to diminish the importance of getting the economic essentials right. It was to say a government could be a conscientious economic manager without pushing all other human sentiments to the margins. That was not only the lesson of the 1890s. It was Curtin's lesson through the war years, and Churchill's. It was Roosevelt's in the 1930s. In the 1950s, issues of heritage and identity, spiritual health, national cohesion and progress were central to all our lives, and happily coexisted with economic questions. If Paul Keating decided to revive their status in Australian life the last people to complain should have been those for whom R.G. Menzies was a hero. No-one manipulated symbols better than Menzies, including the Australian flag which he made official by an act of parliament without referendum or public debate. In the half century preceding, three flags had flown in Australia's name in peace and war—the Union Jack, the Defaced Red Ensign and the Defaced

Blue Ensign. The Blue Ensign had flown at Gallipoli and on the Somme, the Red Ensign at the liberation of Changi, the Union Jack here and there throughout. Had they been asked to choose between the three officially approved flags of Australia it is likely the people would have chosen, as Menzies did, the Blue Ensign in preference to the red one or the flag of Great Britain. Even if Menzies had offered alternative designs, including some without the Union Jack, Australians probably would have voted for the one that defined them as Australian Britons. But that was 1954.

Political memory is conveniently short and grows ever shorter. The conservatives heaped rage and abuse on Keating for lacking patriotism and also for resorting to it like a scoundrel. The polls confirmed that the public liked their flag more than they liked their prime minister. Labor members in marginal seats were aghast and depressed, none more so, we heard, than Kim Beazley whose electorate of Swan was home to large numbers of British migrants. It was probably a tactical mistake, and reacted badly with the more substantial issue of the republic that Keating was soon to raise. Yet by raising the flag as he did, Keating drew out his first new allies in a decade: sections of the intelligentsia, radio commentators, dormant republicans, people from the arts community, trendy advertisers and designers—even some old soldiers wrote in support. Graphic artists of all kinds, advertising agencies and schoolchildren from all over the country sent in their designs. It was remarkable that the great majority of them depicted the landscape—the sea, the land, the rock in the centre, the Southern Cross above. One had a silver-haired Hawke-like figure adjacent to the rock.

A debate about Australia's symbols and history and the shape of its future got going. All sorts of old prejudices, buried facts and new ideas were aired. And no-one was seriously injured or thrown out of work.

The economy and the big statement continued to be the main story, of course. It was the same in the Prime Minister's Office, where all hands were at the economic pump. But the government was throwing a reception for the Queen and the

Prime Minister was obliged to say a few words. The PM thought the first draft was a bit strong, so with the judicious aid of Ashton Calvert the speech was pared back to something everyone thought appropriately polite and to the point. After congratulating Her Majesty on the fortieth anniversary of her accession to the throne, the Prime Minister referred to certain fundamental changes which had occurred in that time:

> These days we must both face the necessities of a global economy and global change of often staggering speed and magnitude. We must also face regional realities. Just as Great Britain some time ago sought to make her future secure in the European community, so now Australia vigorously seeks partnerships with countries in our own region. Our outlook is necessarily independent. That independence was in part reflected in your becoming, in 1973, Queen of Australia. In 1992 it is reflected in our growing sense of national purpose: in our conviction that we must move quickly to make the most of our human and material resources and seize our opportunities in the world. We must do this so that Australians will be assured of the same freedom in the next century as they have enjoyed in this.

The politicians gathered in King's Hall with canapes and bubbly hoping for a chance to shake her hand. If she had been his mother the PM could not have been more of a gentleman with Her Majesty. A night or two before, over dinner at Kirribilli, he had lamented the loss of Carlton House with her, and discussed the architecture of the palace. Now he gallantly shepherded the Queen among her varied subjects, introducing Liberals and Nationals and their spouses with no less warmth than he bestowed on some equally humble and obedient Labor colleagues. His arm had extended to the small of her back, as if protecting Her Majesty from her over-zealous subjects. From where Ryan and I stood it looked like the sort of arm a gentleman would extend in such circumstances; and if he touched her at all it must have been with little more than the epidermis of his fingertips. When he made his short speech Her Majesty did not blink. Half an hour later, life in the office had resumed in full.

But before the crockery was cleared from King's Hall John Hewson shot out of Parliament House to tell the media that Keating had made a political speech and failed to show proper respect. He, John Hewson, had learned respect, but this prime minister plainly had not. John Howard bought in: the reception was 'insultingly low key', he said, and managed to add something to the effect that the 1950s had been a splendid period in Australian history. Next day news arrived from the old country that the tabloids were up in arms: Keating, was dubbed the 'Lizard of Oz'. He had compounded his wife's insolence in failing to bend her knee at Sydney airport by putting his arm around the Queen in King's Hall. 'Hands orf Cobber!' they said. There were front-page photos of the offending limb encircling Her Majesty as he introduced her to none other than Bob Menzies' widow, Dame Pattie. It was amazing news, and almost entirely welcome.

On the afternoon following the King's Hall reception, the PM, half his office and his department secretary, Mike Keating, flew to Adelaide to farewell Her Majesty and His Royal Highness at the airport; or rather, the PM farewelled her while his staff remained on board the plane writing the last of the speech to accompany the big economic statement. There were arguments about whether to include the actual amount of the depreciation allowance and every economic and statistical embolism a speech could suffer without actually dying. Because the market reaction was seen as the one which mattered most, and television coverage demanded that the speech run for exactly 28 minutes, there was little room for inspirational rhetoric, or even forms of words which would make the government's meaning clear and unmistakable. On my suggestion it had been decided to call the thing One Nation. On seeing this in print David Epstein, the chief of the National Media Liaison Service, reminded us that the Nazis had employed an identical slogan. As well, he pointed out that contemporary opinion tended to the view that the nation state was in decline. The second point was at least contestable but the first, which I simply had not thought of, made my marrow go cold. All this four years before Pauline Hanson decided to give the same title to her xenophobic project.

At the time, however, One Nation was consistent with the intention of getting beyond the economy and instilling in the country a sense of pride and common purpose independent of sporting conquests and foreign military endeavours. It suggested links and free-flowing arteries and bonds that the Prime Minister had described with the telephone and its cord. It suggested strength and 'inclusiveness'; not by the sound of marching feet, but by virtue of such ambitions as raising the number of young people in vocational education from 20 per cent to the average for developed countries, which was 50 per cent. And 'One Nation' was better than the alternative—'Rebuilding Australia' did suggest that the previous nine years had been spent in acts of demolition. The Prime Minister liked it. I didn't know and he may have forgotten, but he had used the phrase himself in the Placido Domingo speech more than a year before: 'We occupy a continent and we're one nation and we're basically a European nation, changing now to adapt to the region.'

The day began well. Peter Barron phoned Keating in the morning to say that he should call it 'the greatest one night hit on unemployment in the nation's history'. As unemployment was expected to rise before it fell (and as unemployment *did* for the next twelve months) the remark was bound to serve the Opposition much better than the government. It might have been 'the recession we had to have' all over again. In the general excitement surrounding the government's first big strike, and the general concern about market reaction, no-one saw the danger. Political salvation rarely comes in the shape of Athena or an angel of mercy but that does not rule out divine intervention. There is no way of saying why sometimes we have the thought we need and at other times we don't. This time I had it, as I went out his door. Being still uncertain of my status, I asked Mark Ryan if it wasn't mad to claim for the statement what we knew it would not do for at least twelve months. He sent me back to tell the Prime Minister that the line was bound to come back and bite him. There is no way of saying if the line would have made a difference. What *is* certain is that such moments of percipience are a joy and a boon for the political adviser who is blessed with them.

The little problem of the recession was resolved in the first few lines: 'For a government which took pride in creating 1.6 million jobs this recession has been a bitter blow. Far worse I know has been the blow to a great many Australians.' A speech is an act of persuasion and cannot reveal uncertainties underlying it. One Nation had to describe a broad path, not the knife edge on which it was created. When the Prime Minister announced that the government would spend $300 million on a one-off payment of upwards of $125 to all families receiving the FAS, and said that it would help kick-start the economy, he of course did not mention the fear expressed by some in his inner circle that it might cause overheating. The $2.3 billion overall cost of the package, or 'fiscal shot in the arm', emerged from an admixture of quasi-scientific economic calculations, self-interest, social need, political necessity and simple hope that it would prove neither too hot nor too cold but just right. You cannot sell dilemmas, only decisions: the speech did not describe the policy predicament between fiscal responsibility necessary to ensure long-term recovery and more popular short-term measures required to salve wounds and win an election.

In the end, neither the speech nor the document rose to great heights of imagination or rhetoric and more than one commentator remarked that the whole thing was uninspiring. Ten minutes after the Prime Minister sat down from delivering it Don Russell was found peering at his Reuters screen. Consistent with the unreality that surrounded the preparation of the document, the markets were at first spooked by the scale of the proposed spending and serious economic commentators went on television to declare that recovery was already underway and this was dangerous and unnecessary stimulation, or that the forecasts were implausibly optimistic. It was bold to the point of recklessness; timid to the point of paltriness. Business was more positive than the press, which was flat, suspicious, cynical. ACOSS, the social welfare lobby, applauded what was in the statement but said it was not enough.

It was not a political king hit. However, with One Nation Keating could now enter the argument. In future he could say that he was for social investment and Dr Hewson was opposed to it. His document had low inflation, industrial peace, tax cuts and no GST: Dr Hewson had 6 per cent inflation factored into Fight-back, industrial confrontation and a GST. Keating's statement document was extensively figured by Treasury and Finance; Dr Hewson's had not been modelled. With '93 measures designed to increase output, competition and flexibility, to better train our young people, to rebuild our transport infrastructure, and to give us one of the most competitive business tax structures in the world', the Prime Minister had a position on Australia: Dr Hewson, he would say, had a position on accountancy. When John Hewson said the government was trying to spend its way out of trouble, Keating replied that Dr Hewson was the only person in Australia who believed that nothing should be done about the recession and that his entire response was 'nothing more than a litany of reasons why Australia could not succeed'.

The stimulus was not so great as to either frighten the markets for very long or satisfy the welfare lobbies. This left the way open to steer a course through the middle where the political dynamic was; one day assailing the dries for their gloom and their failure to recognise social need, the next setting about the wets for their refusal to accommodate economic reality. If it fell short of being an icon to inspire them, it changed the mood of caucus and was at least a text to work from; and for Keating it was a blunt but serviceable instrument with which to belabour Fightback. And Labor's polling indicated general approval—especially of the title.

The next day Keating made the mandatory visit to the National Press Club to begin the task of selling One Nation. He went with a half-written speech and scraps of notes, many of them in answer to the morning press. He went knowing that he had jolted the government back to life; that if he had not given Simon Crean and the left everything they wanted it had been enough to satisfy them for now, and in doing it he had given the government the edge in some key areas—wages policy, industry policy and social policy for a start. He had wrenched the initiative back from the bureaucracy, defused the tension in cabinet, enlivened a caucus which had all but given up.

He also went to the Press Club with a joke in mind. He had come to the office that morning with the thing half-formed but already bursting with potential: he would say he wanted to put Hewson and Howard in a diorama at the new constitutional museum as relics of the fifties. By the time he got to the Press Club the joke had grown more elaborate and picked up a punch-line. On the way in he said he was happy not to have a speech. 'It's how it's always been,' he said, 'downhill, one ski, no poles.' He winged most of it and was effective enough to even get away with imitating John Hewson's little speech defect—'Real Reform for Austraya'. Back at Question Time he got the Dorothy he'd been waiting for and followed the agreed response for a while: he'd put them in the museum with the Morphy Richards toaster and the Qualcast lawnmower and heavily protected slippers and other relics of the 1950s and the Liberals would bring their children to see it and the kids would look up and say, 'Gee, Dad, is that the past?' And Dad would say, 'No, son, that's the future.' The Labor benches guffawed happily.

But Keating had more in mind than anyone knew. What followed was the first of many instances in which an observer could be forgiven for thinking the two men provoked in each other the memories of childhood battlefields where all the most indelible lessons are learned. Or had it triggered ancestral memories of the civil war, what Elias Canetti calls 'the first lethal clash'? Hewson's reaction to what Keating believed was a perfectly proper speech to the Queen had touched a nerve. It was a deep insult, and almost certainly intensified by the press reaction to Annita's missing curtsy. And it probably awoke another half-buried memory, that of his father's brother who had been captured at the fall of Singapore and murdered on the Sandakan death marches. He berated the Opposition.

I was told I did not learn respect at school. I learned one thing:
I learned about self-respect and self-regard for Australia [this much
had been agreed upon—the rest was entirely unexpected]—not
about some cultural cringe to a country which decided not to
defend the Malayan peninsula, not to worry about Singapore, and
not to give us our troops back to keep ourselves free from Japanese
domination. This was the country that you people wedded yourselves to, and even as it walked out on you and joined the
Common Market, you were still looking for your MBEs and your
knighthoods, and all the rest of the regalia that comes with it.

One reporter said that his words produced 'the most visceral roar'
to be heard on Labor's back benches for years. It also produced
from other quarters the most astonishing yelps. The London
tabloids went barmy again. The *Sun* ran a poll, 'Do Aussies Make
You Sick?', Kylie Minogue was reported as saying she wouldn't
hear a word against England, and Les Paterson as advising the
Prime Minister that 'you have got to have a bit of chat with your
Queen before you stick your hand up her frock'. Three years later
Keating was still receiving letters from RSL members claiming
that he had said British troops had run away at Singapore. From
people whose opinion had more weight came savage denunciations: he was rewriting history, they said (the same people who
four years later were complaining about political correctness). Yet
much in what they said suggested ignorance of history, or at best
a partisan reading of it. Keating was not the first Australian prime
minister to complain about British unwillingness to adequately
defend Singapore—that distinction fell to Menzies, in 1941.
Indeed, there is hardly a history of the war, including the one
by Churchill, that does not substantially support Keating's interpretation of those events. True, his outburst lacked nuance and
detail, but Question Time in the House is not the place for the
exposition of subtle historical arguments. Nor was Keating's a
specifically Labor view. As someone remarked, the Prime Minister
was only expressing a judgment you might have heard in any RSL
club after a few beers had gone down.

As the dust settled, Alf Garland, the RSL chief, having hurled insults at him for weeks, asked for and was granted a meeting with the Prime Minister. As we trooped into the PM's sitting room, Guy Nelligan, standing stiffly at the door, said quietly, 'Give it to him, suh!' But the brigadier who had declared that every soldier ever to fight under the Australian flag was insulted by the Prime Minister, and within a month of this meeting would call him an 'Irish bigot', was mouse-like. After half an hour of shillyshallying the Prime Minister said, 'But Alf, I thought you'd come to give us a serve about Singapore and all that business you've been making a noise about.' The brigadier denied it: he said, 'it was all the press, you know, Prime Minister'. It was 'perception' of things. The Prime Minister said he was disappointed, he had been looking forward to a bit of an argument. Since there was not going to be one, what could he do for him? The brigadier said he wondered if the influence of the RSL might be restored at the War Memorial. To this the Veterans' Affairs Minister, Ben Humphreys, said something along the lines of 'For God's sake, Alf, we're not talking about that'. 'Is that it, then?' asked the Prime Minister. The brigadier indicated that it pretty well was, except that there was this do coming up in London for leaders of ex-servicemen's organisations and he put it to the Prime Minister that it would be appropriate for the government to sponsor the attendance of Mr and Mrs Garland.

One learned to live with strangely altered behaviour among friends and acquaintances. The historian Geoffrey Serle, who I had known well for twenty years, cut me with startling intent at a function in Melbourne. When I addressed his turned head, he looked at me fiercely and said, 'You're keeping bad company.' At the same function another friend, shaken it seemed with an uncontrollable animus, told me, 'Tell him to stop it.' I chose my company more carefully than before, narrowed the range of my acquaintances and the risk of verbal assault. It was not all the identity debate: one had to argue foreign policy, economic policy, arts policy. Very often people would put the very case I had put all week, and I would find myself putting the case to them that had been put to me. All week was spent in first gear going forward, and the weekends engaged reverse. It was tiring and dementing, but it helped me understand why politicians sometimes go strange.

The new front of history, identity and symbols could not be closed even if we wanted to. It was called Pom-bashing, Irish republicanism, political opportunism, the last refuge of a scoundrel and, over and over, a cynical diversion from the economy. In fact if it was any of these things at all, it was only incidentally. Keating believed the last symbols of Australia's colonial past were inimical to a clear-eyed appreciation of reality. He wanted it to be universally understood that the country had to make its own way. On that perception depended the courage to make radically new choices about the future. He thought from this clearing of the national decks might come the energy to make the whole Australian experiment exciting again. Once started, he was not going to let up on it for long: he took it everywhere as a natural accompaniment to economic recovery, micro-economic reform, the environment, the arts and Aboriginal issues. He took it abroad, especially to Asia where he thought we'd do much better if we went 'sure of who we are and what we stand for'.

The political landscape had been changed beyond recognition and the catalyst had been the Queen. The new front was opened because it was perceived as good policy as well as good politics. Some in the Prime Minister's Office never agreed, and there were times when pointy heads and bleeding hearts alike wished we could go back to the main game where there was less heat if not more light. But we could not stop it if we wanted to, and when it turned out that this new front created more difficulties for Dr Hewson than it did for us it was easy enough to grin and bear it. Especially when in April, despite depressingly high unemployment and mixed economic signals, and continuing daily thundering against Keating's intention to create a republic and change the flag, the social researcher Hugh Mackay reported that his focus groups were 'astonished by the turnaround in their own feelings about Paul Keating', and that he now had 'an excellent chance of leading Labor to yet another election victory'.

CHAPTER 5

It is a feature of strongly held dogmas that they steadfastly resist not only unpalatable truths but even the faintest suggestion of the barest possibility of the most tangential reference to an unacceptable fact. Better that men should die and cities be overrun than that the sacred teaching should be found wanting.

NORMAN DIXON, ON THE PSYCHOLOGY OF MILITARY INCOMPETENCE

A SPINNAKER WAS always going to be out of the question, but One Nation did raise a modest sail for the government, and in March 1992 it got some wind in it. Four weeks after the big economic statement, Newspoll put the government ahead and the Morgan, which in Hawke's last week had the government twenty points behind, now had it closing steadily. Had the election been in sight just then, momentum might have carried Keating there. It was remarkable. Even people in the party's focus groups found it hard to understand the change in their feeling about him. He had done something to them and they did not know what. Yet it was not so surprising. One Nation was a sign that he knew they existed, after a year in which everything pointed to the pursuit of his own interests. He had offered a faint indication that he, the one they took to be the architect of the recession, was the man most likely to know how to fix it. It was less an affirmation than a suspension of disbelief, but so long as he held this course and remained passably upright he could count himself a chance in an election.

Keating had a metaphor for it: sometimes, he said, you have to pick up a bloody big rock and drop it in the pond. One minute all the frogs are sitting round on their old familiar lily pads, singing the same old songs, thinking the same old thoughts—everything in its proper place in what seems the natural order. And then there's this bloody great tidal wave and when they look around the next time the world has changed. This is what he had done to the political environment. Suddenly there was more than the economy to argue about. There were new pads, new frogs and new tunes. Things looked the same but different.

In just a few weeks John Hewson had taken on a much more problematic cast. Keating's forays into history and national symbols had put his opponent in relief; being matters as much of the heart as of the head, they had for the first time revealed something of the nature of Dr Hewson's soul. Tapes of him from 1989 suggest a personable, modest, genuine liberal. There was no sign of zealotry; rather concern for a country whose economy, he said, had been fenced into Labor's political timetable. He saw the crash coming. Keating, he said, did not understand that without urgent micro-economic reform 'this country's going out backwards'. Now, leader of the Opposition with a program for micro-economic reform and enough of the recession around to prove the need for it, he should have had Keating where he wanted him. But when Keating, who had made the economy the main game of politics in Australia and insisted that this was where the battle must be fought, began to operate on different ground, Hewson seemed unable to think straight. He said it was a sideshow, a diversion. He said the Prime Minister had thrown the switch to vaudeville. But Hewson could not do what reason would have told him: he could not ignore it.

The doctrine of the main game had this remarkable political characteristic: it cut the threads that bind a government to ordinary thought and feeling. It was a regime of emotional austerity which denied government any capacity to work effectively in areas where it must work—the realms of sentiment, spirit, fellow feeling; the realms inhabited by people and their symbols. Bob Menzies, Ben Chifley and John Curtin would never have cut those ties. It was their feel for them which made great leaders of those Keating most admired—Lincoln, Roosevelt, Churchill. That master of sentiments and symbols, Menzies, never ventured far from the Queen, the flag, the British inheritance, the menace of communism, the ideals of personal effort, frugality, authority and cricket. Menzies elevated this panoply of values to the status of a 'natural dogma', of the kind associated with popes and kings. Paul Keating had a current account and the headline inflation rate to keep him company.

This non-economic environment was not always comfortable for Keating, nor always politically profitable. It did get messy at times: it was not always possible to argue about the facts of history or wrestle over the flag and still look like he was concerned about the interests of ordinary people. It was not always possible to have these arguments and look wise or sensible. It made everyone nervous. Once the debate about symbols was labelled a 'cynical diversion' from the country's economic problems it became risky to enter the territory, even when he had to. To stand in front of the flag could appear in the media as a picture of hypocrisy; to offer a view on history which ran counter to the general understanding—or a view which in the general ignorance passed for a general understanding—sharpened a perception of him as a humbug or an anarchist, a dangerous man who would do anything. And it was not easy for him to quickly let go of these debates once they had been started. Meanwhile his opponents could stir the people's anger at a leader who talked about the past when the present was stealing the fruits of their labour and hope.

Yet this world where economics didn't reach never sat as badly with Keating as it did with Hewson. Every time Keating bounded into the republican paddock Hewson steamed and fretted on the other side of the fence. But what could he say? That the national flag was both unimportant *and* sacred? That a nation could not concern itself with the economy and its identity at the same time? Keating might not have been Renaissance Man, but his tactic made Hewson resemble a relic of the Reformation. As the year in politics and in rhetoric went on, the thoroughly modern Hewson revealed not only a mean-spirited and pious side, but a deep streak of fogeyism. For Keating, playing the republican card ran the risk that people would take him for a cunning, even unscrupulous politician. The risk for Hewson in responding was that they would take him for an inept or incompetent one.

Much against his will, early in March Keating went to Adelaide to be seen among the arts community at Writers' Week and launch a novel by Rodney Hall, the Chair of the Australia Council. He was reluctant to go to Adelaide at the best of times. But to a book launch! He hated book launches. Peter Barron, who had driven down to Canberra in his Lexus as if to give prime ministerial advisers not just the benefits of his wisdom but a fore-taste of the political hereafter, said the Prime Minister ought to be visiting a factory instead. There were people in our office who felt the same way, and no doubt felt it more intensely because Barron felt it. Ryan and I thought it was a chance to widen him, and to make some friends among people with a voice in the nation's affairs. In the plane the Prime Minister read the speech I had given him. He liked the speech, but he was not sure that he could get away with it.

Hundreds gathered outside the Adelaide tent to welcome him. They clapped and cheered his speech, and laughed when he said his hard-bitten advisers reckoned he shouldn't be hanging around arty turns. He congratulated Hall for the brilliant reviews he had received in the London *Times* and the *Financial Times*, but 'you haven't really been reviewed until you've been reviewed in the London tabloids'. It was a perfect environment to keep the debate alive. He said his 'greatest pleasures' included European architecture and music. 'But I am not British or French. I'm Australian. It's the land I know, the people I know, the resonance I feel.' He didn't think there should be any compromising Australia's identity. Australians had been saying as much for a century, yet in the last few weeks we had seen how when a contemporary political leader says 'these simple, unexceptional things' it still draws 'quite extraordinary' responses.

He would support the arts, he said, because he loved the

arts. And in fact he did: anyone who has been moved by music or some other great creative work knows what I mean, he often said, and then he would say that that is why governments must encourage them. In Adelaide he told his audience that a country is 'healthier when the arts flourish'. They tell us who we are, he said. He wanted to see Australians come to terms with Aboriginal Australia. If they didn't there will 'always be a feeling among us that we don't quite belong, that we're not serious, that we're just here for the view'. He didn't want us to remain 'what Manning Clark called Austral-Britons'. The audience clapped and whistled. The next day they threw a splendid lunch for him. He gave an equally splendid interview about the arts on ABC television and went home happy.

In Melbourne a few days later he returned to his themes: he told a St Patrick's Day gathering that Australians should 'reclaim their history'. The literal meaning of these words may not have been clear even to their author. That they had sufficient meaning to bring on applause, excite uncritical comment and give Keating's persona a dimension it had lacked was entirely due to the events which followed his speech in the presence of Her Majesty. It was because Hewson and others had so vehemently denied his right to have a view on history that Keating continued with his argument about it. Their response had smacked of toadying, it was wrong in fact and it had as its central premise the silly view that there could be but one interpretation of Australian history and conservatives owned it. Keating was even less likely to retreat so long as their rebuttals came with the scent of educated snobbery. John Hewson was more matter of fact than most. In April 1992 he said Keating had derived his anti-British attitudes from Jack Lang: 'He knew nothing before he met Jack Lang—his formal education was particularly limited—and he learned nothing after Jack Lang.' 'He was a graduate in common law of Osuna, but even if he had been of Salamanca, as many think, he would have been just as mad,' Cervantes said about someone else with a good CV. Hewson, as Keating told the media, had 'gall'.

Politics is a game of the emotions, it is psychological war and is therefore very difficult to keep the child from stepping up on behalf of the man. Again and again Hewson would ruin his argument by lurching into the invective he learned at school. In the House he took to sledging. In a voice loud enough for Keating to hear, but not the House microphone, he called him 'loser'. He turned his back and spoke to his colleagues, or at least pretended to, when Keating had the floor. It was worth reminding the Prime Minister as he left for Question Time that his opponent might have such a hatred of him, an outward show of calm, or humour, a big smile—anything that suggested Paul Keating was at home in the Prime Minister's job—and Dr Hewson's hatred might, for all political purposes, consume him. 'That's right,' Keating would say as he went out the door, 'and you know I don't hate *him*. He's just a poor dumb bastard, that's all he is.'

For all its little Keynesian heresies, One Nation had not killed off the puritan economic ethic on the government side. But it had helped to neutralise the bad news. That was the key. By a combination of policy activity and comparisons with Hewson's right-wing radicalism the government could get back in the race. And those heresies, combined with others concerning the nation's symbols, helped: not only because they gave the Keating Government a human face, but also because they frequently drove Hewson into an undignified frenzy of righteousness.

Arts, history, Aborigines and national symbols were useful for now, but both sides knew that in the long run the issue would be decided on the economic side of the fence. In between times the government lived a shaky existence, knowing that at any moment a new set of figures could knock it over. Even if Keating picked up points for bravery in debates about the war, or won a round or two in the House, knocked holes in Fightback, recited a hundred benefits of One Nation, the economy lurked. A little advantage might be squeezed out of low inflation figures, or the statistical proof of growth's existence, or an improvement in the participation rate of the workforce—and then unemployment would rise by another 0.5 of a per cent, another fifty thousand closer to a million; or Treasury would quietly inform the office that growth was insufficient to meet the forecast budget deficit. And the government would run off the road.

Every few weeks there was a mugging of this kind. The recovery was there but it wouldn't show itself. In the comedian John Clarke's words (speaking as Keating of course) it was 'a recessiony sort of recovery'. The government's policies were working, the government said, but only a very special kind of government person could discern this.

Political leaders are wise not to take their own psychology too seriously. It might suggest weakness, damage or self-obsession or run counter to the need for all leaders to be 'forward looking'. Leaders are the opposite of Proustian; they must put everything, including disappointment and their mothers, behind them. It doesn't do for them to resemble candidates for the analyst's couch. They are supposed to speak for the needs of the country, and their mood should reflect the public's not their own; the more profound their own needs are, the more consuming their own moods, the more they must be sublimated. This may be one main reason why some of them become eccentric or age prematurely.

'The dogs may bark, but the caravan moves on,' Paul Keating was fond of saying. Publicly, he used it to mock backward-looking opponents, but privately it might have been an expression of personal loss. Forward movement is everything and no-one will vote for a cot case. They are equally disinclined to vote for someone they don't know, so a politician must have a story. If they don't, the media will soon enough provide it. Voters also require wisdom in their leaders and, as there cannot be wisdom without experience, leaders are obliged to bring the past with them on their journey forward. It comes usually in the form of ennobling deeds and cautionary tales—or telling comparisons: 'They are like the Bourbons,' Keating used to bellow at his opponents, 'they've learned nothing and they've forgotten nothing.' And everyone behind him would laugh and the point was always made, though it is not certain that everyone knew what it was.

Keating was never inclined to put his private life on public view. His own childhood, like that of his children, he considered precious. John Hewson, by contrast, told Laurie Oakes on Channel 9 how as a child he had stood up to the school bully. One day on the way home he had decked the brute. He meant by this that we should think he was the man to stand up to Keating, but it is likely that most people took it to mean the man was still a boy. Given his propensities, it might have been a blessing for everyone that Hewson didn't know that at roughly the same age Paul Keating snatched a hat from a Protestant boy's head and threw it up a tree. It would not have been uplifting to hear him charge Keating with it in the parliament. The national parliament is among other things a sign that we have left the playground, and to some extent we judge parliamentarians by the degree to which they appear to have given up their childhood. This is why political analysts who enter the arena with psychoanalytic tools should expect resistance, and there is a case for saying that it will be the best politicians who resist most fiercely.

Among politicians the word 'psychological' is nearly always followed by the word 'bullshit'. The derision is generally greatest among the politicians who practise psychology to the point of torture on their opponents. But you can't hide your mother forever. Paul Keating and Bob Hawke both had powerful, fiercely loyal mothers, the sort of mother you expect to see in a John Ford film; warm-hearted, hard-headed, indomitable, tough-as-boots mothers who in one way or another have never stopped feeding their boys. Such mothers are admired for what they have given unbroken, not for what, inevitably, they had to take away. It is not therefore surprising if the psychology of politics often seems closest to that of a western: political drama is played out on a constantly changing frontier, where high ambition competes with dire experience, where the future is carved out and memory is swept aside and a man's past is his own business.

For all that, the past won't go away. 'The awful thing is,' as D. W. Winnicott said, 'nothing is ever forgotten.' Even as they speak of what lies beyond the sunrise it grips them, as a comforter, as a symbol, as a source of coherence, as an inspiration, as a bludgeon for one's opponents. No-one has ever calculated the use-by date on guilt in politics. John Howard's failures as treasurer in the Fraser Government still had some currency in 1989 but, as Keating found, in 1995 they had lost all potency. Albeit with some difficulty, Keating's support for a GST in 1986 could be brushed aside in 1993. The tag the 'guilty party', which the Liberals applied to Labor in Victoria, worked for two elections but not for three. It's a fine judgment: at some indefinable point the party holding its opponent accountable for the past looks fraudulent and without a case to put.

Some characters and events from history defy time's passage. Judas, Napoleon, Macbeth and Custer are perennial political bywords. The lessons of Munich are clear and immutable to all but the rankest fools and may be scornfully applied to anyone who at any time suggests a policy of conciliation with anyone on anything. It matters not if the circumstances are wholly dissimilar, one's bargaining position much weaker, one's aims very different or the thing at stake is not the enslavement of Europe but the market for woollen products—Munich can be very hard to get around. The name Billy McMahon, the prime minister who succeeded John Gorton and was defeated by Gough Whitlam in 1972, is also potent and unmistakable. Billy McMahon means a leader without respect or credibility and certain to lose whatever election he contests. The name is shorthand for folly, decay and defeat.

Despite the boost from One Nation, the ALP's research was always salutary or depressing, depending on the sort of person you were. It was negative even when the polls were good. You could pass it off as expensive proof of what any intelligent observer could deduce from sniffing the air. But sometimes the view from outside the Prime Minister's Office would suddenly overwhelm you: a conversation overheard in a Melbourne tram, a taxi's talkback radio, something your children said—and you would find yourself sick with fear. It was after a succession of these incidents that I said in an advisers' meeting that Paul Keating's standing had ebbed to a point where we could any day expect comparisons with McMahon. I am sure it was true—in fact it was obvious. So obvious that once I had uttered it I lived in fear that we would hear someone on the Opposition side say the same thing. It didn't happen with McMahon, but a couple of years later when I wrote in my diary that the Prime Minister seemed to share certain psychological characteristics with Ned Kelly, Bronwyn Bishop turned up in the papers a few days later saying the same thing. That McMahon was not used against us in the low points of 1993 was doubly fortunate because three years later it was available to Keating when he wanted to put Downer away. 'I am not saying the Leader of the Opposition is a racist,' he said over the din in the House. 'I am saying he is the most foolish Leader of the Liberal Party since Billy McMahon.' Some of the commentators reckoned it was devastating. The only cause for regret was that everyone knew any politician who can be plausibly compared to Billy McMahon is bound for extinction, whoever you compare him with.

If the past is sometimes used as a truncheon, it also comes as a mantra, a chorus of disapproval. Just as the bureaucracy resists all things without precedent, so politicians—and bureaucrats—resist everything for which something resembling a precedent has been judged a failure. The past is a curtain to be dropped on stray and unwanted ideas which find their way on to the political stage. It smothers them. It works in two ways, each as stupefying to outsiders as the other. One—the more obvious and common version—takes the form of collective wisdom or dogma. It says to those who come bearing suggestions: silly fellow, it was tried before and failed dismally, go away. It is often accompanied by mutual back-slapping and derision among the Druids, and a mental note is made: *that person is a dickhead and need not be taken seriously until he learns what is true.* The second is a dogma held to by a single individual—a prime minister, for instance. It is like a bone or teddy bear that cannot be let go or changed in any way. First uttered at a moment in the past when it was both the right and the perfect riposte, it has been internalised and continues to reverberate delightfully inside. The pleasure derived from repeating the words, including presumably the pleasure of seeing the frustration they yield in others, surpasses reason and makes argument pointless. In the end it can only be treated as an eccentricity or psychosis.

Paul Keating had an aversion to the idea of a national museum. 'The last thing we need is another bloody great mausoleum by the lake,' he would say. At other times he would preface this with, 'I said to Lionel Bowen in 1987 [or thereabouts] and I won't be changing my mind'. Nothing could persuade him. It did no good to say that there would be no mausoleum, or any other kind of public building; that we would build half of it in cyberspace and put the rest on permanent tour. A virtual museum linked to every community in the country, every school and public meeting place. It would have found favour with the general public, the new information industries and the old intelligentsia; it was an investment in technology as much as heritage; it combined the national with the regional; fostered a sense of national unity and greater understanding of Australia's history; it was postmodern in the best way possible—and in all this it was a perfect fit with government policy.

Over three years the concept for a national museum evolved into a brilliant fusion of technology, democracy and imagination—a masterpiece on which any prime minister would love to hang his hat. But Paul Keating snarled at it, stonewalled, elided all reference to it in speeches. Late in 1995 he finally submitted, but before the new Keating-style museum could be started he lost the election. The new government demolished a hospital (killing a bystander in the process) and on the site built, if not another bloody great mausoleum, another bloody big building by the lake.

In politics—possibly at any level—words become passwords or talismans. Certain areas are sealed off if you don't know them. Like other passwords, of themselves they don't make sense—they are essentially functional rather than meaningful. In 1992 the words 'no RED schemes' worked in this way.

RED schemes (Regional Employment Development) were devised by the Whitlam Government as a cure or palliative for unemployment in the 1970s. They were work-creation schemes. In the spirit of the Great Depression projects, but more generous, they put young people to work on community projects all over suburban and regional Australia. It was believed that the experience of work, together with the benefits to communities, was preferable in every way to the dole. Although no analysis of RED schemes ever demonstrated that their net result was failure, this became the almost universal belief. Many communities and individuals must have profited a little, and the product of the schemes may still be seen in pleasant town landscapes and sporting facilities. But the wisdom was that these good works were bad. The wisdom was they wasted money, created little more than densely forested traffic roundabouts and, through bringing young people into contact with each other and putting money in their pockets, gave an unprecedented stimulus to cannabis consumption.

RED schemes became a symbol of all that was wrong with the Whitlam Government and the embodiment of Keynesian follies. It was a hallmark of Hawke–Keating Labor that there were 'no RED schemes'. Like 'picking winners' and other 'discredited' species of 'industry policy', they were a blasphemy against the neoclassical economic doctrine, and they remained so when unemployment reached 11 per cent, when a large proportion of the million unemployed were long term, when the life chances of a generation were slipping away from tens of thousands because the accident of a recession had cut them off from work and training. Even when there was rage and despair, there would be 'no RED schemes'. In Innisfail in Queensland, the town's taxi driver told me he had been put out of work not by the recession but by government policy on the environment. He had been a timber cutter. He was more fortunate than scores of others in the district who had not been able to find jobs. He wondered whether it would cost the government less to pay these men to replant the areas they had cleared than to keep them and their families on benefits. He said they would be happier and healthier and the kids would have a better chance in life. It seemed obvious to him—as it did to millions of others around the country. But there would be 'no RED schemes'. And no national service schemes either, although I was not always sure why not.

These talismanic responses create a kind of deafness. If you've forgotten the password, no-one is going to listen to your reasons. If you say: but we are the government, a Labor government, we have to do *something*! They say: squandering money planting trees in nature strips isn't going to help. How many roundabouts can the nation stand? You are trying to cross a border but the guards are laughing at you. You say, let's rope business into it, and the States, come up with schemes which have a chance of working. 'No RED schemes' comes the reply—meaning we did not create this supply-side paradise to have it soiled by the likes of you.

Little in human history suggests that people without degrees in economics are more feckless or daft than people with them. No-one in the Prime Minister's Office was suggesting the re-introduction of RED schemes. No-one thought that they were a practical solution, or that they would wash in the media. No-one thought there was a quick fix. Everyone knew equally that there was *no* quick fix—but this didn't stop some people saying it endlessly and avidly to others. It was tempting to say that while RED schemes had not spectacularly succeeded, similar programs conducted in the thirties here and in the United States had been judged as at least partially successful; some respected commentators, indeed, have said that they saved a generation. But this only invited the people with economics degrees to say that one was possessed of a burning desire to recreate some impossible era when huge amounts were spent in building dams or pyramids. One was alleged to be talking Mickey Mouse stuff.

Mickey Mouse was a name to be feared by all advisers. To be touched by those two words was poison. 'Bleeding heart', 'froth', 'fairy floss' and 'Creanite' were others—a Creanite was someone who sympathised with industry policy of the kind advocated by Simon Crean. These names were dreaded in the way

Trotskyist, 'revisionist' and 'tendencies' were dreaded in another time and another place. You knew your economic credibility was shot. You could try to postpone or deflect it by declaring that some other minister's office was full of bludgers and incorrigible bleeding hearts and the minister himself would not get off the pot—and perhaps spitting in a corner. You could mock the whole thing by asking if the economy was expected to be still growing at Christmas, and when they said they couldn't say for sure, ask how they expected the rest of the office to organise a strategy for the flag. You could outflank them on the right by advocating a wholly deregulated labour market *and* universal national service, but neither the econocrats nor my closest ally, Mark Ryan, had the stomach for national service.

At an impromptu meeting in Don Russell's office in mid-March 1992 the gun was pointed gingerly at their heads. It proceeded from the revelation that the economists were agreed growth was too slow for unemployment to improve. The inflation figures were good, however. Try to imagine the day, the bleeding hearts said, when unemployment passes a million. The day in its political dimension. And all the days before it when our opponents say, it's coming any day now. Who will be the millionth Australian? Every day between that one and this, someone somewhere will make you pay for unemployment. Most often it will be Hewson, but there will be many others including the media, the churches, the caucus, the welfare lobby, the public at large including Labor's own supporters. What will you say? That the inflation figures are good? That exports are improving? That the economy is growing? That the recession is over? But if you say the recession is over—please don't say the recession is over! You can't even say that things are looking up—because if you say they're looking up, Hewson will ask if they're looking up for the 27,384 who have become unemployed since the end of last month, or for the umpteen hundred thousand who are long-term unemployed.

It didn't stop the Prime Minister. He told the House the recession was over. The figures had been showing growth for a year or more. Hewson of course asked the obvious questions. With his miniature Australian flag beside him, and sea of miniature Australian flags all around, day after day he asked the Prime Minister if the recession was over for the likes of Joe Smith aged seventeen of Coburg North who, although he had applied for 114 jobs, had not had work for eighteen months and was now being treated for depression. Or Lucy Jones and her twelve workmates who had been laid off from the only industry in Woop Woop, now closed owing to the government's crippling interest rates. And so on, all the way to young people who had committed suicide because of the recession.

Stephen Smith had been urging Keating to make jobs and recovery his buzz words wherever he went. Stephen was a great mate of the ALP national secretary, Bob Hogg, who was a great mate of the incomparable pollster, Rod Cameron. Stephen believed politics had to be played by the polls. Whatever the focus groups are most impressed by, repeat. Whatever the focus groups say they want, say you'll give them, say you're 'committed' to it. Whatever they don't like, you don't like either. The terrible thing about this tactic is that, on balance, it probably works. When the Prime Minister was on his way to a speech or a press conference or Question Time, as he went out the door or hurried down a corridor or jumped in a car, Smith would say, 'Mention jobs, mate. Jobs and recovery.' Keating all too rarely did, and it was probably because Smith so incessantly told him to. Speeches were subjected to the same kind of judgments. The principle was to never leave the strategy. Jobs and recovery always had to be at the top of the speech: that was the message, and nothing else in the document, nothing else said that week, nothing else between whenever it was and the election, should get in the way of the message. If someone did have an idea, Smith would usually say, 'We've got Hoggy's polling on Friday. Let's wait and look at the polling.'

Some people thought it was a barmy approach and sometimes it surely was. Polls incline towards the bleeding obvious, but they are not the same as commonsense. Not always, at least. Keating could not win without policy initiative and political surprise. It was, in any event, the way he functioned. He could do no other. From this rose much of the surface tension in the office and between the office and operatives outside it. Stephen Smith was an admiring and unfailingly loyal adviser, but his instincts were different from Keating's. That didn't make him any less right about jobs. So long as it did nothing, or seemed to be doing nothing about unemployment, the government could expect to be routed at the polls by a party vowing to lower wages, remove the safety net and introduce a 15 per cent tax on everything including food.

I talked to Stephen Smith and Mark Ryan about the idea of a national summit. RED schemes aren't going to make any difference to the unemployment numbers, the economic advisers said—they always talked about 'numbers' or the 'number'. They also pointed out that Hewson's new tax was hardly likely to improve things for the unemployed. Once we narrowed Fightback down to higher taxes and lower wages, voters would begin to turn our way, the econocrats said. We said—but how can we do that when all their minds are on unemployment? And why *shouldn't* their minds be on unemployment which was terrible and getting worse? On the other hand, we said, if the PM announces that he will hold a national summit on unemployment with enough lead time to seek solutions from all those people who have been blaming him, he can dodge some of the flak, he can pull the community into him and Hewson will have to either come with him or play spoiler. A summit bursting with community representation might draw focus on the nasty centre of Fightback. Why not do it? We might even avoid what now seems assured—political defeat. And who knows, there might be some solutions.

But they will be RED schemes, they said. One way or another they will be RED schemes. It's no good doing things which haven't worked in the past; it's no good Paul going outside and saying stupid things; hand-wringing is not an option, they said. Was it by this tactic and reasoning that they conquered their enemies and reformed the economy? It owed a lot to Kafka. We haven't enough time to get a big enough policy ready, they said. It will raise expectations we can't meet. It will be a rod for our backs, they said. But which rod would you rather, we asked: the one you fashion yourself, or the one half the population want to apply?

Many weeks passed and the unemployed numbers grew higher before the Prime Minister and his pointy heads relented and announced an August national meeting on youth unemployment. Advice and ideas would be sought from business and community leaders, youth leaders, trade unions and other interested and expert parties.

'Ideas do not drop from trees,' sixties Marxists used to say, 'they are rooted in experience.' Early in March the ALP business lunch needed a speech which described the virtues of One Nation and the iniquities of the Fightback. Speeches of any substance were circulated among advisers before a penultimate draft was given to the Prime Minister. On this occasion the political adviser, Stephen Smith, recommended that a sentence describing John Hewson as a 'man with no heart' be deleted. The ALP polling, he said, indicated that 'they don't like it when we biff Hewson'. An argument followed. Smith's compromise was to say 'a man with a policy with no heart'. Don Russell suggested substituting 'an Opposition with a policy with no heart'. If you couldn't say Hewson was heartless, what could you say, I asked. Ryan spoke to the Prime Minister at the Lodge and on hanging up announced that the word was now 'heartbeat'. Hewson had no heartbeat. Were we saying he had passed on? 'Opposition', Ryan said—the speech would say the Opposition 'only follow the textbook, only obey their ideological reflexes—there is no heartbeat in any of them'. It had been a bruising debate for such a paltry result. On his way to deliver the speech, the PM rang from his car. He wanted 'Opposition' changed to 'Hewson'.

Ten days later, in a speech to the Victorian branch of the ALP, he leapt clean over the polling and said Hewson was 'a cold fish washed ashore by the recession'. I heard it on the ABC news. It was a line I had offered but did not expect him to use. It produced a roar in the auditorium, but doubtless a sinking feeling in Stephen Smith. The line was intended to convey the image of something primeval, a leftover from an extinct species disgorged by chance, a mutation of the New Right. It owed something to Charles Darwin and something to *The Blob*, and something to the notion that it might articulate a view for Hewson's potential opponents in the Liberal Party. The media ran it everywhere, some of it in the negative context of political name-calling. But the Prime Minister believed that he had hurt Hewson and that the name would stick.

It was like this on and off all through the year, a visceral, savage, exhausting brawl. They were like two brothers locked in mutual loathing which no-one, least of all the antagonists, could properly understand. Perhaps they *were* like brothers—and each saw in the other too many reflections of himself. Hewson, Keating said, was a real wolf in sheep's clothing, unlike Andrew Peacock who had been a sheep in sheep's clothing. And it was uncanny how to Keating and those around him Hewson came to look like a wolf, or a coyote, once the Prime Minister likened himself to his favourite cartoon character, the Road Runner. In the House Hewson began to regularly lean across and call Keating a 'creep'. No doubt this is how he looked to Hewson and others on that side. And no doubt he had people on his side designing insults for him, as we designed them for the Prime Minister— though whether he had 'three researchers' working on the task, as Phillip Knightley, author of *The First Casualty*, a book about truth, alleged of Keating in the British *Independent,* we did not know.

It is the last thing anyone in the game will admit, but many things in politics are imponderable. They defy prediction and analysis. That is why smart practitioners stay out of the debate when they don't know the answer. It is better to be silent than to be caught on the wrong side. One part of a political life is spent exercising influence, another equally large part is spent measuring and recording it. You will hear them telling each other how he or she had warned against a course of action which recently turned out badly; or recounting how other operators had counselled against an initiative which just proved a stunning triumph. Some, especially those with public service backgrounds, zealously write file notes which may be brought to prove that one's wise counsel had been followed or ignored, depending on the consequences. Experts at this practice can subtly blend two streams of advice into one—so that, for example, if the election is lost in March posterity will record that a certain soothsayer in the Prime Minister's Office had recommended holding it in the previous November; and if it is won there will be a document showing that the selfsame prophet had declared for March against the November trend of thought. Alternatively, one imagines it is not difficult to write two contrasting file notes and destroy one as events unfold.

In politics, whatever the wisest heads may say, only the rankest stupidity has entirely predictable consequences, and sometimes even that goes unpunished. On 9 March the Prime Minister addressed the United Nations Development Fund for Women which was celebrating International Women's Day with an 8 a.m. breakfast in Brisbane. It was never the best time of the day for Paul Keating, who was semi-Churchillian in his morning habits. His voice was never strong at 8 a.m. He was also an unknown quantity on the subject of women, although it was widely known that he liked them. He had with him a speech I had written in consultation with Anne de Salis in our office and Craddock Morton in the office of the Minister Assisting the Prime Minister on Women's Affairs, Wendy Fatin. The Office for the Status of Women (OSW) also made a contribution and, for the information of the Prime Minister, myself and others living in darkness sent to the PMO three typed pages headed 'General Rules of Addressing Women'. Among other recommendations they urged us to abolish from all our written and spoken communications the term 'man-made'. Instead we were to say 'artificial' or 'constructed'. Also, we were not to say 'man hours' or 'man power'. Do not say 'sportsmanship', but 'fair' or 'sporting', they told us. Do not say 'to master an art', rather say 'to become skilled'; do not say 'man the desk' (or boats?), say 'staff' them; do not say 'maiden speech' or 'maiden name', or 'the man in the street', or 'no-man's land', or 'every man for himself'—say 'everyone for themselves' (and hang the grammar). 'Ladies and Gentlemen' is appropriate in a speech if you have a mixed audience, but if the audience is primarily women, use 'Friends'. 'Do not use Men and Ladies in sentence [*sic*] together.'

Paul Keating's maiden speech in the House of Representatives was notorious among feminists for advocating policies which, contrary to the trend under the then conservative government, would encourage women out of the workforce and back into the home and child-bearing. There was nothing unusual in that for a Catholic from the Labor right—or for a Protestant from anywhere for that matter. Keating's views on the 1975 Family Law Bill would have tested a feminist's patience, without necessarily exhausting it. In the House he spoke in defence of 'good conscientious' women and 'faithful and conscientious' wives: 'It is not espousing the interests of women today to say of a conscientious woman who is trying to preserve her marriage and is doing the right thing by her husband and family that because her husband does not want her companionship any longer, and she is freed from the house, she must go to the government and receive social services.' Thus he defended women against inconstant men—and modern women. Better to force the man to meet his responsibilities than to subsidise his escape from them. He thought some contemporary thinking was 'hogwash' and that it was 'time many of these trendy women's groups had a good look at themselves'.

He was also untrendy about abortion: in 1979 he told the parliament that Australia was 'losing the impulse for social advance. Instead of maintaining the family it is killing it off to maintain living standards.' Abortion, he said, 'threatens the nation through the destruction of its children'. It was the Catholic view. The Labor part of his position was contained in his attack on those anti-abortionists on the other side of politics whose principal motive in opposing it was to 'tie up the Catholic vote'.

Cant and falsity produce unease and resentment in balanced minds, but zealots will welcome the most shameful performance if they know it is to appease them, and find hypocrisy to be no bad thing if it is also capitulation. No politician, including Paul Keating, ever got through a career without saying things he or she didn't believe or knew to be only half true. Like many others, no doubt, Keating dreaded this kind of dissembling. It was possibly his most consistent fear to be taken for a man with a mask. He was not an actor performing a script, which is why he did not read speeches with much confidence. He could only perform from conviction. Without conviction he lost credibility, and without credibility he was done for. This is not the same as saying that everything he said was true; like all storytellers he was prone to exaggerate, add colour for the sake of the point, stretch the boundaries of probability to the point of snapping. But at some fundamental level, even perhaps a mythic one, the words had to be true to him. It was one reason why working for Keating was exhausting: you had to make him believe it before he would say it. This could take a long time, and before embarking on the project advisers, whose own credibility was also at stake, had to decide whether it was worth the effort. The need to persuade him possibly served as a form of risk insurance: no doubt it meant sometimes he did not say or do things, or go to places which might have caused him grief. But it is likely just as often advisers chose not to lure or chase him in directions he really should have gone. The history of governments is to a substantial degree the history of these unrecorded calculations.

He did not go unwillingly to address the women in Brisbane, but he would not go with a speech full of the expected pieties or renunciations of his past beliefs. And no-one in his office wanted him to. The speech made no attempt to hide the stamp of his past thinking or pretend that it had much changed. After paying the usual respects to the honourable work of his hosts, he said, 'I have a feeling, an inkling, that I am not widely regarded as a feminist.' He was, he said, 'that most conservative of creatures, a family man'. He gave his audience an account of himself and his thoughts about women and politics which was cogent and matter of fact. It was a speech of the 'here I stand' kind, but with substance and an earnest undertaking to serve the cause of women in Australia.

His approach had been and would continue to be practical: 'I have always thought that the crime in politics was not thinking the wrong thought, but not doing enough.' He listed the specific measures of the previous nine years, which were substantial: trebling the number of child care places, a 60 per cent increase in average payments for long day care and a 200 per cent increase in those receiving it; the Family Allowance Supplement for the low paid and their dependants; supplementary payments for low-income workers; the Child Support Agency; the National Women's Health Strategy; a Sex Discrimination Act; an Affirmative Action Act; a National Committee on Violence Against Women; a National Agenda for Women.

However, he insisted, the greatest benefits to women had come through the success of national policy initiatives: 60 per cent of the one and a half million new jobs had gone to women; when the school retention rate doubled it meant two out of three girls now finished secondary school; more than half the higher education places were filled by women; where in 1983 women earned 67 cents for every dollar earned by men, they now earned 84 cents; and all those changes to the economy would in the longer term make Australia a better place for women. He described One Nation in much the same way he had described it to business gatherings—as a program to build links and partnership, as an effort to make the country stronger, and as reflecting a philosophy of social inclusion. He pointed out that as women became increasingly part of the mainstream of society—in the workplace, education, politics and community forums—it was not always possible or appropriate to single out policies for women from policies for the society at large. But all government policies, he assured them, would continue to be 'assessed in regard to their impact on women'.

He said that by expanding the economy, creating 1.5 million jobs and extending both opportunities and services to make it 'easier for people to plan their lives with confidence', he believed that as treasurer he had done 'things of great benefit to women'. That was still his view, but as Prime Minister he wanted 'more windows on to it'. He wanted to increase the influence of women in national policy-making, social development, the culture of the country. 'I incline towards inclusion. I want to lower the drawbridge,' he said.

For a man who had been raised deep in the bosom of the Catholic Church, and whose personal life was as reasonable a manifestation of its philosophy as it was possible for a worldly man to achieve, he could hardly be accused of failing to make concessions. But the speech was honest, unpatronising and free of the OSW's dire language requirements. OSW had drafted a message for the Prime Minister to record for UNIFEM breakfasts across the country. As usual, it was written in the verbal equivalent of putty. The message referred to 'our new agenda called "Shaping and Sharing the Future"'. It was an agenda, they said, which 'renews our commitment to the women of Australia to continue to place a high priority on ensuring women are able to participate as fully as they choose in all areas of our society'.

The feminist critic, Dale Spender, said the Prime Minister's Brisbane speech was patronising. We could not see *how* it was patronising, but many who were close to the women's movement, Wendy Fatin and others with attachments to the government, thought it was alarming that Spender thought so. The scene following the broadcast of her criticism resembled a field of budgerigars after a shotgun blast. In no time, the Assistant Minister, the women in the Labor caucus, several women advisers and several men as well, along with some of the chaps down at ALP headquarters, all seemed to be thinking the same thought: namely, Keating had blown it and the women's vote so assiduously pursued and won would now be lost.

It was difficult to see how the speech was patronising without accepting as true the premises the speech opposed: that, for example, economic policy should not be discussed with women; that women were to enter the mainstream but be addressed as a minority. Ultimately, it was not the feminist interpretation of Keating's words that was so disturbing or instructive, it was the flight from them when a well-known lobbyist took exception. John Hewson should have made a note.

It settled down as quickly as it had begun. By nightfall the Minister Assisting had been told that the government sought the women's vote and not the feminists' necessarily. Other advisers, ministers and caucus were told to read the speech and get out and support the Prime Minister. Months later an occasional voice could be heard muttering about 'his UNIFEM speech' as if it were a notorious thing. But it was immaterial by then. The Opposition must have taken some pleasure in this but their celebrations were not too rowdy; possibly because John Hewson found little joy in the prospect of an alliance with Dale Spender, and possibly because he had plans for OSW which did not include its continued existence.

Late in February I had suggested that the Prime Minister ask Anne Summers if she would be prepared to return to Australia from New York and join his office. It seemed a good idea because it would signal immediately that he took the women's vote seriously—and, what was more important, provide some gumption and broad experience we badly needed. A first-rate journalist, an effective networker and, having run OSW in the first three years of the Hawke Government, an experienced operator in government and bureaucracy, she would bring energy, ideas and nous to the office mix. She would make the office less of a bunker, and the debate more robust, less precious, slogan-riddled and ideological. In New York, where she had been editor-in-chief of *Ms.* magazine, she was attacked by both the Moral Majority and the feminists for her liberal editorial line. Summers loved, even needed, proximity to power. She also had a passion for the country. When I phoned, she hesitated. Was it true the New South Wales right had all sorts of vile influence, as the rumours reaching her suggested? I said that most likely they were just the same old Fairfax rumours. She wanted to come. She would wait for the Prime Minister to ring her. The Prime Minister was keen, but not so keen as to phone immediately. It took him several weeks to make the phone call. His wife, Annita, was keen, for the same reasons as I was. Mark Ryan was keen. Don Russell and Anne de Salis were half-keen, then rang one cold Saturday afternoon when I was cleaning autumn leaves out of the spouting, and while I sat on the roof seething with discontent told me on the new-fangled mobile phone that Summers might be trouble—her public profile might be resented, she might irritate the Prime Minister and raise expectations he could not meet. I said it was a worthwhile risk, particularly as the same could be said about several other people in the office, including me. Eventually they agreed, eventually the Prime Minister rang her and eventually she came.

Russell and de Salis were partly right: Summers did attract a lot of media attention, one or two in the office did resent her, some at party headquarters disliked her aggressive, publicity-generating manner, and the PM occasionally complained about attempts to shunt him into feminist positions. But he was more fun when Summers was around, because he liked women, and women—from everything I saw—liked him, even when, contrary to OSW rules, he called them not only 'girls' and 'ladies' but 'sheilas', 'old boilers' and 'love'. Summers had a laugh like an Australian bush bird that you could hear from one end of the office to the other; she stormed up and down the corridor in miniskirts, white stockings, high heels and startling vermilion lipstick; she would complain bitterly about not getting his attention, and more than once she threatened to resign. She could drink old-fashioned quantities of red wine. And she networked and researched and cajoled with extraordinary vigour and made a difference to his fortunes. Despite the protests of the pointy heads that Keating would never do the things Anne Summers wanted him to do, he did announce reforms to child care in a major economic statement rather than a 'women's' statement; he did make significant legislative changes for women; and he did appear on the front cover of *Rolling Stone* in a pair of Ray Bans. In the month that Summers arrived a Morgan poll showed that only 17 per cent of Australian women approved of Keating. Nine months later Labor got 50 per cent of the women's vote—the first time ever. There were plenty of reasons why and the GST was one of them, but if Summers only took 10 per cent of the credit it would still be the difference between winning and losing.

The government bounced along from a set of encouraging economic figures to a set of bad ones; from an exhilarating spurt to a depressing stumble; from good poll to bad; from good news to gruesome. You would read the press clippings at 9 a.m. and feel confident, then read the media summaries at 10 and feel it was hopeless. A kind of progress was made but satisfactory and reliable traction was never achieved. So much emotional turmoil is at least as addictive as it is destructive. Sometimes there was nothing, as if a frame had been cut from the film: everything stopped in mid-stride, instant doldrums, as if one had walked into a black hole in a familiar corridor, and a few strides later the depression—if that's what it was—would lift and the drama would start up again.

In mid-year John Hewson began referring to the Prime Minister's Office as 'Keating's Republican Guard'. This no doubt suited his designs on that large body of Australians who reckoned in their straitened times that any republic was about as useful as a club foot, and one imposed on them by Keating quite insufferable. 'Keating's Republican Guard' was a good line in the tradition of bogey-creation. It was also deeply flattering. The Prime Minister's Office resembled a republican guard in the way *Duck Soup* resembles *Hamlet*—which is to say that generally things were more farcical than tragic.

The PMO was a problem which never went away. It is not as unkind as it sounds to say that it wouldn't go away so long as it was the office of Paul Keating. There are many theories of management and organisation and many people have persuaded industry to give them many millions of dollars to organise them along their particular model. The PMO had no model and very little management or organisation. If a model could be drawn from any of the more popular theories it might be Peter F. Drucker's model of a company which is about to go under. For the mindset of the PMO was welded to the past, fixed on its traditional product rather than prepared to cannibalise it before its competition did, refusing to give up on that which was no longer profitable—like neoclassical economics, like 'main game' thinking, like spinning the same story day after day—instead of finding the new opportunities and 'zoning in on them'. And as Drucker would say, 'reassess, reassess, reassess'.

The Melbourne consultant, journalist, and former adviser to John Cain, Michael Richards, had an early go at helping the PMO escape from chaos. By day Richards talked to every member of staff and almost became part of the team, and at night he marvelled with Ryan and me that the place actually worked at all. He recommended that people be put in jobs for which they were competent and confident, and those who were in the wrong places be moved to more appropriate ones; that an adviser be appointed to deal with social policy; that the office be reconfigured so that the Prime Minister could get to them with greater or less ease according to their need and his desire. The new door connecting him directly with Don Russell obliged needy advisers to congregate inside or just outside the principal adviser's office. The door between Keating and Russell saved a lot of time and internal travel—it cut about fifteen metres off the trip—but it also created an alternative means of escape for a Prime Minister who sometimes felt and looked like a rat in a cage. There were occasions when it was necessary to lie in wait for him with all three exits blocked. The poor man could not scratch his head without being seen on the monitors beneath Russell's desk at one end and Peter Robinson's desk at the other. The former Treasury economist Robinson had the horrendous job of managing the Prime Minister's timetable and movements. Should the Prime Minister be seen on the monitor putting on his coat the word went out that he was leaving, whereupon scurrying would be heard in the corridors as his staff rushed to take up positions at the exits. The time to worry was when you couldn't see him on the monitor, and often at the moment you began to worry you heard the squeal of tyres on the tiles in his courtyard as Jimmy Warner the driver hightailed it away to the

Lodge, the Prime Minister looking like Houdini grinning grimly beside him.

He was unshakeably stubborn, chronically wilful. He would not be co-opted except by strenuous effort. Put an open gate in front of him and he would not go through it; put a fence and he'd try to jump it. In so many things an adviser to Paul Keating was like a sheepdog with a refractory sheep. He'd stamp his foot and petulantly bleat, he'd turn and face you with his head down and when you weren't looking he'd bolt. He was like a prima donna who never goes on the stage without a tantrum, or a brawl or some mysterious illness, or with anything resembling mastery of her lines, and then after a peerless performance has to be dragged from it while a team of lackeys gather up the flowers. Or a child who will not get into the car to go on a Sunday drive, wrestles with his harness, gets car sick and complains all the way there and then doesn't want to come home.

His staff felt his moods most acutely because with the staff he was less disposed to hide them. It was not the bouts of anger and frustration—they were to be expected, were probably therapeutic and, in fact, less common than displays of joie de vivre: the debilitating mood was the one when he seemed to be saying that the job meant less to him than it did to us. It was trying to find signs of enthusiasm in him when there were none visible. It was trying to not let his 'black dog' eat you.

Management theory was for business to play around with. It was a necessary element in the great drive to make Australian industry competitive. It was a key to world's best practice, the essential stuff of international benchmarking. None of those new companies on the frontiers of the brave new world could do without it. And not just private industry; the public service took on new management systems and were very proud of them. A lot of them were silly. Some very successful business people still run their companies according to instinct rather than theory or systems. A political office probably has more to learn from these examples than from total quality management. Some things in politics can *only* be done by instinct. Systems run counter to the unexpected, including the need to do it occasionally.

Sometimes, however, the office seemed devoid of both organisation *and* instinct. Too many of them had given up politics for ideology. Instinct had been replaced by a pattern of political responses arranged by habit around the regular release of economic data. Instinct was useless when the bounds of politics were so circumscribed. It was remarkable that, Mark Ryan apart, no-one seemed to have given more than a passing thought to what the job entailed. Yet the political opportunities for a prime minister are almost limitless, and the advantages of the office without measure. It was puzzling, therefore, that the perspectives from within were so narrow and could only be widened at the expense of one's dignity and everyone's peace of mind. One had to be a pest sometimes, even a rival prima donna. One had to make a fool of oneself if necessary just to stir the place into action.

The failure of computer equipment half an hour before a speech was to be delivered in some far-off place frayed my nerves, even if Nina or Cheryl or Anna remained ice cool like good soldiers in a tight spot. The computer was like the potato in that the more absolutely life depended on it the greater the disaster if it failed. After several near calamities, one day in Adelaide a forty-minute business speech was stuck fast in a machine which, despite public service assurances to the contrary, was not compatible with our equipment. Well past the time we were supposed to leave for the venue it seemed almost certain that the Prime Minister would not have a speech to deliver. I said to him that we had to do something about the office systems. Could we not get a bit of quality management into the place? Just a bit of quality? He shook his head sadly and said, 'I know, mate, I've been trying to get a bit of quality into it for years. Just a bit of quality.' 'It's like the bloody Keystone Cops,' I said. 'That's right, it's like the bloody Keystone Cops,' he said. It was a comforting irony that speeches such as the one stuck in Adelaide almost invariably contained exhortations to business to adopt 'best practice' and better management principles and recitations of the benefits to flow from the government's deregulation of the economy. The PMO would not have lasted a week in a deregulated environment, and we would say to Don Russell—you pointy heads who talk so warmly about the marketplace would starve if you ever had to live in it. Even John Edwards, having said in the first week of March that the office was working very well, said in the third week that changes were urgently needed.

Ashton Calvert, who was very careful with his words, said privately that he was concerned the Prime Minister was getting 'very narrow advice'. In May we discovered the office had not replied to hundreds of letters that had been sent to Annita since the beginning of the year. In airport lounges chief executives and their secretaries asked me what the hell was going on in the Prime Minister's Office—they don't answer letters, they don't return calls. By June it was a media story. The *Canberra Times* reported that ministers and senior public servants were complaining that the PMO was 'an incredibly narrow funnel', that it played a role 'more significant than cabinet' and that its operations had thrown the government into 'utter chaos'. A senior member of the Australian Embassy in Japan said that he had heard the place described as 'a living example of the free market gone too far', and there was truth in that, because it *was* as if we believed that everything would be resolved by unseen forces.

The Prime Minister continued to find new ways to confound his advisers, and his advisers, it seemed to a couple of us, found new ways of not confronting him about it. The Prime Minister would often arrive late and leave before certain essential tasks were completed. Nothing and nobody could make him sign letters until he was ready and, what with all the accumulated pressure, he might not be ready for six months after the letters were written. He would not commit to an engagement unless all possible avenues of escape from it had been closed off. Invitations sent in February were not responded to by April. He would agree to attend functions without really agreeing and then quietly tell Peter Robinson to cancel. He kept the Japanese Ambassador waiting while inside he watched John Button in the Senate defend his interest in a piggery. The piggery—that was another story. He had borrowed money to buy a half share in the joint venture between the Australian company Brown and Hatton and the Danish company, Danpork when he was on the back benches and thought his political life might be ending. It was a promising investment and with reasonable luck he had every reason to think it would make him a lot of money—reasonable luck and a reliable partner and an Opposition prepared to leave alone what was a legitimate business venture.

The New South Wales Liberal Premier, Nick Greiner, had warmly welcomed the project when it was announced in April. He and his agriculture minister promised Danpork 'fast-tracking' through planning and environment controls. In press releases they said it was in keeping with the State's export strategy, especially its ambitions in Asian markets; it was a 'major boost' for the Hunter Valley and the State, it would create 200 new jobs, 'underpin the future of the State's pig industry and give an enormous boost to grain and fodder producers'. But in June the Liberals changed their tune and the attack had still not ended nine years later. Keating had no luck with it, and got no peace, and the partner proved less than ideal.

Late one night in March, encouraged by Ryan, I rang the PM and said that if things didn't change I was leaving. I said that, along with the chaos and inefficiency, the work was unfairly distributed and too much of it was landing with me. A couple of nights later he held a meeting with four of us at the Lodge. He described each of us in Formula One terms. He himself was like Alain Prost—fast in the straight, brake into the corners. Stephen Smith, he said, kept the brakes on all the way around the track. Ryan would brake in the corners but sometimes also in the straight. He described my problem as being an inclination to never brake at all. Don Russell he said spent his time thinking about building a new track. Foolishly I began to venture the opinion that perhaps it seemed different to me because I had come from outside the culture, and nothing I had ever experienced anywhere before . . . 'God!' the Prime Minister exclaimed. 'You can't complain, mate! Jesus! You've been made welcome!

God! You've got in here a bloody sight quicker than anybody else ever did!' 'That's right,' said Russell, as if at last someone had nailed me for the ingrate I was. 'Christ!' said Keating, 'You were the one who started all this, and if you don't like it when we've made these changes you want, well frankly, mate, you'll have to go. You're a prima donna, mate,' he said, 'an organisational prima donna.' It did not seem worth finishing what I had begun to say which was that nothing I had seen ran so incompetently or perversely as the PMO, unless it was the old parcel shed at the Victorian Railways. And despite the changes we made in the next few weeks, so it pretty well always remained.

Only some of Richards' recommendations were adopted, but even so it was like a revolution while it lasted. People were moved here and there and given new tasks, new systems were engaged to deal with correspondence. Mark Ryan moved into the main office and Greg Turnbull, who had been an ABC journalist, took over in the media office. Mary Ann O'Loughlin became the second woman senior adviser in the PMO and gave a great boost to the humour, intellectual breadth and general humanity of the place when she was appointed to look after social policy. She stayed until the end, a main engine of the training and employment programs and the extended social wage which gave the Keating Government much of its character.

Guy Nelligan was delighted by the revolution. He hoped it might lift the professional standards of the office somewhere closer to his own. Guy was an unlikely character at the end of the office populated by laconic Commonwealth policemen and drivers whose chief occupations were killing time and representing to those who might have forgotten what real people were like. Guy dressed in a Fletcher Jones version of a morning suit that suited his fastidious character. He was feisty, moody and eccentrically proper, and sloppiness in the nation's highest office caused him intense irritation.

Change had been essential and some of it worked. But the culture couldn't be changed. Some people were doing the work of three while others spent half their lives doing languid laps of the Parliament House pool. A month after meeting at the Lodge on a day when things seemed as diabolical as ever, Ryan told Russell that he had given up trying with the office, he was sick of nagging. Russell's insouciance knew no bounds: 'That's right,' he said, 'nagging is counterproductive.' I repeated my threat to resign, but then that too was probably counterproductive.

And yet there were times when the 'house style' not only seemed to serve the PM and the government well, but in ways quite beyond the reach of any sophisticated management theory. The chaos on some days seemed to create a kind of logic which no-one else including the Opposition could follow. If an economic adviser should one day seriously suggest that the Prime Minister make a pleasant Sunday afternoon fundraiser in the working-class electorate of Dunkley the occasion for a speech on mid-term economic prospects, the sheer madness of the idea might inspire other advisers to come up with something of a much more political kind. It might have been recognised as creative tension if the tension were not so often unbearable. It was more like an extension of Keating's 'rock in the pond' theory.

Late in March the Prime Minister went to Question Time armed with a good joke but one which required a bit of telling. In essence it likened John Hewson's followers to people who had bought a ticket on the Hindenburg—Fightback obviously the doomed airship. They were all on their way to what we called the Hewsonburg Disaster. He didn't have the story quite clearly enough in his head to relate it without reference to his notes and Tim Fischer was heard to call out, 'Lost your place in the Gillies script!' Such slights never worried Keating when he knew he'd made his point. Indeed, so enthused was he a few minutes later he jumped up and began to answer a question that had been directed to the Treasurer. It was hard to tell whether this kind of mockery took much of a toll on Hewson; it was more likely that the sense of chaos Keating created, the feeling that things were never quite under control, destabilised his judgment. With the Hindenburg still in the air, Keating went ill-prepared into the House where he made a dud reply to a Dorothy Dix question about the GST and, perhaps trying to make up for the missed opportunity, called the leader of the Opposition a cheat and a fraud. The leader of the Opposition demanded an apology. The Speaker claimed that he didn't hear the words the Prime Minister used. The Prime Minister assured the Speaker that the words were not unparliamentary, which the Speaker not unexpectedly accepted. Chaos naturally followed. It was difficult to believe that the Prime Minister's victory was other than pyrrhic and that it might have been much easier and more fruitful to withdraw.

Yet this exercise in unreason produced a worse one from Hewson. He brought on a censure motion declaring that Keating was part of a criminal mafia whose political arm, if not its actual hub, was the New South Wales right. A bundle of old clippings about the New South Wales right, believed to have come from Hewson's office, began to circulate in the House. Keating called a press conference and demanded in the usual way that Hewson repeat the claims outside the chamber. He made the stronger point that the cleanskin had resorted to foul play. And that is how it played politically. Hewson had put himself in the place he had always said he was above, and he only compounded his folly when he told Laurie Oakes on the Sunday following the story of how he had floored the school bully. By then everyone including the Prime Minister and his office had forgotten the point of the Dorothy Dix question with which the episode began—it had been to demonstrate that a basket of average household goods would cost substantially more with a GST.

CHAPTER 6

They create illusions and call them facts, and between what they are said to be and what they are falls the shadow of all the useful words not spoken, of all the actual deeds not done.

GORE VIDAL, 'THE HOLY FAMILY'

BOB HAWKE HAD resigned on 24 February, the eve of One Nation. In normal times his seat in Melbourne's working-class northern suburbs would have returned a Labor candidate as a matter of course. But in abnormal times Wills was just the kind of seat to cause the government heartache. There was more than 10 per cent unemployment. Many small businesses had gone to the wall. Not only the government awaited judgment in Wills: economic rationalism in general and the tariff cuts in particular were on the line. The electors of Wills would be the first Australians with a chance to send the government a message. Their task, however, was complicated by the policies of John Hewson. Labor was in no doubt that the people of Wills were of a mind to deliver the 8 per cent swing which would throw them out of the seat. There were plenty on the government side who wanted a fundamental reassessment of economic policy to meet the needs of people precisely like the people of Wills: namely, abandoning the notion of the level playing field, more government support for local industry, a more concerted attack on unemployment and above all, at least a two-year moratorium on tariff reductions. But how could the electors of Wills tell Labor what they thought without signalling approval of John Hewson who advocated everything Labor advocated but in larger measure and with fewer compensations? The Prime Minister's line drew a very wide arc, in the shape of a ring road to be built with One Nation money: 'We just make the point,' he said, 'that those huge semis [semi-trailers] running through Pascoe Vale Road and all that noise and thunder that goes with them, and pollution, won't be removed by taxing your Weet-Bix.'

'A fair field without favour' was President Grover Cleveland's description of the tariff-free America he conspicuously failed to create at the end of the 19th century. Sharing Cleveland's belief that the tariff corrupted the polity as well as the economy, created class divisions more than it mitigated them, and never acted in the long-term interests of workers, Paul Keating was anti-tariff in his bones. And unlike Grover Cleveland, he did something about it. But in 1992, no politician still wishing to survive could ignore the public's passionate belief that the field was not 'fair' and it was wilfully stupid to think otherwise.

As treasurer in March 1991 Keating had announced the last phases of a tariff reduction program begun by the Hawke Government in 1988. This would mean, he said, an 'end to the high tariff wall which had done so much to diminish Australia's potential in the postwar period' and the completion of 'the transition to an open economy'. A year later the temper had changed a little. In late March 1992 he told the Economic Planning Advisory Committee (EPAC) that tariff reduction had always been a means of industry 'restructuring and adjustment rather than elimination'. He acknowledged that the car industry could 'not function at zero protection'. In fact he'd said so in 1990. The car industry became a significant player in Labor's 1992 strategy. More than once and at crucial times Keating jockeyed himself to the high ground and declared Hewson's policy would bring disaster on the industry. Labor had brought tariffs down from the order of 90 per cent to 35 per cent, on course to 15 per cent by 2000. Hewson, surely very foolishly, described this as the path of 'wimps'. He would bring it down to 5 per cent or zero; but, the argument went, with 'the bigger incentive' of faster micro-economic reform. Given that a small fluctuation in the exchange rate might easily wipe out most of the 10 per cent difference in the two positions, the argument was at least as symbolic as substantive.

But neither Hewson nor his shadow industry minister, the rural patrician, Ian McLachlan, could ever resist the heroic position. Keating, they said, was a hypocrite, a backslider, a political opportunist who was compromising the long-term national interest. They came forth with old fiercely anti-tariff quotations from the Prime Minister. If it had been their most earnest desire to help Keating they could not have done more for him. Under intense pressure from his own side to 'pause' or scrap the policy, with the community hardening in its view that the cuts were a root cause of unemployment and folly into the bargain because no other country was doing it, tariffs had the potential to be Keating's undoing. Instead, more often than not, they made his day. He might never be able to persuade the electorate or their talkback hosts that other countries, including Asian countries, were cutting tariffs, that a more level playing field *was* being made and that Australia stood to gain in great measure from being a good free-trading citizen. With Hewson's help, however, he could hold the policy line, defy the backsliders and yet seem moderate. And he could etch even more deeply his portrait of Hewson as heartless and unbending. He called him 'Captain Zero', but it was not this which gave him his advantage: it was that these 'moderate' reductions seemed to have done precisely what had been intended by them—namely, they had assured investment, brought dramatic productivity improvements and, with the addition of an export facilitation plan, increased the industry's exports from 370 million to over a billion dollars a year. Toyota had just established a new car plant in Melbourne. Mitsubishi was exporting cars made in Adelaide and, like GMH, had invested in new plant. When Nissan abandoned its manufacturing in February 1992, the employment consequences played badly for a few days, but it also helped the government to demonstrate the folly of protection. What point in governments propping up a multinational car maker the country manifestly did not need?

Both as big employers and benchmarks of Australia's new international economy, the vehicle industry offered Keating a rare opportunity to remind the electorate of astute, successful and socially responsible policy. There was even a positive message to be conveyed about the advantages of foreign investment and the benefits of the global economy. It was one of the Prime Minister's better April moments when he visited the new Toyota car plant in Melbourne; even though the commercial media made the story his failure to wear a seatbelt when—for their cameras—he drove a new Toyota down a ramp from the plant.

The principles applying to the car industry applied equally to textile, clothing and footwear, where government policy was to reduce tariffs to 25 per cent by 2000. Around the world developed countries restricted imports in these labour-intensive industries, so it was argued that the higher tariff would not reduce the ability of local manufacturers to become internationally competitive. Within the labour movement all through 1992 there was pressure for a 'tariff pause'. In the PMO Stephen Smith was echoing opinion in the caucus, in the party polling and probably at ALP headquarters when he advocated a two-year moratorium. Late in May at a meeting with the ACTU, George Campbell of the Metal and Engineering Workers Union declared for an eighteen-month pause to give manufacturing time to recover from the recession. Keating refused: he said too many people would want to make it permanent and too many others would be tempted to agree. Bill Kelty agreed with Keating.

I was at Melbourne's La Trobe University with Bill Kelty in its first four years but I don't recall ever speaking a word to him. Students marched in the streets, staged endless mass meetings, planned all kinds of rebellion and even revolution, wrote manifestos, read Marx and Lenin, got stoned. Conscripts burned their papers by the campus moat. Kelty was never seen in any of it. He was known on the campus, but only by reputation as a brilliant economics student. Like many La Trobe students he was of the working class. He grew up in Brunswick. When, nearly twenty-five years later, I met him at Don Russell's send-off dinner at the Lodge, he was a famous and very influential Australian—national secretary of the ACTU, a member of the Reserve Bank board and a principal architect of Labor's rule. The reformed Australian economy was as much his legacy as Keating's and Hawke's. The Accord, the shift to enterprise bargaining, the lower incidence of strikes, the improved profit share and all the pro-capital measures to make it so he had approved, helped or conceived. If Keating was Groucho and Hawke was Chico, the mop-haired, inscrutable Kelty was Harpo. In startling contrast to Hawke's charisma and Keating's hubris, he looked and sounded like he had been drawn from the depths of Labor's well, which may be why he appeared to be a stranger to vanity, narcissism and greed and found these qualities more curious than odious in others. A lot of people with half his talent earned ten times more than he did for work in private enterprise that was a hundred times less complex and consequential. He flew economy, stayed in budget hotels, drove a Commodore, ate at the City Baths cafeteria and every Saturday throughout the football season watched Essendon with his family from the outer. He had the only rising inflection I ever heard with menace in it. Like a true Labor tribesman, Kelty was deeply attached to the traditions of the clan—including the traditions of loyalty to friends and savagery to enemies. I said to him once that all Paul Keating's worst enemies seemed to be former friends. He reflected for a moment or two and replied that it was much the same with him. He told me how twenty years after he left La Trobe University, he was sitting at a dinner in a Melbourne hotel banquet room. The man beside him introduced himself. The name was the same as the one on the monthly government letters Kelty had received as a student on deferment from conscription. He asked the man if he had ever worked in the old Department of Labor and National Service. It happened that he had. Kelty told the man that one of them would have to leave. The man left. Until then I did not know that Bill Kelty had been conscripted, or that when he had finished his studies he went to court and acting as his own counsel proved himself a conscientious objector.

Kelty had not brought the union movement as far as he had, or played such a part in Labor's deregulatory program, without paying a price in the affections of his colleagues and members. And the members were not as numerous as they had been. There were plenty who blamed Kelty for the decline. The relationship with Keating was built on hard-earned mutual respect and genuine affection. There were times when they seemed to delight in each other's company—they had nothing in common except the big picture and the ideas it comprised. It was enough. But Kelty had gone out on a long limb so many times for the government one could not be sure about what he would do if ever he felt taken for granted.

Bob Hawke gave no sign he was ready to make life easy for Keating. In the middle of the Wills campaign he wrote in a news-paper column that the new PM had insisted that his valet, Guy Nelligan, wear a morning suit. What sort of republican, asked Hawke, put his man in the dress of the English butlering classes? Hawke knew that Keating would not have cared much if Guy Nelligan had worn thongs. He also knew that if Guy Nelligan put himself in a morning suit it was because Guy was like that. He knew it because Guy had worked for him in the same morning suit. Hawke also chose the Wills moment to declare that Queen Elizabeth II should remain Australia's head of state until her death or abdication, and that any money Paul Keating was proposing to spend on establishing a process for his republican ambitions would be better spent on achieving reconciliation with Aboriginal Australia. From a former Prime Minister who had sidelined Aboriginal land rights and the republic this was rank provocation and his successor was duly provoked to jump on the radio and launch a counterattack. The next time the Prime Minister bowled into the office Don Russell and Mark Ryan asked him if brawling with Hawke in the last week of a by-election was not unwise, and if it might not undermine the good work he had recently done—we had *all* done—and draw attention away from some recent encour-aging economic figures? 'He took four years off me!' the Prime

Minister said, and he asked if we didn't think he deserved what he'd just given him. Besides, he had enjoyed it. And then he laughed. And everyone else laughed because it was impossible not to laugh when Paul Keating laughed, and his eyes shone and his gums showed and his face came apart as if it comprised two separate hemispheres hinged at the ears. When you saw Paul Keating's gums, reason was abolished, indignation vanished, your game was up.

It didn't matter in the end, John Hewson was always there to bail us out. To all those concerns that the voters of Wills had about the deregulated economy, the absence of protection for their manufacturing industries, the foreign ownership of Australian companies and of course the unemployment in their community, John Hewson offered them just stronger medicine. By the last week of the campaign the Liberals were not a factor, and would not have been even if they had been promising some Keynesian New Deal. They had put up a candidate named Delacratz who promptly declared the seat unwinnable. Whether he was speaking his mind or practising psychology will never be known because within a few days no-one took him seriously enough to inquire. For it soon emerged that he had not long before written to his local member, Mr Hawke, urging him to suspend government subsidies for a disabled workshop which was competing with his factory—and it emerged around the same time that his factory which he had said was in Wills was in truth in another electorate. Then Laurie Oakes asked John Hewson if he knew anything about the three independent candidates in Wills who appeared to be members of the Liberal Party. John Hewson said he didn't, but it's probable that by that stage of the interview a lot of people weren't taking John Hewson seriously either.

The only independent candidate who mattered in Wills was Phil Cleary, a semi-legendary Coburg footballer and a 1970s graduate of La Trobe University with a beard as residual evidence. Cleary was a sort of self-styled working-class hero who brought the perfect mix of populism, economic nationalism and local identity to win the election in a landslide. Labor and Liberal both lost heavily, but the Liberals lost the most. In the *Australian* Glenn Milne wrote that their failure to make ground in Wills was a sign that under Hewson nothing had changed for the Liberals since the 1980s when they could not 'get disillusioned voters to cross directly to the Coalition rather than the halfway house of Independents'. That was probably being polite. Wills showed—or at least Phil Cleary did—that so long as Hewson would not bend from his economic orthodoxy he could be beaten. And this was the more likely if Labor was prepared to bend a little. And if Labor bent a little, it was becoming increasingly obvious, Hewson would be that much less inclined to bend at all.

For his part, the Prime Minister gave little outward appearance of concern about the result. At a doorstop interview he told journalists that plainly the people of Wills were concerned about unemployment and that was something the government was also concerned about.

Ashton Calvert said and the Prime Minister agreed that he should make himself better known in the world, and that his attention should be directed first to that part of it in which Australians live. Perhaps Keating did once say that Asia was the place you fly over on the way to Europe, but what he thought was very different. He did not need educating to the view that it was in Asia that Australia's future substantially lies or that it had been the crucial economic factor in Australia's recent past. Asia was where the great epoch-making boom was taking place. No prime minister with half a grip on reality could fly over Asia. Indonesia is Australia's nearest Asian neighbour, the fourth most populous country in the world, and the relationship with its government was the one most in need of attention. On his first trip abroad Keating would go to Indonesia.

Indonesia had been a strategic and moral dilemma for half a century. In the 1940s the Australian Labor Party and the unions had offered moral and material support to the independence movement. That was not a sentiment shared by everyone, of course, and Australian attitudes to Indonesia in particular and Asian anti-colonial movements in general remained divided for the next several decades. The Indonesian archipelago was in the nature of a screen across Australia's front door and on it over the years the rents in Australia's collective consciousness were imprinted. Indonesia was Asia's numberless hordes. In Sukarno's last years that dread was allied to the equally potent fear of communism. It reminded Australians of their extreme isolation from the world they trusted and knew and of their suffocating proximity to one they didn't. It drove a wedge through our moral certainty. Suharto came to power in a horrifying bloodbath, but he came at the expense of the man we had come to fear, Sukarno, the architect of Confrontation and the friend of communist powers.

If not actually admiring Suharto, Paul Keating had always thought his ascendancy was Australia's historic good fortune. He had thought this, he often said, from the day he read about the bloody coup which brought the general to power in Jakarta. Whatever offence it gave to Western notions of democracy and civil rights, Keating maintained that Suharto's regime had brought priceless benefits to Australia in the last quarter of the century. To appreciate this it is only necessary to ask what would have been the cost of chronic political instability in Jakarta; or a communist regime or one strongly influenced by the communist powers; or one susceptible to the influence of religious extremists; or a *more* brutal, dictatorial or corrupt regime along the lines of the dictatorships of Latin and South America or Africa; or a regime under which the Indonesian economy and society, instead of experiencing growth and relative order as it did under Suharto, regressed into greater poverty and greater chaos. Make real any of these quite plausible alternatives and Australia's history in the last quarter of a century becomes a very different matter. Imagine the difference to the defence budget to begin with.

Under Suharto, Indonesia's economy grew, modernised and integrated with the region and the world. As it did so it developed what trade officials like to call 'complementarities' with the Australian economy, meaning it created trade and investment opportunities. The Indonesian standard of living rose markedly.

Literacy rates dramatically improved. Indonesian society, spread across the vast archipelago, was remarkably stable and, examples of brutal repression notwithstanding, Indonesia's polyglot religions and cultures enjoyed a substantial measure of tolerance.

It was largely because of Suharto that old Australian fears of Asia had been allowed to fade—and partly from that followed the transformation of the old Australian xenophobia of the 1960s into pride in multiculturalism, tolerance and openness that sometimes bordered on the sanctimonious. If it is true that the perceived threat of Asia shaped the national character, 'racialising' and 'masculinising' it, as the historian David Walker says, then it is quite possible that Suharto's ascendancy helped reshape it. Keating believed that before Australians turned their backs indignantly on the Indonesian regime they ought to acknowledge these dividends. It was not a position that the expatriate Australian writer John Pilger or many on the left of the Labor Party approved, but Keating thought Pilger's work was humbug, and the left he reckoned were too inclined to substitute moral outrage for intelligent effort. He was convinced, quite independently of his foreign policy advice, that the policy approach so often quoted was inescapable: Australia could not allow the relationship with Jakarta to be determined by a single issue, even one as painful as East Timor. He would say two things about Indonesia that no other prime minister had: that Suharto's new order had brought profound benefits to Australia, and that no country was more important to Australia than Indonesia. He would thus put Indonesia on an equal footing with our most important ally, the US, and our most important trading partner, Japan. Even after the massacre of East Timorese protesters in Dili in February 1992, the rule still applied—Australia would not look at Indonesia 'through the prism of East Timor'.

Not everyone in the Prime Minister's Office, and certainly not everyone in the government, was as certain as Paul Keating and Ashton Calvert were about these matters. In some hearts, even those most faithful to him, there was often a flicker of disquiet. The Dili massacre made it more so. For the four years of the Keating Government, whenever I visited my local supermarket in Melbourne, Callisto, the East Timorese proprietor, told me more stories about people he knew who had recently disappeared, who had been admitted to hospital and never come out, of what he said was indisputable evidence that the Indonesian military wanted to 'get rid of everyone'. He was a friend of the East Timorese leaders, Jose Ramos Horta and Xanana Gusmão. Callisto fought with the resistance before escaping to Australia with his family. Now he ran a supermarket which was part of a chain whose head office squeezed his margins and gave him no leeway on his weekly returns. When he was not talking about East Timor he talked about how hard it was to keep the business viable. He voted for the Labor Party and thought Paul Keating was a good leader. But he thought he was wrong about Suharto. It was pointless to tell him that Paul Keating found Suharto to be a supporter of Australia's interests in the region. And I never told him that when we took a business delegation to Jakarta, one of the four businessmen who travelled on the Prime Minister's plane was the owner of the supermarket chain.

We had grown up with a faint awareness that we owed the Timorese something for the support they gave Australian troops in the war against Japan, that there was a bond which our recognising Indonesia's claims had broken and betrayed. That we also owed Indonesia something was a possibility never much examined; and that some other policy would have persuaded Suharto to our point of view was not advanced in any plausible or coherent way. Furthermore, a myth had emerged that the Australian Government had approved Indonesia's military invasion. The myth made the murder of five Australian journalists by Indonesian soldiers a crime for which the Australian Government was substantially responsible. More persuasive than the historical argument, however, was the undeniable evidence of Indonesian repression. Whether one believed, as East Timorese in Australia told us, that the Indonesians were engaged in a genocidal campaign or, as the Department of Foreign Affairs maintained, that there had been sporadic unwarranted but inevitable instances of violent repression by Indonesian troops, East Timor cast a shadow on the relationship with Jakarta. The relationship was steeped in guilt and moral confusion. It was, in other words, the sort of relationship which countries of independent mind and making their own policy often have with one another.

The word most often used by critics was 'appeasement'. The lesson was meant to be: 'appease' the Indonesians and they'll take more and more, like the Germans took all Czechoslovakia after Munich gave them part of it. Despite the fact that no-one ever suggested Indonesia intended to precipitate a war, conquer and enslave its neighbours and exterminate six million of a race, the comparison continued to appeal particularly in those forums where moral virtue is never threatened by necessity—or in this case historical veracity. Those like Churchill who opposed the 'appeasement' of Hitler were not dealing in moral absolutes, but absolute necessities. That is why they urged a deal with the other totalitarian, Stalin—to contain the more menacing of the two evils. Keating, who had made himself more familiar with that decade of European history than any other, brought the same logic to his thinking about Indonesia. Keating's view was traditional Realpolitik. National leaders have to deal with other national leaders regardless of what they think of them. Furthermore, they fail in their duty if they let anything, including moral outrage, blind them to their country's interests. Keating pursued the relationship with Suharto on just this basis—not to give or imply moral assent to his regime in East Timor, but to further the interests of Australia's security. 'We have a continent to ourselves and a border with no-one,' he said, and he believed that it was a minimum requirement of every prime minister to ensure that this benign fact would continue to obtain.

While many in the Labor Party could not think of the relationship without a sometimes overwhelming sense of guilt, Keating approached it with an overwhelming sense of duty. Indonesia was the one big fact of Australia's geopolitical reality and it always would be. Nothing would be gained for Australia—or East Timor—by refusing to deal with Jakarta, or having the relationship clouded with ambivalence. Instead, much would be lost. Everything that Keating knew about history and everything he thought about leadership told him that his duty to creating security in the region far outweighed any he had to East Timor. Furthermore, he thought that if he drew Suharto towards greater engagement in the politics of the region, and particularly the politics of APEC, it would be of incalculable value for both Australian and regional security. He also believed, and experience had continually confirmed it, that what little prospect there was of changing Indonesia's attitude to East Timor only existed so long as the relationship with Jakarta was active, extensive and friendly.

Early in April, by way of setting the scene for his forthcoming trip, he gave a speech for Stephen Fitzgerald's Asia–Australia Institute at the University of New South Wales. The title of the speech, 'Australia and Asia: Knowing Who We Are', was shorthand for the central theme—the Keating Government would make an intense effort to integrate Australia more fully into the region and its starting point would be the assertion of an 'unambiguous' post-colonial identity. Keating did not pretend that he was the first Australian prime minister to venture seriously into Asia, but he was determined to venture more seriously than any before him. If his opponents reckoned he was claiming more than his due, as always, it only added to his pleasure. Over the next four years they would protest that Menzies had gone there first with the Colombo Plan; that it was Jack McEwen who had done the trade treaty with Japan in the fifties, and the same man got Australian wool into Red China; they even insisted that a Liberal government had abolished the White Australia policy. Keating's preoccupation with the region made Tim Fischer cranky because he had been to most of these countries more often than the Prime Minister. When Keating talked about Indonesia, Fischer would say Burma has been badly neglected. If he talked buoyantly about the future of multilateralism Fischer would say our unilateral relationships were being shamefully overlooked. Then Downer would aver that Keating had abandoned our traditional relationships with Europe and America, and someone else that he was ignoring opportunities in India, and another that he had an 'obsession' with Asia and what our foreign policy needed was 'balance'.

It was curious. Here was Keating embarking like Magellan for the new world, determined to secure his country's future interests, and most of the talk was about history. As usual, the excitement of the enterprise might have been more generally shared if the Prime Minister had less of a reputation for overstating the significance of his undertakings and his opponents were not so predictably inclined to prove that Keating was a humbug. The Prime Minister wanted to signal that, all previous initiatives notwithstanding, this venture into Asia by his government was the definitive one. Nothing done by past governments had made Australia's position unequivocal. Neither the countries of Asia nor the people of Australia were convinced that the relationship was more than one of convenience or uncomfortable necessity. Keating wanted a seismic shift which no-one could mistake for posturing or symbolism. Australians had to reform their 'outlook', he said: they had to understand as John Curtin had asked Australians to understand in 1942, that 'On what we now do depends everything we may like to do'.

In his speech in Sydney he argued that the colonial relationship with Great Britain continued to exercise 'a subliminal influence' on Australian thinking, 'persuading us that someone or something else will do it for us'. He compared it to the pre-war period when Australia blindly followed British foreign policy. As well, he compared it to the cultural obstacles economic reform had had to overcome in the 1980s: the task had been to turn the economy towards the world, away from protection and vestiges of the days when it was conveniently interlocked with Britain's. He was conscious of public trepidation and public scepticism about the consequences of this new engagement with Asia. He understood the reservations an older generation of Australians might have, and was aware of the perception that this engagement with Asia might compromise Australian democracy. The reverse was true, he said. Many things had and would continue to change; change was inevitable and necessary if Australia was to take its place in the region and the world. However, he said, 'Australia's democratic institutions and traditions are non-negotiable.'

The point so obvious to Keating, but obscure to most of the electorate was that Australia would have more influence in the region and be better able to pursue all its interests if the countries of East Asia were confident that Australia spoke as they did—with an independent voice. The noise that Keating had been making in the previous couple of months had been in part calculated to send this message. Even if the record could be made to show that others had been down this path before him, Keating wanted to make it clear and unmistakable. 'That is something I think Australians must realise,' he said to the Asia–Australia Institute: 'That we don't go to Asia cap in hand, any more than we go, like Menzies went to London, pleading family ties. We go as we are. Not with the ghost of Empire about us. Not as a vicar of Europe, or as a US deputy. But unambivalently. Sure of who we are and what we stand for. If we are to be taken seriously, believed, trusted, that is the only way to go.'

Ultimately the task of establishing warm and profitable relationships with regional leaders, even sceptical if not hostile ones like Suharto and Mahathir, proved easier than persuading the Australian public that such relationships were both worth-while and unthreatening. There was never as much to be gained politically from success in Asia as Keating sometimes imagined. Always a doubt seemed to linger in a corner of the public mind that his efforts were a part of a broader assault on those intang-ible things which tend to go under the aegis of the Australian Way of Life.

The argument was nonetheless compelling: the geophysical reality of Australia's position is not going to change; we cannot be half in and half out; we can't have more than half our trade there but the great majority of our other interests elsewhere; if our strategic interests lie in the region we can't have them dependent on someone somewhere else. It was not to say that Australia had to abandon all its traditional ties with Britain, the Commonwealth, the US and Europe, but rather that we had to establish better linkages with the countries on our doorstep. The other reality which was not going to change was trade: 60 per cent of Australian trade was with the countries of East Asia, the proportion was growing, and the opportunities for growth were greatest there. In 1992 those countries were growing at twice the world average, and they maintained that rate throughout the four years of the Keating Government. In 1992 Asia represented a truly historic opportunity, one which no responsible government could fail to grasp. Australia had to become part of the Asian economic miracle. To stand back and watch, to hedge bets with old allegiances or with a sceptical electorate, to be in any way half-hearted about the project was, in Paul Keating's view, pure dereliction.

Keating set out to establish cordial and open relationships with all the countries of the region. He talked about 'broadening and deepening' bilateral relationships, creating 'structures' and 'threads' and 'webs'. The real dividends of these efforts turn up in new trade agreements, business contacts, information and technology transfers, ministerial dialogues, cultural exchanges. In Cambodia it was hoped the return on a major investment in diplomatic effort would be peace. The political settlement agreed in Paris in October 1991 had been largely the work of Gareth Evans in concert with his Indonesian counterpart, Ali Alatas. Implementation of the agreement would be overseen by a contingent of UN defence force personnel to which, in April 1992, Australia contributed 495 from its own forces and the commander, Lieutenant General John Sanderson. With the country divided and in ruins and the Khmer Rouge one of the parties to the settlement, it was a very fraught affair and Evans was never going to drown in praise from his fellow Australians, not even when he was nominated for the Nobel Peace Prize. The Prime Minister made the obvious point to an electorate which was not visibly impressed: Australia had for once played the role of independent broker in Asia, brought leadership to a region where a generation earlier it had dispatched troops to satisfy the putative requirements of the American alliance, and it had done these things in the collective interest with Indonesia.

At the same time the aim was to build multilateral structures that would at once set the region on the path of liberalised trade and collective security. That is why Keating invested so much in APEC—he believed that nothing else could contribute so much to underwriting Australia's future. It was as simple a concept as duty, which meant that sometimes it seemed to him beyond the reach of argument.

A more popular view might have gone like this: if two-thirds of all our merchandised exports are going to Asia like you say; if the ASEAN countries are now bigger markets for us than the US or the EU; if our manufactured exports are really going to Asia at twice the rate of our traditional primary products—what's the problem? Why change things? Why all this talk about cutting our old ties? If it ain't broke, why fix it? If Australia is on its own as never before, why give up on our old friends? If we're on our own why make it worse?

It was really not an argument that Keating had much hope of winning, especially when it seemed remote from the pressing immediate needs of people and communities. To prime ministers the only politically useful instruments of foreign policy are wars, including cold wars. Trade agreements, multilateral structures of one kind or another, dialogues—the rewards of such things are too distant and too hard to identify. Keating and the Foreign Affairs Department and all manner of learned people might fear the creation of an East Asia economic bloc 'in rivalry with Europe and North America', and they might decide that APEC, by drawing North America into the East Asian sphere, could be the means of preventing this event, but that argument was not likely to move the general public. Even if the polls showed that they thought he was good and conscientious about Asia and Australia's future, even if they thought he had some 'vision' in this regard, they never thought it had much to do with them, and on balance they probably reckoned it was yet more evidence that he was 'out of touch' with their real concerns.

In truth the Prime Minister did not much care what they thought were their real concerns. He would have been happier if there had been a vote in it but, Burkean as he was in these matters, he let virtue be its own reward. APEC became Keating's grand obsession. It took hold slowly, in the first conversation with George Bush and then in the 7 April speech in Sydney when he proposed 'a process of periodic heads of governments meetings, say every two or three years'.

In mid-April the Prime Minister escaped from the burden of his duties and the noise and dust of the House carpenters who were creating the new doorway between his office and Don Russell's, and took what he reckoned was a well-earned rest at Port Douglas. Speeches for his forthcoming trip to Indonesia and Papua New Guinea meanwhile were prepared under the direction of Ashton Calvert. Privately Dr Calvert said he had never worked with such an 'unprofessional rabble'. But he did not say it to the Prime Minister or anybody responsible for the rabble. The Prime Minister reviewed the speeches in their various drafts as they were sent to him by fax, and he telephoned back the amendments he thought desirable. On these occasions he had a tone which no sensible person could mistake: it said, why are you ruining my holiday? Don't you know how badly I need a rest? In the circumstances we thought it impolitic to pass on to him reports received by Dr Calvert that large numbers of New Guinea highlanders had sharpened their spears and strapped on their penis sheaths and were already on the march to Kokoda where the Prime Minister would be in a fortnight's time.

The Prime Minister dragged himself away from his friend's apartment and the dazzling white sand and blue water of Port Douglas in time to catch the Rubens exhibition at the National Gallery before going to Jakarta. 'Wasn't he a star?' he asked rhetorically, and sadly. Sometimes he wished he had been an art dealer. Anything would be better than the drudgery he was presently putting up with. He meant the endless demands on his time; the imperatives of political debate: not that the people should necessarily share his view of things, but it was so tedious to be reminded that he had to persuade them. If Stephen Smith told him to 'mention jobs and recovery' again he would knock his block off! He would! This was the night before he flew out to meet Suharto. Of course he was talking about drudgery and alternative careers and things which mattered more than the mission he was embarked on. It was always the way.

Loaded with department secretaries, deputy secretaries and real secretaries, numerous doctors of philosophy in advisory capacities, a doctor of medicine, a photographer, media advisers, policemen, the Prime Minister and his wife of course, and down the back, like sardines in a can or jackals in a cage, quantities of journalists—the thirty-year-old Boeing 707 ground down the Canberra runway and at last with a mighty roar angled aloft. The 707, the Prime Minister often observed, had a 'beautiful wing on it'. This was all it had to recommend it. The RAAF said they were fantastically reliable, but we found it hard to forget that the sister craft to the one we flew in had dived into Bass Strait shortly after bringing Bob Hawke home from his last official trip. Some international airports would not allow our plane to land or take off because it made too much noise. When it sat on the tarmac in Asian climates for long periods the interior became clammy and dripping wet. Some people called the old thing the Black Pig. There was an office on board where it was customary for speech-writers and secretaries to labour with advice from Foreign Affairs personnel. The final products were copied and distributed to members of the press, usually as the plane descended over paddy fields and the secretaries quickly packed the computers away and the staff got back into their suits and ties and the Prime Minister spruced himself up and everyone else downed the last dregs of the Petaluma red or riesling and buckled themselves in. Sometimes the RAAF would feather the landing in the manner of commercial aircraft, and sometimes if the tarmac was wet they would hit it in the military style, with a teeth-snapping jolt.

Huge hoardings with pictures of Mr and Mrs Keating had been erected in Jakarta by way of welcome. The *Indonesian Observer* said the mission might demonstrate that 'Paul Keating is not Bob Hawke. Unlike his predecessor who, like the historical white rajahs, wanted to dictate conditions before consenting to visit, Paul Keating arrives with none.' It was a grand welcome. At the banquet in his honour on the first night in Jakarta two songstresses sang American tunes. Keating and Suharto talked earnestly through an interpreter. Here, and earlier that day as he stood beaming with his hosts in the palace, it was impossible not to wonder how a man could seem so indifferent to it all one evening and so engaged and engaging the day after. This was not the only paradox alive in the room that night. The other one concerned East Timor. If Keating made no gesture towards the Dili massacre and Indonesia's response to it, or if he made one that could be too easily deemed inadequate, he could expect a sound thrashing from the Australian media for moral infamy. If, on the other hand, his gesture caused offence and he got a rebuff from Suharto, the media would thrash him just as fiercely for diplomatic failure.

Keating had prepared the ground a little in an interview with the *Australian*'s Greg Sheridan before leaving. Michelle Grattan had interviewed the academic Indonesia specialist Jamie Mackie who urged Keating to take a 'let's maximise our agreements and minimise our disagreements' approach to the question. Mackie's view was much like the government's: East Timor would always be a bind for Australia and it was better not to pursue arguments for self-determination or overstate the matter of human rights. The best interests of Australia and East Timor would be served instead by promoting aid programs in the province, and above all by developing a closer relationship and deeper mutual understanding with Indonesia. Mackie feared that in the wake of the Dili massacre xenophobia had been reborn and a simplistic stereotype of Indonesia had taken hold. It so happened that these were precisely the tendencies Keating chose to address.

He opened by calling Suharto 'the region's undisputed elder statesman' and congratulating him on his election to the position of chairman of the Non-Aligned Movement. He pointed out the common interests of the two countries and the areas of cooperation in which they had recently engaged—Cambodia, APEC, the

Cairns Group, the Timor Gap. And he said: 'These substantive links have enabled our government to maintain a frank and constructive dialogue, especially during the past few months, following the tragic events in East Timor last November.' That was all he said on East Timor in his official speech. He went on to say that while the Australian nation and identity had been forged from values which were 'in both spirit and substance, anti-Asian', these were now being reshaped, and the last vestiges of Australia's colonial past were being discarded. And he said that for both countries the other was the 'best test of how effectively we will be able to deal with the social and political diversity, and the rapid change, which will mark our region and the world in the 1990s'. He hoped that his visit would be seen as 'a signal of Australia's determination to pass that test'.

The story of the night, however, had already been written. It was written even before Keating rose to speak. Suharto wrote it when he said in his speech of welcome that Indonesia was open to criticism 'expressed in a brotherly manner', but that 'comments and criticisms . . . only to exaggerate weaknesses in our national development efforts and tending towards interference into our internal affairs are another thing'. By the time Suharto sat down the Australian press had decided that this constituted an official rebuff. The Indonesian Foreign Minister, Ali Alatas, assured the Prime Minister's staff that the President's words did not contribute a personal rebuke, but were a recital of his standard position as leader of the non-aligned nations. The Prime Minister's staff spent half the night attempting to persuade the press that this was the case.

The Prime Minister's visit to Indonesia, which later took in Surabaya and the famous temple at Borobudur, was as close to an unequivocal success as anyone had reason to hope. At a press conference before leaving Keating said that it didn't 'get much better than this'. Ministerial forums were established, defence cooperation agreements agreed; a fisheries cooperation agreement, a double taxation agreement, an extradition treaty aimed at narcotics trafficking, an agreement on science and technology cooperation, and a memorandum of understanding on a water supply and sanitation project in East Timor. Most importantly, in the longer term Suharto offered support for the idea to hold regular meetings of regional leaders. Beyond establishing a good relationship with Suharto, the trip served a significant educational function. More than once Keating made the point that Suharto's administration was 'one of the most significant and beneficial events in Australia's strategic history' and this was not widely enough acknowledged. He stressed the fact of geography: the countries were neighbours with no territorial designs on each other and wished to live peacefully. The great task was to create a broader and stronger relationship so that if one part came under pressure the structure would still hold. Creating as 'many struts and structural members as we can' through closer commercial, cultural and political links would be a preoccupation of foreign policy under Keating. And there was scope for developing defence links. The effort had implications for East Timor. By pointing out the benefits to Australia of a vigorous and creative relationship with a stable Indonesia, Keating hoped he could oblige Australians to put the Timor issue in a broader context and recognise that it should not determine Australia's relationship with Indonesia overall. There was simply too much at stake. The change in the media's tack was something of a measure of Keating's success. On the way to Jakarta they asked: is Indonesia's response to the February massacre in Dili credible? The Indonesians had not accounted for the dead; they had not released the names of the responsible army officers; and they were intending to send thirteen East Timorese protesters for trial. At the end of the trip, the media were either praising Keating for his courage or lambasting him for talking about the Australian flag.

Keating had proved himself adept in the role of prime minister abroad. He had been everything those who knew him knew he could be. But he was still the other thing as well. He decided to tell a press conference in Surabaya that the Australian flag was an inappropriate symbol for Australia in the present age. 'I'm sure in this part of the world people wonder about Australians representing themselves with a British flag in the corner of our flag,' he said. 'That must change and should change.' You couldn't help but love him for it. Of course the Coalition loved him for it too. He had denigrated the flag in a foreign country, they said. He had proved himself unfit. Australians would be ashamed of such a prime minister, John Hewson said. When Keating arrived in Port Moresby, Hewson was already there rehearsing his presence at the Anzac Day ceremonies. That afternoon he had presented the PNG Prime Minister, Rabbie Namilu, with his very own Australian flag 'under which so many brave Australians fought and died, and which I, for one, will never denigrate'. *And*, we were told, he had then gone jogging along the lower stretches of the Kokoda Track. It promised to be a splendid struggle for the moral high ground. At the state dinner at the PNG parliament that night resentment was etched deep on John Hewson's face. He seemed unable to look in Keating's direction and sat motionless as he spoke.

As if he knew that Hewson's sense of his own virtue could be excited to the point of bursting by the merest hint of sin on his own part, the next morning the Prime Minister arrived at a dawn service after the sun was up. Hewson stood in Bomana cemetery with a face like stone. In front of him by the cenotaph a soldier went through a heartstopping ballet with his rifle on the catafalque. All the crowd—the veterans, the politicians, the diplomats, the soldiers, the locals—stood silent. The rising sun glinted on the white gravestones. And just when it seemed the PM would never arrive and the whole expedition would come to spectacular political grief, his car appeared. He had forgotten his speech and had to go back.

John Hewson read a prayer. Alf Garland read something else. A New Zealander with a mighty limp read another thing. The Last Post was played. Keating strode gracefully to the microphone and began: 'This is ground made sacred by the bravery and sacrifice of those who lie buried here.' It did have a ring to it. Later that morning he delivered the big Anzac Day address outdoors in Moresby. Hundreds of residents watched from the trees. It was very hot and some of the military personnel fainted, most of them during an address by a New Zealand cabinet minister. Alf Garland spoke again and the New Zealander with the limp. The US consul left the proceedings in protest because he had not been given the chance to speak. He had a point. Keating's speech was mildly inflammatory. The Anzac legend binds Australians and 'defines us to ourselves', he said. But legends 'should not stifle us. They should not constrain us when we have to change.' Anzac did not 'confer on us a duty to see that the world stands still'. Curtin understood this when, after Singapore fell, he turned to the US; 'We know that Australia can go and Britain still hold on. We are therefore determined that Australia shall not go,' he said. For Keating, the young men who fought and died in New Guinea and other parts of Asia and the Pacific fought for 'the future they believed their country held'. That night all the journalists I spoke to except a very drunk one said what a good speech it was. The very drunk one said it was 'shit'.

It was not always possible to say with certainty what Paul Keating was thinking, although there were times when he clearly wasn't thinking what his words might lead one to believe he was thinking. He was always thinking something, one knew that, and guessing what it was—what he was up to—was one of the pastimes of employment. But it was silly to imagine that there might be an art to it. The Prime Minister flew to Kokoda in a Hercules separate from his media and political advisers. He had a professor of history, David Horner, with him, an expert on World War II. No Australian prime minister had been to Kokoda since the battles there in 1942—the battles which halted the Japanese advance on Port Moresby. The graves Keating had seen in Bomana cemetery were those of Kokoda's fallen. Many of them were just eighteen years old.

When Paul Keating was born on 18 January 1944, the Allies had still not landed in Normandy and the Philippines had not been retaken. John Curtin had eighteen months to live, a little less than Billy Keating, Paul's uncle, who was a prisoner of the Japanese in Sabah and would die in the Sandakan death marches. Curtin became prime minister a week or two before Pearl Harbor.

Keating became prime minister a week or two after its fiftieth anniversary. The coincidence was significant for both men. For Curtin it meant that he would forever be identified as a wartime prime minister—an admirable, even heroic one, but not the one who built a great society on the lines of his Labor dream. People make history but not as they please. Curtin would have much preferred to be a great peacetime prime minister. For Keating, the war's consequences were of course less profound, yet among Australian prime ministers probably only Curtin made more speeches about World War II. The war washed through Keating's prime ministership like reflux. It was not because he had a great passion for history, or a fixation with military conflict, but because there is scarcely a country between Australia and Japan that does not have a cemetery with Australian graves in it, or a monument to the sacrifice of Australian servicemen and women. When, in accordance with his mission to secure Australia's interests in the region, Keating visited almost every country in East Asia at least once, invariably these places of indescribable sadness became the backdrop for ceremonies commemorating the fiftieth anniversary of the war.

Paul Keating made so many of these speeches we feared that he might eventually have to revert to the platitudes with which such occasions are generally observed. Insofar as we avoided this, it made for better speeches, but also for controversy sometimes. He was on sacred ground: any departure from the customary words and gestures would always offend someone. When offence was taken he was unrepentant. He was speaking for a war in which his father's brother died; brutally murdered with two thousand others in an episode that history, politicians and the platitudes had almost entirely ignored. How could the sacrifice of his parents' generation be understood if he did not attempt to invest it with contemporary meaning? How else would their deeds live on? For the whole four years of the Keating Government the war was there, a memory stalking the set, pulling focus from the main game, the real issues, the vision thing and the future in cyberspace. Even the media's unsleeping pursuit of the daily truth or a comment on the current account deficit could be brought to a standstill by a rendition of the Last Post in the vicinity of a foreign battlefield. Darwin was the first of these events, but it was at Kokoda that he cast the die.

Kokoda is a telling place for an Australian to go to, there among those highlanders in costumes beyond surreal. This most foreign of places is the site of the most profound reality Australians have ever had to face—the possibility of invasion by a foreign power. They were fighting for the place they had built; the democracy, the wheat crop, the wool clip, their families. Somewhere on the flight from Moresby to Kokoda, as he talked to David Horner, Keating decided that he should make a gesture which would do justice to these events—an act of some kind which would indelibly mark Kokoda in Australia's collective memory, as perhaps Gettysburg was marked in the American mind by Lincoln. So when he reached the modest memorial at Kokoda, to the utter surprise of everyone around him, including Horner, Keating dropped to his knees and kissed the ground.

The press thought his advisers had put him up to it, but the advisers they came hurrying towards had not even seen it happen. Standing beside him, Professor Horner was said to have thought that the Prime Minister had suffered a heart attack. Even by Keating's standards it was a remarkable act.

Old diggers of course had at best mixed feelings about this svelte creature in his Italian suit blessing their ground. The press at the time were divided between saying it was a stroke of political genius and a very strange thing to do. Some of them mocked it, a few saw it for the solemn thing it was. Inevitably, RSL spokesmen were critical: to them it continued a pattern in which Keating was ascribing more glory to some battles than others and more to some soldiers than others—though, blessedly, no-one demanded that he now kiss the ground of every battlefield he visited, and obliged all subsequent prime ministers to follow suit.

Amid the bemusement and mortification, Keating was quite unfazed. He was confident that the simple power of his gesture would long outlive the criticism. He also believed that he had delivered another kind of message, namely that custom would not restrain him. A children's choir waving Australian and PNG flags stood in a circle at Kokoda and sang the PNG national anthem and 'Advance Australia Fair'. And no-one had a dry eye. The PM went around the kids patting their heads and shaking hands, so at ease he said to one of them, indicating the Australian flag, 'Don't worry, sonny, we'll get you a new one of these soon.' He didn't see the sound boom hanging over him. Nor did he care when on the flight to Lae we told him that the remark had been recorded. In Lae he was mobbed and cheered. By the edge of the cemetery at the end of the twenty-one gun salute a branch snapped in a large tree and a dozen Papuans plunged laughing to the ground. Keating told the luncheon in his honour that it had been the most moving day in his entire public career. The RSL curmudgeon Bruce Ruxton told the media that for degrading the Australian flag the men in the Bomana cemetery 'would have got up and pulled him down one of those holes'.

CHAPTER 7

Politics, as a practice, whatever its pretensions, had always been the systematic organisation of hatreds.

HENRY ADAMS

THERE IS NOTHING like a trip overseas. Keating returned in splendid fettle and tore strips off them in Question Time. The Opposition benches were now bedecked with little Australian flags. Tim Fischer asked the Prime Minister to kiss the flag just as he had kissed the ground at Kokoda. Hewson said Keating had 'made a mockery of the country . . . and demeaned our nation in the eyes of the Indonesians'. Somewhat incongruously, standing in a sea of Defaced Blue Ensigns as he was, he added that the flag should be seen as 'nothing more than a distraction from the main game'. News came in that the visit to Indonesia had gone down very well in the region. In his favourite Indian restaurant in the nearby suburb of Deakin, where the PM would sometimes retreat with his staff for lunch, it was whispered that Suharto had been very impressed and some in Jakarta had compared it to the relationship Sukarno had struck with JFK. It seemed that Keating had gone some way to proving his seriousness about engagement in the region. 'Keating is seen as a new leader with a new direction,' Greg Sheridan reported. 'The countries of the region like his nationalistic, pro-republican campaign.' The Prime Minister was remarkably equable for the best part of two and a half days. He welcomed the US Secretary of Defence, Dick Cheney, with a neat little speech and listened to Hewson make a tense and clumsy one. The difference between them might have been related to the poll that showed Keating had passed Hewson as preferred prime minister.

In the House, John Hewson's jaw grew tighter, his responses more churlish. His tactic of turning his back rather than face the camera when Keating was speaking became a chronic habit. He also referred loudly to his 'joke writer'. So badly was Hewson going, joke writing had indeed become a necessary part of political life. With Terry Counihan, the erudite polymath in the office of the Minister for Aged, Family and Health Services, Peter Staples, a little cottage industry of mockery sprang up. A Shell scholar at Cambridge in the 1970s, Counihan had abandoned his academic career to work in mainstream Labor politics. It could not be said of all advisers in Parliament House that their competence easily outstretched the demands placed on it, but it could be said of Counihan. His mind was broad, rigorous and playful. He would drop round and say: do you realise Hewson has a shadow cabinet of forty which is a Commonwealth record; or, here's an article on economic rationalism and *Alice in Wonderland*; or what about a Dorothy on Fightback using the *Monty Python* sketch about a dead parrot? He was adept at social policy, economics and industrial relations, and equally skilled at feeding the more influential journalists who respected his intelligence. For reasons which seemed to have something to do with his personality and education and something else to do with mainstream Labor parties, Counihan never found his way into a senior minister's office. He was one of the government's most undervalued talents.

Defying Chinese displeasure, the Prime Minister welcomed the Dalai Lama to his office. Good works of this kind, putting his foot in the warm water of liberalism, confounding the centrifugal force of pragmatism, always made Paul Keating happy. Then, as if he liked sport as much as the next man, he addressed the Olympics people, and even attended an Australian football match.

With momentum on his side and signs of depression and panic on the other, it was one of those times, rarely lasting more than a week, when one was tempted to think that now he had the bit between his teeth and would not easily let it go. And then he would say he was exhausted, that those trips take it out of you, that it's been all 'go' for so long, and that it was not so good 'up there' (meaning the Lodge). The warning was unmistakable—don't think I'm yours to do what you want with.

He came in furious one morning brandishing an article by Geoffrey Blainey. It said that Keating had his history wrong; that among other things he was wrong to say Menzies had ignored Asia. The article was patronising in the way of the Melbourne history school, biting in the way of a wounded animal. The Prime Minister was infuriated enough to want to draft a reply. But Blainey is an impossibly difficult opponent, as many historians found in the previous decade. The Prime Minister decided not to reply. He said he wished Manning Clark were alive. In the *Australian* several historians expressed delight that Keating had put Australian history into the contemporary political debate and applauded his willingness to question Australia's myths and symbols. David Horner even said he was right 'in substance if not in all detail' about Singapore.

History was not the main game, of course. By some measures, the main game was picking up: a little growth, low inflation, there was even a day when we worried that the Prime Minister's statement on Indonesia might have the unwanted effect of diverting attention from signs of improvement in the economy. So pervasive was the optimism in that week or two, those who played the main game agreed in principle to undertake a serious effort to reduce unemployment and alleviate its human effects. In retrospect it is also possible that their agreement was secured because it occurred to them that announcing something so visionary and bonnie might camouflage a little the news that the budget deficit had blown out by $2 billion. It was news, the *Financial Review* reported, which 'calls into question the government's ability to deliver the large tax cuts it has pledged in its next term of office while fulfilling its promise to return the budget to surplus by 1995–96'. It was all there in One Nation, the tax cuts without a GST and the heroic last lines: 'Within four years the Federal budget will return to surplus, we will have created another 800,000 jobs, clipping 3 percentage points off unemployment. We will have made up our loss in economic growth four times over . . .'

In the daily struggle to assert politics over economics or commonsense over rationalism, or whatever at its heart the tug-of-war was about, bad news sometimes had benefits. When, in the second week of May, the economic advisers began to backslide on unemployment programs, it was possible to suggest that their qualifications were questionable. Yet it always felt bizarre to have to argue the case to them. They worked their collective way through the usual lines about hand-wringing not being an option, and they looked superciliously aggrieved whenever it was suggested that *not* doing something was also not an option. Good intentions were not enough, they said. It would be the recovery which carried us through: only the recovery would cure this malaise which some of them ventured was not as terrible as the figures suggested, or rather, looked at in a certain light, was not as grave as the layperson possibly thought. The same was true of the alarming heights of foreign debt. At the end of September 1992 it was $201 billion, up $29 billion on the last year, up $13.9 billion on the last quarter, which was more than a billion a week and a very large sum every day for those predisposed to figure it. Treasury did not have the language to placate the feelings these numbers generated. The Prime Minister would say that the debt servicing ratio was down 4 per cent, that the country now had a greater capacity to pay. He would say that Commonwealth debt to GDP was 12 per cent or so now, compared with more than 21 per cent a decade ago; that gross general government debt was much lower than the OECD average. He would say that more than half the debt was private; that increasing Australian investment abroad was balancing the equation; that Australia had always needed to import capital—it was that kind of country; that foreign investment was *good*. But one always had the feeling that so long as the Prime Minister was the former treasurer, foreign debt was like any other debt and any debt was *bad*.

It seemed for a moment that our economist colleagues reckoned the political task was to persuade the population that 11 per cent wasn't 11 per cent, or that 900,000 was something less than that. Why should we listen to you? we would ask. You are the authors of the great middle-class tax cuts and the budget which can't pay for them. Still they said about the unemployment programs, it's no use promising what we can't deliver.

It is remotely possible that one's life in the Prime Minister's Office consisted principally of a furious assault on egos like Keating's and Russell's, as if trying to forge in them the separation between self and other—read self and mother—which the rest of us have suffered. Self-interested or motivated by a species of sibling rivalry though this might be, the same drive makes for credible politics. Isn't it untouchable pride and arrogance which people loathe in their leaders? Isn't it that in these diffuse democratic times people value respect more than power, and loathe politicians most for exercising what they don't want and denying them what they do? Why then would a political adviser not try to tell his leader to at least *act* as if the people's trials are his also, and people's voices are the ones he listens to and not some distant drum that only he can hear? Yet people who find such huge egos deplorable or strange should remember that political leadership demands them. They need something to protect them against both the critics and the flatterers. The paradox might be that, having fewer personal doubts to distract them, leaders with indomitable egos are most able to govern for all. The distant drum they hear above the popular tumult is the signature of leadership. The balance we seek and never find is between the leader we want to look up to and the leader we want to shoot down.

The budget deficit blow-out slowed the government's momentum. Then an affair involving Graham Richardson emerged like a ghoul from the dark and a week later, when it had at last been ushered away, all sensations of forward movement had become a distant memory. Graham Richardson was then Minister for Transport and Communications. He was Keating's close colleague, a legendary hard man of the New South Wales right, 'the senator for kneecaps' Bill Hayden called him, competent minister, very astute politician—and priceless scalp for the Opposition.

We might have had a very good debate about unemployment in the office during the last weeks of autumn if it hadn't emerged that Richardson had got himself into what looked like a compromising position with the husband of his cousin, one Greg Symonds who was then in gaol in the Marshall Islands. As it turned out the June balance of payments figures were the best for ages: record export earnings, current account down, imports steady, building approvals up nearly 10 per cent and Westpac's inflation forecast down from 2.5 per cent to 1 per cent. These good figures just might have counteracted the budget blow-out. In the office we might have found the common ground we were still looking for, a balance between the logic of allowing economic growth to create the jobs and the need to educate people to fill them.

Graham Richardson could not be surrendered lightly. Apart from his powerful powerbroking role in the party he had proved himself a very capable minister. As minister for the environment in the Hawke Government it was said that he had delivered the Green vote without which Labor would have lost the 1990 election. As Minister for Communications in the Keating Government he was charged with responsibilities as fraught and as crucial as any except perhaps the Treasurer's and the Prime Minister's. The introduction to Australia of pay TV, for instance, was Richardson's responsibility. Richardson wanted a guaranteed maximum of 35 per cent of pay TV for the networks, with a maximum of 20 per cent for any one network. His opponents said that this was a gift to the only man with a network who could afford 20 per cent— Kerry Packer. Pay TV was soon to become a big issue for the Keating Government, though it was always a minor issue for the public—and as it turned out, for Graham Richardson.

Greg Symonds had been gaoled on charges of fraud over the promised provision of passports to Chinese investors in the Marshall Islands. In the past he had appeared as a crown witness in a case in which the principals of a company for whom he had worked were sent to gaol for tax fraud. He had also been involved with two companies which had gone into receivership with what the *Age* called 'massive losses'. The minister, who had known Symonds for twenty-five years, had provided him with a business reference; then, following his arrest, had phoned the President of the Marshall Islands—an action which the Marshall Islands Attorney-General considered improper.

As these events came to light, the President of the Senate, Kerry Sibraa, became a figure in the drama. Sibraa had written to the Australian Embassy in Washington asking them to arrange meetings with US officials who might assist Symonds to mount his defence. As Richardson pleaded his innocence, his critics suggested that his mates were making Sibraa the scapegoat.

Richardson put his position to the Senate on 7 May: 'I knew that he had a business immigration scheme in the Marshall Islands, but as to having knowledge of his business affairs, I have none.' On these words his case rested—and on them also the Prime Minister was hung out to dry. For on Friday 15 May a letter dated 18 September 1991 was faxed from DFAT to Don Russell's office. It was from Symonds to Richardson and it described his business interests in the Marshall Islands in detail.

Margaret Thatcher would have ascended to a great height and drowned him in boiling oil. Stalin would have shot him. Richardson, it seemed to us, had put his friend and leader out on a limb which might easily have broken. He had, at least on the face of things, misled both the Senate and the Prime Minister. The Prime Minister would not sack Richardson. He asked him to deliver by Monday an explanation of his behaviour.

Meanwhile, as if Richo and the budget deficit were not enough, the Opposition charged Keating with something tantamount to hindering a royal commission into the commercial activities of the former West Australian Labor Government. As treasurer in April the previous year Keating had refused a request from the principal solicitor for the commission for information from the Australian Tax Office, and subsequently rejected another request from the commissioner, Ian Templeman QC. Why, the Opposition asked, had Keating refused an inquiry into a Labor government when on a previous occasion he had agreed to supply information from the Australian Taxation Office to the Fitzgerald Commission in the National Party's Queensland? Because, said Keating, it was on the advice of the Taxation Commissioner, and the advice was that the two cases were different. Furthermore, the Taxation Commissioner now said, the West Australian inquiry had other means of approach.

The Prime Minister told his advisers that he would bring Templeman before the House as Menzies had once brought two journalists before it and put them in Goulburn Gaol. 'You can't do that,' we chorused predictably. 'My oath I can,' he said and produced the handbook. 'This is the ultimate court,' he said. 'Menzies did it. I can do it.' 'It wasn't the most *popular* thing he did,' we said. 'But he had a lot of fun doing it,' said the Prime Minister. It was the only bright moment in a fortnight.

Rumours circulated. When one passed on a rumour to Keating—and one always tried to be selective—he would listen silently and as often as not say nothing at all. He might have been storing it in his memory, or putting it out of his mind. He never said anything much more than 'Is that right?' or 'I don't think that's right'. As the weekend passed and we waited for Richardson's report, a federal politician who knew them both well reckoned that Richardson and Peter Barron were very dark on Mark Ryan and Stephen Smith—and would be fearfully dark should the minister be sacked. 'I don't think that's right,' the Prime Minister said. Another old powerbroker and mate from Sydney reportedly said that the minister was 'safe'—that a government could not allow trial by media. The Prime Minister said nothing.

He gave a press conference on the West Australian royal commission and sounded off about all the QCs filling the front seats of Ansett Airlines. It was a passable performance, but it didn't remove the look of collective agitation which the press had about them. They were hunting in a pack. On the Saturday Michelle Grattan wrote in the *Age* that Keating's honeymoon was over. No-one could remember him having one. The government looked as embattled as the old Hawke Government had in its dying days, she said. When on the Monday Richardson announced his resignation in a long letter to his Prime Minister it made little difference to the general mood or the objective state of things. The Opposition had a prize scalp and inflicted a real wound in the government's side. Keating had not been obliged to decide whether or not to sack Richardson, a serious minister, factional brother and backstop. But spared the decision, he had been left without the moral authority attached to making it.

Richardson said he had never seen the document that described Symonds' business interests and his misleading the Senate, therefore, had been entirely accidental. He was resigning because: 'for twenty years the Labor party has been giving to me. Today it's my turn to give something back.' It sounded very convincing but most of the gallery said it was an act. 'He always gives the impression of candour, no matter how implausible the words,' Mike Seccombe wrote in the *Sydney Morning Herald*. 'He will never come back, not in this or any other Labor government,' Alan Ramsey thundered. Grattan said that you'd swear he was about to be nominated for sainthood. Just as predictably perhaps, P. P. McGuinness said that Richardson was the victim of a press feeding frenzy.

If so, their appetite was far from sated. In a week of forlorn inactivity in the Prime Minister's Office, the press piled cliché upon cliché about decay, rot and the beginning of the end. The Coalition shot six points ahead in the polls. Hewson was again preferred PM. And the Prime Minister had to watch as Richardson's successor was chosen according to a factional deal done in 1990. It delivered up a left replacement, Jeannette McHugh, for the right vacancy. The Prime Minister had wanted the redoubtable member for the Northern Territory, Warren Snowdon. The press duly noticed Keating's inability to get the replacement he wanted. To compound the disaster, McHugh's seat of Phillip had been abolished and she wanted Leo McLeay's seat, Grayndler. It was all 'symptomatic of a tired government', just as the journalists said it was.

The Prime Minister was silent, glum. We wondered if he would have sacked Richardson had the minister not run on his sword. The consensus was he would have stuck by him to the end. He said that Richardson was 'too soft headed', and it is likely that he did not think his old friend was guilty of much more than this. When Mark Ryan had walked into Keating's office with the damning document and said what he thought was the obvious thing—that Richardson had to go—Keating had asked why. Because it means he misled the parliament, and misled you, Ryan had said. Keating said he wasn't sure that this was so. If Richardson had not gone Ryan would have resigned. His position was impossible. In Richardson's office he had been painted as the culprit; the one who had urged the minister's sacking and who since his resignation had been telling the press that he went quietly to avoid being pushed. But he and everyone else knew that when he wasn't talking to Ryan and his other advisers the Prime Minister talked freely to Richardson. It was a test of loyalty: Barron and Richardson and old friends against Russell and Ryan and new friends. Whatever the Prime Minister did, one side was likely to feel betrayed.

Perhaps the press were right and it *was* the beginning of the end. Out of the factional struggle, the demands from State branches and the increasingly obvious paucity of talent, a Queensland member, David Beddall, found himself in the junior ministry. His appointment had been urged by the Brisbane *Courier-Mail*. David Beddall was destined one day to play a role in the demise of the Labor Government.

The best candidate was neither left nor right. Senator Bob McMullan had youth, talent and credibility on his side, and because his election to the cabinet might have been read as an assertion of Keating's authority over the factions in the interests of a wise middle way, he also had logic. But Keating would not have had McMullan in cabinet even if he had had the power to put him there. He was always suspicious of McMullan for reasons that might have been less mysterious had he not been so trusting of some truly suspicious characters. So McMullan languished and Jeannette McHugh became Minister for Consumer Affairs.

We considered various ways to regain momentum, though not John Edwards who was confident next month's figures would be adequate to the task. John did not think like most other people; sometimes it seemed he did not breathe the same air. Certainly he was never tuned to obey the same imperatives. He would agree to write a speech, write an elegant half draft and then he would toddle off for a swim or a jog, telling you as he went that you had better check the figures, which usually meant the figures were wrong—that he had got them, perhaps, from *Fortune* magazine while waiting to have a tooth filled. In his favour it must be said that no-one in the office read more widely, or had such clear ideas about the shape and direction of the new economy and what the social implications were. To work with Edwards was to be consistently reminded of the historic dimensions of the task—indeed, so long as he was there hardly a week went past when I did not think of Robespierre or Lenin.

With Stephen Smith buzzing about trying to satisfy caucus and his own old-fashioned Labor instincts by garnering support for a two-year moratorium on tariff cuts; and Mary Ann O'Loughlin travelling the country enjoining business and welfare groups to support a national meeting on youth unemployment, there was plenty of fodder for John Edwards' contempt. The youth unemployment program was ready to be announced as soon as the Prime Minister could be persuaded to do it. We considered an advertising campaign, but Bob Hogg said that the party had no money. Keating said Hogg was asleep at the wheel and probably would never be woken.

By now Anne Summers had arrived from New York and very soon her picture was in the papers. Just as quickly some people complained about her tendency to claim for herself more than they felt was just; or her self-promotion; or the 'Clinton for

President' badge she wore around the corridors. Some bore old resentments, and some suffered from plain jealousy. But she put some hooks into the world outside, gave Mary Ann O'Loughlin some moral support and, most importantly, brought to the Prime Minister's Office and the government at least the fleeting suggestion that they had the will to renew themselves.

If it looked bad from outside, inside it looked even gloomier. Within days of arriving Summers was asking what was wrong with the place and everybody in it, and especially what was wrong with *him*. Peter Barron said it just six weeks after he became Prime Minister, and Anne Summers said it two weeks after she arrived in the office: he sometimes did not seem to want the job he had always coveted. Mary Ann O'Loughlin had within the space of six weeks developed the look of puzzlement that comes with being unimaginably close to the kind of influence that will make your dreams come true, and yet unable to touch it. To end the most miserable month of the government's short life—more miserable because it had started so propitiously—the Minister for the Environment, Ros Kelly, was obliged to withdraw a school booklet that had been issued by her department and endorsed by her and contained some deeply silly Green propaganda. The Opposition mauled her savagely in the House. Counterattacking, Keating rose and delivered a revised version of the famous Monty Python sketch about a dead parrot that Terry Counihan had been urging on the office for weeks. In the original, a pet shop proprietor attempts to sell John Cleese a parrot which is plainly dead. In the Keating version the parrot was Fightback. The Prime Minister read it before going to Question Time and thought it hilarious, but understandably he wondered if he'd get away with it in the House. In the event he didn't quite, though the point was well made. The next question was to the beleaguered Kelly who that day was wearing a very bright outfit, and as she rose, of all people, John Howard said loudly, 'There's your dead parrot.' It was a very black day. In the evening the President of Yugoslavia told Keating that it had been worth coming all the way to Australia to hear the Prime Minister of Australia speak as he had that day in the House about Bosnia. And the evening news was led not by the humiliation of Ros Kelly, but the mortar attack on Sarajevo.

A snare was set for the Prime Minister. An adviser was placed at each of the exits from his office and others at each of the monitors. Rugged up against the night, he slipped in to Don Russell's office for a last word before going home and found himself trapped by his staff. He started back but Russell had blocked the door. The Prime Minister looked at the clock. I said, we have to talk about the youth thing. 'What youth thing is that, mate?' he said. 'The speech I gave you yesterday,' I said. 'I'll take it home with me,' he said, 'and read it.' 'I've read it and it's fine,' said Donald. The Prime Minister stared. 'Is it, mate?' he said. It had taken two months.

For no logical or discernible reason, both his mood and the media pendulum swung back. He opened a railway on the Gold Coast which had been completed with One Nation money. He addressed Aboriginal leaders and came away enlivened. He charmed a Sydney Olympic bid breakfast and gave them $5 million. He met a delegation of academics led by Sir Ninian Stephen from UTS and told them he was determined to seize back Australia's past from the conservatives who had stolen it. In an article in the *Australian* he urged a renewed sense of common national purpose to go with the economic restructuring which had linked Australia to the rest of the world. When, in June, the Liberals released a silly scaremongering, poll-driven, US Republican Party-inspired pamphlet about the threat of violence to decent home-dwelling people, he asked with undisguised pleasure if the Coalition's laissez-faire economy and the GST would do much for the cause of crime fighting. Between one speech and another in Brisbane he rang from the Botanic Gardens full of confidence and bright ideas and sounding like he was within a few hours of giving his enemies the slip forever.

There was a moment at the beginning of June when the germ of a great idea began to form. It was not quite visible and it was never described, but its presence was enough to create energy which had not been there before. For a few days the real nature of the project took shape. The dry economists did not see more wisdom in the arguments of their opponents, but reckoned it was wise to accept them for now; and their opponents began to see, if not the sense of economic rationalism, the virtue that accrued from seeming to. It was not quite what Marxists called praxis, but in my head at least, Don Russell's notion of a 'virtuous circle' seemed capable of completion. The exhilaration this epiphany inspires may also be known to football coaches and conductors of symphony orchestras, but I doubt if they know all the dimensions of the political experience. It is the pulse you feel when the impossible obstacles to progress suddenly seem capable of negotiation; history's direction becomes discernible; and the force of your strategy feels irresistible. When you feel that you have both the power and the collective intelligence to make something so tangled and multifarious work it creates a kind of religious ecstasy. It can last for as long as two days, but two minutes is more common.

As an interviewer, Channel 9's Laurie Oakes is a minimalist. If you concentrate you can see a trace of a smile sometimes, the lips *do* move. Little else shows. He sits there as still as a frog on a lily pad, while his subjects buzz in the spotlight. He rarely strikes; it's enough to know that he can and, if he wants, he will. If it is newsworthy, whatever you say in your interview with Laurie Oakes at 9.30 runs all day and night on radios and TV and often uncontested in the Monday morning dailies. The show can also be used for changing policy or announcing policy in a concerted way. In an effort to seize back the initiative, this is what Paul Keating did on 30 May 1992. Without consulting cabinet or the caucus, he told Oakes that it had been decided to sell the government-owned Australian Airlines to Qantas and privatise two-thirds of the merged company; to introduce pay television under regulations that allowed 45 per cent ownership of the entire system by existing TV networks with a limit of 20 per cent per network; and, to hurdle State government intransigence, set up a Commonwealth vocational education system.

It was a policy Big Hit. Inevitably, many said that it was typically Keating in style—but whether that meant typically bold and visionary, typically reckless, or typically offensive to Labor tradition and sensibilities, depended on one's point of view. Selling more than 49 per cent of the government airline was a breach of party policy and bound to cause anger in caucus. A pay TV policy which seemed calculated to satisfy the existing networks, particularly Kerry Packer's, and a plan for vocational education that might start a brawl with the Labor premiers of West Australia and Queensland was not going to make them any happier.

To the first two criticisms he could point to harsh reality: why have two struggling airlines when it is possible to have one paying its own way? Why deny Australians the delights of 200 pay television channels and fibre optics with 'interactivity' and other technology we had never heard of, and thousands of jobs, all for the sake of narking Kerry Packer? It was true that few Australians gave a hoot about pay TV; inside and out of the Labor Party it was commonly thought better to do nothing about it than offer it up for the greater wealth and power of people who were already too wealthy and too powerful; from other quarters came predictions that pay television would mean only more American and less Australian content—perhaps worse, that the day would come when Australians had to pay to watch sport. And yet it was impossible to imagine how any government, much less a beleaguered one, could ignore pay television while insisting that jobs were its highest priority and new technologies inseparable from them, and that it still had vision, imagination, energy and all those other things its opponents and the press were anxious to say it lacked.

Keating went to the cabinet meeting happy and confident that he would persuade them to bypass the party's platform on Qantas. The newspapers had praised his brave effort to regain the initiative. 'Keating is gambling . . . that the ALP can only retain office if it extends the will to continue its market-based policies,' Glenn Milne wrote in the *Australian*. The party would have to follow or face defeat, Michelle Grattan said. The boys in the office walked up and down with the old swagger. Even the normally taciturn pointy head, Ric Simes, couldn't help telling the bleeding hearts that if they ever got their youth unemployment meeting up it was going to look pretty small after this. The Prime Minister booted the air with his patent leather slip-on and declared that one had to kick goals in this game. 'Hawkey never had the ticker for this,' he said, and in cabinet he won the day, and somersaulting brilliantly won it again in caucus.

With caucus, compromise was inevitable. It was decided that all of Qantas would be sold and, by way of a trade-off, the networks' share of pay TV would be kept to 35 per cent; foreign ownership would be limited, no individual could have more than a 20 per cent stake. 'Everybody is tired of the old faded and jaded players,' the Prime Minister said. It doesn't matter who owns it, Ken Davidson wrote in the *Age*, pay TV 'will undermine Australian popular culture to the point of destruction'. In both meetings Keating was dynamic. Cabinet members were said to appreciate the degree of political discussion he encouraged, the *esprit de corps* he called up from the decade of experience. In cabinet at least he was the first among equals. One member of the caucus described the speech he made to them as 'lethal'; he had 'everyone laughing and feeling terrific and hating the Liberals'. The South Australian senator, Chris Schacht, said anyone who wanted to know what Keating had meant by 'a touch of excitement' should have seen him selling the pay TV deal. In the House he was 'potent and intimidating'. The *Financial Review* called it all a 'spectacular display of pyrotechnic politics' which had 'wrenched the government's political future back from the brink'. As for the backflip, hubris pumping in his veins, Keating said it was the political equivalent of the great diver, Greg Louganis, on the high board. Only a few remembered when Louganis, trying for the impossible, caught the board with his head on the way down.

No-one was sure the new policies were actually good policies or bulletproof, but the surge was irresistible and the media pendulum had swung back with astounding force. Could it be just a week since Graham Richardson resigned? Then we saw the

Liberal senator, Michael Baume, standing in an empty chamber talking about the Prime Minister's business interests and his failure to lodge a company annual return. Keating watched the tape and muttered darkly, but didn't seem too worried. We watched and wondered if we should be. It cast a shadow on a bright night. We had no idea how long the shadow would prove to be. Watching Baume and wondering was to become part of one's life. Answering Baume's questions in the Senate would become part of Gareth Evans' and John Button's lives. Counterattacking, Mark Ryan got some people in the Labor Party to look into some people in the Liberal Party. They found something.

In *Crowds and Power*, Elias Canetti wrote a memorable analysis of the way one animal captures, kills and devours another. The hand on the flesh, anteroom to the mouth; the mouth, the prison; swallowing, the act of incorporation. He might have been describing Keating that day. The Prime Minister went into the House armed with a Dorothy like an animal that knows every habit of its prey. He didn't have to wait for the Dorothy. Andrew Peacock rose, transcendentally smug, and asked if the failure of a company of which the Prime Minister was a director to lodge an annual return was not evidence of an alarming decline in standards.

Keating got to his feet in a camouflage of seriousness, as usual buttoning and unbuttoning his coat, as if everything was as nature intended. He admitted his error, conceded that it should not have been made. Then he baited them, drew them towards his maw: what was his small investment of half a million dollars in a piggery, compared to Hewson's 365 GTB Ferrari, his Lamborghini Mira, his three Mercedes, his Rolls-Royce, his $3 million house in Bellevue Hill and $1 million house in Bowral? He suggested that Peacock ask his leader 'how he left here in 1983 as an officer serving the treasurer and came back here in 1987 with $5 million worth of assets and how he worked all sides of the streets throughout the portals of Sydney business to advance himself'. The words went to the bowels on both sides. There was mayhem. He began on Michael Baume. Baume had voted against Labor's Bill requiring members to make a full declaration of their interests. Baume was involved in the Patrick Partners share market scandal of the 1970s and escaped prosecution. The Opposition could not contain their (partly feigned) outrage. He made them feel so sure of their moral ground. Then Keating said that he'd done a few checks of Hewson's companies and one of them, of which Carolyn, his wife, was secretary, had failed to lodge an annual return. Over the roar from the government benches he said that he had also looked into Peter Reith's company and—and the camera homed in on the shadow minister—Reith's company too had been fined for failing to lodge an annual return. It was childish pleasure of course, like watching the villain get his comeuppance in a pantomime, or a big balloon go blurting into the air. But at that moment, as the camera panned along the Opposition benches, politically speaking, to be alive was heaven.

There was romance in serving one's prime minister in Canberra's season of frosts and fogs: to crunch through the long grass and gravel in the early hours of the morning, speech in hand, eyeballs chilled and red; drop the thing off with the guard at the Lodge gate. There was a speech for the NSW State Conference on the Saturday morning. Afterwards someone told the Prime Minister, and he told me, that it was the best speech a Labor leader had ever given to a State conference. The standing ovation went on for so long, the PM reported, that he sat down and then he had to stand up again.

But what he said and the way the brothers cheered him to the rafters of Sydney Town Hall was never reported. He had arrived to learn that the National President, Senator Stephen Loosley, had resigned over the matter of the sale of party headquarters. This became the news. The line between triumph and despair is narrow in politics. What propels you one moment blows back in your face the next. The great policy push of early June rushed the government on for a fortnight and a moment later it was becalmed.

The summit on youth unemployment was announced on the tail of the aviation reforms and pay TV. Mary Ann O'Loughlin had dredged up no end of support from the community. The desire to be heard by the highest office in the Commonwealth is limitless. Ring a CEO and tell him that you're from the Prime Minister's Office and he'll see you; ask him for his ideas in a nutshell and he'll give them to you by the wheelbarrow load; thank him for giving you a moment of his time and an hour later you'll be wondering how you will keep your next appointment. Cynics say such people are driven as much by self-interest and vanity as patriotism and goodwill, and nothing you say or do will persuade them to vote Labor. The cynics have a point. This is not the real hardship, however. The problem with soliciting the advice and participation of business is that, wise though they may be in their chosen fields, they know nothing about politics and have no need for its disciplines. Their *can-do* mentalities do not necessarily meld with the *can't-do* or *not yet* realities of government. They are liable to welcome the government initiative on arrival at the meeting, and on their departure heap on it buckets of contempt. They are inclined to raise public expectations far beyond the government's capacity to deliver. Add to the mix the welfare lobby, including its most sanctimonious and its most sophisticated extremes, and it is not difficult to understand why politicians do not thank those who organise summits on youth unemployment. In the 1980s Bob Hawke had mastered this kind of summitry, principally through the force of his own personality, but this was just another reason why the Keating office economists were hostile and the PM less than enthusiastic.

The youth unemployment summit was not inspired politics but essential politics, an essential gesture to the community and to the caucus. In some quarters the big policy push of 30 May had been called the Free Market Bastard Son of One Nation. The summit would confirm that Keating had indeed cut himself adrift from free-market ideology, and could fight on several fronts. In addition, the possibility remained that from all these deliberations the young unemployed might gain some benefit.

And now there was Mabo. In June by a majority of six to one the High Court quashed the doctrine of *terra nullius,* finding that a Native Title to the land existed and had survived European settlement. The court determined that the doctrine used to legally sanction European occupation and the dispossession of the Aboriginal people was bogus. Australia had not been a continent empty of people. The historic significance of the decision was obvious to everyone, except all those who either had no history or something else on at the time. As this meant about 80 per cent of the population and up to 90 per cent of the gallery, panic and excitement took some time to set in. The decision raised certain fundamental questions about land tenure. Where else in Australia beyond Eddie Mabo's island in Torres Strait did Native Title exist? Who was secure from it? Anyone? Yet Mabo spilled into the political debate with little drama and few howls of protest. The *Age* put it on the front page, 'Key ruling boosts blacks', but as second fiddle to a pay TV headline. On 4 June Keating told the House that the Mabo judgment had quashed 'the outrageous notion' of *terra nullius* and thus 'the foundation of discrimination and prejudice has been kicked away'. However, he said, the judgment 'does not challenge the granting of freehold title over much of Australia and does not interfere with private property rights of this kind'. There were no visible signs of alarm.

The Prime Minister's Office went back to the bitter struggle about the face on the five-dollar note. Having withdrawn the two-dollar note from circulation, the Reserve Bank announced that the Queen's image must now adorn the five-dollar note, which left the pioneer philanthropist Caroline Chisholm without a note to grace. This was not at all consistent with the government's position on matters of Australian history and identity; nor, it appeared, with popular feeling. A TV vox pop found widespread support for retaining Chisholm. Even John Hewson wanted Chisholm to stay where she was, or judged it wise to say that he did. The House passed a resolution in favour of it. But it was the rule: the Queen's face shall appear on the lowest denomination of paper currency, which was now the five-dollar note. Bernie Fraser was adamant that the rule would apply, and as they had much bigger fish than this to fry with him, neither Keating nor Russell was prepared to push the point for long. The debate provoked the British tabloids to say Australia was Pom-bashing again. Bashing was the wrong word. We were only trying to ignore them.

No-one on either side of the argument felt that the five-dollar note was important in the grand scheme, but it did maintain the beat of the national drum. We had tried, some of us, to get into the public mind the idea that Australians were all of the one tribe. We hoped that such a sense of fellow feeling might propel the country towards new goals, give us the impetus to keep going and throw aside those who opposed our progress. It was the same principle which applied to the Labor Party and bicycles, as the Prime Minister told the NSW ALP State Conference—they both fall over if you stop pedalling.

'Our big picture has people in it,' he told the conference in the unreported speech. We have proved ourselves capable of profound change, he said, and in this way given ourselves a chance in the world. Fightback was a throwback to the days before the change: in a society 'with one of the most sophisticated and effec-tive social security systems in the world they want to introduce measures characteristic of societies in decay', he said. He meant the cuts to welfare promised by Fightback; the move away from collective bargaining towards individual contracts in the work-place; the Thatcherism inherent in Fightback and the GST. It was a rallying cry for the faithful. When the speech wasn't reported the Prime Minister asked that it be sent to all ALP branches.

It was easy to make a persuasive case against the Opposition; possible to make a logical case for the Government; but very difficult, in the face of the economic data and the realities of life after the recession, to sustain political momentum. The recovery was said to be 'patchy'. Unemployment, by contrast, was constant and general. A Westpac survey found business confidence was rising. It also found consumer confidence in retreat. Car sales and building approvals were down. In the media habitually hostile and sympathetic economics writers alike declared that the One Nation growth predictions were too high and would have to be revised, that the government's budget options were narrowing, that unemployment was unlikely to fall before the next election. When inflation fell by 0.3 per cent in the June quarter, Keating said the 'inflation stick' had been 'snapped'. Hewson said the figure only proved that the economy was 'dead in the water'. Keating began to talk about a 'low inflation sustainable recovery'. Hewson said he smelt 'a double dip recession'. Keating reminded people of the virtues of low inflation and explained that it was essential to the country's trade prospects, but it was easier for the electorate to believe Hewson. Keating explained that continuing high unemployment was a reflection of 'productivity gains', that companies had learned to produce more with fewer employees, but as the economy expanded they would 'reach a point where they would have to employ more people'. It was still easier to believe Hewson. The OECD joined in with a 'downbeat assessment' of the world economy that predicted economic growth would be only 1.8 per cent, not 2.2 per cent as earlier advised.

It was open to Keating to draw comparisons with other countries where growth was just as slow or worse than Australia's. Britain was still in recession. Canada had virtually zero growth. France had just recorded a record unemployment figure. The US was slowing. Japan's leaders had just agreed on the first of several monster sums to revive the economy. The Australian people were not visibly comforted by the knowledge that other countries were in a similar pickle. They held their own prime minister responsible for their own difficult times. Gloom and cynicism prevailed, and John Hewson assiduously went about his business of turning it to gold—so assiduously he failed to see the risk he ran. The risk was that Keating would cast him as the enemy of hope: here we are, he would say, like other countries, struggling free of a recession and into a new world order and my opponent seeks only to belittle our efforts—*your* efforts. Why, it lay on the very cusp of un-Australianness.

Before he could get to this position, however, Keating had

to earn the electorate's trust, persuade them that he was defending their interests and not his own record. That was why it was mad for him to go on playing treasurer. Why continue to wear the ignominy? Why remind the electors at every opportunity that this economy was his? It was like watching a man on a treadmill. Ignoring the fatal risk to my credibility, I suggested that a speech to the Companies Directors Association might depart from Treasury-related matters for a time and consider, of all things, multiculturalism—the contribution of European and other migrants, their entrepreneurial spirit, their loyalty, the flesh-and-blood drama of capital accumulation. In one aspect it might be a hymn to the bold, adventurous spirit of enterprise. I thought it would make a change to talk to these business people about the psychological roots of their core business; and about culture, history and philosophy including the Prime Minister's own.

The economists were aghast. The company directors would think he had lost his mind, as plainly I had lost mine. The detailed plan of what such a speech would look like made no difference. They might be interested for a change, I said, even a little flattered that he should talk to them as citizens, as intelligent men and women of Australia and not mere suits. There was a line to run on multiculturalism which might appeal to businesspeople who had not traded on their ethnicity but become both rich and patriotic—entrepreneurs like Frank Lowy, Richard Pratt, John David, Peter Abeles, Arvi Parbo and Bruno Grollo. There were plenty of postwar migrants among the Australians who felt that multiculturalism had left the path of reason and become a species of political correctness. It was not necessary to suggest that Australia was in danger of becoming Balkanised, but a partial, reasoned evacuation of multiculturalism in its ideological form would address the growing community hostility to entitlements for minorities.

That was one good political argument for it. It put Keating in the mainstream. It was consistent with the need to sell Keating as a man of hard-headed commonsense. And there was always the possibility that it might drive John Hewson to try outflanking him on the right. Keating may have only needed to go as far as he went two months later in an address to a conference of the Federation of Ethnic Community Councils: 'We don't support particular cultures for their own sake. We do it to keep the barriers down. We take the view that these policies are an extension of our democratic tradition.' If he had told these company directors that the government thought cultural pluralism was a great thing for the country, but not as great as personal freedom, or the ties binding all Australians, or equality real and perceived, he might have been heard in places where Australians were not listening— and Hewson just might have been provoked to say the Liberals were going to scrap the whole multicultural idea. And then we would double back.

It is one of the countless anomalies of politics that a pursuit which demands extreme agility and willingness to compromise and innovate gives rise to chronic pedantry and the rule of pre-cedent. Those poor company directors were going to get the economy and nothing but the economy. The price for being players of the main game was a diet of gruel and no fun. It could have been such a good address about the economy and history and democracy and national development and culture and the sort of man the Prime Minister was. The economists would hear nothing of it. I told one of them that he was the Khmer Rouge of political thinking. On that very day, according to Simon Balderstone, we had managed to destroy the Australian music industry by exposing it to cheap CD imports. Bob Hogg and Rod Cameron were sympathetic over dinner. You're doing everything right except the flag, they said. Drop the flag for now and change it after you've won the election. I would have dropped everything just then. The next day I was offered a much better paid job by a team of consultants, but by then leaving was unthinkable.

Through all these weeks we survived on flickers of hope. Much of the energy came from the doctrinal folly of Hewson. Much of the exhaustion came from fighting the same doctrine in the Prime Minister's Office. Barry Jones became national president of the ALP and told the press that the party remained under the malign influence of neoclassical zealots. Keating gave the company directors a familiar economic speech off the cuff and it passed unnoticed into the void. Just nine days after he strode triumphant from the House and was hailed as the master of agile political thinking, he had regressed to the old fixations. He was stuck like a fly. Even Don Russell was for a time persuaded that speeches on the economy were not doing the Prime Minister any good. This reversion to the Good Old Story, which he trotted out again in an interview with Geraldine Doogue, generally coincided with a retreat into his familiar lassitude and obstinacy. Even in the more sympathetic environment created by the announcement of a summit, when she asked him about youth unemployment he could not help saying that there was not as much of it as people thought. Likewise the recession. Likewise the hardship that people at least imagined they were feeling. There were times when it seemed the Prime Minister thought no-one was doing it as hard as him. The story, that which he had done; the economy, that which he had made his own—these were his comforters, his transitional objects, like his music and his other beautiful things. He could not leave them alone for long.

Telling no-one, he cancelled speeches his office had formally agreed to: the Australian Writers' Guild (AWGIE) Awards because it was the night of the day that he returned from the Pacific Forum in the Solomon Islands; the Australian Book Publishers' Association annual dinner because he was 'not really a book person'; and a meeting I had arranged with the historian, Henry Reynolds, to talk about the implications of the Mabo judgment, because it was 'low priority'. He bought some suits and felt better. I was a 'fuming old nationalist', he said. In fact it was a day when I wanted to emigrate. There was a row. He retreated saying that he just reckoned there were too many 'arty-farty events'. To this one might have replied, none of them so arty-farty as your concept of the economy. Instead one asked if his great leaders in history—Washington, Lincoln, Roosevelt and

Churchill—surrounded themselves with economists? Did Churchill have economists crawling over him? Economists should be kept in cupboards and consulted only for a set of figures. Why now did we have to listen to their predictions and their revised predictions and speak their non-language, and make that impossible leap of faith to believing they knew something about lived lives, or even what it was like to run a small business? It was not the task of a leader to run an economy, it was to run a country, a community, an empire if need be.

Although he was said to exercise the principle brilliantly in cabinet, in the broad electorate Keating did not seem to understand the meaning of *primus inter pares*. It was as if the idea was foreign to him. Of course we were all equal—we are born equal, we die equal and are equal in the eyes of God. But *primus inter pares* is a principle of leadership, and Keating understood leadership to mean *doing* something, not *being* something. Being was his business: his being, his family's being, these things were properly beyond the eyes and claws of politics. Judge him on what he does, not on what he is: what he does is manage an economy, because the economy will decide the issues for you and your children. First among equals—humbug! Perhaps he sensed the patrician in it. Keating always recoiled from the patrician. He had few traces of it in himself and loathed it in others. He was no Augustus. At crucial times he also affected to recoil from leadership. You could shepherd him into new fields for a time, but he was a man managing an economy when it came down to it. He relented on the arty-farty speeches and flashed his gums to heal any wounds. A day later he complained about the program and the arty-farty speeches again. The Liberals hunted him over the piggery. The *Sydney Morning Herald* did a job on him on its front page.

It was strange to hear the office described as a bunker, impenetrable to outside influence, when those inside knew that they competed every day with advice he took on the telephone— about the wisdom of identifying with the arts, for instance. The arts were for the elites. The arts, nonetheless, also received wide coverage in the press and Keating looked at home in their company. Had he been as comfortable with sporting heroes we would have thrown him among them and few would have escaped his smiling embrace. But he was not Hawke or Menzies. He had no passion for sport. More than that, he thought its pre-eminence in Australian culture was a threat to the nation's collective intelligence and maturity. The diffidence showed, sometimes painfully. It was much wiser, therefore, to put him among artists, musicians and film-makers and let him be photographed in a non-combative attitude. Let the public see another dimension to his character.

Very occasionally the Prime Minister participated in a staff meeting. It was intriguing to observe him. Would he enter with a galvanising sense of purpose, or the bored and care-worn look which warned his tormentors off? Keating the political predator frequently looked like the prey. John Edwards made a suggestion, at once so ingratiating and shrewd and in such shameless defiance of the known truth about his employer's work habits nearly everyone grinned and at least two advisers copied it down. He said 'You're going to be pretty ragged with the program through to the budget. Have you given any thought to taking a few days off?' It turned out that the Prime Minister had. Within minutes, official visits to Tasmania and Queensland had been postponed, and into the timetable went a few days in Port Douglas. Various other troublesome inconveniences were solemnly noted and before long we had a happy prime minister. Dr Edwards' humane concern had so revived his spirits the youth initiative was upgraded from a 'meeting' to a 'summit'.

There were limits to his goodwill, however. Ashton Calvert had tentatively scheduled a visit to Japan and Korea before the end of the year. The PM mused. He did not want to visit more than one country at a time—two at the most. He was not keen, therefore, to add Korea to the Japan trip, though he recognised that the Koreans were important trading partners. Dr Calvert looked aggrieved. It was a long flight from Japan to Korea, mate, the PM ventured by way of apology. It was two hours, Ashton said. There being no other convincing explanation, it is possible these were exercises in mere impishness, attempts such as he might have made in childhood to see what he could get away with.

The Prime Minister descended into what seemed to be a form of depression. The pressures on his family life had much to do with it. Being treasurer was nothing like this: there had not been all these demands that Annita make speeches, pose for photographs, lend her name and influence to good causes. Now it seemed barely a week went by without her doing one thing or another. With him it was a matter of principle that the public had no call on his wife's time or the children's. He could not readily accept the scale of her public engagements. When they kept her away from the children he worried. When it meant they were both away he worried more, and to some extent this considera-tion shaped his own program. More disconcerting was the coolness of relations between his mother and his wife. Develop-ments of this kind are no less knotty and painful because they are common, if not inevitable in marriages. Privately, for Keating, this relationship sometimes seemed a deeper concern than the Oppo-sition or the press. He was always at least outwardly confident that in the end he would round up his opponents as he had with Hewson and Downer and would with Howard if they allowed him time. But he could not bring the same bravado—or the same skills—to this private puzzle. In such low spirits he was prone to heed the voices of rebellious minorities and zealots and say to buggery with the consequences. So he went to Bankstown and told his audience (again) that about one in ten of Australia's youth was unemployed, not four or more as some claimed. The media were there and duly lambasted him—first for denying the figures, second for practising bad politics. An article on his private affairs in the *Sunday Age* so infuriated him he rang and berated the editor, who threatened to publish the catalogue of his abuse. To the media he looked like a wildebeest on its knees. You could hear their barking and their drooling.

In horror the Minister for Social Security, Neal Blewett,

rang from Sydney. He had flown up from Canberra with the Prime Minister that morning. The Prime Minister had proffered the opinion that the government should be saying that high unemployment figures were proof its policies were working. Restructuring was proceeding satisfactorily. Companies were making productivity gains, which was to say they were becoming more profitable by shedding labour. They were gearing up for the modern world. The economy was being transformed on the lines intended. This view, which put some bleeding hearts in mind of Stalin's figuring on Ukrainian peasants, had also been expressed by Dr Edwards. We were confident he had passed it on to the Prime Minister who in his troubled mood was prepared to buy it. They had apparently decided that if the government was going down, they would go down pure. The Minister was assured that it had all been in the nature of speculative analysis and would not form part of our strategy.

Don Russell thought that the proposed visit to Japan was politically unwise. His reasoning was easy enough to follow: there is an element of political danger in all overseas trips and a large element of it in uncertain times. On overseas trips the media pack plays the parasite to the prime ministerial host, it sweats on him day and night. Was anything that might be gained in Japan worth the risk that they might turn nasty—by reporting, for instance, that he and his staff were living it up at the Imperial Hotel, where a hamburger cost $60 and a suite at least $1000, when his fellow Australians were struggling to survive? And why risk unpleasant comparisons? Despite the first signs of weakness, in 1992 the Japanese economy was still regarded as a miracle, and there were people bursting to say that its success had nothing to do with free-market economics.

Keating went because Japan was Australia's biggest trading partner and the country above all others on which the Australian economy depended. A visit to Japan could be made symbolic of strength and hope. Beyond the immediately political, there was another agenda which the Prime Minister could not responsibly ignore. On Japan depended his growing ambitions for APEC.

If Australia intended to play a major creative role in East Asia and the Pacific, pursue its trading interests there and more thoroughly integrate with the region, a visit to Japan was an obvious priority and one which could be sold as crucial to the national interest.

Indeed there was a case to be made for extending the trip not only to Korea, but to Vietnam and Cambodia. All other things being equal, being the first prime minister to visit Vietnam might mark out his economic strategy even more clearly. It might say this is where the future lies and so vigorously am I pursuing it, I will go there regardless of the US position or that of any other country. If the trip drew criticism from Australia's Vietnamese community, Australia's veterans of the war or from the Coalition, it was a debate worth having and probably one Keating could win. In Cambodia, Australian soldiers formed part of the UN force whose commander was an Australian. The peace had been largely conceived and brokered by Australia. It made sense for an Australian prime minister to visit Phnom Penh and show his country's support for their efforts and have Australians see him do it. But all other things were not equal. Other things went too badly for a prime minister to be out of the country for so long. He would not go to Korea or Vietnam.

Very occasionally, there was a day in the office when nothing seemed to happen at all. It was a disagreeable feeling akin to quitting smoking. If you turned off the fluorescent lights and created a warm bath of light with a normal lamp and played some music you could create a thin calm veneer and work within it. It was some defence against the overflowing urge to get up and tell someone of a thought that had come into your head, to go and stop something happening, or make something happen, or make sure that what was meant to happen had happened, to discover if it had gone well or badly, or to check that nothing was happening in your absence. One needed to know to be reassured; to have a fix or know that one was coming. Politics is ritualised addiction to influence. It is like being in love or having delirium tremens. Because possibilities seem limitless when one is very close to power, the most common feeling is powerlessness. The next most common is the perception of inertia in others. In this heightened, some would say distorted, reality it often felt as if, of all the players on the field, only a couple were actually moving. And in the early hours of the morning when Parliament House was deserted and the only one was me writing speeches and a security man bringing cups of tea it was easy to lose contact with the reality of all other lives.

In fact acute consciousness of others was the key to success in this environment. Don Russell said that he understood the Prime Minister like no-one else, that there was a kind of symbiotic relationship between them. Russell and Keating shared both the experience of the great reform story and a belief that they understood the relationship between politics and economic reform like no-one else alive. They may have been right, but that was less important than the powerful glue of mutual admiration which the belief inspired. It was set the harder because it was a teacher–pupil bond, for each had taught the other about economics and politics and the relationship between them. Keating loved Russell if not as a son then as a younger sibling. He often reminded us that when he first came across him the now very bald Don Russell had been a long-haired middle-class hippie who just happened to be as well a Treasury official of impressive natural intelligence and impeccable academic qualifications. The Keating version had him leading this unworldly second-generation academic economist into the mainstream of politics and to the great reform adventure. As Russell broadened Keating's economic knowledge and honed his mastery of economic language, Keating encouraged Russell's political instincts. By the time Keating became prime minister, it had become a kind of double act. It was second nature to them, to test each other's reaction to every move on the screen—economic or political. To decide jointly what to say, what not to say, what the tone and volume should be. Politics and the economy were virtually as one for them. All else was a matter of shoring up enough support to get the party re-elected so the reforms could continue.

There was something undeniable and impressive, even noble, about it. It was not an equal relationship—Russell was always respectful, proper and dutiful—but there was equality of respect. The relationship lived off mutual regard for the qualities of dispassionate intelligence, courage and duty each saw in the other and held as the chief virtues. Beneath Russell's insouciance and Keating's languor—and what was perceived almost universally as arrogance—there was passion for a great cause. They felt sure that no-one had done it this way before, and they were probably right.

The problem was that the act didn't work as well for a prime minister, particularly a prime minister who had made the economy his personal province and now had to explain why it was floundering. Keating needed to create evidence of renewal, but his act was passé. It was like doing vaudeville after television came. Yet there was no sense in trying to fracture the relationship between Keating and Russell; better by far to broaden it, to insert into it other perspectives, if not other personnel. It required a circling movement; to employ a Keatingism, one needed to 'draw down its strength'.

The starting point was to recognise Keating's unique qualities. The government had no better warrior, no more persuasive advocate, no mind as powerfully creative and no-one with a prouder recent record of achievement. Keating was sometimes wilful and self-absorbed, occasionally full of mad rage, damn near uncivilised. It had something to do with the blessings of his childhood leaving him without much fear of judgment, and to that extent without some of the normal boundaries of behaviour. He was never worried about enemies. In his early twenties, Jack Lang told him he was going well because already so many people did not like him. Put it to Keating and he will agree that it was the boundless affection of his mother and grandmother that left him with so little need to be liked by anyone else. Yet he was also governed by an instinct or a calculation (who can say which?) telling him that not all human action derives from or responds to reason: there is an impulse to war and self-destruction, a need for faith in things that are not rational, and a tendency to chaos— perhaps because chaos has cleansing or redemptive qualities. Chaos resets the equation. Keating's wilfulness was in part a corollary of his determination to remake the world, a partner to his heroic impulse. It was a heroic 'tactic'. Achilles was governed by similar instincts. And Keating did have the hero in him, or enough of it for those who suffered most from his moods to remain the most devoted to him.

Railing and despair, to which I was occasionally prone, achieved nothing. You cannot change him, my wife used to say; you can't change anyone over forty. Better to try thinking the same way, and having won his trust, lead him into new pastures. But it was like trying to get a sheep to go through a gate; it was like Sancho Panza trying to persuade Don Quixote to give up his quest and go home. It was only possible so long as you lost neither your temper nor sight of all there was to admire in him.

As a diversion I tried to analyse him. A psychologist friend directed me to books that seemed to say: wherever we go, we go as a very young child; and everything is a reminder of the earliest days, and has the potential to be hostile or benign, and must be dealt with either by coping or aggression. I'm not sure if his moods—or mine—had anything to do with his childhood, but this tactic proved an aid to bonding and forgiveness (forgiveness is essential in politics), and a barrier against panic and despair. Politicians who must forever pretend that they are in control of themselves and the circumstances around them have huge demands placed on their capacity to perform, to act. It helped to remember that Keating had been performing at high levels for a long while: verbal brilliance, balancing acts, magic tricks, hair-raising risks—performance had been the essential element in his success. No wonder he was exhausted.

Some frustrations were beyond the reach of analysis. One would be in the middle of an argument and sensing a decisive victory and Anne Summers would walk in and say that Brett Whiteley was dead, or Stephen Smith might rush in and tell you that the Premier of New South Wales had just resigned. And seizing the opportunity the Prime Minister and his followers would speak dolefully or with delight and the thread would be lost and another raft of policy would drift out of reach.

CHAPTER 8

*All war supposes human weakness, and against that it is
directed.*

CARL VON CLAUSEWITZ, ON WAR

THE AUGUST BUDGET was being prepared—an election
budget but with scarcely any means of making it a vote-
winner. In the House John Hewson attempted to draw a
link between the Prime Minister's recession and the rising rate of
youth suicide. The Prime Minister said this was a squalid tactic
and asked Hewson if cuts to welfare and education, a nine-month
limit on unemployment benefits, or a 15 per cent consumption
tax would make a difference. Gruelling as the times were, Fightback was always there to help out.

The Royal Commission into Aboriginal Deaths in
Custody delivered its report. The commission had investigated
ninety-nine deaths. A further thirty had occurred since it ended.
It was impossible not to conclude with them that there was a
connection between that statistic and these others: Aborigines'
average yearly income was about half the national average; their
participation in post-school education was one-fifth of the
national average; their mortality rate among all age groups was
three to six times that for other Australians; infant mortality was
three times higher; and 29 times more Aborigines and Torres
Strait Islanders were in custody. The commission found that the

deaths of Aborigines in Australian gaols was ultimately the consequence of two centuries of dispossession, prejudice and neglect. In a statement to the House, Keating announced that despite the tough economic times the government would spend $250 million on programs to combat the problem. He also pledged an effort by the Commonwealth Government to deliver justice by the end of the century. He called on all levels of government to become involved with the new programs in education and training, employment, pre-schools and industry development.

He reasserted the government's faith in the principles of self-determination embodied in ATSIC and its sixty regional councils. Change could not be imposed, he said. There can be no change 'without the energy and will' of the people. He expressed his hopes for the new Council for Aboriginal Reconciliation which, he said, 'offers Australia its greatest chance of learning that there is no true loyalty or affection for this country which does not include respect for Aboriginal and Torres Strait Islander Australians'. Most newspapers reported the speech on their front pages, and no-one at that stage even politely demurred. But who can say if something dark did not stir in a Queensland or Kalgoorlie heart?

In the broad swim, neither side was able to make much sense or headway. Labor was dragged down by bad figures, bad luck and bad management. Attempting to say something interesting about the country, the Prime Minister told an interviewer that it would be a pleasant change if Australia was more often represented by some of its clever and cultivated achievements and less often by a shrimp on a barbie. Soon after, he used the word 'yobbo'. These appeared to be derisory references to the mightily successful advertising campaign starring Paul Hogan, famous throughout the world as Crocodile Dundee. It was alleged that the remark offended everyone who loved Paul Hogan, including Paul Hogan, and all those associated with the advertisements which had been credited with the foundation of the modern Australian tourism industry. At least a fortnight was spent trying to repair the damage. It was fortuitous when the *Far Eastern*

Economic Review appeared with a beer-swilling Australian and the message, 'Australia—time to get serious', on the front cover, but it was not a total cure.

There were supporters out there. Anne Summers and I talked to Donald Horne about the republic, an Australian equivalent of the US Endowment for the Humanities and a national cultural policy. Soon after, Horne publicly endorsed Keating's effort to develop a broader image for Australia. Hugh Mackay, the social researcher, spoke glowingly of One Nation. These were fringe issues, but they did give the government some definition which the big policy push of early June had failed to do. In fact by mid-winter the big policy push had been identified for what it was—a brave, but hasty and inevitably flawed attempt to regain the political initiative. Cabinet ministers complained to journalists that Keating had missed a chance to do something 'integrated' about unemployment. This was another word for industry policy. These cabinet ministers, according to the newspapers, reckoned that the Qantas takeover of Australian Airlines would cost thousands of jobs, as all things done in the name of 'efficiencies' do. They reckoned the pay TV package was rushed and chaotic and devoid of plans for local software production and domestic content. They despaired, it was reported, of the 'cyclical approach' to unemployment which was the Micawber principle by another name. They also complained that Keating's inner office was driving policy, that cabinet was excluded, that he was habitually late for cabinet meetings and that he had abdicated in favour of Dawkins from the Expenditure Review Committee, the budget watchdog. If this kept up, they were alleged to be saying, the consequences for the election would be disastrous. They were therefore watching progress on the youth summit with 'intense interest'.

The PM thought the figures were the big problem. If only the One Nation forecasts had been right we would have been home and hosed. Some of us, fools that we were, could not see that One Nation ever needed forecasts. Some of us reckoned leadership, not forecasts, would get us home. But at the mention of leadership the Christie's catalogue came out.

The speech to the Australian Booksellers and Publishers' Association pushed the economy to page two. Keating shared the stage with the British writer John Mortimer and praised him for his willingness to co-mingle with such a notorious Pom-basher as himself. Of course he was no such thing, the Prime Minister said. He sought nothing beyond making Australia's interests clear and its image less ambiguous. He regretted that the popular image of Australia and Australians' own self-image tended not to include some of the country's most notable achievements; in social progress for instance, and he quoted as an example the fact that no country surpassed Australia's record for contemporary legislation to advance and protect the interests and rights of women. He quoted the words of two senior Australian historians in support of his objectives—the foreign policy expert, W.J. Hudson, and the Ernest Scott Professor of History at the University of Melbourne, Stuart Macintyre. In an article published just a few months earlier, Hudson compared Australia to the child that even as an adult will not leave home. Indeed mother 'was moving out and not taking him with her'. Macintyre had written about the lack of a 'civic dimension' in Australian history and a similar absence in the contemporary culture. 'The new citizen,' he said, 'swears an oath to abide by the laws but these are not spelt out nor is there any elaboration of their guiding principles or the ethos they encompass.' Keating proposed replacing the Oath of Allegiance with an Australian Citizenship Pledge. The oath required persons wishing to become Australian citizens to swear by Almighty God that they would be 'faithful and bear true allegiance to Her Majesty Elizabeth the Second, Queen of Australia, her heirs and successors according to law' and faithfully observe the laws and fulfil their duties as Australian citizens. The pledge, as it was eventually resolved, made God optional and the Queen obsolete. The first version was written by the Minister for Justice, Michael Tate, after a conversation he had with the poet Les Murray: it pledged 'loyalty to the Australian people, whose democratic values I share, whose diversity I respect within the one community of Australia, and whose constitution and laws I promise to uphold and obey'.

After reworking in the Prime Minister's Office, the version put to cabinet said: 'From this time forward [under God] I pledge my loyalty to Australia and its people, whose democratic beliefs I share, whose rights and liberties I respect, and whose laws I will always uphold and obey.' Cabinet deleted 'always'.

The change was announced in December 1992. Soon after, many letters arrived from people who said that until now they had been unwilling to take out citizenship, and indeed we heard that the numbers participating in ceremonies had increased. The Opposition said the Pledge would not help the unemployed, that it was a republican ploy and the Prime Minister was dancing on the grave of Charles and Diana's marriage. Alf Garland was 'disgusted'.

In that mid-year speech to the booksellers and publishers, Keating called for a definition of multiculturalism which left no doubt that 'the first loyalty of all who make their home here will be to Australia'. In subsequent speeches he sharpened his critique. Each time the multicultural bureaucrats resisted, but his ethnic audiences applauded. He insisted multiculturalism was never meant to be an ideology, nor a guarantee of any entitlements beyond assistance consistent with need, cultural tolerance and freedom from discrimination. He had no desire to shed the concept of a multicultural Australia; but, he said, the ideals and ambitions of multiculturalism had to be compatible with the nation's ambitions and ideals. This was the point of the new oath he proposed. New citizens would proclaim their loyalty to Australia and to the nation's notional ideals of liberty and toler- ance—the very things which made multiculturalism possible.

Mere froth such thoughts might be, but multiplied a few times they begin to resemble leadership. They also begin to take a prime minister a little further from the tar baby embrace of his opponent. Pledges are hardly 'on strategy', but they do work on sentiment and imagination which can hardly be banished from politics. Yet in hard political times sentiment is often the last thing you want to hear. A letter in the *Age* from the historian Noel McLachlan says it is outrageous for a Labor prime minister to have an interest in a commercial company worth $2 million. On ABC radio Terry Lane interviews a man who describes foreign ownership of Australian companies as if the Black Death was abroad. A taxi driver tells you he used to drive a Visyboard truck but he got laid off. His car radio has a shock-jock on it railing against your leader's arrogance. These things subvert your confidence, upset your equilibrium. You want to shut them out.

Over lunch at the Indian restaurant in Deakin on 1 July 1992, the Prime Minister told Don Russell, Ashton Calvert, Mark Ryan and me that he wanted to formally propose an Australian republic within the next couple of months. He wanted to say that a second Keating Government would put it to a referendum in its next term. In his office later that day, he told the secretary of the Department of Prime Minister and Cabinet, Michael Keating, and the deputy secretary, Sandy Hollway. The meeting had been called to discuss ways by which we might conduct a competition to choose a new national flag. Keating added the republic as if he were asking for another cup of tea. He was light-hearted. He told stories about conversations with Her Majesty which he thought revealed how essentially uninterested in Australian affairs she was. Sandy Hollway said he converted to a republic's cause during his time in Hawke's office, when a letter arrived from the palace referring to Australia as one of Her Majesty's realms. The feeble reception she received on her February visit was noted. Keating said if he had to take it to cabinet, cabinet would leak. It was decided that a green paper would be produced. The trick would be to proceed gracefully and subtly and not resemble, at one extreme, a runaway train, or at the other a government looking for a place to hide from its own invention. The Prime Minister for one was quite unaffected by the momentous decision. A couple of hours later he wandered down the corridor loudly complaining that he never got to see the news.

Fightback was beginning to crack and at times Hewson looked like he might too. Bob Hogg and Rod Cameron thought the Coalition might drop both Hewson and the GST before the election. All the more reason for the Prime Minister to wish he could go early. But the economic figures were not good, and once again the government was slipping in the polls. When Keating told his staff that only the bad economic figures stood between him and an early victory over Hewson his staff wondered what could be put between him and the media, because if he put this view to them nothing could be put between the Prime Minister and a severe drubbing. The remark had all the requirements of a fatal faux pas, yet there was a point to it. He had demonstrated his superiority in the parliament, even if his style was not universally popular. One Nation programs were now visible. He had opened a new debate about the nation's identity and future. He had seized the initiative on policy, including, in the first week of July, a Superannuation Guarantee Levy requiring employers to pay 3–5 per cent on top of their employees' contribution. John Bannon, the South Australian Labor Premier, said his State could not afford the impost and the Opposition insisted that it would cost jobs. Keating and Dawkins said it was rich for parliamentarians on extremely generous super packages to begrudge modest benefits to workers. Besides, it was integral to wages policy and maintaining low inflation and the only means of affording a reasonable standard of living as the aged population doubled over the next twenty years.

I thought he had his lines wrong. He insisted on referring to 'dead-end jobs', meaning jobs with no future or a limited one, as opposed to jobs typical of the emerging new economy, requiring skills and training of the kind the government had set itself to provide. The policy point was undeniable, but with such high unemployment, who could be fussy? It verged on insulting those who were in the jobs, those who provided them and those who sought them. The Prime Minister was also prone to make more of the rise in school retention rates than people were inclined to give him credit for. This too was a better policy point than a political one. School retention rates had indeed more than doubled since 1983, but one never escaped the impression that the public suspected keeping kids at school was a means of keeping the unemployment rate down. Another section of the public, who were regularly represented among the talk-show calls and newspaper letter writers, believed their diligent, deserving children were suffering because children who were only *fit* for 'dead-end jobs' now remained at school to disrupt classes and drag down standards. It was not Keating's nature to deal in shades of grey. Moreover, it was not his political philosophy. He spoke in black or white and then held out against contrary evidence or sentiments for as long as reason allowed—sometimes longer. The approach pushed policy to the forefront of politics. It eliminated much of the nicety of debate which is popularly taken to be a hallmark of democratic civilisation. Being more tribal, Keating preferred to play politics on a battlefield which, among other advantages, meant that the people were never in much doubt about where he stood. However, it also meant that more often than perhaps was necessary they reckoned he stood against them, and that he cared little about their lives.

For much of June and July he was like a man with a tin leg. The thought arose that he would lose the election not because the people could not forgive him for the recession, but because he could not admit to them the fact of it. He had a Horatius complex; he was forever defending bridges which ought to have had no need of it. In this constant state of war, when his heart was in the battle, his advisers could not resist the temptation to acquiesce in the folly. We might have been galloping gaily hither and thither; instead we fought valiantly with our backs to an imaginary wall, all the while beseeching the Gods to send us reinforcements in the shape of some decent figures. That would bring us victory *and* prove the rightness of our cause. It was hubris. It was Churchill's axiom perfectly demonstrated: 'However beautiful the strategy one should occasionally look at the results.'

Without the heat of battle, Keating's pulse slowed. Years of death-defying struggle had given him the metabolism of a cornered rat—he could not get excited until the stakes were very high, preferably a matter of life and death. Only when he felt his skin creeping and his hair standing on the back of his neck did it seem worthwhile. At other times he found it hard to even sound interested. When the tide ebbed in Keating everyone felt an absence. Even when he was overseas, at the South Pacific Forum in the Solomon Islands, for instance, one could sense his spiritless, contrary mood. It was debilitating. After a while you would swear from the polls and the radio that the people sensed it as well, as if they knew his moods and when he didn't care.

What was more dispiriting, John Hewson proved himself more beatable with each day that passed. He had, moreover, a party and policies which guaranteed his weaknesses would show. In the first week of July the Liberals held their national convention. It opened with US-style razzamatazz replete with a 107-voice choir, school band and massed displays by young people with flags. The press described them as dancing girls. Dr Hewson said they were no such thing. He said they were kids with flags. He said they had made one of the most moving sights he had seen for a long time. John Hewson had turned very dark on the media and on business which he said had been intimidated by the government and the unions and wouldn't support him when he 'called it the way it is'. He was churlish and preppy. Referring to Labor Senator Chris Schacht, he said he didn't know whether to pronounce his name 'shat' or 'shot', 'but I'll say shot because shat isn't very nice'. Hewson seemed to be at the mercy of some hormonal excess: with circumstances entirely in his favour he decided to open entirely unnecessary battlefronts. Having fired at the Reserve Bank board, the environmental movement, business and journalists, soon he would set his sights on less robust targets. He seemed to think that his qualifications for the prime ministership were self-evident, as if he believed that a Johns Hopkins degree actually counted for something in politics. 'He despises anyone who doesn't have an MBA,' Keating said. And it was true enough—any public doubting of his wisdom galled him terribly.

In the course of their convention the Liberals released their policy on youth. If this was a strategy to counter the government's forthcoming youth summit, it was a dismal failure. The Liberals' youth policy was a cameo of free-market ideology. It did Labor the kind of service it could never have done itself, mainly because it made Labor's biggest problem the Coalition's too. More gratifying still, it was based almost entirely on the premise that unemployment was the product of high wages. This gave Labor undreamed-of room to move. The Coalition proposed a $3.00 per hour wage for fifteen-to-eighteen-year-olds and a weekly rate for workers which was only $8.10 more than the dole. By failing to address the possibility that youth unemployment might be less the consequence of wage rates than weak demand, technological change and productivity improvements or efficiencies, the Liberal policy left the way clear for Labor to come up with policies which were not only more compassionate, but more credible and sophisticated. The Catholic Social Welfare Commission was among the first to object. One journalist, Geoffrey Barker, said the Liberal policy reflected 'a shrivelled concept of justice and dignity'. The new Liberal Premier of New South Wales, John Fahey, thought so little of his party's policy he refused to endorse it because it had no training component. The churches and the welfare organisations denounced it, and then calculations were made to show that many young workers would have their wages substantially reduced; and all this drew attention to the intention declared in Fightback to cut a billion dollars from welfare and labour market programs.

The Coalition policy made training a Labor strength, and by doing it so early handed over other advantages; a mission in life was not the least of them, and one consistent with the decade-long program of economic and social transformation. In training at least Labor could be at ease with its conscience and at one with the direction of the world. And the Opposition were now easily cast as deaf to reason and compassion—the more so because their policies followed in the wake of their own highly publicised public forum on jobs. It created the perfect environment for the government's own youth employment summit.

The Prime Minister turned up late on the opening morning of the South Pacific Forum and thus managed to conjure bad news from what was essentially a political free kick. The press said it was an insult to the smaller nations, inept and bullying. Then came the really bad news. In the middle of writing that speech for the Australian Writers' Guild Awards—the speech he had never wanted to give—loud groaning came from the office corridor. Everyone knew what it was—unemployment had gone through 11 per cent. It was 11.1 per cent to be precise, a rise of 0.6 per cent to a postwar record. This would be the backdrop for the Prime Minister's speech about his ambitions for Australian arts and culture, on the night of his return from the Solomon Islands.

It said much for the times we lived in that the first thought was to drop the ballooning budget deficit on top of the unemployment figure and get it all over at once. This done, the second thought was to put our backs to the wall and sound such loud and general alarm that people would become confused and join us—those whom they wished to annihilate—in defence of all they held dear. It was an unlikely strategy, but history teaches us that stranger things have happened.

If the point was to radically change the people's perception, an 'arts' speech was not, on the face of it, the ideal vehicle. It did seem to be a very bad time for an 'arts' speech, after that groaning; and a very bad time to be the bleeding heart who had insisted that the speech be made. Cancelling, however, was obviously not an option: so, knowing that the PM was about to be held responsible for a national crisis, before he and his principal adviser reached Canberra I wrote a new opening paragraph which directly confronted it.

As expected, upon his arrival in Canberra the Prime Minister was assailed by a media pack for whom a 0.6 per cent increase in unemployment meant a 100 per cent decline in the Prime Minister's credibility and moral character. Some called out, 'Will you apologise? Will you apologise to the Australian people?' The Prime Minister sagely chose not to reply. He said the solution was economic growth. Later, at a press conference he acknowledged the human cost but drew the line at 'an act of contrition', as suggested by one journalist. 'What have you got in mind?' he asked. Should he be contrite about the One Nation spending which was plainly the right policy, though the press and his opponents said he had abandoned fiscal discipline? The journalists asked, hadn't the union leaders, John Halfpenny and George Campbell, urged them to drop the One Nation tax cuts? Keating said yes, but the tax cuts were not for 1992. He promised an employment budget, including direct spending on unemployment through labour market programs. Much of the unemployment was cyclical rather than structural; it was not, principally, a product of policy—whatever the press or the Opposition said. And whatever they said, the one thing he would not be doing was panicking.

But panic had already been decided upon. With 963,500 people unemployed and a budget deficit of $12.3 billion, why not? The next day the headlines would be uniformly ugly. 'Australia hits the wall!'; 'National disaster!'; 'an unprecedented unemployment tragedy and a budgetary crisis of a magnitude rarely seen since the Great Depression'; the Government was now 'clinically dead'.

On the flight from the Solomon Islands, Don Russell and the Prime Minister had reassessed the arts speech. Arriving in the office, Russell gave a new draft to his assistant Nina for typing. As Nina was also my assistant the vandalism was quickly discovered. Everything of any value or elegance had been deleted. The new paragraph acknowledging the grievous unemployment figures and calling the nation to battle was also scrapped. It was 'too defensive', Donald said. Too defensive to acknowledge 'the economic setbacks of the last couple of days and the human cost which those unemployment figures spell'?, I asked. The paragraph said that 'for as long as it takes every government effort will be directed at turning the tide'? Insofar as this meant fundamentally turning the tide of the economy and getting investment and growth back it was hard to see what was defensive about it, or ideologically unsound for that matter. The paragraph also said that we intended where it was sensible to create new jobs and to make the best possible provision for those without them. This was no more than a statement of existing policy. Unthinkable as it seemed, something in Donald's reaction suggested panic.

Gone also from his new draft were the words to appease Paul Hogan. Hogan, we had been recently advised, was about to tip a very large bucket on the Prime Minister for his remarks about yobbos and shrimps. The national museum was also gone, but that was expected. What was unexpected was Don Russell's aggression. The hour before the Prime Minister left to give the speech in Melbourne was intensely rancorous. Donald had overstepped and got it wrong, I said. It was a grave day, the Prime Minister said, meaning that the tone of the speech should be grave. The speech acknowledged that the day was grave, I said: that was why it referred to the human consequences. It was also why we were having a national meeting on the consequences—a meeting that he and Russell had opposed—because the days were grave. Russell had produced a non-speech, not a grave one, I said. Mark Ryan supported this interpretation. The Prime Minister said it wasn't as if I hadn't usually got my way: I had 'a high strike rate', he said. Donald said he knew what the punters expected. We might have said, if ever you met a punter who knew your story it might very well be the last punter you ever saw. But tact is needed to conquer a salon. This was the old treasurer's office in half-conscious shape reasserting itself. It was better to simply snort. Over the next half hour the two speeches were merged—the Hogan material went back, and the opening paragraph about unemployment.

In all the mayhem the Prime Minister told me privately what works he had done for our friends in the Pacific. And now this! He was stuffed and he wobbled his knees with a grin to illustrate the point. But, while a good deal of what Russell had removed was reinstated in the speech, it was now a dull and ugly compromise. I asked Donald if this was to be the new practice, that he would rewrite speeches as he saw fit? What examples did he have of speeches or press releases or notes for parliament or press conferences prepared in the usual way by me and checked by others which had done us damage? 'Yobbos' had done terrible damage, he said. But 'yobbos' did not come from me, I said. 'Yobbos' occurred in an interview when the Prime Minister was travelling with Donald.

On the flight to Melbourne the Prime Minister told Mark Ryan and me that Donald had a splendid political mind. So why did the PM take so much advice from Tom Mockridge and Peter Barron? He said he didn't. He and Donald thought almost identically. But this, we said, was poor political judgment. In fact every bit of wind in the government's sails had come from non-economic areas. We poured forth our case. The Prime Minister would concede nothing. We did not expect him to.

The Prime Minister's tiredness was visible and he did not perform with much zeal. The news, however, could not have given the speech better coverage. Channel 9 led with his unemployment opening line, the other channels led with his arts initiatives, the newspapers included his reparations with Paul Hogan and all referred to the great reception he received. As he often did in such circumstances, the Prime Minister made no mention of the good press. But he did speak to Mark Ryan, and Mark passed on the message to me: Donald's authority was not to be assaulted again.

A friend from Tokyo told me that the Japanese found Australia puzzling. What we call restructuring they saw as destructuring. The deputy ambassador told him that we never had an answer to the question: but what do you intend to do? To them it seemed we had stepped out of a leaky boat into the sea, and they wondered why we had no plans to build even a raft. The Tokyo friend also said that Australian businessmen he had spoken to reckoned the Prime Minister's Office was shambolic and the advice it gave to the Prime Minister narrow and unworldly.

Criticism of the office appeared in the press. For a day or two, no-one was beyond suspicion. For a couple more days as the Canberra frosts grew thicker, as wounds were licked and grievances quietly aired, and preparations were made for the budget and that Keynesian malefaction, the youth unemployment summit, an effort was made to lay the foundations of a cultural policy for the nation. The Prime Minister foreshadowed it in the Melbourne speech, using the Paul Hogan business to lead him into it. He had been treasurer, after all, and he knew better than most what the boom in tourism had done for Australia, and he knew how much the country owed its 1980s icon, Paul Hogan. But he wanted to broaden the canvas, which really meant nothing more than doing justice to more of the reality of contemporary Australian life. That front cover on the *Far Eastern Economic Review* had said: 'Australia—time to get serious'. That was what he wanted to do. Much that seems to 'live exclusively in the realms of politics or economics and seems to demand a purely political or economic solution', he said, 'also demands a cultural one'. To make economic, political and social progress, 'we have to make parallel cultural advance'. He thus began a theme. Cultural policy was important enough to be brought into the mainstream of policy-making. He announced the government's intention to establish an advisory panel to help the government develop a national cultural policy. Among other suggestions, he recommended that the panel address itself to private funding for the arts; the best ways to take the nation's arts and heritage to the provinces; and, in the interests of enlivening the marketplace of ideas, an endowment for the humanities. He said cultural policy should be part of the vision laid out in One Nation and the general effort to call on all our national resources and all our people. The arts policy was a political policy, an economic policy and a republican policy. It was also an industry policy. It was one answer at least to the Japanese question: but what do you intend to do?

Dr Russell said an early election was not out of the question. The economy was sinking towards the bottom and there was nothing we could do to stop it. If this, his 'pessimistic scenario', came to pass, in a couple of months all our cards would have been played and the government would be left with nothing but a slow drift to oblivion. It was a reasonable argument, but then so was Mark Ryan's question: 'If you were wrong when you said the figures would be good, why should we believe you when you say they'll be bad?' Most conversations with Donald were good-humoured. He was a truly happy man. His ego appeared to be unassailable. For these reasons he recovered from the most bitter encounters with no apparent wounds or ill-feeling. For all the arguments, neither Ryan nor I wanted to undermine him, or the relationship he had with the Prime Minister. We took the view that if Keating needed Russell, which he did, we needed Russell too. The most bitter attacks were never more than acts of persuasion. But this time Donald flew the flag. Every birthday was celebrated in the office. We would gather among the computers and telephones while Guy Nelligan, in plastic gloves, expertly carved up a cake and poured sparkling wine and a speech or two was made and Happy Birthday sung. Donald made John Edwards' birthday the occasion of a short speech which firmly put his view that the Prime Minister's Office was a continuation of the former treasurer's office and disputatious new members of the outfit ought to know their places, and be grateful for having places at all.

Like many other human activities, politics is frequently compared with sex. Politics has some of the same frenetic, visceral characteristics. It mixes love, loathing and treachery, triumph and tristesse in similar proportions. It is not uncommon to deal with one's colleagues in politics as Harry Angstrom sometimes contemplated making love to his wife in John Updike's 'Rabbit' novels—that is, while also contemplating braining her with an ornament on the mantelpiece. But of course with sex it is not possible to lose your virginity more than once. That is what took so long to understand about the office economists. They had lost it repeatedly over the years, yet at every new step they dug their heels in as if protecting their honour. They would number among the examples of a transformed economy Kodak's exports of film to Asia, yet you would hear them lament the Hawke Government's decision to spend $60 million to keep Kodak in Melbourne. They said it was bad policy, and insisted that private capital would have filled the void if the company had decamped. The road of the Labor Government was pocked with impurities like this—a bit of industry policy here, a bit of something very like it there. And then there was One Nation. Keating had been willing to say: 'Call it Keynesianism if you like, it's just commonsense.' Whatever else they called it, it was not supply-side. We had quite a few industry policies, but we didn't like to say so and we tried to call them by other names: except the cultural policy, which we preferred to call industry policy so people didn't get the idea it was a hand-out to the arts. Nevertheless, each time a need arose—political, economic, social or commonsensical—the argument had to be had again. In fact it was not so much an argument as a Punch and Judy show. We were not demanding that they give up their virtue or disown their admirable discipline, but it was part of the drama for them to act as if we were.

One might put an argument of this kind: in our next big speech let us try to give the people grounds for hope in the future of the Australian economy, particularly as unemployment is, as you say, sure to grow, and the public are becoming aware that the increased competitiveness we offer them as encouragement comes with the near certainty of ever more unemployment and less job security. At this point they might nod their heads and say: yes, let's us get on to the front foot; in fact, the front foot is justified by last week's forecast. Encouraged, we would say: let us therefore vigorously and visibly clear the impediments to new industries, identify areas of the economy which can grow, and if we cannot actually make them grow, let's make it clear that we are trying. Let's biff the banks for their oppressive borrowing requirements, for instance; or look again at ways to get super funds invested in regional infrastructure. We know it won't at once resolve the problem. It might not resolve it in a thousand years. But let's at least *appear* to be on the case—so that we have some counter to the incessant drone every hour of every day on radio and television about dumped cheap imports, foreign ownership and foreign debt. Because all the evidence suggests that the people are depressed about Australia's future, and even if they are wrong, these things deepen their depression. This is a political office, we would say. We must think politically. We are not asking you to be wanton, but merely to help us address the public mood. And the office economists would smile their economists' little smiles as if to say: you poor benighted bleeding hearts, don't you know where it will lead? To a new tariff wall. Or more industry policy.

Or buying back the farm. Closing off foreign investment. To Whitlam-like chaos and defeat. We only wanted to bring economic and political realities into alignment. But they would smile and say: Ha! That's where it always starts!

It took eight months to erect the first unmistakable sign that the government was concerned about the consequences of unemployment and not just the fact of it. The youth summit signalled something else just as important. Being a national summit it said that unemployment was everyone's problem, not just the Commonwealth Government's. Somewhere hidden in the symbolism was also a sign that not all the blame for unemployment could be laid at Paul Keating's feet. The summit opened the door a little on the reasons. It took the politics out of unemployment for a moment and made it a social issue, an intellectual issue. It did not ask who is to blame, but what is to be done?

Two young people spoke before the Prime Minister. One said that there was 'a staggering feeling of worthlessness out there, and if these powerful people can't find solutions then they will think they might as well give up'. The other was Aboriginal: she said Australian society should be built on the Aboriginal principle of sharing.

The Prime Minister said unemployment was not the 'shock absorber', 'the buffer at the end of the station'; he said no group should have to carry the 'adjustment burden of an economy in transition'. The first necessity was economic growth. There was no future for employment unless Australia continued to develop a modern economy integrated with the world economy. The micro-economic reform program had to continue. The second necessity was training. Youth unemployment rates, long-term employment prospects and remuneration all correlate directly with training levels. Training was everything for young people, and for a competitive economy. The day before the summit the government had announced that it had established the Australian National Training Authority (ANTA). In One Nation, Keating had called vocational education and training 'the weak reed' in Australia's education system. Now, after months of arguing with the States, it would become, as he had promised, 'a strand of equal strength'. Training was the pathway to secure employment. The third necessity was material assistance for the unemployed and five days after the summit, Keating and the minister, Kim Beazley, announced a youth training and employment plan, and Landcare and environment programs (the well-named LEAP schemes) which would create 96,000 training and employment opportunities for people aged 15–19. Together with the 75,000 existing labour marketplaces, no-one among the 120,000 unemployed young people in the country was denied an opportunity for employment, training or both.

The summit was not the answer and no-one thought it would be. Its virtue lay principally in the way it posed the questions, and the opportunity it gave the government to demonstrate good faith with the community. By doing that it sharpened other debates and it is worth recording that, long after the press and public had forgotten it or even dismissed its worth, programs which had been devised at the conference were assisting thousands of unemployed young people. Not that the Prime Minister was ever going to be entirely convinced. After everyone had gone away a little more confident that with cooperation, goodwill and hard work the problem could be overcome the Prime Minister appeared on Derryn Hinch's television program. Hinch asked him what advice he would give his teenage son if he were facing unemployment. The Prime Minister paused for a second or two and then said that we needed economic growth and he proceeded to explain why. He would not give it up, not to anyone.

We never knew if we were just behind the break and waiting for a wave or slowly drowning. At 3.00 a.m. with the frost lying all around, the Parliament House boiler blowing steam and an enormous silence under the stars, it did sometimes seem possible that we were dead and didn't know it. The Olympic Games were on in Barcelona and Mrs Keating was there to watch them. Her husband had gone to north Queensland where there were seats that needed winning. He had gone telling Ashton Calvert that he wouldn't go to Cambodia. Ashton was ropable, but no-one much doubted that a little time and patience would see the Prime Minister relent. It was encouraging in a way because often this sort of thing preceded a big performance. He was curiously predictable. Perhaps it was the prima donna syndrome: because a big performance demands a radical personal transformation it is a necessary part of the mental preparation to seem entirely incapable of carrying it off. Perhaps he was rebelling against control, stifling control, like mother love. If he was going to do what *we* wanted, did he feel he must before or after make a show of doing what *he* wanted. It was no disorder, but a natural reaction to the unnatural business of political performance. Would that we could always keep it in our minds for comfort.

In Townsville he spoke from notes for fifty minutes and received a standing ovation from the Labor Party audience. Earlier in the day at a government-funded port development he did forceful and eloquent press conferences. And at Innisfail in the dark warm fog among the cane fields he visited a school, a Skill-share centre, a foundry, a sugar mill and he spoke to a full town hall over lunch. Afterwards he went into a pub run by two marvellous women who charged $3 for a counter lunch. There were two or three men in the bar, and one of them fell off his stool when he saw the man in the Zegna suit beside him. The man in the Zegna suit crossed the road and entered a bus full of tourists and shook their hands. As he left the town a woman with a stud in her nose and a three-year-old child told us to tell the Prime Minister to round up all the whingers and put them in the army.

The Prime Minister suspected that we might congratulate him on his brilliant exhibition and ask him to make a habit of it, or take advantage of the good mood he had displayed on the road, and set about thwarting our ambitions. As we took off he regaled us with a stream of consciousness about aeronautics. Once airborne he quickly followed with a description of the cold virus that was at that very moment invading his chest. When there was nothing more to say on this subject he pointed out Great Keppel Island. They had built houses on sand down there apparently, and they all slipped down the hill. Then it was Stephen Smith who had been giving him too much to do. Then he spoke fiercely against the banks. And just when he'd run out of tricks and we were about to ask him what he was going to say in Brisbane, he told the pilot to fly over Shoalwater Bay. He pointed down to it. There! See the big wound in it. That's from sand mining. That's what Garrett wants us to save. Churlishly I cursed the Greens and said they wouldn't have let Innisfail be built if they had been around at the time. 'That's right,' he said. 'They wouldn't have let it be built.' It was clear that he had decided to save Shoalwater Bay. Two nights later in Brisbane, he gave, if not the best speech of his first year, the most important.

In the Brisbane hotel room before the speech, Ryan and I told him that the hall would be packed with party faithful. They want to see a leader, we said, the whole country does. That's what the speech should be about. Gloomily, he said he didn't think so. Leadership is largely bullshit, he told us: as he had fifteen years earlier, when people were calling him a populist, and he told the journalist Craig McGregor, 'You have to be with the consensus, not ahead of it'. 'I don't believe there should be heroes running the government', he told him. In the hall in 1992, however, Premier Wayne Goss introduced a leader. He called him 'a fiercely proud Australian and a man of vision'. And, almost despite himself, it seemed as he spoke that the Prime Minister rose to a leader-like plane. Of course in the same interview with McGregor he *had* made claims about getting the Labor Party off the hook, and his demeanour *had* put Bob Carr in mind of the young Churchill and persuaded a lot of people that he was bound to be prime minister one day. There had always been a lot of hero about him, deny it as he may.

Referring only occasionally to a few notes, he spoke about the difference between a Keating Government and a Coalition Government. A Keating Government believed in a free-market economy open to the world as the best way to create jobs and opportunity for all. But a Keating Government also believed in a social safety net. Hewson's Australia would be a hard, dog-eat-dog place where the strong prospered and the weak had to fend for themselves. Heaven help anyone who fell off the back of a truck in Hewson's Australia. But Labor saw things differently, he said. Labor believed that if you fell down, the government should reach out for you. Labor would reach out 'a caring arm' and lift you up. And the Prime Minister actually acted out his words. He reached out a caring arm. Silence reigned for several moments and then the hall erupted in applause for a prime minister who had thrown away reserve. It was a big gesture, and the meaning of it grew wings and echoed all the way to the election. Reasserting Labor's belief in the social safety net was not the same as changing tack on economic policy, but that one unrehearsed phrase changed things fundamentally. From then on everything the government said or did could be judged against it, including economic policy. It was an official sanction of the new rhetoric and it was amazing how much clearer everything seemed afterwards.

Keating began a speech to the Committee for the Economic Development of Australia (CEDA) by denying the rumour 'that the government is run by fanatics, pointy heads and zealots. These people do exist but they are not our people.' The 'caring arm' speech in Brisbane, the youth summit and the CEDA speech marked a turning point. The last of them did not happen without a fight, but this time Don Russell and the Prime Minister were on opposing sides. No doubt political necessity more than reason forced the issue, but it was decided that the story of the CEDA speech would be that our story was one of sensible creative reform. Labor had never sacrificed people to ideological purity and Labor never would. Rather, Labor darted in and out of the economy, reaching out a helping hand and offering good ideas as industry needed them. Ideological purity belonged to the other side of politics. Or so the story was to go. John Edwards was the first to object but he soon gave up. Then, an hour before he was to catch the plane to Melbourne and give the speech, we found the Prime Minister at his desk with his big black Mont Blanc carving through the paragraphs. With the plane due to leave Fairbairn at 5.45, at 5.30 the Prime Minister was up to page three.

The travelling party put down their bags and took off their coats. The sticking point was a paragraph which said that Australia's economic growth was coming 'sizeably' from 'planned' sectors of the economy. 'Planned' was never going to survive, but the PM's pen had run through the whole paragraph, several times. He called in Dr Russell to behold the sacrilege he had just excised. To the Prime Minister's astonishment Donald declared that paragraph should stay. It was true, he said. It was bullshit, the Prime Minister said: growth would come in the deregulated sector, he said. Yes, said Donald, but a lot of the growth we boasted about was coming in elaborately transformed manufactures, and a lot of them were growing under government industry plans. Dr Russell stood firm and, shrewdly, he stood behind the PM's shoulder. The Prime Minister stared in disbelief. Mark Ryan's face had a huge grin on it; so did Russell's. It was very hard not to giggle. The PM looked around, he looked at the page, he looked around again. He was being verballed. It was like the invasion of the body snatchers, except they weren't Martians in those suits, they were Creanites! Industry policy types.

Outnumbered, he decided to wear it, but he would not suffer the word 'planned'. 'Planned' became 'areas the government has shown an interest in'. The plane left an hour late. As we flew down to Melbourne, the PM offered the opinion that it was not a bad speech. The economists and businessmen in the audience were told that now and always Labor believed there was a role for government in the new deregulated economy. 'Where we have thought it sensible to intervene, we have intervened. Where we think our responsibility stops, we will stop there,' the Prime Minister said. 'We have an eclectic view,' he said, 'not an ideological one.' He went further and into territory where, as a rule over the past decade, Labor only went during election launches and speeches to the party or the unions. Labor's mission was to establish a healthy social democracy. That was the end, and economic reform was simply the means to it. He told them that right from the start Labor's pursuit of a competitive Australian economy had been inspired by the knowledge that this was the precondition of a good society. He was not rewriting the story but he was changing the emphases, bleeding the eighties into the nineties, the economic into the political. An economy did not exist in the abstract. Economic reforms were the result of human agencies and they had human consequences for good or ill. 'There are costs for people in the process, social and psychological, and they can never be left out of the economic equation.' It was Labor's passion for a viable expanded social democracy which had produced these great reforms: 'nothing we wanted to do could be done without it'. It was where the will had come from. It was true—it was how Hawke, Keating and Kelty had persuaded their constituencies.

Despite the patchy growth and the still rising unemployment, the twin deficits and the general gloom, it was not difficult to produce evidence that the 'eclectic' approach had worked. Keating could continue to preach the notion that Australia was now on the path of a 'sustained low inflation recovery'. He could draw the lines connecting the social safety net to wage restraint to the higher profit share and the lowest level of strikes in thirty years. It was not hard to make a persuasive case for the claim that the economy was heading in the right direction.

It was by no means certain, however, that any of this answered the questions on the public mind. Industrial relations reform might well have been the most constructive step the country had taken since the war, but memories of strike-torn Australia were fading, the Accord was taken for granted, and the wharves remained a notorious obstacle to progress. The same could be said about his other stories: floating the dollar had given exporting a chance, lowering tariffs had given manufacturing a chance. If all these reforms had given the country a chance, as he claimed, how come all people saw was opportunity narrowing? They saw it wrong; there were no 'ifs' about it; we've given the country the best chance it ever had. And—he would say—we're coming out of this recession with one of the lowest inflation rates in the world. We came out of the last one with the rate above

10 per cent. This also gave the country a chance—even if the bastards weren't celebrating.

In the CEDA speech Paul Keating began to provide new evidence that there were grounds for hope. It was not yet cause for general satisfaction, but in the past decade both service and manufactured exports had tripled. In 1991, for the first time in the country's history, the value of exported manufactures exceeded that of rural products. Then there were those ETMs— those motor vehicles and vehicle parts, computers, scientific equipment, pharmaceuticals, telecommunications equipment, machinery. Of all the export categories, ETMs were growing fastest and something like half of this growth came from industries 'where the government had shown an interest'. And where were they going? To East Asia, where the government had also shown an interest.

The political winter of 1992 might have been as bad as any government had experienced since World War II. Keating was pronounced dead a dozen times and just as often began to breathe again. He would go to battle against the Trojans again, and again retire exhausted. The gods would not smile on him. The economy would not revive. Even after a year of growth, all the indicators that mattered, which means all those that measured the human dimension or that humans understood, continued to point in the wrong directions. Politics was rabid and spiteful. Only Hewson's obsessions and loathing of all who could not see that he was right and Keating manifestly inferior, wicked and wrong gave Labor a chance. It was reminiscent of Muhammad Ali and George Foreman. Hewson's work rate was ten times Keating's, but Keating just kept ducking the head shots and absorbing the body blows and, as with Ali—Keating's great hero—every now and again he would land a blow solid enough to give us hope that we still had a chance, that he had not given up, that he knew what he was doing.

Now, just a few days before the budget he had begun to pull his story together; at last it had a political dimension to it, it had begun to address the contemporary reality, and it was even possible that some social good might flow from it. As the budget approached and the arts lobby rang regularly to complain about rumoured cuts to their funds, the Prime Minister said he wanted to take the Brisbane speech and the CEDA speech everywhere he went.

Anne Summers reported that her focus groups of women found the Prime Minister 'cold, aloof and even repellent and they hated his suits'. The government climbed a fraction in the polls. In fact the PM seemed to have found his range a little better and he began advocating optimism—or was he just simply projecting the state of his own emotions when he told an ALP gathering in South Australia not to get 'maudlin'? There were promising signs, but they never seemed to last.

It was agreed that the issue of the flag should be laid to rest for the time being. The dry section of the office—Edwards and Simes, and Russell on every other day—believed the same should be done with the republic. The influence had waned dry. John Edwards complained to Keating that he could not get a hearing with him. It was obvious and the polling confirmed it: Keating had not established his credentials as a leader. When we talked about attempting to project his human dimension, the pointy heads protested, as if making him appear human would make him appear to be what he was not. There were two difficulties with this view. First, the Prime Minister could not win when he was so disliked; second, the PM was in fact quite noticeably human. The trick was to broaden him into what he was. If that meant making him an enigma or even a contradiction, it was better to have the electorate curious than full of loathing. It also meant pulling focus to those qualities which the public had only glimpsed—his devotion to the family, his feelings for his wife and children, his genuine if old-fashioned concerns for the problems faced by women, his love of the arts. It mattered less that not everybody liked the things he liked than that the people knew he cared about *something*.

At the same time it was necessary to magnify the perception of his strength. The research always showed that people believed

Keating was strong and that he would usually achieve what he set out to achieve. The story of his prime ministership was in part about persuading the people that he used this strength in their interests. Keating was never more than a couple of breaths away from earning the country's respect: a word, a gesture, a gummy smile away from overcoming their distaste. But it may as well have been a hundred miles dividing them so long as they thought what he did was for his satisfaction rather than theirs. Perhaps it was something more subtle and more elusive. If it was respect they ultimately craved, all too frequently in Keating's language and persona there were signs that he respected the abstracted beauty of an idea, or a building, or a suit, or power itself more than the reality of ordinary lives. Why else did the media think it worth tracking him through the streets of Paris or Berlin when, if he had an hour off, he went looking in antique shops or admiring old buildings—'corkers' as he called them? Where should he have gone? To a fish market? To a factory? For a power walk?

So often it seemed to require such painless concessions. Anne Summers' focus groups of women expressed the same outrage at his foreign suits as the press expressed when he brought to the Lodge a table made of Thai teak. Why should they be urged to buy Australian-made products if the country's leader thinks they are not good enough for him? Keating's answer was that he had never willingly urged anyone to buy Australian products if the overseas brands were better. That was the whole point of free trade and the deregulated economy: Australian manufacturing standards would improve and Australians would be able to buy the best wherever it is made. Insisting that Paul Keating buy Australian made no more sense than telling Bob Menzies to drive a Holden or smoke Australian cigars. Even so, life would have been a great deal easier had our prime minister bought a table of Tasmanian blue gum and a Fletcher Jones single-breasted suit.

The Prime Minister prepared for Question Time at his desk which was in places half a metre deep in unsorted files. As advisers

Matt and Paul.
Courtesy of Paul Keating

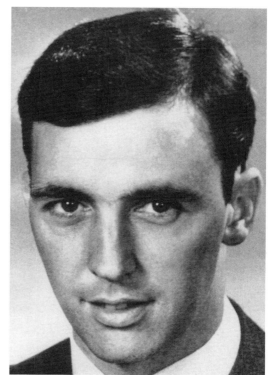

Minister for Mining and
Energy, 1975.
Courtesy of National Library of Australia

At a joint press conference with Bob Hawke, on the devaluation of the Australian dollar, 1983. *Courtesy of Brett Thomson, News Limited*

The great economic reformers: Paul Keating with (left) Bob Johnston, Governor of the RBA and (right) Bernie Fraser, Secretary of the Treasury, 1987. *Courtesy of Paul Keating*

National Press Club. *Courtesy of Andrew Chapman*

National Press Club, 1988. *Courtesy of National Library of Australia*

On Sydney radio, 1990. *Courtesy of Fairfax Photo Library*

King's Hall, Parliament House, Canberra, 1992. *Courtesy of Fairfax Photo Library*

Question Time, 1992. *Courtesy of Paul Keating*

Talking to Aaron Link at celebrations to mark the 1993 International Year of Indigenous Peoples in Redfern Park, Sydney.
Courtesy of News Limited

With Bill Clinton at the 1994 APEC meeting in Jakarta. *Courtesy of News Limited*

With Suharto in Bali, 1995. *Courtesy of Paul Keating*

Labor Party launch, Bankstown, 1993. *Courtesy of Andrew Chapman*

Acknowledging the workers on the Macquarie Tower, Sydney, on Election eve, 1993. *Courtesy of News Limited*

Don and Paul on the last day of the campaign, 1993. *Courtesy of Don Watson*

Left: The PM makes a last call, election eve, 1993.
Courtesy of Don Watson

Below: John Miner, Anne Summers, Mark Ryan, Greg Turnbull, the day after the 1993 election.
Courtesy of Don Watson

gathered before him he ate his lunch and drank the tea Guy brought to him. Guy's moods were difficult to read. One day he served the Prime Minister two small birds. 'What are they?' the Prime Minister, a napkin under his chin, asked Guy. 'Poor little quail,' I said. 'They are spatchcocks,' said Guy, and abruptly marched out. Guy was a stickler for form. He served everyone according to rank, even when the rankings were unknown to those being served. A few days before the 1992 Budget he told the Prime Minister that he had devised a better backdrop for the traditional cabinet photograph. 'Have you, mate?' said the Prime Minister. 'I think one can have a more natural setting without exposing oneself to every passing lout in a motor car or truck, sir,' said Guy. The Prime Minister occasionally wondered if Guy was the best man for the job. But of course he was. His high tone act was a perfect parody of Keating's own aestheticism. To remember the Prime Minister is to remember Guy.

Ross Gittins described it as the gloomiest pre-election budget in living memory. The cartoonist Bruce Petty portrayed it as the last shot in the locker. Bernie Fraser of the Reserve Bank supported the fiscal stimulus it contained and even conceded that, with hindsight, it might have been used earlier and more vigorously. The Prime Minister said it was a 'real Labor budget'. John Dawkins' first budget drove the bumpy middle road and survived the rocks thrown from either side. Nothing in it was so predictable as Max Walsh, who said it was almost criminally expansionary, and Ken Davidson, who said it was almost criminally mean. The more telling criticism concerned the growth forecasts which for weeks everyone knew would have to be revised downwards, as it turned out from 4 per cent to 3 per cent. The Prime Minister's heroic March remark—'If we can't run the place at 4 per cent we should give the game away'—gave the media a rope with which to pursue Dawkins and Keating, but no-one came close to getting it round their necks.

The Prime Minister and his treasurer were helped a little by the OECD's decision to revise their forecasts down as well. Bob

Hawke came closest to unseating his old colleagues by saying with perfectly disguised venom what the Liberals had been trying to say with much passionate display, namely that the figures did not add up. If the government was to pay the 'unwise promised tax cuts' in One Nation, and return the budget to surplus in 1995–96, it now had over its head the threat of further business taxes, Hawke said; and indeed the budget statement foreshadowed 'a domestic interest withholding tax'. This became the 'secret tax'. John Dawkins could valiantly say that these new taxes were little more than remote possibilities, but it did seem for a while that Hawke was right and the government had squandered its advantage over the Opposition on the tax issue. Hereafter, John Hewson would be able to say that Labor had a secret tax agenda— a GST in the bottom drawer; that the personal tax cuts Keating claimed he could pay without a GST would be paid for either with one, or with something like it.

John Dawkins' budget lost a wing with the 'secret tax' but it was still able to fly a bit. Although the deficit came in at $13.4 billion, $14 billion or more had been predicted. Ten per cent unemployment was forecast for twelve months' time, but anything lower would have defied belief. The Opposition said the $1.2 billion allocated to employment and training, much of it through local government, would create queues of better educated unemployed. It was throwing money at the problem and it would fail, they said. But it is possible that in the electorate not throwing money at the problem did not recommend itself as a solution either.

One of the reasons a week is such a long time in politics is that so much of it is predictable. For the Greens, the welfare lobby and the Democrats it is always heartless and lacking vision. For the Opposition it is beyond redemption, a vote-catching exercise, a cynical ploy, a dud. For Tim Fischer it was always another occasion for mixing metaphors with whatever came into his head: 'it's really absolutely tinkering on the *Titanic*, we're heading towards the icebergs and there's not much hope for getting the economy into substantial recovery mode', the Deputy Leader of the Opposition said. It did nothing for ordinary taxpayers, the Taxpayers' Association said. It did nothing for small business, the Small Business Association said. Why should the people believe you? the media said. Because under the Liberals, tax was optional for the rich and it's not any more, the Prime Minister said. Because business has low inflation, low interest rates, a competitive exchange rate, a high profit share and wage arrangements which will keep inflation below the rate of Australia's trading partners. Because the work-force is 25 per cent bigger than it was in 1983, whereas in New Zealand, which Dr Hewson admires, it is actually smaller. Labor has Australia growing, whereas the UK, which Dr Hewson admires, is back into recession. Labor has maintained reasonable wages and developed high quality health and other security benefits whereas the US, which Dr Hewson admires, pays workers $3 an hour and has no safety net. The Opposition failed to sink the 1992 Budget because the government had at last picked the public mood: taxes were not the issue, unemployment was. This much was clear from the budget decision to raise the Medicare levy. No-one complained. They seemed to think better hospitals were more important than lower taxes.

In an interview on the ABC the Prime Minister was asked, if the government could graft a massive education and training scheme onto the nation's economic goals, why could it not graft industry policy onto them? The Prime Minister answered that the government had done just that. Industry policy was there for all to see. For the first time in the country's history manufacturing had surpassed agricultural and mineral exports. There had been huge growth in services—education, health, finance and tourism. Huge growth in elaborately transformed manufactures. These were the results of the government's industry policy. In the same interview, the Prime Minister said that from now on the ideological differences between the Government and the Opposition would become more apparent. The public would see their options in sharp relief: the Gordon Gecko, 'greed is good', Thatcherite philosophy of the Coalition, on the one hand; on the other, a liberal free-market economy but one in which government strategically intervenes, sophisticated social services, a civilised industrial relations system. The lines would be very clear.

In his address in reply to the budget John Hewson came up with a powerful climax. He asked the Prime Minister to contemplate all the unemployed linked arm in arm. They would stretch, he said, from Melbourne to Newcastle. Keating and Dawkins, he said, should go along the line and 'look them in the eye'. These people, and people who had had to sell their homes, and the farmers who were paying 25 per cent interest rates had paid the price of Keating's political expedience, he said. 'The people will never forgive you,' he told the Prime Minister. And they would never forgive him for this budget which put his own job 'significantly ahead of everyone else's jobs'. Hewson was no lettuce leaf. His rhetoric often had a sting in it and usually he sounded like he meant it. Yet his desire to defeat Keating in argument was often overwhelmed by his greater desire to reduce him to dust. The loathing dissipated his power; his words fell like rain in the tropics and the effect soon evaporated. There was something American about it. The passion was symmetrical, the rhythms, like the sentiments, predictable. It might sting but it rarely pierced the skin. No-one was really listening at the end, but I heard him say it and the morning *Hansard* was confirmation of the treasure he had delivered us: 'I remember you saying not long ago that when they fall off the pace you'll reach back and pull them up,' Hewson had said. He glared fearlessly at the enemy. And then he said: 'What you mean is you'll pull everyone down to the lowest common denominator.'

Nothing Keating said in 1992 was as good as this. John Hewson had defined himself as Gordon Gecko. The Prime Minister would never quote it back in the awkward form of the original. He would say, 'John Hewson says if you reach back for them, they will drag you down.' Six months later he had developed such a way with the line you could sense a surge of shock and anger in the audience. Just as remarkably, you could sense it in yourself.

CHAPTER 9

We have got to exert ourselves a little to keep sane and call things by the names as other people call them by.

GEORGE ELIOT, MIDDLEMARCH

C ANBERRA'S ENVIRONMENT is restful, close to nature; its plain living and work ethic admirable; its basic amenities without equal in Australia. A resident of many years once told me to leave the moment I began to like living there. If you don't, she said, you'll wake up one morning and find you've spent your whole life here. It is easy to be seduced by Canberra, but just as easy to feel that some hollowness might devour you. Canberra is the abyss in thick disguise. It is affluent, informed and civilised, yet it feels a lot like a gimcrack suburb or a declining country town. Canberra is a democracy; everyone's opinion is as good as the next. Hell is to be caught in a Canberra taxi with the driver telling you the country's going to the dogs.

Canberra is like no other Australian town or city, yet no other town or city is more Australian. On the roof of Australia in Banjo Paterson's country under an enormous sky; sprawling suburbs set among the gum trees, the bush and the birds omnipresent. The light is brilliant, the air crystalline. It's only right that the people who live in Canberra should have such an inspirational setting for their labours; they are there, after all, in the interests of the peace, order, progress and good governance of the

Commonwealth. And, indeed, if one had just assisted in contriving some overdue improving policy or transforming speech, trudging to bed down Canberra nature strips while squawking cockatoos ripped flowers from the gums, one might have felt that there was unity there, a unified purpose. But one didn't.

Because it was an illusion. Go out to Yass, just forty miles away and under the same sky. There are only a couple of thousand people in Yass. The hinterland does not thrive like it used to. Salt is eating away the foundations of the buildings. The highway connecting Sydney to Melbourne no longer runs through the town; the trucks and their drivers now refuel in a giant McDonald's-dominated 'service centre' on the freeway. Yass struggles against the tide of history. But the people who live in Yass count themselves as real and typical. *They* are not the deracinated ones. *They* haven't lost touch with their roots or the truth about things. They know shit from clay. It's the people in Canberra who don't. Living in Canberra between the two great realities of the suburbs and the bush, the Australian Government is present in neither.

I would walk up the grassy hill in the morning and down at night, dodging sprinklers in the summer, in winter slipping in the frost. Over the two wide circle roads around the House to the old Presbyterian church on the corner—the only sign between Parliament and Queanbeyan that Canberra had a history before the Commonwealth Government took up residence there. It is a relic of religion (and pastoral capitalism) surrounded on all sides by godless technocracy and gimcrack. Canberra Avenue runs down from the church towards Manuka, the Paris end of Canberra with the coffee shops. The avenue passes a Jewish centre and a statue of Robbie Burns. There are also paddocks. Burns' statue can be found in all the unlikely far-flung places the Scots went in the world, but nowhere can he look lonelier than this. He's seated, thinking, staring across the paddock towards the new Department of Foreign Affairs and Trade building. It became a sad monument to exile and writer's block. A little further on there is another statue in the front yard of an unprepossessing, deeply shaded weatherboard house which serves as a meeting room for returned soldiers. As few people pass on foot, its presence is all but unknown. Yet the statue is drawn from one of the most famous of all Australian images: the photograph from World War II of a blind, wounded soldier being guided down a jungle track by a Papuan carrier, a 'fuzzy wuzzy angel'. It might be an illustration from the Gospels for children: the right arm of the blinded soldier is draped across the shoulders of the 'angel', and with his left hand he supports himself on a staff. The 'angel' has his arm around the soldier's back, bearing his weight, guiding him to salvation. It is an icon of suffering and sacrifice. It is also an emblem of the debt we owe the Papuan people for their assistance in the war. But where the first is now in the realm of the semi-sacred and teeters on the edge of bathos, the second is alive and real and therefore unresolved. The soldier died a few days after the photograph was taken. The angel was still alive when Paul Keating visited Kokoda in 1992, and with his fellow angels wondering when Australia would pay him for his services.

Those three monuments—the church, Burns and the Good Samaritan—became daily symbols of the concoctedness of Canberra, its lack of provenance; its remoteness from the smell and confusion of reality; the inadequacy of efforts to transplant a culture there or grow a fresh one. And yet they were reassuring. Irony is a primary source of reassurance in Australia.

The fuzzy wuzzy statue came to represent the challenge for a speechwriter. How to make that dead soldier step out of the stone and, as it were, speak to the living. He needed pulling back not just from empty sentiment but from meaninglessness. How many under forty, after all, know the story of the Good Samaritan? If they don't know the story of the war, what will they know of the New Testament? And if you take away the New Testament and the Old, what is there left for oratory?

And there was the other less straightforward challenge of interpreting the angel. The thing was pregnant with postcolonial possibilities, but most of them could not be uttered. How could one find room in politics to debate who or what the fuzzy wuzzy

angel meant in Australia's history? 'One of the great humanitar-
ian acts of the war' we called it in New Guinea and left any other
meaning for academic forums beyond the public view.

That statue was a daily measure of the task. How to take in
words that would move people—as sometimes they visibly did?
How to describe complex, subtle, near-invisible meanings in words
that could be understood on first hearing them? How to interpret
the country without offending other interpretations? How to
avoid cliché, pedantry, sentimentality and yet never venture too
far from the familiar? How to advance the argument, pull the
audience beyond what they knew to what they didn't know?

One would walk this way along the almost carless freeways,
crisp white grass, snow on the blue Brindabellas, imagining our
opponent already at his desk; heart, lungs and muscles all stretched
by vigorous exercise; exalting in the knowledge that Australia's
first rational man was on the cusp of seizing control; his advisers
in their places and knowing what to do; the day's press releases
already printing, lines agreed, doorstops arranged. Meanwhile,
just a mile away *our* man would just as likely be rising from his
slumber, shuffling round the house in his pyjamas, feeling the
friction in his vertebrae, thinking of the death that awaits all living
things, the possibility that there is no meaning to it all. Our bloke
will be putting on the Bruch Violin Concerto, standing in front of
the speakers, stroking his thinning hair.

He is still there two hours later, which means we have to
travel at 120 km/h to get to the War Memorial in time. It doesn't
matter, he loves speeding and so does Jimmy Warner. He smiles at
Dame Beryl Beaurepaire with the warmth he reserves for women
but is less polite to the equally deserving deputy director, Michael
McKernan. He admires the new Kittyhawk in the Pacific War
display, and talks quietly to 'Buster' Brown, the man who flew the
aircraft at the Battle of Milne Bay. He reads a speech which he
picked up for the first time only twenty minutes earlier. He says
the memorial allows us to see how those who died in war had 'a
love of country from which we can all learn; a hope for the future
that was denied to them, but which we have a duty and a reason

to maintain'. A veteran with a tattered RAAF moustache takes his glasses off and wipes away tears. Some of these people had at first refused to come, in protest at the bastard who wanted to change the flag. The Prime Minister tells Dame Beryl he will double the funding of the Pacific War gallery. It is not in the speech. The room applauds.

Back at the exhibition he has his photo taken with the veterans. The press are gathered, not to report on the event but to ask him about the falling dollar. He agrees to a doorstop and tells them the market will look after itself and they would do everyone a favour if they showed a little interest in the Battle of Milne Bay. He proceeds through schoolchildren and says to them, 'How're youse goin'?'

Later the Prime Minister invites us to lunch. He stands by the Lodge pool complaining about what Hawkey had them do to the wisteria. He goes inside, puts on Elgar's 'England' and opens the window so we can hear it while we eat al fresco by the pool. He talks about the bastardry of the Bundesbank strangling growth, the flaws in the international trading system, the perennial problem of the current account. He plays Heifetz playing Bruch, Saint-Saëns, Sibelius, and Vaughan Williams' 'Lark Ascending'. When we get back to the office the pigeonholes are full of Hewson press releases and furious denunciations.

Don Russell says the States can't agree about where the new National Training Authority should go. Does the Prime Minister care? Not so you would notice. John Dawkins is on the evening news looking battered and exhausted after a week defending his budget. Hewson, Howard, Reith and Ian McLachlan have all been after the government with fanatical vigour. But Keating, you would swear, had entered some kind of trance, mourning lost wisterias and letting the music of Saint-Saëns take him down its mysterious passages. Next morning in the *Financial Review* Geoff Kitney said the government was 'as good as dead', and in truth, the office was like a morgue.

Then the moment shattered. Don Russell walked into my office with a copy of the *Australian*. The front page of it had Ian

McLachlan telling the car industry that it must 'revamp or perish'. The Coalition, the minister said, would go all the way to zero tariffs by the year 2000. The Prime Minister wandered in complaining about something he had seen on *Four Corners*. He was shown the front page. This is the best news we've had, said Russell. The PM pondered, went to a meeting. When he came out he was handed some notes and sent off to do an interview on the ABC about Dr Hewson's narrow ideology and the fate that awaited the car industry under a Hewson government. In the interview the Prime Minister said Dr Hewson would rip the car industry to shreds. On the following day he flew to Adelaide to talk to the management of Mitsubishi and assure them that under Labor the tariff which had been massively reduced since 1983 would remain at its present level.

It took a week or two but the car tariff was another turning point. It gave concrete expression to the sentiments expressed in those two pre-budget speeches. And as usual the Opposition howled loudly about Keating's perfidious backsliding. Some of the journalists howled with them, remembering all those lectures he had given them about the necessity for low tariffs and for governments brave enough to do what was right rather than merely popular. In the *Sun-Herald* Peter Robinson said Keating was a coward. Ian McLachlan looked at Keating from the Opposition benches with outraged eyes, as if thinking that the last time he saw something like that he'd shot it. It was all to the good because the lines were becoming clear.

A week after the Prime Minister went to the War Memorial, Michael McKernan phoned to say that the visit had gone beautifully and not a few of the diggers present had undergone at least partial conversion. It was another speck of gold with which to lure Keating to the belief that hope if not salvation lay in letting the public get to know him, connecting to national sentiments and thus making himself less a hostage to the economy.

He went to the twentieth anniversary of the election of the Whitlam Government and told the gathering of veterans of that famous campaign that all the charges that his government was run by economic rationalists were false. It was not now and it never had been. Rational yes, but not like Thatcher, Reagan or the New Zealanders. He quoted the one and a half million jobs created since 1983, the massive investment in secondary education, the national health system, the family allowance supplement, the legislation for women and all the rest. And in his own brief term the nation-building reforms in rail, road, electricity supply, aviation, education and training, youth employment schemes, the budget which reflected the twin threads of government policy to seize the economic opportunities of a rapidly evolving global economy and to care for those who were hurt by the transition. To give them the wherewithal to at least catch up.

At a lecture in Bathurst to honour another legend of the party, Ben Chifley, he pursued the same theme, that his government was in the great tradition. It was a respectable argument, and in time would become a difficult one to deny. There were the emblems of old-style nation-building in the infrastructure investment. Chifley, he said, 'had served in the wartime government which through cooperation of business and the unions and through calling on the best feelings of Australians had set and achieved national goals'. One Nation he said was in that tradition, so was the Accord, so was the effort to diversify industry, raise skills and expand savings through the Superannuation Guarantee Levy. Indeed the government 'had done things in social, industrial and economic policy beyond the compass of Chifley's imagination'. He described Labor's philosophy as 'social democratic', meaning, he said 'democracy of the broadest kind, the maximisation of rights and liberties, the extension of both individual opportunity and social justice'. The history of the last half of the century, he argued, proved him right. The successful economies were free-market economies. The successful societies were those which combined these economies with sophisticated social programs and investment in their own cultural development. And he said that 'it would be derelict of such a government if we did not give the people of this post-imperial multicultural Australia the opportunity to choose those institutions and symbols which reflect their sentiments and their reality and not those of a bygone era'. He said it would 'energise the country' and 'see that faith in this Australia, this liberal democratic tolerant diverse independent Australia has a chance to grow'. He said all this without mentioning the words republic, flag, oath, Britain or Queen because that was the agreement in the office. It had said something for the government's dilemma that, even without these words, the argument fitted snugly into the picture the Prime Minister was painting. Not that it changed the general perception that week. Melbourne's *Sunday Age* reported that the message had gone out, the government now thought of the republic as something 'years off'.

Whether he mentioned it or not, whenever Keating spoke on republican themes in the broad Labor electorate he met with applause and excitement. But it was no substitute for a reason to hope that Labor might win an election. While the government could compile long lists of initiatives and achievements, of themselves none of them was worth votes. There is nothing more gratifying to a speechwriter than to fill several pages with the good things a government has done—and only a long list of promises is less persuasive. Creating one and a half million jobs in ten years might look like a heroic achievement to a political leader, to the public the figure is at best worth a nod, at worst it merely prompts the question: how come none of them went to the unemployed? In the middle lies the feeling always that this is not a triumph of government, but the fulfilment of a minimum condition which makes the claim 'a boast', a typical politician's exaggeration—and therefore quite possibly a political net negative. The family allowance supplement might be a fine thing, but it is taken for granted by those who receive it and resented by many of those who don't. Even Medicare had entered the same region of entitlement.

Every time governments crow about their achievements they imply that what their constituents hold to be a right is in fact a privilege. In one sense every such claim is heard as an abuse of power. To boast is to show a lack of respect, and not to show respect to the people inverts the popular understanding of the democratic relationship. The media, particularly the electronic

media, live off the tension surrounding these two perceptions—
the politician's and the people's. When, three years later on John
Laws's show, Paul Keating exclaimed in frustration, 'What are
people going on about?' he was surrendering to that tension. It
was the ultimate gaffe because it was the ultimate withdrawal of
respect. More and more in the course of the Keating Government
this became the nature of the political discourse. The more
Keating claimed for the government's record, the more policies he
developed, the more success he had in melding the story of his
government and Hawke's into one persuasive narrative, the more
he seemed to alienate the public. In part it was because no story
could be told which did not leave some significant part of the
public out of it, and another part feeling that their anxiety had
been represented as happiness, and another that their hardships
were not regarded as bona fide. It is an easy choice for people of
sound mind to make: either the politician is lying or they are.

Working against Keating, of course, was an economic
recovery which would not deliver its bounties in ways that the
public could measure. Their chief asset, their houses, did not rise
in value. It did not feel like a recovery. Inflationary booms might
be economically destructive, but psychologically they may represent a reward for surviving the recession that precedes them.
When Paul Keating said, as he did hundreds of times, that the
government had raised the number of young people completing
secondary education from three in ten to eight in ten (and soon
it would be nine in ten, he'd add) he believed he was describing
an unarguable good. Policy experts would agree. It fitted the
story of progress towards a modern, competitive, skilled, high-
waged economy replete with jobs that were not dead-end; but
parents and teachers thought it was a mixed blessing at best and
many in the universities said, with some justification, that the
increase had not only dramatically lowered their own academic
standards but also destroyed institutions which had been the foundation of the nation's research and knowledge, if not much of its
more civilised life. Over the four years of Keating's Government
the better the story got and the more policies that were built upon

it, the more it seemed the voters interpreted them as a sign that they had been disfranchised, or denied 'empowerment' as it had come to be called. It was as if unwittingly everything Keating did contravened the axiom: when in hole, do not dig.

John Hewson was a blessing because by promising to demolish the cornerstones of the government's record he made a case for their retention when Labor no longer could. Perhaps because he felt so certain of victory, Hewson appeared to have no tactic other than to dissociate himself from everything Labor or his own Liberal predecessors had done. All before him had been wrong. All before him had been weak. They had sown the seeds of weakness and wrongness. He could see the harvest of their misdeeds in welfare, multiculturalism, trade unions, protected industries. 'The Labor Party of Australia has only ever had two ideas,' he said. Bureaucracy was the first and tax increases was the second. Whatever gratification such lines gave Dr Hewson, they were almost certainly more useful to Labor than to him. He often seemed to be at the mercy of his personal myth. The myth was of a man who, unaided by the state, the community or anything but his own resolve dragged himself up to the commanding heights of Bellevue Hill. From this he drew the conclusion—or Keating said he did—that Australia would only be a successful country if it was made of the same stuff as he was, and the only way to make Australia of the same stuff was to reduce the people to the same social impoverishment as he saw himself as coming from. Hewson didn't know the boundaries of political debate, Keating told Paul Lyneham. There might have been some truth in this. It was just as likely true that, believing he was certain to win, Hewson was pushing the boundaries of his coming mandate as wide as possible.

The climate created by Hewson's zealotry and Keating's mood swings and cartoon humour was a constant stimulus to the imagination—not to say, in private, hysteria. Mark Ryan and I decided one evening that Keating should parody Fightback as Hewson's patent remedy for everything. We would dub it ACME Fightback, a reference to the Prime Minister's favourite cartoon, *The Road Runner Show*. Keating identified with the maverick, indestructible, counter-punching Roadrunner; he identified John Hewson with Wile E. Coyote. The word ACME was pasted on the Prime Minister's copy of Fightback and thereafter this was the copy he displayed in the House. Hewson became the Mad Doctor in his social laboratory trying to sprout little Hewsons. He was the Loaded Dog. He was the wind-up ideologue, the sado-monetarist. He was what Bob Ellis suggested—the feral abacus.

It is not likely that any of these indulgences did much to help the electoral cause of Labor, but they helped in the way it helps people working in asylums to occasionally act mad. It is probably true that substance matters more than satire, but in Question Time the lines were blurred. In the first week of September Keating dominated proceedings on trade, tariffs and other policy matters. But it was the manner of doing it which exhilarated his staff and caused journalists to say 7 September 1992 was the best day for the government in memory. Hewson and his colleagues had been driven to suggest that there was less difference between the parties on basic issues than the government was suggesting. This made life easy. The front bench seemed to rally. The Attorney-General, Michael Duffy, who had been silent all year, got to his feet and delivered a performance piece so elegant and witty he might have been Barry Humphries. Keating topped off the week by producing a poster for 'The Gordon Gecko Ball' staged by the Bond University Business School. The motto for the evening emblazoned on the poster was 'Greed Is Good'. The dean of the Business School at Bond University was Ashley Goldsworthy and Ashley Goldsworthy, the Prime Minister pointed out, was the national president of the Liberal Party.

On a roll, Keating went to the National Press Club to deliver a long speech intended to knock the stuffing out of Fightback. It had been an agonising all-night preparation as the economic advisers found words to put the government's case. The speech was not his most electrifying performance and it was made harder by a disbelieving press who, whether consciously or not, were bound to resist the notion that the Opposition might be put out of business. Keating was careful, as he had been for some time, to mock Hewson rather than savage him, and to criticise him for his values rather than his character. It had long been obvious that he lost the advantage every time he was drawn into a clinch and in recent weeks he'd resisted all temptation. He did make the point that Hewson and Fightback were inseparable. Fightback was the word of Hewson. 'I am the word and the word is Fight-back,' he said. The Liberal Party, he said, could not get rid of one without the other. But the press were not listening and he was still on the first page. He worked up the line that Hewson had uttered a year before—that nobody has really tried rational economics properly. This did seem to cast Thatcher and Roger Douglas as wimps and Hewson as the only man prepared to go to the limits with his experiment. The Commonwealth Public Service was shifting to enterprise bargains, to provide a model for private sector workplaces. The Prime Minister stressed the difference between his model, which had the support not only of the unions but of BHP's CEO, John Prescott, and the Hewson labour market deregulation without limits variety.

It was a useful exercise but it was far from a triumph. The press were not in the mood for a triumph, and in fact found some-thing to blow furious about when the PM prefaced an answer to a question from a female journalist with green hair: 'Kieran, it's only that colour coordination of yours and that wonderful hairdo that encourages me into giving you a very nice reply because you always put the most charming questions.' Feminists groaned. Men who had not previously been recognised as feminists now declared themselves. Channel 7's Dennis Grant came out. He was heard to say that Anne Summers' good work had been ruined by a gratu-itous sexist remark about a journalist's hair. There had been a patronising tone in the Prime Minister's remark but this seemed rich. The Opposition Shadow Minister for the Status of Women, however, agreed with Grant: the Prime Minister was an unrecon-structed sexist and Anne Summers may as well go back to New York, she said. Failing dismally to appreciate the dimensions of his crime, the Prime Minister went to Question Time where John

Hewson asked why if he thought Fightback was so flawed did Keating not call an early election. Because 'I want to do you slowly,' he said, and brought the House down. He returned to the office full of muscular good humour. What an election it would be to win, he said: to come from nowhere and do it. We told him he had to ring the journalist. He seemed surprised.

Now there was a feeling around that the election could be won. Don Russell phoned around worried MPs and bemused journalists, including a couple who'd only a week or two before said we were dead meat. The journalists wanted to know what exactly the Prime Minister had in mind.

He was an enigma, a paradox, an oxymoron on legs, a contradiction. People were always saying it. How could a man who was so brilliant so much of the time do such foolish things? Early in October he told the House that the recession was over. It had been over for a long time, he said; and what was more the Labor Government had 'saved' Australia. The Opposition roared, the press poured scorn. In the House it became a gruelling spiteful struggle as the Opposition made all the capital it could from Keating's 'callous rhetoric', as Glenn Milne called it. They would ask Labor frontbenchers if they thought the recession was over. They would ask if the recession was over for this particular unemployed person of this depressed place, or this bankrupted small business, or this couple who had lost everything they had worked for.

Once again Keating had raised the bar for no particular reason. Once again he'd made what everyone agreed was a blunder. And once again it was not one he would admit to. His public defence was that what he said was literally and unarguably true; a recession is defined by negative growth in two consecutive quarters, or more sensibly, when an economy is contracting. The Australian economy was not contracting and had not been for some time. In fact it was growing. In private, he said the election cannot be won unless we establish this fact. The Opposition can't be allowed to go on saying the country is in recession without the claim being contested, and they can't be allowed to say that Labor had led the country to ruin without it also being said that Labor had saved it. It was the usual conundrum about Paul Keating. Was it wilful or brilliantly considered? Did he see further than his advisers could? Or his ministers? Or was it because, on his trip to Japan, his only economic adviser had been John Edwards? Who can judge these things?

A few days later John Button told Laurie Oakes on television that the budget growth figures might be 'optimistic'. Button's gaffe, as it was inevitably called, set off a cacophony of jeers and groans across the country which at least drew attention away from the Prime Minister's gaffe.

Fired by the prospect of success, and a successful trip to Japan, Keating decided to remind us that he was not yet what we intended to make him: he said he thought he might call Hewson a scumbag in the House, just quietly, just so only Hewson could hear it. A few days before he had roared about 'Advisers! You spend half your time working for your advisers!' He complained that Anne Summers was not doing him any good because everyone thought he couldn't do anything for women without a 'professional hairy leg' telling him what to think. We knew he didn't mean it. It was just his way of warning the rest of us away from his patch, keeping his self-respect. It was a sign that he was on his game. We knew this for sure when, while preparing for Question Time, he rang 'Leaping' Leo McLeay, the embattled Speaker of the House, and told him he had to stop the orchestrated laughing of the Opposition when he was not saying anything funny. Leo McLeay fitted the position of Speaker like Caligula's horse fitted the Roman Senate. He was not comfortable and it showed. Mike Steketee wrote in the *Australian* that Keating ought to sack him, and the truth was a more venerable-looking speaker, preferably not from the PM's own faction, might have brought more discipline and dignity to the House which was, for the most part, Keating's best environment. Between mouthfuls of lunch, the Prime Minister spoke to McLeay softly, as a mate, as if the understanding between them was ancestral and beyond the reach of anyone outside the clan. The Speaker was complaining that the government's Dorothy Dix questions were beyond a joke, the answers too often in breach of the standing orders, that Steketee had turned the heat up on him and he was going to have to do something about it. The Prime Minister reckoned there was no need for that. 'No, mate,' he said. 'You'll be right. You stay tucked up in the vortex, mate.'

In the landslide that everyone knew was coming, the intriguing almost charismatic Liberal, Jeff Kennett, was elected Premier of Victoria in October 1992. Labor's loss was as gruesome as it was predictable, but for the federal government the sorrow was mixed liberally with relief. There was even a little optimism. No-one quite knew to which side of his political personality the new premier would play, but Labor hoped it would be to the one for which Jeff Kennett had long been known—the less rational, erratic sometimes bullying one.

Kennett was a conundrum for the Labor Government. The Prime Minister was comfortable with his radical aggression, his good-natured larrikinism, his inclination when it mattered to serve the national interest as much as the parochial one and his dislike of John Hewson and John Howard. For these personal reasons, in a good world, Keating might have thought twice before pursuing Kennett into territory where the Premier might be vulnerable. In the bad world of politics he would have thought twice and done it. But there were good political reasons for holding back; namely, Kennett was popular and Keating was not. Worse, it was difficult to attack Kennett and at the same time avoid association with the widely despised Labor Government which preceded him. There was hardly any more to be gained from a seeming alliance with the Victorian trade unions who led the resistance to the new government. For all the protests, Victorians had voted in overwhelming numbers for Kennett and if Keating wanted to win seats in that state he was obliged to tread carefully with the man they had chosen with such enthusiasm. Kennett of course did not feel so constrained. Premiers always prosper from blaming and abusing Canberra and, for all his singularity, Kennett was not immune to the temptation. So while each of them confessed to, and sometimes publicly displayed, a soft spot for the other, one often felt that Keating's was softer than Kennett's. Or, rather, that all head-kicking legends to the contrary, Keating was far more inclined to want to believe the best of someone he instinctively liked and, because he needed to trust his instincts, to go on believing in them for longer.

Policy areas were different. Kennett's most aggressive early act, his industrial legislation, was a convenient issue for the Commonwealth Government because it came as a practical demonstration of federal Coalition policy. There was no better measure of Labor's revolution in the eighties than that industrial relations should be an argument they stood a chance of winning in 1992. It was also, of course, a comment on Dr Hewson's belief in his own invincibility and the free-market cause. While the Accord had not become a universal article of faith in Australia, the word had come to signify more general goods like cooperation, common-sense, progress and industrial peace. The Coalition could paint it as a sweetheart deal between the government and the unions and talk malevolently about an industrial relations 'club', but people were not necessarily hostile to sweethearts and clubs. They could say that Australia did not need an Accord, it needed deregulation of the labour market—the tough part of economic reform that Labor had wimped for the sake of its trade union mates—and when they said this, on balance it was good for Labor. The 'social wage' was not a well-understood concept, but its components were—Medicare, family allowances, child care, pensions, pharmaceutical benefits, unemployment benefits. The Industrial Relations Commission was not on everybody's mind or lips, but people did understand the idea of an umpire, and abolishing the umpire did not seem likely to encourage harmony or fairness.

It was called deregulating the labour market, or continuing the micro-economic reform agenda, but Labor only had to call it the 'law of the jungle' to make its political point—that everyone would be less secure in their work and those already insecure would be in dire jeopardy, that the weakest would be exploited, wages would be lower, conditions worse, rights diminished. The Coalition could say it would mean less unemployment, but that was not an argument for those who were employed and they were the vast majority. Labor's position was as strong as political arguments get: they had both tradition and progress to point to—the tradition of the 'fair go' and the progress of the past decade. 'Why would you wreck what has taken so long to create?' Labor could say. 'Why go back to the bad old days?' As it happened these words masked the fact that the Accord was in fact the last link to those days of regulation and arbitration. As sometimes happens in politics, the most powerful argument might have gone unspoken. In the event, Labor never had to make the case. When Jeff Kennett introduced his industrial legislation and workers flooded onto the streets, it was made for them.

The beginning of the spring of 1992 was a good time for Paul Keating. He had momentum. There were times, it is true, when in the House it seemed as if he felt that he must destroy his opponents totally, physically; that he thought his duty would not be done until they were all strewn on the floor, or slumped across the benches, massacred like Penelope's suitors and impaled on their little flags. No-one would be spared. It was not easy to insert into this kind of frenzy an incisive thrust or two which might disarm his opponents and make the victory less bloody. For days he carried the lines in his brief: 'Yes, I once believed in a consumption tax. It is also true that I once believed in Santa Claus. But in both cases I learned that the things I desired came by other means.'

Eventually he uttered the words, but the timing was out and they had no visible effect. Not that comparisons with Santa Claus would undo the fact that Keating had once done everything in his power to persuade his party and the country to the consumption tax he now so stridently opposed. It was always a potent weapon for Hewson and something we would have to live with. In politics, chaos theory tends to apply: you can never tell when a line will do the job intended, or come back and bite you; or whether it will change your opponent's angle of approach or touch some cranky nerve in him, and who knows what the effect will be. The 'caring arm' was proof of that; even in November

Hewson was still so offended by the notion that he could not help saying that certain forms of 'giving' were 'suffocating'. No-one could say how John Hewson got on the path which led him to say that one had to wonder what sort of man Bob Carr was, and whether he was really a 'red-blooded Australian', because Bob Carr didn't have children. And no-one could say for sure if on that day had Keating announced a major policy or uttered a deathless line that Hewson's line would have made the news. As it turned out, the entire political debate up to October 1992, every punch and counter-punch on every issue, suddenly seemed like a waste of energy as all the newspapers and all the radio and television beat Hewson mercilessly for the remark until, utterly humiliated, he apologised for it on Jana Wendt's program. Nothing Keating had called him would stick to him like those words and the picture of him recanting.

It all went to make Paul Keating a happier, more hard-working man. He agreed to broaden his canvas. At the Australian Film Institute awards he mingled with the smart things gathered round for Baz Luhrmann's film hit *Strictly Ballroom*. Annita wore a 1920s dress he had bought her for the occasion. Despite some misgivings, he said he would argue in cabinet for lifting the ban on gays in the armed forces. 'You know me,' he said, 'some of my best friends are cats.' He was much more excited about the prospect of buying a swag of dirt cheap F-111s from the Americans. He delivered a speech of welcome to President Mary Robinson of Ireland with more charm and smiles than anyone had seen that year. He had regular acupuncture which relaxed him mightily. He flashed his gums more often which cheered his staff and, we thought, demoralised his opponent.

He went to Bankstown and in the boardroom of the Sports Club sat down with old mates to prawns, oysters and beer—he in his double-breasted Zegna, they in their green blazers. It was remarkable, one of them said to me, how he still knows the names of everyone in the electorate and remembers their kids. On leaving the boardroom he said he needed a slash, and while we waited outside one of them remarked that it was strange how he had known the bloke since he was a kid but he felt he really couldn't go in there and stand next to him at the urinal now he was prime minister. And everyone laughed. That night he addressed the local Federal Electoral Council of the ALP—at length—and then answered questions for an hour and a half while his staff drifted off into the vast poker-machine labyrinth. At midnight he told his driver to take us on a tour of Bankstown; past the shed at Bankstown Oval where he joined the ALP and went to meetings every Monday thereafter and made many speeches like the one he had just given at the Sports Club. He took us past the family house and nearby the house he had lived in with Annita; and Black Charlie's Hill where MacArthur's headquarters had been. And with the police following, through the shopping centre where all the shops he'd known as a kid by their Irish and English names were now called Bin Thong and Hung Phat and Thung Tung. And his constituents were always telling him that they should be put on a boat and sent back to where they'd come from. That's what I'm up against, he said. And then we drove at last to Bankstown airport and flew back to Canberra in a small plane beneath an incredibly starry sky which reminded the Prime Minister of his days in the Riverina when the night sky was 'this close'—the length of his nose—to your face. Everyone gazed out the windows at it and it would not have surprised if the Prime Minister had told the pilot to fly on to Deniliquin at least.

It was curious how Paul Keating's good moods always took him back, not quite to his childhood but to the birth of his political life and to what was hopeful and innocent or beautiful and unchanging. Not quite so curious, perhaps. The good mood was almost certainly due to the prospect of an election—so far had the pendulum swung—and an election was bound to provoke deep reflection because an election was a matter of death or resurrection.

People rang from various parts of the Commonwealth to say that they had heard rumours. John Hewson announced that there would be an election before Christmas and he did it on the very day that the office met with a former Hawke adviser, Geoff Walsh, to discuss the tactics Hawke's office had used with success in 1990. Walsh believed that 1990 was Labor's best campaign—it had to be to win with interest rates at 17 per cent. Hawke had been thoroughly scripted and made to keep to it; all danger had been minimised if not eliminated by tough and thorough 'advances', meaning reconnoitring of the road ahead and the people, well and ill-disposed alike, who lie in wait; the itinerary was tight and aimed directly at the media, which meant no night-time appearances which meant less fatigue and therefore less risk of blunders; and the Prime Minister was kept well away from the advertising. This, apparently, was crucial. It was depressing to think that all our efforts would reduce to something so mean. Nonetheless, one woke in the night thinking wouldn't it be lovely to have it over by Christmas. And we decided that all future prime ministerial travel would be rehearsals for an election.

Hewson challenged Keating to a debate. Keating said he'd be there 'with bells on', and flashed a smile. 'It's a great tactic to smile,' I said. 'You may as well be relaxed,' he said and flexed his shoulders loose. 'They don't know what you're thinking when you smile,' I said. 'That's right,' he said, 'they wonder—what's the cunt thinking?' 'That's right,' I said. 'Bad things,' he said; 'that's what I'm thinking. Bad things.'

We heard that Glenn Milne was about to say in the *Australian* that Peter Barron was the Prime Minister's most influential adviser and the 'power intellect' of his office. Russell was too narrow and Ryan too young. Readers would learn that the Prime Minister and his advisers often gathered round the phone to listen to the former Hawke heavy. The former Keating heavy, Tom Mockridge, rang Milne and told him it was bullshit. No-one was in much doubt that the story was connected with Graham Richardson's feelings about the PM's office. We thought it might have had something to do with Barron as well. And we thought it the more when he rang Mark Ryan and, in a tone no less patronising for being conciliatory, told him that the Prime Minister should get out and talk to some real punters—but he must be well prepared, mate. We wondered how we had managed without gathering round the phone to Peter Barron.

Bob Hogg said he hoped Anne Summers didn't think she'd spend the campaign travelling the country 'feminising Australia'. Down at Curtin House they were not keen on any pushy, trendy, publicity-seeking bastard, male or female. Hoggy, Gary Gray, Ian Henderson and David Epstein all had a tendency to speak with their mouths shut tight. At least half a dozen times in the first meeting about an election each asked the other what he'd said. Everyone seemed to think that we could have the election before Christmas, but no-one said that we should. I ventured that our main concern was our failure to persuade anyone that we were a new government, not the old one in its dotage. We had lost control of the agenda in the autumn and had survived on Hewson's mistakes pretty well ever since. Everyone agreed, but no-one suggested how we might proceed. I went back to Don Russell's office and said we needed to come up with some agenda-setting program, possibly involving superannuation funds, industry policy and regional Australia. Dr Russell said it couldn't be done. Our program is very complex and subtle, he said. John Edwards, bless him, said we had plenty to say about the next three years. And Ric Simes, bless him as well, said we didn't.

Jeff Kennett abolished leave loading and penalty rates and sacked 7000 public servants. In one twenty-four hour period he voted pay increases for parliamentarians and abolished penalty rates for nurses. Then he decided to take his entire cabinet to the Melbourne Cup in tails and, we were told, twice prevailed on the Governor to join them. There was a moment's hesitation before the Prime Minister did a doorstop on these developments because the dollar had just dived through 70 cents. The Prime Minister was undeterred: he said he'd tell them that the dollar went down and the dollar went up—and he did. A man ran amok with a gun near Terrigal and killed six people, and that was the news.

Kennett's extraordinary actions injected great enthusiasm into the Labor movement. At a dinner attended by Keating, Bill Kelty, Hogg and Anna Booth, Jenny George said that Kennett had made this election a matter of life and death. Hoggy had a couple of drinks and put his arm around Keating—possibly for the last time. Keating told the women they should be in politics. There was fight in the comradely air. Later, Don Russell warned us that this could be like 1975 when all on the Labor side mistook their own passion for the public mood.

The pollster came and told us that Western Australia was bad and getting worse; South Australia bad but getting better; and Victoria bad, but that was pre-Kennett. She also said that no-one liked the Prime Minister's suits. We said, get on with it. Listening in his suit, brown eyes smiling, the Prime Minister said that just now all he wanted to do was climb all over Kennett. The Opposition had run a smokescreen for their rampant Victorian colleague—an allegation that Dawkins had known Joan Kirner's Victorian Labor Government figures were shonky when a short-term loan was extended to medium term. They called it the 'Loans Affair' to echo the last days of Whitlam and set up a Senate committee of inquiry. Kennett, however, was not waiting for smokescreens. Howard and Reith felt constrained to criticise him for introducing industrial relations legislation different from that which he proposed before the election.

It was not quite manna from heaven, as the press said it was, but it was certainly welcome. However, there was nothing to suggest that the outrage in Victoria went much beyond the union movement, and nothing to say that voters who had only a month before demolished one Labor government would now come to the rescue of another one.

In the House, the Opposition took to staring at Dawkins and drawing their fingers across their throats. Hewson called out that the Treasurer was 'dead meat'. Keating was overheard telling Hewson that he would 'take care of him'. Into this challenging environment on that same day the Prime Minister introduced a Sex Discrimination Bill.

Bill Clinton was elected President of the United States, an event which Keating greeted warmly in the parliament but not without adding some lines of his own about the fine qualities of George Bush. For reasons that were perhaps not entirely logical,

Clinton's election encouraged the Keating office in the view that the world was turning against the conservative, supply-side policies which John Hewson was advocating for Australia. With Clinton ascendant in Washington and the Conservatives in decline in London, it was possible to imagine that, far from being in its dotage, the Keating Government suddenly had history on its side.

Full of confidence and fight—and freshly acupunctured—Keating went into the House on 4 November in dazzling form. There were times when the old adversary, John Howard, served him better than any adviser could—the sight of him jogged his memory, providing him with an historical context he could feed off. On this day Howard had given notice that he would introduce as a Matter of Public Importance the question of the 'Loans Affair'. The Prime Minister took into the House Budget Paper No. 4 of 1984–85 and waving it about proceeded to paste Howard in language that was horrible or Homeric depending on your taste. As treasurer in the Fraser Government, he said, Howard had let the Loans Council 'haemorrhage all over the place'; it had 'blurted out the back' of the public sector. And these people who had taken Loan Council authority over State borrowings from 95 per cent to 25 per cent and let the system 'run amok' expected a minister from the government which brought Loan Council authority back to 100 per cent, a minister from the House of Representatives, 'to wander over to the unrepresentative chamber and account for himself'. They had to be joking. 'Whether the Treasurer wished to go there or not, I would forbid him going to the Senate to account to this unrepresentative swill over there.' The most intriguing response to this came from Alexander Downer, who was heard calling out over the uproar that the Prime Minister should have his mouth washed out with soap and water. The damage had been done, or rather, the damage inflicted on the Opposition had been undone. Howard moved his MPI and hammed it up, comparing Keating to the last days of Whitlam. Keating put on a great display but nothing was going to distract the press from 'unrepresentative swill'.

Back in the office, the Prime Minister was almost entirely unrepentant. He agreed that he had gone a bit over the top, but they were not talking about a 'Loans Affair' any more were they? They were talking about swill. I searched for words or precedents which might lessen the impact—not least on Labor members of the swill. Hadn't Churchill or Lloyd George or someone used this expression? A swill is 'a thin soup'. What is so offensive about thin soup?

The next day the Prime Minister came to work absolutely determined to say to Hewson: if, as you say, the Senate will obstruct your GST, let's get rid of it. He would. It was impossible not to smile. Mark Ryan talked him out of it, if he was ever serious, and from this rather unlikely discussion sprang a fateful decision. He would tell Hewson in Question Time that Labor in opposition would *not* obstruct a GST in the Senate. Labor would *pass* a GST. No-one spoke. He would do it that afternoon. He would chain the Coalition to the GST, and the country would realise that they could not have one without the other. The election would be a referendum on the GST. We nodded. Greg Turnbull expressed the concern that the rest of us, including the Prime Minister, doubtless felt—that it might be interpreted as capitulation, that voters would understand it to mean the opposite of what was intended; that effectively there was now no difference between the parties on the GST.

The effect on both sides of the House was truly remarkable. 'I say to the Opposition that, in the unlikely event of its becoming a government, the Labor Party would not obstruct the passage of the GST legislation in the Senate.' There seemed to be a moment or two of silence and then the Opposition called 'Hooray!' and delirium broke out on that side. Behind the Prime Minister, government members were so obviously stunned Reith called out, 'Look behind you! Look behind you!' The Opposition hooted and howled in triumph. They slapped each other's backs and laughed and did high fives and any other gesture of celebration they could think of. Watching in the office we wondered if the whole game had been thrown away in one lunatic moment or if it was something heroic—the Prime Minister standing there, staring down the ridicule in front of him and sensing the great hole of incredulity and horror opening up behind. He said afterwards it was the most hair-raising moment of his career. You had to marvel at the way he stampeded over his own doubts. 'There will be no hiding behind the Democrats,' he repeated. 'Laugh with your silly feigned giggle,' he said to Hewson, but 'You, in your own silly way, understand the deadliness of that remark.' 'Bye-bye, Paul. Thanks, Paul,' they called. It would be 'branded' on them now, the Prime Minister said, 'G full stop S full stop T full stop'. Hewson would be like 'a cow at a cattle branding'. He sat down at last, though not before referring to the 'pansies' in the Senate and causing more uproar. Reith rose and thanked him for conceding the game and letting the people know that 'a vote for Labor is a vote for the GST'. But some people said they saw worry creep across John Howard's face.

In the circumstances his next performance was just as remarkable. Betraying not a sign of the general mayhem he had just created, he answered a Dorothy Dixer about television violence. Keating hated violence. *Braveheart* was too violent for him. His youngest daughter had been frightened by something she saw on television and he had been horrified when he saw what she had been watching. We showed him an episode of *The Simpsons* in which Marge, like him appalled by the violence depicted in her children's favourite cartoon program, *Itchy and Scratchy*, mounts a national campaign and takes the issue to Congress. The Prime Minister, who had never seen *The Simpsons*, laughed uproariously at Itchy and Scratchy as they tore out each other's eyeballs and sawed each other in half. Cartoon violence was different. Wisely, he made no reference to the show in his answer: he told the House new censorship classifications would be introduced to prohibit the screening of certain violent material before 9.30 p.m.

By mid-afternoon from the press gallery came reports that a consensus was growing in favour of Keating's GST tactic. That evening he told the ABC's Jim Middleton that while everyone had been looking on one side of the street he had just hurled a big piece of meat to the other side and tomorrow that's where they'd all be.

Mike Richards rang to say the tactic was a masterstroke, that we would win up to ten seats in Victoria if we held the election before Christmas. The press began thinking along similar lines. As the day wore on and Hewson and Reith began to sound lame, rumours flew about—Keating was going to see the Governor-General, he was on his way, he had already been. In one short lunch Mark Ryan's phone rang half a dozen times. The last call was from Bob Hogg: the party was in no shape to fight an election, so what was all this about Paul going to see Bill? In fact Paul was rugged up at the Lodge sniffing Vicks Vaporub and drinking sage tea from my mother-in-law's recipe.

Bob Hogg didn't want an election, but his two deputies, Gary Gray and Ian Henderson, came to the PMO urging us to hold one. Dawkins wanted an election. Don Russell wanted one on 19 December. The odd backbencher dropped by to say go for it. Peter Barron sent a note saying he would argue against it, but he was not committed to the position. Brian Courtice, the indefatigable north Queenslander, put his head in the door and said something about the Shenandoah Valley—let's go and burn it, like Sherman did.

I was for it in the morning and after lunch against it. The turmoil in Victoria; the near certainty of unemployment getting worse; the uninspiring economy; the momentum we seemed to have; what Don Russell called the 'spell' we appeared to have cast on the electorate so that with 11 per cent unemployment they thought we were the ones who cared! And then there was the fear that the Coalition would drop or draw the sharpest teeth of the GST and perhaps substitute Howard for Hewson. That was why I wanted an election in the morning. But then there were the bad polls in Western Australia and South Australia; and the difficulty of picking Victoria; and the incompetence of our office; and elections at Christmas kill retail trade; and above all this hung the spectre of an electorate which wakes up one morning and says to itself, he has to be joking! He gives us a recession and 11 per cent unemployment and then he tries to fox us into voting for him. He's pulled his last stunt. It was the spectre of the spell breaking which drove me into the don't do it camp.

The unemployment figure probably decided it. It was hard to imagine a snap election after it came in at another postwar record of 11.3 per cent. Hewson told a doorstop that the country was drifting towards Depression. I told the Prime Minister he may as well call this 'treachery', and in the House that afternoon he did on several occasions. It was odd—as if the pendulum was at the top of its arc and not yet started on its descent—in the midst of the economic bad news he received extraordinarily good press for his campaign against TV violence, and even for a speech to the Test cricketers down at Manuka Oval. Mark Ryan and I asked our economic advisers what his line on unemployment should be. Perhaps they could write it down. One of them wrote, 'Unemployment is clearly not coming down.' We all laughed, including Don Russell, who then suggested, 'We are not out of the unemployment woods yet.' John Edwards smacked his lips and said actually the figures weren't so bad, what with the improved participation rate. I was panicking, he said. I said I was merely asking them if thought of a more creative kind was possible. Edwards said it was obvious that I wanted to go back to high tariffs. I said I didn't, but I did want to know how people who had been wrong so often could maintain the demeanour of the Popes. Could they show us a little evidence of their infallibility, even if only for six months or so? They agreed that unemployment would not be falling in that period, and perhaps not for a year.

The papers said the unemployment figures swept away any thought of an election before Christmas. Glenn Milne reported that a rush of blood had taken Paul Keating to the edge of an election, but wiser heads, including Don Russell and Mark Ryan, had pulled him back. It had been decided at a meeting at 9.30 that morning, 16 November, he said. There never was such a meeting; but it was true that there would not be a 19 December election. The right must be taken with the wrong and the good with the bad: towards the end of November a television journalist rang Greg Turnbull to say that he had footage of very expensive cars turning up at a Liberal Fightback function do in Sydney. That afternoon in Question Time the Prime Minister duly provided the words for the vision on the evening news. Not that the journalist could be accused of bias; immediately after the expensive cars with Keating voice-over he firmly endorsed a question Hewson had asked in the House. Anyway, everyone said that what he had done to the Coalition, he would do to us if it suited him.

I had a telephone conversation with Don Russell and immediately afterwards wrote it down. I suggested that a gentle re-embrace of Keynes might win us the election.

> DR: Actually I found my copy of *The General Theory* moving house today.
> DW: It's propitious. It means you are to re-read it and apply it. Am I right in saying that what the Prime Minister described to me when I first came as 'asset price overhang' is in fact what Keynes called 'debt deflation'—meaning that your debt remains the same but your assets are reduced?
> DR: Right.
> DW: And you spend all your wages on retiring your debt?
> DR: And you don't spend it on anything else.
> DW: So if they're not spending any money, what is the obvious solution?
> DR/DW (together): That we spend it.

Russell came to work the following morning with a copy of a speech Keating had given in New York in 1988. It was intended to convince me that our Prime Minister had never been an economic ideologue of any variety, including economic rationalism. I believed him, but it was not me he needed to persuade.

The Prime Minister had agreed to make certain announcements in a speech in Sydney: one was the Citizenship Pledge, another was a feasibility study into a new national museum (not a mausoleum by the lake) for which we had arranged $40,000 from the department. As press copies of the speech were printed in the Sydney office, Russell rang from the Prime Minister's car as he drove to the place where the speech was to be given. The flu-stricken Prime Minister wanted the national museum removed.

Cursing him we took it out and started printing again. Russell rang again to say the Prime Minister wanted the Oath of Allegiance out too. The Pledge was there to trump Hewson's recent attempts to buy into the citizenship debate; with the national museum we hoped to swing the focus of Keating's nationalism towards things we knew were much more generally approved than the republic and the flag. It was plain dumb to change the plan—and bad-mannered to demand it minutes before the speech was delivered. Mark Ryan, whose baby it was as much as mine, managed to find the cool within him to do what was necessary and get the revised speech in the hands of the press. I, by contrast, departed in a rage leaving Russell a filthy note.

Two hours later he rang me on my mobile phone and told me I was off my head. It got terribly heated. He did what the Prime Minister often did and put it all down to my 'nationalism'. I said that in that week I had written speeches on Aerospace, the economy, cricket and one for Annita that, like the other three, had nothing to do with nationalism. I had also written his lines on unemployment and Kennett and, in all, provided the copy for five good headlines in as many days. There would have been more from this speech if they hadn't vandalised it. My contribution was appreciated, said Russell, but I should recognise that I was privileged to have such access to the Prime Minister. It was, he said, making me famous. I said fame was a goal I had put aside for now. Two cars collided in front of me, and the drivers stood in Oxford Street abusing each other.

The speech was stillborn; they buried it or led with the republican stuff we had intended to screen behind the new Oath of Allegiance and the national museum that would not be a mausoleum by the lake. The jaundice lasted for days—as long as the Prime Minister's flu. If we were winning it was despite ourselves and you would have sworn some people wanted to win that way. Don Russell called it 'getting our story right', but for what and for whom were unanswered questions. John Button came saying we needed to do something positive, that instead of worrying about the story Russell should start looking forward.

Outside, the flowers were in bloom, above the rattling flagpole the evening sky was steel blue, the evening star brilliant. Inside, walking down the corridor it suddenly seemed hopeless. We were going to win by default, the people who had sat on their hands and counselled inactivity and self-congratulation would be vindicated, the feckless and uninspired would claim as much (and have a right to) as we who had belted on the doors in frenzy or tortured our brains all night searching for the right words or the right actions. And we heard that the Prime Minister was listening 'sympathetically' to Conrad Black, the Canadian newspaper magnate Labor had let into Fairfax in 1991 and who now had an application in for more. The Opposition had no objections. Would Labor also have no objections? Would Keating listen to his devoted advisers or to outsiders, including those who said ad nauseam, keep it simple, stay on strategy. It must have been frustration and disappointment but it came in waves of what felt like unspeakable boredom.

Most Monday mornings on the plane to Canberra, a Jewish businessman sat in business class among the politicians, consultants and civil servants. He had a heavily thumbed Torah in one hand, the *Financial Review* in the other and the breakfast he brought himself on his knee. One morning late in November I found myself sitting next to him. He told me business had never been so hard as the last couple of years, and now these unions in Victoria—they were mad. I found myself saying, but the GATT breakthrough this week is good, and the figures for job vacancies are the best for a long while.

CHAPTER 10

'Nay Francesco,' said Machiavelli, smiling . . . 'The secret of oratory lies not in saying new things, but saying things with a certain power that moves the hearers . . .'

GEORGE ELIOT, ROMOLA

T HE *ECONOMIST* IN October had said that the end was not nigh. The international economy was not about to plunge into some tragic equivalent of the 1930s. Nevertheless, the journal's panel of forecasters felt constrained to revise their estimates of world economic growth in the coming year. They revised it downwards. The Australian Treasury said the government's predicted 3 per cent growth rate for 1993 was 'on track', but hopes for anything above that were 'fading'. It was Kerry Packer's view that the current economic environment would remain the same for the rest of the decade, which was to say, 'tough'. The government pointed to Australia's 'world's lowest inflation' rate, 'world's best' growth prospects and strong export growth as encouraging signs, while continuing to insist that the changes made in the previous decade had made the economy stronger and reshaped it to fit the world. The Opposition said the inflation rate was a 'bitter legacy' of the high interest rates of the late eighties, the growth an illusion and the export growth dwarfed by the current account.

That was in October. At the end of November the worst monthly current account deficit for three years was announced.

Exports fell. Growth was lower than expected. Foreign debt rose—again. It was uniformly believed that unemployment would rise before it fell. Dr Hewson said all this was due to structural problems in the economy which Fightback—and only Fightback—would solve. The Reserve Bank chief, Bernie Fraser, said the government's approach was generally right, but there was great confusion in business and the community. He recommended a study which would set directions for the next two decades as the 1945 white paper had done for the postwar period. He was right about the confusion; and into it Paul Keating had to insert something trickier than a white paper—he had to hold an election.

Cabinet met in late November and voted to lift the ban on homosexuals in the Defence Forces. The ban breached Australia's human rights objectives, the Attorney-General reported. We heard that Kim Beazley and Ros Kelly both spoke in favour of retaining the ban, but our man spoke in favour of lifting it. He told the press that the decision 'brought the ADF into line with the tolerant attitudes of Australians generally'. Alexander Downer said the Defence Minister ought to resign. The Vietnam veteran, Tim Fischer, said it was a sad day. A veteran of a more ancient war, Sir Roden Cutler, said: 'When you are fighting next to someone you need to have confidence in that person and how can you be confident of someone when they have made suggestions to you?'

One day in mid-November the Prime Minister rang and asked me to have lunch with him at the Lodge. I abandoned my fish and chips. He was in his tracksuit, slippers and stubble. While he talked we ate borsch, omelette, ice-cream and fruit. He had not called an election because he was not of that school of thought which held that Labor could only hope to minimise electoral damage. We could not have won, he said. The figures were too bad in Western Australia and South Australia. He intended to win the election and the best chance would be as early as possible in the new year.

Bill Clinton, the US President-elect, interested him. He thought he might borrow one of his techniques in the election and travel to unlikely places in swinging seats. He would write to him, offering not just congratulations but ideas about the Asia-Pacific and recommending that he abandon plans to extend NAFTA into South and Central America. He thought Clinton was a 'real chance': he had brains and he understood power. Power, Keating said, had to be exercised constantly. It had to be moved around. The Victorian ALP was a good example of an outfit that did not understand power. The Victorian ALP were 'boarders'. The New South Wales ALP were 'repellers of boarders'.

Keating does not anticipate precisely what one is about to say, but when it might have too much point or import to easily ignore. It is an essential political skill; without it a politician would never escape from an auditorium or press scrum, or from his advisers. Sensing a threat to his own pleasure or his command of the floor, Keating deflects the subject or changes it, or says 'that's right, mate', and repeats one's last line aloud. Or he might go and get some entirely unrelated object—for example, a photo album with pictures of Annita in full bloom. I try again. He asks me if I'm a tyke. I say I'm not. I'm Presbyterian, can't you tell? He says, it doesn't matter: 'You think like a tyke. You've got that view of the world. It's different.' I take it as flattery and start again, but he gets up and leads the way to the 'brown room'. We sit in front of giant speakers and listen to two versions of a moment in *Tannhäuser*, then Kempe's version of the opening of Strauss' Alpine Symphony, then von Karajan's. He likes the Kempe. He says the greatest moment in the history of twentieth-century music was the premiere of Mahler's Eighth Symphony.

The children are home from school and eating sandwiches. He hugs and kisses them. By the time I get back to the office he has been on the phone to Linda, his secretary, and complained bitterly about having to go to Melbourne tonight and the 'fucking tyranny' of Mark Ryan who arranged it. He is going to speak to two thousand young people and their families in the Melbourne Concert Hall, and to hear the Australian Children's Choir sing a new version of 'Advance Australia Fair'. The author of this strange addition to the prime ministerial timetable is Pete Steedman, boss of Ausmusic, former Labor MHR, maverick member of the Victorian socialist left. Steedman reckons Keating owes him—no-one quite knows what, but it's enough to get the Prime Minister to something which is likely to fall well short of Mahler's premiere. Yet on the plane to Melbourne he is in good spirits again; and he addresses the audience charmingly, and later does not join the chorus of derision from his staff about the truly awful new rendition of our national anthem we have had to sit through. On Channel 7 the next day, Dennis Grant contrives a story from the event: the Prime Minister, he says, is off on a new crusade; now he wants to make 'Waltzing Matilda' the national anthem. It is not true. The Prime Minister said quite plainly that he thought, like the Americans, we had a national song and a national anthem and we should stick to the arrangement. But Grant coolly quotes the speech out of context to give a false impression of its meaning. The Prime Minister doesn't seem to notice. He's in Sydney, talking about his piggery, we think.

It was remarkable. In some of the mid-November polls Labor was well ahead. Jeffrey Kennett helped by sacking teachers, closing schools and getting people demonstrating in the streets in numbers not seen since the Vietnam War. Everything he did seemed to confirm what Labor said about industrial relations under the Liberals. The federal government took heart. It was one of the more decisive actions of Keating's first year as prime minister: he announced that he would use the Commonwealth's external affairs powers to enable Victorian workers to escape the Victorian industrial relations legislation into federal jurisdiction. Bryan Noakes of the Australian Chamber of Commerce and Industry declared it 'the most blatant grab for power since World War II'. State premiers from both sides of politics blustered about this encroachment on their jurisdiction. But Keating's plan would save Victorian workers from the Kennett regime of individual contracts and give them the protection of minimum industry awards set by the Industrial Relations Commission. More than that, the move would bring a halt to the strikes and demonstrations in Victoria which must soon begin to hurt Labor, and it would lend some passion and vigour to the Keating Government's cause.

All the major lobbies by now had been addressed: reminded of Labor's work on their behalf, instructed in the risks that went with contemplating even half-hearted approval of the Coalition. Hewson had touted himself as the honest broker who had sacrificed his career as a merchant banker to enter the rotten world of politics to do what needed to be done. He was, he said proudly, not a politician. In that case, Keating said, Dr Hewson should not be in politics. One expected one's dentist to indeed be a dentist, a plumber to know about plumbing, and one had an equal right to expect those who represented the people's interests to be competent at politics. When Hewson began talking about his desire to 'break the mould' of Australian politics Keating found the proof of his argument. Watch out, he said; this man does not understand politics, or the nature of Australian democracy, or the link between the mould of politics and the mould of society. Or does he? Could it be that his talk about breaking the mould of politics is sign language for breaking the social mould? Isn't that what his policies threaten to do? This was a polemic of some quality. It was a flexible, all-purpose stick for beating. It could be deployed in arguments of considerable sophistication and power with dark intimations of other twentieth-century 'anti-political' politicians. But argument was purely optional: so long as the audience kept hearing that Dr Hewson wanted to 'break the mould' the job was two-thirds done.

There were demonstrable hurdles to get over. Mick Young told us that South Australia was grim, although nothing, he said, an industry policy wouldn't fix. Then the Industry Commission declared support for certain aspects of Fightback and torrents of invective flowed from behind the Prime Minister's door, most of it concerning the IC's Professor Ross Garnaut. The Prime Minister's piggery remained discomforting. For reasons that were possibly related, the Prime Minister contemplated telling the journalists gathered in Sydney for the annual Walkley Awards that Conrad Black had confided to him that John Hewson had confided to Black that if elected he would give him 100 per cent of Fairfax. Foreign ownership of Australian companies sporadically loomed as a major issue: the airwaves buzzed with outrage when John Dawkins revealed that the way had been opened for the American company, Campbells, to buy the iconic Australian biscuit company, Arnotts. By way of balance, the government declared that the Coalition had no chance of selling Telstra for the $20 billion they claimed unless they sold it to foreign interests—and they couldn't sell it to foreign interests without timed local calls, reduced services and mass sackings. And if they couldn't sell it for $20 billion, all their figuring in Fightback was bogus.

Yet none of it mattered so much. Not even the bad BOP figures at the beginning of December mattered, or the chorus of business groups complaining that micro-economic reform was proceeding too slowly. The truth could be seen in Hewson's face and in the sound of his voice. He'd grown cantankerous. The news summaries from all over the country were a measure of his dedication and phenomenal energy, and a daily source of depression in the PMO. But a day came towards the end of the year when one looked at them and thought, there is hope in here. The listeners must be sick of him. His bounding energy and passionate belief in himself will be making them feel tired. He sounds like a man who signed up for Billy Graham and never really got over it. In November one felt that they were halfway to deciding that Fightback was unfair. It could be seen in John Hewson's face—the first signs of rejection. In the House he complained about Keating's 'smart lines' being no substitute for policy. No-one saw it at the time, but it was probably the first sign that reality was penetrating Hewson's mind. There was an election coming and it was not going to be a walkover. A certain amount of virtue was bound to be lost.

On the eve of a general election John Hewson and Paul Keating fought a phoney war. They stalked the country under different flags, each bludgeoning reality into the rhetorical shape which best suited him. So different was one interpretation from the other, some disinterested person might think that if they were both looking at the same reality, one of them must be deranged. It might be argued that whereas Don Quixote described what, in his madness, he actually saw, Keating and Hewson saw the same things as everybody else and merely put a spin on them to help us see it in a certain light. Yet Don Quixote's madness also began with nothing more than a wish to see the world in a certain light. Political leaders, similarly, reach a point where even to see the other's point of view as credible, much less concede its worth, threatens their very existence. The further one extends the comparison the more difficult it is to say whether politicians are mad or Don Quixote was an early archetype of modern political wisdom. In either case there can be no doubt that Sancho Panza and voters have a lot in common.

Keating told the parliament, the press gallery, the radio, the television, reporters, factory workers, party faithful, the Business Council, forums of women, migrants and small businesspeople that the economic figures were indicators of prosperity and reason for hope. He told them that such problems as the country had would not be remedied by Dr Hewson's tax 'switch' (from income to consumption). 'Switch' was a very useful word: it could mean a silly, pointless thing sometimes; a sleight of hand at others. To much the same forums, though much more often, Hewson insisted that the economic figures measured pervasive gloom and despair. Keating said the previous ten years was a story of bravery, imagination and collective goodwill which had saved Australia. Hewson said the last ten years had not saved the country but wasted it. If the people continued to believe in this story—the 'inclusive' story, the big picture with people in it—Keating said they would be rewarded. Hewson said they would be mugs. If they believed in this story and the emerging story of an Australian republic in the Asia-Pacific, Keating said they would be rewarded twice over. He said the two stories were really one. They joined somewhere in the middle with the recession, but the recession was not so much a chapter as a diversion, a lengthy footnote or appendix. The enemy in Keating's story was Fightback. Fightback could undo all the good work. Fightback was the enemy of hope.

Hewson's story went like this: Keating mocks the Menzies years, yet if when we were growing up in them someone had told us that before we were very old Japan, Taiwan and Singapore would 'outperform' us economically and match our living standards we would have thought them mad. But that was what 'you guys' have done, he told Labor in the parliament. The same guys had squashed individual freedom and individual choice under government regulations and welfare dependency. Labor had settled for a second-rate Australia. Imagine if Allan Border had that attitude—if he had come back from a Test series and said, 'Well, guys, we lost the series but we made more runs than we did last time.' Or if our Olympians had been content with coming second. Choice, incentive and the individual were among Hewson's favourite words, and no-one who heard him utter them could doubt his passionate conviction that they conveyed truth as inviolable as Scripture. That was why the terms 'you guys' and 'these guys' did not serve his cause so well—somehow they spoke for an unanchored soul, a man of passing fashion, an American derivative, a yuppie. The more he talked this way the more it irritated, and the more it irritated the more resolve it inspired. Hewson was a leader who always gave his opponent a hint of a chance. Such hints can easily lead to fantasies about unlikely victories and these to false hopes and spectacular defeats. Equally they give rise to unjustified but powerful surges of morale—and in battle, as Clausewitz said, morale is often the decisive factor.

By December there was little or nothing Labor could do to change the argument. The various elements of the story had been refreshed: women had been promised remedies for domestic violence; families would be protected by new censorship classifications for film and video; ACOSS was reminded of the government's 'commitment to social justice' and the Coalition's commitment to 'cold charity'; the ethnic lobby was promised a new Oath of Allegiance and a strategy for turning cultural diversity into a means of breaking into foreign markets; all audiences were told that great strides had been made, the recession was a stumble, the country was performing better than most people realised, better indeed than just about any other country, and it would be egregious folly to elect an outfit whose GST and cuts to expenditure and wages would dampen demand just when the country was recovering. It was a matter of finding the best possible words and repeating them. Tedious as the prospect of doing it was, the fundamental task would be to defend the status quo.

Given John Hewson's propensity to make war on nearly everyone, it was also desirable for the PM to make peace wherever he could. This included the press. At the Walkley Awards for journalism the Prime Minister told the journalists that he liked them. They were an integral part of the political culture, or the 'mould'. He told them he thought there should be less opinion and more reporting, and that 'the bears should hunt in a bigger circle—the bigger circle of Australian democracy, the provenance of our institutions and traditions and ideas'. Nevertheless he recognised their dilemma: he knew that under the daily pressure of events, journalists, like politicians, needed to make sense out of what were nearly always uncompleted stories. He also spoke of their common cause, the great Australian democracy. He thought that was why he liked journalists, because 'I actually like democracy'. He liked to see in journalists what he liked to see in politicians—and press proprietors: toughness, passion, the courage for change, an understanding of power. Gently he pushed his opponent beyond the pale where people did not understand these things, or pretended to because it was part of their political strategy to prey on the public's distrust of politics and politicians. They talked about breaking the mould of Australian politics because they did not understand or care for its democratic stamp. Real politicians like himself and good journalists, like those in front of him, by implication, did. It was necessary to keep them at a distance, to flatter without being ingratiating. That was why he called them grizzly bears: only when he had acknowledged they were big, fierce animals was it safe to embrace them.

On 10 December 1992 the Prime Minister made a speech to launch the Year of the World's Indigenous People. On the same day he made a speech to a business audience. We could not be sure which of the two events would attract more publicity— the speech to an Aboriginal audience in Redfern, or the one at the *BRW* Business Awards in the CBD. At the business awards he would put the usual case for an optimistic interpretation of the economy, and press the banks to introduce for the benefit of their business customers what went by the name of 'closer relationship banking'. The idea was that they might begin to more closely resemble bankers.

Redfern is that sad inner-city suburb visitors to Sydney sometimes pass through on the way to the airport. It has a large, depressed, angry indigenous population. A group of Aborigines sometimes phoned the PMO late at night to tell us in vehement terms that things were bad and getting worse and the government was useless and Keating no good. They always began by saying they were ringing from Redfern. Redfern is not a place to dissemble about Aboriginal Australia. The PM gave the speech outdoors, in Redfern Park. For the first few minutes there were intermittent catcalls from the back, and later when I listened to the tape I wondered if they were the people who made the calls at night.

The speech was made to a black audience but its core was an appeal to white Australians. We cannot say we have succeeded as a nation or a society if we have not solved the problems arising from the dispossession of Australia's indigenous people. White Australia cannot give them up without giving up its own most deeply held values. If Australia had reached out for the poor and dispossessed of Europe, how could it not reach out for its own people. The catcalls continued. But then he said—just in time, it seemed:

It begins, I think with that act of recognition. Recognition that it was we who did the dispossessing. We took the traditional lands and smashed the traditional way of life. We brought the diseases.

The alcohol. We committed the murders. We took the children from their mothers. We practised discrimination and exclusion. It was our ignorance and our prejudice. And our failure to imagine these things being done to us. With some noble exceptions, we failed to make the most basic human response and enter into their hearts and minds. We failed to ask, how would I feel if this were done to me? As a consequence, we failed to see that what we were doing degraded all of us.

The catcalls stopped. They were not cheering as Martin Luther King's audience did when he described his dream, but there were murmurs—and occasional shouts of approval.

A month later I read in a collection of essays that thought of Vico's: historical knowledge is less like knowing the facts of things and more like knowing what it is to experience them— 'what it is to be poor, or to belong to a nation'. The words seemed to describe the difference between the technocrat's task and the speechwriter's: it also describes the difference between what a speechwriter and a prime minister can be easily content with, and what they might attempt. The first principle of the Redfern speech was that the problem could only be solved by an act of imagination. The country had to acknowledge certain notorious facts—indisputable facts, not hedged about with doubts and qual- ifications, nor as elements of a partisan agenda. There was no hope of useful debate if the truth was not acknowledged and consequences of it imagined. The consequences were trauma, alienation, anger, despair, suicide—and much else that reduces Aboriginal Australians and feeds white Australians' racism and neglect.

'Satire is a sort of glass, wherein beholders do generally discover everybody's face but their own,' Swift said, and he might also have said prejudice. Redfern was a 'Hath not a Jew eyes?' speech. It was a political gesture of a deliberately simple kind, and one no different in essence from acknowledging that Australians of previous generations had suffered in war and peace. If the facts, motivations and behaviour were more complex than the speech recognised, so they were with the First AIF. If it did not tell the whole story, the story of Anzac is not the whole story. If it was a bleeding heart speech, pure and simple, it afforded to one group of Australians what the other group had been demanding ever since the recession and would continue to demand throughout the decade—recognition, that primary human need.

The speech could not afford to be bleak: it had to convey resolution, confidence, hope. Comparisons with Martin Luther King being inevitably invidious, rhetorical fireworks and high senti-ment were not attempted. The Redfern speech tried to be hopeful in a matter-of-fact way, as if we believed we would succeed, not because we had a dream, but because we had our share of humanity and a tradition of social justice. The speech did not say that our history was a story of unutterable shame. It said shameful things had been done and it assumed—perhaps wrongly—that no-one would infer from this that Keating thought they were the only things that had been done, or that similar deeds had not been done elsewhere. Had the speech been subjected to office scrutiny, doubtless some would have insisted on a caveat to the effect that Australia's history is no worse than anywhere else in this regard, and indeed is better than most. The office did not see it, and the Prime Minister expressed no such reservations. He read it with his breakfast and went to Redfern Park with every word intact, and I think knowing better than I did what it would mean to say them. He said nothing before the speech to indicate he had any doubts, and everything he said—and did—later was proof of his conviction that such a state-ment was due and appropriate. Perhaps he did feel some unease: in the plane to Sydney he pointed to a headline on the front of the *Canberra Times* which quoted him uttering a line of mine, the 'filleting of Fightback', and said: 'Look at that. You'll be able to say that you were the puppet master for the highest puppet in the land.' His car stopped at Redfern and he walked into the largely Aborig-inal audience while the rest of us continued to the Sydney office to prepare his business speech.

The problematic word turned out to be 'we'. From 'we' the inference has been drawn that the present generation of

Australians is responsible for the actions of previous generations. This was not intended. Nor was it anywhere implied that the modern generation does or should feel guilt about what had happened. '[T]here has been no shortage of guilt, but it has not produced the responses we need. Guilt is not a very constructive emotion,' he said. If anything, the Redfern speech began from the premise that where unconscious guilt is present, confronting the source offers the best hope of purging it: if the sins of the fathers are to be visited on the children, the children have a right to know what they were. 'We' no more meant that we are guilty of the crimes of our forebears than saying that 'we won the Ashes in 1938' means 'we' actually did it, and not Don Bradman's team; or that when we say 'we' brought civilisation and rabbits to this country, we mean you and I did.

The Redfern speech was the media story. Perhaps because the facts were not as well known as we thought, the public response surpassed everyone's expectations. It was headlined on news bulletins and newspaper front pages across Australia. Aboriginal leaders from all over the country phoned to express their gratitude. It was a good start, they said. In the *Sun-Herald* Peter Robinson praised Keating for being 'blunter, more decent and humble than any other Australian leader has ever been'. Radio and television news replayed sections of the speech over and over. In particular they played that part where the catcalls and booing were replaced by silence and then by applause—the part when Keating refused to be knocked off course. It was one of those moments when to write for him was an unqualified privilege.

Mark Ryan organised a book of the Prime Minister's speeches. A few days before its launch Don Russell asked whether it contained any 'speeches of substance'. The implication was obvious but we asked him for a definition. Did he mean the speech to the Business Council? It became one of our worst arguments. Had he noticed that Hewson's mooted changes to Fightback were a response to sentiments in the community which some of us had been trying to address all year. He denied that he had ever opposed me. I said I had his opposition on

292 | *Recollections of a Bleeding Heart*

record. He said he had a record going back five years, *proving* how clever he had been. I said I was glad to hear him say this with witnesses present. Later he came to my office and asked why I had taken such offence. I told him. He wagged his finger in my face. I threatened to hit him—a bizarre suggestion given his height advantage. If it was a power struggle, it was a very primitive one. Donald reminded me of the biggest boy in the sandpit telling everyone else what their names were, what they were good at, and where to stand, and pushing all invaders from his patch. At other times his blithe other-worldliness reminded me of those interest rates which had 'snapped' the economy. It was not a matter of blaming him; it was needing to see a sign that he knew what it meant to have your life's work 'snapped' by the same forces.

All through October and November the reports came in that the Liberal Party director, Andrew Robb, and Andrew Peacock and Petro Georgiou were trying to persuade Hewson to soften his policies. Every day we wondered: would they sack both Hewson and Fightback, or keep Hewson and draw the policy's sharper teeth? Would they have the courage to do to Keating what Labor had done to Malcolm Fraser, and drop John Howard into the leadership at the last minute? Hawke himself thought they might. Laurie Oakes thought not because the rancour would run too deep. It was clear by the beginning of December that either they could not bring themselves to do it, or they had told Hewson to change or face the sack. Then Hewson and Reith began having meetings with the sort of folk they had recently scorned—people like Merle Mitchell of ACOSS. Hewson told the country he was listening to the people, and that he would attend the National Press Club on 8 December to apprise Australians of certain modifications to Fightback.

The question was, how much compromise could their zealous leader stand? Wouldn't the humiliation unhinge him? Wouldn't it undo the assiduously maintained image of a man who was not for turning? Would anyone believe in Fightback with a human face? And how would they get their figures to add up?

Yet we dreaded it. On the morning of 8 December it was reported that Dr Hewson had spoken to Archbishop Holling-worth of the Brotherhood of St Laurence and the Church of England. The Prime Minister told the press that the 'lowbrows' were back in charge of the Liberal Party—the cynics. For obvious reasons this was not a line he could pursue very far without suggesting that his own criticisms of Fightback had been of the same low order. For ten days we had tried to second-guess and discredit the man who was above politics playing politics so cynically. When at last he did it at the Press Club he looked like a man who felt God see into his soul as he spoke, and who knew that His tremendous ear was bent to him and detecting every atom of hocus-pocus and bad faith. Rivers of sweat rolled down his cheeks. The nation blushed, as the Prime Minister later said. Yet it was impossible not to think that every bit of carefully calculated largesse swung the odds in his favour. We mocked his somersault, his transparent deceit, the hollowness of those words about his listening to the Australian people from the man who habitually charged Labor with compromising policy and sacrificing the national good in pursuit of votes. Why should anyone now believe him, the Prime Minister asked? We said it was clear that Fightback had been nothing more than a diversion. He could not fillet Fightback and leave himself with a backbone, the Prime Minister said. The leader of the Opposition only discovered his heart when he felt fear in it, the PM said, and it ran on the news five minutes later. We said some *very* telling things. But we knew that Fightback Mark II had raised the bar.

The keys to it were the removal of the GST from food, and the establishment of a $3 billion Rebuild Australia Fund. The latter, the *Financial Review* said, was 'not a very sensible piece of window dressing', but the same flagship financial journal admired Dr Hewson's 'powerful combination of short-term pragmatism and opportunism and genuine medium-term reform', a review that should have left its writer as embarrassed as Dr Hewson. The *Sydney Morning Herald* praised the new Dr Hewson and its chief correspondent, Geoff Kitney, said that with Fightback Mark

II, 'Hewson the politician was born'. The Prime Minister called it 'Crawlback' and privately expressed amazement at the uncritical treatment the altered document received. He threw everything at it, but two weeks after Hewson capitulated to the lowbrows Newspoll showed Labor's lead halved and Saulwick had the Coalition climbing 9 per cent to a seven-point lead.

With TV crews waiting for them on the beaches, US Marines invaded Somalia and knocked Dr Hewson's backflip off the front pages for a day. The Palace announced that the Prince and Princess of Wales had separated and knocked the latest employment figures off the front pages for a day. We thought of asking if Dr Hewson would protest at this diversion from the main game. It was revealed that the Speaker of the House, Leo McLeay, had received $65,000 in compensation for injuries he received when he fell off a Parliament House bicycle. The Prime Minister was in his office and feeling good about the world when we told him. The matter had been raised in the House as he strutted back after one of his very best days in Question Time. Who can say what makes someone who has already been elevated to unlikely station, salary and privileges seek even more from the public revenue, and to do it knowing that his actions will imperil the standing of the government and the prime minister who put him there? That exaggerated sense of entitlement which often comes with public office? There is also the creed of the NSW right which no-one on the outside can hope to understand. We saw the PM shake his head and his face darken when we told him, but no-one in his office knew exactly what the Prime Minister later said to his Speaker, or what others in the faction said to him. Would he get the blowtorch to the belly or find a dead animal in his bed? Not likely, much as we might hope. We got the feeling he was addressed more in sorrow than in anger, as if it were a lapse. What were brothers for if not to forgive lapses—even lapses which seemed to prove John Hewson right and it was indeed a government staggering towards oblivion.

There was no sorrow in the community. Talkback radio had a picnic. So did John Hewson. In the week before he announced his changes to Fightback the government increased its lead in the polls. Two days later Hewson, in some of them, was comfortably back in front. We saw it on the billboards on the way to Adelaide 'Hewson Surges in Polls'. A *Quadrant* poll had his popularity increasing by no less than 20 per cent. The Prime Minister was going to deliver the government's environment statement in the Botanical Gardens and to test what Hoggy called 'themes and rhetoric' in those seats we needed to win. It was a dress rehearsal for the election. The party faithful packed into halls in Unley, West Torrens, Kilburn and Henley and Grange. In front of pictures of Her Majesty, British and Australian flags and honour rolls from the World Wars, he told them how the government believed Australia should be a place where wealth was shared and those who fell behind were looked after; whereas John Hewson believed in breaking the mould of Australian society and creating a world of dog eat dog. He had tried to slip his own leash with the Fightback flip-flop but John Hewson would always be John Hewson. The crowds cheered. Outside half a dozen youthful demonstrators chanted about the rights of the 'young unemployed'. The Prime Minister excepted, they were the best dressed people in West Torrens. There is no disguising a Young Liberal's haircut.

In rooms adjoining a darkened bingo hall with a blue ice-cream container on every table he saw representatives of Adelaide's Greek community; then he saw the Greek archbishop at his home; then he had his photo taken with a couple of families who had gathered on the street outside, as he had with the proprietor and staff of the fish cafe together with a passer-by who thought he may as well; and everywhere saying hello, good on you, that's right. Good on you, love! That's very nice of you, love. Stick with us, darling.

The Wilderness Society chanted 'No woodchips! No woodchips!'. In the presence of the minister, Ros Kelly, Simon Crean, various South Australian Labor MPs, people from the department and the Murray–Darling Basin Commission, and all the green lobbies, the PM stood among the foliage in his Zegna and gave forth on the government's intentions for the Australian environment. Ros Kelly's polling showed that these days people were more interested in 'brown' issues like pollution, salinity and soil degradation and less interested in 'green' ones like trees, and the statement indicated that the government had taken notice. The National Farmers Federation approved the government's direction, but the environment lobby's leader quickly hived off to other trees and ran through their complaints with the media. That night Tricia Caswell, formerly of the union movement, now of the Australian Conservation Foundation, told the ABC that it was a great pity no political leader had a vision for the Australian environment like Al Gore had in the United States. The Prime Minister rang Caswell from a fish restaurant and scolded her severely. In doorstop interviews he described the perils to the environment from salinity and feral animals. He said the environment movement no longer had leaders, just people 'matching press release for release'. The lobbies thought they had a 'moral lien' over the environment, but they had no such thing, he said—the issue belonged to the nation. But that day he was more determined to say that Dr Hewson could not sell Telstra for the figure he had nominated without introducing timed local calls. We waited to see if the press would bite on 'Dr Hewson's telephone tax'. They didn't, but it was a start. The Prime Minister wished everyone a happy Christmas on the radio, and flew home feeling confident that his rhetoric had worked and that there were plenty of people out there who liked him. He took with him a dog, a German pointer pup, which he had picked up for the kids from a breeder in Prospect. It had a pedigree as long as your arm, of course.

The Hewson surge continued. Three days before Christmas a meeting was held at the offices of John Singleton's advertising agency in Sydney. We flew up grumbling about the Greens and the failure of the press to subject Hewson to any critical analysis since his backflip, including funding holes in Fightback Mark II. Graham Richardson was there, Bob Hogg and the amazing Singo himself who remembered me from the days when I wrote satire for Max Gillies. In 1983 he put a stop writ on an item by Stephen

Sewell in one of our shows and every night a heavily built man would stand at the back of the Nimrod Theatre to make sure that the offending words were not uttered. Gillies stood in silence for as many beats as the lines would have taken to speak and then resumed. He was nervous driving home.

At the Sydney meeting the Prime Minister was eloquent: 'They want to slit us,' he said, 'they want to slit us badly.' He demonstrated the productivity–unemployment equation with an elastic band. 'We are in the mature phase of the deregulated economy,' he told them. He explained the model: a modern, smart, educated country hooked to Asia. 'We are the people from *Terra Australis.*' Nationalism was a big plus for us. We are good at bigness, he said. We are also good at the community, I ventured, and suggested we stick to the One Nation rhetoric which had gone down well in Adelaide. Someone handed John Singleton a note and he reported that there were press crews out the front. Bob Hogg said the research groups were looking quite good: the negative campaign would be relatively easy, the positive one was harder. The Prime Minister put it in the following terms: 'We've got back the blue-collar base vote and the arty-crafties; we've got to get the middle-class vote and Hewson's tax might help us.' I left before the others and walked straight into a media crew. Some of them thought I was Bob Hogg and wanted to ask me questions. I spent Christmas dreaming about answers I might have given them.

Singo was on the plane that afternoon when I flew back to Melbourne. He waited for me in the terminal and offered me a lift into town. He was almost irresistibly warm, friendly, genuine and amusing; so much good nature and, one couldn't help thinking, the menace in proportion. He told me that one of his executives at the meeting was a Liberal who had volunteered to work on Labor's campaign because he was disgusted by Hewson's flip-flop. Paul Keating phoned me and said that Singo was basically a decent bloke who had taken a while to discover the party he belonged to. But there was one character there he didn't trust, he reckoned he was a Tory and he wanted him off the case.

At the office Christmas party he got up to the microphone, wobbled his knees and said, 'Jesus I'm rooted.' He then spoke in kindly fashion about each and every person in the PMO. He was very funny. He talked about what a 'nice' little group we were, as Don Russell had in an earlier address. The Prime Minister also said that we had been too narrowly economic. In the eighties he liked to be up there casting down the lightning bolts. But there was more to it than this. Economic rationalism was dead. Some people cheered and stamped their feet. He danced happily, while Annita told me how annoyed they had been with Mark Ryan because he was always so gloomy; and I told her that Mark was as devoted and loyal as anyone could be, but he was the one who always had to tell him the truth, say 'No' to him, put him in the way of political necessity, and suffer the rebukes. Was not her husband prone to gloomy bouts himself? I asked. It seemed strange, but just then, watching him groove on the dance floor and gaily flash his gums, gloominess seemed as unlikely as the judgment of two friends of mine, Lacanian psychoanalysts who admired him, but reckoned he was a phobic.

The Prime Minister must have very quickly identified with the new dog: two days after Christmas he left a message on my answering machine, 'I'm just up here wagging my tail. Give us a ring.' He was thinking about recalling parliament for a week so he could 'really get stuck into' Hewson. This Quixotic display was a response to a front-page story on the piggery in one of the Sunday papers. In the course of the year there had been claims of unaudited returns, breaches of corporation law; claims that he had paid $430,000 for a half share in the company that was valued at $4.2 million just six weeks after he bought in; and now, on 27 December, claims that the piggery was facing an action in the Supreme Court relating to $250,000 in unpaid workers' compensation premiums. Keating was furious. Both Hewson and Michael Baume waded into the fray. A fortnight later Keating sued Baume. But there was little he could do publicly: it had long been obvious that while he could hit harder, counter-punching usually hurt Keating more than Hewson. That was why every time he did the smart thing and stepped out of the public image of Paul Keating street fighter, the Liberals tried to drive him back to it. It was the story of the first year: Hewson trying to make Keating be Keating, and Keating trying to make Hewson be Hewson. It was the story of the first weeks in January, and the results were predictably ghastly.

While wagging his tail at the Lodge the Prime Minister wondered if the coming task would be made easier by a book about Hewson soon to be published by Pan Macmillan. It had been written by Christine Wallace, a Canberra journalist. We all strenuously hoped it would reveal some scandal about Hewson. As my wife was publishing at Pan, I got to read the book in manuscript over Christmas. Alas, in the sordid circumstances of the day, no scandalous malpractice was revealed: but there was enough there to consolidate the impression of a hungry fellow; and perhaps a rather hollow one. More striking than the account of how he had made his fortune was the chapter about his growing up. It revealed that dominating the landscape of his Baptist youth was a Catholic church on a hill. The circumstances in which he separated from his first wife were described but, contrary to a common public perception, relatively few people in politics and least of all Keating, would consider drawing attention to them. I sent him a note summarising the contents of the book and adding, among other equally futile and inconsequential suggestions, that he get some coaching in speech delivery; build a high-tech fibre optic national museum in cyberspace; do something about the condition of refugees in the detention centre at Port Hedland, at least by insisting that the department speed up the processing of applications; take 'recognition' wherever he went in the forthcoming campaign, and try to get beyond both John Hewson and Paul Keating and speak for the nation's vision. I knew he wouldn't reply.

He had had mixed reviews over the past month. On the ABC's *Lateline*, Kerry O'Brien had subjected him to an unmerciful end-of-year interview, discrediting One Nation and particularly its forecasts and its promise to return the budget to surplus. In the *Bulletin* Laurie Oakes scored it 'a disaster' for the Prime

Minister. A week later the same Laurie Oakes said in the same column that Keating had 'performed wonders politically'. Perhaps it was Christmas spirit. At an end-of-year caucus gathering in Parliament House, unlikely colleagues like Michael Duffy and Barry Jones cheerfully acknowledged the transformation he had wrought in the electorate, in the party and, Jones said, in himself—Jones thought he was now broader. Graham Richardson was reported as saying that never in Australian politics had there been as big a change as Keating had pulled off in the last twelve months. It was true, a year earlier the Coalition had been eighteen points ahead in the Morgan poll: they were now three points behind. It was 'amazing stuff', according to Richardson. Ramsey said Labor had 'climbed up out of the grave . . . on the back of Keating's political skills and political leadership'. And Peter Robinson declared that Keating had claims to being 'that rare creature, the all Australian political leader'. While he had 'a ruthless, sometimes repulsive, political instinct', there was in the broad sweep of his behaviour something to suggest 'a man who not only has nothing to hide or distort, but who is emotionally and physically incapable of distorting'. Robinson thought him rare in his ability 'to deal with the sweep and currents of national evolution. And he does it with passion, elan and raw honesty.'

On the face of things it was strange, therefore, that scarcely a month later the party's national secretary, Bob Hogg, painted a dismal picture of Keating's leadership. He told the *Australian*'s Glenn Milne that the party would not be 'hiding' the Prime Minister in the forthcoming election campaign, but Keating did not have the edge over Hewson that Hawke had over Peacock three years earlier. Keating came 'warts and all'. It might have been the years spent dealing with political pollyannas and egomaniacs, or the permanent wound of their ingratitude, or a manifestation of the personal disappointment implied in his journey from the party's left to its national pragmatist, or tiredness and depression like Keating's own, but by 1992 Bob Hogg was accompanied everywhere by a cloud of grim pessimism. The Weltschmerz went with a persona which appeared to disdain both cultivation and self-interest or ego. He was one of that category of successful political operators who are known, and like to be known, for calling it as they see it. This is an admirable trait, and much to be preferred over the tendency of scoundrels to call it as they don't. It remains true, however, that both categories retain the option of choosing what to see, and what to call and when. No-one is divorced from motive or judgment, even someone as inscrutable as Bob Hogg. It was not easy to see why on the verge of an election he told the media that Keating was less of a leader than Hawke, unless he was already looking for ways to excuse the defeat he expected.

Defeat was certainly on the cards. The first few weeks of January did not go well for the government. A National Australia Bank survey found the recovery sluggish and unemployment likely to reach as high as 12 per cent. This, as usual, was a sufficiently gloomy prospect to offset the government's good news that the One Nation investment development allowance had brought project applications from the private sector in excess of $60 billion; and even Bernie Fraser's prediction that the new Australian economy emerging from recession would sustain a decade-long boom with annual growth in the region of 4 per cent and inflation at 2 per cent or less. The government and the unions agreed to Accord Mark VII, which tied wage rises and superannuation benefits to the aim of creating 500,000 new jobs in three years—an aim which, like Fraser's prediction, was realised. Voters, however, do not have the benefit of foresight.

In an attempt to further prepare the electoral ground and freshen up the government's economic story and credentials, the Keating office and officers in the Department of Prime Minister and Cabinet secretly prepared an economic statement, called Investing in the Nation. It was to be pitched primarily at business, but after overcoming stiff resistance from Michael Keating and others, Anne Summers secured a substantial offering to women and working parents. Business got a company tax rate reduced from 39 per cent to 33 per cent—distinctly competitive, as the economists were prone to say, with our rivals in the region.

Women (and working parents) were to receive a 30 per cent rebate on their child care fees, collectable at Medicare agencies.

As best it could with little money to throw around, the statement sought to emphasise the positive amid the gloom, point the way in all the uncertainty and encourage the view that between us and our destination it was not far now. A McKinsey Report into Australian manufacturing suited these purposes admirably. It showed that an increasingly large proportion of the country's export growth was coming from the manufacturing sector, and particularly from a new, post-protection breed of companies making sophisticated products specifically for export. These companies were the future—born of new technology, free markets and the global economy. The McKinsey Report was in a small way heaven sent, with flecks of gold to show there was life, hope and reason to believe. Two years later it still helped underpin Labor's 'themes and rhetoric'. For now it helped the Prime Minister in his effort to say that he captained a ship with the new world in sight. He was as conscientious as ever, still active and expert. It would be madness to mutiny now, just as a new Australia became visible on the horizon.

While the main game was played behind a curtain of secrecy, everything else was politics. All the debates the government did not need found their way to the surface. The Camilla-gate tapes were published, but it didn't help the government's cause to have people talking about an Australian republic because the next King of Australia had once fancied himself as a tampon. The London tabloids stirred up the Singapore debate again, and Geoffrey Blainey and like minds in the RSL joined the fray in Australia. Tim Fischer took a redneck swipe at what he called the 'guilt industry', meaning those who shared the sentiments of the six High Court judges who found that Native Title existed, or those of the speech the PM had given at Redfern. The Coalition demanded and got a judicial inquiry into Leo McLeay. It was a measure of the government's bad luck, it seemed, that when the bicycle disintegrated beneath him, the Speaker had not been thrown headlong into a cement truck on its way to the site of the new Foreign Affairs building. Had he been poured into the slab of a building as unpopular as he was, would it have been a less likely chain of events than the one now causing the government such grief? No-one really wished such a fate to befall him of course, but after the inquiry was called, for a couple of days no-one felt kindly when McLeay refused to stand down. Some wished the Prime Minister would sack him and say that Australians were entitled to be sure that politicians were not enjoying privileges they lacked. Twice in that first year when members of the right seemed set to put their own political interests before the Prime Minister's and the government's, the Prime Minister chose to mainly grin and bear it. When finally McLeay took the same unselfish course as Graham Richardson and stood down, the days of his intransigence seemed all the more pointless—even more so when the payment made him was judged legal and proper by the inquirer, Sir Laurence Street.

All through January the Prime Minister was in a state of profound political agitation. This was masked somewhat by an interview with Michelle Grattan in which he said, a lifetime of politics notwithstanding, his true profession was 'aesthete'. Accordingly the photograph caught him, not on the hustings or among the hoi polloi, but alone on the grand staircase beneath the dome in Elizabeth Bay House. Flying back from Sir Paul Hasluck's funeral in Perth, with Mahler's Fifth Symphony playing, he agreed reluctantly to take instruction in speech delivery from Baz Luhrmann, and to give a modern American dual autocue a trial. We asked him if he had seen Hewson at the funeral. He had, and there he was, he said, true to form, helping some poor old crone across the road for the benefit of the cameras. We asked what he would do if he lost the election. He said he would tell the Australian people that they were idiots and resign. It would be the most ungracious speech in the country's history. He wanted Dawkins to succeed him, because Dawkins had ideas and wouldn't be bought by the tiny minds of caucus. Some of Dawkins' ideas were mad, but they were ideas. And what if he won? Move the navy out of Garden Island in Sydney Harbour and move the national parliament in. It would be there where it always should have been, ready for the republic. It was a wonderful flight. The next morning we saw the picture on the front pages—Dr Hewson outside the church in Perth helping Dame Pattie Menzies across the road.

The *Sydney Morning Herald* ran a pre-publication extract from Chris Wallace's book about Hewson. It described how the Baptist proto-missionary for Christ became a full-blown missionary of the markets and how, in the course of becoming moderately rich in the previous decade, the leader of the Opposition managed to consistently pay tax at only 15 cents in the dollar. He had done it by tax minimisation practices which were strictly legal (and very common), but which were condemned both in Fightback and in a speech Hewson had given to the Press Club as part of a 'tax cheat mentality'. When the extract outlining Hewson's history and methods appeared in the *Sydney Morning Herald* on 27 January, Keating felt he could not let it pass. He accused Hewson of 'dubious and slick practices', and soon after the newspapers reported that the Prime Minister seemed certain to recall parliament and expose his opponent's record before calling the election. It was also said that Keating would use the nation's parliament to launch the critical attack on Fightback Mark II that the media conspicuously had failed to do.

It was true, Fightback Mark II had not been analysed in the press; its credibility went unquestioned while journalists wondered aloud how Keating could hope to beat the new 'political' Hewson. And how could Keating not be tempted by the chance to make it known everywhere that the man who wanted to impose a consumption tax on everybody else had done everything possible to minimise his own tax. He had lectured the country on the iniquities of a system in which PAYE taxpayers bore the burden while others incorporated themselves and paid next to nothing on property deals. You have this dreadful unfairness, he had declared, when you have such a gap between the company and the personal rate. Yet he had enriched himself by exploiting the system. He could say fairly that what he did was legal. But he would put a consumption tax on those who spent everything they earned, while the well off would, as he had, pay 'as needs be, upon advice from a tax accountant'. The essential point was Dr Hewson's 'philosophy', he said. Although he did not throw it wildly, it was a punch he had to throw. Unfortunately it landed on a tar baby.

The Liberals said Keating had reduced the tax on a $4 million profit in the piggery to zero; and Keating had no sooner furiously denied this than Alexander Downer said he had 'sunk to new depths of hypocrisy', and Peter Reith said he had got down in the gutter again. Keating said he had never placed his Elizabeth Bay house in company ownership to minimise tax and claim repairs on it against tax on other income; that his was not property speculation like Hewson's had been, but investment in the kind of world class export industry the country needed. Hewson said that 'quite frankly' he was not going to be part of such wickedness. 'We're all out here trying to re-build Australia . . . If he wants to stay in the gutter, that's fine.' Then he went on television to say that Keating might have 'personally benefited' from government decisions; and when questioned about it in Brisbane the next morning demanded that the reporters stick to the real issues like unemployment. Coalition members never mentioned the Wallace book, but played it as if Keating had dredged up the stories himself. It was a travesty and very clever and it went very well for them, as Wayne Swan, adviser to the Queensland Premier, pointed out to us when he sent us a poll from the seat of Moreton.

Parliament was not recalled. On 7 February the Prime Minister called a press conference. Amazingly the journalists seemed not to know why. It was because that morning he had got in his wife's car, a humble burgundy Magna, and driven himself and two of his daughters out the gates of the Lodge. Not a single photographer or journalist had thought to follow them. He drove to the Governor-General's residence in Yarralumla. Now he told them that a federal election would be held on 13 March. Everyone had decided that it would be 27 March. Bob Hogg was among them. The party was not ready, the advertising was not ready, the 'themes and rhetoric' were not, in his view, ready. Furthermore, Keating had contrived a campaign in which not one but two sets of employment figures would be released, the second of them in the last week before the poll. Hogg was appalled, the more so when he learned that an economic statement had been prepared without his knowledge. But Keating was happy, and not only because he had fooled the press. Each last day of the phoney campaign had been alienating the public, confusing the issues, agitating caucus and dissipating the government's confidence and energy. He would throw the rock in the pond, and the next day everything would be different.

'Themes and rhetoric' mean lines repeated until the point is reached when the person uttering them can scarcely stand it any more. It is at this point, some experts say, that the people begin to get the message. In the end it all reduces to a slogan—a battle cry. But what sort of battle cry is this? 'We have unemployment because, rather than investing, corporations and financial institutions have been strengthening their balance sheets and reducing debt levels accumulated during the excesses of the late eighties!' Alan Greenspan described the same thing in the US just the other day. So take heart! The good part is that the Opposition, gripped by the same need to simplify, will hardly be pausing to tell people that business investment in December 1992 was 33 per cent down on the March 1989 high, and investment in non-dwelling construction was down 39 per cent on September 1989. So lose heart!

Victory was not going to be decided by an argument about corporate debt/equity ratios. True, they were falling; true, having tightened their lending guidelines the banks must soon loosen them again, and move to lending to new businesses on cash flow rather than relying on property values; true, the process of debt restructuring must soon be completed. But it was not going to win an election.

CHAPTER 11

*But obviously man is a political animal in a sense in which a
bee is not, or any other gregarious animal. Nature, as we say,
does nothing without some purpose; and she has endowed man
alone among the animals with the power of speech.*

ARISTOTLE, THE POLITICS, BOOK I

PAUL KEATING DELIVERED Labor's 1993 election campaign
address in his electorate of Blaxland in Sydney's working-
class west—a stone's throw from the houses of his childhood and the first years of his marriage. In the Bankstown Sports
Club he stood in front of a cobalt blue curtain that the film-maker
Baz Luhrmann had chosen because it took the 'greens' out of the
Prime Minister's Spanish colouring and softened his features.
To achieve a similar effect Luhrmann's little team of postmodern
whizzes added blue to the Max Factor he carried with him and
often applied himself, and insisted on suits of a lighter colour.
Luhrmann wanted those soft brown eyes aimed at the camera
where people could see, admire and (it was our fervent hope) trust
them and so, to lift his gaze, he raked the seating in the hall.

That was all Luhrmann did. His original design had the
stars of the Southern Cross on the curtain. He showed the model
to Anne Summers, Mark Ryan, Bob Hogg and me in a room at
the Ramada. It was modest in size, simple in design, utterly arresting and breathtakingly bold. At first sight it caused eyes to well
tears and veins to bulge with national sentiment we did not know
we owned. It was the most perfect and least prolix statement of a

country's hope, aspiration and promise; a glimpse of what could be in a new world country not at the mercy of the past, or prey to fear, prejudice and manipulation. As soon as we saw it we knew it was hopeless. Hogg was first to say so. Australians would think Keating was standing in front of the flag he intended to impose on them. And if they did not think this, the Opposition would certainly tell them that they should think it, and the flag would be the media story for days, and at the very least we would have a huge distraction from the main issue which was the Opposition's goods and services tax. And all this would make us look very stupid, which always compounds the penalty for political mis-judgment. No-one needed persuading. Baz's stars were beautiful, but impossible as politics. So Paul Keating stood in the Banks-town Sports Club with a plain blue Presbyterian sort of curtain behind him, and before him a cheering audience of six hundred. They cheered and cheered. He had the speech on the lectern but he couldn't get started over the din. The speech he was about to read began this way.

> Let there be no mistake. This *is* the most important election in memory.
>
> Today we stand against radical right-wing proposals which are hostile to fundamental Australian beliefs and Australian institu-tions and all that we have achieved in recent years.
>
> Not new proposals but old ones.
>
> Proposals which have been tried in other countries and which in every case have failed—at great social and economic cost.
>
> Dr Hewson says these other countries did not try hard enough. He is nothing if not zealous. In this election there is Dr Hewson —Dr Hewson and Tim Fischer—or there is Labor.
>
> I ask every Australian to think about this:
>
> When you wake up on March 14, whoever has won the election, there will still be unemployment. There will still be problems to solve.
>
> If Labor is re-elected there will also be an Accord between the unions and the government, guaranteeing industrial peace, low

inflation and a continuation of that spirit of cooperation. There will still be Medicare . . . There will still be . . . [Here other significant social programs were listed, before the crescendo]

And there will be every reason to believe that we will continue to succeed in our ambition to become a great trading nation, a great Australian social democracy, a proud and independent country, united and cohesive—and able to deliver to all our people living standards and a way of life unequalled in the world.

If one had written stage directions to follow this they might have said: long pause, scan audience with piercing gaze, speak slowly and distinctly on the downbeat.

And there will be no GST. [over the roar] No miserable 15 per cent tax on virtually everything you buy.

It was fifteen months since Keating had deposed Bob Hawke as leader. Now Hawke was up the front and staring balefully like Banquo's ghost along with other past leaders of the party, including Gough Whitlam and Neville Wran. Senior members of his cabinet, party officials, trade union leaders, rank and file of the Australian Labor Party—the whole glum, rancorous, triumphant thing holding itself together for one more go at the prize, waiting on Paul Keating to make them believe the hope was not forlorn. Not a few were still waiting to be convinced that the execution of Hawke would yield a political dividend.

A little more than thirty years ago, just down the road, aged fifteen, Paul Keating had joined the Labor Party. The party had been split then: not formally in New South Wales, but psychologically broken apart by the struggle over communism. It had been like this all through his childhood and youth. The gruelling anti-communist movement beginning in his father's day with Jack Lang's mad, doomed crusades against the federal party; the fight with the reds for control of the unions; and then the long campaign to reunite Catholics with the party. Paul Keating had grown up with it. It was the way of the world. Things fractured and things were put back together. Malice and spite were normal. Brutal acts were necessary. So, all the more, was the love of a family necessary, the moral order of a church, the gentleness and warmth required to knit the broken bones and make them whole again.

His family was sitting in the same front row: his mother, Min, his wife Annita and their four children. His father wasn't there, and it's a fair guess Paul Keating wished he was. Matt Keating had died not far from where Paul now stood and did not see his son become Treasurer of the Commonwealth of Australia and then Prime Minister. Paul Keating would always be sorry about that. He was also sorry because relations between his wife and his mother were not as he wished them to be. He talked about it frequently: how he sometimes felt as if he were being forced to choose between the family in which he had been born and nurtured and the family he had made with Annita. Wider family contact and occasions together were less frequent than he would have liked. The seeds of the problem had very likely been there from the start; but Paul Keating believed the rot set in during those years when he was trying to drive the government and get the job off Hawkey at the same time. This personal dimension to the 'three lost years' made it all the harder for him to forgive Bob Hawke. The pressures of the treasurer's job had been heavy enough, and much of the work had come home to the family's rented house in Canberra where Annita raised the children uncomplainingly, rode the blows with him, urged him to keep going when he wavered. That pressure they had survived. But when Bob broke those unbreakable undertakings about the leadership and he had to fight to take it from him, and all the time he was carrying much of the government burden Bob should have been carrying—that was when, it seemed to him that his marriage was put under a considerable strain. He lived with the sense that something in his personal life was shifting. The warm bath of familial affection he had long enjoyed and perhaps taken too much for granted on some days felt more like an obstacle course. And they were all there in the front row.

To put the task facing him into perspective he had as usual spent much of the morning listening to music. Against Richard Strauss' *Metamorphoses*, Heifetz playing the Bruch Violin Concerto, Klemperer conducting Mahler, a speech was a speck of dust. He was never one for elaborate rehearsals, but that morning he seemed particularly distracted and was unable to muster enough concentration to do more than browse his way through it. If Paul Keating had been a horse in a mounting yard no-one would have backed him. Early that morning Baz Luhrmann had gone to Kirribilli to rehearse his delivery, but he never got past the Mahler. Later at a motel in Bankstown, as he waited to go to the sports club, I suggested that the PM read it aloud once more, to see if there were any glitches. Better to iron them out now, I said. He re-read the first couple of pages, including the emphasis on 'is' in the opening line, but that was all. It was not so surprising. Often he would not react to a serious challenge until he felt the shadow of the axe above him. It would be the same before the Press Club performance, three days from the election. As Jimmy Warner waited in the car outside the Lodge, he was in his office poring over revised plans for buildings along East Circular Quay. The buildings were too tall. They had been lowered but he wanted them lower still. He had asked Ric Simes to bring the drawings up from the PMO. Nothing could persuade him that the Press Club cause was greater. On the wall, the Italian mezzo soprano Cecilia Bartoli smiled down from a portrait she had signed for him. We gazed at the prima donna and practised breathing.

He said later he had been quite unfazed at the time, but when he finally rose to speak at Bankstown it is possible that he felt more than the usual pressure of a big political moment, more than he was conscious of, perhaps. He had only learned an hour before that Hawke would be sitting up the front. And there were Annita and Min. At the motel he had felt the chill between them. It is just possible that somewhere in his mind the thought was stirring that his happiness was held together by the most fragile threads, that disintegration always threatened. That might have been why, when the crowd would not stop cheering, he said,

'Aren't you nice'. He said it five times. 'Nice' is a favourite Keating word. We all worked in a nice little office, more of a family than an office he would say, and we ran a nice little show rather like the one we hoped Australia would become. Nice puts everyone together. Nice is the opposite of strife. It comes after the war and the din—like neoclassical architecture and a Mahler adagio.

Not every sentence in that speech now reads as felicitously as it should. There were cloying bits around the social measures which themselves read like a shopping list and begged to be heard as pork-barrelling. In the patches of dull phrasing there were signs of the committee process which necessarily bears down on all policy launch speeches, and the exhaustion of energy and imagination which also afflicts them. A policy speech presents more problems than any other speech principally because it is such a test of stamina; the final test of your ability to say for the thousandth time as if it were the first, why one exists, why one ought to exist, why one has more of a right to exist than one's opponents—and to hold off the ennui and self-loathing long enough to do it. A policy speech is written to be read aloud, before a well-primed audience, and before television. Immediately after the last word is delivered the process of cutting it to TV replay length begins, the arguments about it begin. The Bankstown speech in 1993 was like any other policy speech in these essentials. It was a performance piece, but it took account of the performer's unwillingness to engage in theatre or histrionics. To work satisfactorily the speech needed only a low level of attack—enough to leave no-one wondering what he meant or whether he believed it.

For the first minute or two, however, Paul Keating seemed to be ambushed by emotions. He ought to have anticipated the heady enthusiasm of the audience—it happens at campaign launches—but it seemed to catch him by surprise. If those vagrant thoughts did indeed weigh in, it was perhaps a wonder that he could speak at all. Some people cry at times like this. Actors have been known to 'dry'. Some of us find our tongues seem to thicken and the words will not form in our mouths. This seemed to happen to Paul Keating. He stumbled on the first five words: 'Let there be . . .' sounded very like 'Let there me', and he uttered the second sentence without the emphasis on 'is'. There was no appreciable conviction in any of the first two dozen lines. He said 'March the fourteen' and, instead of 'continuation' (it should not have been there anyway), he said 'continuity'. As Barry Jones said later, he sounded sibilant. No-one had seen him so nervous as he seemed in those first couple of minutes. Despite the applause on cue from the audience, he did not even attempt the desired crescendo. The equally desired diminuendo therefore also languished. He became steadily more fluent, but only in the last five minutes did he deliver the lines with precision and confidence. Throughout his tone was soft, almost lilting—almost *Irish*. There was none of the famous aggression; instead, a kind of artless sincerity, as if he was aiming not to inspire so much as to heal. But this was a staged political event and the audience would hardly sit in judgment on the tone of things. They cheered every policy announcement, every good line and every half-good one, regardless of how he delivered them. There would be a guarantee of training or a wage subsidy for those who gave jobs to the long-term unemployed; an easier assets test for pensioners and cheap pharmaceuticals for low income non-pensioners; free basic dental care for 2 million low-paid or welfare-receiving Australians; an increase in the Dependent Spouse Rebate; fee relief for occasional child care; 10,000 private hospital beds would be made available for public patients; a Department of Regional Development to address uneven growth and employment across the country; young people in regional Australia would be able to listen to the rock station JJJ; everyone would be able to use a portion of their superannuation to help them put a deposit on a home. In all, $1.1 billion worth. It always seems a pity to reduce politics to material bribes, but such things reveal the truth about the system which vision things never do. These are the organ meats of politics—the essentials to some minds, offal to others.

The speech attempted a kind of incorporation of the

people. It was the people who had made the revolution: 'The Australian people are bringing into being a new Australia.' If what that presumed was not quite an irresistible tide, it *was* a sense of shared ambition, with the government doing little more than the people's will or the desire of their collective unconscious—and that was some presumption. But by this means he came at last to the grand moment, and when he said that a second Keating Government would move the country towards a referendum on a republic, the applause was deafening and sustained. 'It's time,' he repeated over the din. At the end they were exultant; who knows if it was because they had just seen a politician without a mask or any other artifice. They cheered Paul Keating to the rafters and when his family came on stage, albeit in an awkward operation, his happiness was palpable and infectious. And when his speech-writer, watching it all on a screen in an adjoining room, tried to say something to a colleague he found that he could not get the words out. His tongue appeared to have swollen in his mouth.

In the media, we probably broke even. TV comment varied from the noncommittal to the arch and dismissive. Yet the sight of a kind and strangely humble Keating was probably good for Labor's cause. In the newspapers Geoff Kitney said the speech was 'unusual for its earnestness and depth of content', but it was hard to think other than that it might have been 'a reluctant valedictory'. Under the circumstances—namely a nine-year incumbency plus a million unemployed—it was, said Kitney, probably the best he could have done. That was the general opinion, though not everyone put it as generously. Tom Burton said it was 'his first and probably last' campaign launch. Steve Burrell, the economics writer, said he should have dropped the tax cuts—and Hewson should drop his as well. Some of the opinion pieces were scathing. Glenn Milne, who might have had a word with the national secretariat, said the mention of the republic was 'conceived in desperation' and risked being seen as a 'cynical diversion' or a 'personal indulgence', and was driven by Keating who 'privately carries republicanism like a torch', and by his office. The headlines talked in the familiar way about 'grab bags of promises'. Almost as familiar was the complaint that it lacked a vision—as if a vision was not a promise and had no consequences for the budget. Because it contained a number of promises—as nearly all such speeches do—the *Sydney Morning Herald* headlined their first edition 'Pork Barrel Republic!' 'Low key', they said in their editorial; also 'ambitious, politically dexterous, costly, provocative and risky'. Their chief political reporter, Mike Seccombe, said Keating had delivered a 'stirring' speech which 'struck the perfect balance between contrition for all that had gone wrong, recognition that recovery would take a long time . . . and hope for the future'. We couldn't have put it better ourselves.

The contrition issue had dogged him all year. Time and again the PM had been hectored and urged to apologise for the recession, the bankruptcies, the unemployment, even the rate of suicide. He had always refused to apologise and he was not apologising now. But he did recognise his 'responsibility' for the problems the country faced. He conceded that 'Governments in Australia in the eighties were not always as prudent or wise as they might have been.' He also recognised that with some of the essential economic gains had come social hardship—in particular, productivity gains in business and industry were adding to the numbers of unemployed. He took responsibility for the bad with the good. Contrite perhaps, but on more favourable terms than any the media had demanded. It was in the shape of an embrace. In the great project to remake Australia there had been casualties and casualties are always to be regretted. But, he was almost saying, casualties are no reason to abandon our cause. On the contrary, if their sacrifice was not to be in vain we must go on. That was the unspoken message. We've been through so much together, let us go on together. Let us make the change that Australia needs but let's not upset the apple cart, as Dr Hewson would have us do. Let us not break the mould.

His message was strength through unity and cooperation, a society and a nation of shared values and ideals, a pervasive sense of shared responsibility. In an era of change, he said, 'the watchwords of government should be care, support, cooperation'. He had learned that in Bankstown. In tough times you stick together. Under that ordinance he placed Labor's great initiatives—the Accord, Medicare, education for all, extensive social services and all the other elements of the social wage developed in the previous decade. This was Labor's 'inclusive' society: a social democracy sustained by the wealth-creating power of free markets and economic integration with the world economy, and made strong by a practical ethic of social cooperation and fair distribution. In the story itself there was strength—and optimism. It was a 'remarkable' story. From there it was an easy—if politically risky—segue to the republic. What was an Australian republic if not the natural expression of the country remade? Everyone was welcomed aboard. Any who fell back would be gathered up again. As Seccombe noted, the recurring words were of the 'caring', 'community' kind. Free markets were mentioned only once. But the speech pointed to the signs that the economy was improving, and that it was a different kind of economy; a more efficient, robust, varied and competitive one; and that this was due to Labor's deregulatory initiatives was not left open to doubt. The recovery had indeed been slow, but now Australia was growing faster than any country in the OECD. The new export economy would be so much stronger and so much better equipped to succeed in the world—especially the fastest growing part of it, the part in which we lived, Asia and the Pacific.

The election speech was almost identical in theme and tone to the speech that launched One Nation a year before. It was bound to be, if only because in those twelve months the economy had refused to give an unambiguous sign that it was firmly on the mend. For every good figure there had been a bad one. There were reasons to be confident and reasons to be worried. It was also because Hewson's radical right blueprint for the country had breathed new life and meaning into Labor's traditional social alternative. Not that Labor in the eighties had abandoned the language of social justice and improvement; it was just better known for what it did than what it said, and much of what it did was in the name of free markets. Labor has always talked about such things while doing what was necessary or possible to reconcile free enterprise with the general good. Leftists and Labor people of days past might baulk, but Keating Labor was concerned with 'civilising capitalism' in much the same degree as Billy Hughes and Andrew Fisher were, or John Curtin and Ben Chifley, albeit with less formal (and pointless) obeisance to the socialist ideal. Critics from the same school said that privatisation breached Labor's most fundamental principles: Keating and his colleagues of the past decade could reply, but Medicare fulfils them as none of our predecessors did, and so does the Accord and the Family Allowance Supplement and all the other components of the modern social safety net. Critics said that deregulation of the economy was the antithesis of Labor: Keating said that socialisation of the economy had once proved all but the *end* of Labor, and revisited it would be—once and for all.

For eighteen months John Hewson had every right to believe that the prime ministership was in the bag. But Keating did to Hewson what he and his colleagues had done to the Liberals for a decade—he drove him further and further to the right. It wasn't hard: in the course of the year Hewson's enthusiasm and self-belief took a near-fanatical turn which the public found disquieting. At times he seemed interested only in doing the impossible. If he won it would be despite himself; above all, it would be despite a 15 per cent GST on everything except food. The election was not quite a referendum on the new tax, but it was the dominant issue. Hence the theme of the speech—all these good things the people could have, and no GST. John Hewson's GST. The government's glucose drip. It sustained us through the darkest times, all year long.

For the election slogan, Bob Hogg's suggestion, 'Let's Advance Australia', did not grab my imagination; and when I suggested 'Advance Australia *Fair*' it did not grab his. I also suggested 'Community and Nation': it had a no-nonsense old-fashioned ring to it, it played to the disaffected provinces, and 'community' flagged our rather poorly apprehended interest in the lives of ordinary people. Hogg did not like it. Community was a word that Joan Kirner had made much of and in some ALP quarters that was proof of its inefficacy. When the election was called we still had not agreed on a slogan—unless you called 'No GST!' a slogan. By contrast, the Opposition were armed with the catchy 'Labor's Got to Go'. They opened their advertising blitz with television images of faces in a crowded street picked out at random by a telescopic gunsight. The notion was derived from research revealing that unemployment was the most widespread fear in Australian society. The sight settled on an innocent face, viewers heard the gun cocked, a flicker of fear ran across the face and a voice said: 'Don't be next. Labor's got to go.'

It was curious, then, that 1993 is remembered as the election Labor won with a scare campaign, the more so given that in the month before the election John Hewson and the Coalition sounded alarms wherever they could half-plausibly do so. There would be a double-dip recession. The Reserve Bank did not have enough reserves to support the Australian dollar. Unemployment would go to 12 per cent. But their advertisements called Keating 'the scumbag of scare'. Such epithets were widely employed in the campaign: the *Financial Review* of 1 March reported that 'independent market research' found business had turned savagely against Keating, that its representatives had called him variously a 'viper', a 'gutter rat', a 'boorish oaf', an 'undertaker' and a 'gutter brawler', and reckoned he was 'running scared' and 'looking like a loser'.

On the first day of the campaign Paul Keating was locked up in a studio in Sydney with a camera in front of him and an Australian flag behind him. He spent a whole day there at Acme film studios with Richo and Singo and Hoggy, reading scripts to camera for Labor's free-to-air advertisements. He was told that the scripts had been written by his speechwriter and scrutinised by Don Russell and Mark Ryan. We three were indeed in the same building, and we were indeed working on scripts under the sporadic supervision of Bob Hogg, but the scripts we worked on and the scripts Keating was asked to read were not the same. Nor were we aware that the notorious campaigner for a new

Australian flag was about to go to air with the old one draped behind him, Union Jack aggressively to the fore. At the end of the day we were taken to meet our master and view the rough cuts. It was like a Hollywood nightmare. The Prime Minister resembled a kidnap victim who had just endured a day of torture, and the 'advertisements' looked more like forced confessions. His eyes were dark and haunted, his yellowy green pallor clashed horribly with the red, white and blue backdrop. Surely he can't have the flag behind him, we said: our enemies will manufacture a storm of protest against his hypocrisy, and nothing he says—for the little it is worth—will be heard. His captors were unsympathetic: we were going to get a lesson in political reality whether we liked it or not. The words he had been given were as banal as the images were inappropriate, and the rendering of them painful. Driving back to Kirribilli, the Prime Minister, looking like a man at the end of a campaign rather than the beginning, woke from the nightmare and tried to phone Bob Hogg.

So, from the first day the relationship with the national secretariat turned dirty. There were bitter arguments and accusations of incompetence. The hardheads of the party like to get together with the hardheads of the press and nod sagely and mutter great oaths about what is Realpolitik—and so it was inevitable that the disputes would find their way into the newspapers. It was said that the Prime Minister's Office was trying to run the campaign as no campaign had ever been run, and yet the office was inexperienced; incompetent, arrogant and lacking in battle-hardness, according to some 'senior cabinet members', one report said. It was true that no-one in the office had ever run a campaign before; it seemed just as true that no-one outside it knew how to run this one either. To bridge the divide the amiable and non-aligned Bob McMullan was asked to be an intermediary, working between the PMO, the secretariat and Singleton's. McMullan had been the party's national secretary in the eighties and parliamentary secretary to the treasurer from 1990 to 1993. Although McMullan's unvarying caution sometimes provoked explosions and reckless threats in the PM, the arrangement worked tolerably well. The lamentable free-to-air advertisements were never used, and the press took this as another sure sign that Labor was unprepared and probably on the ropes.

The truth was neither side had much reason for confidence, and both had much to fear. A swing of 0.9 per cent in just five seats was all the Coalition needed to win. The polling suggested they would do it, but not in a way that left Labor without hope. The fear for Hewson was losing the unlosable election, failing to pull back the miserable 1 per cent he needed to wrest power from a government with a recession and a million unemployed on its conscience. Keating's position was no less delicate: he could buoy himself—we all could—with the delicious prospect of snatching victory *despite* the unemployment horror, the huge electoral deficit he inherited, the nay-saying of the press and the Schadenfreude of various parties on the Labor side. But in proportion to the hope was the dread of failing and the certain knowledge that if he did, judgment would be savage. They would say that Keating was the man who overthrew Labor's most successful leader and delivered government to a barely competent, far right novice promising a 15 per cent tax.

As much by accident as design, Labor's first week was extraordinarily high tone. The economic statement was preceded on the Monday by a speech on Australia's relationship with Asia and the Pacific. The PM said the government would make employment growth through an improved trade performance a priority. A Labor government would strengthen APEC—'a market of 2 billion people producing half the world's output, bound together with harmonised trade rules, harmonised investment rules, harmonised standards and certification'. It was not traditional election material—the speech had been agreed to long before the election was called—but it was no bad thing to start above the ruck and remind everyone, including the Prime Minister, that great works remained to be done. 'I am utterly convinced,' he said, 'that our prosperity, our national wellbeing, our ability to maintain and build a good society, depend on our . . . moving boldly to integrate our economy with the economies of East Asia.' His economic statement was mainly praised in the Sydney media and mainly derided in Melbourne and the other capitals. In Melbourne one commentator said he looked like a man on Mogadon, in Sydney they said he looked remarkably relaxed. Close-up he looked like both. Some said the child care scheme would be welcomed, some said it was middle-class welfare of the kind Labor had spent a decade rooting out. Keating said that it marked his government's recognition that child care was henceforth, like aged care and education, a right not a privilege—a universal right because working women were a universal reality. It could not have come from very deep in his heart, but he said it.

Small business organisations said the economic statement did nothing for them, and some people pointed out that the drop in the company rate would encourage the sort of tax minimisation schemes for which Hewson had just been roasted. It was better than promising not to tell lies and encouraging South Australians and Territorians to believe he would build the Alice–Darwin railway, which was what Hewson did in the first week. Keating did not have a brilliant first week, but Hewson's was thoroughly ordinary, and it remained to be seen whether Australians were impressed by his conducting roadside interviews in shorts and singlet and dripping with sweat. He ran on Cottesloe beach with footballers, he crutched sheep in the dust, he played soccer in the rain, he got down among the throng because, in his own words, John Hewson was a politician who would 'look you in the eye'. Whether Australians wanted him to do this remained arguable. He dealt fearlessly with hecklers and still kept to his lines: 'They send people like you along to scare me,' he shouted at them. 'You know the most scary thing? Another three years of Labor.' Michelle Grattan, for one, was very impressed by all this.

It is very doubtful if Paul Keating had run ten metres in twenty years. Blearily watching Hewson on the evening news, he reckoned it was further proof that his opponent was dangerous, if not a creature from another planet. There were signs of obsession in some of his own performances, however. Sometimes he suffered a relapse of that old condition which had him imagining he was still the treasurer; and, as one journalist observed tartly, there were 'too many eye-glazing explanations of why we are so lucky to have him'. But no-one could accuse him of carelessly expending energy and, unlike Hewson who shamelessly borrowed his from Bill Clinton, no-one could say Keating's campaign style was less than all his own. He was regularly late, frequently distracted, sometimes uninterested and often opaque when his staff badly needed to know what he was thinking.

In the first week the annual tide of school-leavers pushed unemployment through a million. Labor was wounded but, because the seasonally adjusted rate fell from 11.3 to 10.9 instead of rising as predicted, it was thought not fatally. Hewson said 'you can't seasonally adjust people', which was glib and predictable, but probably the best he could do with it. And who were we to talk? In fact the campaign coincided with a series of encouraging economic statistics: profits, exports, industry investment and job vacancies all improved. It made life a little easier for Labor, but everyone knew the telling statistic would be the one which measured unemployment in the last week of the campaign.

Election campaigns are politics reduced to its most grue-somely banal and its most vividly poetic. Day after day is spent chasing the best photo and the best sound grab. No plan survives contact with the enemy, as the military strategists say; but in polit-ical campaigns everything is planned and nothing must throw the campaigners off strategy; yet everyone knows unpredictable things will happen and sometimes they will *need* them to happen; and everyone knows that it is pure folly to stay on strategy if the strategy is not working, or if something comes along which is better than the strategy. History suggests that for every good strategy there are at least ten bad ones and, good or bad, every strategy is also an idée fixe. Like many other human calamities, the first battle of the Somme was fought according to a strategy and so was the second one. It is strange when history contains so many failed strategies, and so many which achieved the opposite of their intention, that in modern politics no-one ever says, 'Let's not have one this time. Let's just play it by ear.' The death of Fred Hollows, possibly Australia's best loved citizen, was not on strategy and it was not predicted to occur during the early days of the campaign. But both leaders attended the state funeral at St Mary's, Sydney, on 15 January and the front-page photographs of Paul Keating kissing Hollows' widow, Gabi, were probably the best taken of him during the campaign. It would not have been possible to manufacture such a photo or such an opportunity, and it was not possible then or now to look at that photograph of the passionate prime minister and the beautiful widow without thinking it must have been worth VOTES.

Manufactured opportunities never fail to look manufactured. Stunts, as every experienced campaigner knows, are always recognised as stunts and untold numbers of voters think them odious. It is axiomatic in politics that the only stunts people remember are stunts that go wrong. But there never was a campaign in which both sides didn't try them. Early in the 1993 campaign John Hewson and State Coalition leaders got together and pledged to abolish payroll tax. Labor said it was a stunt. On commercial radio in Western Australia John Hewson accepted Howard Sattler's challenge to pledge himself to tell no lies in the campaign. Keating refused it—he said it was a stunt. Throughout the campaign Labor visited all sorts of shops and workplaces to drive home the point that the GST was discriminatory, anomalous, inflationary, unworkable or fiendish. Some were riskier operations than others, few if any significantly improved Labor's chances and a couple were disasters. All of them combined did not come close to helping in the way that events in Canada helped. Two weeks before the poll the Canadian Prime Minister, Brian Mulrooney, resigned: the 7 per cent GST his government had introduced (which, when sales taxes were added, made it comparable with the Coalition's) had lifted inflation by 3 per cent which led to interest rate rises which led to more unemployment and prolonged recession, which led Mulrooney to resign. The Prime Minister of Australia was campaigning in Bendigo at the time. Better news had never reached his ears. He climbed into it and all over it. He did a doorstop and said it was 'a message in a bottle' which had arrived just in time to save Australia. Countries rarely 'got this lucky', he said. The GST had 'flattened Canada' and Australians would now not have to live out the same 'pointless tragedy'. He rang radio stations and told listeners that 'the place will be trauma-tised and stunned, and . . . we will step back into recession'. No stunt was ever this good. And it was on strategy, indeed it helped get us on strategy after the confusing effect of talking about more than one issue in the campaign launch.

Three television debates had been agreed to. The first, on 14 February, was a gruesome affair for all parties including the voting public. One journalist wrote that it was 'a debate in search of real human beings'. Chaired by Kerry O'Brien, with Michelle Grattan, Laurie Oakes and Paul Kelly asking the questions, both leaders were wooden and unconvincing. The PM was palpably nervous at the start and never got into stride. Hewson was no more impressive. Channel 9 screened the proceedings with the addition of an electronic 'worm', the new gadget which measured a studio audience's reaction. Its most spectacular act was a vertical dive when Dr Hewson attempted to enlist Australia's more successful Olympians as at least tacit supporters of his cause, proving yet again that sport and politics will not mix. The worm scored it 54–53 in Keating's favour, but with Labor now behind in all polls and the Prime Minister in dire need of a decisive victory, the score did not matter. Hewson came out of the debate a relatively credible, if not especially attractive, alternative.

The Prime Minister had spent the afternoon preparing for the ordeal with Peter Barron at the Lodge. At dusk he invited his staff up. We trooped in pathetically as the sun set and magpies settled in the trees. Barron looked at us with that dutiful conde-scension jockeys and trainers show owners in the mounting yard. The riding instructions had been decided by people who knew one end of the horse from the other. We were allowed to make suggestions, but we were essentially an element to be humoured. From this demeaning and thoroughly unproductive experience, the Prime Minister went to the debate in the worst possible state of mind—tense and almost preternaturally conscious of the need to remember his lines but deeply uncertain about what to do with them. He was bound to either forget them or repeat them mechanically. There was another tension—he had to assert his superiority without being aggressive. He went in like a man in armour. The One Nation rhetoric, the all-encompassing vision, had been erased and with it the capacity to outsmart and out-charm his opponent. With nothing else to feed on he was bound to go back to the old economic seed ball. He did, and he looked very awkward pecking at it, though one commentator pointed out that the whole thing lifted when he smiled.

Labor's advertising got under way. The concept—scare the pants off them—was admirably primitive with its old-fashioned cash register going 'ding' and announcing 10 per cent on an endless series of basic items. The strategy became irresistible as industry lobbies joined in. Book publishers and sellers said the tax on books would send businesses to the wall, authors and educa-tionists said it was a tax on knowledge. Sporting clubs said it would send them broke and the Prime Minister said the effect on sport would be a 'crime'. Dr Geoff Chapman of the Sydney (Horse) Trainers' Association reckoned the GST meant 'genocide for the horseracing industry' and the horseracing industry was, he claimed, 'the third highest employer in the land'. In north Queensland the Prime Minister said the tax would 'devastate' tourism. It was a tax on knowledge, a tax on pleasure and a tax on jobs. It was a 'monster of a tax', he said. And then he got the Peter Barron line going: 'Whenever you put your hand in your pocket Dr Hewson's hand will be in there too.' The effect was not immediate. At the end of the second week Morgan and Newspoll both had the Coalition six to seven points ahead. We planned a quiet start, we said. One out and one back is the best position, the Prime Minister claimed. We were timing our run. We were also putting a brave face on it. None braver than the photo of our prime minister in Ray Bans on the cover of *Rolling Stone*.

In the course of the campaign Leo McLeay was exonerated

by the inquiry into his compensation claim and the amount was declared 'appropriate'. No-one seemed to notice. McLeay said he had been the victim of a 'vicious campaign of lies' and went back to campaigning in the seat of Watson, which in the end he won comfortably. A report by Salamon Brothers valued Telecom at $10.6 to $12.2 billion; a report by Goldman Sachs put the figure at $13 billion. In either case, said Keating, the Coalition had a $7 billion hole and could not abolish payroll tax—unless, he said, they stripped out half the workforce and introduced timed local calls. Out in the backblocks of South Australia where such things counted for double, John Hewson failed to kill off the idea of such a radical 'restructuring' and the story ran on front pages across the country. But the story didn't last very long; not even when the Democrats said they would not pass legislation for the sale of Telecom, which the *Financial Review* pointed out put the funding of Fightback in 'extreme doubt'. In Melbourne a crowd estimated by some at 95,000, the biggest since the Vietnam moratoriums, marched in protest at Kennett's industrial relations legislation. It was news for a day; even after John Howard appeared to concede that under the Coalition's proposals new entrants to the work-force would suffer penalties. The Australian Bureau of Statistics released figures which indicated that growth was much stronger than previously thought, and might even reach an annual rate of 4 per cent. No-one was much interested. The PM gave an educa-tion speech in company with Kim Beazley, but we made sure the media coverage was minimal. We did the same with the environ-ment. Meanwhile, a huge bomb exploded in New York's World Trade Center, killing several people and injuring hundreds—and that was the news.

But the GST lasted the whole campaign long. Through good days and bad the GST kept coming. It was a miracle of a campaign issue because it could not be made to go away. It was a silent juggernaut, it was like yeast swelling the dough in the bowl. More to the point, it was like poison, and we laid it wherever we could, and put aside any old hopes we still had that the campaign would decide between competing visions for Australia.

In the second week of the campaign Keating told a Newcastle radio audience that he had accepted an invitation from Channel 9's Mike Willesee to a second debate, and he hoped Hewson would agree. Hewson had no choice. The preparation was minimal, the strategy no more complex than this: risk everything to get the campaign's focus on the GST. In the *Australian* Kate Legge said the Prime Minister 'demolished Hewson by sheer jaw power'. He had 'tasted the flesh of the Opposition and tore it off'. It was certainly not subtle or pretty. He ground out the lines about a 'lifestyle tax', a 'monster tax', a tax on 'the essentials of life'. He was aggressive and agitated and someone said 'twitchy'. He was like 'Lucky Starr on speed'. Hewson said he had a plan and Keating said 'Yes, but it's the wrong plan, dear boy'. But when it was over he told the press that Hewson hadn't let him finish a sentence. The press went into contortions of analysis, opinion and posturing as they always do when politics is presented in the raw. It was necessary to condemn him for his shameless scaremongering and street fighting, and just as necessary to see the smart political strategy behind it. It was necessary to report from a great moral height, and to report from ringside where you could see the blood. Glenn Milne said Keating had sacrificed the prestige of the office, but he had triumphed—Keating the street fighter had saved Keating the Prime Minister. The Liberals flooded the talkback shows to say that the Prime Minister was feral and arrogant—they hated 'dear boy'—and Hewson was cool. Newspoll scored it to Hewson by a small margin. It felt worse than that, but bravely we maintained our official view that Labor had managed to get 35 minutes of prime time television dedicated to the GST, and we were forcing the campaign towards our terms—which were, Hewson defends the GST and criticises the country's record and performance; Labor attacks the GST and implicitly defends the country. Keating is positive, Hewson is negative.

A policy speech is written by a committee through the medium of a speechwriter. Every serious operator in the party and some outside it fancy they deserve a say; ministers reckon their portfolios must be represented; most lobbies want to muscle in on pain of electoral execution; everyone who wakes in the middle of the night with a brilliant line seems to find your phone or fax number. And why not? The campaign launch is the sum total of the political movement gathered into one leader with one twenty-seven-minute speech in his hand. Because it is the moment when the whole party visibly and noisily projects itself onto the leadership it is also the moment when the leader's dependence on the led is most obvious. The campaign launch is the occasion when some leaders might feel most powerful, and others most vulnerable—and some might feel terribly powerful and terribly vulnerable at the same time.

The first draft of the 1993 speech was written in a hotel room high above Circular Quay. The Ramada Renaissance, which catered principally for Japanese tourists, became the campaign office, and the floor above, the honeymoon suite with a four-poster bed, was dedicated to the construction of the big speech. Kirribilli lay on the other side of the harbour; one could see it through the window—like Running Bear and Little White Dove. We made Sydney the base because in a campaign the politician must go to where the people are, where the connections are, where the real centre of the country is. And we stayed at the Ramada, as I understood it, because the rate was cheap; the club sandwiches, however, were diabolically dear. The ferries chugged in and out of the Quay, through rain and sparkling Sydney sunlight, in golden dusk and lit up in the wonderland of the Sydney night. Through another window workers steadily made their way up the side of the new Macquarie Tower, putting windows in it.

The task for the speech was to create a receptacle into which all necessary items could be dropped—and good lines like Bob McMullan's, 'when you wake up on March 14 . . .' you will still have everything that Labor has given you and more, and no GST. It might be as well that everybody pitches in to the campaign launch speech, or it might reflect the natural cycle of political activity, because the speech always seems to be written at the point when it feels most like there is nothing left to say—nothing fresh, at least, nothing that does not sound just like everything else we'd been saying for the past few years, or cloyingly parti pris or pork-barrelling or plain cant. Then there is the matter of making the campaign message the unmistakable message of the speech, which means leaving out anything which might get in its way, or if this is politically impossible, making it inconspicuous. Campaign speeches must be 'on strategy', of course. They must also contain a number of discrete 'grabs' for television, and for advertisements very often, and to facilitate the TV cut-up. A campaign launch speech is painstakingly composed to look like the most natural thing ever.

Two nights before the launch the speech was still a dog. It was all economics for some reason and quite devoid of inspiration. There was not a cannon left to fire. I went to Brisbane to meet the Prime Minister and his team. I sat down with Russell, Ryan and McMullan in the Sheraton restaurant and ate a steak. No-one that night thought we had much chance of winning. Everyone had agreed that our only slender hope was attached to a negative campaign against the GST and other lesser monsters. The logic was irresistible: the lesser monsters must not be once allowed to draw attention from the GST, and under no circumstances must any extraneous issue enter the landscape. In flagrant contravention of this strategy, Ryan and I had agreed in advance to mention the R word. If we were going to lose, we said, we shouldn't go without putting a proposal on the table. To ignore it would invite charges that the republic had indeed been a diversion, or that a victorious Keating would impose his republic on the country, that we would look at best very lame and cowardly and at worst deceitful.

It was plainly off strategy. The much safer position was simply to drop it and to say in response to any accusations that the monster tax was the big issue and nothing should divert the electorate's attention from that fact. But that night we persuaded Russell and McMullan that a proposal for the republic should be in the speech. It was some time before the Prime Minister could

330 Recollections of a Bleeding Heart

be told of our deliberations because he was on the phone to the social researcher, Hugh Mackay. All year his speeches had been informed to some degree by Mackay's *Reports*, but the Prime Minister did not know this. When he finally hung up half an hour before midnight he proceeded to relate many of Mackay's soft messages with which the rest of us had long been familiar. Nonetheless, the conversation with Mackay reinforced the idea of a social contract which Keating had been grappling with on and off all year. Mackay's words were useful for another reason; he told him that there would very soon be a big swing to the government and thus gave him hope to cling to. At six the next morning I returned to Sydney to dictate furiously all day while Don Russell consulted with constitutional experts and drafted an acceptable form of words for the republic proposal to which the Prime Minister had half-convincingly agreed at 1 a.m. when his bed was beckoning. Ryan knocked on his door at 7.30 a.m. Our leader was still in his pyjamas. They were half an hour late getting to Lismore.

With the speech still full of lumps and holes we went to Bankstown Sports Club for a rehearsal. A certain snarliness had invaded the atmosphere. Ryan had a snarl with Hogg—an inevitable one when the national secretary told him that Hawke would be attending the launch. What else could Hogg do but invite him? And what else could Ryan do but snarl, or the PM do but say that Hawkey was bound to make a bastard of himself? Like an attempt at the Lodge three days earlier, the Prime Minister's rehearsal was predictably desultory, which probably didn't help the general mood. The general mood was only helped by the unreality which seemed to have descended on the whole campaign: here in Bankstown—Ballarat and Melbourne's eastern suburbs had been considered—with Baz Luhrmann and an unfinished speech and a Prime Minister determined to not be seen trying.

To a fiendishly hot little office back at Kirribilli we went to finish the thing. As he often did in moments of crisis, Don Russell entered a dreamy kind of mood and dreamily sketched out a 'jobs plan' for inclusion. Following his example, the Prime Minister dreamily read the draft and marked it with his big black pen;

I wrote a dreamily 'poetic' ending and a big 'poetic' sentence on Labor's golden vision to go between the Coalition's negatives and the ALP's positives. Everyone became very good-natured, including Cheryl Griffiths who sat typing all night. Shortly after midnight Ryan mentioned the R word. He said we had no choice but to include it and moreover we had agreed upon this twenty-four hours earlier and nothing had changed since then. Nothing except the Prime Minister's mind. The dream sequence ended with the R word. The Prime Minister said he thought we couldn't, mate. He asked Dr Russell whether he didn't agree, and Dr Russell who had spent most of the previous twenty-four hours preparing a very credible proposal for a republic, replied that he was nervous about it. Predictably, we two chorused our astonishment. 'No-one wants it more than me, mate,' the Prime Minister said, 'but . . .' and he put the perfectly reasonable case against. We repeated our arguments from the night before: if Paul Keating was in favour of a republic but not in favour of doing anything about it, and, when the crunch came, not even game to *say* he was in favour of it, how was Paul Keating an advance on Bob Hawke? The answer was, no advance at all. And win or lose—but especially lose which remained the most likely possibility—this was how Paul Keating would be judged. It might have been this argument which did the trick, for suddenly he interrupted, saying, 'Well if we're going to do it, let's call it by its right fucking name' and he pulled off the cap of the big Mont Blanc and scrawled on the speech a 'Federal Republic of Australia'.

Dr Russell retired to an antechamber for a nap. The PM continued to work on the 'poetry' of the second last paragraph, which he felt was very good inspiring stuff—mate—but not quite right. When it was fixed he went to bed and more hours were spent attending to the detail. We crossed the bridge as sunrise turned the harbour apricot and sparkled on the new windows in the Macquarie Tower.

At 8.30 I crawled under the veils of the four-poster bed for an hour's sleep before the trip to Bankstown. At 8.50 the phone rang. It was him. He couldn't find the speech. I told him where it had been left and hung up. At 9 he rang again. 'You've cut the pages, mate,' he said. 'We always cut the pages,' I said: 'You like the pages cut.' 'But this one's got a different lectern,' he said: 'I need pages that aren't cut.' I asked him if Baz Luhrmann had arrived. He told me that Baz had been there for an hour and a half. I went down to the office and asked for a copy of the speech with uncut pages and large print to be sent to Kirribilli, and then I went back to bed. Five minutes later the phone rang again. 'There's a paragraph missing,' he said. 'We had to shorten it to make it fit the television,' I said. 'I know, mate,' he said, 'but you can't leave out this paragraph.' It was a paragraph designed to satisfy the economic commentators and financial markets. I went downstairs and got another version made with large print, uncut pages and the missing paragraph restored and it went off with Mark Ryan across the bridge to Kirribilli. I went back to bed. Arriving at Kirribilli around 9.30, Mark Ryan found the Prime Minister fairly seriously unprepared, and the film director bemused. The Prime Minister's wife complained that the Prime Minister had spent the morning listening to music instead of preparing. The Prime Minister swore to Ryan that he had done no such thing and went off to read the speech in another room.

If writing a campaign launch speech is one kind of singular experience, travelling this continent and writing them every day and night is another. In Adelaide 26 February we stood in drizzle in a park outside the Mitsubishi car plant as sausages sizzled and a few workers and Gordon Bilney and Nick Bolkus listened to the Prime Minister declaring through a megaphone that the factory would close if the Coalition were elected. In a spasm of rebellion against his minders he was wearing a dark sports coat and dark slacks and, we worried, looked like the prince of darkness again. From Mitsubishi he went to a party function in Hindmarsh where they cheered and then he took himself off to a house in the suburbs where his German short-haired pointer had been bred. We waited outside. With the news from Canada we should have been happy but we weren't. The polls were not good and the effort of the campaign launch had taken a toll. Still, the arts policy launch in Sydney on the day following shaped as a wonderful event—or so I tried to persuade him as we flew back to Canberra. For some reason there seemed to be only two of us on the plane.

We had a 'statement' for the arts which had been in preparation before the election was called and necessarily became a party document thereafter. The thrust of the policy was to move the arts into the mainstream of government decision-making, and into the cabinet. This had been the thinking behind establishing the Arts Advisory Council in mid-1992. It was not explicit in this first document, but some of us had in mind that the arts needed a broader definition, or at least to be nudged into the broader creative environment of communications and the new media. It was a strategy to politically liberate the arts from its reputation for elitism and give more recognisable meaning to the claim that the arts were useful and even profitable pursuits. We would say that from the arts Australia already drew much of its identity, and the bigger the arts pool the deeper the well of creativity on which to draw—and this was an era when creativity was a priceless national resource.

As we sailed above the Riverina, Keating was in that limbo between melancholy and aggression. Earlier in the day I had tried to persuade him to tell an audience that voting for the GST was like voting for influenza. He liked the idea but he wanted to say cancer—that it would eat the white blood cells of the country. He wanted to say that the GST would be the 'killing fields' of the Australian family. He stuck with cancer. He talked about cancer on the plane. He reckoned people of our age were in cancer country. We were also in heart attack country because we were driven people and we'd reached the age when it strikes. He recalled Chris Higgins, and his father and Peter Wilenski. He also told me that I should get out of Melbourne because Melbourne—like cancer—would eat me up. Get out of politics and get out of Melbourne. He knew what course his own life must take: get the economy ticking over like it should with the new motor Labor had given it, get the republic, get reconciliation, get everything wrapped up into a really nice little society to go with the economic motor, get the engagement with Asia into the sort of shape that would make it a permanent part of the country's life—and then we would enter the world of the senses. Oscar Wilde had it right, he said, though not his sexual preferences, mate. The most beautiful thing in the world was a woman's body, and the next most beautiful things were made in the late eighteenth century. All he wanted, he said, was pleasure. Including music. And owning beautiful things. But Eden was spoiled, and had been for some time. It seemed to him that life had not been the same since Annita began to fulfil her duties so conscientiously. It also seemed to him that she was not quite as she had been. All year, he said, he had been struggling with the pall of this perception. He looked very miserable and gazed out the window at the night. I said that there would be a huge crowd tomorrow in Sydney and it might be a great cheer-up. The difference between me and Hewson, he said, is that Hewson wants to make life harder for people and I want to make it softer. That's what the whole purpose of public life is, he said, to make life easier not harder. I said that he sounded like Manning Clark and his two categories of people, the enlargers of life and the punishers or straiteners. Is that what he said? he asked.

His passion for the arts was real. The lack of both a classical education and the regular companionship of creative genius made him no less inclined to view the world with an aesthetic eye and value the imagination. As with political leaders, he did not think it was worthwhile to pretend that one artist was as good as another, or to fudge the line between honest endeavour and real excellence, or excellence and genius. Confusing crafts with the arts, or the second rate with the first, he thought was the antithesis of what the arts concerned and fatal to arts policy. He was not passionate about all the arts equally. Music, painting, architecture, design, dance he loved, but theatre held little interest for him, film even less. He read history, but not novels or poetry. It was the areas of aesthetic and educational underdevelopment, presumably, which prompted the Australian critic resident in London, Clive James, to declare the Prime Minister an 'ignoramus'. James was hardly in a position to know. In the arts, however, as Keating was aware, it's not what you know, but what your opinion is. The arts were ripe with poseurs and awash with envy and paranoia. The arts, like no other form of human endeavour, spawned mediocrity and bureaucracy, and mediocrity and bureaucracy were the natural enemies of art. Knowing this, he also knew that, just as works of art and conversations with artists could be incomparably uplifting, they could also be diabolically boring and pointless. The Prime Minister was not the Minister for the Arts—the West Australian, Wendy Fatin, was—but if the Australia Council reduced the funding for a dance company in Adelaide, or a rumour was heard that the government was going to reduce funding for the Australia Council, it was to the 'arts loving' Prime Minister that the representations were invariably made.

In the PMO Simon Balderstone had been responsible for the arts, but he had more than enough to do, and early in 1992 I became the one who took the phone calls, answered the letters and tried to coordinate the Prime Minister's part-time interest and absolutist attitudes with his minister's general, and generally forgivable, uncertainty—or, rather, with what Craddock Morton, her adviser, could make of it. Only in the arts portfolio did one regularly meet people who conceived of a personal slight as a national issue. In the arts a performer might demand that the Prime Minister speak to the general manager of the ABC about his dispute with an arm of that organisation, and if the Prime Minister's intercessions failed to produce the result desired, the performer might declare that the Labor Government was closing ranks behind the general manager, had sold out the nation's talent, abandoned itself to the cultural cringe and no longer stood for anything worthwhile. If it was not a pianist it might be a poet or a playwright, alleging the rankest conspiracies against native talent. Correspondence and phone calls of this kind were never received from disgruntled swimmers or cricketers; small business-people, who complain a lot on the radio and in the letters columns, and who are even more numerous than artists, much less commonly waged these kinds of wars.

The arts were sometimes hard to like, arts bureaucracies even harder. It was true, as their advocates said, that participation in the arts was far more general than people recognised, but it was not participation of the kind that showed up in opinion polls and elections, and therefore it was not something to carry much influence in cabinet, caucus, the Expenditure Review Committee, or for that matter with the Prime Minister, nine days out of ten. In time it became part of the received political wisdom that Keating's love for the arts led him away from the real people and their real issues and into the arms of the despised elites. You would think from some reports that daily he lay around with his advisers discussing the relative merits of the great tenors or how to fund an ALP chamber orchestra. You would also think that lavish sums were spent on the arts in Australia. It was never thus. As his unofficial adviser I invariably went to him on arts business wishing that I had something else in my folder. Apart from a couple of weeks in 1994 when the cultural policy was prepared, the arts were never even close to the centre of his political consciousness, or the PMO's, and it is fantastic to think that they might have been. It was a political office and the coins of value were those that counted politically. One might cautiously venture when the ERC was meeting that the annual budget of the Australia Council, responsible for the arts throughout this vast continent, was less than one-tenth of the annual appropriation in the City of Berlin. They would still talk as if cuts to the arts budget would make a mighty difference to the deficit, and even if it didn't there was the inherent virtue in getting a few more snouts out of the trough.

For all the mean political reality and the confounded nuisance the arts could make of themselves, Keating loved artists and believed that encouraging the nation's imagination was his profound responsibility. He believed the arts were good for the country's heart, as they were good for his. They were good for the character of the place, and if nothing else an essential balance to the sports obsession. He agreed that they fused with the government's economic, regional and constitutional ambitions and needed bringing into the mainstream of national policy-making—and in that difficult manoeuvre he succeeded for a while. He was open to this way of thinking from the start, but he was much more easily persuaded of it after the astonishing reception he received in Sydney on 28 February.

Sydney's State Theatre was packed. The Hermannsburg Aboriginal Women's Choir sang; Jane Rutter played the flute; Bangarra danced; there was circus, comedy—it was probably the greatest live performance in Australia that year. It was followed by tirades against the GST's effects on books in particular and the arts in general, letters of gratitude and praise from current holders of Creative Arts Fellowships ('Keatings') and torrents of praise for the Prime Minister from Bryan Brown, Sam Neill, Robin Nevin and others. The Prime Minister and his wife took their bows on the stage to tumultuous applause. Arts for Labor, a coalition in which Anne Summers played an early instrumental role, had attracted actors, writers, agents, theatre and film producers whose affection for Keating was unalloyed and totally surprising in its intensity. Elites they may be, but the Prime Minister could not stop smiling and bowing. He told them of his ambitions for another term—the economic motor, the links with East Asia, the republic, the Aborigines, the unemployed and the arts. He said the Coalition could never understand the meaning of all this. They did not understand the meaning of the arts because they could not see or understand the synergy between the arts and the economy, how they sprang from the same creative instincts. That was why he would put the arts into the mainstream. And how great our arts will be, he said, when we are as one with indigenous Australians, when we say sorry and mean it, 'when we say sorry for the murders and dispossession and mean it, and not just write a cheque off the budget'. But these things to the Coalition were 'like a wooden cross to Dracula'. Because there were two types of people in the world—the enlargers of life on the one hand, and on the other the punishers and the straiteners.

Between Adelaide and the arts launch came news that the general manager of Mitsubishi had written to John Hewson saying that he would work as happily with a Coalition government as a

Labor one. The blow was heavier because it had been expected: all week Don Russell warned us that the general manager was anxious about appearing to support Labor because Mitsubishi dealers found it hard to sell cars when customers thought the company, deprived of tariff protection by the Liberals, might be about to leave.

In Perth it was hot. We listened on phones to Hewson's campaign launch: phones connected to phones in the Canberra office pressed against TVs. We heard the hoopla borrowed from Clinton's campaign but it was difficult to get a mental picture of it. Staff explained from Canberra what was happening as half a dozen 'ordinary Australians' were brought on stage to tell their tragic stories. It was straight out of Clinton's campaign textbook. There was the woman whose husband had lost his job; then their car was stolen; then their house was burgled; then their marriage collapsed. Hewson had said to these six Australians that they were 'today's forgotten people'—which was straight out of Menzies' campaign textbook. 'I look you in the eye,' Hewson said, 'and say we can solve your problems.' That it was all happening in Sydney's Wesleyan Mission added to the atmosphere of evangelical kitsch and bathos. Laughter came down the line from the Prime Minister's Office. 'This one's got a bandaged neck,' they said. 'John' not only had a bandaged neck, he was on a walking stick and he was alarmingly short of breath as he told his story. Hewson then told his story—at least that part of it which had not already been told by his wife in introducing him and the party's bio-documentary which had been screened as an audience warm-up. He told—just as Clinton had—of the poor folks he had met on the campaign trail. And how he would look them in the eye and solve their problems. He talked about all the hidden taxes in the family home, as if taxes caused emphysema and burglary. It was shameless and gruesome and we were scared it would work. He said he would appoint a team of six eminent Australian 'special advisers' on matters of 'fundamental importance'—Dick Smith, Arvi Parbo, Ita Buttrose, David Penington, Judith Sloan and Charles Perkins—and we put out a press release saying that these names did not appear on the ballot paper and were only there to hide the real forgotten people, namely Hewson's front bench. The Prime Minister lingered at a barbecue in the seat of Perth that Stephen Smith was trying to win and left the staff and press sweltering and cursing in the plane on the tarmac for two hours. On the way to Cairns we passed over Uluru at dusk and the extraordinary sight of it caused a hush, the Prime Minister pausing in his description of crawling all over Hewson like a black widow spider and nailing him—with one hand raised as if holding the nail and the other mimicking a hammer putting the nail in, 'not just half in, I mean all the way'. He lay on the 707's bed, arms outstretched in the crucified position, martyred to the cause, and when we stole a look half an hour later his hands were clasped on his chest like a monk in a coffin. I told Annita that he was far from happy. There were not many outward signs of happiness between them though it's true they were always very private. The core of the travelling party comprised the Prime Minister and Mrs Keating, Russell, Ryan, Greg Turnbull and me, Nina England and Cheryl Griffiths, the police, and down the back of the 707 the press in whose tired, disgruntled faces we tried to read our fortunes.

Whatever else Hewson got out of his launch, he timed it well enough to knock the good economic news off many front pages: record exports which took $1.12 billion off the current account, put .75c on the Australian dollar, made cutting interest rates a certainty, and even raised the possibility that the government's forecasts might be accurate. The recovery, Keating told the press, was gathering pace. Why would anyone want to stop it in its tracks with a monster tax?

In Cairns the Prime Minister talked about tourism and the GST to the press, and the ruination of the old town by high-rise development to his advisers. I mused about setting up regional councils to encourage and if necessary coerce local government authorities to control development and preserve what was left of the built environment. We heard that John Laws had given Hewson a terrible time on the radio, as caller after caller asked him questions about the GST, some of which he could not answer. Dr Hewson said he wanted calls on unemployment. He angrily accused Laws of doctoring his listeners' faxes. He called a press conference but the press asked him if he could not explain the GST how could the public be expected to understand it. This dovetailed beautifully with the line George Gear gave Keating in Perth: 'If you don't understand it, don't vote for it; because if you do understand it you certainly won't.' Hewson appeared on the Willesee program and found that he couldn't say whether a child's birthday cake would be GST-free, or parts of it would or all of it. It was national news.

Leaving the press on the tarmac in a plane with a broken wing after a luggage bus backed into it, the Prime Minister's team flew down to Mackay in an old Hawker Siddeley. Everyone slept except the Prime Minister who over the din of the engines sang for me some of the great songs he had sung as a lad at Labor Party gatherings. No-one woke as he sang 'Shenandoah', 'Deep River' and 'Anything Goes'. It ended in the familiar melancholy as he explained how his vocal chords had been ruined by overuse and tension.

On the ground he bubbled with enthusiasm for the chase. Bob McMullan counselled caution as ever, and every time he did Keating suggested some even more absurdly bold strategy. Not too much personal abuse, we would say, knowing this would provoke great spates of it—and then it was less likely to be uttered near a sound boom. He had to attend an investiture of school prefects. I asked him if he had ever been a prefect. No, he said, we hated them. The worst thing you could be was a prefect. It wasn't worth living if you were a prefect. I was a prefect, I said—a head prefect. 'Were you, mate?' he said. Cane toads flopped about in the motel garden while Nina typed a speech on tourism. The tide was miles out, a container ship at anchor just beyond the sand on which billions of tiny blue crabs scurried in swarms like sheep. A little after midnight we heard the journalists' plane come in.

We were due to go to a marginal seat south of Sydney and, to make the most of Hewson's problems with the GST and cakes, it was arranged to visit a bakery in Bomaderry. The Labor local member, the unusual Peter Knott, took the PM to the premises whose owner he believed to be sympathetic to our cause. Alas, while the Prime Minister held up a cake the owner told the press that he had recently expanded his business and could expand it further and employ another two or three people were it not that he had to pay $45,000 in payroll tax and wholesale sales tax on icing, candles and piping bags. This became known immediately as the Great Pie Shop Disaster, the stunt that failed just as momentum was flowing our way. The PM did another arts function in Melbourne in the Playbox Theatre with a huge crucifix, a prop from the current play, hanging above him. When he told the audience that Hewson had said the poor will drag you down if you reach back for them there was a groan of anger and horror, and to their astonishment some of Keating's advisers who'd heard it a hundred times before felt a lump in their throats. In the bus outside, Geoff Kitney and Michelle Grattan sat with expressions of blank indifference and it was impossible not to feel a ripple of despair. You could see that they had given up and were beyond the reach of persuasion.

In an effort to see that voters did not take the same course the Prime Minister proposed to say: 'Voters may wish to punish Labor. But they must be careful not to punish themselves.' We advised him not to, believing it invited the headline, 'Don't Punish Me Pleads PM'. He rang Peter Barron who told him he should use it. He did. On the Monday morning the front page headline in Melbourne's *Herald Sun* was exactly as we described. It was curious and ironic. The line implied that they had a reason to punish him, a thought he had resisted fiercely for more than a year. He was willing to publicly concede that there had been mistakes. A few days later he said, 'governments are not infallible and this one has had its share of mistakes'. He even acknowledged that 'with hindsight' interest rates might have been reduced at a faster rate before the recession struck so brutally. As he said these things a large part of the year-long tension vanished like smoke and we were suddenly, if all too late, so much freer. Barron was right. Conceding responsibility was not enough, conceding the people's right to punish him was like offering them the blood that alone would satisfy.

Modern politics tends towards an ever-tightening circle. It may reflect a primitive fear—all that media, all that public opinion, all that baying for blood. There are savages out there and ravening wolves. Only a brave politician or a desperate one will try to break out because he is conditioned to fear that, even if he is not cut down, he will never get back in. The aim is to be still alive at the end of the day (it is probably no accident that 'the end of the day' is now a favourite political cliché) and the end of the day is usually about 6.15 p.m. when the commercial channels are finished with the political news and everyone can relax. In the second last week of the '93 campaign it suddenly seemed absurd to have remained in the circle for so long. Nervously we had dropped the republic into the campaign and held our breath. Two days later it was part of the landscape. So long as our position was known it was so much harder to imagine it as ghoulish. Now it seemed that had we gone abroad acknowledging that unemployment was in part a consequence of past mistakes we could have much more easily turned the debate towards the remedies and the causes of unemployment which were indeed beyond the government's control. Paul Keating was understandably reluctant to be made the whipping boy for events over which he had no power. Yet the more persuasive factor was every politician's unwillingness to concede ground in the daily battle not to be seen to lose at the end of the day—for you never knew where the rot would stop: and never to let the story get into the other side's hands. It was as if some instinct in Keating told him that he could best confront the third and last debate, and the final unemployment figure just two days before the poll, if by a subtle shift in the discourse he could gently disperse some of the public anger. And if he could remove some of the anger he could begin talking about hope. Whether it was instinct or intellect, by the beginning of the second last week Keating had reached ground where he could talk about the promise of the future while John Hewson talked about the past. It would be too much to say that all blame and anger towards Keating was now in suspension, or that more than a few people thought his recent candour ought to be rewarded, and yet it was just possible that at the last moment, not Keating but Hewson would become the target of public frustration. Perhaps it was both simpler and more subtle still: perhaps it came down not to strategies or advertisements or hoopla, but to gumption. Not in every case, but consistently over the last two weeks, Keating demonstrated gumption which Hewson in proportion seemed to lack.

So much ran Labor's way, as well. In a new book Professor John Head of Monash University wrote that the economists he had assembled to analyse Fightback disputed all its major claims; one of them calculated that 66 per cent of households would be worse off if its proposals were implemented; and another, a Coalition adviser, John Freebairn, found that abolishing payroll tax would have 'no positive impact on employment'. These findings were reported on the front page of the *Financial Review* and widely elsewhere.

Elsewhere it was also reported that one of the 'ordinary Australians' who had come forward to be looked in the eye by John Hewson at the Liberals' campaign launch had also appeared in Liberal Party advertisements in the 1990 election, and another three of the six were on social security programs which the Liberal Party planned to abolish. Then Bob Hawke came forth in Kim Beazley's narrowly held seat of Swan and declared that, contrary to his earlier prognostication, Labor could now win.

On the last day of February Melbourne's *Sunday Age* published a poll which showed Labor ahead, and just as significantly, that only 17 per cent of people believed they would be better off with a GST. Rushing to create momentum, Keating said the more people learned about the tax the less they liked it. It was amazing, he said, that John Hewson had got people into the streets to demonstrate in favour of a new 15 per cent tax. The Saulwick poll showed Labor closing fast; Morgan had Labor within 1 per cent on the primary vote; Newspoll had Labor 3.5 per cent behind, which was still a virtual dead heat on two party preferred.

Hewson's campaign to dislodge a long-serving government was modelled in every detail on Clinton's overthrow of the

Republicans, employing the same symbols of youthful energy, high passion and melodrama, staged spectacles full of balloons real and metaphorical, even the same phrasing in speeches, the same hoarseness. As the campaign reached its close he was like a man on a mad treadmill. Where Keating, though tired and riddled with doubt, could employ instinct, commonsense and sometimes even the element of surprise, Hewson worked himself into a predetermined lather. Keating went to the final debate better prepared in that he was now thinking on his feet. Wearing his light grey suit and suddenly looking relaxed, he trounced Hewson mainly by emphasising the positive. 'We're off—we've turned the corner,' he said, referring to Australia's economic growth rate which was just then the highest among developed nations. Dr Hewson was obliged to say that we weren't off, that we hadn't turned the corner, that things were bad. Keating said they would be worse with a GST. Hewson said Australia might go back into recession. Keating said only a GST could slow the present momentum, and somehow it did seem as if Keating had the momentum with him. Some people on Hewson's side believed Kerry O'Brien had favoured Keating. We thought it fair to say that our man had not been significantly disadvantaged.

Increasingly, the case for voting Labor looked like the safer option. A vote for Hewson was a vote against Keating, but it was also a vote for a GST. A vote for Keating was a vote against a GST and a vote against leaping into the unknown with a strange man.

The uncertainty, which perforce contained the prospect of both victory and defeat, did not spur our Prime Minister on to surpassing feats. His mood ran from gloomy introspection to bad temper, to torpor, to sporadic bursts of courage and brilliance. He was not helped when Bob Hogg took it upon himself to tell the press that Labor would lose. Hogg came from that school of political thought which believed this pessimism was tactical, that it applied pressure to voters who thought they could get away with a non-Labor vote. From where the Prime Minister was sitting it applied pressure principally to him, and it dulled the spirit and slowed the momentum. Hogg's move sent Keating into an entirely predictable rage and then into exhaustion and gloom from which it was difficult to raise him. Hogg had more than strategy to motivate him. Labor's pollster, Karen Luscombe, thought Labor would lose: she phoned me to suggest the sorts of issues Keating might raise in his last major speech at the Press Club on the Thursday before the election. I asked if her opinions derived from a view that Labor could win, or a view that Labor should try to cut its losses. It was the latter. We could not win, she said. She expressed sympathy for what Bob Hogg had done. It would be poison for us to look like we were winning, to behave in any way to suggest that we imagined some hope existed. Then the Queensland Labor Premier, Wayne Goss, a member of the same strategic school as Hogg, announced that Labor would lose seats in Queensland. Doubtless they all thought they were calling it as they saw it and did it without spite. But we saw it as throwing sand on the campaign's embers. We saw it as a body blow to the person, like him or not, who had to lead Labor across the line. Just when Keating should have been powering through the last week of the campaign he sank for twenty-four hours into gloom.

Hewson decided not to address the Press Club which left Keating with an opportunity to parade himself as the one candidate open to serious cross-examination. While his opponent shouted slogans and whipped himself into a carefully orchestrated frenzy at rallies around the country, our man would approach the ultimate democratic test in the orderly and traditional way by subjecting himself to the hard scrutiny of our free and independent press. No-one knew how Hewson's rallies were really going down. The hope was that Australians would recoil from techniques of hoopla and mass hysteria; that they'd be saying by now, 'he's mad, the bastard', and allowing themselves to think that Keating had turned out the bearer of peace, reason and democracy. And yet as the last week began he was glum and full of doubt. He said he couldn't read a speech to the Press Club, he would have to ad lib it. In fact no-one ever *made* him read a speech. And he insisted that he would need briefing notes for an interview he had coming up. He was *always* given notes. At

3 a.m., in the usual way, notes were slipped under his and the advisers' hotel doors. He took them to the first interview of the morning, but he was like a man on Largactyl: asked what he would be telling the workers in Whyalla later in the day, he seemed unable to think of anything, and unable to read the notes in front of him. One of the notes contained a variation on the Barron line. We had spent some time thinking of popular, even semi-sacred social preoccupations which would be subject to the GST—sport, religion, children, dogs and cats. One of the lines he took to Whyalla was, 'Next time you take your dog to the vet, Dr Hewson will have one hand on the leash.'

I stayed in Adelaide dictating a speech for the Press Club which I knew might not be used. Peter Barron phoned. He put his case forcefully—as, he said, Bob McMullan had told him to. It went like this: Keating and his advisers had dispensed with Graham Richardson, who had got Keating into the job and had six times more brains than any of the advisers. If Labor lost, Keating would have his arms ripped off, and Don Russell's and Mark Ryan's with them. The truth, Barron said, was that Keating did not want to be prime minister. Keating had never got over his own proposal for a GST and he still wanted one. His tariff policy was stupid, as Barron had been telling him for years. His doorstop interviews had been calamitous because his advisers had not got the lines into his head. When Labor lost people would say—as Kerry Packer recently said to Barron—how could you lose to John Hewson with a 15 per cent GST? The campaign had been a travesty, and mainly because Richo had been left out of it. I ventured that Richo had been present at the great Acme advertising studio debacle and did not particularly distinguish himself. Wrong. Hoggy had authored that shemozzle. That day Hoggy had not only frozen out Keating's staff, he had also tried to freeze out Richo. And Hoggy had come up with the previous night's lines about losing the election all by himself.

Mark Ryan phoned to say that the Prime Minister had failed to spark in Whyalla and left his audience perplexed when he told them, 'Remember, next time you take your vet to the dogtor,

Dr Hewson will have one hand on his leash.' When they returned, I recited Barron's various communications. In accordance with Barron's peculiar power to intimidate, there was a visible blanching and deep swallowing in some quarters. In Hindmarsh that afternoon, Keating rose to the occasion of a rapturous reception. And later he came through a fiercely hard interview with Paul Lyneham as perhaps no other politician in the country could have. Some thought it was his best performance of the campaign.

In these last few days he began to talk about 'massive social dislocation, confrontation and division', if Hewson formed a government. And a Clinton campaign adviser, Derek Shearer, said on Australian radio that while Hewson had done a shameless imitation of Clinton's campaign, Clinton's program was much more like Keating's: it had been modelled 'much more on social democratic governments . . . and not on Thatcherite programs'. In every interview and at the Press Club Keating sharpened the argument. And at every shouting foot-stamping rally Hewson tried to do the same. Hewson's campaign reduced to 'Labor's Got to Go'. And the more it was shouted the more Keating could extend, and sound sage and dulcet doing it: 'Let me give the oldest advice in the world to people who are contemplating the big jump,' he said. 'Don't do it.'

He went to the Press Club on the day the unemployment figures came out. Eleven point one per cent was terrible, and yet nothing much more than a reminder of what everyone knew to be the case. And somehow there was still enough political room for Keating to say in response to them: 'Australians can vote for a GST or they can vote for jobs. But they can't vote for both.' The transformation was all but complete. The man they had called the architect of the recession now called himself the man for jobs. The irony was probably lost on Keating because irony is for those who know that their demise is certain or accomplished, not when victory and salvation are in prospect. It did not matter whether he was the man for the recession or the man for jobs, so long as he was the man. So long as he was the one spinning the story.

It was agreed that the PM should read the Press Club speech.

In the hectic last week, the more precise and measured he sounded the more dramatic the impression of chaos surrounding Hewson, we thought. I handed over the speech an hour before he was due to deliver it. He was not yet in his suit nor any frame of mind to deliver so much as a limerick. He was looking at the East Circular Quay plans. It was not the tense Keating, or the one with a face 'veiled in apathy' as someone once described Disraeli's when he was obliged to listen to someone he did not want to hear, such as an Opposition member in the House. Paul Keating often had that look about him, especially in those circumstances, but this look was not affected: it was the genuinely dissociated Keating; the one who had taken himself somewhere else and might as well have been in Paris. When at last he got into the car with the thing in his hand I suggested he read it as if he had an urgent appointment with Cecilia Bartoli on the other side of town. The idea was that speed might create a sense of drama and still the gallery's urge to see him as a spent force. There would be no harm done if he also sounded like a man with much to do before the weekend.

He rattled it off at a great rate and no-one called it anything worse than an 'appeal to pure animal fear'—which was rough justice to the speech's subtleties, but a gratifyingly long way from implying he had thrown in the towel. He made the point that he was fronting up to the press while Hewson was staging a rally. Hewson believed in 'American razzamatazz and hoopla and carefully staged passion plays and bunfights'. He didn't believe in it. He thought it was rubbish. He thought leaders should 'face the music—scratchy, discordant, unpleasant music though it may be'. He didn't agree with Wayne Goss, either. If it had been a tactic to predict the loss of seats in Queensland, it was a bad tactic.

The election was a perilous moment in the life of the country. Hewson was the most extreme radical right-winger to propose himself as Prime Minister in the country's history. Keating conceded the government had made mistakes, interest rates stayed too high for too long; but in their desire to punish the government, the Prime Minister said, the people must be careful not to punish themselves. The real choice they had to make was between the prospect of recovery and the prospect of losing it. To whom should they trust the recovery—the devil they knew or the devil they didn't? Rarely in the previous twelve months had we understood that the purpose of all our labours, all the expressions of high sentiment and visionary policy and all the furious struggle came down to this pedestrian ritual—the one by which even the basest governments seek to get themselves returned.

It was still a formidable task, of course, because the devil many voters knew was the veritable archetype of devils. In the last week of the campaign Keating revealed every element of the paradox that defines him. He was depressed and exuberant, remote and fiercely engaged. Until the last two days every gesture and expression seemed to conceal its opposite. When everything bore down on him, he was reflective: when the sailing was smooth, he stormed. In a reflective mood he told me that he was different from his mates in the New South Wales right. Once they reached the top end of town they were swallowed up in the long lunches, the Hawkesbury weekender and all the other seductions of Sydney. But Paul Keating was not seducible: he went back to work or home to his wife and children. He told me again how he had sat in the train outside the tunnel near St Mary's and decided that if a tyke like JFK could be president of the United States, a tyke like PJK could be prime minister of Australia. From that moment he always thought he would succeed. Now that he had the job, however, he found that he hated the publicity. He would have been very happy if someone had said, 'Paul, you can be prime minister, but we won't tell anybody.'

In the last hours of the campaign there were a couple of interviews, a piece for the newspapers about why people should vote for him, a press release about why they should vote for him and a press conference on the same theme. The theme was— don't do it, don't jump into the unknown. For the press conference we drove the 300 metres from the Ramada to the Phillip Street offices. Mark Ryan told the driver to stop twenty metres before the car park, by the footpath where the press had gathered for one last photograph. The Prime Minister said drive on, drive past the bastards, they've had enough. And the front page of every election day newspaper, we said, will have a photo of Keating with his head down slinking into an underground car park in a Commonwealth car. The driver stopped. Grumbling, the Prime Minister got out. High on the Macquarie Tower, workers were calling out. 'What do those characters want?' asked the Prime Minister. We might have said, they're wondering if they should leap into the unknown. 'They're workers,' we said, 'they're saying, "Go Paul!"' 'Is that what they're saying?' he said. It was. 'Good on them,' he said, and acknowledged them with a wave and a sunny smile. And when they cheered he gave them the victory salute. It was the best photo of the campaign—he looked confident, charming and warm, a real man of the people, a real leader—and it was on several of the election day front pages.

Only Sydney's *Telegraph-Mirror* editorialised for Labor, and only two senior members of the press gallery, Amanda Buckley and Chris Wallace, along with the academic psephologist Malcolm Mackerras, predicted a Labor victory. As Hugh Mackay pointed out, with 15 per cent of voters declaring themselves undecided with only a few days remaining it was pure folly to call the result in advance. In the *Financial Review* Tom Burton wrote that Labor would lose, and that when Labor looked back at last Thursday's unemployment figures, Bob Hogg, Graham Richardson and other wiser heads would be vindicated in their judgment that the election should have been called a fortnight later. Like a din is to a person with a headache, every word was another tiny hammer blow. It was torture in the current environment; it would be poison in the future. The gallery, and even more the newspapers—the same newspapers which had backed Menzies when Keating was a boy—had turned on Labor. They were supporting a half-baked conservative tyro against the man who had given the country a modern economy and supplied them with first-rate copy for a decade. In the last week of the campaign the press put the poison in Keating's soul. It never left. He would never be able to forgive them.

Yet three of the four main polls had Labor in the lead on

the last day, and there was no good reason to think that all was lost. At Susie Carlton's Bellevue Hotel in Paddington on the night before the vote, Keating put his case as he had never put it before. With the final judgment certain and upon him, he found unprecedented eloquence and irresistible coherence and meaning in all that he had done. He departed in triumph, leaving the gathering of Sydney cognoscenti agog and full of hope. They were Arts for Labor people and he had gone to thank them for their efforts, and so they could raffle various donated items, including his tie and a copy of the policy speech, to defray the costs of their campaign. It is almost certain that at that point in their lives, none of those present realised that they were members of a politically unconscionable elite. And because no-one on his staff was aware that the Prime Minister was going to make his best speech of the year, his words were not recorded.

It went like this. Labor had the economics and now the country was beginning to perform accordingly. Soon the motor would be ticking over sweetly and things would be set fair to create one of the nicest little societies anyone ever saw. We would make the most of the great bounty, the continent we had to ourselves and our proximity to the booming economies of Asia. Australia would thrive in the twenty-first century; the place would buzz for generations and grow very strong. And we had been busy bundling this in with a set of social policies that would look after everyone who fell off the truck or had ground to make up; and these we were tying in with a republic, reconciliation with our indigenes because we could never say we had succeeded until we had done that, and we would also give the arts their due and pull them into the mainstream because a country needs an imaginative life; and we were going to wrap all this up into a nice little package and wrap it so tightly the others wouldn't be able to get into it with an oxyacetylene torch. That was if we won, of course. We might not win; the figures might still beat us. The voters were pretty sick of us and they wanted to teach us a lesson, a dirty big lesson—but then again they didn't like the look of the other bloke, and we might just scramble over the line.

Later that night he offered the same perspective to his staff who had all gathered in The Imperial Peking restaurant down by Circular Quay. He talked about the country knowing itself better, and making peace with the Aborigines 'to get the place right'. This 'bigger view of the place', that we had worked on all year, had got Australians interested. 'They think this is a bit different. This is better than just economics and social policy, it's something else wrapped around it as well. It's got a binding around it.' And then he said: 'We are the entrepreneurs of political life and are the people who dream the big dreams and do the big things. There are no bigger dreamers than in our office. It's a mixture of econocrats and bleeding hearts. But together we make a pretty powerful combination.' If we win, he said, I reckon that we'll do more things here than any other Western government will do in the next three years.

If we won. It would be the 'win of the century' if we won. That night he said he had a sneaking suspicion that we might. But next day, on the way to Bankstown for the count, he told Mark Ryan that he thought the unemployment and the ten years would probably bring us undone.

At Sydney Town Hall and every voting booth across the continent we have to ourselves, not a single sign said 'Vote for an Australian Republic' or 'Vote for an Australian Social Democracy' or 'Vote for Keating's Vision'. We had a couple of dozen 'Keating is Right' badges made, to echo Jack Lang's 1931 slogan and all the love and loathing that accompanied his demise. But the 1993 slogan was 'Jobs not GST', or sometimes simply 'No GST'. It was everywhere like confetti, and the Labor people distributing how-to-vote cards intoned it to all constituents—'No GST'.

Peter Harvey told us as we left for Bankstown that the exit polls looked good for Labor. While it was better than being told that they looked bad, it did not relieve at all the burden of—what was it? Fear, morbidity, guilt? One could say that we had a chance, even that we would win, and in some part of one's brain believe it. *Feeling* it, however, was quite a different matter. On the ground floor of the Bankstown Sports Club many hundreds of punters played the poker machines. On the balcony upstairs and in the boardroom the local faithful and the Prime Minister's staff mingled at the bar and around the prawns and watched the screens. The campaign team crunched numbers in adjoining rooms. By 6.30 Labor had won two seats in Tasmania that it had to win. Keating looked grim. The test would be to see if we could win enough in the east to withstand the backlash in South Australia and the West. For a moment around 8.30 it seemed unlikely—the Queensland sugar seats did not seem to be holding. For twenty minutes no-one seemed to speak, or if they did no-one answered. The truth dawned on everyone at much the same time. It took a while for the disbelief to wash away. Tom Mock-ridge took my elbow and said very quietly, as if he didn't want to trigger a stampede or avalanche, 'You've won.' Tom was an ace number cruncher. 'What about the west?' He said, 'Not even a debacle in the west could lose it.'

Now as we realised that we had won, we also realised how profoundly we thought that we must lose. The dread was in the marrow. The hand of the hangman had been stayed, but it felt more like the rope had snapped. Is it part of our design that as a sentence of death concentrates the mind so powerfully, some other part of us withers and dies of neglect? We had been in denial for so long no-one noticed that somewhere in our minds we had given up the ghost. That night it felt less like survival than rebirth. We could have our life over again. The moment of victory was wonderful; it was also a species of trauma.

Through it all the poker machines, like real life, kept dinging and buzzing and rattling. The Prime Minister looked at some notes I had given him—victory notes—and scrawled some himself. Don Russell counselled humility and modesty. Tom Mockridge, Mark Ryan and I chorused, 'No! Claim it!' He went downstairs with Annita and they walked out on to Baz Luhrmann's blue-draped stage to cheering. Suddenly there were no pokies. He said: 'This is a victory for the true believers; the people who in difficult times have kept the faith, and for the Australian people through hard times, it makes their act of faith that much greater.'

He left no doubt that he was claiming it, in fact he might have been still campaigning. 'It will be a long time before an Opposition tries to divide the country again.' It was a victory for Australian values over a party that wanted 'to change Australia from the country it has become'. In a sense he was right; in future, programs of this type would not be loudly advertised in the way John Hewson had advertised them. Yet some people thought it was not appropriate to make such points in a victory speech. The Melbourne broadcaster Terry Lane said later he found it 'chilling'. In truth Keating was more generous to those who voted against Labor than reporting and memory of the speech allows. It depended on your point of view. Bob Carr rang him before he stepped on to the stage and urged him to be 'humble', and later he described what he heard as 'one of the great Labor speeches'. The result, Keating said, would 'go to the heart of the Government and the Labor Party'. He made a pledge to the unemployed: 'If we can't get people back to work we'll sure as hell look after them.'

It was stirring stuff for his supporters. He said so many of the things we had urged all year and he said them with natural and absolute conviction. He left at 1 a.m. with punters swarming round chanting for some reason the English football refrain, 'Here we go, here we go, here we go'. And then it seemed they went back to the poker machines.

For now and for some time afterwards the victory speech would be the guiding light, the inspiration, the high tide of our ambitions. When we were in doubt, we thought, we will have the victory speech to turn to. But Don Russell had been right. He should have been more modest. The sound bite should have been humble. Instead, only the opening line was remembered, and for much of the next three years we would battle the perception that the words meant his victory had only been for the faithful and the rest of the country could go hang. Later it was hard not to think that just as they were going to put the axe back in the woodheap the people of Australia heard him say on the television, 'This is a victory for the true believers,' and they decided to leave it at the back door ready for next time.

CHAPTER 12

I say sometimes, that all goes by wager of battle in this world;
that strength, well understood, is the measure of all worth. Give
a thing time; if it can succeed, it is a right thing.

THOMAS CARLYLE, ON HEROES, HERO WORSHIP AND
THE HEROIC IN HISTORY

T HE DEMOCRATIC POLITICAL process works according to a system of relatively benign corruption—relative to an undemocratic political process, that is. The corruption exists in the dissemination of information by the media and in the efforts of governments and oppositions to manipulate the process to suit themselves. It is inescapable and ineradicable. It falls well short of propaganda because it is a free-for-all: for every opinion there is a countervailing one; for every lie there is at least an opportunity to correct the record; for every cover-up there is the prospect that the truth will be exposed. It is anarchy with threads of order. The French nature film, *Microcosmos*, might be a useful parallel: creatures of all descriptions hunting each other, laying trails and traps for each other, posturing and making positive spectacles of themselves for each other, grunting and whirring and jabbering at each other, fertilising each other, eating and being eaten by each other. But the naked eye sees only a tranquil meadow—or in our case, a democracy that works tolerably well. Then there is the pendulum which swings like the seasons. There are long dry spells that leave one wondering if relief will ever come, and then what comes is not relief but a flood. There are feral episodes. And there is the occasional political leader who wanders through like a Vandal and throws a big rock in the pond. Still, the natural order survives: it evolves constantly and it is modified, but the basic dynamics are unconquerable. It is permitted for a politician to bellow at an editor or shut out journalists and stories that offend him; and a farmer may bellow at the sky or do a rain dance, or try to stamp out grasshoppers. In their different cultures, both are common forms of behaviour, and both leave the order unchanged.

It is nonetheless essential to the proper functioning of democracy that the corruption of the system is understood. When ordinary citizens are libelled or misrepresented in the media they are outraged and seek redress, sometimes through the courts, sometimes through the media itself. Which course is a matter for judgment: depending on the dimensions of the offence, the degree of hurt or rage it has provoked, the cost of litigation, the chances of success relative to both the cost and the adverse publicity which a court case or media storm may bring. Politicians and governments are misrepresented every day, almost every hour of the day. Sometimes it is deliberate, sometimes accidental, sometimes the result of carelessness or incompetence. And every day politicians and governments have to make those same decisions. Naturally, only rarely is litigation contemplated: the crucial decisions, usually mediated by staff and media advisers, concern truth or accuracy relative to political damage. If I complain about a false or unfair allegation will I succeed only in drawing more attention to it? Will a journalist's opinion be lent more credibility if I publicly take issue with it? Because there can be no sure way of knowing the answer to these questions, and because the consequences can be disastrous, countless distortions and falsehoods are allowed permanent entry to the political landscape. It would of course be physically impossible to stop them all—and politicians seen attempting it are immediately identified as fools.

The alternative, universally practised, is media management. Media management is a bit like Landcare or biodynamic farming. One works with the natural order rather than in conflict with it.

One becomes part of it. Hungry journalists need feeding. The bigger ones need bigger serves and more. Friendly ones need occasional rewards, unfriendly ones inducements to come over. The food is stories. Stories contain varying degrees of fact and interpretation. Many require modification, known as spin. Some require both spin and lunch. Sometimes they need to be exclusive; but every exclusive feed has an attendant risk of retribution from those not fed. That is why the usual and essential feeds, apart from written press releases, are press conferences and doorstop interviews, which Joh Bjelke-Petersen famously called 'feeding the chooks'. These are open slather. The politician needs to be reasonably articulate, but as Bjelke-Petersen demonstrated, that is less important than looking confident and in control; and looking confident is less important than getting your message across in the form that fits a news grab. The politician must do this even if he is not asked a question on the subject. Then he must get out from the scrum before he is asked questions likely to confound, confuse or anger him, or lure him to some indiscretion. This is not always easy: there is always the temptation to respond to some harmless-sounding question thrown from left field, a curly one, or one containing a slight or some other poisonous bait. One never knows what is lurking in a doorstop until one's leader is safely in the car.

Just as surely one can never be sure what the media will run with. Not at least on normal days. They can be directed up to a point; dissuaded from prejudice, injustice and folly sometimes; foiled by the creation of a smokescreen or the setting of a hare. But no technique is foolproof and nothing works forever. Even when the momentum is with you and right is manifestly on your side, you cannot insure against a maverick in the pack. And there are days on which one *can* be sure what they will run with. If the budget deficit goes through the roof or tax cuts out the window, nothing will prevent a universal onslaught.

These feeding frenzies are not always so predictable—like earthquakes they come from nowhere and strike at random. Like tornadoes they appear to feed upon themselves, gathering force as they go—even to the point at which their principal justification appears to be the failure of the government to stop them. As if they are saying, as you cannot control us why should we not hold you in contempt? Once started, no human agency can stop a feeding frenzy. They must be ridden out. Yet there are precautions available to us well before the moment arrives when there is no option but to get in the bath with a mattress over our heads. Risks can be minimised by care, restraint and good management and, above all, by staying half a step ahead of the game. To be chronically reactive is to invite disaster. It is also best practice, of course, to be on good terms with the media—while always exercising a proper dignity to treat them as equals, mates, people with rights. Never forget they are as much a part of nature as the prime minister himself.

It was reasonable to imagine that Paul Keating's second government would begin life free of doubt and charged with spirit and ideas. The election had granted him a new canvas. He had little more to do, it seemed, than decide where first to apply his brush. He had the authority of popular election. By proving himself against his critics and opponents he had put his power in the party beyond question. And in trouncing Hewson, furthermore, he had put paid to an entire alternative ideology. He had been right to say on the night that no-one would ever go to the people with such policies again. In future, stealth would be employed. For as long as anyone could see, the Coalition would be working their way back to scratch from whence they might start again. While they laboured with that task and dealt with the awful disappointment of their loss and the equally awful recriminations, Keating was free to follow his quest for the big picture. Most of this, including basic steps towards the creation of an Australian republic, he had described in the previous year; and so, together with his power, he had a mandate as unassailable as Hawke's had been in 1983 and just as much his own. Readers of the *Bulletin* were told that it was now 'The Power of One'. 'We have won an inspired victory. One of the really great victories of our history,' he told the State ALP

Conference in Sydney in June. He pointed out that ten years earlier social democratic parties dominated the European political landscape, but not any more. In the eighties the need to 'confront new realities and yet keep faith with traditional principles' had proved too much for them. If they kept their principles and neglected the new realities they were run over by free-market conservatives. If they attended to the realities but neglected their principles they lost first their integrity and then their supporters. But Australian Labor had survived.

In that speech he laid out his plans. He had authorised an organisational review of the party to open it up to ideas, attract new members, and select better candidates. He had set up a high level inquiry leading to, in the first half of 1994, the first white paper on employment since 1945. He had established a new Office of Regional Development and a taskforce led by Bill Kelty to pull the regions into the national mainstream. In that speech he stressed the need for collective effort. Full employment depended on the country deciding it wanted full employment: not just governments but business, unions, schools and colleges had to take up the cause. Similarly, the regions' problems would not be addressed with drayloads of Commonwealth money: it would be less a question of what the Commonwealth could do for the regions, more one of what, with Commonwealth assistance, the regions could do for themselves. He urged the Labor Party to back Mabo and reconciliation as a 'true Labor cause'. Over the next couple of years he wanted 'to build among Australians a more general sense of identification with national aspirations'. A broader consensus on social democratic ideas and achievements, the republic and reconciliation. Labor would maintain the pace of change. It would keep both its principles and its zeal. It would be both nimble and immovable, 'both the mammoth and the mountain goat'. He laid it out in front of the party, in front of the country. It was all theirs, all his.

But no democratically elected leader ever begins with a clean slate. While Keating had won with a handsome majority, his victory was clouded with the suspicion (it was very nearly a fact) that the vote had been less for Paul Keating and Labor than against John Hewson and the GST. Some of the baggage was obvious, some disguised. Paul Keating would always be Paul Keating, which meant extended smooth sailing was out of the question, even if circumstances were favourable. No-one, including very likely the journalists themselves, could predict the mind and mood of the press gallery. Insofar as they are governed—or govern themselves—by a pendulum, the honours they bestowed upon him now made it probable that later they would raise the bar. The gallery sometimes tries to even up the game. They begin to award penalties that have not been earned and they would not normally award, and the contest ceases to be one in which rewards are proportionate to achievements and rules apply equally to both sides. To compound matters, the press had been wrong about the election. It was silly to imagine that we would see in the wake of their mistake a collective effort to make amends. If it was not in Paul Keating's nature to be contrite it was even less in theirs. They might look and sound a little bashful for a month or two, and shake their heads and say they got it wrong, but being nothing if not intensely human, in their hearts they were resolved to have their judgment vindicated. It did not help that Keating was unwilling to let them forget their error. Who could blame him? They thundered so righteously; they wrote him off and tagged around for the last two weeks without listening or seeing. Keating saw this not only as professional failure, but as betrayal. If politicians had done as badly as the media, the media would be 'baying for their blood', he told a press conference soon after the election. Next time any of you are absolutely certain about something, he said, ask yourself, 'Can I be as confident of these views as I was about the election result of 1993?' Nothing in his nature, including a streak of sadism, it sometimes seemed, would allow him to forgive; even when it was clear that his contempt only made their spite and revenge more certain.

Canberra's trees were turning bronze before our eyes, and patches of gold flecked the landscape north of the Divide, where the farms lie in the valleys and the houses sit sadly by the sandy roadsides. It never failed to make me forlorn. As we flew down over the Brindabellas through the air pocket which often lies in wait for planes, over the pool above the bridge on the Goodradigbee River where twenty years before I hooked and lost a monster trout on a small green lure, the poplars were yellowing. It was autumn in Canberra. We needed spring.

The first signs of our grim future appeared on the day after the election. They entered into the very triumph. As people continued to grin and drink champagne in the hotel rooms which had been the campaign office, I waited for the lift across the corridor. I was going back to Melbourne where great celebrations were promised. The doors opened to reveal three men in suits, all carrying briefcases. The middle one was the department secretary, Mike Keating. As the lift descended I wondered what formalities needed to be observed so urgently, and why it took three of them. It was reality calling: early evidence that victory had come at the expense of certain freedoms. The new Labor Government was born entwined in creepers whose roots were in its own past, and half its life would be spent avoiding suffocation.

The men had come to talk about the numbers; specifically, to tell us that the government could not afford to pay the tax cuts. The revenue expected when the ingenious plan was hatched and on which the cuts depended had not materialised. Growth had been too slow, fiscal drag inadequate to the task. The figures had double-crossed us. Now we would have to double-cross the people. There were nasty implications for Keating's authority in caucus, though no-one was looking that far ahead—they sat there spectrally, like bandits on the horizon where the August budget also lurked.

Sufficient unto the political day is the evil thereof. A new cabinet had to be appointed. It is a cruel thing to follow on a triumph. A competent minister, the Victorian left's Peter Staples, was left out. Less competent and less deserving people were put in. Then there were the near imponderables. Who should be the Minister for Industrial Relations, the pivotal portfolio for a government that balanced on the twin traditions of a fraternal alliance with the unions and a proven will to reform, and knew that it must very soon turn the latter on the former? Some on the left and in the unions wanted Bob McMullan, but Keating reckoned McMullan was an equivocating character and the last man he needed in the job, or in the cabinet for that matter. He favoured his old mate from the NSW right, Laurie Brereton—'Dangerman'—who the left and the unions reckoned was a man without honour and nearest thing to their natural enemy as anyone could find in the entire labour movement.

Then there was Richo. Should he resume his place or go to London where he might be just the man to tell the Palace that Australia was cutting the painter? Keating was adamant: Richardson had served his time, he wanted his job back and he had a right to it. Who would be the Minister for the Arts? For twenty-four hours it seemed likely to be the New South Wales left in the person of Frank Walker. And Ros Kelly might be Minister for Women's Affairs. Keating took little persuading that Walker fell well short of expectations in the arts community and he decided that Kelly's style might not reflect the element of ideological purity and gravitas which women's affairs are thought by some women to require.

Briefly, the Prime Minister proposed taking both portfolios on himself, as several artists and women had requested. He would need a reliable minister assisting in each case. For arts he thought the Tasmanian senator, Nick Sherry, might do the job—it was reported that his father was an actor and his mother a stage designer. This, with his coming from a place so far from Sydney, made him almost perfect. But apart from rapture on the day that he announced it, what would be the Prime Minister's reward as Minister for the Arts? What can you do with idealists except disappoint them? Within six months half Australia's artists—and three-quarters of those who claimed to be—would feel betrayed, and half of them would say so. And meanwhile, as the artists grow crankier, the minister, our prime minister, is asked to attend the opening of a new arts cooperative in Lismore, or a ballet in Brisbane, or the launch of a book about Brett Whiteley and sign approvals for gallery purchases, film funding and tax exemptions of one kind and another. It was unimaginable. And women—for every insufferable political torture the arts offered a prime minister, women offered two of a crueller kind.

Long into the night the discussion went on in the office while the Prime Minister slept at the Lodge; and still Don Russell would not hear of expanding the cabinet from eighteen to nineteen and making the nineteenth McMullan. He would not hear of it because the Prime Minister would not hear of it. But in the morning we all awoke with the same thought—that it was pure madness to leave the competent, plausible, new and unaligned McMullan out of the second Keating cabinet. Russell had found his cat dead in the backyard and this seemed to galvanise him. He went to the Lodge and told the Prime Minister that Richardson should be dropped and offered London. He returned to say that he had not seemed averse. Then the Prime Minister turned up in the office thoroughly averse. Richo did not want to go in disgrace or even with discredit—and, said Keating, why should he? Putting justice to Richardson aside, and Richardson knew that politics often requires it, removing an old factional mate for a new unaligned non-mate could only have stamped Keating's authority more vigorously, and acted as at least symbolic assurance that the second Keating Government was not tied to the past or any person, faction or doctrine. The decision to keep him may have been fair to an old friend and ally and sometimes invaluable servant of the government, but it was also the first strong whiff of staleness, and possibly of weakness, and it came just a few days after the election.

The compromise was to put Bob McMullan into a cabinet of nineteen and give him Administrative Services, Arts, Women and the assistant treasurership. Word came immediately from Dawkins that he didn't want his assistant in the cabinet, so the last of the portfolios was dropped at once. Then McMullan told Summers and me that he was happy with the first two but he didn't want women. He said it was a political mistake. I said it was important to get these things up to cabinet status and the chocks under their

364 | Recollections of a Bleeding Heart

wheels with a credible new minister. He was adamant. Sometimes I found myself in awe of the good politician's capacity to act decisively in his own interests. In the same position the great majority of people would take what they were offered and try to look grateful. Perhaps he did think it was a 'political mistake'; but more likely he reckoned it would be very rough-going for a man to be looking after the women's portfolio, that we may as well toss him to the wolves. If I had been Bob McMullan I would have let myself be tossed. Having spent days urging his promotion, and risking credibility in doing it, it seemed to me outrageous that he should now be choosy, but the outrage overlay a sneaking regard. Anne Summers was thoroughly aghast at McMullan's refusal; but just then she was also on the phone frenziedly trying to persuade the ALP secretariat to pay for that night's True Believers Ball, and she could only convey her feelings by such random aghast looks as this drama allowed. Don Russell walked in and out of these strange proceedings like a dog that can't remember where it buried a bone. Earlier in the day, Mark Ryan told me, seconds after I had left his office Russell had thrown his briefcase after me and shouted that he would resign. Perhaps the Prime Minister also saw something to admire in McMullan's baulk: when told of it, he did not even consider casting him back into darkness, but merely reminded us of his reservations about his colleague and made Rosemary Crowley the minister assisting him in the women's portfolio.

When Anne Summers suggested a great celebration of the election victory, the PM had encouraged her, but a few days before the great event, like just about everyone else, he was having second thoughts. This was not the United States: it was Australia and this was the Labor Party. At $100 a ticket, plus airfares and accommodation, rank and file members and ordinary supporters were effectively excluded, while the famous and well-heeled who perhaps made a statement or put in a couple of days for the campaign would turn up in droves. Some people boycotted it, some approached it with dread.

The Prime Minister and his wife entered the hall to a standing ovation and music from Holst's *The Planets*, and as they strode between two long rows of tables smiling and looking regal in an antipodean sort of way, Dinny O'Hearn, the Melbourne bon viveur and critic who was dying of leukemia, said Keating should have been riding on an ass. Bob and Hazel Hawke were there. The former prime minister looked agitated when he arrived, and grew even more agitated when the Prime Minister spoke. In his speech Keating said, off the cuff, that there could not have been a fifth Labor victory without someone winning the first four. Thunderous applause followed and Hawke stood and took a bow. Later the two couples embraced and appeared to make up, but when I asked Annita if she thought all was forgiven she smiled and said she didn't think so. It might have been, as many said, a US-style elitist wank as offensive to ordinary Labor people as it was beyond their financial reach. For those who were there, however, it was a great night for dancing and reconciliation. The Aboriginal band, Yothu Yindi, played the songs that had made them famous, the lights and camera moved among the revellers and caught Ros Kelly in a dazzling gown dancing with a boisterous Gareth Evans. Wherever one looked someone was embracing someone he or she had been fighting with for months—or years. I chose Bob Hogg to embrace—indeed I think we chose each other—and we laughed about the whole thing. I would not say with certainty that in that moment true reconciliation was achieved, though I am confident it was mutually desired. Political friendships are as fragile as any others and wounds take as long to heal as they do in any walk of life. The difference is that political life cannot be sustained without these makeovers, and possibly there is as much to learn from this as there is to condemn. At the very least it is a lesson in human survival.

When Don Russell threw his briefcase and threatened to resign it was the only suggestion to that point of change in the office. The first advisers' meeting was a replica of all previous advisers' meetings. The second one was distinguished by the presence of a very bored-looking Prime Minister not long back from a rest at Port Douglas. He had reason to be disgruntled with his staff. The Fairfax journalist Max Suich had been given the

transcript of his speech at the Imperial Peking the night before
the election. It was a misjudgment by those who gave it to him
and everyone else who knew about it and failed to intervene or
tell the PM. The Prime Minister read it in the *Financial Review* in
Port Douglas. He was furious that the press had been given an
inside, uncensored look at his thinking and words and sentiments
to which he might be held in future. It flew in the face of all political commonsense. It is also likely that the fury overlay feelings of
betrayal. It had been a private affair, after all, and the thoughts
revealed had been privileged. But the affair was not mentioned:
instead he announced his intention to establish a roster of ministers for Question Time in the House and that, governed by this
roster, he would attend only some of the sessions.

He had to give a speech to the Institute of Company Directors. What did he intend to talk about? He thought he'd tell them
about how we had got inflation out of the economy and how
before that we had deregulated the financial system, floated the
dollar . . . and now we had a low inflation recovery. But wasn't
this a new government, and all that the story of the old one? we
bleeding hearts asked. Well, what do you want me to talk about?
he asked. It was not that he did not have ideas in his mind, rather
that he had not got round to thinking about them. To fill this (we
hoped) temporary imaginative vacuum an uninspired speech was
cobbled together from bits of social democratic sentiment,
commitments to the unemployed and other 'inclusive' undertakings in the victory speech, and the usual economic pieties laced
with optimism.

The only new element was a vigorous statement of
the government's intentions for Australian workplaces. Principal
among them was extending the domain of enterprise bargaining:
the Accord was to stay; the safety net was to be kept 'in good
repair'; and the IRC would remain, though less to exercise its
powers of arbitration than to help employers and employees agree
on enterprise bargains. It was signalling the government's answer
to a question posed in various ways and by various interests ever
since economic deregulation began. It went deeper to the heart of

Labor than any other deregulatory measure, and for that matter deeper to the heart of the country—it went to the principle of centralised wage fixing, that not the market but an impartial umpire should determine what was a 'fair and reasonable wage' for all workers. This was one of the pillars of Australian civilisation, the institutional expression of the Australian democratic ideal and the 'fair go'. It went beyond Labor to the national consensus that Paul Kelly called the 'Australian Settlement'. But the settlement was already unstuck. No-one was arguing for White Australia, and business would have been justified in saying that if tariffs were on the way out awards should go too, because that was the old deal—minimum wages and conditions in return for protection. But the real question was less philosophical than practical. One school of hardline rationalists, including the *Economist* magazine, believed Australia began deregulation at the wrong end—the government should have started with the labour market and moved on to the financial markets later. But whichever end it began, how could it be stopped once started? Each reform created pressure for another. Once competitiveness became the essential condition of success, how could labour be quarantined? How could the government talk about micro-economic reform as essential to national success, if it did not make the micro reform that counted—deregulation of the labour market? That had been the refrain from business and from the other side of politics for years. When he retired as governor of the Reserve Bank in 1989, Bob Johnston was at pains to recognise the social and political difficulties: it was a 'nice question', he said, 'how ruthlessly this process should proceed'. Press too hard and the regulated areas would resist: press only softly and 'the fruits of financial deregulation may be lost'. Johnston came down on the harder side, but with 'education and persuasion and . . . advance planning to soften the pain'.

Four years later, at the end of the speech to the Institute of Company Directors Paul Keating put his government's answer to that 'nice question'. The new industrial relations model only came after the business elite had been urged to pursue social ends and the national interest, think again about mass retrenchments as the means to productivity and join in the general effort to fight unemployment. These were words less for the edification and comfort of his audience and more for public consumption. It was difficult to find anything new to say to these forums of Australian businessmen, because the substance of all speeches was always some variety of obeisance to the view that the historian, Jacob Burckhardt, noted among French businessmen in 1848; namely, that 'the state should be no more than the protective guarantor of [their] interests and of [their] type of intelligence, henceforth assumed to be the main purpose of the world'. Talk about unemployment and social responsibility and the national interest was perfectly acceptable, but it would never be mistaken for the bottom line. It was, as our own economic advisers never tired of saying, window dressing—worthy but essentially decorative. In this instance they might have said camouflage.

However, the words did not escape the notice of the union movement. They noticed that under the government's model the safety net 'would not be intended to prescribe the actual conditions of work of most employees, but only to catch those unable to make workplace agreements with employers'; that the government intended enterprise agreements to cover 100 per cent of people under federal awards and that the agreements should not be 'add-ons' to awards, but 'full substitutes'; and that the Industrial Relations Commission would be reformed to administer this new non-adversarial system with 'clear, substantial and easily enforceable penalties for breaches'.

It added up to dramatically narrowing the compass of centralised wage fixing. In line with thinking that only a few years before was confined to the right, the Labor Government now wanted the great majority of wages and conditions to be negotiated in workplaces by enterprise bargaining. The role of arbitrated national awards, a principle as old as the Australian labour movement itself, would be reduced to providing a safety net. Some said the government was betraying Labor principles. Others believed that the semi-decentralised model it was seeking might deliver the worst of both worlds—one with many of the odious social consequences of the US system, but less of the productivity benefits; and one equally inferior to the efficient fully centralised systems of the Scandinavian countries, but without the social benefits. The government argued that it offered both the flexibility needed for new business to adopt new work practices and new technologies and thus make the essential improvements in productivity, and the 'fairness' demanded of an Australian industrial relations system. Some said, and no doubt many others suspected, that it dislodged the Accord's main foundation. On the contrary, the government was disposed to say, here was a step in the evolution of Australian industrial relations which only the Accord could deliver.

Almost a decade later it sounds unexceptional, but just a month after an election in which the unions had thrown themselves behind the government, the speech was bound to be disquieting. It may have been as much in the tone and timing, and the conjunction of the uncompromising words with the appointment of Laurie Brereton as minister, but just when unions thought they had renewed the old passionate partnership, Keating seemed to be telling them that for him the heat had gone out of the affair. The speech was a slow-acting poison: for the next three years it sat there like an abscess on the brain of the old alliance, draining it of vigour and erupting every now and then with awful consequences. It was tactical on Keating's part. With, among others, John Edwards, who had responsibility in the office for industrial relations, Keating wanted to let the unions know early in the piece—and let business and the business press know—that this long-awaited micro reform was coming. He calculated that the unions would quickly judge it wise to accept the change on the much more favourable terms of a Labor government. It was to be a signal consistent with the appointment of Brereton, and the unions read it without difficulty. Some of them may have read it in the *Financial Review,* to which the speech was leaked from the PMO. They demanded to know what it meant, and it had to be explained in sweeter terms. Long after the Keating Government had fallen, the speech still lingered in Bill Kelty's mind as a sort of primal insult. And the thought lingered in mine that both the intention and the tactic were mistaken; that the speech betrayed the influence of euphoria and concussion, both of them occasioned by the election victory, and that had any one of three or four of us thought clearly, had it not taken the whole of one night just to extract a few sentences from the economists, a single idea from the full office complement, we might have seen that the passage on industrial relations would be read as mugging our most loyal allies. We might have calculated the effects and insisted on something that would do more good and less damage.

In politics, when hope dissipates on your side there is a fair chance the other side will restore it for you. The Liberals began to talk about 'inclusion' and 'inclusiveness'. Ian McLachlan, of all people, used the words on television. Bronwyn Bishop, who had burst on to the scene and was pursuing Hewson like a hobyah, preferred to say the Liberals needed policies with 'heart', but that was another Keating word. 'Inclusive' had become a catch phrase for all sides. A Sydney newspaper reported that while many of the Prime Minister's words and phrases began with his speechwriter, the word 'inclusive' was all his own. He was welcome to it. If there is one word of which I am ashamed it is 'inclusive'. It is like being the author of 'enhance', or 'commitment' or the rabbit plague. But since the Liberals had taken it up, it seemed reasonable to raise the ante. It was therefore put to the Prime Minister before a television interview that he describe the republic he envisaged as 'the ultimate act of inclusion'. He nodded and went off to make-up. Sometime later a newspaper reported that Mr Keating believed the republic would be 'the ultimate act of conclusion'.

Not only were the Liberals talking about 'inclusion', they were talking about the republic. It irritated the Prime Minister, as well it might seeing that they had until now called the idea a cynical distraction. With Don Russell on holidays and contemplating his future, a little team from the PMO met a larger one from PMC to discuss the government's next steps. Bill Blick, who was always clear and practical, recommended that we dedicate ourselves to getting the simplest form of a republic agreed by a referendum first, and only take on more complex constitutional change later. The simplest form of a republic was a polity virtually unchanged but with an Australian head of state. Blick's colleagues agreed and so did we. Michael Keating argued that the Constitutional Centenary Foundation should be co-opted to develop a discussion paper. His team generally agreed. A respected former governor-general, Sir Ninian Stephen, was head of the CCF and the Melbourne constitutional lawyer and academic, Cheryl Saunders, was a prominent and we understood, pro-republic, member. The CCF would bring bottomless expertise and respectability to the process and help dispose of the widely held view that the republic was little more than an effort by Keating to impose his personal obsessions on the country and set himself up as president.

It can be said without doubt that Paul Keating's ambitions did not encompass the first presidency of the Australian Republic. He was not and never wanted to be a symbolic figure, much less a 'mirror to his people'. The second he knew was laughable. The first was too morbid a concept—to be reamed out like a stuffed animal, with the trappings of power but none of the drama. From the beginning he insisted that no new power should reside in the office of head of state. What use was such an office to Paul Keating? Being to the republic what Henry Parkes was to Federation was of no more interest than the presidency. He wanted to be the man who got it there, it is true, and he would take all due credit for it; but for Keating the satisfactions of public life were in the doing, not in the memorialising. He did not want to be the father of the republic, he wanted to be the architect. His mind did not lean towards posterity: posterity was death, and such a poor imitation of—or substitute for—the truly eternal.

None of this altered the fact that the republic was a cause needing momentum to succeed, and to this the CCF did not recommend itself as ideal. The CCF had other barrows to push; it was less than streamlined in design; it had members who were not known to be republicans or friends of the Labor

Government. The CCF might very well make a welter of the task. Constitutional committees are famously cautious and slow, not to say a little timid. It was natural that those who urged the issue to this point and risked a great deal in doing so were unwilling to surrender carriage of it to the lawyers. Keating wanted a republic by the end of the century. He had decided to call on the Queen and personally tell her that this was the ambition of his government. He could not do this if the fate of the project lay too far out of his control.

On the day that the PMO met with PMC, Malcolm Turnbull phoned. He told me that it was on his advice that John Hewson had not made an issue of the republic during the election: were he to win, Turnbull said he told him, as prime minister he would find himself opposing an increasingly popular position. Turnbull wanted the government to move quickly: a referendum six months before the next election. He also felt the CCF might dither. It was clear by the end of that day—the last day in March—that Malcolm Turnbull would have a hand in the drafting of the government's republic discussion paper. And so he did. The Prime Minister had a meeting with Sir Ninian Stephen and asked him to chair the committee, with Turnbull as his deputy. Sir Ninian, however, was heavily engaged in the Northern Ireland peace process and politely declined. Keating also met Cheryl Saunders to discuss her role in the process. He was not impressed. She left him phone numbers to ring, but when he called, he said, she did not answer. He thought this was strange. 'I am the bloody Prime Minister after all.' So Malcolm Turnbull, who promised to get the job done, was made chair of the Republic Advisory Committee.

On the Friday night of the republic meeting I flew back to Melbourne with Ian McLachlan sitting in the window seat beside me, and Andrew Theophanous across the aisle. It is rare to sit between such social extremes in Australia and possible in few places outside the business class end of aeroplanes at the end of a week when parliament is sitting. Theophanous munched noisily on his in-flight pork and read Michael Gordon's *Paul Keating:*

Prime Minister. McLachlan declined the meal and read 'The Tragedy of the Commons' in Cato's *Journal*. I wondered if any republic could include both these men. I wondered whether I should speak to Mr McLachlan, the more so because that night I was having dinner with a mutual friend, the grazier and writer, Jim Morgan. Friendship with Jim had dampened at least the more puerile reaches of my hostility to the squatting classes and I felt no animosity to McLachlan, yet I thought I might give up something valuable by attempting a friendly exchange and decided to stay behind the political battlements. I said nothing. Better to remain the anonymous adversary, keep the animus intact, better not to risk the ardour of conviction. So not a word did I speak, even as I thought how crass and hollow it was, and what churls politics makes of us. When we landed the peanuts between us shot forward and as we both grabbed for them, as if in a game of Snap, the palm of Mr McLachlan's hand—it had not crutched a sheep for many years—found itself on the back of mine. As our paws separated we exchanged a little smile. It was better that way.

In so many ways life with the new government was very like the old. The same sub-plots kept running. The Prime Minister agreed to launch a new book about the Burma–Thailand railway, written by two academics from ANU, Hank Nelson and Gavan McCormack. Too late, Ashton Calvert objected. He did not like McCormack and when Ashton didn't like a person, no-one was left wondering. It was a useful mirror on one's own soul. Dr Calvert was a breath away from being Australia's ambassador in Tokyo where the splendidly named but non-Japanese speaking Rawdon Dalrymple was moving on. His heir-apparent spoke the language fluently, had a Japanese wife and was expert in Japanese affairs. Calvert not only thought it a mistake for the PM to launch a book with McCormack's name attached to it, he thought refer-ences in the speech to Japanese atrocities likely to offend Japanese Prime Minister Miyazawa, who was about to visit Australia. Miyazawa, who had recently been through a bruising exchange with Clinton over trade, needed particularly careful handling because he was crucial to Keating's APEC aspirations. Keating's view would be: no trade arrangements which exclude or penalise Japan. We would support the US on the big issues, but not on this and not on any notion of managed trade.

The speech was duly adjusted and caused no offence to Mr Miyazawa. Even before he arrived back at the office, members of the audience phoned to say what a splendid thing it was and to order copies. The Prime Minister had again made the point, that the soldiers on the Burma Railway were a kind of advance guard for Australia's strategic interests in Asia. It was a reasonable historical point made with prejudice to no-one, living or dead. John Howard, however, was aggrieved, as were some of his colleagues, or at least they pretended to be, and they joined with the RSL leaders Bruce Ruxton and Alf Garland in charging Keating with variations on the ancient themes of heresy and sedition. He was playing politics with the Anzac legend, they said.

These were tiring and strangely distressing arguments, possibly because there was a faint taste in them of the witch hunt which characteristically contains the shadow of the dark force it pursues. I could not believe these people really thought that history was beyond interpretation and review, that it was not open to interpretation, that the meaning of events did not alter with the passage of time and generations, that accepted interpretations were often inadequate and wrong. Yet they called this perfectly orthodox view of the discipline of history 'rewriting' and 'politicising' and 'divisive'. They meant heretical or worse. They meant to imply that there was something undemocratic and dictatorial in Keating's interpretation of history; but of course it is in the notion of history as immutable that one hears an echo of real dictatorships. In this democratic era these are not conversations one can have with the press, the parliament or the electorate. In all those places, the need to win is greater than the need to reason, and ignorance far outweighs understanding; the debate, therefore, quickly takes on the farcical characteristics of the Inquisition or the Marx Brothers. Nor is there much comfort in an office permanently dedicated to the demands of the next twenty-four hours. They are conversations to be had only in one's head, and for sanity's sake they are best not had there either.

It was to be a perpetual theme of Keating's prime minister-ship: again and again he would be charged with 'dictatorial' behaviour. Every time he 'thought anew' and spoke aloud or hastened with what he thought the country needed urgently, his opponents or the press would say he harboured a desire to impose his own perverse agenda on the nation. It was nearly always a gross misreading. As anyone who depended on them should, Keating understood and valued the institutions through which he worked and was always ready to defend the principles on which they rested. It was not from disrespect for the principles and insti-tutions of Australian democracy that he could call the Senate 'unrepresentative swill', but because, as he saw it, the Senate was not truly of the democracy and essentially did not respect it. Strident speech and unruly behaviour in the House, so often portrayed as contempt for the institution, were in reality a reflec-tion of its true function—which was not to practise politeness but to engage in the battle of ideas on whose outcome depended the wellbeing and character of the country. He would never be able to persuade Australians that these were deeply held beliefs and that his behaviour was consistent with them; that sophists and legalists did more damage to democracy than he would ever countenance, and that the media's manipulative or inadequate reporting of the national debate was a still greater menace. The republic caught him in precisely the same quandary: a republic was a logical and necessary step for the nation and the radical in him insisted that he take up its cause, but the cause had the potential to subvert the foundations of Australian democracy and the conservative in him counselled caution.

The more he thought about the republic in the two months after the election, the more he thought he must hasten slowly and take great care to keep control of it. To move quickly ran the risk of frightening the country into resistance; to dawdle allowed the possibility of a worse disaster. For much more than the defeat or indefinite postponement of a republic, Keating feared popular demand for an elected president. Popular election of the head of state was in violent opposition to the diffusion of power in the existing system; it would give the president more power than the prime minister and the parliament, and the time was bound to come when it would be exercised. Popular election would replace a foreign monarch stripped of power with a political president possessed of it. He was unchanging in his view that ideally the president should be appointed in the manner of the present governor-general—by the prime minister and with the same mutual powers of dismissal. But, as he said, who was going to let Paul Keating, for instance, appoint their president?

He was equally conservative about the matter of codifying the reserve powers. To republicans who could not bear the thought that Keating's ideal republic would leave the head of state with the same powers as Sir John Kerr had exercised against Whitlam in 1975, he insisted that there was no choice. Codifying the powers was impractical and counterproductive; they could not be codified without upsetting the balance of a system which worked well. And there was a severe penalty for misuse of the dismissal power. Kerr had paid it in public loathing and virtual exile, and his example would not be lost on any future president.

All these considerations led Keating to conclude that the republic should proceed under a tight rein. He was saying so a few hours before giving the speech that announced Malcolm Turnbull would chair the government's Republic Advisory Committee. But holding to this conservative 'minimalist' position did not diminish his enthusiasm for it. As we took off for Sydney in Canberra's beautiful autumn light, he said, 'These are amazing things we're doing.'

It was, of all things, the H. V. Evatt Memorial Lecture. When he announced that Turnbull would be the chair, 400 diners at the Wentworth Hotel alternately applauded, groaned and laughed. But with Turnbull it would not take until the end of the century to come up with a model. And Keating felt that Turnbull was by conviction close enough to his own position, and would not be subverted either by arcane legal argument or some form of populism. He wanted the minimalist position reached by firm and unequivocal decision, although in the speech he was candid enough to concede that he did not know the details of what constitutional changes this required. Turnbull's intellect and prodigious energy were the surest guarantees of this. There were obvious disadvantages to the appointment: not everyone could run up against his ego without bruising; he was Sydney to his marrow; he was rich and plainly destined to get much richer; he could not always hide his impatience for people with greater doubts and lesser minds. He made it easier for opponents of the republic to cast the movement as elitist; though harder, one would have thought, to convincingly call it Irish—Turnbull is a direct descendant of Governor William Bligh. But six sea green incorruptibles were appointed to share the duties with him: Lois O'Donoghue, the Chair of ATSIC; Professor George Winterton, a Sydney constitutional expert; Nick Greiner, a former Liberal premier of New South Wales (some people thought it should have been Llew Edwards from Queensland); John Hirst, an Adelaide-born, Melbourne-based, conservative revisionist historian; Susan Ryan, a former minister in the Hawke Government; and Mary Kostakidis, a broadcaster from the Special Broadcasting Service. It was hoped that they would bring broad representative opinion and respectability to the process and restrain Turnbull's more egocentric tendency, or more realistically the impression of it; but not so much, it was also hoped, as to allow the thing to stop or run off the rails. And three seats on the committee were left vacant for John Hewson to fill with his nominations. Hewson declined to fill any of them.

It was a rather lacklustre affair in the end, an anti-climax, or perhaps it was bound to feel that way seated next to the toplofty reporter P.P. McGuinness. That night one felt the media were determined not to share the Prime Minister's excitement, and it would not be the last evening to feel this way. They were in general not unkind, nor, with the exception of the *Australian*, very enthusiastic. The Liberals were discomforted for a couple of days but soon made sport with it. The premiers threatened trouble: in Western Australia Richard Court even threatened to secede; because, he said, it was fundamental to the Commonwealth that it be 'under the Crown of the United Kingdom' and, furthermore, no West Australian was on the committee and he had not been adequately consulted. One heard about this letter from him, and then one heard that the Prime Minister had phoned him and 'settled him down'. The Prime Minister was more worried about Wayne Goss' reaction. He was not sure that Wayne Goss wasn't disposed to make a bastard of himself—you could never tell with Queenslanders. Kennett might also be a spoiler, but you could never tell with premiers either, but with premiers you had to be optimistic or go mad. In the hope of shaming Hewson into support, or silence at least, Keating spoke soothingly in the House, and urged him and other well-disposed Coalition people to join with the government in this great enterprise. A few days later Hewson said Keating had a secret plan to leave the British Commonwealth of Nations. He had no such thing of course—'more's the pity!' we might have chorused, because soon the Prime Minister would have to go to Cyprus for CHOGM. It was like this for months. Of course Hewson would pull out his furphy. Half the population thought the Commonwealth did not have republics, and just as many were oppressed by the thought that there would be no more Commonwealth Games, no more bags of gold medals. And of course if no less an expert than Sir Harry Gibbs thought that there were only two free and democratic republics in the world (the United States and Switzerland), then the media would provide space for him to say so. It was hard to stay calm in the face of this and confident that we could hold everything together.

Preparing the ground to remove a monarch is traditionally nerve-racking. Very soon after setting the plan in motion issues of a less controversial nature, like unemployment, regional policy, industry policy, the budget, began to seem like safe havens. The Prime Minister had an election night promise about unemployment to fulfil. He remained averse to the idea of industry policy, but that had not stopped his government and Hawke's from having several. What government, furthermore, could let the information revolution pass without a policy for it, and what would that be if not an industry policy? And if the information revolution was recasting industry, the shape of the economy and the future of employment, how could industry policy be separated from the question of unemployment? Why should it be? And if it was acceptable for the government to establish advisory boards and commission reports and think very hard about information technology and the global economy, was it not also acceptable to think about a policy for the food industry—especially as that might tie nicely with the global economy, export opportunities in East Asia, sustainable development ambitions and, furthermore, have a bearing upon both unemployment and the other people the Prime Minister had pledged to help, the people of the rural regions. Indeed it remained very difficult for some of us to see how unemployment could be quarantined from industry, except in ideological terms. But we knew it was best to remain very circumspect, or else be accused of favouring job creation schemes or 'trying to pick winners'.

In the Evatt lecture Keating said that reducing unemployment would be his government's 'primary aim'; that success in this would be 'the measure of our success as a society'. Just then, however, unemployment occupied his mind not half as much as Mabo. He returned from the first meeting with Aboriginal leaders passionate about it. Soon after he told the minister, Robert Tickner, that sentimentality was not enough. There had been two centuries of sentimentality, and to proceed now with the sentiment that all of Australia's titles and leases could be made subject to Aboriginal veto would only compound the folly. If Tickner made a mess of the portfolio, he told Balderstone and me, he would go and see Hayden and get himself sworn in. He had told Tickner, he said, 'Don't come telling me you've got a ten-pound fish on the line. I only want to know about the one you've got in the boat.' Soon after this exchange Tickner rang me at home to say that while he respected the Prime Minister and admired the things he had said about Aboriginal matters, he felt he should warn me that our leader was 'backsliding', that the promised 'big package' was about to be abandoned.

It was odd to receive this 'information' from the minister just a day after the Prime Minister had again urged me to attend these Mabo meetings, and expressed disappointment to Don Russell and Mark Ryan that so far I had not done so. Ryan said it was because he reckoned I had put him in this position and he wanted me to see what he was up against. Russell fancied it was because I was the house historian. It may have been a combination of both; but in any case Mabo was Simon Balderstone's job, not mine. Moreover, I did not want to give any sign that Mabo was my one true cause—or that I thought it should be the Prime Minister's. I did not know all the implications of the High Court judgment, or trust my ability to read them right. I could not trust myself to tell him to backslide when possibly he should have been o'erleaping, or leaping when he should have been backsliding. Sandy Hollway could be relied upon to assemble the best advice and give it wisely; Simon Balderstone, belting on his keyboard and yelling into his phone, maintained a generally useful environment of perpetual, if perplexing, agitation. But in Mabo as in most everything, Keating would lead the negotiations and make the decisions. It would be his intellect and skills, and his moral universe that determined the matter—his and the Aboriginal leaders. If one could make no useful contribution, all other functions—judge, confessor, conscience, court historian—were even less attractive. All the rest, especially 'historian', were politically debilitated categories, like 'bleeding heart'. Historians were, by definition, outside the main game.

Keating was always fascinating to watch in meetings, but the pleasure of politics is visceral, not voyeuristic—voyeurs are the world's great losers. The only pleasure is in doing it. But now I wish I had been there. With Aboriginal groups lodging Mabo-style claims over mining areas, like McArthur River in eastern Arnhem Land, and metropolitan precincts including Perth; Richard Court rejecting the Commonwealth's jurisdiction in the matter and threatening to hold a Mabo referendum in WA; Kennett threatening to go it alone with legislation in Victoria; Goss insisting on protection for Comalco's giant lease in Queensland; miners, bankers, business leaders and pastoralists all in states of agitation and demanding action to protect their holdings and investments, the government negotiated under intense pressure. Much of the concern was understandable and reasonable, but there was also much ugly hysteria. At least one farmer on the Murray River cut down the old 'canoe trees' on his property, he thought to protect himself against Aboriginal claims. The right-wing industrialist, Hugh Morgan, declared that it encouraged Aborigines to 'think of themselves as separate and distinct from their fellow citizens. It promises racial tension. It guarantees economic stagnation.' It was all because of the 'guilt-industry people'. They couldn't accept that 'cultures are not equal, that some cultures will wither away, and some cultures will expand and grow'. With its echoes of Marx and social Darwinism, the Prime Minister had a point when he said that Morgan's was 'the bigoted voice of the nineteenth century'. Tim Fischer was also fond of talking about the 'guilt industry', and suggesting one minute that Mabo represented great threats to the national economy, the next that he was all for peace and reconciliation—and how dare the Prime Minister accuse him of encouraging fear and resentment. Ian McLachlan referred to 'Aboriginal industries' and agreed with Howard Sattler, the right-wing West Australian broadcaster, that a lot of people who said they were Aboriginal might not be Aboriginal—but to say such things, he said, was 'regarded as not being politically correct these days'. Fischer and McLachlan no doubt knew what they were doing: what they picked up on their travels beyond Sydney, Melbourne and Canberra, or from the mining and pastoral lobbies, was there for anyone to hear on talkback radio. The fear and resentment that confronted Keating when he appeared on John Laws's program in June also ran through Labor's polling. 'Why do it?' was one expression of the general feeling. 'How dare you do it?' was never far away. Or 'It can't be done'. It was an ugly nexus of pragmatism, self-interest, provincial paranoia and racism pure and simple.

For Keating it was the big chance to make a difference, a chance that Hawke had squibbed in 1984. He saw it as one of those generational opportunities. If he could come up with national legislation enshrining the Mabo judgment, it would lay a new foundation for Australia in the twenty-first century. To do that he would have to combat not just the Liberal and National parties under the entirely negative leadership of Hewson and Fischer, but the States, the industry lobbies, the Democrats and Greens, the Aboriginal groups very often and the majority of the Australian people who, the polling showed, thought the Prime Minister's efforts were more evidence that he was out of touch. What was most forlorn about broad debate was any awareness that these were waters mature people might have to navigate—as they had in New Zealand and North America. Among all those cries of complaint no-one seemed to ask, 'Why should it be so easy?' It was as if Australians reckoned they ought not to be made to go through such difficult processes. It was a bloody nuisance, a waste of bloody time. Inevitably, caucus was wobbly. So were many in the cabinet. But in September the draft legislation was released, and despite criticism from all sides, including some in the Labor Party, he won caucus support for it. It was really just the start: he still had to get it through a Senate in which he needed every Democrat and Green vote, and win them over without losing everyone else.

CHAPTER 13

The fact is that the public have an insatiable curiosity to know everything, except what is worth knowing. Journalism, conscious of this, and having tradesmen-like habits, supplies their demands.

OSCAR WILDE, THE SOUL OF MAN UNDER SOCIALISM

I N POLITICS IT is not essential to be known as a person who prefers a fight to a feed, but it can be useful. Threats of actual injury are not unknown but rarely necessary: most people instinctively shy even at the prospect of a fight, and will do what another wants just to keep the peace. Intimidation is practised in all sorts of ways, some of them very subtle and invisible. But this is the tyranny of the strong over the weak. As Oscar Wilde said, the greater tyranny, and the only one that lasts, is that of the weak over the strong. Fear ceases to work the moment it runs up against someone who cannot be frightened; flattery, by contrast, works on the fearful and fearless alike. 'I had found that negotiating with men's vanity gives one the best bargain, for one often receives the most substantial advantages in return for very little of substance' Alex de Tocqueville wrote at the conclusion of his brief engagement in politics. The theme is as old as politics itself. Flattery, not fear, is politics' original sin. It is astonishing what powers we have inside us once we delve—and what susceptibility.

We had been to New Zealand, watched as our Prime Minister endured a haka and nose rubbing in heavy drizzle at a marae, and stared down Jim Bolger, their Prime Minister, who did not want him to visit a memorial to the Labor Party founder of their welfare state, Michael Joseph Savage. There was nothing of the welfare state left in New Zealand—they were very modern, not to say global, now. You could get sushi where just a few years before they sold only fried oysters and paua burgers. It is difficult not to conclude that New Zealanders do not like Australians much: they have long tended to think us uncivilised, too big for our boots and morally backward. Now we were also insufficiently deregulated. Nonetheless their Prime Minister stuck with our Mr Keating from beginning to end; stuck like a paua burger sticks to the stomach for the press it brought him. He never left his side all the way down to Queenstown, where the Australian journalists who might have been cranky at the lack of news the trip had generated were tamed by the grandeur of the mountain scenery, the lake, the steamer and the sauvignon blanc with the asparagus nose. There was hardly a hiccup once a lousy economic speech sank without trace—like a lead balloon, the journalists said— in Auckland on the second day. At 3 a.m. the lights were out in Queenstown and it was six kilometres back to the hotel. Show us your free market now, we said to Dr Russell, and out of the dark appeared a validating miracle—a seven-seater for the seven of us.

Chaos had accompanied us across the Tasman. Just before leaving, the Prime Minister gave instructions to cancel a five-day visit to China which Ashton Calvert and the department had been preparing for months. Nick Greiner, we learned, had warned him that if he went to China, and then Sydney lost the Olympics to Beijing, much blame would fall on the Prime Minister's head. This did seem to be a long bow; it was more likely that the Prime Minister just didn't want to go. It was understandable that Calvert and the department were depressed by his decision. They were still trying to persuade him to change his mind when we landed in the night at a military airport near, we thought, New Plymouth. Wellington could not accommodate the mad but beautiful RAAF 707, so the Beijing debate was continued in an NZAF plane with propellers. It was foreign policy on the pay TV model, but with their usual dullness of mind the press did not imagine that Beijing was the issue as we droned on towards Wellington. There in a hotel the Prime Minister agreed to a compromise—he would make a three-day visit to China.

It is a measure of the way New Zealanders bring Australians together that our press behaved delightfully on this trip. Don Russell was also in rare form. He had decided to write a book about his seven and a half years as a Keating adviser and the idea, particularly as it meant elbowing aside other literary contenders like John Edwards and me, seemed not only to cheer him but encourage the broader and more reflective side of his nature. It could only be good for the Prime Minister and the government. One had to ask if history was not the main game, after all?

Russell, however, had other plans. He disappeared one day shortly after our return. When he reappeared Mark Ryan asked him what he thought he was doing, clearing out when there were important decisions to be taken. Russell said that he had been to see the Prime Minister and told him that he intended to resign. He would announce it the following Sunday. He would look around for another job, and write his book.

The news was unwelcome. It was not that Don Russell was indispensable, just that no-one could replace him. As if to demonstrate the point in case we missed it, Donald at once suggested as his replacement two people who plainly could not have filled his shoes. He could hardly have chosen a less convenient time, with the republic, Mabo, the unemployment statement, the budget and much else bearing down on the government. It was not possible to think of anyone else capable of providing the Prime Minister with the support he needed on all these issues. Donald did not argue with this assessment but, he said, these days he was simply 'treading water'.

In truth, no-one was likely to step forward who had the menace to win with the bureaucracy and the ministers; the ability to handle several portfolios; the depth of corporate knowledge running back into the Hawke Government; or the intimate, mutually reinforcing relationship with Keating. It was that relationship and his unequalled capacity to influence the Prime

Minister, the quality so widely resented within and outside the office, that would be our deepest loss. He was the one reliable conduit to Keating's mind. Where he went there went one's own influence. The Prime Minister said he would not stand in Donald's way or try to bribe him, but he could not understand why he was going just when all they had done together was about to bear fruit. He gave his blessing to all reasonable efforts which might persuade him to change his mind.

One Saturday morning the Prime Minister rang me in Melbourne before I was out of bed. He repeated what a blow the 'big bald bastard' had landed on us. He intended to approach the Treasury economist, Greg Smith, who he said was as bright as Russell and had a better sense of humour. Was he as dry? Drier. As broad? Not as broad. I said I had been trying to gently persuade Donald into staying, but perhaps it was time to be nasty. He thought this a wise change of tactic—'and you can be nasty, mate'. Naturally I was inspired by this spontaneous endorsement. I lay there pondering nasty ways to serve him. In Robert Skidelsky's biography of Keynes I had read recently how the great economist thought the most essential thing was to understand the nature of the times. Economists must be aware of the signs of change and change themselves accordingly. As the sparrows twittered in the half-naked birch outside I decided that I would not be nasty to Dr Russell, but say instead: 'Your career, which has done so much to create these times, has not ended, but is poised on the edge of a new phase. And, remarkable as your career has been, it will not be judged remarkable unless you are there for the years which will bear the fruits of your labours. The Wright brothers would be remembered only half as well if they had just built the plane and employed someone else to fly it. Not even half as well.'

It was flattery of a high order, inspired no doubt by the Prime Minister's compliment to me. (That's another thing about flattery, it is infectious.) Confident in this new strategy, my hand was reaching for the phone when it rang. It was Donald. He said I might be interested to know that the Prime Minister had just offered him the position of Ambassador to the United States. 'When did he do this?' I asked. 'Just now,' he said.

It seemed odd. One minute the Prime Minister was telling me to stop at nothing in my effort to talk him out of leaving, and the next he was telling him that he could have the best job the government had to offer. Whatever provoked his sudden change of heart, it was bad for me. 'It's a good job,' said Donald, 'and I could write my book and do good works with APEC and things like that.' The ante needed upping. Fear needed to be added to flattery. And if you go, I said, history will regard you as the narrow economic rationalist who gave the country its worst recession in sixty years, then cheated an election victory against an incompetent opposition—then walked out. But if you stay and things pick up and we broaden the policy effort, and the second Keating Government becomes a famously good one, Don Russell will be remembered for much more. Don't think your memoirs will make any difference to your place in history—not when Edwards and I are writing ours too. Go and be forgotten. Watch a less competent successor take the credit. But if you stay . . . I could not in conscience say it, but I hoped he might envisage himself going down in history as another H.C. Coombs at least. It might have been the sparrows in the birch outside but I imagined I could hear him thinking.

It went on for a fortnight. The Prime Minister would murmur, 'Have you done any good with our friend?' And I would say that yesterday I put my arm around him and said, 'Once you take your hand off the levers of power, Donald, you will never get it back on again.' And today I told him he would be a hopeless diplomat, yet his skills were peerless in economics and politics and the marriage between them; that he was a rare, even eccentric, master of these disciplines and wasted on the palaver of diplomacy. 'But my capacity for flattery is not inexhaustible,' I'd say to Keating. 'No, mate,' he would say, 'it's not inexhaustible,' and slide off down the corridor.

Speech after speech, press releases, letters, articles; five or ten thousand words a week in the Prime Minister's voice, many of them written while the plane circled the high plains waiting for the cloud to lift from Canberra. The children faxed their homework to the office for revision. Winter came and the lake looked like thick beef broth, snow lay on the mountains and the valleys were once more stuffed with fog. My uncle, a veteran of Tobruk and New Guinea, died of a heart attack at the pump by his dam. He had been depressed about the election result. Dinny O'Hearn was lying in his bed with leukemia, still talking bravely, but his body was a ruin and his hopes were gone. And we were still trying to talk Don Russell into staying.

COAG (the Council of Australian Governments) met in Melbourne in June and suddenly the press became very interested in Mabo. The Prime Minister issued a press statement in advance, urging participants to understand that it was pointless to stake out extreme or unworkable positions, to misrepresent the facts or the High Court's judgment, or to think that the problems would go away because they were difficult. The press, having been slow to pick up the significance or the detail of the judgment, and like everyone else not yet sure of its implications, may have projected some of their own failings onto the government. They were determined to report a disaster. The premiers could not resist the opportunity to provide them with one. Jeff Kennett staged a walkout, which some thought an entirely contrived show of despair. Keating had hoped that the meeting would at least agree that Native Title was now a common law reality and that the next step was to find the means by which the 'who and where of Native Title' could be identified. He hoped the meeting would agree that the country needed to 'move quickly to a new land management regime'. If anything, by the meeting's end the country might have moved a little in the other direction.

John Dawkins, Mike Keating, Hollway, Balderstone and Russell stood around in the Hyatt wondering if we should not give the States an old-fashioned beating. The Prime Minister stood to one side watching the ABC's new documentary on the Hawke Government, *Labor in Power*, and like a bird with a mirror in a cage, animatedly renewed the arguments.

Once he knew that his old adviser was determined to go, Keating had offered him the ambassadorship because, he said, he owed it to him for years of service. In the same spirit I suggested that no-one was indispensable. 'That's right, no-one's indispensable,' he said. 'The office will just have to fill the gap,' I said. 'But Don's pretty close to indispensable,' he said. He wasn't doing us any favours going, the PM said. He was a bastard, really. He, the Prime Minister, was much more tired than Donald. He was nearly worn out. But it was a politician's lot to see his advisers come and go like this. And Donald would make a good ambassador. He would do well with Clinton, and that would make him very useful to us with APEC. As was the case more often than the public recognised, Keating exercised personal decency, sound political reason and courage in making his decision: courage, because he knew the Opposition, DFAT, many in his own party, some on his staff and most of the media would say it smelt of cronyism. Keating would resist them all. Far from demeaning the Washington position, the appointment of his key adviser and a person of intellect and ideas illustrated the importance Keating attached to it. That was the truth of the matter—that and his disappointment—and he would live with both.

Overseas travel is good for the soul: it helps us forget and refreshes our patriotism. We went to South Korea, which had built a massive steel industry with Australian iron ore and coal, and more besides—automotive and electronics industries with international brand names. Their economy was almost exactly the same size as Australia's. Paul Keating thought it was a very impressive show. But wasn't it all done with industry policy? Wasn't that shonky? Or were we planning a new approach? 'You're a miserable bastard,' he said. 'You never stop.'

The PM was impressed with the newly elected President of South Korea, Kim Young Sam, who gave his support to an APEC leaders' meeting. We seemed to get on well with the Koreans, who according to one of the diplomatic staff were down-to-earth people—though not without a sense of style if the Harley

Davidson police bikes were anything to go by, and at the official dinner the food and chamber music, like 'Advance Australia Fair', were rendered in polished Western taste. At the usual business luncheon our man tried to excite Korean interest—and regional interest generally—in APEC. The Korean next to me asked me why Australia prohibits the entry of Asian migrants. It continued to be DFAT policy not to mention White Australia, but on tours of Asia, officials and businessmen one found oneself sitting with regularly raised it. The middle-aged in Asian countries remember what they were taught at school. At a press conference later that day, Keating was asked the same question and answered as emphatically as he had in Singapore a year before.

At the DMZ an American soldier delivered a seamless twenty-minute briefing about the border we were visiting, and concluded, 'Please do not make anti-communist gestures. Remember you are a target.' Entering the hut through which the border runs we become part of a sad pantomime: a North Korean soldier watches through the window and gestures belligerently when anyone comes close to the line drawn on the floor. We can see the 'Propaganda Village' on a hill and hear the ranting coming from it. The Cold War has boiled down to a farce. You can't help thinking, the Americans are barmy but thank God they won. That afternoon in streaming rain we climbed to view a magnificent Buddha. It was remarkable that the Prime Minister looked so much at home among the monks it was almost as if he belonged in the monastery.

If we get it right in Asia and we get APEC running well, Australia will be set up. On the way from Pusan to Beijing, the PM called half the gallery up from the back of the plane to drum it into them again. He was energetic, flushed with success, the way he often was after a foreign visit. Beijing's streets were lined with signs saying 'Olympics 2000' and declaring a 'more open China'. An intimidating guard of honour faced us lined up in the Great Hall of the People while a nineteen-gun salute rang out from Tiananmen Square. Then the Prime Minister introduced all of us to Li Peng, the Butcher of Beijing, and we trooped off to a meeting with the Chinese Premier, where the Prime Minister would encourage him in the view that APEC offered China its one chance to sit down with the leaders of what would soon be the world's most powerful economic grouping—the word 'bloc' was to be avoided. The Prime Minister felt that if China could be made a strong supporter of an APEC leaders' meeting, President Clinton was more likely to hold one. After the meeting he told journalists that he still held out hope.

At the state dinner that evening, while the Prime Minister chatted to Li Peng, a little further along the head table the ambassador-elect contemplated a dumpling bigger than a golf ball on the end of his chopstick while the translator in front of him explained what one of his companions had just said. At last he put the ball of dough in his mouth and for three or four minutes chewed his way through it, the great goitre in his cheek slowly reducing to a few bits on his teeth which he picked with the end of his tongue. His dining companions and the translator waited. When Donald was feeding Donald, nothing outside could disturb him. Li Peng suddenly rose. Keating rose. The dinner had come to an abrupt end, apparently when Keating mentioned to his host the matter of human rights.

He raised the same issue at Beijing Film Studios, where some of the world's best cinema was made in dingy buildings on a run-down lot. The young director Chen Kaige, who had been under house arrest and whose film *Farewell My Concubine* had been banned in China, escorted the Prime Minister to a bleak meeting room filled with his Chinese colleagues. I asked Ashton Calvert if we could make this visit after I had spoken to Nicholas Jose, the Australian writer and Chinese scholar. On the way to the studios the journalists muttered imprecations about the pointlessness of the expedition. But Keating spoke wonderfully well about the need for freshness and renewal in societies, and on his way through the film lot groups of actors and gymnasts put on fantastic displays for the press cameras and the Prime Minister met and engaged in mock combat with the peerless kung-fu exponent Lie Luan Jie. Next day the photographs ran in all the newspapers.

There are few things so blissful as a press coup, even a very modest one—and even if we heard a week or two later that Chen Kaige had been put back under house arrest soon after we left.

There was a little interest in the human rights story; a little more in the Shanghai meeting with Zhu Rongi. At every meeting he put the APEC case. With such huge existing trade, and such huge growth and the potential for so much more, the chance had to be grasped. With the region at peace, the world's biggest trade community ought to be established before parochialism of one kind or another, especially in the US, China and Japan, sank the idea, or the region fragmented into smaller regional trade blocs. For Australia the stakes were massive—enmeshed in an open trading community like the world had never seen, the nation's prosperity was guaranteed for a century. So also were the prospects of regional peace and stability much improved. Keating wanted leaders' meetings because only leaders could bring to APEC the executive force it needed to seize the moment.

The trip had been flawless and successful. It was a pity that among all the good news the ABC's Jim Middleton reported that on the flight from Pusan to Beijing, in a conversation about Mabo and the premiers, the Prime Minister made unflattering remarks about Wayne Goss and called his adviser, Kevin Rudd, a 'menace'. The Prime Minister confronted Middleton in the foyer of the Shanghai hotel and told him that he had broken a confidence. He probably had. But we wondered then, and we would wonder again and again, why so often when the Prime Minister travelled overseas his good works were punctured by bad domestic stories.

In his Evatt lecture Keating had talked about courage; how new world countries made much of it because much of it had been needed. 'Between the conception and the execution there is faith, hope—and courage.' He said that countries fail for the lack of it. But, he said, it is never the people who let their countries down, but governments that 'lack heart', politicians who 'imagine things but don't do them', bureaucrats who 'thwart initiative'. The minimum responsibility of government, he said, is 'to at least have the courage of the people'. 'I mean,' he said, 'the courage of a person who starts a business or a farm, or the person who migrates and makes a home here, the people who have gone to war for us, or in peace laboured to create the wealth we now enjoy.' It was of course partly intended to underpin that which he was about to launch—the journey to an Australian republic which, like journeys of exploration and discovery, journeys of migration, needed courage. It was to say that by this act of boldness the government was keeping faith with the people. It was satisfyingly powerful on the night, but it wasn't reported. Perhaps the thought was too complex, or out of keeping with the press image of Keating. If we are bold, he said, and faithful to our beliefs, the 1990s would be a watershed in our history as the 1890s had been.

That was the point of the republic: it was 'important that the reality of our having to go it alone is matched by our ability to go it alone', and that depended on 'our shared consciousness of the task before us' and other qualities of collective mind and spirit and unity. But hence also the need for vigorous government activity in the economy and the society. How else to come up with a robust social democracy, or an innovative industrial culture?

So why, within weeks of this announcement, were the Prime Minister and his office in a state of seeming paralysis?

In the office it was excitement mixed with disenchantment and frustration. Away from the office it was just disenchantment. It was like Siegfried Sassoon when he was in England recuperating among friends and not across the Channel where the men and the guns were: as foul as the battle was, it was infinitely better than life in the wash of public opinion. Especially perhaps, Melbourne public opinion, which to me seemed always at least tinged with antipathy. To venture wider, into family events in country towns, was to sense it even more. Rarely would they tell you that you were keeping bad company, but you knew that was what they thought. An aunt was frank enough to tell me that Keating was an ignorant, stupid man and not even educated.

After I appeared on an ABC television show I received a letter from a seventy-eight-year-old veteran of the 9th Division who said that he was surprised to hear me 'speak well of Keating'. The PM seemed to him a 'school drop-out with the arrogance and hubris of an illiterate'. He much preferred someone of 'knowledge and vision' like Barry Jones, and he attached a long list of useful things a good government would do. A farmer told me that they didn't understand anything in Canberra. But wasn't the constant battle for markets, including agriculture in the GATT, building a stable and fair international trading environment—weren't these worth anything to farmers? Not really. Didn't it indicate some understanding of farmers' needs? No. Wasn't the lower dollar better for exports? The trouble was the politicians didn't listen. But weren't they elected to govern? Did people want to spend their time talking to politicians? Yes. Bloody oath. He would love to tell them what he thought, he said. I do believe that some constituents came to think of Keating in the way that some of those who made feeble attempts on the life of George III thought of their monarch—not that he was bad or mad, or brought harm to the country, but he wouldn't *speak* to them and they could not speak to him.

It was not that public opinion was wrong; it was that it did not know. It was unbearable to engage with people who did not know what it was like, and could not understand if you tried to tell them. And to try was somehow to betray the whole endeavour. One wanted to be with one's troops. Driving them to greater effort, or madness if necessary. We had a lunch meeting to consider Don Russell's replacement. There were four of us. Guy catered and even produced a menu, a kind of à la carte record of the event. The Treasury's Greg Smith had declined the job. The new candidates included a deputy secretary from DFAT and Allan Hawke from PMC. The DFAT man appeared to have several bitter enemies, though it seemed that everyone from DFAT had several bitter enemies. Hawke was a jovial robust chap who wore a beard, aftershave and a bright green suit, any one of which would normally have disqualified him in the eyes of our Prime

Minister. He also had a PhD, like most people in the Prime
Minister's Office, but his had been on the subject of grasshoppers,
which on the face of it was even less useful than one on history.
Nevertheless, Hawke was confident and lacking all affectation, and
he came with a strong recommendation from Mike Keating who
said he was a good manager and a tough negotiator. These were
useful qualities and there were no visible signs of any psychological fracturing. By the end of the meeting we had agreed that
Allan Hawke should become the new principal adviser.

Dr Russell blushed a good deal at this meeting. We were still
in the habit of flattering him and by now he knew. Nearly
everyone in the Prime Minister's Office blushed. Blushing was
probably inevitable in a political office where no-one is without
sin and everyone knows it. People blushed for what they knew
and for what they knew was known. Sometimes they blushed for
the unblushingness of others. Not surprisingly, the only two who
didn't were John Edwards and the Prime Minister.

Every winter of the Keating Government seemed to be worse than
the one before. It was true that progress was made with Mabo; the
republic now had rails on which to travel; the unemployment
white paper was being prepared; a regional development taskforce
established. And word came from Washington that Bill Clinton
intended to give his blessing to an APEC leaders' meeting. The last
was truly historic and the press called it 'Keating's APEC triumph'.
And yet there was a sense of mystifying inaction. The budget was
bound to be bad and the tax cuts would cause us to bleed. All the
more reason, some of us said, to gather momentum where we
could. In truth it might have had less to do with industry, employment, regional development or any other policy, and more to do
with words and signs. For twelve months in the previous year the
Prime Minister had been urged to say that a great national effort
must be made to find employment in the new order of productivity. He had finally said it during the election campaign. But he
would not say it now. Bill Clinton said it, but Paul Keating would
only talk about participation rates and the need for growth. He

would not venture into hazy ill-defined areas that might deliver high-sounding phrases but poor policy. He had a point, of course, but it was not a political point, nor a rhetorical point, nor a point that would lead the public mind towards our white paper which itself presupposed that growth was not the only answer and increased participation rates the only explanation. He would not say 'national unity'. When the premiers fought him over Mabo, he would not seize the high ground the Commonwealth afforded and call on them to put the national interest first. His language seemed still to be derived from those days in Treasury when they talked about pulling levers, and occasionally biffing an opponent or a colleague was the only relief from routine. To the less patient sometimes it seemed that this diminished language governed policy as much as it described it. What had been surrendered was the potential of words to create calm as well as excitement; to suggest hope, to create a sense of travel but without chaos or rancour. We seemed to use such a small part of the language, and such a deracinated part, in our conversations with the people. Half a dozen more phrases were all he needed to convey to the people that he needed them in concert with his vision, that what he did he did for them and for the country.

The Melbourne political scientist, Judith Brett, wrote in the *Age* that modern Labor was much more skilled at language than the Liberals. They were better with cultural metaphors, she said. She described the Liberals as 'philosophically bankrupt'. Brett's article fitted perfectly with my efforts to persuade him to deliver a strong philosophical speech about national unity before the looming horrors of the budget. The Prime Minister read it differently: he rang pleased with the article and said he would use it to 'biff' John Hewson.

Language may not have been the reason, but just four months after winning the election the government was trailing a seriously divided and 'philosophically bankrupt' Opposition in the polls. In the media they described Keating as the 'part-time' Prime Minister. They said he was 'the phantom of the Lodge'. Some commentators suggested that he wasn't up to the job; it was rumoured that colleagues thought he was pursuing Mabo, the republic and APEC for the personal glory he imagined they contained, rather than the issues which 'mattered to Australians'. It was said that he did not live up to his rhetoric, that he could not talk unscripted about issues beyond economics and antiques. In substance, these allegations were untrue. In substance, the enormous Thai teak table he had purchased for the Lodge for what he reckoned was a tenth of its actual value was not an issue either, but it was an issue on talkback radio which meant it was a political issue. The same could be said of his investment in the piggery at Scone. It went with the absence of signs that he had a genuine interest in the lives of the Australian people. The gallery were vermin, he said. They are wrong about the substance, I said, but they're right about the perception. He didn't agree. This conversation took place on 26 July, just before the budget, a couple of days before a Press Club speech in which he had to announce that only half the promised tax cuts would be paid.

Keating was strangely quiet through all the budget preliminaries, quiet as a mouse in the Troika meetings, someone said. Then Dawkins announced that he would bring in a deficit of just $16 billion which meant that certain election promises would have to go. It also meant that the One Nation tax cuts would have to be financed out of revenue; but the revenue was not there. It was those intransigent growth figures again, and the cut in the company tax rate had not helped. As we went to the Press Club with a speech that attempted to finesse the tax cut flip-flop, the Prime Minister said that it was a good one, 'too good for the bastards' in fact. He also said that if Dawkins kept up his wilful behaviour he would have to knock his block off.

It *was* a good speech: it began with a quote from Menzies on the death of the last king which, he said, reminded us that the Commonwealth was united not by legal bonds or 'fine spun constitutional theories, but by a common and all-powerful human emotion which discards form and penetrates instantly to the substantial truth'. Precisely, said Keating. If only Menzies' successors understood this. National unity and national sentiment were all-important to our future success—as an economy, as a cohesive society, as a player in the region and the world. Specifically he used the Menzies analysis to put pressure on the Opposition and other opponents of his Mabo legislation. The Liberals, and Hewson in particular, he accused of playing spoiler in what was a great challenge for the nation. He had a point: Hewson's attitude to Mabo might have found a consensus of sorts in the 1950s, but in the 1990s it was regressive, myopic and ultimately divisive. Did he mean to say that *terra nullius* should be reinstated? Did he disagree with the court's judgment that the development of Australia was underwritten by the dispossession of the original inhabitants, or that Aboriginal customary law and tradition were properly a source of Australian common law? Or did he accept the judgments, but believe that the consequences should not be addressed? Did he believe that there was no need to address them just then, or that they never need be addressed? Of the consequences of Mabo, Keating said, none of them 'exceeds our capacities as a community and a nation'. No amount of 'sophistry or denial or lies' would help deliver Australia from the truth or the judgment of the world.

It was never going to work. 'In the old days, men had the rack; now they have the Press,' as Oscar Wilde said. They sat in silence through the jokes, and through the passion about Mabo, and one or two later observed that it was a good speech, but they were waiting for him to utter the inevitable words. With growth continuing but 'stubbornly slow' it was appropriate for the government to provide some stimulus: on the other hand it was imperative to reduce the budget deficit in the medium term. Therefore, to provide the immediate stimulus, the first tranche of the tax cuts which were to be paid next year would now be paid this year. And to reduce the deficit and 'secure the savings task', the tranche to be paid in 1996 would be put back—perhaps to 1998. This had the added advantage of bringing the tax cuts back to the proportions intended—namely, encompassing fiscal drag— whereas to pay them all on the dates legislated would be to pay 'substantially more' than fiscal drag, owing to the better performance on inflation. 'In this way,' he said (one might have thought it was a triumph), 'the incidence of income tax will not rise, savings will be boosted, and the economy will receive a fillip at a time when it's still needed.' It was damn near perfect. 'These tax cuts will be delivered in full this financial year. They will be L-A-W—law. And what is more, they are R-E-S-P-O-N-S-I-B-L-E—responsible law.'

It did not matter that many finance writers had been urging the government to drop the cuts for months, and some in the Labor Party had also wanted them thrown out. By bringing forward half the cuts and paying them immediately, with the promise of the other half later in the decade, the government was attempting to marry fiscal responsibility with electoral integrity. It was the responsible thing to do, even if it might have been a little more responsible to do it before the election. But of course the media wouldn't buy it. They wanted revenge for the election they got wrong and for the penalties he had made them pay. And, like the caucus and the radio listeners, they were getting the messages from the Opposition. How does he bring forward $3.4 billion worth of tax cuts without damage to the current fiscal position? How could he justify the fact that the cuts went to people on incomes of more than $50,000 while people on less than $20,000 got nothing, less than nothing if the cuts were paid for by increased indirect taxation? Why would anyone believe him when he said that the second tranche would be paid in 1998? And why would he 'effectively derail' a medium-term savings strategy by promising to pay them?

The journalists went after him like jackals. Disloyal as it seemed, one couldn't help thinking that it might have been less the fault of the press than the fault of the promise. There were still a few who thought the tax cuts had won the election for Labor, or at least that it could not have been won without them. It's possible that the Prime Minister did, but he defended them on moral and economic grounds: they offered middle income earners what they hadn't received in the last round of cuts negotiated as part of the Accord, and they would kick into the economy. Churlish and recriminatory, I said one day soon after the Press Club that the tax cuts had poisoned the March victory, whereupon Don Russell produced a note he had written to the Prime Minister at the beginning of the election suggesting that it might be sensible to abandon them immediately. Recriminations are never helpful but they happen, and when they do frequently they draw out specks of submerged truth that would otherwise leach into oblivion. It was soon after this that Don Russell flew out to Washington, leaving the office with a large hole in the middle.

The Prime Minister was as constant as the moon. He went into shadow and then he would shine. He came out of a cabinet meeting looking like a man who had flown fifty missions in a Spitfire, but aglow because he fought the good fight on Mabo and carried the day. He went to Corowa down on the Murray where a hundred years before a conference had been held that led on to Federation, and he delivered a speech about the republic so well and answered questions so beguilingly you could feel the tension in the room as all the National Party minds tried to fight off his seductions. They didn't know that flying down he had complained about all the dams Australian farmers dug in the landscape and 'bloody ruined it'. He had pointed out to his fellow travellers that just near here was a piggery much bigger than his own and discharging much more effluent than his ever would; that the NSW Liberal Government was holding out on giving his operation an environmental clearance while Michael Baume milked it in the Senate. Tim Fischer, with the rather blank eyes and staccato speech, welcomed the Prime Minister to his electorate, and the Prime Minister with no visible trace of irony made the eyes go blanker by saying that Fischer was a friend and such a good fellow that on the Labor side we often thought he really belonged with us. To what was likely great surprise among the local audience, for a moment it seemed possible that Paul Keating was as nice a bloke as Tim Fischer, and when, getting into the spirit of it, Tim thanked Paul for making his new wife welcome at Parliament House, the whole thing got very warm and foggy.

In his speech the Prime Minister employed agricultural metaphors: to the effect that the anti-republican 'if it ain't broke, don't fix it' line overlooked the fact that there were any number of ploughs, harrows, carts and jinkers lying unused in paddocks thereabouts not because they were broke but because, like the concept of a British monarch being Australia's head of state, they were obsolete. The venerable former governor-general, Sir Ninian Stephen, was there and did not seem outraged by Keating's speech. The Prime Minister mingled amiably, his staff were well behaved, he did not swear or act inappropriately. He seemed very civilised really, nice, charming. It seemed possible that next morning as roosters crowed and dogs stretched themselves and the first rays of the sun glinted on all those dams round Corowa, many good citizens lay in bed wondering for a moment if the night before they had not been tempted into some nameless enormity. It was another reminder of Paul Keating's capacity for grassroots politics. The next day he said that he wanted to get out more among the people. Every time he went out among the people he said he wanted to go back and every time, for some reason, I believed him. But this was one political light he hid under a bushel, and the longer he was in office the harder it became to persuade him to go out into the provinces.

The budget was the horror that everyone expected. And yet in sundry ways much worse than necessary. To protect the environment, they had decided to raise the tax on unleaded petrol. Quite rightly, the people read it as a tax on the poor. We were meant to cheer because the tax would 'upgrade the national fleet', as if those who could not afford fuel for an old car would somehow find the money for a new one. In addition to this unmistakable sign that the government was out of touch, optometry was cut from the list of Medicare benefits. Wholesale sales tax was extended which gave the Opposition the opportunity to say that it was a GST by stealth. Promised child care benefits were not delivered. It was a political monster of a budget, and what seemed most remarkable, it had appeared out of an office close to our own, in fact in combination with our own, and yet it bore no resemblance to anything we'd hoped for or expected. It was a mystery how it came to be, a booby, a freak of nature. Old ladies jammed the office phones at night; the faxes clogged with hostile messages from optometrists and builders and women's groups. Owners of old cars abused us on the airwaves. The newspapers tore shreds from us. The ACTU and people all over the country who had voted Labor and cheered when Paul Keating said he'd look after them talked about 'betrayal'. The Democrats had a field day on the high moral ground, and swore they would extract their usual pound of social justice. The Liberals enjoyed a temporary revival and said Keating had lied his way back into office.

Some people in the PMO said it would soon pass, that caucus would be savage for a while but soon they would go home and, away from the heat for a day or two, they would calm down. It is true that parliament has a certain demonic agency: it is governed sometimes by the same principles that operate in henhouses—there's a lot of strutting and muttering and posturing. Stephen Smith, the same one who had been Keating's political adviser just a year before, turned up on the television, standing outside the parliament saying why caucus was in rebellion. The Prime Minister phoned him and told him that he and Wayne Swan could forget about finding places in this or any future Keating ministry. He told us that he would call the caucus together and give them a dose of what he'd just given Smith. We said it was a bad idea, although it was difficult not to have some sympathy with his view that they were people of little faith and short memories. Caucus did not settle down. The rebellion simmered for months. It was still simmering after the '96 election. Paying only half the tax cuts was the merest ripple compared to the backwash on the budget.

If they thought that their government had misled them and betrayed their trust, the people were right. It was surely not so profound or uncommon a crime as the Coalition, Democrats and

Greens, the caucus and the media almost without exception said it was. The government had not introduced a GST or cut pensions or done anything in shameless breach of promises. The sins were piecemeal and small. But they were symptomatic of something else. The budget appeared mean viewed against the Prime Minister's election campaign, and especially that promise of his to gather everybody in. It wasn't a convenient lie, but it did look like one. It was the same with the tax cuts—it was not the loss of the dollars but the use that had been made of them. At the heart of the protest against the Budget of 1993 was the feeling that Paul Keating had made bunnies of the people. Close up, it was bewildering. How had the politics been so abysmal, so stupid, so unconsidered? The awful haunting truth about the budget was that not once in the Prime Minister's Office did the advisers meet with the Prime Minister to discuss the politics of taxing unleaded petrol or breaking promises on Medicare. Like all great political and military blunders, the harder one looked at this one the more inexplicable it seemed.

What could he do, except meet Cheryl Kernot and talk about compromises; hope that an overseas trip would make a difference; pray that when he addressed the ACTU the delegates would not boo and hiss? When he went to see them after the election he received a standing ovation. To be booed by them five months later would mean something very like the end was approaching. Keating was standing as usual with his back to the wall: 'sometimes it's better to work in saltpetre than in sand,' he said.

He was watching a documentary about Maria Callas at the Lodge. 'Look,' he said 'they clap her as she leaves the church in a coffin.' If he saw it as symbolic he didn't say so. He said he would get Mabo out of the way, go and see Clinton and then he would tour the country and leave the Liberals in his wake. The thought as usual crossed my mind that this was just another sign that he believed all I needed was reconciliation and a republican anthem every now and then. When a day later the caucus revolt intensified, he said that he would now have to rebuild himself once again from the ground up—for the sake of all those pricks who in March were going to the guillotine with their heads bowed. Richo wanted to come around for a talk. At least Richo always said we'd win, the Prime Minister said. It's not what he told the journalists, Mark Ryan said. And it wasn't what Peter Barron told me. But Richo came around anyway.

Chapter 14

Out of Ireland we have come,
Great hatred, little room,
Maimed us at the start.
I carry from my mother's womb
A fanatic heart.

W. B. Yeats, Remorse for Intemperate Speech

DESIGNING A LEGISLATIVE response to Mabo was a moral imperative and a political death trap. There were three options: hedge, backslide, prevaricate—and live with the ignominy; go the long way round—and perhaps get lost and never reach the other side; or wade straight in—and risk disaster. Keating waded in. From that moment we could never be sure that he would not sink irremediably in quicksand or reach the other side in triumph, but alone and stranded. Mabo had all the elements of political horror. The legal sticking points made it irresistible to lawyers and pedants. Its moral and emotional content attracted the sanctimonious and hysterical, in addition to more sober bleeding hearts. It concerned money and property, so the venal and the paranoid would not stay away. It was an argument about history so it was open to all sorts of mischief. It set black rights against white so encouraged racists and cranks. And because it was a national issue, the States felt they had a dispensation to be mad.

By the end of July 1993 the people working on Mabo displayed signs of exhaustion, and those working around them, who had long given up hope of understanding the issues, had also given up listening. In this the PMO was possibly a microcosm of the nation. Keating's political courage and skill, and his innate feeling for the subject, would get his country a Native Title Act, but he would pay a large political price for it. Because it was a matter of high principle and old sentiment, some people—including many in the labour movement—would never have forgiven him had he failed to do the right thing. But because there were no new votes in it, only the potential to lose old ones, other people—including many in the labour movement—were quick to say it was an obsession, an expression of his vanity or hubris, an excuse for not concerning himself with the lives of working Australians. For these people his pursuit of the Mabo issue was the clearest evidence yet that he was out of touch. And then there was a third category of people: those who said it was right to pursue it but impossible, those who applauded him as he went into the morass, but when he began to sink shook their heads and clicked their tongues and said I told you so.

Whenever he rang from Washington we thought Don Russell sounded a little homesick. He sent a photograph taken in the White House when, with his wife Lisa Barker and their new baby, they met the President. It stayed pinned up in the office until the end. It was simply impossible for anyone to fill the gap that Russell left; no successor could hope to learn the way that he had of talking to the Prime Minister, or earn the respect that Russell had earned. Indeed, all advisers, if to varying degrees, laboured with the same deficiencies. Allan Hawke, the new principal adviser, kept up with the administrative requirements of the job, but he would never enjoy the authority to resist or otherwise influence the Prime Minister, or to resist or influence others on his behalf. That it was hopeless was obvious from the first week; thereafter all that remained was to admire Hawke's courage and good nature in the face of what might otherwise have been humiliation. The Prime Minister, meanwhile, took such advice as he wanted to take and when he wanted to take it. Perhaps only Ashton Calvert was consistently successful. It is true that there are fewer choices and fewer political traps in foreign policy decisions, but Calvert had earned Keating's respect as a good and courageous thinker. Those who had to advise him on social policy or politics had a harder road, not because Mary Ann O'Loughlin or Mark Ryan were lesser minds, but because everything in their areas was contestable. They could never rely on a conscientious hearing from Keating or be like-minds as Don Russell had been—at least not without sacrificing the responsibility to give their best advice. Nor could the economic advisers push their way into a Russell-like position. The conundrum was the same for them: if you did not have his confidence your advice was worthless, but how could you gain his confidence and yet tell him things he did not want to hear? It was more than a conundrum, it was a chronic and exhausting condition. Always good advice had to be weighed against the possible deleterious effects on his mood and your influence. What good was the right advice if it made him glum or encouraged him to avoid your advice in future, or worse, if it impelled him to do the contrary thing? One would never say, for instance, 'be statesmanlike' as he went into the parliament: one would say, 'Smile, it makes them angry' or, 'I imagine they'll be desperate to tear us off the high ground today. I imagine we'll be wanting to keep it'—and grin. Similarly, if he was assailing the reputation of his treasurer for loading him with a dreadful budget, one would no more discourage him than ask him why he let Dawkins have his head for so long: instead one would welcome the admission that the budget was a dud and the energy implicit in the complaint that as usual Paul Keating would have to pick up the pieces left by the incompetence of others. One would try to channel the aggression. The segue from such exaggerated outbursts was often the fuel of political progress; almost as if polit-ical reality was built like a coral reef upon countless tiny living scraps of truth and untruth.

If Mabo was a sign that he was politically disconnected, what price a round-the-world trip including Ireland? We could see him trooping around his ancestral home, or the Queen's at Balmoral, while the foundations crumbled in Canberra. We decided on a little strategy to rebuild credibility and respect at home before he set off to see President Clinton and the Queen of England and Australia. Mark Ryan would brief whatever journalists were likely to listen to the effect that the Prime Minister's Mabo statement, to be made the following day, represented the courage and vision of a political leader determined not to let a generational opportunity pass. He would explain to the nation that the Native Title Act was his government's response to a challenge issued by the High Court's judgment; he would remind them of the principles on which the government had acted and assure them that from now on the detail would be passed on to officials. Having persuaded the press that the Prime Minister's handling of Mabo had been both principled and politically astute, Ryan would assure them that his man was also attending to caucus. Indeed, on the day following Mabo he had scheduled a television appearance with Laurie Oakes to talk about unemployment. He would tell Oakes that he had called for an interim report on the unemployment white paper to be handed to him immediately on his return from overseas. He might even go so far as to say that the government would consider all options, including the introduction of a job development levy.

In fact the Prime Minister was opposed to the levy, as he was to anything which upset his tax scales. Some of us—Ryan, O'Loughlin and I—thought it worth announcing that he would consider it if only to gain the political initiative and pacify the caucus. He would not hear of it. Those tax scales, he said, are 'like the product of a medieval science. I put my arsehole into them.' We asked him what alternative he fancied, given the continuing high unemployment and his continuing free fall in the polls. Whatever it was it was not a new tax: he had just delivered cuts to both the personal and the company rate, and then been flayed alive for raising indirect taxes in the budget. We urged him to at least make the point again that if Australians wanted full employment, but not US-style wage regimes, this was the kind of option that had to be considered. He could say a levy looked desirable on the face of it, but there might be better options. In the end that was what he told Oakes, though not with much conviction.

Keating believed that a levy would be ineffectual and counter-productive, that it was simply bad policy because it did not address the reality behind the figures. The reality was this: if participation in the Australian workforce in 1993 had been of the same order as 1983, unemployment would have been about 5 per cent. This was a salutary statistic but the public thought it was humbug. The public universally believed the unemployment rate was a measure of people, hardship, lost opportunity and social breakdown and attempts at explaining this failure by reference to some other success was an insult to their intelligence. They wanted solutions, not explanations. In fact the Prime Minister had a solution in mind, one that sprang from the reality the statistics described, a systemic solution but one that he could not publicly utter. For the statistics showed that among all those new entrants to the workforce in the eighties there was a significantly higher proportion of women than men. In some contexts—when addressing women, for instance—he would hold this up as one of Labor's considerable achievements. In other contexts—in his office as dark descended on a winter's evening—he might voice the thought that the solution to unemployment was persuading women to leave the workforce. Of course he could not go about the country urging women to go home, but he did continue to believe, albeit in ways modified by experience, that the home was the ideal place for women with children. He thought that the Home Child Care Allowance might be raised to encourage such a development— though he knew, and sometimes it agitated him, that his government's new child care scheme encouraged its opposite.

Our media strategy did seem to stabilise affairs a little. The press response to the Mabo statement was in general grudging, but not particularly unkind. Caucus, whose mood and attitude had become almost indistinguishable from the media's, fell back into a solemn truce, but the bitterness never dissolved completely. The damage was entirely to Keating. Dawkins and Richardson would soon leave. So many were leaving. Button and Blewett had gone. Russell had gone from the PMO and Calvert, Edwards, Ryan and de Salis were soon to go as well. Ros Kelly would go a year later.

It was Keating who suffered the accusation that he didn't have his mind on the job, and in anger from time to time he said they didn't know just how far off the job his mind was. When Richardson told him that he must be seen about the branches, the Prime Minister told him that there was no way he would be conscripted to the barbecue circuit. He told Richardson, so he related to Ryan and me, that he'd walk out on the party if the caucus kept their budget rebellion going. He'd do a Theodore. Just as Theodore said he was more interested in a gold mine in Fiji, Paul Keating would tell them he was more interested in his piggery. He did have a point: the politics of the budget had been poor, the tax cuts manoeuvre was always going to be ugly, but much had been delivered since the election and in difficult circumstances: the gallery and the caucus might stop hounding him for a moment and ask themselves where else in the world was a government doing better with the jobless recovery? Which countries were getting more growth? Where were they putting more into solving the unemployment problem; where had they found the answer to the perverse consequences of productivity improvements?

Despite the threats, while all around the ranks of the old guard thinned, Keating stayed. Every few months he would talk about resigning, but it was never more than talk. He was angry some of the time, but more often he was gloomy. He preferred his own counsel and maintained a barrier against those who offered theirs—a sort of thick hedge through which our voices could be heard but dully and were easily ignored. Rarely did he come to ask what we thought he should do, or what we ourselves were doing. He came mainly to talk about his troubles and every so often about the ingratitude of friends and colleagues. With Russell gone, our conversations became more frequent and lengthy, and while almost invariably I spent much time listening and waiting frustrated for an opportunity to make the subject politics rather than his private life, I also felt that listening was essential to the cause.

We were off! In the old 707 with the faded RAAF livery, roaring and belching down every inch of the runway, chock-full of advisers, support staff, departmental secretaries and their secretaries, police, the protocol officer, Norm the photographer, Graham the doctor and the press corps—all, apart from the journalists, seated in rows according to rank. We were going to see Bill Clinton, John Major, the Queen, Dublin and a little town in Galway from whence the Keating family came, and the battlefields of France and Monte Carlo where Sydney's bid for the Olympic Games would be decided. We wondered why the gallery doyen, Alan Ramsey, had decided to come along for the ride, and found out later when he ridiculed the number of staff who had come along for the ride. Indeed there were always one or two superfluities from the public service, but you couldn't turn up in these places looking undermanned and scrappy.

My doctor said I shouldn't go because I had Barrow trauma in both ears, but a dagger in both kidneys wouldn't have kept me away. Dr Killer's Drixine might have stopped my head exploding for all I know, but it did not get rid of symptoms of inexplicable rancour. At Arlington, though the US military band did their best with our national anthem it sounded more like a dirge than ever, and worse when they played the 'Star Spangled Banner' with electrifying verve. It has to be said for 'Advance Australia Fair' that it puts a brake on excessive patriotism abroad. From Blair House we watched on television and heard the voices coming live from the ceremony across the road where Yasser Arafat and Yitzhak Rabin reached across Bill Clinton and shook hands. We feared the Middle East agreement might consign us to obscurity, but Bill Clinton and Paul Keating liked each other at once and emerged from their meeting like old friends to conduct a remarkably warm and cheerful press conference. Educationally and culturally they had nothing in common, but they were very much alike politically. They were big-picture, economic liberalisers from left of centre. They were trying to perform the same trick, namely to be seen as the leaders best able to manage a free-market economy in such a way as to maximise wealth and opportunity, and yet, in the tradition of the parties they led, the most determined to deliver a good and fair society. Both were trying to take their parties into low tax, low government spending, supply-side economic territory traditionally occupied by their rivals. While their personal styles were very different, they shared reputations as formidable politicians who had sought power because each had a transforming perspective and a will sufficiently precocious to impose on the certitudes of an older generation.

Keating saw Clinton's election as a stroke of luck for his own ambitions. The President was a trade liberaliser, an anti-isolationist and a pragmatist. He could be persuaded away from the east coast Cold War view that America's international interests principally concern peacekeeping in Europe and the Middle East, rather than trade in the world's fastest growing region, and the region where US trade was growing fastest—East Asia and the Western Pacific. Clinton's support for the Seattle APEC leaders' meeting to be held in December; his success in extending China's Most Favoured Nation (MFN) status; his support, against fervent opposition, for the Blair House accord which would lower farm subsidies; his brilliant advocacy of NAFTA as the way forward, all suggested he might be the ideal President for the times as Keating saw them. These were the principal matters raised in their meeting—free trade and the Asia–Pacific. How to make the Seattle meeting a success; how certain Australia might be that the Clinton administration would attach a higher priority to trade and foreign policy in the Western Pacific; how deeply he would commit to APEC; how much they could do jointly to thwart the French and successfully conclude the GATT round by 15 December. The Prime Minister was satisfied with the answers he received. He emerged from the meeting with 'a deeper conviction that Mr Clinton is putting United States on the right path. A path west to the Pacific.'

In what they said at their press conference, and in the exceptionally warm and relaxed demeanour of both men, it seemed very clear that Keating's judgment about Clinton had been right, and that he now had in Washington a friend and supporter. 'APEC equals growth equals jobs,' the Prime Minister told the joint press conference, doing the equation in the air with his hands: 'NAFTA equals growth equals jobs,' he said and the President said he could not have put it better. The President spoke eloquently—almost as if he had just been briefed and could not wait to tell the White House press corps—about the remarkable opportunity that Indonesia and its 180 million people offered as a potential partner in the global economy. The *Australian* journalist, Laura Tingle, said it was the moment that symbolised the success of the visit.

Advisers and officials who had accompanied both Hawke and Keating on overseas missions observed Keating to be more sensitive to culture and personality, a quality which served him particularly well in dealing with Asian leaders. Some of these officials said they had never been to meetings that were so candid, friendly and illuminating. Keating possessed great charm and an acute sense of personal space. His attitude implied both confidence and respect. He picked up the substance of an argument and articulated it with rare speed and finesse. And of course he was a masterly salesman. These qualities, which made him very effective in all meetings, served him brilliantly in meetings with foreign leaders.

He would throw out most of the checklist given him by DFAT and raise just a couple of ideas, putting them with the salesman's knack of recognising the customer's need perhaps even better than the customer recognised them. He understood their problems and happened to have, right there, the solution to them. After a 1994 meeting in Ho Chi Minh City, advisers reported with astonishment how Keating had managed to transform the attitude of the Vietnamese Communist Party leader, Do Muoi. Grim and taciturn when the meeting started, the expression on his face changed to interest and amusement as Keating told him that he should consider following the example of the ALP and back away from state ownership of business and utilities that might as well draw their capital from private sources, and leave governments to fund the essential things like schools and hospitals. At the end of it, Keating said he thought he had made a friend and there is evidence to suggest that Do Muoi thought the same.

So it was with Clinton. Not only the officials, but old hands among the gallery said they had never seen signs of such instant rapport as there were when the two men stepped out of their meeting in Washington. Watching the two of them was, as one journalist said, 'compelling'.

Naturally triumph at the beginning of such a long trip spelt trouble. How to keep the media entertained and interested as the journey wound down to vaudeville; how to keep the content up as the gravity of each succeeding engagement diminished, the days and miles slipped by, the hangovers and sleeplessness intensified and the pendulum swung back? In New York he was down to speak to the Asia Society, a tired old outfit by all reports. Then it was London where there was nothing much to occupy idle media minds but the republic; and then Ireland where there was little more than sentiment, and much of it republican. The speech in New York concerned the predictable matters of growth in East Asia and Australia's desire to see American participation in the trade and politics of the region, the excellent discussions he had had with President Clinton on these matters, the transformation of the Australian economy and Australian society in recent years, and of course the hoped-for conclusion to the Uruguay Round of the GATT. But with an eye on the need to keep our press onside, we agreed to conclude with the following words: 'Tomorrow I go from New York to London, from a country which scarcely notices the presence of an Australian prime minister to one whose popular press is driven to an orgy of insults by his impending arrival. There it was recently written that I was among other things a "barbarian" . . . that I was bent on taking Australia towards "some hellish Japanese future".' We hoped to provoke such a Fleet Street storm of abuse and anti-Australian loathing, our media would get on their high horses and rally to our cause. 'I expect it will get quite abusive when I arrive,' he told the New York audience, and offered the generous thought that it was the British people who deserved pity for having to put up with it every day.

High over the Atlantic the Prime Minister sidled down the aisle and Mark Ryan whispered, 'He's come to suck up to you.' Near death in Washington, in the genteel perfection of Blair House during raspberry season, I had complained to Ryan that I had no room to work in without half the travelling party gathered round telling jokes and drinking beer; that half of them had only come for the duty-free shopping, and that having given the Prime Minister a substantial part of his philosophy and most of his rhetoric, including the speeches that we knew Clinton was reading, and having given Ambassador Russell contacts which he was now using, arranged the gifts for the President and his wife, and helped Ambassador Russell do the seating for his official dinner, I thought I was entitled to a larger and quieter room and an invitation to the luncheon with the President. It was boorish, shameful; but having said it I could not take it back and at the Carlisle Hotel in New York I was given a suite of almost obscene proportions, and it was the same wherever we went thereafter. And now here was the Prime Minister settling down beside me with some catalogues he had got from a friend in the New York antique trade, explaining to me the characteristics of a good Second Empire clock, and telling me what a great speech it was that I wrote for the Asia Society, and how Clinton had told him that upon reading his speeches he had been impressed by the similarity to his own. The Prime Minister wondered how the US President came to have copies of his speeches, and when I told him that I had arranged it through Derek Shearer because I thought it might give the President some insight into our philosophy, he got that that far-away look in his eyes. Later, an hour or so before a steep descent into Heathrow which, if noise is an indicator of these things, threatened to pop every rivet on the plane and destroy my eardrums forever, he offered yet more soothing words and Annita told me rather crossly that I should be on Vitamin C. I replied rather crossly that I had been taking it by the drayload. She said I did not push enough in the office. You must push more, she said. Just then it would have taken little to persuade me to push them both through a window.

Britain really turned it on. In the middle of the night the Australian Prime Minister stepped from the old plane not onto a red carpet as was customary in foreign countries, or even to a handshake with a senior minister, but into a British press crush— a melee. When at last our federal policemen had forged a path from the tarmac to the old Daimlers, a driver closed the boot of one of them before Ashton Calvert had withdrawn his head. 'Sorry, old cock,' the driver said. We sped off to the first roundabout where- upon the leading car, carrying the Prime Minister and his wife, braked suddenly, and the last car ran into the back of the one in front. No-one was hurt, though Ashton Calvert was still mopping blood from his crown. On the motorway I lost consciousness. I woke to hear the cockney driver announcing with condescending pride that we were in 'the Royal Borough', and there was Harrods, and this was Knightsbridge and that was the most expensive bit of real estate in the world. He should have been bludgeoned, but we soon arrived at the Inn on the Park where my suite—the Welling- ton Room—spread across a substantial slice of Mayfair and, despite its military motif including a full-sized cannon, tranquillised me.

The London tabloids quoted the PM's remarks in New York, but insisted their insane reaction had nothing to do with it. We took that to indicate the opposite was the case. Some of the Australian journalists agreed and privately complimented us on our clever tactic, and clever is the best thing you can have them think about you. The tabloids *were* vile—obnoxious enough to make that sympathy for the British people Keating described in New York thoroughly well founded. Everywhere he was the Lizard of Oz. In the *Sun*, Annita was the 'witch' whose refusal to curtsy to Her Majesty had been 'pathetic' and who would shortly be 'prancing round the grouse moors dressed like Ruby Wax'. The abuse in the press and at the airport was duly reported in Australia, and provided the best possible setting for the PM's extraordinary visit to the grouse moors. It was also the perfect environment in which to compose a speech to the Irish parliament. I had read Sean O'Faolain's *The Irish* on the plane and felt entirely compe- tent to deal with it.

In his speech commemorating the seventy-fifth anniversary of Australia House, Keating said it was not because of any loss of affection, friendship or admiration for the culture and institutions we inherited from Britain that we were now 'considering the option of becoming a republic'. It was because for many Australians the moment in our history had come. He thought if the question were put to the British people that they would agree, and he thought that if Australians did choose to become a republic our relationship with Britain would be the stronger for being more mature. He echoed recent remarks of both the British Prime Minister, John Major, and the Foreign Secretary, Douglas Hurd, who had said both countries would be driven by the imperatives of their own very different circumstances, and if Australians decided that those circumstances warranted a republic, this would constitute 'no threat to the strength of our friendship, the memory of shared experience or the future of our exceedingly healthy trade and diplomatic links'.

Among the journalists there were some who felt the Australia House speech was a bit rich coming from such a well-known Pom-basher. It was a lie, we said: Churchill was his hero, Joseph Chamberlain was high in his esteem and he liked Elgar. He had said as much at the end of the New York speech. Britain was an important trading partner, firm friend and a source of Australia's culture and institutions. The historical ties were unbreakable, even though 'the game changed a long time ago'. The symbolism of Australia House had been perfect—opened by King George V at the end of World War I (who said it would 'call to mind for all those who pass by the immense opportunities and limitless resources of the great continent under the Southern Cross'), it had been the first point of contact for hundreds of thousands of British migrants to Australia, and embodied an era when Australians saw themselves as an extension of the British Empire and the British 'race'. The republic got the headlines, particularly the suggestion that the British would bless our going. When Keating went on to 10 Downing Street, John Major uttered a word or two of regret about the sordid excuse for a welcome Her Majesty's Government had dealt him at Heathrow. Our Prime Minister thought Major was not a bad bloke at all, but the game was over for the Tories in Britain and, although it was an amiable meeting and the pictures were reassuring, little of substance was reported from it.

In Scotland, in the evening, Her Majesty drove the Australians herself in her Range Rover to a hunting shelter that her great grandmother had erected for the Prince Consort, and they had a barbecue there in the Australian style. In the late afternoon, before this excursion, the Prime Minister met the Queen alone and told her that her government in Canberra had begun a process which he expected to culminate in a referendum to decide the future of Australia's ties to the British monarchy. The Australian people would be asked if they wished to substitute for the Queen of England an Australian head of state and become a republic. She could not have been more gracious. Later the Prime Minister made a note for file in which he wrote, *inter alia*:

> The Queen told me the room in which we met had been Victoria's favourite and was as Victoria had left it. Furnished in the manner of William IV, the last gasp of classicism was falling prey to its decoration ... In the poignancy of the moment the Queen sat with her dignity and the long history of her family. I sat there with the aspirations and live mandate of a people. I wanted her to understand how and why Australia had changed ... that our position was not unlike the one Britain found itself in ...
>
> Australia had to find its security in Asia not from Asia just as Britain had to find its way in Europe not from Europe ... I reminded her that on our doorstep stood 200 million Indonesians, the largest Islamic country in the world. Australia had to be relevant in these places ...
>
> I said we were going to the region as the Australian nation with all of our hopes and aspirations, yet were going with the monarchy of another country. With a monarchy for whom a great number of Australians, especially of non-Anglo descent, felt no

particular association . . . I explained how much people appreciated her efforts throughout the years. I said it was not my wish or
the government's to involve her in any way in the current debate
in a manner that would be detrimental to her personally or to her
position as Queen of Great Britain. I said I would do all that was
possible to remove her from the fray . . .

I made it clear to her that the matter was not about me. Some
people might have told her this but it was not so. I said I had been
given the rump end of a long government which I had managed
to extend by winning another term but winning six elections
consecutively would be difficult. I said, 'You may not be dealing
with me but the issue will not go away.' . . .

When I finished my remarks, she said to me that she and her
family had always tried to do their best for Australia. I said I knew
that. She said that she would, of course, take the advice of
Australian ministers and respect the wishes of the Australian
people . . .'

He told the Queen that it would be wise to let him say this
publicly, because this would elevate her 'above the battle. But if the
debate focused on her and her family as the surrogate for what is
good or not good about Australia's constitutional arrangements,
she must lose and maybe not only in Australia.' This was quickly
agreed with Sir Robert Fellowes. 'I think we then both had a
whisky,' he said.

Grasping a press release they had drafted to this effect, Mr
and Mrs Keating, Calvert and Ryan joined us on the plane in
traditional Highland drizzle at Leuchans. Short of an actual
instruction to secede at once, or an official blessing on his endeavour, the PM could not have hoped for more from the visit. Now
that the Queen had proved entirely grown up about the subject,
we imagined a more grown-up environment for debate at home:
one in which it would be very much harder for opponents of an
Australian republic to exploit popular affection for Her Majesty
and that general desire not to offend a woman many loved and
nearly everyone admired. And having plucked our emissaries from

the fastnesses of Scotland, we fled to Dublin with our document, polishing it as we went.

In his address to the Dáil (the Irish parliament) Paul Keating drew an analogy between the nineteenth-century Irish emigrants to Australia and a government embarked upon economic reform. Both were acts of will and imagination. In opening Australia to the world, the Labor Government 'did what the emigrant does—we confronted necessity. Had we not done this, the modern world and the opportunities it offers would have passed us by.' Sometimes it felt as if one had gone to sea in a boat without oars. Sometimes mutiny threatened. Sometimes one had to fight off the doubters and the temptation to turn back. Just like those voyages in those old sailing ships, one day you might be tearing along with the sails threatening to rip apart, the next would find you in the doldrums; another, finding yourself horribly close to the rocks. 'And then of course there are the days when the ship is immaculately on course and travelling at a manageable rate and you are thinking not of home, nor even of the journey, but of the destination.' The destination, obviously, was an 'internationally competitive economy' and all the blessings it would bring. And why had Australians chosen to make this journey? For the same reason the Irish emigrants of the nineteenth century—and all emigrants before and since—have made their journeys: to break free of history, to give themselves and their children a chance, for the prospect of a better life in a better country. At its bottom it was a speech about leadership. As well as the transformation of the economy, he talked about the social wage, the Accord, the Native Title Act, multiculturalism, and the republic which might 'put a border round the tapestry of our national life' and acknowledge 'the values of a people who have been willing to imagine something better'. He quoted Sean O'Faolain's estimation of Wolf Tone, the leader of the 1798 rebellion: 'that his laughter and humanity would have blown away orthodoxy, sectarianism and cant', and defined 'political liberty not merely in terms of comfort, but of gaiety and tolerance and a great pity and a free mind and a free heart and a full life'.

And so it was that Australia, when it opened its heart, could do what Tone might have done—welcome people from suffering poverty or persecution and, with the blessings of liberty and independence, 'winnow from their hearts and minds all the ancient bitterness and unreason'. That was what Paul Keating was doing for Australia, making it open-hearted. It was, on reflection, a speech from the dreaming of Paul Keating, and it did not fail to mention the remarkable coincidence that several of Wolf Tone's fellow rebels were transported to New South Wales, and eventually took up land south-west of Sydney 'in such numbers as to earn the place the name of Irishtown. It is now called Bankstown and it is where I grew up and spent most of my life. It is my home town and the heart of my constituency—and the most obvious ethnic groups these days are Vietnamese and Lebanese.'

I heard him saying these things on a radio in a shop in Grafton Street. The MPs were laughing at his jokes. In a pub that night three men argued about it. One said it was a better speech than JFK's thirty years before. Another said it was a good speech, but not that good for Christ's sake. A third said it was a better speech, though not so well read. The first asked the third how he could make such a judgment, seeing as he could hardly have been weaned at the time Kennedy came to Ireland.

Even in Ireland there had to be a business speech—even in 1993 before Ireland was modern. John Edwards wrote a draft which contained severe strictures on the Irish position on agricultural trade. I suggested to the Prime Minister that the tone was bullying and out of tune both with the spirit of our visit and the more conciliatory attitude he had taken in the US. He agreed and told me to delete the passages. But Edwards would only delete some of it. He said I was imposing my ideological opposition to free trade on the speech. I said I was imposing what I thought was the appropriate tone on the speech and it had nothing to do with ideology. In fact I was in favour of free trade, but it was hard to imagine what good would come of hectoring the Irish about protection, even without reference to the Corn Laws and the famine. In any event, with the smell of Ireland in his nostrils, the

Prime Minister was not in the mood to be nasty. The offending passages were removed. We flew around Ireland in a very large helicopter and landed here and there on hurling pitches thronged with dignitaries and schoolchildren. At Thurles in Co. Tipperary he made a speech in the town square in praise of Ben Chifley whose forebears had come from these parts. Jim Middleton said loudly, 'I thought Chifley was just a trier.' We smiled. We couldn't tell him that the Prime Minister was in Tipperary making a speech about Ben Chifley because the department had somehow been led to believe that the Keatings came from here, and only discovered after arrangements for the visit had been made that the ancestral home was actually in Galway—Tynagh, to be precise. It was rare luck: who knows what we would have found to say in Thurles if the Chifleys had come from Donegal or Sligo?

Galway FM radio broadcast the Tynagh proceedings live. The streets were packed: the hall, the pubs and the cemetery almost too crowded to enter. Loudspeakers boomed 'please observe decorum and allow Mr Keating to pay his respects at the graves of his forebears'. It was raining and the people, many of whom wore the name 'Keating' on their coats, were drenched. In the hall he began his speech with a line cooked up as we helicoptered in over the fairy rings and the remnants of the old road by which his great-great-grandfather had very likely left the district a century before. 'I have always been proud of my Irish ancestry. Today I rejoice in it.' It was a good start, but as his ramble got under way it produced better lines—about the Irish hatred of class distinction, about the Catholic Church teaching that we are all equal when we're born and equal when we die, and equal in the sight of God, and this was the principle which guided him in politics—and he received waves of applause. In an earlier interview on Irish television he said he had 'probably' come to be a republican by the same process, not because he was Irish but because he was Catholic. For this he was rebuked for flirting with sectarianism by Tim Fischer and John Hewson. In the *Sydney Morning Herald*, the journalist Tony Wright was also scathing about the remark. No doubt it was in some way an indication of the

resentment Keating felt about real and possibly imagined exclusion of Catholics in the Australia of his childhood and before. It
was artless and unwise, but he would say he did nothing more
than account honestly for the origins of *his* Labor and republican
views—views he shared with Protestants and atheists and, for all
he knew, people who owed theirs to Darwin or Confucius.

As he left Tynagh, the crowds gathered behind wire fences
and the voice on the loudspeakers promised everyone a refresh-
ment as soon as Mr and Mrs Keating were on their way. We rose
above the sea of faces—the kinds of faces we have not seen in
Australia since the Great Depression—peering up as Paul Keating
peered down, and no-one could say what he was thinking. Never
had the journalists been so contented. Perhaps it was the brass
bands and the Irish dancing, the scenery, the air, the Guinness, the
night at the Dromoland Castle. Ireland tamed them with its
miraculous charm—the miracle being that heathens, Protestants
and cynics without a drop of Irish blood in their veins all seemed
to feel that they had found home. Whatever it was, they laughed
and sang and, Alan Ramsey aside, wrote glowing articles.

Early in April 1918, at Villers-Bretonneux, a little village over-
looking the Somme valley, the 3rd Australian Division halted the
seemingly unstoppable German offensive and saved Amiens. On
24 April the 5th Division lost the town, but recaptured it in
terrible fighting which cost 1200 Australian lives. It was a turning
point and the French have always recognised it as such. The town
hall at Villers-Bretonneux carries the inscription, 'Never forget the
Australians'. After a ceremony at the great monument nearby, the
stone pocked by bullets fired by the retreating German army in
1945, the Prime Minister gave a speech about the war in the hall.
Later, while his staff competed for Moët and savouries with
townsfolk who very likely had grown accustomed to visits of this
kind, he slipped away to do a doorstop with the travelling journalists. He had been inspired, apparently, by the spectacle of the
Australian graves and the insensitive remark of a French deputy.
No doubt he also had on his mind the GATT, and the recent

French attempt to undermine the agricultural provisions of it and the solidarity he had just enjoyed with President Clinton. He strolled up to the morning tea looking very pleased with himself and related happily how, having dealt with questions about John Dawkins' recent threats to resign for lack of caucus support on the budget, he had told the journalists that with 'the flower of many countries' youth' buried here in French soil, French intransigence on the GATT was evidence of a lack of gratitude. Seven years was long enough, he said; it was time for 'plain speaking'. But he was not so tough on the Irish, the journalists said. 'I said exactly that to the Irish,' he replied. Was it fair to raise the matter of World War I in a current trade negotiation? 'More than fair,' he said. The world ought to be a better place, but it couldn't be while the Europeans were so self-centred and selfish.

It might have made a useful, hard political point after three or four days of republican 'vaudeville', and better to make it on a flying visit to France than in tiny Ireland. If Sydney did not win the Games in Monte Carlo, his remarks might have served as a patriotic smokescreen in the Billy Hughes mould, even if they drew criticism from the French for rudeness and bad taste—*better* maybe if it drew criticism from the French. The PM's point was simple: what meaning obtained in the injunction to never forget the Australians if the French Government discriminated against Australian interests? What was the use of saying 'Lest We Forget' if it was not a reminder of obligations? There was nothing wrong with the argument or the instinct.

The French agriculture minister regretted these 'bombastic statements' and said they would not help the GATT negotiations, but that was not the problem at the Australian end of things. The problem was the figures. Whichever way you looked at the transcript the figures were wrong, and irremediably so. He had said that in the war we 'lost nearly 10 per cent of our population'. One in a hundred was nearer the mark. Perhaps he had calculated roughly that one in ten of all who served had died in France, but even that did not fit. It was not possible to find a construction to save him— or his historian speechwriter—from mockery. What was worse, our opponents both in politics and the media leapt on his mistake as an example of Keating rewriting history to suit his political purposes.

He had stayed in the Grace Kelly room in the Shelbourne Hotel in Dublin and now here he was in Monaco. Something about the coincidence promised success. Of all the Hollywood stars, he loved Grace Kelly best. In Monte Carlo the bid team were growing in confidence, but seemed unable to convince themselves that victory was possible. It appeared that many people had travelled considerable distances in yachts to be present at the contest, but we wondered if it was just the time of the year. Sydney and Beijing were the two prime contenders, with Manchester an influential third party. Republicans had not refrained from drawing attention to the fact that at least two members of our monarchy had lent their support to the Manchester bid, but quite rightly the bid team were less concerned about this than getting their second round votes. Istanbul (or was it Ankara?) was also in the contest, and one of its supporters had come in a truly *huge* yacht, but the word was that he knew the score and the party would go ahead regardless. To signal the beginning of the countdown, a squadron of French Mirages came in low from the south and roared over the balconies and, if I remember correctly, later there were fireworks.

The Prime Minister might not have approved of all his wife's public activities, but she performed them flawlessly. She worked for the campaign against breast cancer, for the arts, the Sydney Olympics and the Australian fashion industry. Wherever she accompanied him, both in Australia and abroad, she lent her husband grace and confidence. She looked the part. She was multilingual and modern. She sometimes did more in public than the PM approved, but, she kept enough in reserve to remain interesting nonetheless. And despite his reservations at the time, the same PM is the first to suggest that no Prime Minister's wife in living memory has filled the role more successfully. In Monte Carlo she distinguished herself with a splendid multilingual presentation to the IOC. To everyone's astonishment and delight, Sydney won. The New South Wales Premier, John Fahey, leapt half a metre in the air and thus assured himself of a large share of at least the superficial credit. His wife's performance and the federal government's generous contributions to the bid allowed the Prime Minister to bask in some of the glory. He told the press that it was a great opportunity to see out the old century and welcome in the new with the world's attention upon us—and how much better, he said, if we did it as a republic. For inserting this political note he received mixed reviews. The same people who, after Villers-Bretonneux, said it was scandalous to associate the name of Anzac with the interests of Australian trade were doubtless also among those who felt that the Olympic spirit was a thing of too high an order to be joined with a republic. We had advised him to leave the republic out of it and talk more broadly about the boost to national unity and confidence and what the Olympics might do for the economy. He was unconvinced, a reflection of his belief that one cannot warrant the truth of one's position by succumbing to the prejudice of fools.

CHAPTER 15

*We get into a vicious circle, we do nothing because we have not
the money; but it is precisely because we do not do anything
that we have not the money.*

J. M. KEYNES

THE PRIME MINISTER flew home not so much covered in
glory as spattered by it, and the Olympic thrill evaporated
in an instant. A disgruntled electorate, a caucus still in
revolt, the ACTU stiffening its resistance to labour market reform,
a high-minded refusnik Senate, all lay waiting for him. Resistance
to the budget had not ebbed as some predicted. The Senate
blocked passage of the Bill, and the Prime Minister was to find
himself obliged to suffer the indignity of negotiating compromises
with Cheryl Kernot of the Democrats and the Greens from
Western Australia. Persuading the country that he would devote
himself to unemployment and other matters which rated highly
in the polls was his most urgent task. No-one wanted to think
about Mabo or the republic and, what was more, we wanted to
avoid the merest suggestion that it was on the Prime Minister's
mind because we knew the public would think it very nearly a
crime and were on the lookout for signs.

Unfortunately, the Republic Advisory Committee had
concluded its report and the Prime Minister had no choice but
to receive it, and have them all to morning tea and a photo
opportunity. When the formalities were over members of the

committee took themselves to the public gallery of the House of Representatives to watch Question Time. The Prime Minister went with a Dorothy to acknowledge their presence and their services to necessary constitutional reform. He went with a grin on his face because he also had in his pocket some remarks Robert Menzies had made about obstructive Senates—to wit, they were obnoxious to good government. He was grinning because he knew what would happen when he uttered the name Menzies. Sure enough, they were driven to a frenzy. Sadly, Ralph Willis lost his way for a moment and contrived to say in blatant contradiction of his Prime Minister's position that one should not be held accountable for everything one said in the past. This produced such uproar Kim Beazley advised Keating to suspend proceedings for that day and Keating did just that. Immediately he gave a press conference to say how deplorable the Opposition's behaviour was, but the media nevertheless directed most of their criticism at the Prime Minister. The Republic Committee went home denied both their moment and two-thirds of the parliamentary entertainment they had come to see.

If the timing was less than perfect, the report itself was much as the Prime Minister had hoped. The model was essentially minimalist. After canvassing various means of electing an Australian head of state the committee recommended that the requirement be a two-thirds majority at a joint sitting of both Houses of the Commonwealth Parliament. Popular election, they said, would make the position (and the election of people to it) political, and was likely to invest it with considerably more power relative to the legislature. Given the need for referenda to pass not only with a majority of the people but in a majority of the States, the report left the way open for States to remain monarchies, 'however unlikely or anomalous'. The committee thought the name Commonwealth of Australia should be retained by an Australian republic. It thought the powers of the head of state (who might be called 'president', or 'governor', or 'governor-general' or 'head of state') should be the same as those of the present governor-general. And, contrary to the Prime Minister's firm belief, it thought these powers should be codified. Australians were assured that their country could become a republic without threat to any of their 'cherished democratic traditions'. In delivering it the committee expressed the hope that from now on debate might be more informed, rational and free of scaremongering—a futile hope if some of the responses were any indication of public sentiment. Senator Bill O'Chee of Queensland was prompted to say that the thing would likely lead to bloodshed of the kind recently seen in Russia. John Hewson and John Howard said the report failed to say why Australia would be better off as a republic, which we thought feeble seeing the committee was not asked to say so.

It was nonetheless an unavoidable weakness in the government's proposal that the report did not paint a picture of a republican future. Australians were not encouraged to reflect upon the prospect of greater contentment and happiness. Yet it was possible to take the argument beyond the appropriateness of Australia having an Australian head of state, even when that argument was attached to heightened national purpose and self-esteem or greater respect abroad. These were good arguments but they were never going to inspire everyone. Furthermore they kept the republic somewhere between the romantic and modern borders of the nation state, when an Australian republic ought to be postmodern, in the sense that its characteristics would be those of contemporary Australia—pluralist, complex and various; not oppressive or prescriptive but light, ironic, free—a republic on a human scale. The Prime Minister hinted at such a vision, putting the case for a republic in keeping with the contemporary reality; but that encouraged opponents to say, why change it? In the most ideal circumstances it was going to be difficult to persuade the populace of such a subtle argument—that a republic would confirm rather than diminish the Australian achievement, and offer a more accurate reflection of the way we live our lives. And the circumstances were far from ideal.

The people were not interested. Indeed, for many Australians the republic was one of the more infuriating indications that their Prime Minister was interested in everything except their concerns. One would urge him to explicitly address the ordinary people and their needs. Even if they could not have roads, bridges or money in the quantities it was generally believed they craved, could he not give them recognition? It was plain to everyone that Mabo and the republic were alienating votes. Could we not pursue those issues just as resolutely without talking so much about them?

One Saturday morning the butcher told me that he had seen a newspaper article alleging that I was the person responsible for driving the Prime Minister from the proper interests of Labor towards these high-flown 'elitist' interests. It ruined the day. At about the same time I began to see reports that, through me, the late Manning Clark had become the dominant ideological influence on the Prime Minister. Putting the most common allegations about the historian with those about the Prime Minister, an uninformed observer might conclude that Clark was a politically correct Irish republican Tammany Hall anti-communist with a taste for Second Empire clocks and other affectations beyond his social and financial reach; and Keating was a politically correct pro-Soviet romantic with an aversion to the middle class. Both were caricatures, and poor ones at that, but no more misguided than the notion that Keating's vision had been defined by Clark. Clark had recently been viciously attacked in the press by the man who published him for thirty years, knew him intimately and let him think that he was his friend. In publicly defending Clark, I wondered if by doing so I was not confirming the new prejudice against both him and Keating. The campaign against Clark and the little McCarthyist micro-climate it produced ignited helpless fury and black despair all at once and was one reason why the thought that I should find some decent means of resigning took up permanent residence in my mind, co-tenant with innumerable mainly fruitless schemes to prove that the Prime Minister was *not* Clarkian or elitist and could easily commune with ordinary Australians. And these two streams of consciousness coexisted with a third, encouraged by friends outside the office, who said that all we were doing would end in our demise.

In Sydney one such friend gently advised me to decamp before my reputation went the same way as Keating's. And Keating, I was told, would soon be toppled to make way for Beazley; that Barron was in league with Hawke on this and if Richo did not soon find some influence in our office he would join the putsch. It was a commonplace in these circles that Keating had been led astray by people without nous or the strength to pull him into line. Mabo was a case in point. When early in October the Aboriginal leaders walked out of a meeting and told the press that they had suspended negotiations because the government was acting in bad faith the word came flooding in on the tide—Keating had set the bar too high and now found he couldn't jump it. He would fail at the attempt and the government with him. On a plane between Melbourne and Sydney, Gareth Evans told me that he always knew you couldn't put the miners and the Aborigines together and get any kind of result. Therefore the Prime Minister's efforts were destined to end a noble failure. But hadn't Evans put deadlier enemies than these together in Cambodia? Yes, he said, but there was a core of common interest in Cambodia.

The critics did not always say what they would have done in the same circumstances. Keating knew the issue was acting like acid on his government. He might have used signs of uncompromising belligerence on the part of Aboriginal leaders as the excuse he needed to get free of the matter. Instead he told them that he had offered the best deal they would ever get from an Australian government; they had seats at the main table which they could choose to make permanent or return to the margins. Like everyone else in the government, and in the country for that matter, he had grounds for frustration and complaint—but not for abandoning the cause. And it was curious that while we heard of many people in the party, including Gary Gray, saying Keating had made a mess of Mabo, no-one was heard to say he ought to sell out Aboriginal Australia. Not in so many words.

Moreover, those who carped about persisting with Mabo did not seem to ask what would follow from not persisting. The answer was another split in the caucus, more disaffection in the electorate, more punishment from the media and a profound loss of face. Just then the media were pursuing him for bad politics— how much worse to be pursued for bad faith and lack of courage. Courage was Keating's hallmark and his stock in trade, as for some good politicians it is nous, charm or practicality. Keating had these other attributes, but they did not define him in the way that courage did. Courage was the prime element in the Keating mythos and a sign of weakness or a failure of will which in other politicians might be passed over was for Keating deadly evidence that the aura had shattered and the game was over.

Sometimes he came out of Mabo meetings raging against the Aboriginal leaders and the left in his own party and muttering various threats. The whole deal was sinking, he would say. One got used to it and thought the more he raged the more likely that agreement would be reached.

There was a limit to compromise in any direction. When in the face of the States' intransigence the Prime Minister spoke of one form of compromise, the widely respected Phillip Toyne, a former Australian Conservation Foundation chief and the government's special consultant in the Mabo negotiations, threatened to walk out on proceedings. When he spoke of another form of compromise, the Aboriginal leaders did walk out on proceedings. In August the Queensland Government was threatening to introduce its own legislation to protect mining operations at Weipa against a claim by the Wik people, even in contravention of the Commonwealth Racial Discrimination Act. Or it would be the Farmers Federation, and when they were satisfied the Greens weren't. The miners were at least reliable: they would never be satisfied until their leases extinguished Native Title, even though they did not extinguish freehold title. The law in Western Australia said: 'When a mining tenement expires or is surrendered or forfeited, the owner of the land to which the mining tenement related may take possession of the land forthwith.' Not if the owner was Aboriginal, said the mining industry. It would create 'uncertainty'. It threatened national development. Better to have racial discrimination built into the law.

The National Farmers Federation took a different view, or at least their leader, Rick Farley, did. Farley would not accept the government's recommendation that pastoral leases granted since the introduction of the Racial Discrimination Act should NOT be held to have extinguished Native Title, even though it was believed that, when tested, in 99 per cent of cases involving valid leases extinguishment would be proved. This approach, Farley said, guaranteed a dramatic increase in common law actions, actions which could take years to resolve. It would create uncertainty and destroy confidence in an already battered pastoral industry. And it may not stop at the pastoral industry, but involve residential and mining leases. It would be a bonanza for lawyers and disaster for everyone else including, he suggested, the Aborigines. In a letter to Sandy Hollway, Farley wondered 'if Aboriginal leaders had thought through the ramifications', given the advice that nearly every action was bound to prove Native Title had been extinguished. Noel Pearson, the young Aboriginal lawyer from Cape York, was one who had thought it through. Pearson discussed with Toyne the idea that Aborigines forgo their claims over pastoral leases in return for the right to convert Aboriginal pastoral leases, and other land which in future may be available for purchase—possibly through a Commonwealth land fund—to the equivalent of Native Title. The plan removed the uncertainty from the pastoralists' position and gave to the Aborigines something more concrete and hopeful than the pursuit of 'slender and uncertain rights' in the courts. Toyne discussed it with Farley. On the afternoon of Monday, 18 October, Keating spoke to Farley who told him he could not accept anything short of extinguishment. Cabinet met at 5 p.m. and Keating persuaded first that meeting and then, over several hours, the Aboriginal leaders waiting in his office across the corridor to accept the deal. At 10 p.m. Keating rang Farley. The deal was done.

Twenty-four hours later the deal was announced and acclaimed as something of a triumph. At the same time the Prime Minister also secured the passage of the budget by means of a $144 million deal with the Greens and Democrats. It was a great day. The newspapers announced that Keating, who was about to leave for the Commonwealth Heads of Government Meeting in Cyprus, had pulled off a double. Farley was a hero of the Native Title legislation. It is probably also true that only Toyne, with his negotiating experience and the trust invested in him by both parties to the deal, could have kept the flow of goodwill and ideas going when it might otherwise have dried up; and Simon Balderstone's friendship with Toyne, his noisy zeal and unquestioned integrity made a vital difference. Remove any of these elements— and Pearson, of course, or Lois O'Donoghue or half a dozen other Aboriginal leaders, or add to them someone weak in mind or spirit—and the legislation might not have come to pass.

Yet Keating was the essential player: not because he had all the ideas, which he didn't; or because he was the supreme advocate and negotiator, which he was. It was because of the authority he brought to all negotiations. It was the prerogative of his office, but more important was the use he made of it. It came from what he called 'weight'. In this case it was a mastery of the brief which was not bureaucratic or legalistic, but imaginative and empathetic. He was helped by excellent advice, not just from Balderstone and Toyne, but from the public servants Sandy Hollway and Mike Dillon. In this way he brought the 'weight' of the office with him. And there was that charismatic vernacular which gave his arguments lustre and genuineness at the same time. I went to a meeting between the Prime Minister and the Aboriginal leaders on 14 October. There had been a stand-off owing to what each side believed had been a breach of faith on the other's part. Keating looked exhausted with those truly startling huge black rings which sometimes formed round his eyes. But he had new proposals to accommodate their concerns about the Racial Discrimination Act. That was the first essential step. The second one was to tell the leaders that it was no good fighting for something that could not be: legislation which we knew the States would take to the High Court; legislation which the Greens and Democrats would want amended in ways the others could not agree to. The settlement could not be perfect but it could be just.

He called on them for support. They had to stand up for it as he stood up for the republic. They had to barrack for it. Noel Pearson said that if it was just and workable they *would* barrack for it. After that meeting it seemed certain that the legislation would prevail—not because the principle had been compromised to the point where it was no longer the same principle, but because the principle had been given a shape in which it could survive, and hope with it. People could barrack for it.

The Commonwealth legislation was set down to be introduced in the parliament on 16 November. On 4 November the West Australian Premier, Richard Court, introduced legislation of his own which extinguished Native Title and replaced it with 'rights of traditional usage'. The proprietary title in the common law that the High Court found to exist was thus to be replaced by a statutory right—a conferred right, as Keating said, would replace an inherent right. Ian McLachlan supported Court's legislation and backed Geoffrey Blainey's suggestion that the High Court should either explain themselves or resign. McLachlan said the WA legislation was the 'start of a process of reversal of the Native Title decision'. As the Prime Minister said, the Liberals were prone to stand by the rule of law and sanctity of private property only when it suited them.

Just as significantly, the Liberals' deputy leader, Michael Wooldridge, said McLachlan's views on race had been tried out in the 1930s; two former Liberal ministers for Aboriginal Affairs, Ian Viner and Fred Chaney, said the WA legislation was unacceptable; a Liberal shadow cabinet member (and with several others including Bronwyn Bishop, an increasingly blatant noisy aspirant to the leadership), Alexander Downer, said that morally the High Court decision should not be reversed; and the Victorian Liberal heavyweight, Peter Reith, said in a classic example of his craft: 'In terms of the Coalition's position in respect of the Richard Court legislation, obviously we're going to examine that.'

The States would resist, but how could the Commonwealth govern in good conscience if the States were *not* resisting? As for the charge that the Prime Minister had made statements that neither he nor the country could live up to, when the mayor of New York, Mario Cuomo, received the same criticism he suggested that Americans should disown the Declaration of Independence.

The triumph coincided with news that a senior cabinet colleague had fed the *Bulletin* a story that was critical of the Prime Minister and his office. I told Keating what I'd been told in Sydney about the rumours of a push against him despite the risk that it would excite him to unhelpful anger and frustration. There was of course also a chance that I was telling him no more than he knew. He wove down paths of passionate commitment to his government's cause one minute, the salvation of his family and his marriage the next. Much that he did, including his efforts to retain an interest in a piggery and make it profitable related—though not always directly—to his desire to prove to those he loved that there would be a reward when he was finished with politics. Later he bought houses which he could not really afford for the same reason.

Some of the Aboriginal leaders, including Lois O'Donoghue, and the left's Bolkus, Tickner and Warren Snowdon gathered in the Prime Minister's suite to celebrate. Snowdon, who was someone I believed, said he'd never doubted Keating. Not everyone in cabinet and caucus could say that. O'Donoghue radiated happiness. She seemed then and has seemed ever since to be a person of such transcendent warmth, if Australians ever got to know her they would want her as their Queen. Tough as the negotiations had been, Keating had steadily built trust and respect among the Aboriginal leaders and increasingly he returned it. That had been one of the great benefits of the process—both sides learned new skills. Never in Australia's history had black and white Australians worked together in such a sustained way, at such a level and with such effect as they did in the eighteen months after the High Court judgment. As they gathered in the Prime Minister's suite for a drink, and the PM made his short speech of thanks, Graham Richardson walked down the corridor saying to Simon Balderstone as he passed, 'I hope you're right. I hope you're right.'

Like Ned Kelly, the Governor brothers, the Wild Bunch and other fugitive souls, our Prime Minister liked to stay ahead of his pursuers, but not so far that they could not discern his contempt for them. Pleased about his Mabo agreement, he went into the House and called the Opposition 'vermin'. He flew off to the Commonwealth Heads of Government Meeting in Cyprus unrepentant, and doubtless felt vindicated when, shortly after his departure, John Hewson tried to fire up his own troops by referring to 'Labor spivs in Armani suits'. The very notion that this uneducated larrikin should represent his country abroad seemed to wound his vanity. Keating called on Suharto on the way back to urge more progress on APEC and, cheered by the meeting, he spent much of the time between Jakarta and Canberra explaining to the RAAF crew how he wanted the old plane reconfigured to provide more room and comfort for the journalists.

Employing what had become a familiar tactic, Hewson said that anyone who opposed the government on Mabo was labelled a racist by the Prime Minister. This, he said, was contemptible. John Howard used to say the same thing about people who opposed him in the debate about Asian immigration in the late eighties. Disguising or justifying racists in their own ranks and among the electorate at large was only one attractive feature of this ploy. Another was to paint advocates of liberalism and tolerance as illiberal and intolerant—or politically correct. The tactic was to make the aggressor the putative victim. Keating had not called all opponents of the Mabo agreement racist, even if by calling the Liberals vermin he had helped to make their smear stick.

The Liberal strategy was to poison the well before Keating reached it. We suggested a radio campaign explaining the principles of the agreement, reassuring those who were nervous about its consequences and rebutting Hewson's calumny. Mabo was going to take a lot of selling. As usual, John Laws was recommended as the starting point. When I suggested that the PM start in Melbourne, that he was working Sydney too much, that the rest of the country including the second biggest city were wondering if he knew they even existed, to my amazement he agreed. Sydney had become too much the focus of Australian public life, he said, and to counter this insidious development he intended proposing to Kerry Packer that he buy a radio station in Melbourne and put John Laws on it.

These were the days when to some people it seemed obvious that the government must push on rapidly into areas of policy which were at once 'visionary' (and in that sense definitively Keating) and local, regional or communitarian. It was not that Mabo, APEC and the republic were unimportant or by now even avoidable. It was rather that they did not mean much to most Australians, and what little they meant frequently annoyed or alarmed them. Regional development programs seemed to some of us an antidote to most of the charges of arrogance and isolation and the practical effects of globalisation and the new 'productivity' which eventually stripped the Keating Government of legitimacy and power. They also seemed a relatively simple undertaking and an easy fusion of policy and rhetoric. Yet for reasons which even now remain mysterious, the idea excited nothing better than derision and alarm in the cabinet, the PMO and for a long while the Prime Minister. In October 1993 Bill Kelty was saying that the Keating Government could ride regional development to another election victory. But to most Labor people around Parliament House the idea brought on sighs, shrugs and other familiar scornful signs of the economic idée fixe that had debilitated debate about policy options in the previous year. Regional development was, as far as one could tell, a 'big spending option', smacking too much of industry policy or even Whitlamite decentralisation; perhaps there was something Keynesian about it, something hostile to the dictum that capital flowed of its own accord to the places where it would flourish and should never be forced into barren ground. Over the next two years the pendulum swung, but much too slowly to give the government the advantage it might have had or the regions a little of what they needed to prosper.

Just before Christmas 1993 Bill Kelty released the report of the federal government's regional taskforce, *Developing Australia:*

A Regional Perspective. It might not have been the ideal time for the launch; by the time consciousness returned in the New Year the drier economists in government, the bureaucracy and the press had decided the report was a blueprint for pork-barrelling, a recipe for budget disaster, a heresy against the economic policy he had helped to make the orthodoxy. Kelty never really got a chance to argue his case; instead he saw his work, not to say his intelligence, traduced and his report pushed towards the realms of invisibility. In the course of this process Kelty's loyalty was stretched beyond its limits.

His central premise was that regional and rural Australia had in general suffered most from the economic revolution of the eighties and enjoyed the least benefits. The most obvious measure of the disadvantage was unemployment. Like the unemployed, the regions could not reach their potential without assistance, and if the regions did not reach their full potential Australia could not. Kelty had toured the regions with his unlikely friend, the transport millionaire Lindsay Fox. 'In none of our journeys did we ever find the fiscal fairies that could provide to a country unlimited expenditure,' he said. He proposed instead a massive injection of public money, tapping the burgeoning superannuation funds through expanded tax concessions for infrastructure bonds and the creation of pooled development funds; the sale of major airports to fund the development of regional ones; an increase in petrol tax directed at road development; and replacing the 1.5 per cent training guarantee levy with a 1 per cent increase in company tax to pay for 75,000 new traineeships. The Opposition said they did not believe in increasing taxation to assist regional Australia, and eventually the government decided on the same course. Those of us who thought that for political and other good reasons regional Australia ought to be assisted wondered how it would happen without additional taxation—and we wondered more when after two years the bureaucracy in Canberra could not invent an instrument that would attract private investment or the superannuation funds.

Among Kelty's proposals was massive investment on the

national road system, including a dual highway from Cairns to Adelaide developed over thirty years—not as exciting as the Snowy Mountains, he said, but just as 'practical'; fast train links in the eastern states; improved port and airport facilities; extended metropolitan telephone zones; bringing a regional focus to industry policy; pricing energy to provide cross subsidies in regional Australia; and the establishment of Regional Economic Development Organisations (REDOs). Investment in infrastructure, he said, would address a forty-year decline and create employment for people whose own communities had long since lost all capacity to provide it. Kelty had met hundreds of people who struck him as open-hearted, dedicated and capable; what he saw and what they said reminded him of the waste of lives and resources, the loss of regional identity. It gave his thinking a high degree of passion and vision which he never found matched in the government—not even when he pointed out to them that this was the issue of the era, the one most likely to take Labor into another term. In a significant sense, Kelty was recognising the failure of free markets to deliver nationally: he was recommending, as it were, a social wage for the regions. It looked like a massive Keynesian program on the lines of the New Deal, which was doubtless a reason why it frightened people, but its solutions were essentially market-based. The challenge would be finding some way to get the market working where it did not want to. The Industry Minister, Alan Griffiths, said the Kelty report would be the most important source of government thinking on regional policy. But that position would not always prevail. The Industry Commission had a report to deliver, and another had been commissioned from McKinsey and Company. For many in the cabinet it was very welcome insurance.

Spending revenue is, like gathering it, entirely at the government's discretion. Regional development presented the standard equation which boils down to doing those things that you cannot afford not to do, and doing them to the degree you calculate as the necessary minimum. The grist of politics is marrying public needs and expectations to the political and financial realities—and this is the principal function of rhetoric. Regional policies might have constituted big or small spending as the government saw fit; indeed a government at the height of its powers can make small spending a proof of its virtue, not that this was such a government. If regional development sounded uncomfortably like industry policy, then so did much else in the platform on which the government was re-elected. It was difficult to see how the government might live up to its promise to assist people on the margins if it was not prepared to direct capital to those places where manifestly capital would not go freely. Within the Prime Minister's Office the argument was very like the one about unemployment: one had to tread carefully or risk being branded an advocate of reckless spending and unmitigated folly. Sometimes it seemed as if the notion was too seductive and must perforce be seen through a dark glass, or pushed out of sight altogether. Late in 1993 when, not for the first time, I suggested that the Murray–Darling basin might be a case worth taking up more vigorously, the Prime Minister said he preferred the idea of developing Darwin.

Paul Keating had already decided that the next election would be his last. If he lost he would go; if he won, he would leave within a year. With the story of the new table at the Lodge running all week and effectively countering the other story that the Liberal Party was tearing itself apart, I asked if it would not be prudent to bring the election forward as far as he could so we could all leave quickly.

The table, manufactured from a quantity of Thai mahogany by a Sydney furniture maker, had been ordered by the PM through his friend the Sydney antique dealer, Paul Kenny. A magnificent monster in the Georgian style, it had been installed in the Lodge dining room. I dined with him at one end of it one night, unaware of the storm it was about to create. He showed me the extraordinary detail in the legs. It seemed capable of seating an entire symphony orchestra. I asked him if he ever had so many to dinner. He said no, but it was a 'beauty', that was the point, and an excellent addition to the national estate. Unfortunately, when it was brought to their attention, many Australians seemed to believe that the table was an addition to Paul Keating's estate, and they resented paying for it. Australian furniture makers complained that, like his suits, it had been made from foreign materials, and environmentalists expressed their anger about logging in Thailand.

In the midst of this he strolled into my office to talk about a program on Creation that he had seen on TV the night before. I said I did not live comfortably with the Big Bang, but preferred my childhood's canopy of stars with God and all good people who had gone before looking down. It was no surprise that he agreed. He reckoned that if there was nothing more to it than a big bang one may as well just go after antiques and beautiful women full-time. I told him how Manning Clark had been fond of quoting Dostoyevsky in *The Brothers Karamazov* in which it is said that if the Christ story is not true, existence is nothing but 'a carnival of devils'. The PM was much taken by the phrase. He laughed and sucked air as he often did, and wandered off repeating it, 'a carnival of devils—that's right'.

Just then it might have seemed to him a reasonably accurate description of his own life. In the Senate and in the press he was accused of abusing a female public servant on the telephone; in the *Sydney Morning Herald* an editorial charged that he had abused Admiral Beaumont, the Chief of the Defence Force; in the *Age* Michelle Grattan claimed he had bought prints by John Gould for the cabinet room through his Melbourne 'clock dealer'; in the *Canberra Times* a public servant declared that three members of his staff at the Lodge had been dismissed because it was 'not a happy place'; and somewhere else Brian Toohey savaged him. He had never abused a public servant, he said, and he never would as a matter of principle. He had never had a telephone conversation with Admiral Beaumont. He had never done business with the Melbourne dealer, and the Melbourne dealer did not sell clocks. His relationship with the press gallery was in poor repair: he would impress them with a grand act, like precipitating a meeting of the leaders of Asia-Pacific including the three biggest economies in the world, or visit the Queen in her castle and tell her she might soon not be needed, or take on the impossible and win on Mabo—and they would give him a good headline and then attack him for three weeks about a table.

But he could not help himself with Michelle Grattan. He rang in a rage: 'I've abused politicians and I've abused you,' he said, 'but never a public servant'; and he proceeded to outline her other errors. Ten minutes later he was telling her that what she needed was a nice eighteenth-century commode and a good painting at one end of her sitting room and someone to bring her slippers to her when she got home at night.

Those who saw themselves as guardians of the nation's military glory continued in their enmity. An invitation to deliver a speech on the occasion of the interment of an Unknown Australian Soldier came despite strong opposition from people in the RSL and at the War Memorial. Some of the same people wanted to call the soldier whose remains had been removed from a site in France, the Unknown Warrior. Mercifully, on both issues the director and deputy director of the War Memorial, the admirable Brendon Kelson and Michael McKernan, prevailed. In overcoming the reactionaries for a while Kelson and McKernan did considerable service to Australia's military and cultural traditions. The grand ceremony on the steps of the Memorial was televised live across the country and appeared to make a great impact. The Prime Minister read the speech with dignity and feeling. Tears were shed. The papers published the speech the next morning and for a short while the people who were normally driven to a frenzy whenever the Prime Minister said anything about the country's military history were silent.

Soon after, on 15 November, he delivered an address to the nation on television. He told the people that the country was within reach of 'an enlightened, practical response to Mabo'. He asked the people to recognise that no Australian government could in conscience fail to give legislative effect to the High Court judgment. 'What sort of country would we be?' he asked.

'How could we say we stand for the fair go if we were to wipe away a title to land which has lasted through thousands of years of occupation of the continent and 200 years of European settlement?' He explained the complexity of the issues thrown up by the judgment, reminded people (if anyone had ever heard it the first time) that Native Title had survived on only a very small proportion of land and reassured them that the threat to private land and the national economic interest was negligible. He was in effect establishing a fair and efficient system of land management. He was providing 'certainty . . . a single, uniform national approach' and one to which seven of the eight States and Territories and the National Farmers Federation had agreed. Now he was asking the people to sign up to it as well.

It was the usual thing in politics—fuse the moral imperative with good old self-interest and call the hybrid a fair go for all. Sandy Hollway and I worked on it most of the night before, including a couple of hours with the Prime Minister. The text no longer speaks for the work that went into it, but the reviews were gratifying: the *Sydney Morning Herald* expressed whole-hearted approval, and noticed a 'remarkable similarity' to the Redfern speech. 'Consistency' would have been more appropriate, although he did make a few of the same points. One of them concerned the question of guilt. At Redfern he said it was not a useful emotion. In his national address it was that we had 'no need . . . nor any use' for it. 'This generation cannot be held responsible for the cruelty of previous generations. But to ignore Mabo would be the final cruelty, and we *would* be held responsible.' It didn't matter how many times he said it, some people would go on insisting that the whole effort was driven by guilt, and was indeed part of a 'guilt industry'. Whether fewer people said it after the Mabo national address we could not know. Certainly John Hewson was not persuaded, but John Hewson was like a drowning man. Only one thing drove him madder than Paul Keating presuming to know as much or more about economics as he did, and that was Paul Keating presuming to have an equivalent or higher moral sense.

We put it to the PM very tactfully: 'They'll be wanting to tear you down from the high ground you've been occupying, we imagine; and we imagine you won't be willing to descend,' we said. 'I don't know how long I can stand it up there,' he said as he left for the chamber. But, fearing inundation in a wave of popular acclaim or foolish respect, in Question Time he told Hewson that he had no taste. The Opposition leader had chosen to ignore Mabo and the forthcoming APEC leaders' meeting and ask about the new table at the Lodge. The Prime Minister declared that Coalition members were 'shocking Philistines' and it was all in the end a 'snide reference to art'. They were 'gauche nouveau riche characters' who thought you could 'write a cheque for taste'. Well, you couldn't. If you did not understand it you could never acquire it. He had seen the Opposition leader on the television gardening program, *Burke's Backyard*. He had seen him lined up 'in the green gumboots, à la the back of Wiltshire . . . and with the French boxed orange plants, and a screen of the worst Tuscan order columns . . .' at which point Tim Fischer took a point of order and the Speaker asked the Prime Minister to conclude his answer and the Prime Minister did; but not without making a point about 'the Ralph Lauren shirts' and another reference to the 'forest of the crookest looking Tuscan order columns . . . in a place that you could have done better drawing up on a kid's pad'. With taste like that the Opposition leader was well advised to leave the arts—and Georgian tables—well alone.

It was funny so long as one could believe that the irony was conscious; it was justified to the extent that the matter of a table at the Lodge was puny in comparison to his achievement with Mabo, and their attitude to Mabo had been puny as well. But the diatribe and his demeanour that day were out of proportion to the bait; they seemed to issue from a well of anger and malice that he could neither control nor understand. The media flayed him. Peter Robinson and Laurie Oakes both asked the question in their columns: why did a man with such talent and capacity for leadership so often behave like a mug lair? I asked him the same question on the way to Seattle for the APEC leaders' meeting—

446 | Recollections of a Bleeding Heart

the best concrete example perhaps of his talents and capacities. Many good questions were put to him in aeroplanes because there was little chance of escape. This time for once he owned to some regret about his performance in the House. It was a result, he said, of a 'dry liver' which had since been corrected by acupuncture.

Before Seattle he gave a speech in Orange County, California. It was called 'Present at the Creation' and it pitched the case for APEC and US engagement in a new order in the Pacific. As half a century ago the postwar order was created in Europe on the back of superpower rivalry, now with the end of the Cold War 'we are present at the creation of quite another configuration in world affairs'. This one would be built upon the prosperity generated by free and open trade, and it would reflect the emergence of the Asia–Pacific Economic Community to match the successes of the European Community. On American television Bill Clinton was uttering kind words and paying tribute to his opponents in the debate on NAFTA which he had just won. As we watched Clinton, we drafted a press statement about Hewson's mean-spirited response to Mabo. We called it 'shameful', and if playing to the fears of the electorate at the expense of logic, principle and respect for the law of the land was the measure, shameful it was. 'In good faith we have all bought homes and farms and opened mines and businesses,' he said: 'So while Aboriginal people want the land they are entitled to, other Australians want to be sure that they do indeed own their home or their farm.' He played to every popular anxiety and stretched the boundaries of moral sanctimony. The Prime Minister's press release pointed out the 'distortions, misconceptions, untruths and downright lies' and said Hewson had portrayed Mabo as 'something beyond the reach of Australians' intelligence and goodwill'.

In Australia's adversarial political system Keating was the most adversarial of all. He refused to give his opponent anything, ever. He would rather resign than give them credit, he said. Nothing could have been further from the American style, particularly the Clinton style. And nothing was further from Keating the mug lair than Keating in Orange County, where his performance drew much praise and was described by one member of the audience as 'a class act'.

When Bill Clinton agreed to the first APEC leaders' meeting in Seattle the Australian press billed it as 'Keating's APEC triumph', and in many ways it was just that. For the first time in history the leaders of the East Asian and Northern Pacific countries met, and when it was finished, lined up in leather jackets provided by the host country, they declared that they would meet again next year in Jakarta. They issued a statement declaring that APEC was henceforth a new voice for the region in world affairs, calling for a successful conclusion to the GATT round, and announcing that a committee had been formed to address certain trade-inhibiting regulations in customs procedures and competition policy. It did not sound like a great deal, and it might be true that the bilateral meetings held concurrently with the summit produced the greatest benefits. For example, when Clinton met the Chinese leader, Jiang Zemin, it was the first contact at the highest level since Tiananmen Square. The Seattle meeting was a symbol of cooperation and unity in a region which had never known or imagined them. It did not seem naive to expect a certain amount of concrete good would come from the gathering. It was a very promising beginning. This optimistic view proved to be the right one: while in Seattle the APEC ministerial council, which met before the leaders' meeting, decided not to set a target date and timetable for free trade in the region; a year later in Indonesia the leaders' meeting did just that.

No-one could estimate the long-term benefits of a geo-political kind that flowed from the discussions. It was a great achievement for Keating and, even if Australians had not yet fully grasped the dimensions or the nature of it, he should have earned their respect. Instead the Seattle meeting was followed by outpourings of public anger and even contempt. He left Seattle as the first storm of winter blew in. Before driving to the airport he gave a doorstop interview. Allan Gyngell, the Prime Minister's new foreign affairs adviser, got in the car wearing a slightly bemused grin. It had been a good doorstop, he said, but he was not sure how one of his remarks would play. Irritated by persistent questions about the Malaysian Prime Minister's failure to attend the historic meeting—the only refusal among the fifteen regional leaders invited—Paul Keating had replied: 'APEC is bigger than all of us—Australia, the US and Malaysia and Dr Mahathir and any other recalcitrants.'

In the House on his return he was splendidly statesmanlike. We wondered if the journalists' lament about his squandered gifts had taken effect. Perhaps it would have, if not for that momentary blossoming of hubris outside the Boeing hangar in Seattle. Perhaps Mark Ryan would have delayed his plans to resign, and others might have stopped thinking about resigning. But as usual, just as he rode tall in the saddle onto a patch of open ground, a snare he had laid somewhere back in the thicket tightened round his neck. Free trade in the Asia–Pacific. A forum for unprecedented dialogue between leaders in the region. It counted for nothing. The Malaysian Prime Minister took umbrage at the word 'recalcitrant' and his cabinet agreed to meet and consider trade embargoes against Australia. Greg Sheridan of the *Australian* almost invariably applauded Keating's trade and foreign policies, but on this he said the Prime Minister had been 'idiotic'. He was no more impressed when on national television the Prime Minister referred to Mahathir's 'feigned outrage'. The Malaysian affair fitted neatly into the paradox the press had been pondering for weeks—Keating's wilful waste of his abilities.

'Recalcitrant' was hardly the worst thing Keating had called anyone, but this was unlikely to pacify Mahathir or persuade him to stop mining the political lode Keating had handed him. Keating was, as one newspaper described him, 'incandescent with rage', and only under extreme duress was he persuaded to say in a Laurie Oakes interview that he had not intended to cause offence and if offence had been caused he was sorry. Mahathir was not satisfied. More threats were made. The cabinet meeting approached. A great wave of public rage and loathing swept the Australian media. Snap polls showed the vast majority thought Keating should apologise.

The fact that Mahathir was a minor Asian authoritarian of the kind other polls would likely show they neither liked nor trusted meant nothing in this case. Nor did the less obvious interpretation register: namely, that Mahathir was aggrieved by Keating's relationship with Suharto, hostile to his assumption of a role in the region and determined to spoil the APEC party. That he was indeed manipulating a minor affair into a crisis is unquestionable. It was extraordinary that for such a minor infraction of diplomatic nicety an Australian prime minister should be expected to grovel to the leader of a country not a quarter of our economic strength. But Mahathir was able to create a crisis because his reaction played not only on his own electorate but the Australian one where frustration about Paul Keating was endemic. In punishing Keating, Mahathir was doing what many Australians wanted to do. 'Keating's mouth got us into this, Keating's mouth will have to get us out,' John Hewson said and for once expressed the public mood perfectly. We wondered if our Prime Minister was not having fleeting fantasies about F-111s thundering towards Kuala Lumpur. He had some cause for anger, but then he also had cause for calling Mahathir a 'recalcitrant'. He drafted a letter which explained to the Malaysian leader why he had been irritated by his position: Mahathir had protested about US domination of the forum, and that it was too big, but on the eve of the Seattle meeting he pushed for the inclusion of Chile, which would hardly make it smaller. Then, declaring that this was sometimes the only way for a small country to make itself heard, he boycotted Seattle where the chance to be heard was unprecedented.

In a flat in the suburbs of Canberra, while writing a speech in honour of Weary Dunlop and spelling out the government's domestic and regional ambitions, I heard the hysteria on the radio. Contracts would be terminated, investment halted, jobs lost, companies bankrupted, lives ruined, the national interest betrayed—and Keating had done it all with that tongue of his. With thumping heart I walked to the House. The Prime Minister had fought with advisers and officials all day long about his letter. He said he would alter nothing more, the aggressive unrepentant tone would remain. The advisers and officials had given up. A morgue-like silence pervaded the place. I found the PM and reported what the media were saying. His reaction was entirely predictable: he would not be governed by their opinions.

Talking to him in the corridor just then was like being caught in a mangle. The gist of my argument was: I agree with what you say but I will fight to the death to stop you saying it. If, as is certain should you send the present letter, the issue does extend to trade embargoes, you'll be out of a job within a month. You are sending your enemy the ammunition he craves, gift-wrapped—*and* you are fatally misreading community opinion. Why would you let Mahathir be the man who defeats you?

At last, with John Edwards' help, he was persuaded to make certain relatively simple changes. A sentence was added to the effect that, as PM, he believed Australia's relationship with Malaysia was more important than the present issue. A paragraph which was not material to the case but likely to inflame the situation he reluctantly agreed to excise. Eventually, a letter that was still decidedly firm but harder to construe as offensive was dispatched and soon after Mahathir was reported as saying that he was inclined to accept Keating's regrets. No sanctions were applied. Honour was apparently satisfied. At the Weary Dunlop lecture Keating said again that any offence was unintentional and regretted. People who had been at the lecture rang to say how impressive the Prime Minister had been. Then word came that the Indonesians were much impressed by the way he stood up to Mahathir. It was hardly a triumph, but the same might be said about Gallipoli.

In the wake of the crisis came relief and even celebration, yet it was not quite enough to banish the thought that more might have been gained if Keating had been allowed to do what his instinct told him and call Mahathir's bluff. If he had turned his back on Mahathir and forced the Australian people to decide if the Malaysian was right or their own prime minister, all sorts of mayhem may have followed but a more profound lesson might also have been learned.

It was always the nature of our progress to be fighting hostile circumstances, and of these our enemies' most zealous and strategic endeavours were usually the least daunting. Bad luck and our own follies were much stronger against us. And human nature for which there is no accounting. Offered the gift portfolio of Arts and Communications, a new and patently advantageous combination of the creative arts, the media and the new technologies, and in fulfilment of the Prime Minister's promise to bring the arts into cabinet and the political mainstream, Michael Lee refused to take the arts part. Was it unbecoming to a hard man of the NSW right? Did it matter if he knew nothing about it? Graham Richardson had been Minister for the Arts in the Hawke Government—and a very successful Minister for the Environment. Lee was considered by the Prime Minister to have great potential, even to be leader of the party. Months later, Wonder Boy, as he had become known, accepted the dual portfolio, but his initial refusal was the sort of thing which preyed on your mind and left you wondering if you—or Keating—were not swimming in an altogether different pond. The cabinet reshuffle, forced by the resignation of John Dawkins but convenient anyway, saw Willis become Treasurer, Beazley Finance Minister, Bob Collins Primary Industry Minister and Laurie Brereton added Transport to his Industrial Relations portfolio. Simon Crean took on Education, Employment and Training.

Few proceedings in the Australian parliament have been more dramatic than the passage through the Senate of the Native Title Bill. The principal provisions of the Bill, passed in the House on party lines, with not one Liberal dissenting from John Hewson's blanket opposition, were these:

All existing freehold and most leasehold titles were secure;

To prove Native Title Aborigines would have to prove continuing association with the land;

Claims would be heard in either a state tribunal or through the Federal Court;

Commonwealth and State governments would share

compensation costs where Native Title was extinguished;

A Land Acquisition Fund would be created to help Aborigines who had been dispossessed but who did not benefit from the Bill; and

Except for validation, the Racial Discrimination Act would have primacy.

As Christmas approached, the protests of the mining industry grew louder, the Greens played ever harder to get and John Hewson and conservative State leaders urged the Prime Minister to 'delay' the legislation until the new year. Keating said by 'delay' they meant 'destroy'. He said no Opposition 'tag team of filibusters' would stop passage of the Bill. The Senate would sit until Christmas Eve if necessary and return on Boxing Day. Hewson's blanket opposition was an extraordinary error of judgment, which required his colleagues to vote with the Greens and Democrats against amendments demanded by industry groups. Well before the Bill passed, a sense had developed on the Labor side that by alienating the sympathy of both the wets and the dries in the Coalition, Mabo might spell the end of Hewson. With the pressure on to get the Bill through before Christmas or risk the whole thing unravelling, the Democrat leader, Cheryl Kernot, played a crucial negotiating role. The Greens at last succumbed to the same argument that Keating had put to the Land Councils—this is the one chance to get across the tryline. As Pearson said later, he distilled it to 'them and us', good and evil— now or never.

It fell to Gareth Evans, who had told me a few months before that Keating was attempting the impossible, to carry the Bill through the longest debate in the Senate's history. With one or two department advisers nearby at all times to verify or explain each detail, the debate lasted for sixty hours. Evans was on his feet for forty-eight of them. It was the kind of tour de force he was born to deliver one day. Heart, mind, body and the Melbourne improving ethic working all in harness, he might have been William Wilberforce or Alfred Deakin or James Stewart in *Mr Smith Goes to Washington*. Evans lent the occasion not just resolute intelligence but a kind of heroic theatre. The Opposition moved not one amendment. Many said it was a shameful performance. It was also bizarre. Determined to demonstrate that the legislation was so bad as to be beyond improvement, the Opposition voted against government amendments negotiated with industry which, had they passed, would have seen the Bill voted down by the Greens. It was an abject folly of meanness, pig-headedness, foolishness—and then Dr Hewson underlined his failure to grasp the meaning of what had just happened by describing it as 'a day of shame for the Australian Parliament', a 'disaster for Australia' that would 'divide Australian against Australian' (*sic*). Perhaps it was just his way with words: he said that the challenge of the High Court's judgment had been to deal with Native Title 'in a way that was fair to Aborigines and fair to our major industries'.

In front of a packed public gallery the Bill passed just before midnight on 21 December after the government moved the guillotine. The scenes which followed were probably unprecedented in the parliament's history. As Evans and Kernot embraced, the gallery, full of those big rodeo hats which had become part of the scenery in Parliament House over the past eighteen months, rose and applauded. The happiness was palpable and infectious—people *wept* with it. The press joined the applause. The Labor side stood and applauded the gallery. In offices and other places all through the building there was cheering. And, in striking contrast to the demeanour of his Coalition partners, the National Party Senate leader, Ron Boswell, who had opposed the Bill, rose and wished the Aboriginal people well.

No-one on any side of politics believed that passage of the Bill through the parliament meant it would sail smoothly in the world outside. There were bound to be problems. But the Act did what Paul Keating had said it must do—it gave legislative expression to the High Court's judgment. It meant Australian law reflected the truth of Australian history rather than a lie about it. Without the Act there could never be reconciliation. Everywhere they said it would stand as a monument to the Keating Government and to Paul Keating himself. It does. It is almost certainly true that no-one else in that government, or for that matter in any previous one, would have got the legislation through. It was a monument not only to his political skill and integrity, but to his belief that sometimes it is your duty to be ahead of public opinion and to ignore it, whatever the risk. He said later that the Bill's passage was a blow against racist feeling in Australia, that while most Australians opposed it, after it had passed more of them felt better about themselves. Credit was paid to many people, but no-one deserved it as much as Keating and everyone knew that. The *Age* said in an editorial that the Act 'may yet be judged the most profound achievement of Paul Keating's political career'. Yet the Aboriginal leaders were no less the heroes of the legislation. All the ignorance and malice thrown at Keating landed on them as well—as if their grievance was not as real as the mining industry's; as if they were there for a handout; as if the legislation did more than assert the rights of a few Aborigines in the remote parts of Australia to the remnants of a Native Title proved in law. The Act acknowledged and enshrined in law the fact that every other title held by Australians over 200 years had extinguished the Aborigines'. At the very moment the law asserted the rights remaining to a few, it confirmed the permanent dispossession of the vast majority. As much as it was a triumph for Aboriginal Australians, the passing of the Native Title Act was another reminder of their unending forbearance.

Mark Ryan left. Malcolm Turnbull offered him a job running the Australian Republican Movement from his offices in Sydney. Feeling that he had done all the good he was ever likely to do with Paul Keating, and that he no longer had enough respect and influence at the Lodge to be useful, Ryan decided to accept it. He went with a degree of disillusionment, but completely without bitterness; and, practical to the end, he suggested that he use his departure as a pretext for suggesting to Allan Hawke that he also leave as part of a broader reshuffle. Anne de Salis left. So did John Edwards. They all go in the end and they all have a right to, as Keating saw it. He did not miss them all equally, of course, but along with departing cabinet colleagues it intensified his sense of isolation and loneliness, and pushed nearer to the surface the thought that he must soon go as well. His resolve, his energy, the intensity of his vision were not lost but unquestionably diminished. He had girded his loins for the Christmas party, nevertheless, and told the staff that as the 1980s had been given to remaking the Australian economy, in the 1990s Australian society would be remade.

CHAPTER 16

The first thing which strikes one about the pack is its unswerving direction; equality is expressed in the fact that all are obsessed by the same goal, the sight of an animal perhaps, which they want to kill.

ELIAS CANETTI, CROWDS AND POWER

IN JANUARY 1994 Paul Keating celebrated his fiftieth birthday with a party for fifty people at Kirribilli House. It was an elegant Baz Luhrmann bud-lit affair on the lawns and nothing was more elegant or charming than his short speech. He considered himself very lucky, he said, to reach such an age when so many did not, and to have such friends—and it was his wish that because they were his friends there would be friendship between them. In some instances at least it was doubtless a vain hope, and so was the suggestion that before he left Kirribilli an Australian president might reside in Admiralty House next door. It was unlikely that the two Leos—Schofield and McLeay—would ever become great mates; or Bill Kelty and Al Konstandinidis, or Richo and several other people. Not even Geoffrey Tozer's virtuosity on the piano and David Hobson singing 'Nessun Dorma' could do that. But Paul Keating's words, unscripted and seemingly unrehearsed, were calculated to do what Paul Keating could do better than almost anyone else—they warmed all the souls there and it is likely that every one of them went home that night feeling some kind of love for him.

As 1994 began, Paul Keating had a right to feel in tolerably good political shape. His government trailed in the polls, but often he had trailed by more depressing margins and he remained preferred prime minister. The risk was, as he said, a sudden surge for the Coalition when the inevitable happened and the Liberals replaced John Hewson with a more palatable leader. But in the meantime Keating could make hay. He had a recovery on his hands. To simple minds this seemed to mean that the radical reformer in him had some chance of finding expression: and with a cultural statement, an industry statement, the unemployment white paper, a regional development statement and a May budget all in the policy pipeline he had plenty of means for it.

The economic recovery and the policy surge we expected it to underwrite were not, however, matters for simple minds. Late in January the Prime Minister told some of us that now the recovery was undeniable, the press would become less interested in unemployment and more interested in reducing the deficit to less than 1 per cent and deregulating the labour market. The commentators would adopt what had been the government's position, namely that growth was the answer to unemployment; they would assume that which they never let the government assume—that unemployment would take care of itself. Business, Keating said, would follow their example and forget that their record profit levels had not a little to do with government policy. No-one who blamed the Labor Government for the recession would give it credit for the recovery. Therefore, the Prime Minister said, the government must itself claim credit; and, moreover, tell business that they should be supporting Labor and keeping the 'goon show' in Opposition. The country must be told how much the recovery owed to the stimulus provided by One Nation. He thought it likely to be very difficult keeping 'social justice' issues alive in this new orthodoxy. Ralph Willis had to 'get his head straight' and ignore the deficit argument for now. There had to be 'a poultice of revenue out there' and the Prime Minister wanted it pushed into infrastructure and unemployment. He expressed a wish to be seen somewhere in outback Australia driving a silver spike into a new rail line funded by One Nation.

In a long discussion at the Sydney office he told four of his advisers that he had already spoken to Bernie Fraser and the journalist Paul Kelly, and he would be telling the 'media dinosaurs waiting in the knackery paddock', and the business honchos who were cleaning up but still voting Liberal, and he would be telling the nervous nellies in the cabinet—it was better to spend the proceeds of recovery on unemployment, education and infrastructure than on another housing and development boom. As it happened, a personification of that unlamented boom, the Governor Macquarie Tower, was just then blocking out the light in the window behind him, and with a snarl and an angry wave of his arm he indicated that such 'monstrosities' would have no place in the coming age.

Such an expansive social program naturally had implications for the union movement and Labor's core support. It depended on low inflation and the elimination of labour market bottlenecks which had impeded progress in the eighties. It meant another 'eight dollar sort of deal' would have to be stitched up with Bill Kelty. Laurie Brereton must get the whips cracking on enterprise agreements for which the government laid the foundations in legislation before Christmas. And the white paper would have to find radical solutions in education and training to get the workforce up to scratch. It was all about micro-economic reform which, in lay terms, means eliminating the barriers to economic progress for individuals, companies, communities and nations. It was One Nation with a human face—in close-up. Kelty's report on regional development was a starting point but, for Keating, a worrying one. It set the hurdle far too high and the government had to avoid any sign of obligation to the measures it recommended. 'Bill is only two-thirds reconstructed,' he said. But he thought some of his road, rail and port proposals were possible.

Geoff Walsh, formerly Bob Hawke's adviser, had agreed to take over from Allan Hawke as principal adviser. With his arrival the direct line to Peter Barron was restored. Walsh was what is known as a smart operator—smart enough to need a lot of persuading before he returned to political life. He saw his major task as pacifying caucus, something in which we had manifestly failed. He knew the vagaries of the public service, was well connected in the press gallery, respected at the Labor secretariat and, coming from Melbourne, knew that the reaches of politics extended beyond Sydney. The last ideological scales had long since fallen from Walsh's eyes and he was deeply unsentimental about politicians and political leaders. Yet he was breezy rather than cynical, and for a while his sense of humour and bottomless store of jokes perceptibly altered the mood of Keating's jaded and depleted office. All that we needed in addition was a revival of his old enthusiasm for the work.

The Prime Minister gave Walsh the low-down on his piggery interests. Each charge brought by the Opposition had been proven wrong, he said, and the last had ended in a writ on Michael Baume. Even if he wanted to sell, and Walsh like the rest of us wished he would, he could not until the result of an environmental impact study was known, and he had it on impeccable authority that the NSW Liberal Government was doing its best to stop this happening. Keating was always persuasive about the piggery; his account of its history and the bastardry of his enemies rarely failed to make us feel a little less anxious, but never were the fears dispelled. There had been horror stories in the media about the smell emanating from the operation in its existing state and it was difficult for laypeople—Alan Jones's listeners, for example—to imagine that the expanded 90,000 pig version would not smell much worse. With the likes of Jones and Baume on Keating's back we knew that no case he could make for the piggery, and no case in natural justice was likely to save him, his office or the government from political torment on the issue. The piggery was an ulcer that nothing would heal. He could always make a case for his right to have such an investment, even if it did not satisfy everybody. But there seemed to be always something else: the loan from the bank, the environment, the conditions for the pigs, and what seemed like incredible negligence in the day-to-day management of the company. The questions kept coming and the PM and his Senate representatives were obliged to answer them. It ate at his time, patience and energy. It darkened his mood and debilitated his relationship with his office. It would subside and then Jones would say something, or Baume would ask a question, or an article would appear in the *Sydney Morning Herald* and the effect would be like acid because it was not only a slur on his integrity but an implied denial of his rights. For Keating the piggery was as much a right as his opponents' inherited wealth was a right. It could even be seen as an extension of his war against them.

Walsh said Alan Jones and Laurie Oakes both suspected there was a bigger story to be told: and despite our desire to believe that what our leader told us was the whole of it, so did we. Then he had to stand down the Industry, Technology and Regional Development Minister, the young Victorian from the right, Alan Griffiths, for a financial disclosure matter. Oakes asked ominously at a doorstop if this meant no minister should have investments of this kind. In industry, Griffiths had a portfolio with rich potential, and all manner of political capital to make from succeeding with it. No ministry was more central to the government's ambitions and, according to Keating, Griffiths had pleaded to be given it. The serial changes to the cabinet which his departure precipitated were of much greater significance than the loss of a minister whom Keating said—miming a gold prospector peering into an empty pan—had so far yielded not a speck of an idea. He told Griffiths that a vacancy would be left for him, but like Richardson and McLeay, he would have to fight his way back. In the meantime, Simon Crean was proposed for industry. Keating wished it were otherwise: he did not like what he called Crean's 'deal-making' approach to the job, or his liking for 'sectoral' industry policy, and there was something in his attitude that went back to Simon's father Frank, who had been Gough Whitlam's treasurer. Frank Crean might have taken the young Paul Keating a little too much for granted. In any case, he believed Simon Crean was better advised to stay with Employment, Education and Training and claim the credit for the forthcoming white paper that might revolutionise education and training and mark the beginning of the end for unemployment. Then we heard that while Crean had not rung Keating about his plans, he had rung Hawke, and Keating said it was a pity because he had just begun to like him.

Crean went to Employment. Despite Richardson's objection that he could not sell the white paper, Peter Baldwin retained Social Security. Keating liked Baldwin because he had ideas and was dedicated to nailing down policy after it was announced. As for 'selling' the white paper, said the Prime Minister, 'I'll do the selling.' Michael Lee might have got the nod for industry over Crean, but Lee wanted communications, and had he wanted anything else Keating would not have given it to him because he had refused to take on the arts. Then there was Carmen Lawrence, wanted in Canberra but still languishing in Perth. John Dawkins tried to persuade her to take over his seat. Lawrence might have become the education and training minister but no-one wanted her to stand for a federal seat in the climate Griffiths' resignation had created. And even if she had, the cabinet vacancy had been promised long ago to Queensland—specifically to Con Sciacca, an energetic right-wing MHR. Failure to honour this promise, we were assured, meant certain war with Wayne Goss and a brawl at the next national conference. Insofar as he had the potential to go much further as a minister than Sciacca, Wayne Swan had a better claim on the vacancy. Swan, however, had disgraced himself during the budget fracas: the Prime Minister told him at the time he was a fool to publicly reprove a leader who believed in giving youth a chance. And so it was all resolved to honour pledges, reward loyalty and settle scores. Griffiths' resignation worked like a mild purgative and on balance made the cabinet somewhat sturdier. Bob McMullan's move up to become Minister for Trade helped in this, and at the same time created the opportunity for the Prime Minister to tell Michael Lee that he would be adding to his communications portfolio McMullan's old job of Minister for the Arts.

Bronwyn Bishop's tilt at the Liberal leadership had stumbled badly enough for there to be little prospect of recovery.

The writer Bob Ellis was entitled to take much of the credit for her demise, and doubtless did. He had harried her mercilessly for months and when, to move from the Senate to the House of Representatives, she stood for the seat of Mackellar, he stood against her. Ellis had found the humour and energy to undo her where the Labor Party could not. The Labor Party did a fair imitation of a rabbit in a spotlight: it was bizarre that anyone should have thought Bronwyn Bishop could win the Liberal leadership and then a general election, yet so low was Labor's confidence in Paul Keating, and so great their awareness that they had governed beyond the normal tenure, they were prepared to believe that anyone who lined up on the other side would necessarily blitz them. Anyone but John Hewson, of course. What was true of the Labor Party was also true of the press gallery. In some ways it was a pity that Bishop fell over because it brought John Howard a step closer to the leadership. For a while the gallery had taken Bishop seriously. Soon they would take Alexander Downer seriously. They were wrong about both of them, as they had been wrong about John Hewson. However, they were right to believe, and the pessimists and curmudgeons in the Labor Party with them, that to win a federal election the Liberals did not need an outstanding leader or even a highly competent one. Someone halfway credible would do.

In the meantime the government had the chance to make hay. Defying the opprobrium from all the expected quarters, the Prime Minister proceeded with his plans to organise Question Time on a roster system, and to his staff he vowed that he would spend the extra time available out in the broad electorate, or on the media explaining his plans to the people and making news. We hoped he would explain the conundrum of the times: how in a period of growth there were so many symptoms of decline. Why 'downsizing' continued even in growth industries and people felt ever less secure in their work and in the future of their communities. He needed to explain in terms that no-one could fail to understand that the government was addressing a revolution comparable in its effects on daily life to the industrial revolution:

that this was behind much that he did, including the coming white paper on employment. The green paper, called Restoring Full Employment, had been delivered by Mike Keating in December, after much writing and rewriting of its philosophical base. Saying where we stood on full employment had been the hard part. The *Sydney Morning Herald* took our words to mean that the government had abandoned it as a national goal. The Prime Minister told the media the words meant that if Australians wanted full employment they must reaffirm it; employers, unions, educational bodies, communities and all governments must take the necessary steps. That was the message he needed to take to the country every day.

I took an Australia Day speech over to Kirribilli, arriving by one gate as Prince Charles left by the other. The Prime Minister felt a bit sorry for the Prince and had made what he believed was the truth of things as palatable as he could. The truth was that as the only monarch to visit Australia, the Queen had a special place in Australian hearts and she would always be welcome, as would the Prince. But the generation who were adults when she came so memorably the first time were now in their seventies. The old affections were fading. Australians knew their destiny lay elsewhere, and some believed that we would be better off pursuing it without this baggage round our necks. For his part, the Prince said that Australia was dear to him because he had been partly educated here. The Palace had always done its best to look after Australia's interests. He left the draft of a speech for the Prime Minister to read. This we did as the moon hung above the harbour, the fruit bats set out on the evening's hunt and the ferries glittered on the water. We agreed that the Prince really hit his straps on the last page, where he said that in a mature confident democracy like ours debate on constitutional change was welcome, and if Australians decided that they wanted a republic the British monarchy would not stand in the way. We agreed it was good that he had come.

Later on this sublime evening, from the window of the hotel I watched the boats chug up Darling Harbour, ferrying people to see the Prince deliver his speech. It was a beautiful scene, and beautiful politics. I commenced a speech and had a page or two written when Ric Simes rang to say that someone had fired a gun of some kind at the Prince, and on the television moments later I saw it happening—the New South Wales Premier and the Australian of the Year both leaping to protect the Prince, followed by the British security officials, followed by the Australian Federal Police, followed by the New South Wales uniformed police. The Prince, betraying only the mildest discomfort and very superior breeding, adjusted his cuffs as his assailant, an Asian student, was gang tackled to the floor and a cap gun wrested from his hand.

We immediately wrote a press release and in it called the Prince a good friend of Australia. Call him an 'exceedingly good friend', the Prime Minister said. We decided on 'very good friend'. On radio a talkback person took the opportunity to say that all the talk about an Australian republic was nonsense when Australia had so much foreign debt. We were, he said, like a small child that had left its parents and taken the credit card, and run up these massive bills and now it wanted the parents to let it go. It was always a mistake to listen to the radio: the caller's idiotic words kept me awake all night.

Yet all the news was positive in January 1994. The Americans had growth. We had growth. Even the morning after the terrible Charles incident the newspapers brimmed with good news. The piggery remained discomforting, however, and it looked likely that Ros Kelly would be run to ground over a matter involving the allocation of money to sporting bodies in marginal seats. Yet never had we had so few reasons for gloom. Feeling more secure for the presence of Geoff Walsh and the renewed connection to the old gang Walsh gave him, the Prime Minister talked boldly about many things. He thought he might put all the forthcoming statements into one big all-conquering thing. It was not the absence of feasibility which impressed, but the presence of confidence.

It was in this summer that he formed a satirical idea. He had become fond of describing John Hewson in Jack Lang's terms, as a political typical skyrocket, the type who went off in a shower of sparks but fell like 'a dead stick' to the ground. Now it occurred to him that the Coalition was like cracker night. Howard was one of those 'flower pots' that used to sputter and spit, and just when you thought it had gone out, it would sputter and spit again and go out again, this time you were sure for good—but again it would burst into sputtering life. Bronwyn Bishop was a catherine-wheel—the one you hung on a nail, and when lit it spun and fizzed and invariably came off the nail and shot across the yard, and set fire to the dog and went out. And there was the three-penny bunger which you lit full of expectation that a mighty bang would follow, watching and watching, but it never went off. This was Ian McLachlan. He resolved to wait for the appropriate moment.

In Question Time a few days after this brainwave, for some reason the Opposition put their pastoralist Ian McLachlan up on the piggery, and we thought the Prime Minister might reply with his threepenny bunger. Instead he took the opportunity to publicly reflect on the Member for Barker's extensive family interests, and at last defended his investment in terms that had been urged on him for two years: he had invested in a growth industry; an export industry; a value-adding state-of-the-art, international best practice industry; an industry that would create new jobs. Where was the crime in that?

We expected another dose a day or two later and, for ammunition in the counterattack, the Prime Minister went armed with a dossier on John Howard's historic failings. The back bench had been revved up to provide as much covering fire and chaos as possible. Again for reasons no-one could understand, John Hewson aborted Question Time by moving a censure motion on the Prime Minister, and as had become his custom proceeded to lay about his enemy with grotesquely exaggerated rhetoric and flourishes. His awful exhibition might have made an unlikely victory for the government had he been heard in silence. But Labor's back bench faithfully followed their orders: they bellowed and guffawed, and when the other side joined in Hewson began to look strangely valiant. The chaos left Keating with only seven minutes to reply and he failed to fire even half his ammunition. He was laughing about the simple-minded back bench when he came back to the office, like a toreador who enjoyed being gored a little. He said that in future he would have to wear a plastic suit to Question Time and we would have to hose him down at the end of it.

The Prime Minister was relaxed. The economy was growing and it was marvellous what a good set of figures could do. On 12 March 1994 the *Economist*'s economic indicators showed Australia leading the world in GDP growth and also leading it with the *Economist*'s forecasters. At a conference in Canberra hosted by that magazine, the Prime Minister pointed out that in the week the dollar was floated in 1983, the same indicators showed Australian GDP growth as the lowest in the developed world, and Australian inflation among the highest. The inflation rate was 9.2 per cent. In the US it was 2.9 per cent and in Germany 2.6 per cent. Now, in March 1994, Australia's inflation was lower than both those countries. Between the figures at either end of that decade, the Prime Minister said, 'lies a tale'. And he was very happy to tell it then, and many times thereafter.

The moment glowed with political opportunity. Then Geoff Walsh came back from a meeting with the bureaucrats working on the unemployment statement saying that the lack of verve and vision had depressed him. Bill Kelty rang to say that he did not want much on his regional development study, but he wanted a lot more than he was being offered by our office and the bureaucracy. And then Ros Kelly resigned—I could see it in her face as she walked out of the Prime Minister's doors.

Laurie Oakes wrote in his column early in 1994 that Geoff Walsh's appointment should level out the 'highs and lows' in the Prime Minister's performance, which was exactly as Walsh had described his mission to me—and doubtless also as Peter Barron would have described it. At about the same time Paul Lyneham announced on radio that a couple of the Prime Minister's recent interviews were evidence that with Walsh around Australians would see a more warm and cuddly Paul Keating. With Walsh in the office, Barron was in the office; no bad thing if it gave our prime minister the reassurance of experience, a direct line to the top end of town, and proven political nous. It should have been ideal, and it did work well sometimes, even if it was hard on those who were employed to give him advice on the same matters. It was not particularly wise, however, to imagine that one could have a Keating without highs and lows. Keating without highs was just another, lesser, politician—and for every high there was bound to be a low. How we had all hoped and believed his temperament could be changed, and we went on hoping when there was no hope. It would never happen. The only solution to the highs and lows of political life under Keating was replacing him with someone who did not have highs.

The levelling project aside, Walsh's main interest in these first few months was persuading the Prime Minister to decide between politics and his private life, in particular the piggery. Seeing the corrosive effect on his political effectiveness and standing and feeling the strain of dealing with various increasingly cantankerous, unreliable and feuding parties to the enterprise, by now Keating was saying privately that he was prepared to abandon it. This, naturally, was everyone's hope. Selling was one possible option: there was also talk about putting his interest in a blind trust; about getting someone credible and competent to manage it. However, even when he reached the equable frame of mind in which he could surrender the rewards of a legitimate investment and concede the Coalition a rank victory, there were daunting obstacles. Finding a buyer was one of them. Ensuring the Danish joint-venturer, Danpork, was not scared off was another. If Danpork went, and the venture collapsed, the Prime Minister would be left owing the Commonwealth Bank several million dollars. Then it emerged that his partner, Al Konstandinidis, was engaged in a legal battle with an old friend. The old friend's depositions were not flattering to Konstandinidis, which was likely to prove useful to Paul Keating's opponents.

--

Rather like a skyrocket, as quickly as Paul Keating's spirits soared, they dived towards the ground. From the Hobart Council of Australian Governments meeting came pictures of him starting a penny-farthing race in his familiar 'casual' tartan shirt. He looked happy in the photo but in the flesh he was tired, almost haggard. The Ros Kelly saga made it worse. There is something about the undoing of a high-profile woman in politics which excites a more vicious kind of popular contumely. Forced to defend herself every day in the House, Kelly had been brave but under pressure her manner resembled an admonishing schoolmistress, which seemed to at once goad her tormentors and alienate the electorate. Her end was certain when she revealed that the allocations of money had been worked out on a whiteboard in her office. As decisions are always worked out on something I never could work out why this produced such a bout of ridicule, but Kelly could not withstand it and resigned in March. She was defiant and dignified at her press conference. It was galling to have given them her scalp. Keating appeared to be emotionally shaken by the episode. Suddenly in extremis again, he took on the hungry defiant look of a dog on the prowl—a 'don't you try and stop me' look. He had too many office faces—some of them unfamiliar—staring at him, itching to give him advice he did not want or need. Nigel Ray, the new economic adviser, and Tom Wheelwright, the new political adviser, each spent about a year in the office and he rarely listened to either of them.

In the days following Kelly's resignation, the PM might have been trounced: he had lost two young ministers, his Question Time roster was everywhere being flayed as undemocratic and cowardly, the piggery nightmare continued. One day in the first week of March he arrived for his briefing three minutes before the bells began to ring. We expected the worst, but we should have known better. Be 'steely' rather than 'flamboyant', I suggested. Be cold not hot. He turned in a performance that was all heat and flamboyance. And quite deadly. He savaged Howard's consultancy with Clayton Utz, slammed Downer's personal interests. Hewson's face went scarlet and his teeth appeared to lock together. We wondered if he feared Keating would turn on him next, or was trying to disguise his pleasure at the discomfort of his colleagues—and rivals. It was all wonderful for us to behold, although we knew only the parti pris and parliamentary buffs would share our pleasure. And it was yet more evidence that in domestic politics Keating now performed brilliantly only when he felt his life was threatened. Anthropomorphism is unavoidable in politics. He was a cornered rat and a prowling dog; he was feline; he was a spider skulking in a corner of the web, rushing out every now and then to furiously bind and paralyse his victims. If you must be a spider, I said, be a spider that lives in the centre of the web.

Having decided not to sell the piggery precipitately, and to proceed with his parliamentary roster, and therefore to lend some credibility to the view that he was only half-interested in the prime ministership and less than half-interested in the people, the Prime Minister needed to prove his virtue by other means. He needed to go beyond the castle walls to the marketplace and in all the variety and self-interest find the common good—and speak for it. More media appearances, not less; more travel round the country, more mall crawls; more exposure of Annita and the family—a concerted friendly entry into the lives of the ordinary people. It meant a perpetual conversation with them, and policies appearing to flow from this rather than from the presumption of Canberra's wisdom or Paul Keating's vision. We thought it worth trying to effect a kind of political climate change by creating the impression of a ministerial team; with the great helmsman securely in the Lodge, but all around him experienced, capable, genial ministers. The tactic envisaged less delegation of new responsibilities than more joint press conferences with competent ministers whose personalities were less troubling to voters than the Prime Minister's. We thought the likes of Kim Beazley and Ralph Willis might cast light on some of Keating's shadows. If we left it to Willis and Beazley to explain the figures, and if instead of expressing our own enchantment with them we went to those difficulties in people's lives which the figures contradicted, then

470 | *Recollections of a Bleeding Heart*

we might be prime ministerial. If we let the public see that Keating had such men about him as Willis and Beazley, proven performers like Evans and Crean, and credible characters like Lee, Collins, Lavarch, Cook and McMullan, people might begin to see that for all the efforts of the Coalition to make Keating the issue, it was a government they must vote for and the government was a good one. There might even be some benefit we thought in building up Beazley as Keating's natural successor. Where Keating was loathed it might dilute the poison.

These things were discussed from time to time in the first half of 1994 and it is hard to see now why such reasonable plans were never attempted. The truth is, most likely, that in the Prime Minister's mind they existed much as Singapore had in Winston Churchill's. And yet they were not peripheral, but central, urgent. Keating was an unusual prime minister in no stranger way than this: he seemed not to understand that he would make himself more popular and trusted if he played sometimes to the hollow centre of the job—to the ceremonial, sentimental, clichéd dimension of it. It was as if he would not let himself think such thoughts. He disapproved of Hawke for thinking them, and succumbing. Hawke believed Keating did not have the breadth of personality, the common touch, to make a successful prime minister. Keating would say sometimes that Hawke's common touch was not an expression of understanding or kindness, but personal ego. He believed Hawke was too inclined to make the government his personal sideshow.

These were not positions he held to absolutely. No-one knew better than Keating the value of personal persuasion, and no-one was better at it. He also knew that Hawke's personal popularity had been essential to his government's policy reforms. Yet Keating recoiled from the pursuit of popularity and trust, which is to say from the essence of politics. It was expressed in outbursts of loathing for the mundane tasks, in the way he resisted nearly every simple gesture of communion with the populace and in his own exhausted, alienated persona. For every sign of his resistance, only rarely were his objections obvious. But perceptions do not require proof. The perception was that Keating operated essentially alone, counted his own time as more valuable than theirs and his own taste as much superior. Keating was anything but a fop, yet the Zegna suits were enough to create that perception, just as certain other characteristics of his behaviour created in other minds the perception that he was a vulgar brutish head-kicker.

On 24 March he told the House that he had sold his interest in the Parkville piggery. It was a relief to hear him say so, but the Opposition were soon asking the obvious new questions. For how much did he sell it and who was the buyer? And there was nothing to stop them asking old questions as well. Was the Commonwealth Bank's loan to Paul Keating's enterprise the sort of loan any Australian with comparable assets might have had approved? It was sold but we did not imagine it would go away. Less of his time would be consumed in its always troubled affairs, but the press would continue to ask questions and write stories on its operations as if the Prime Minister were still involved. And those responsible in the Senate would still have to be regularly, painstakingly briefed by the PM before each Question Time.

He gave a speech in Perth at Notre Dame University. Mary Ann O'Loughlin said my speeches these days made her cry and Keating said that the audience of Catholics had been touched. I said something about words that link things—thoughts and objects—being stronger than the things themselves. I had read it somewhere, perhaps in Marguerite Yourcenar whose book, *An Obscure Man*, made me dream of death for weeks. We would visit these places to give and to receive. The radios would be saying one thing about the meaning of our arrival, and the newspapers would be saying another. The local ALP would tell us that these were the issues, the local talkback reactionary would say it was something else. On this uncertain basis we prepared for the media, and then gave a speech of a higher, we hoped, transcending, order. We went like a doctor with a syringe, drawing off blood from the over-heated body, hoping that it was physic for both of us.

Returning from the west the Prime Minister was often at his most voluble and unrestrained. He told lewd jokes. He told stories of his adventures with the new rich. He hated the old money, he said, but liked the spirit of the nouveau riche, like Warren Anderson. Sometimes it did not seem improbable that Australians reckoned Keating was some kind of Jacobin who coveted their homes, their art, their furnishings.

In Fremantle, Carmen Lawrence won the seat of Fremantle and Keating said it was proof that the Australian people would not be influenced by smear campaigns. He had another line for Laurie Oakes—don't ask me how I'm going or how the government is going, the country is going very well. And he began to talk about rekindling the spirit of Australian youth. We suggested to Malcolm Turnbull that he pursue this theme next time he spoke about the republic. But the republic seemed unable to break new ground. Keating spoke about a referendum midway through his next term, but before that happened public opinion about the kind of republic it would be had to be changed. The republic needed a new look which the usual speeches by Turnbull, Whitlam, Wran, Robert Hughes—or Paul Keating—could not give it. The thing had taken on the appearance of a permanent benefit for some of Australia's—and particularly Sydney's—unbridled egos. We would talk about getting the Prime Minister into the debate and just as quickly give up on the idea. The republic did not need more speeches; it needed an education campaign. It needed devolving from Sydney to the other capitals. It needed bipartisan support.

We expected John Howard any day. No-one thought Hewson would lead the Coalition in the next election and, despite the baggage he would bring with him, Howard seemed the only credible candidate. When we got to the front in the polls it did not count for much because any new Opposition leader was bound to overtake us again. As much as one expected Howard, one expected a colleague to slip up and let the Opposition into the race. Graham Richardson obliged in part when he discovered that Aborigines were living in shameful conditions and recommended that the Commonwealth spend vastly more on their health. In his best public service conspiratorial tones Nigel Ray told me that the Prime Minister had set Richardson the task of persuading the colleagues to a 0.4 per cent increase in Medicare to fund this spending. But it was stupid, surely. Use Medicare to raise taxes? Get white Australia to pay huge new amounts for Aboriginal health when white Australia believed (with some justification) that throwing money their way only made the problem worse. It was madness. He's setting Richardson up, said Nigel Ray. He's giving him the green light knowing that Beazley and Willis will knock him over. If this was in fact the strategy, it did not do much for our cause. Richardson's gift (parting as it turned out) was to put the government in double jeopardy: it drew attention to the failure of Labor's past policies and it recommended essentially the same policies on a larger scale as a solution. The government was left with a choice between meanness and stupidity. Then Richardson announced that he was leaving parliament.

And, as they always did, though it was no particular fault of Richardson's, things went suddenly awry. The Prime Minister seemed to have found his way out of the piggery, which promised to be a great blessing for everyone, but the good news came with the prospect of a Senate inquiry into the affair. Any matters involving the Senate usually upset our leader's equilibrium. This matter threatened to make his anger totally ungovernable. Furthermore, he had advice that the Opposition were in possession of Commonwealth Bank documents and he would have to deal with their questions in the House, as Evans would in the Senate. In the press, meanwhile, Richo was lamented by people who two years earlier reckoned he was a scoundrel. Scoundrel or not, now they said his departure would leave a 'gaping hole'. And what would he do to the government once he was outside it?

An 8 per cent swing against the government in a by-election in Bonython was not so bad seeing only 3 per cent went to the Liberals. However, apparently unsupervised, the Prime Minister conducted a doorstop in a red denim stone-wash over-sized brand new shirt, and still sounded arrogant. He was angry with the press for the way they edited his comments. Then he was angry with Wendy Guest for encouraging Annita to be away so often. Wendy Guest was politically experienced and astute, and dedicated to the Prime Minister's vision. She had valiantly served Labor in the 1993 election, and became Annita's adviser soon after. When I told him that Wendy wanted only to serve his interests; and if discreetly informed would advise Annita to stay home whenever politics demanded it, he got angry with the world.

Bill Kelty swore he was finished with the government. Nothing had been done to implement his regional development proposals in the white paper. For weeks I urged it on Ric Simes and Ric urged it on the public service. But the resistance to Kelty did not abate. At every level it had been decided that his report was a noose for the government's neck, a rod for its back, a pit to fall in. It had become proverbial—and therefore irremediable. As he left for an Easter holiday Kelty told his assistant that the game was over. His assistant told me, and I told the Prime Minister to ring him at once, which the Prime Minister did. But why would Kelty not be furious? Brian Howe, Deputy Prime Minister and Minister for Regional Development, had made it clear to the press that the government set more store by the McKinsey Report than Kelty's. After Keating had spoken to him and told him that he was doing what he could to get a few of his 'generic things' into the statement, and that he was concerned that Kelty might think his friendship questionable, Kelty told me to tell Keating not to worry about the friendship but to do a few decent things for the regions. He added, however, that Keating ought to spend a couple of hours on the phone one Sunday, talking to the people who had helped him in the past. Tell him not to leave it for ten years like Bob Hawke did with George Slater, he said. Or some of them might hang up on him.

We had two good weeks, then we had angst and mess. There was a biblical dimension to it. Brothers, wives, mothers. It was as if he—and we with him—were cursed like Job. John Cain rang in the middle of it and told me that the government's economic policy was as lousy as ever, its achievements minor, Mabo the only worthwhile thing he had done. Cain was more frank than most on the Labor side outside the office. Out of politeness or self-interest or because their faith held up, others said nothing. But one could tell. By the end of autumn 1994 it was clear even from my reduced circle of friends that the Keating Government was in danger of losing touch even with the true believers. There had been such expectation, and now there was disappointment on an equivalent scale. Writers I knew would say it, or make their meaning just as plain by not saying it. I came to think it was the great insight of democracy that the wisdom and judgment of intellectuals does not exceed that of an uneducated voter.

The white paper on employment was to be the circuit-breaker, proof that the people had momentarily lost touch with the government, not the other way around. The document, which was finally called Working Nation, was conceived in the Prime Minister's Office, and delivered there, but it spent much of its life in the departments where for a time it seemed likely to be defined mainly by what it could not do. Later the Prime Minister's and other offices attempted to squeeze into it what they could through a narrow door. As usual it was a three-way contest between the socially desirable, the politically necessary and the fiscally responsible. But it was also a contest between imagination and pedantry; between thinking anew and thinking in the past; between politicians deciding what the country needed and demanding that the public service find the means of doing it, and the public service deciding and telling the politicians why it could not be done.

Nothing in politics, including the demolition of your opponents or the fear of being demolished, brings such pleasure as doing something tangible, measurable and good. Obviously there had been whole rafts of these political pleasure seekers in the Labor Government of the eighties, albeit some of them got their pleasure from the more austere measures, the denial of comforts, the punishments they inflicted. 'We will build the Glebe Island Bridge,' is one of the few sentences I remember writing, because after I wrote it I saw it being built, and ten years later every time I drive over it I recite the words, 'We will build the Glebe Island Bridge.' Now with Working Nation we could remake the employment and training landscape for the country; we could remake working lives; change the outlook for millions in the suburbs, in the towns, on the farms.

Because politics offers such opportunities to do good, it is perverse to find people in positions of influence dedicated to preventing good things from happening. Caution, balanced judgment, the wisdom to foresee unwanted consequences; these are essential skills in a policy-maker. Unfortunately, they are also among the easiest for the untalented, timid and meretricious to affect. The line between prudence and self-interested arse-covering is blurred. Wrinkled brows and grey beards can suggest wisdom but just as easily disguise total mental atrophy, or a prac-tised imitation of some retired superior who was genuinely wise. Among such public servants, as with political officers, homilies and platitudes abound. If they have not mastered at least two-thirds of the whole typology of the culture—who and what is to be respected, who is conspiring and who is paranoid about conspiracies, who is proven and who is doubtful, who wins their fights and who loses them—it is not safe to go to work.

In the political culture there are people of energy, imagina-tion and enlightenment, and yet more often you hear the voice of those for whom life is a tragic negative, an endless repetition of cynical laughs and groans. It shows in the empty tortuous language . . . 'you will be advised in terms of the outcome in due course'. Or in the time it took to do something: Rod Cameron would say polling on the republic will take three months, but in the department they would say six. Their documents defined the problem of their lives: they were designed for people by people who had nothing to do with ordinary people's lives. They were like Florence in *The Good Soldier*, 'a real human being with a heart, with feelings, with sympathies and with emotions only as a banknote represents a certain quantity of gold'. One tried not to be angered by them by trying to feel sorry for them—it must have been their childhoods, some trauma had occurred and they could not bear to see something happen as a consequence of something they had done.

Yet just who 'they' were I could not say. Most of the public servants I met were bright, agreeable, informed, professional and dedicated—some more than others to be sure, but hardly any could be called genuinely incompetent. And some were exceptional and easily surpassed many of the ministers in competence and drive. 'They' means the culture, the habits of mind and industry. For all the modern managerial revolutions, the beast was essentially unchanged. Perhaps it is the difference between executive and bureaucratic power, but I could never understand why for many of them the power in their hands did not animate them and rouse their imagination. Instead they carried it like a dead weight for dropping on the toes of enthusiastic people.

Just before leaving on the Prime Minister's tour of Thailand, Laos and Vietnam in April I saw an old rerun of Kenneth Clark's *Civilisation* on television. Sir Kenneth stood on top of an ancient viaduct and talked about the Romans' 'confidence'. It reminded me of One Nation—naturally—and that the Prime Minister would be opening a bridge across the Mekong between Thailand and Laos. The Friendship Bridge created the first road link between Thailand and Laos, thus linking Laos to the port of Bangkok, Thailand to Vietnam, Singapore to southern China. The bridge had been built by an Australian company. It was symbolic of cooperation and progress in the region and of Australia's role in it. It pointed to greater prosperity generally. Before we left, the people from the Murray–Darling Commission told me about the life-saving skills in irrigation and salinity they had to sell in South-East Asia. On the face of it there really was limitless possibility.

It fed one's hope of getting a Roman sort of confidence into our deeds and words. As the person responsible for the words, I wanted to move gently away from the mantras of modern Labor ideology and revive older concepts of citizenship and reciprocal obligation. On this trip I fancied we could employ a kind of bridging language—in the same speeches stressing for local Asian audiences so-called Australian traditions of tolerance and liberal-ism, and for Australians reading the reports, collective values and responsibilities. I imagined we could conjure a new perspective, a sense of possibility as much as a sense of continuity. We might open the oyster, rather than just throw another one on the midden.

The first draft of the white paper, which was handed to us on the way to Bangkok, made it clear that this perspective did not exist in the departments. Much of it concerned what had been done in the previous decade, and a considerable quantity addressed itself to the matter of what could not be done now. Some of it comprised a résumé of what was happening and another part concerned itself with what we might expect to happen. Not many measures were proposed. Nothing of a stimu-lating kind was written about what the Australian Government might do. It was without any obvious political value. It was written in verbless, prolix sludge.

The Prime Minister was not too distressed. As we flew to South-East Asia with the usual bulging complement of staff and journalists he told Geoff Walsh and me for the first time that he had in mind the possibility of a defence treaty with Indonesia. It would, he said, occupy the space left by America's withdrawal, signal that Australia had stepped up to the line as a creator of regional security.

Through Laos, Thailand and Vietnam Keating took the message of Australia's new engagement with the region. It was this vision of the future he wanted to sell to the leaders he met and to the people at home. But the journalists at the back of the plane had other ideas. In a bar on the first night in Bangkok, while a woman sang in the style of Sarah Vaughan, Peter Charlton from the *Courier-Mail* grew maudlin and let us know what he thought of the Prime Minister's decision not to visit a battle site in Vietnam. He had written an article called 'The War Keating Forgot'. Charlton had been in the Australian Army at the time of the Vietnam War, and it was easy to understand his feelings on this subject. But the other journalists gave no sign of sharing them. We—Walsh, Turnbull and

Wendy Guest—explained that there was no war cemetery in Vietnam. There was, we knew, Long Tan where nineteen Australians had been killed in battle—nineteen of the 501 to lose their lives in the Vietnam War. There was said to be a cross permanently erected in the village. But there was no monument. Even if there had been, an Australian official visit would be asking considerable forbearance of the host country whose government was comprised of the former enemy, whose dead numbered millions and whose people still lived with the devastating consequences of the war, made worse by US trade sanctions. It was the first visit by an Australian Prime Minister since the end of the war. The mission was to set the relationship on a sound footing, one favourable to Australian strategic and commercial interests. In the circumstances to expect the Vietnamese to cooperate in a ceremony honouring our invading troops was to compound gross insensitivity with needless folly. In future perhaps a ceremony might be organised, perhaps a monument would be built, but it was not appropriate now, we said.

The next day the Prime Minister visited the perfectly kept war cemetery at Kanchanaburi where the Australians who died as slave labourers on the Burma–Thailand railway are buried. About one in five of the 13,000 Australians who worked on the railway died, along with many thousands more from Britain, India, the Netherlands, New Zealand, Malaya, Burma, Java and Thailand. The vast majority of Asian labourers—300,000 of them—died. The images of emaciated survivors at the end of the war shocked a generation of Australians when they first saw them, and they are just as shocking now. At Kanchanaburi Keating described the Burma–Thailand railway as 'one of the most evil acts' of the war. But Australians had learned to draw a positive message from it, 'to think less about the cruelty and more about the means men found to endure—and help their comrades to endure it'. And, especially through the work of Edward 'Weary' Dunlop, the heroic doctor of the camps, we had learned the value of friendship with the countries of Asia.

He spoke also about Vietnam. The Australians who fought and died in Vietnam had been justly honoured in Australia and for the same reasons—for the sacrifice they made, the faith they showed. By including them in the ceremony at Kanchanaburi, Keating meant to leave no doubt that they occupied the same realms as all other Australian servicemen, living and dead.

Three journalists approached me afterwards and said how clever it had been to mention the Vietnam soldiers. We flew up the Kwai Valley in a military helicopter feeling moderately secure. Hellfire Pass, where Australian and other Allied prisoners of war died in large numbers cutting a rail line through jungle and rock on the Burmese border, is a sacred site of Australian history. It is this country's Dachau or Hades. Thinking of a man I knew who survived the experience, I was walking on ahead of the main party when I came upon the Channel 7 reporter, Dennis Grant, telling a camera that this was a place Australians must never forget. It did not seem appropriate to the man's memory. Soldiers stood in the bush lining the pass as if guarding against remnants of the Imperial Japanese Army. In the sweltering heat the Prime Minister walked in a ludicrously tight phalanx of officials. He muttered as he went past, 'There's no need to say anything is there?' I said no, but in fact the press had been promised a doorstop—perhaps the worst-taste doorstop in the history of the Keating Government. As the press assembled I was talking to Tom Burton. He told me that only Charlton had a problem about Vietnam, and now that his piece had been published we would hear no more about it. I stood on a rock and watched as the Prime Minister tried to answer the usual questions about how it felt to be in a place where thousands died in slavery. Then Tom Burton asked why he would not be paying his respects in similar vein in Vietnam.

It should have been obvious by now that we were being drawn into a war with the journalists. But because the case they were making was absurd, neither our foreign affairs people nor our media advice took it seriously. I went for a stroll around Bangkok with the Prime Minister in the afternoon. He was deter-mined to go incognito and without a police escort, but several tourists recognised him and one introduced herself as a true believer. The Thai police saw him buying an overnight bag in a little store in a back street. They closed off the street to traffic and we returned to the hotel in a tuk tuk accompanied by six motor-cycles with their sirens blaring.

The press told Greg Turnbull that they needed a grab of the Prime Minister to run in their morning stories about his visit to Vietnam, so before attending a dinner at the Australian Embassy he gave a doorstop outside the hotel. Peter Harvey asked him why he was not commemorating the soldiers in Vietnam. He replied that he did not think the veterans expected him to, and, 'Frankly why should they?' His tone was testy. At drinks before dinner the PM was fidgety. He jangled coins in his pocket. I thought it might have been the doorstop but when I asked him he put it down to a private matter—which might have had some bearing on the doorstop nonetheless.

The transcript of the doorstop revealed that the Prime Minister had said veterans of the Vietnam War could not expect a ceremony in Vietnam like the one held at Kanchanaburi because there had been atrocities in Thailand, but in Vietnam these things did not happen. The morning press murdered him. In the dingy Hanoi hotel the Prime Minister was furious. He slammed doors and kicked furniture. He threatened to kick all the press off the plane. He gave them another doorstop in a Hanoi garden but it did not stop the rot. I wrote a business speech for Ho Chi Minh City and included a section in praise of the Vietnam diggers, explaining that there was no suitable place and this was not a suitable time to pay the respects due to them. He lined the section in black and said, 'I don't disagree with you very often but I have to on this.' I said it didn't matter that the press would think he had been forced to say the words. He should say them because they were appropriate. He put more lines around the words, but not through them. I said we should tell the media that the subject would be addressed in the Ho Chi Minh City speech. On this I was outvoted by my fellow advisers. But the PM did agree to say in the business speech that in a city which 'for a decade of our national life was synonymous with a war that took the lives of 501 Australians and caused untold suffering and destruction in Vietnam', the greatest memorial would be friendship with Vietnam and peace and prosperity in the region.

Before we left Hanoi Laura Tingle wrote in the *Australian* that in his meeting with the Vietnamese leaders Keating had given them something tantamount to an apology for the war. This was absolutely untrue and a press release was issued to this effect. Keating had told the Vietnamese that Australians were 'saddened' by the destruction that had been done, but he had in no sense apologised and Tingle had been given no reason to believe that he had. The suggestion made a nice fit for their story, nonetheless: Keating grovels to communists, refuses to honour Australian soldiers. John Hewson at once declared that the Prime Minister had 'sold Australia's honour down the drain'. The Vietnam veteran, Tim Fischer, whose political decency was not always as obvious as his reputation maintained, had already leapt on the Bangkok remarks to say that Keating was insulting the honour of the Vietnam veterans and making distinctions between wars. For three days it was the big media story. Travelling with the Prime Minister was Detective Superintendent Bob Heggie who had made two tours of Vietnam with the Australian army. Heggie did not share Fischer's view, or Peter Charlton's. But Heggie was not in a position to say so. Meanwhile the Prime Minister told the travelling press that if any apologies were to be issued they should come from the Liberal Party which had put Australia into the war.

In Ho Chi Minh City the Prime Minister and officials left in the afternoon to visit Australian joint venture sites before proceeding to a reception on a floating hotel where he would deliver the business speech. Later in the afternoon I set off to join the Prime Minister's party at the floating hotel. Some of the press were in the foyer and a strangely sheepish Peter Harvey joined me for a drink. Then I saw Middleton and Grant and cameramen. I asked where they were going. Middleton said it was a 'secret', then confessed they were going to Long Tan. I spent twenty minutes trying to persuade them against it. Grant, whose logic not everyone could follow, said Keating deserved all he got—a man as skilled with the media as he was should never have made the error he made in Bangkok. I said I hoped that they did not have an accident on the way and set off to alert the Prime Minister and his advisers that, whatever he said in the speech, the news would feature a sleepy village at dusk with the sun setting on a makeshift cross, and the four anchormen intoning in turn that this was the place the Prime Minister refused to visit.

It was a farce, of course. We would glide through these Asian cities while traffic banked up for miles to let the air-conditioned motorcade pass. We would see people standing in the stifling heat on the sides of the freeway selling matches or coloured water and we would have in our hands proposals for a harmonised regional trading environment. In Hanoi, as I wrote the Ho Chi Minh City speech, through the hotel window I watched a man with a bicycle pump selling air. On the massive freeway to Bangkok airport I saw a woman drop a large box she was carrying on a bicycle. The contents blew around in the fumes and dust and the thought that the woman's day was ruined interrupted a conversation I was having about how to get the press off our backs. Now I was trying to get through the mad traffic of Ho Chi Minh City, through people carrying pallets of bricks and forty-foot bamboo poles on bicycles, to convey the message that half a dozen Australian journalists were about to do our Prime Minister in the eye.

Mike Costello and Geoff Walsh were aghast. How could they, the bastards! We wove our way back to the hotel where Costello dictated a long statement to Nina England. I rewrote it and dictated it back to her. The process took several hours and in the course of it the Prime Minister returned. He was buoyant because he had heard that Madame Kiet had been told by her husband, Prime Minister Vo Van Kiet, that his talks with Keating were the best he had had with a foreign leader. And indeed, much later, Allan Gyngell said that among many good foreign encounters, Keating's ninety-minute meeting with Kiet, President Duc Anh and Do Muoi was one of two or three that were truly remarkable for their candour and immediate mutual respect.

The press release spelt out again the reasons for the visit, that it was to secure trade, prosperity, cooperation and peace. As always, the Prime Minister had recognised his duty to the past, so he had gone to Kanchanaburi and there made it clear that those who died in Vietnam occupied 'the same esteemed place in our national memory'. He was 'dismayed by the misrepresentation' of his views. Not long ago he had paid tribute to Vietnam veterans at the inauguration of the Vietnam Memorial in Canberra. He had come to Vietnam, the first Australian prime minister to visit Hanoi, to lay the basis of friendship and help heal wounds. Other prime ministers would doubtless follow him, and he expected that one day there would be a memorial at which they could pay their respects.

Keating did not think this press business was important any more. It was a secondary issue. When we finally issued the press release the journalists asked why it had taken so long. They said it was a smart move to put those words about the veterans in the business speech. Turnbull had a fierce little snarl with Burton. Malcolm Farr said the whole problem began with Allan Gyngell's briefing. Gyngell, he said, did not seem to recognise that the veterans were an issue. Sometime before 3.00 a.m. the newsmen returned from their Long Tan expedition. They had not been able to find the cross.

For Allan Gyngell the trip was to advance the prospects for Australia's relationship with these countries and with the region. Beyond that it was the commemoration of events in Thailand of profound significance in Australia's history. But for the journalists the story was not trade, regional security or healing old wounds with a country that everyone believed would become a significant regional player. It would not be anything the government determined. It would be what the media determined. And it was. In the wash-up they declared that Keating's 'bad politics' had drawn the media's attention away from the good work he was doing—as if to say, see what you made us do. The eminently reasonable *Canberra Times* journalist, Peter Cole Adams, said it had been a combination of Keating's ill-advised comments, a press that allowed itself to be sidetracked, advisers who underestimated the sensitivity of the issue and a small-minded and an opportunistic Opposition who took advantage of the situation.

It was a media burlesque yet it forced a degree of historical catharsis. Some veterans came forward in support of Keating. And Malcolm Fraser, Minister for Defence during the Vietnam War, declared that the whole thing had been a 'wasted effort', even if for a just cause. He blamed Liberal leaders from Menzies on for slavishly following the United States into the war without insisting that Australia have a say in strategy. Knowing what he knew now about the terms of Australia's participation in the war he would have opposed it.

Flying back, the Prime Minister was determined to visit the media in the back of the plane. We suggested he refrain. We did not want more trouble. An hour or so later he came back and saw Geoff Walsh down the back with them. If Walsh could talk to them he could. I stood in the aisle blocking his way, telling him not to. He would not relent. When I stood aside I said, if you have to go just speak to the ones who have behaved decently, don't stir up the others. A little later Greg Turnbull sat down next to us and said that the Prime Minister had just called Peter Harvey 'a jerk'. When he joined us I told him it was stupid. He said we had to stand up to them. I said he had left us with another mess to clean up, that was the most offensive thing about his behaviour.

It was the worst of times with the gallery. Not long after his return from Vietnam the Prime Minister cast dark aspersions on Nikki Savva from the *Herald Sun*. Ms Savva was said to be deeply hurt and Laurie Oakes felt constrained to devote his column in the *Bulletin* to savaging Keating's dreadful attack. Meanwhile Paul Lyneham accused the Prime Minister of using the media 'for political purposes'.

Cynicism pervaded the electorate and made life dangerous as well as difficult. If we did not produce a big and bold policy on employment our opponents would make merry. They need only call it inadequate, uninspired, a product of a tired government and the thing would be born dead. They could even go further and call it a 'betrayal' of the unemployed, even a 'cynical betrayal' or 'another Keating lie'.

As a pre-emptive measure, Keating went on television for the express purpose of establishing in the public mind that Hewson was bound to say these things—that he was always negative. The white paper had to signal energy, intellectual weight, compassion, vision and renewal. It had to do this for political reasons. That it should do so for moral or any other reasons only rarely came into it. The constraint of course was money: no proposal, necessary or merely desirable, escaped that judgment. And when the time came nothing would escape it in the media. Yet the process was also constrained by habit, conservative exhausted minds, a failure of imagination, an impoverished language. The task was immense. When measures had been decided and cabinet had approved them, all day and night for seeming weeks the office wrestled them into a shape and language that might be understood. As there was no section on regional development policy, and no sign of one emerging from the department, Iola Matthews who had worked on Bill Kelty's project was brought into the PMO to help me write one. The education and training and social security measures were depressingly complex and defied explanation for days, even from those who devised them.

Perhaps it did not matter that they were beyond the reach of ordinary understanding. On the first day the press would break the statement down into its principal parts—the half-dozen principal measures, the cost, the growth assumptions—and those dot points on the newspaper front pages would thereafter be the statement. For reasons I now wonder at, I thought the thing so many people had laboured over needed a language that might give the public heart. It was essentially a practical document, to be sure, but I thought it also needed to speak in compelling terms for a philosophy. As the government's flagship, it needed to be formidable and inspiring. It had to be the answer. Wasn't it pointless for the Prime Minister to say that the key to Working Nation was the unprecedented degree of personal understanding it brought to unemployed people if the measures were described in words that people could not understand?

In the end, Working Nation was not everything we had hoped, but far better than our fears sometimes allowed—better, furthermore, than the media allowed. No Australian government since the war had delivered such a complex statement on the matter of employment and unemployment. Indeed it was much more complex, and no less definitive, than the famous white paper of 1945. Working Nation addressed employment consequences of the new information age economy, as the 1945 white paper addressed the postwar economy. The 1945 white paper was a statement of Keynesian orthodoxy written with the 1930s Depression in mind. The 1994 white paper owed something to Keynes and something to his successors, but was tied to no orthodoxy and had only the future to guide it. It was intended to be consistent with free markets and the rapidly advancing forces of globalisation. But to these the statement welded labour market programs and social policies that were novel and sophisticated to an unprecedented degree, though also in the long tradition of social melioration in Australia. There was a new 'parenting allowance', for instance: $59 per week for 118,000 unemployed and low income families. Working Nation heralded an awareness of the consuming change upon us in the 1990s and at the same time echoed the first decade of the Commonwealth. In time other governments would take it as a starting point for their own plans.

In his speech at the National Press Club on 5 May 1994, the day after the statement's release, Keating said that whereas the 1945 white paper sought ways to demobilise a million servicemen and women, the 1994 statement set itself the task of remobilising a million unemployed. He quoted Chifley's definition of the safety net: it was like the net beneath trapeze artists, put there so when they fall they can again climb the ladder of opportunity. He portrayed Working Nation as the fulfilment of the promise he had made before and on the night of the last election—that he would not leave the poor behind; and as further proof that in Australia where cultural difference and economic competitiveness were modern by-words, the people stuck by civilised values. He put Working Nation in the tradition of the nation's 'true liberal' founders. He even found eighteenth-century parallels. Working Nation was the policy expression of Samuel Johnson's maxim that 'In a civilised society we all depend upon each other'. Those who said that preparing the long-term unemployed for the workforce would create unfair competition for the short-term unemployed were practising the moral equivalent of transportation: they believed the unemployed had forfeited their right to a place in society. And those who said the cost was too high were imitating the principle of the hulks: keep them in gaol because it is cheaper. But the social and human cost was in fact much greater, and so was the cost to the nation's skills. And to those who argued that the only answer was full deregulation of the labour market, he said that would be to lower the country's gaze, to invite a widening disparity of wealth and greater hardship for more people—all for the sake of matching the US unemployment statistic. If Labor's opponents wanted to fight the next election as advocates of the American social model, Labor would be very happy to do so. In any event, he said, there was no evidence to show that reducing wages would stimulate growth. No comparable economy was growing faster than Australia; and in those regions of Australia without growth a survey of firms found that only 4 per cent counted wage costs as a problem.

The press inclined to say that he had over-claimed. They said it was not in the same league as the white paper of 1945, although cursory investigations revealed they knew precisely nothing about that much more modest document.

The first premise was growth. Growth was the key to employment. The proof was in the 230,000 new jobs created in the previous twelve months—a year of growth. Working Nation assumed continued growth of 4.5 per cent. Therefore Working Nation addressed itself first to achieving levels of economic efficiency and competitiveness that would assure the country of low inflation growth to the end of the century and beyond. But even a decade of growth would not, of itself, eliminate long-term unemployment. Most of the jobs generated by growth go to new entrants to the labour market. The 300,000 long-term unemployed were bound to remain cut off. It meant not just poverty, but generational disadvantage, family breakdown, social dysfunction. It also meant a waste of resources, a drain on revenue, a brake on efficiency. So with Working Nation the government voted $1.7 billion in the next year for programs to prepare the unemployed for entry or re-entry to the labour market. The cost over four years would be $6.5 billion.

The keystone of the policy was the Job Compact, a government undertaking to provide a job or training or both to all those who had been unemployed for eighteen months or more. Most of the necessary 160,000 jobs were expected to come from the private sector, encouraged by subsidies, bonuses and a training wage agreed with the ACTU. Other employment would be found in environment, community service, education and various other projects generated under a scheme to be called New Work Opportunities, and in successful existing programs. To head off the descent into long-term unemployment a Youth Training Initiative provided case management for people under eighteen years of age who had been registered as unemployed for thirteen weeks. For those under eighteen the dole would be abolished and replaced by a job training allowance. The guiding principle was 'whatever it takes' in work and training to make people ready for employment. Private sector and community agencies, as well as a revamped Commonwealth Employment Service, would provide the case management. Training would be integrated with the needs of employers—and with regions.

In all its elements Working Nation was intended to be part of a strategy for regional revival and development. As both Kelty and McKinsey did, those parts of it which dealt specifically with the regions advocated an approach based on the principle that regions would do best if they identified their own problems and found their own solutions. The Commonwealth would do best by the regions if it provided the wherewithal for them to find their own way—finance to audit skills, natural advantages, export opportunities; more liberal pooled development funds and infrastructure bonds; and specific basic capital works from roads to irrigation, environmental solutions, tailored rural adjustment schemes. Some regions in Australia were actually growing much faster than any of the major cities. The aim of regional development policies was to imitate their success in joining up with the national and global economies.

While Working Nation contained a separate chapter on industry policy, the entire statement might have been put under the same heading. And under that heading senior government politicians and officials were wont to say that, if the past ten years were anything to go by, industry policy was one of the government's great successes. How else to explain, for instance, an increase in manufacturing as a proportion of all exports from about 12 per cent to about 23 per cent? To existing industry policy, of which financial deregulation and tariff reduction were the main parts, the government had added greater flexibility in the labour market afforded by the enterprise bargaining provisions of the previous year's Industrial Relations Reform Act, and through the States agreement to competitive markets for electricity supply, gas and water. With the white paper a more skilled workforce could also be added. Among other direct and indirect assistance to industry, Working Nation boosted funding to scientific research, created new cooperative research centres, offered more assistance to emerging exporters and small and medium-sized enterprises and overhauled the machinery of export promotion.

It was a bit like taking Guadalcanal—formidably difficult and chaotic in execution, driven by fear and necessity as often as vision or courage. Yet it left those of us who were there with a rare sense of achievement, more faith in government and an enlarged conception of what governments can do. Working Nation gave some of us a sense of vocation that had sometimes seemed misplaced. In its wake we could reshape the national debate, give the Keating Government a character quite different from any other, including Hawke's. Working Nation was directed at the mass of Australian workers and their families, not to minorities, single-interest groups or elites. It ought to have been the anchor of government policy, the definitive immovable part of it. As much as it constituted necessary micro-economic reform and met an urgent social need, it also answered the political complaint that Labor had neglected mainstream Australian interests. For a moment it rebalanced the equation between government and the people—one felt less at their mercy. And if the people failed to appreciate it and the media were cynical, we could forgive them because like Guadalcanal they could not know if they had not been there.

Working Nation created a desire to do more. If it was possible to conceive of the means to case-manage tens of thousands of young unemployed, it was possible to case-manage regions and communities. If it was possible to re-imagine the way governments dealt with unemployment, it was possible to re-imagine the way they dealt with Aboriginal health. If the government could take on the challenge of the revolution in business and industry, it could take on the revolution in technology. If it could do those things, surely it might raise the level of knowledge and interest in the democracy itself—in its institutions, the ideas from which they derived, in the nation's history. We could move on to civics and education generally. Working Nation was one essential proof of the government's social democratic ambitions, but what was a social democracy without conscious understanding? And how could you have a social democracy if in the higher reaches of politics and the public service people had lost the capacity to talk to each other and the public in a language capable of understanding? Apart from the exhausted sense of triumph, this is the lingering memory of Working Nation—the effort required to extract the meaning. It felt as if, hard up against its most basic ambitions, the government lost the power of coherent speech. Probably the economists had ruled for too long: the collision of their worldview with poll-driven politics had produced a dullness of thought and expression that was actually inimical to the nation's life and prospects. The instinct to do good was still there, the romance of nation-building floated through corridors and gleamed in eyes, the competence remained. But nothing in the political and bureaucratic discourse spoke of the humanist tradition on which the entire edifice ultimately rested. Therefore nothing in the culture spoke of it.

For all that, public servants delivered the white paper and just a week later public servants delivered a budget that business, financial markets, unions and caucus generally approved. On the Laws program the Prime Minister said the people should ignore the critics. They were 'sourpuss commentators' on $200,000 a year and company cars, and they didn't care if 400,000 Australians who had borne the brunt of change should end up on the scrapheap. He was preferred prime minister by a big margin and Labor was five points ahead in the polls.

It was also with the aid of the public service that the government appointed an expert group to inquire into the state of civics education in Australia and provide the government with a plan for a non-partisan program of public education. In June 1994 Melbourne University historian Stuart Macintyre, the director-general of the New South Wales Department of School Education Kenneth Boston, and Susan Pascoe of the Catholic Education Office were appointed to the task. They found abysmal ignorance about Australian democratic institutions, values and practices, and about Australian history. We thought this knowledge would give us a lever on public opinion when it came to persuading the States to accept proposals for a national civics curriculum. Civics was not—despite the insistence of one premier—a propaganda arm of the republican movement. It was nonetheless a necessary corollary of the sharper, enlivened national consciousness that a republic implies. It was the practical stuff of the republic, as opposed to the symbolic. It gave virtue and substance to the debate in the same way as appointing a taskforce on Aboriginal health and living conditions would provide a practical dimension to reconciliation and Native Title. But State education departments resisted civics as they always resist national initiatives in education. As for the appointment of a taskforce on Aboriginal health, it was delayed again and again, principally from the fear that the cost of its proposals would be immense and deliver to the next Labor government responsibilities that could not be met.

--

Then in May after Working Nation and the budget had both met with muted approval, Alexander Downer took over the Liberal leadership from John Hewson. Viewed from the government side, it was a strange decision. It reeked of the Melbourne Establishment, and the Prime Minister quickly made his mission 'hot-riveting the Melbourne Club to Alexander Downer's arse once and for all'. The press gallery reckoned Mr Downer would be a very difficult opponent for Keating: not as ideological as Hewson, more charming; his pleasantness, they thought, would put Keating's aggression into ugly relief. Consequently, when Keating immediately lambasted Downer's upper-class Adelaide background, Downer replied that Keating's connections were with fast money. Keating's riposte came back that by fast money Downer meant not old money, meaning not quite proper money. The gallery said that Keating had declared class war—and Nikki Savva was quick to say he had lost it. Privately, Keating said it was a great joke to have people say he was connected to any money at all, having just given up a first-grade investment in a piggery and devoted himself to public life when he might have been thriving in the private sector. Privately also, he felt exhausted by the prospect of a new opponent. 'I suppose,' he said, 'I'll have to reach inside again and pull out my personality and smother them with it.' He could see no alternative to bloody war. To the suggestion that he try to draw Downer on the republic by saying he hoped the new Liberal leader would take up the issue seriously, he replied that one should never invite the enemy to one's own side because it was a sign of weakness. No doubt the strategy had worked for him down the years, yet it limited his political options and meant he could not divide and conquer. On the Liberal side there was division which his invitation to cross over might have widened. And on the republican side there was a desperate need to be seen as non-partisan. This too, an invitation might have helped to satisfy.

Downer's election caused an extended hiccup, but nothing approaching a convulsion. It would take a while for Keating to find his feet with him and overcome the mourning which seemed to envelop him each time the battle was renewed—not for the life he would take but the part of his own he would lose. Downer was sure to be granted a honeymoon by the media and voters and in some quarters panic and mistakes would follow. But nothing in Downer's record suggested that he would make a dangerous opponent. He had not distinguished himself in policy and had no apparent capacity for leadership. His manner was mildly fey. If Keating was deficient in the qualities of the common man, Downer was even more so. When Hewson and Keating faced each other both saw something of themselves and they raged like Caliban. When Keating faced Downer he felt only an amused contempt. Hewson sometimes regressed and sounded like a schoolboy: Downer gave the impression that he had never stopped being one. Hewson was Keating's natural enemy; Downer was his natural prey.

Within a month of his elevation to the leadership Walsh and I were willing to wager with the journalists that Downer would not last until Christmas. It was not because we did not want him to last longer, or because our Prime Minister had found his range and target, it was that Downer was so palpably inadequate and so certain to have John Howard coming after him. Half in anticipation of the inevitable, Keating said the problem was the party, not the leader—it was not the jockey but the horse.

As if to vindicate their theory that Downer's pleasant disposition would put Keating's nasty one in sharp relief, the gallery chased Keating mercilessly for a fortnight or so. In the *Sun-Herald* Peter Robinson wrote about 'Keating's Twisted Hatred'; Mike Seccombe in the *Australian* and Peter Charlton in the *Courier-Mail* wrote similarly vicious pieces. There were times when Paul Keating brought opprobrium on himself; just as often it appeared the press made up its mind regardless. In a Sydney restaurant my friend, Andrew Clark, the editor of the *Sun-Herald*, shouted at me about Keating's abuse of what he called 'working journalists'. The plight of working politicians whose policy achievements were ignored and whose hard work and public spirit were traduced did not concern him. What was a prime minister to do about slurs on his character and motives? Let them pass as if they were true? Write to the editor, as if slurs were a matter for public debate? If journalists hunt in packs, or justify their judgments against a pendulum swing, or give the undeserving honeymoons, throw up opinion and speculation as reportage, then the country will have the nondescript governments with safe 'populist' leaders the country does not need and the press at other times despise. Clark was not impressed. Keating's was indeed a good government, he said, and Keating was a leader of courage and vision, but he had no right to yell at journalists. It cannot be a good government if its best efforts are ignored or defamed, I said. But the press has always been about news and entertainment, Clark said. On this note, which might have suggested that governments should also be about news and entertainment, the argument faded.

CHAPTER 17

The mystery of esthetic like that of material creation is accomplished. The artist, like the God of the creation, remains within or behind, or beyond or above his handiwork, invisible, refined out of existence, indifferent, paring his fingernails.
—Trying to refine them also out of existence, said Lynch.

JAMES JOYCE, A PORTRAIT OF THE ARTIST AS A YOUNG MAN

I N ENGLAND FOR the fiftieth anniversary of the D-Day
landings in Normandy, the Prime Minister went to the Air
Force memorial at Runnymede and gave a speech in praise
of Britain's heroic wartime resistance to Nazism. It was from
Britain that came 'the most stalwart resistance to tyranny', 'the
courage democracy needed' and the inspiration for 'the free world
and those whose freedom had been taken from them'. He quoted
John Curtin who expressed very similar sentiments in 1944. They
were talking about momentous events in the history of the world:
events that the Fairfax journalist Tony Wright believed required a
certain amount of gymnastic skill for the Prime Minister to
reconcile with his stress on the Pacific War and Australia's modern
relationship with the countries of Asia. But it was not so difficult
to admire the greatness of Britain, or even France, and yet rebuke
them when they set themselves against Australia's interests or
rebuke Australian governments that failed to see or put Australia's
interests first. If people thought it looked awkward or unstates-
manlike that might be because people had an imperfect idea of
what statesmanship is.

Sheltering from the rain at the memorial, the journalists

asked us if this could be the same prime minister who spoke so harshly of Britain's 'betrayal at Singapore.' Indeed it was, we said, and the same John Curtin who confronted Britain in 1941–42 and yet acknowledged the world's debt to Britain in 1944. The point seemed not to register. The media reported that the Prime Minister had apparently undergone 'a staggering change of heart', he had 'buried the hatchet' with Britain. It was a farcical reading of history to complement the farcical belief that Downer was a serious conservative leader. Don't worry, Glenn Milne assured me, the pendulum will swing.

At the dinner that night in the Guildhall at Portsmouth the leaders of all the former Allies (except the Russians) were gathered at a long table on the stage. At tables in front of them, Allied veterans were assembled. Some veterans' widows had been invited and seated prominently near the stage. Opposite me a France Libre survivor told the English widow beside him that he wished they had met when they were young. The Scottish widow on my left said my prime minister should not have been so rude to the Queen and should certainly not have touched her, and on several occasions politely removed from her own shoulder the ravaged hand of a Canadian veteran seated on her other side. When the Queen rose and her strange hooting voice cut through the hall, the Frenchman gasped and whispered, 'I never thought I would see this.'

With his fellow leaders, the Prime Minister had visited Buckingham Palace on his arrival in London. They lined up to greet her and when she reached him she asked how things were going in Australia. He was telling her how we were now in our tenth quarter of growth and unemployment was declining, when jets roared overhead. 'That will be those Canadians,' she said, looking up at the ceiling. The Prime Minister refused to be fazed by this distraction. 'I have a clock exactly like that one behind you,' he said. 'Do you?' she replied. 'I do,' he said. 'Wherever did you get it?' she inquired. 'Melbourne', he said.

They were all gathered again next day at Southsea Common. As warships cruised past and soldiers paraded on the sodden grass, and the commoners sat with their feet in puddles and plastic raincoats on their heads, the royal family, Allied leaders past and present and military chiefs took their seats in the grand-stand. As each leader was announced, the crowd applauded according to the degree of their approval. The Queen Mother, who arrived with the estranged wife of the Prince of Wales, did best and the estranged wife did almost as well. The US President with his puffy eyes and guilty smile did not much better than the Australian Prime Minister, who did poorly without being heckled or booed. On the *Britannia*, crossing the channel later that day, Clinton put his hand on Keating's shoulder and said to those around him, 'I love this guy.'

Keating and Mitterrand liked each other too. Their meeting went smoothly and, as was common with Keating meetings abroad, for longer than usual. It was also broader and included a tour of the Elysée Palace. In Brussels he met with Jacques Delors and Leon Brittain and those present said he performed with his usual impressive charm and skill. But later, off the cuff, he told an audience of French business people in his conversation with the French President he had declared Australia would soon be a republic with, he hoped, a new flag. Some in the Australian media and the Opposition at once declared this an insult to the monarch whose hospitality he had just enjoyed. Once again, they said, he had gone overseas and stirred up trouble at home. Joyfully the Coalition added to the increasingly preposterous portrait of Keating they had recently been contriving. Once again the media had decided what the story was and wrote it in defiance of history and the truth about events they had ostensibly been sent to cover. It is true Paul Keating had given them the shred of an excuse which was all they needed, yet it was also easier now to see why he so often acted as if they or their influence did not exist. Sanity demanded it. In the early hours of the morning, with a Federal policeman scouting the streets ahead for journalists, the Prime Minister and his wife window-shopped for antiques around Rue St Germain. It was always an impossible conundrum. One would implore him to act judiciously with the gallery and not give them an excuse they needed to punish him. And the next day one would passionately assert to one's colleagues that we worked for the Prime Minister, and not as mediators between his interests and the press gallery's.

Kerry O'Brien wanted to conduct a long interview on the ABC's *Lateline*. It would be O'Brien's mid-term examination, which meant that anything the Prime Minister said of a predictive nature would be subjected to merciless scrutiny in his later pre-election exam. At that moment in our progress Newspoll had the Coalition seven points ahead and Downer's nose in front. If the pendulum had swung it was not obvious in mid-June 1994. Caucus was restless again and complaining that the Prime Minister had fenced himself off from their concerns. We heard that many of them thought the overseas trip had gone badly. Bob McMullan was reported to be critical of the Prime Minister's aggression towards Downer. And, defending him in the uproar which followed his assertion that the Australian Constitution had been written in the Colonial Office, Gareth Evans did not disguise his low opinion of Keating's constitutional knowledge. On this last issue the Opposition maintained a relentless parliamentary attack for two days. The Prime Minister of course would not concede an inch. He was wrong in pedantic fact, perhaps, but he had meant it metaphorically and he was right, he said. In *Atlantic Monthly* Garry Wills wrote that there were two kinds of political leader—the Periclean and the popular. It was clear enough which category our prime minister fell into. It was incredible for anyone to think he could cross over to the other kind. But incredibly it seems I did.

O'Brien submitted to us a long list of subjects on which he intended to question the Prime Minister. For the purposes of coaching him, Geoff Walsh called on advisers to consider their portfolios and come up with such information as might prove helpful. On the evening before the interview we gathered outside his door like rabbits grazing nervously at dusk. When at last he arrived the Prime Minister no doubt wished he had a shotgun.

Most of O'Brien's questions we anticipated. Industrial relations—how many enterprise bargains? Unemployment—will it come down to 8 per cent or less? Will interest rates rise? The republic; health; Downer; how long will Paul Keating stay in the job?

And there was the smoky: serial rights for Bob Hawke's autobiography are circulating and it has come to O'Brien's attention that the former prime minister alleges his successor had once called the country he now leads 'the arse-end of the earth'. It was at once too silly to consider and much too horrible to ignore. The Prime Minister told us that Hawke was talking bullshit and he knew it. If he had used the expression he had meant it in the geographical sense—Australia is at the farthest end of things, and isolated. This is the arse-end of the earth, therefore we must do the following . . . This is what he told O'Brien. He performed very well in the interview: he was relaxed and confident and that was precisely what we wanted the press to report. He even talked about investment in regional infrastructure. Then there came the 'arse-end' question, floating on to the political screen like a malignant spirit. The Prime Minister laughed at it, stood on his record as a man who had given more than most to the nation's life, and would hardly have given it if he held it in anything less than deep affection.

The matter was not going to end there, of course. The Opposition got it going in the Senate, and in the heat Gareth Evans said some rude things about Alexander Downer's wife which only made matters worse. Then Oakes put it beyond doubt—in his terms at least. He told the nation that in the book Hawke alleged that Keating had once said to him that if he did not get the leadership he would leave Australia, which was the arse-end of the earth anyway. It was the worst possible context and it had a whiff of credibility about it. The Prime Minister rang Oakes and told him Hawke was wrong, that Oakes was wrong to suggest Hawke's remark was credible. His tone was subdued, hurt. Why had he done it when he knew Hawke's attitude, when he knew his motives? We put out a press release to the effect that the people could believe the record of Paul Keating's service as proof of his affection for the country and devotion to its interests, or they could believe the alleged fragment of a private conversation. Later I was about to go and find dinner, and realised the office was strangely empty. I put my head in Keating's door and found him sitting there alone watching Paul Lyneham do a soft interview with Alexander Downer. 'I am the most honest and open man you'll ever meet,' Downer was saying. Lyneham betrayed none of his famous cynicism. I thought our leader must be wondering what he had done to deserve this, and if it was worth continuing, especially with advisers who go home when he could do with a bit of company.

In the entirely unpredictable way of politics the issue rallied the troops behind Keating, including some traditional Hawke allies. Geoff Walsh reported that caucus was furious with Hawke. Wayne Swan and Wayne Goss both went public, Goss urging the view that Keating was the most patriotic of Australians. We put a similar view in a press release and, principally by taking the high moral ground, managed to partially control the damage. Then Hawke was door-stopped at a casino where, it seemed to some observers, he was under the weather. He told reporters that Downer would win the next election. Later he told reporters that he was prepared to take a lie detector test to prove that Keating had said Australia was the arse-end of the earth. If it seemed to some people that Hawke was sinking into the mire, he was taking Keating with him. In the polls the Prime Minister's popularity dived.

In mid-winter 1994 Paul Keating thought about quitting. Peter Barron urged him to. Geoff Walsh thought it was a good idea. If he stayed, they said, he would struggle to win the next election. In the likely event of his losing, the departure would be not only forced but bitter. Resignation had two attractions for him. He was exhausted in mind, body and spirit. The doctor, Graham Killer, was concerned about his health. His tinnitus was causing him distress. Displaced hips and collapsed arches gave him severe almost permanent back spasms. He was constantly tired. He worked around his condition. He told me how he had learned to hit the ball back with only one-tenth of the effort. He confessed that he stayed away from meetings and the office when he could and, when he couldn't, switched himself off. As much as he could he occupied himself with his interests outside politics. He had developed the habit of not listening. He thought that he might be able to leave it in the hands of Evans or Beazley and depart to a good life and get his health and his happiness back. Happiness was the second good reason for throwing it in. He wondered if this was not his last chance to give Annita and his children lives with less pressure, an existence of the kind he always wanted. He thought they deserved a reward for all the years at the mercy of his political career. When he left he hoped, and they expected, it would be to a good house in Sydney. He was not thinking of resigning to save his marriage, but to revive it, restore some balance to it and be fair to them.

We discussed these things on the way to Indonesia. As he talked to Suharto in Jakarta, in Canberra the Opposition asked questions about the piggery and Australian journalists combed the streets of the Indonesian capital in search of anti-Suharto demonstrators protesting at the recent closure of dissident magazines. That night we dined with the President in a room featuring a large painting of women bathers. A combo played Indonesian and American standards, two men sang 'Waltzing Matilda', and a succession of beautiful women crooned what could only be love songs. More women danced in the Javanese fashion, and then more still in the fetching Sumatran style which allows the dancers to engage the eyes of their audience. Suharto looked happiest then. The Indonesian official beside me said that the President talked about Paul Keating more than anyone else in the world and that the mention of his name animated him and lifted him from his normal introversion. In the hotel room later Keating was enthusiastic about the progress he was sure he'd made with Suharto. He was now sure that the President would agree to a defence pact. It would be the biggest thing since ANZUS. It would mean, as APEC had, that Australia was becoming an architect of policy in the region, that we would design our own trade and strategic environment. At such times Paul Keating had the power to lead his listeners to the point where they could see what he saw. It was easy to see why the journalists had so admired him in the 1980s. It made one's blood rise. We loved him for it.

The Prime Minister decided he would not resign. He had not finished with APEC, the defence pact, the cultural statement, the republic or the information revolution. He wanted to see Working Nation properly implemented. If he went he was not sure that the government would keep its reforming zeal, its policy integrity or its economic discipline. And he wanted to see off Downer. He still had ideas. The information revolution had captured his imagination. Brian Johns from the Australian Broadcasting Authority came to see him with a plan. He hoped Keating would not consider it too grand. Keating listened as Johns outlined it and when he had finished said that it was 'a nice bit of berley' and then outlined a much grander plan.

He would stay and in the meantime satisfy his family's needs by buying John Laws's house on the Hawkesbury River. We urged him to at least postpone the purchase that was certain to create yet another wave of bad publicity. He thought about it and decided to go ahead. I had not wanted him to resign. Somehow I had persuaded myself that he could change, that he could adopt the persona and disciplines of a prime minister. He would give up his indulgences. When we were trying to sell Working Nation it was stupid to have a three-day story about the Cahill Expressway, which followed from a press release he issued condemning the New South Wales Liberal Government for failing to pull it down. The Cahill Expressway is a hideous blight on Circular Quay, but one that it is entirely invisible to the country at large. He would recognise that the second consideration outweighed the first. He would get his office working even if it meant removing four or five members of his staff. He would go out among the people, show them that he was but their instrument, or at least the nation's instrument. By way of starting the revolution in himself he would announce that the republic was open for the Australian people to consider. It is not my republic but the people's, he would say. Every word, every signal from him would say, 'This I do for you. I am of you. I am for your children.' He would come at

Downer with a little less brutality. He would see that he was giving a starving man his arm to chew on. He had delivered a Native Title Act, a Land Fund, Working Nation, APEC leaders' meetings, low inflation economic growth, and the first serious debate on an Australian republic. And there was more promised. Yet he was regularly castigated in the press for lacking vision and ideas, and in cabinet and caucus, we heard, he was seen to lack 'commitment' to the job. The opinion polls told us that this view was held throughout the land. They saw it in the body language; they knew he wasn't hitting the ball as hard, that he wasn't really there for them. Wasn't really listening.

The truth was nothing would change. The hard grind of the last decade had made him a bit eccentric, he conceded. He had taken some heavy blows. Geoff Walsh intended to leave at the end of the year. When he talked to me about taking over his job I wondered if I wanted to be principal adviser to someone who in recognising his own 'eccentricity' might have found a rational reason for irrational acts. Tom Mockridge agreed that he should stay if he could find the heart for it. Mockridge suspected Packer was behind Barron's advice to throw it in. It had been a curious arrangement for a long time. It seemed even more curious that the PM took so long to confide that he was sometimes reluctant to tell his principal adviser certain things, because his principal adviser was close to Barron, and Barron was close to Richardson whom the Prime Minister no longer trusted. Just as curious—and disturbing—was the fact that our Prime Minister was regularly taking advice from a person who wanted him to resign. They were a curious bunch, the old guard of the Hawke–Keating Government, and one of those associated with them in their myriad incarnations warned me not to speak ill of them for fear of 'repercussions later'.

Tom Wheelwright left to become a senator. He was replaced by Bill Bowtell, then a consultant to the Attorney-General, Michael Lavarch. Bowtell had been a senior adviser in Neal Blewett's office when Medicare was established and had been involved in the government's highly successful campaign against

HIV/AIDS. He had somehow avoided the studied gloom and grim portentousness that seemed to overtake other longstanding Labor Party operators. He was spirited and generally optimistic, and not liked by those who in their hearts, if not yet their minds, had given up the fight.

Bruce Chapman joined the staff as an economic adviser. His affable gently subversive intelligence and the wholeness of his worldview made a great difference. His mentors in economics had been the Australian, Bob Gregory and at Yale, James Tobin, the Nobel Prize winner who advocated a universal tax on foreign exchange transactions which might be usefully brought to bear on world poverty. Chapman's economics tended in the same creative direction. He had been the chief designer of the HECs scheme for universities and a consultant to John Dawkins in the late eighties. Before the Prime Minister approved his appointment to the PMO he asked him to come to the Lodge. As he rushed from the house, Chapman's child vomited on his trouser cuff. He arrived hoping that the famously sartorial Prime Minister did not notice the stain or the smell. He sat in the Brown Room facing the Rupert Bunny painting. The Prime Minister asked him what he believed to be the main problem facing Australia just then. Chapman gave the best account he could of some structural weakness in the economy. The Prime Minister listened quietly until he had finished. Then he told Chapman that he had not described the really big problem. The big problem was all the women in the workforce. And all the children in care, or being brought up by their fathers when they should be at home with their mothers. Chapman joined the office and replaced Nigel Ray in the fraught zone of industrial relations.

We thought it safe to presume that the Coalition's research revealed to them something very like what ours revealed to us. Ours revealed, unvaryingly, that while a minority of voters held Paul Keating in high regard and a majority thought him 'strong', the most common perception was of arrogance and aloofness. What strength the government had, he gave it, but he was also the government's greatest weakness. It was for this reason, we fancied, that the Coalition waged such unrelenting war on him. Late in 1994 we heard of rumours circulating about the Prime Minister's integrity, the propriety of his business affairs. By halfway through the following year it was clear that the slander had taken on something of the form of a campaign. People very close to me heard it from their most senior officials: that Keating was corrupt, he had raised money by illegal means, he was a very rich man. To the extent that it regularly produced damaging TV grabs of his counterattacks, the single-minded pursuit of Keating in the parliament succeeded for the Coalition. It made the Prime Minister's behaviour the issue and rarely allowed moments of calm needed for the public to see the government for what it was—conscientious, tolerably efficient and a good deal more talented, member for member, than its opponents.

What remained were only those moments when the tactic drew them to the jaws of hell. Even tired and dispirited as he so often was, no-one could chew up an Opposition like Keating. The sentiments were very similar on the government side. The colleagues could complain, mutter that he was a liability, but no-one made them feel better than Keating on the attack. And no-one cheered them up like he did. He finally delivered his cracker night speech in Brisbane, and right across the country one could feel the side lift. What other politician was able to make half the country laugh with him?

The general perception of a low tone in parliament made regular high tone speeches very desirable. I wrote something of this kind for the opening of the Graduate School at Melbourne University. It was all the more necessary because the official launch of Hawke's book was about to restart the arse-end story. We tried strenuously to arrange for the speech to immediately precede whatever tawdry news flowed from Hawke. The theme was change and inertia, the endless struggle against the formidable foe of 'the do-nothings and the think-nothings'. Keating said that after twenty-five years in the parliament he could not think of 'a single item of reforming legislation—not even the most flawed—

which has damaged the fabric and future of Australia in a dimension comparable to that caused by inaction or regression'. He quoted a recent article in which Xavier Pons asked if there was a connection between 'say, Mabo, the Industrial Relations Reform Act, multiculturalism, the push for an Australian republic and the upgrading of Australia's military cooperation with Indonesia'. Pons thought he could 'detect the premises of an unprecedented cultural shift' as Australia gave up its illusions and faced realities. Keating said Pons was right.

The last page and a half of the final draft amounted to an announcement that the government was handing over the republic process to the people. Mark Ryan and the ARM were very keen on this, as were the officers in the department. In the office Craddock Morton and I thought it would be a boon both to the republic's fortunes and to ours. We had no doubt it would be the story, and we hoped it would be big enough to at least partly smother anything emerging from the Hawke affair. I delivered the speech to the Lodge at 5 a.m. on a frosty morning. There was energy and conviction in the speech, and with it I thought we had neatly closed a chapter. A stage in the evolution of the republic had been completed and with luck Hawke would be thwarted at the same time.

Greg Turnbull reported that the speech went down beautifully. The newspapers quoted generously from it and praised the PM's vision. They conferred their highest honour and said it was also good politics. They meant that the high tone contrasted vividly with Alexander Downer's newest folly. It was Downer, caught hopelessly between the far right of his party and his own more liberal instincts, not the Prime Minister's speech, that drew attention from the Hawke circus. And there was no mention in the press of giving the republic to the people. The last page and a half had been cut from the text by the Prime Minister, who just then was not willing to hand over the republic to anyone. We did not mind so much. Everything, including a republic, is relative to political ascendancy.

Hawke's book was launched with the usual sustained media

blitz, but this one seemed to run forever. For weeks we never knew when he would up the ante on some radio or television show, if he would compound his felony at the National Press Club, throw another spanner in the works at a literary luncheon. The Prime Minister was understandably tempted to say that the book was boring and pointless and not even Blanche had energised it. At other times he wanted to say that Hawke had failed to 'nourish' the Labor Government for years. He and the ERC had 'carried' him. It had been the popular boost from the war with Iraq that gave him the will to fight off Keating's challenge, not anything unpatriotic his rival had said. We thought of saying what a pity it was to reduce a decade of reform to the story of one man's ego. But in every instance it was clear that silence was the best policy. We had to starve Hawke out of the news. The Prime Minister smiled his way through doorstops and refused to be drawn. He gave a speech at the War Memorial that got front-page coverage; went to Gosford and received the warmest street reception he said he had ever had. He negotiated the States to a standstill over competition policy.

This silence had a wonderful effect on him: he was calm, thoughtful, composed and, when he needed it, 'steely'. He looked like a new prime minister, and indeed for the first time he was consistently acting like one. He went to Tokyo to enlist Japanese support for the forthcoming Bogor APEC meeting, and returned confident that they were converted. We learned how much easier it was to run the office with a few less people in it, not to say with a Prime Minister in the same time zone but compelled to be a statesman and out of the political fray.

A devastating drought in much of western New South Wales and Queensland gave him the opportunity to act generously in the interests of his fellow Australians and after a little persuasion he seized it. When Ray Martin devoted his television program to a national appeal, the Prime Minister agreed to match it dollar for dollar. The hour cost the Commonwealth $4 million, but the farmers benefited along with the government. He even went out to a farm in Queensland, in the vicinity of Dingo, west of Blackwater. It might have been India. The landscape was all dust and even the scrub had died and the few remaining emaciated breeding stock stood round the house as if waiting for the hour of their deaths. He was gracious, relaxed and knowledgeable in conversation with the farmers. They told us how impressed—and surprised—they were. The minister, Bob Collins, had a first-rate adviser, Jack Lake, and with Ric Simes from the PMO the department came up with a $164 million package of relief measures which the National Farmers Federation enthusiastically approved. We had erected at least a tent, if not a big marquee, in enemy territory. It was now possible to imagine a Labor government bridging the ground between environmental issues and the realities of successful farming. Sustainable development was the name given it by the environmentalists. Landcare was the thriving organisation funded by Labor and run by farmers with very similar aims. A Labor government might draw the two together in some form of loose alliance. Had it been able to do so, the environment and the farmers would have been the major beneficiaries, but possibly not the only ones. Bruce Chapman suggested a variety of the HECs scheme, a system of income-contingent loans that would provide more relief for more farmers at much less cost to the Commonwealth in the long run. It seemed an ideal form of government participation in the economy, and may even have promoted a species of bonding with alienated communities. A grand plan of environmental and agricultural renewal might have further marginalised the more marginal environmental groups who made life difficult for governments, and established a reservoir of general goodwill that no single issue could easily exhaust. Like several other ideas, I cannot recall why it slipped into the void but I suspect it was because all things slipped into it if one let them go for more than a moment.

Not that anyone thought the farmers would soon be coming over to Labor. They never do. That was why it was difficult to make a plausible case for a prime ministerial visit. Such trips invariably lacked a dimension of mature political exchange and could only be in the nature of a hand-out, gratefully or grudgingly accepted. On the way to the drought areas the Prime Minister was joined on the plane by Ian Macfarlane of the Queensland Grain Growers Association who had a voice like a chaff-cutter or a wounded crow and Don McGauchie of the National Farmers Federation. He talked to them about life on the land, tractors and their implements and, inevitably, pigs. McGauchie allowed himself the impartial observation that the New South Wales Government had been wrong to thwart the Prime Minister's piggery project. Then why didn't you say so, asked the Prime Minister.

Suddenly in all things the Prime Minister flourished. The journalists noticed it, albeit relative to Alexander Downer's accelerating decline. Yet even in his destruction of Downer in the parliament, the Prime Minister was more clinical and amusing than brutal. When he called him a 'sook', he quickly added, 'if that is not too beastly a thing to say'. By August the journalists were beginning to say that with his 'devastating political skills' Keating was savaging Downer out of the game. It was reported that Downer had inspired him and given him new enthusiasm for the job. By mid-September he had distanced Downer in the polls and the government was twelve points ahead of the Coalition. What was more satisfying, 43 per cent of voters thought he was a satisfactory prime minister. Who knows if that included the three who approached us as I strolled with him in Rockhampton one night and, with no sign that they knew who he was, asked him the way to the leagues club.

Downer's demise was surely as rapid and absolute as any in the Commonwealth's history. It was as if any issue of moderate complexity proved an impossible maze for him. He got tangled in Mabo, the Land Fund and gay rights in Tasmania. Laurie Oakes presented our office with a story he was about to break in the *Bulletin* about Downer addressing a League of Rights meeting in South Australia. The League of Rights is Australia's most notorious right-wing and anti-Semitic organisation. Downer at first denied he had been to the meeting; then he said he thought it was a Christian group. Then Oakes revealed he had a tape of his address.

Not even Glenn Milne, who Geoff Walsh said had given him odds of 3 to 1 that Downer would still be the Liberal leader at Christmas, could save him from this. Asked if he thought Downer was an anti-Semite, the Prime Minister might have said, 'No, but I think he is a fool'; but instead he paused and said, 'Well he went there.' That night Milne ran pictures of the Nuremburg rallies, and spurred on by this indication that the public might be persuaded he was the victim of a terrible slur, on the day following Downer brought on a censure motion in the House. He was full of self-righteous fury and when Keating spoke Coalition members created a terrible din. The Prime Minister came back to the office dark and exhausted, while Beazley, with no-one watching, delivered a brilliant satirical analysis of Downer's political style. Keating had managed to insert the line he might have used in the first place: he was not saying Downer was a racist, but he was saying that he was the most foolish political leader since Billy McMahon. That night at Canberra airport I heard the West Australian Liberal, Wilson Tuckey, telling someone in the queue that it had been a triumph for his side. Paul Lyneham said it was one of those days which 'made everyone smaller and somehow grubby'. And on Channel 7 Glenn Milne said, 'It will be a long time before Paul Keating calls Alexander Downer a racist again.'

For Downer it was a lay day on the path to ruin. He issued a statement of Liberal Party directions called *The Things That Matter*. One look at it told us that it might destroy him. It had enough of Fightback to keep the government well fed with opportunities for derision; enough untruths to punch holes in its credibility; and so little of anything else substantial it was almost sunk on the first day when in Tokyo the Prime Minister derided it as Mills and Boon. He said he read it in twenty minutes while eating a plate of sushi. So bad was the document, Downer satirised it himself in a notorious, mind-numbingly foolish speech which included the observation that Liberal policy on domestic violence might be called 'The Things That Batter'. The self-inflicted wound was probably fatal.

For a while the Prime Minister was more sanguine. He talked about the possibility of staying on for another term. But even through this relatively long period of grace, he still thought about retirement. After Gareth Evans returned from a notably successful meeting in Bangkok the Prime Minister urged him to move to the House of Representatives. He did not mean to imply that Evans was the front-runner for the job, but he did want to signal that the job would soon be available. In Evans' case he was also keen to divert his mind from thoughts about a position on the High Court.

Through these good days the office laboured on the government's cultural policy. It was said that the bureaucracy had been working on it in one form or another for five years, but the first draft of the document in 1994 suggested five weeks at most. If anyone outside the Prime Minister's Office believed in the principle behind the statement they seemed loath to show it. Michael Lee's office was enthusiastic to varying degrees, but it was required to be. Perhaps it was the impression that in the end the thing would be what Keating wanted and there was no point in devising something which he might easily reject. But once started we could not make progress and for every two steps taken we took one back. It might be that others did not believe the statement should or could combine the arts with information technology and the new media. Calling investment in the arts an industry policy was not everyone's ideal of an arts policy. It was not Paul Keating's ideal. But if it provided a more generally compelling logic the price was not too high. We would say it was an investment in the country's future, and if people thought this put the arts on the same plane as the motor vehicle industry they would have to live with it.

From the start, personalities and interests seemed to clash. In Lee's office Sam Mostyn was expert, smart and professional, but one had the feeling that people with whom she needed to work in our office resented her presence. Michael Lee wanted to deliver the policy early. We wanted to wait. We wanted to get the new media policy as right as it was possible to get something in the early stages of its evolution. The Prime Minister had come to think information technology was the biggest thing going. He believed it could even win an election. He also had the germ of an idea for at least one major film studio in Sydney. There was the ABC to deal in. And there was cabinet to convince that a cultural policy was more than a conscience payment for the support of a noisy elite at the last election. After an altercation in the Prime Minister's suite about the timing of the statement, Lee left angry both with the PM and me. Later he invited me to his office and it was patched up. I raised a question I had also raised with the Prime Minister. The Australia Council would be asking for extra funding, and on a triennial basis; a Major Organisations Board was being recommended; an Academy of the Humanities was to be established under the council's auspices, and it was proposed to make the council chair a full-time position. As the chair was my wife, I said, it might be argued that a conflict of interests existed. Lee said, as Keating had, that he did not believe a conflict existed and that he would support extra funding and responsibility for the council so long as it was a *reformed* council. As the Minister understood it our domains were separate. In fact no-one who knew anything about reforming the Australia Council would describe it as a process likely to lead to personal enrichment or unalloyed pleasure. And as this conversation took place while my wife was recovering in a Melbourne cardiac rehabilitation ward, she was hardly proof of the job's rewards. But criticism was bound to come eventually. The Prime Minister's advice was let them do their worst. The date for the statement was fixed for 18 October. It was largely written in the six weeks or so this left us—much of it in the last two days.

There were as ever two main concerns: how much would it cost and what would go where? The Prime Minister wanted the National Music Academy in Sydney. Others wanted it in Canberra or Melbourne. The Prime Minister wanted it in Sydney because Sydney would be more attractive to overseas students and, after he had given extra funding to the Sydney Symphony Orchestra and freed it from the benign but ultimately restricting clutches of the ABC, Sydney would have Australia's world class orchestra. The prospect of leaving the Melbourne Symphony Orchestra to languish was alarming to some of us, as was the likelihood, if the Prime Minister prevailed, that every electorate outside Sydney would feel despised and neglected. Eventually he was persuaded to put the academy in Melbourne where the Victorian Government left it to wither for months, as if showing any enthusiasm for it would defeat their strategy of pretending Victoria had been ignored. In fact Melbourne did better than any other city, winning the television production fund, the Australian Multimedia Enterprise, the Academy of the Humanities (called the Australia Foundation for Culture and the Humanities) and the music academy. The Melbourne Symphony Orchestra's extra funding was not equal to Sydney's, but it was given the same opportunity to disengage from the ABC. Like the Sydney Symphony, the Melbourne orchestra has thrived ever since. But Jeff Kennett's political strategy appeared to work: long after the Cultural Statement was delivered and the money flowed to their new organisations, the Melbourne press and Melbourne people were alleging a frightful Sydney bias.

To satisfy Adelaide, a plan arose to put the Aboriginal collection of the National Museum there. We were warned that all sorts of protests would follow. To satisfy Brisbane, a National Institute for Indigenous Performing Arts would be located there. We were told that Aboriginal people would only go to Sydney. To please Perth we planned to move the America's Cup winning boat, *Australia II*, from Sydney, but Sydney people complained and so did Kay Cottee, the first woman to sail alone around the world. To satisfy the provinces we would fund extensive touring by arts companies and proceed with the plan to create a national museum in cyberspace, but the Prime Minister's interest in information technology had not yet overcome his prejudice against the museum. And we still needed something for Hobart.

And then there was the ABC. The ABC was a perfect fit for the cultural policy, straddling as it did the new technology and the nation's cultural and artistic life. Yet we could not find a way to do with it what was needed. Board members had tired of David Hill, the general manager, and rang the PMO complaining and suggesting ways by which he could be overthrown. Hill was seen in Parliament House, smiling and unworried. He was there, we gathered, to lobby the Liberals and Democrats. Various schemes were suggested but all seemed likely to make Mr Hill a martyr to a Labor-dominated board. And ultimately they would make no fundamental difference to the ABC. No board and no general manager would.

In the PMO we hatched another scheme: the government would sack both Hill and the board, keep the Chair, Mark Armstrong, in some role and appoint an Interim Review Board to examine the roles, structure and potential of the ABC, particularly with a view to the new information technology. We would give it so much of a revolution as it needed. Among the possibilities envisaged was a new, independently incorporated element, devoted to production for free to air and pay television and the new media. It would have links to the film schools and, like Britain's Channel 4, generate essential film and television skills as well as high quality product for local and foreign consumption.

The idea had certain obvious political advantages. It would mean a week of brawling and bad publicity instead of six months while the Senate inquiry dragged on. The interim board would be small, expert and efficient and comprise people without political affiliations or agendas. It would investigate the future and potential of the ABC while the Senate raked over the past. The Prime Minister liked the idea, and Michael Lee was two-thirds persuaded to it.

However, the Prime Minister had another scheme in motion. It was not in any way inimical to the ABC proposal; indeed the ABC idea was in almost every way its perfect complement. The Prime Minister had been talking to Rupert Murdoch, and when not to Murdoch, to Ken Cowley and Tom Mockridge, Murdoch's men. He had been pursuing the idea with them for five months. He had also been talking to Bob Carr, the New South Wales Premier. The plan was to establish Murdoch's Fox

Studios on the site of the Showgrounds in Sydney. The Prime Minister believed that only something of this magnitude could seriously boost the Australian industry. In his own terms, it meant 'weight' in the industry: not just little films like *Strictly Ballroom* or *Priscilla, Queen of the Desert*, but big films like *Braveheart*. The little films would feed off the big ones. There would be a considerable dividend in the transfer of technology and skills. It would make Australia a player in the heavy end of the international film industry. And there would be hundreds of jobs. It was a secret plan. He would sneak it up on the cabinet. It would be the bombshell of the cultural statement.

We invited a former Channel 4 executive to Canberra to talk about the ABC. He had been recommended as someone who might head the Interim Board. He was keen and impressive, and also patient as he waited an hour for the Prime Minister to arrive. The Prime Minister was at Rupert Murdoch's Canberra house clearing the way to announce that, under an agreement with the Australian and New South Wales governments, Fox would establish studios and a theme park in Sydney. He remained enthusiastic about the plan for the ABC. But it never happened. It needed more thought and planning than anyone had time to give it. And to announce something so drastic might have meant delivering the cultural policy into a media storm. Afterwards, new political imperatives prevailed. Afterwards, no-one wanted to hear the word culture again. When David Hill resigned in early November it was too late, or at least too messy.

The board sent out headhunters to find a short list for the ABC job. Brian Johns, a former journalist, publisher and head of the Special Broadcasting Service (SBS) and the ABA, was the Prime Minister's preferred candidate. But when Johns eventually won the job, no-one thought he would or could do what needed to be done. Not surprisingly, the challenge of the technological revolution seemed to consume most of his time. If a chance ever existed to refashion the ABC and invest it with new strength and creativity, it passed with the cultural policy.

The ERC was hard but fair. We lost some good projects but

kept others we half-expected to lose. The cost was trimmed to $260 million, a 'non-trivial sum' as Ric Simes liked to say of these things, but it was less shocking when imagined as an industry statement. Because so much time had been spent debating what would go where, and the department seemed even by the worst public service standards strangely inert and indecisive, much of the writing was done in the last forty-eight hours. Craddock Morton, who also had the rare ability to write, dealt heroically with the lobbies, the ministers' offices, the departments and many strangely difficult people therein. Morton would have become chief of staff in the PMO had he not decided to leave Canberra. He wanted to call the statement Waltzing Australia, but the Prime Minister was attached to the theme of 'nation' and the statement became—with an unearthly William Robinson landscape on the front—Creative Nation.

It had been decided to launch it at the National Gallery in Canberra, although Michael Lee protested that this positioned it too firmly in the province of the elites. The Minister was not always easy to read. On the night the statement had to be completed a long-running dispute came to an ugly head. Ric Simes wanted the new media component to be put in the hands of the Department of Industry, Science and Technology (DIST). Sometime after nightfall we discovered this had been written into the document. Sam Mostyn and I believed it belonged in the Department of Communications and the Arts, Lee's department, the one expressly created for the purpose. A war broke out between Simes and his supporters and Mostyn and hers. I had the document slipped up to the Lodge and told the Prime Minister that he must decide. At 1.30 a.m. he phoned back and read out to me a long section on the new media which he had just written. With the information highway it said, 'We have crossed the technological Rubicon'. No-one in any office or department could have written the section better. What department gets the responsibility? I asked. Lee's, was the answer. Everything that had been taken from Lee's portfolio the PM gave back to him. Ric Simes' anger was understandable. What was strange was the Minister's response: when I rang him two days later, he was not aware that his reduced portfolio had been re-enlarged. He seemed to know nothing of the favour that had been done him by his staff, the Prime Minister and a couple of the Prime Minister's staff. The Minister said as he flicked through the pages of the document published in his name but which he had not read, 'I see, how did this happen? Hmm. Good.' Soon Ric Simes would be storming into my office claiming that he was the victim of a conspiracy.

The launch was splendid. Annette Shun Wah was the host. There were Don Burrows and Kate Ceberano and the band of the Royal Military College, Duntroon. Bangarra danced, and the Hunting Party, 'five women eight feet tall', sang 'songs of blood and love' in 'the tradition of minstrels and troubadours'. David Hobson sang '*Che manina gelida!*', Cheryl Barker sang '*Mi chiamano Mimi*', and when together they sang '*O soave fanciulle*' it was possible to imagine that at least a few caucus hearts were melted. Those who came at least; the ones who did not think, with some of the media, that Puccini was some kind of elitist indulgence. It is a familiar attitude, of course, although it was less common and less aggressive a generation ago. Many of the struggling farmers of my childhood loved opera, Beethoven and ballet, although they had neither formal education nor much hope of ever seeing a live performance. Melba and Sutherland were heroes for that genera-tion and the one preceding. The first lover of Bruckner and Mahler I knew had been an itinerant worker for a lot of his life. People of my parents' generation, the women especially, who left school at thirteen, devoured nineteenth-century novels when they found time in their middle age. They created much of the market for modern Australian literature. In truth the charge of elitism was probably made less often than implied; in, for instance, the depic-tion of Keating as a Medici, a King, a President.

Inevitably the commentators said that Paul Keating was repaying the debt he owed the arts community from the last election. Yet it was difficult to reconcile the claim that he was paying his debt to the arts community with the often popular contention that his association with them was political poison. In any event, neither debt nor electoral gain ranked high among his motives, or those of the people who designed the statement. On one level he was attending to the needs of that considerable section of the Australian population who love music, theatre, art, film, ideas and books. On another he was delivering the germ of an industry policy for the information revolution. On another he was, as the journalist Michael Gordon noted, laying some of the ground for a republic in that Creative Nation was part of what the Prime Minister called 'the big identity and cultural round-up' before the end of the century. And on a fourth reading he was giving to the Australian people the equivalent of that bust of Beethoven he had given to his mother. He was putting a bit of class in the national life, he was making life 'softer', and giving substance to the ancient belief that the life of individuals, communities and nations is richer for the play of imagination.

He spoke with a gleam of pleasure in his eye. Creative Nation, he said, did not seek 'to impose a cultural landscape on Australia but to respond to one which is already in bloom'. He hoped that the statement might one day be seen as a final goodbye to the postcolonial phase in Australian history and the cultural insecurity that went with it. It was about looking forward, 'to pull the threads of our national life together, so that we can ride the waves of global change and create our own'. It was to encourage the creative spirit and the flow of ideas. These things were good for an economy and a society. And it was the realisation of the government's ambition 'to bring cultural life into our national life and national decision-making'. No government decision, he said, was without a cultural consequence. 'The quality of our lives, the opportunities for self-expression, the integrity of our heritage, cannot be left to chance.'

It was a $260 million investment. A $60 million television production fund to be based in Melbourne; a $13 million fund for the SBS to make Australian programs; the National Academy of Music in Melbourne. Fox Studios in Sydney; $7 million for the Sydney Symphony Orchestra; an extra $25 million and an expanded role for the Australia Council; the creation of a Major

Organisations Board for the major performing arts organisations, all of which like the Australia Council would in future be funded triennially; $84 million to seed an Australian multimedia content industry.

The papers next day gave it saturation coverage, and on the whole their reviews were stunningly good. The arts community and the new technology gurus responded warmly. There were complaints from Melbourne about Sydney getting too much. Dissident poets complained in the expected way. And the Opposition railed against the absence of a national museum in Canberra.

It was good policy, good for the country. It was a moment when Australian creative achievement meant as much as sport or war. Yet there was immediate unease. After the launch, at lunch on the footbridge outside, Betty Churcher, the National Gallery director, showered attention and champagne on the prime ministerial entourage while every other table went without, and all around I could feel popular resentment looming. It would descend despite our effort to create a cultural policy as democratic as any cultural policy could be. To call it 'elitist' was the obvious angle of attack. One can no more have a cultural policy that is not in some sense 'elitist' than one can have a sports policy or a policy for the armed services—not at least if one of the aims in every case is excellence. Elitism is as much a part of the arts as it is of an agricultural show.

The Prime Minister saw no point in mincing words. He never willingly called the arts an industry, or suggested they were for everybody. Culture was a different matter. Having delivered a Hollywood studio and a theme park, it was hardly fair to call him a cultural snob. But when the Liberals said they would be launching their arts policy in Elizabeth Bay House he wanted to say that putting Downer in there would be like 'dragging a hog into the Sistine Chapel'. We said that to speak thus was, alas, not in keeping with the democratic spirit of Creative Nation. Instead we gave him a Dorothy on the very democratic national museum we proposed. But when they taunted him with questions about his patronage of the pianist, Geoffrey Tozer, he used the hog line anyway, called his opponents 'lice' and added that Tim Fischer was a 'donkey' and a 'nong'. The question on the national museum was never asked.

Hogs were on Paul Keating's mind again. He was contemplating, on the one hand, the prospect of the piggery deal collapsing and leaving him owing several millions to the Commonwealth Bank; or alternatively, and just as bad, the possibility that the venture would succeed, leaving him to watch others make the millions that his initiative had earned. This might explain why he called Michael Baume 'parliamentary filth', and in a pre-record for the ABC said Bob Hawke was a liar. Suddenly his mood had swung. Two months of steady statesmanlike building crumbled in a day. He swore at photographers, cursed them to us, wanted to (and eventually did) fence off the press at doorstop interviews. It was announced that he had bought St Kevin's, a large, gloomy-looking house in up-market Queen Street, Woollahra. Some commentators described it as a mansion. Some said it set a poor inflationary example to the country. Many people wondered how he got the $2.2 million to buy it. He got it through putting down a ten per cent deposit with a two-year delayed settlement, paid out in July 1996 after being fully paid out of the piggery. It was not a rational act for a politician, but Keating was not thinking like a politician when he bought it. He was thinking about life after politics with his wife and children.

The Prime Minister was listening to Elisabeth Schwarzkopf sing Strauss' *Four Last Songs*, or Aaron Copland's Third Symphony, and telling his speechwriter that what he did now he did only for the country and the party, that there was nothing in it for him any more. His speechwriter had ventured to say the prospect of his ever becoming a real prime minister must fill his opponents with dread: listening to him on the twenty-fifth anniversary of his election to parliament it was (as so often) impossible to understand why he let them escape their nightmare. In an extempore speech to the staff he described our mission with compelling, effortless grace, as if to remind us that we were soldiers in a great crusade and the exhausting chaos of politics contained a semi-divine purpose. Yet one member of staff said he wished he hadn't heard the speech because it made him think the Prime Minister was about to give the game away. The Prime Minister was thinking about retirement because he felt his marriage was collapsing. He bought St Kevin's hoping it would shore it up. And he continued with his plan to buy John Laws's house on the Hawkesbury for the same compelling reason.

CHAPTER 18

I was floating along, of course, four or five miles an hour; but
you don't ever think of that. No, you feel like you are laying
dead still in the water; and if a little glimpse of a snag slips by,
you don't think to yourself how fast you're going, but you catch
your breath and think, my! how that snag's tearing along. If you
think it ain't dismal and lonesome out on a log that way, by
yourself, in the night, you try it once—you'll see.

MARK TWAIN, HUCKLEBERRY FINN

S UMMER WRAPPED ITSELF around a deep and delicate
enigma. Paul Keating's opponent was the political equivalent of the outlaw Joe Byrne, a corpse suspended on a barn
door to absorb the public loathing while a new order was established. He was also election bait. What politician would not be
tempted by the sight of him to cheat another term? But if Keating
called a snap poll, might they not drop Howard or Costello into
the leadership and do to Labor what Labor had done to them by
replacing Hayden with Hawke for the 1983 campaign? And if the
Liberals could not engineer a swap, might not such a patently
cynical decision by Keating be the only thing capable of reviving
Downer? It was hard to imagine how Keating could lose to
Downer. Then again, it had been hard to imagine how Bob
Hawke could lose to Andrew Peacock when he called an early
election in 1984—but Peacock nearly beat him. There was also
the problem of finding the trigger for a double dissolution. In late
November, when rumours flew that the Liberals were beginning
to panic about Downer, the best the government had was a
Migration Bill to retrospectively authorise the detention of

refugees seeking asylum and deny them any rights of compensation. It was not much to go on. With a leader who enjoyed only half Keating's approval in the polls and trailing by 7 per cent in the two party preferred, the Opposition must have been suffering. But while he continued to enjoy Downer as a kind of sport or feast, the times were tense for Keating too. In fact an early poll was always more of a dream than a serious thought; it floated tantalisingly by but no-one much wanted to grasp it.

Keating himself thought the risk too high; that it would rankle the electorate and they might turn on him despite their low regard for Downer. He knew it would be harder in six or twelve months' time. Downer would be gone, and his replacement would enjoy a long honeymoon; there were economic obstacles to clear; interest rates would be higher, new taxes might be necessary, a new deal would have to be cut with the unions. Difficult as it might be to win under these circumstances, it would be more difficult without credibility or goodwill. Moreover, when he was not thinking about retirement, the Prime Minister had grand plans on his mind: there was APEC, the defence pact with Indonesia, an industry statement, the republic.

Sandy Hollway said to Geoff Walsh and me one day, you can't be sure about the precise context of the election or who your opponent will be, but you do know your best hope is to be a good government. Should you not make it a minimum that if you are defeated no-one will be able to say it was because you weren't conscientious? And if you do this much, some hope of winning remains should the other lot stumble. It sounds a little heroic now, but Hollway's thinking had the force of commonsense. It gave us a bit of moral backbone, something to sustain hope and dignity as we waited on death row. It was the best if not the only option for a government whose natural tenure was exhausted and whose political skills were less and less adequate to the task. And it gave us something to do: with policy momentum we could imagine we had political momentum as well. For me, and I think for most others in the office, the 'good government' philosophy became a guiding principle, though of course no proof against unexpected follies and disasters, including self-inflicted ones.

In November, Keating did such grievous damage to Downer we heard that a Coalition frontbencher volunteered to Kim Beazley that they were being 'slaughtered'. They were behaving like schoolboys on the last day of term. Reports circulated that Howard and his fellow 'dries' in the shadow cabinet had rolled Downer's idea for a constitutional convention on the republic, and then we watched Howard on television describe such leaking from meetings as treachery. Downer was bad for the Coalition but worse for Labor. If Howard had been the first choice after Hewson, his honeymoon could not have lasted all the way to election. He could not have gone two years without policies. Keating just might have worn him down. In politics—and history—the imponderables are endless, and endlessly seductive. If only Downer had put up more of a fight. Keating knocked him over with only a tenth of the effort he used to put into destroying opponents, and because Downer so often knocked himself over, with only a tenth of the ammunition he had at his disposal. The worse Downer's position became, the worse in many ways was ours as well. If only we could have propped him up for another year. If only he had been half-competent. We knew he would go, and only hoped that it would not be on a day when we had some good news to report.

After much hard work in Tokyo and Jakarta, word came that the Americans might scuttle the idea of a target date for regional free trade at the APEC meeting in Bogor. The Prime Minister got Don Russell on the phone in Washington and told him in words that no eavesdropper could fail to understand that if the US walked away from this the whole relationship with Australia would from that moment change. Then, for the sake of amusement no doubt, he told us he wanted to send a military outfit to Cambodia to capture Pol Pot; and dispatch F-111s to bomb Khmer Rouge camps, if only the F-111s could get that far. That was what the Americans always had over us—they always had 'their flat-tops' to get them where they wanted to go. He went to Question Time a little later and answered questions about Cambodia in a most restrained and statesmanlike way but he did leave his staff, once again, with their sense of life's possibilities slightly expanded.

He was also turning the criticism of the government's progress on micro-economic reform back on the Coalition. It was the conservative States that were dragging the chain on competition policy, he said. But then that's what the Liberal Party was, a set of State branches devoted to State rights. The Liberal Party was not a national party, it had no sense of nation. After fifty years it was 'still a party of six state rumps' he told the House while brandishing a copy of the Liberals' thin policy document, and his tattered copy of ACME Fightback to go with the look on John Hewson's face. And John Howard, the Prime Minister said, 'always gets a bit visionary when there's a whiff of mortality about the leadership'. But it didn't matter who led them, 'the party has had it'. He turned the attack increasingly on Howard. What could the man who had been found wanting in the past, the self-confessed 'most conservative leader' the Liberals had ever had, offer Australia in the nineties? In this, he said, he was only echoing John Hewson who was thoroughly out of sorts with his colleagues and no longer took the trouble to disguise it. Hewson said publicly it was time the Liberals gave up their infatuation with Bob Menzies, a gratifying remark in view of a decision, not popular with everyone in the office, to contribute a Keating critique of Menzies to the press. It was done with the aim of annoying the Liberals at their fiftieth anniversary conference in Albury and driving them into a passionate defence of their Godhead. It seemed to work, and they talked about it all weekend. However, it also provoked hostility from anti-monetarists keen to demonstrate that the nation's wealth was more fairly distributed in Menzies' day than after a decade of Labor rule. Ken Davidson's typically acid attack was a test of one's mettle, particularly when in the first week of November newspapers published figures (albeit misleading ones) that seemed to indicate Labor's decade had coincided with greater inequality.

The Americans did not thwart the APEC enterprise. Despite some last-minute resistance from South Korea, the leaders at Bogor finally agreed to a progressive reduction in tariffs, reaching zero for the developed countries in 2010, and among the developing countries in 2020. Throughout the meeting the news was led by reports that Australian aid workers in East Timor feared for their lives and wanted to get out. But we dreaded most the possibility that while we were in Jakarta the Liberals would dump Downer and steal our headlines. The *Sydney Morning Herald* didn't need another story: with nothing to rival the significance of the Bogor Declaration the paper still managed to give it only the bottom third of the front page. The Prime Minister was not pleased, and spent much of the journey home drafting a letter to the editor. He surely had a point. Bogor was a historic moment in the history of the Asia-Pacific, confirmation of the success of APEC, and a significant feat of Australian diplomacy. It was also a personal triumph for Keating, and it was difficult to avoid sharing his view that this was the reason why they downgraded it. His complaints were not always entirely personal. He had a notion that being the broadsheet of Australia's premier city, the *Sydney Morning Herald* should be the premier newspaper of the nation, and therefore it should be the nation's principal journal of record, and therefore it should respect the record he was writing. He would brutally curse Conrad Black, the 'truant owner' whose share in it he had allowed to be increased, and John Alexander, the editor-in-chief whom he loathed. But there was more than loathing in it—there was profound disappointment and frustration. It seemed he would never be wholly content until the *Herald* gave him his due. One could never persuade him for long that the paper did not matter that much.

Bill Clinton seemed to be in no doubt about the significance of Bogor. Before he sat down to lunch with Keating in Jakarta he told him that after the misery of the recent US congressional elections he had not much wanted to come to Jakarta, 'but the best things we do are often the things we do not want to do'. APEC was a thing worth doing and, he said, it was due to Paul

Keating. He thanked him. The Prime Minister told the President he could go back to Washington and say that it was Bill Clinton who got the US into the big Asian markets, who got a free-trade Japan by 2010, who at a crucial moment got China into a co-operative free-trade regime. He also told him that it was possible to drive your political opponents so far to the right that they fell off the political map, and you could do it while still expanding your constituency and doing good works. He explained to him the Job Compact in Working Nation. The President and his men appeared to be impressed. The President said he shared Keating's views on China and Japan and accepted his view that Mahathir's behaviour was mainly driven by rivalry with Suharto. They exchanged views on radio talkback hosts. It was all very relaxed. George Stephanopolous asked if Australia's population was about 100 million. When we told him it was only 18 million he said, 'Gee, smaller than Canada.'

Later Keating went to see Suharto for his scheduled meeting and cut it short, telling him to use the time on those who still harboured doubts. Advisers returned marvelling at the relaxed cordiality between them. Keating was now more confident than ever about his dream of a defence agreement. When the declaration was agreed and they'd stood in a line in their batik shirts (like Kamahl's fan club, Paul Lyneham said) the Prime Minister gave a press conference. It was the most tangible development in the north–south dialogue for years, he claimed; Suharto's leadership had been outstanding, and all the more remarkable for a leader of a developing country. About Mahathir, he said, 'Ask him not me.' Most questions came from the foreign press. His answers reflected what he called his 'restrained delight', and as the very positive press reports attested he managed to convey some of this to the journalists. The meaning of the agreement appeared to be understood by everyone at the press conference—but not, we feared, by everyone in Australia. Bogor needed from Keating the kind of speech Clinton gave after NAFTA was signed, on the eve of the Seattle meeting—the speech that said, 'I am going to make this work for everyone.' The Prime Minister repeatedly claimed Bogor as a triumph and employed all kinds of historical comparisons and elegant phrasing to describe it, but it never reached the workers or the farmers or the talkback listeners. He said it would be good for people, but he never said, 'I am going to make it good.' It never registered in such a way that, come the election, people would think that they had better not abandon Paul Keating because it would be abandoning the APEC project—which meant abandoning their kids' interests.

We never found a place for the people in the big picture. This was our great failure and a painful one because we always understood the nature of the task. What did the people care about free trade in the Asia–Pacific in 2010 or 2020? What did they care about the deal between Rupert Murdoch and Telstra? No more than they cared that Kerry Packer cared. The Prime Minister would tell us what he told Peter Barron—that Kerry Packer was spending too much time on his polo horse, that he was interested in wealth through extending his monopoly not through competition, that his son was still wet behind the ears. He would tell me that he had personally overseen the agreement between Telstra and Murdoch, show me the document with his amendments on it, including the 'put option' he suggested to protect Telstra. He would threaten to boost Packer's holding in Fairfax to develop a little 'creative tension'. And he would say that Packer wanted too much. And no doubt he did. But I would say, in a way as annoying to him as it was to me, that you had better go to Charleville and sign up for the south-west Queensland rural readjustment plan, and shake a few hands. It will irritate the National Party if you do it. It will play well in the marginals. It's proof of follow-through on the drought, more evidence that your government is concerned about people, and that it gets things done.

Or tries to. The drought ignited an interest in rural restructuring and Ric Simes in our office and Jack Lake in Bob Collins' office worked at the cause with their customary devotion. Then Lake came in one day and told us that of the 3500 farmers eligible for drought relief more than 750 had applied, and in two weeks the Department of Social Security had managed to process just nineteen applications. It beggared belief. It was one more reason why political leaders needed to go to places like Charleville and shake hands with people and if necessary prostrate themselves in the dust and dung. The alternative was to suspend the pay and confiscate the cars of the department's senior personnel until the job was done. No-one would do that of course because no-one could say where it would stop.

The RAAF's menu for the return from Bogor promised 'plated triangle sandwiches' and 'mini pizza swirls', but we got neither because the PM was down the back of the plane holding forth with the journalists and the staff could not get through with the trolleys. It had been a triumph, but the plane ride at the end always felt a bit like farce. There had been a little farce at the beginning too, when an accident-prone member of the PM's personal staff lost the prime ministerial briefcase containing highly confidential papers. Fortunately, after an hour or two of panic it was found in a bus terminal on the outskirts of the Indonesian capital. Ambassador Russell had flown from Washington for the meeting and came back to Canberra. Interest rates were on the rise, a brake on growth that the November national accounts put at 6.4 per cent per annum. One school of thought held that this time the brake ought to be fiscal rather than monetary policy. Russell was not personally opposed to tax measures. He did not object in principle to a specific drought, environment or deficit tax—or some combination of all three. A 10 per cent two-year surcharge on all incomes above $30,000 was another possibility. Not for a moment, however, did we think the Prime Minister would seriously consider such a plan. It smelt cheap. It would upset the tax scales. It would play badly against the tax cuts he had promised that were already playing badly. It would be the most preposterous break with orthodoxy. The Reserve Bank board met and raised rates another 0.5 per cent. Bill Kelty reported privately that there were people on the board wanting a rise of 3 per cent. All through the summer Ric Simes reckoned that a rise of 2–3 per cent was necessary. To those of us who did not understand the singular virtues of applied monetary policy, this presented itself as lunacy. It would be like rat poison. It would kill us systemically. And in truth it did contribute to our death. But to not have economics or the monetarist's faith was to lack both virtue and understanding. Therefore we bleeding hearts lacked the prerequisite of influence. We must wait for the economic decision to be made and then deal with the consequences in whatever portfolio was ours.

For months, by suggestion, circumlocution and irony we tried to lead them to a position where they might contemplate another way of thinking about the problem of saving the recovery from itself—a way that did not look, sound or feel like the 1990 recession all over again. And it could be argued that the case was won, or that sense prevailed. But the case was also lost because the people did not thank Paul Keating for it. It seems remarkable now that he did not say—Christmas 1994 would have been perfect timing—there will be no repeat of 1989; interest rates will not be raised to such prohibitive heights; we will not be repeating that mistake; there will be no recession. As there was no recession, he might have at least got credit for keeping his word. Instead he got the blame attaching to John Howard's inevitable but telling remark on the first day they met across the dispatch box that, under Keating, Australians had enjoyed just 'five minutes of economic sunshine'.

It was not monetary policy that rankled with the Prime Minister as he flew back from Jakarta. It was the feeling described by Menzies when he returned from Britain during the war—that he had been present at a great moment abroad and was going home to pettiness, ignorance and spite. The Prime Minister was not the only one to feel it, but he was the one for whom it mattered most. In Question Time the Opposition would know that his 'restrained delight' made him vulnerable to the opposite— his deep disgruntlement with petty politics. The pettier they were, the more vulnerable he was. One had to tell him, 'They'll bait you,' even though the chances were he knew it and had made up his mind to take the bait and ram it down their throats.

He called Alexander Downer 'the Christmas turkey' and went for the holiday break knowing that his electoral lead was illusory. It would vanish with Downer's departure, whenever that took place. He would go into 1995 as he had gone into 1994, with a new opponent enjoying a glorious honeymoon. The thought depressed him. Bad balance of payment figures in January made the political problem much worse. We were 'sucking in imports' again. The current account to the September quarter had worsened. All the talk was about boom and bust, how Keating had not solved the structural problem, and how the economy was out of control. Unemployment fell below 9 per cent and was greeted as bad news. Interest rate rises were now inevitable, the papers said. The *Financial Review* predicted both higher interest rates and higher taxes. Like the Business Council they wanted outlays cut. In the Prime Minister's Office Ric Simes wanted to raise $2 billion in taxes with one more rate rise; Chapman favoured $1.5 billion in taxes—1 per cent at $27,000; 2 per cent at $38,000; 3 per cent at $50,000 and 2 per cent on the company rate—and no rate rises. Before returning to Washington, Don Russell agreed that more interest rate hikes were only a repeat of the mistakes made in 1989. He had not, however, advocated higher taxes to the Prime Minister. The occasional lonely voice, like Peter Roberts in the *Financial Review*, said higher interest rates would discourage investment which was the only hope of ever solving the problem. He said that if we stuck to the old economic mantras instead of taking large positive steps to boost investment in tradeable goods, we would be forever on the treadmill.

Over summer, people rang me to say, tell him not to do it. Don't be fooled by the figures: in the real world business is still shaky. A Melbourne businessman with Labor sympathies came to see me, to tell me that it would be the end of the recovery and the end of the government. I went up to Sydney to see the Prime Minister on holidays in John Laws's house on the Hawkesbury. We took a ride up the river in an old Scott Fitzgerald-type cruiser. While he pointed out the glories of the local environment I delivered my jeremiad. His credibility depended entirely on breaking the country's boom–bust cycle, didn't it? Didn't we have even less chance of doing it if we knocked off production, investment, employment—and confidence? I was not entirely sure what I was talking about, and if I did not know him better I would have thought he was not listening. I would have thrown him overboard. He pointed to the circling sea eagles; the gimcrack housing on the banks which spoiled the beauty of the place. Why do people want to spoil beauty? he said. He handed me the end of a tape measure and measured the length of the cabin. I formed the impression that he and Bernie Fraser already had an understanding that between 1 per cent and 1.5 per cent was in the pipeline. I told him what Kelty had said—that some of the RBA board wanted 3 per cent. I said that I thought any rise would be the end of the government.

I rang him every other day after that. I quoted business people (in greater numbers than I knew). I quoted Bruce Chapman who reckoned that if we knocked any more steam out of the economy we could not deliver unemployment programs. I quoted Bill Bowtell who had been in the marginal seats where small businesses and home buyers abounded, and concluded that they were blaming the banks for now, but very soon they would blame the government. Geoff Walsh said the research showed people were bemused. Wasn't everything going well at last? What had happened to create this dark cloud? The Great Depression lived in the minds of the people who experienced it for forty years or more. Why should we assume the Great Recession had passed in the space of five?

A meeting was held at the Phillip Street offices. The Prime Minister told me not to leave my holiday: not that I didn't understand the arguments, he said, but he could put them better. It was probably the greatest compliment I ever got from him, but I was not sure it meant he agreed with me.

It would be fanciful to think that decisions taken that day were governed in the slightest degree by the presence in Sydney of His Holiness the Pope. It is true, however, that the Prime Minister had recently met and heard him make a speech about caring for the poor and giving hope to the young. It was a very 'bolshie' speech. In the Pope's presence the Prime Minister had experienced a rare glow of personal approval. The crowds clapped and cheered him on arrival, applauded his speech of welcome and sang Happy Birthday to him. The bishops loved the Prime Minister's speech: Archbishop Little said that he wished he could say things like that. I took it as evidence that I did indeed 'think like a tyke' albeit with a little help from Fr. Edmund Campion. The Prime Minister gave the monsignor copies of both his 'welcome' speech and the one he delivered on His Holiness's departure—which was based substantially on the speech His Holiness gave upon his arrival. It is no more likely that the Pope nudged Paul Keating away from higher interest rates than it was that he broke the drought. But the drought did break: His Holiness and his party had to shelter from the rain. And the meeting at Phillip Street decided that interest rates should stay where they were. It also decided that for the time being there would be no new taxes.

Mike Keating had in mind, we were told, a hypothecated tax which would boost national savings and pay for the baby boomers' old age. It sounded very like superannuation to the uninitiated, but it also sounded prudent, resourceful, conscientious and even visionary. Boosting national savings was the work of a conscientious government. Better still, it sounded like the government was on a different tack from 1989's. This recovery would not be blown away.

We were not blessed. Had we been, Alexander Downer would not have lost the Liberal Party leadership to John Howard on Australia Day. The Prime Minister's happiness, which seemed to grow during the papal visit and the momentary reuniting of his family through the faith, would not have receded again. It would not have been so difficult to find someone to serve as principal adviser in the highest office in the land. Or to persuade Sam Mostyn to join us for half a year and write an information technology policy for her country—or to persuade her employers to give her the time to do it. There would have been fewer good people leaving the office and more good ones wanting to join it. The Prime Minister would not have been able to credibly say that there was no point creating Bill Kelty's business round table because the business people had all gone over to Howard and wouldn't sit at the government's table. We were not blessed and presumably it showed, and when that happens in politics it's like a curse. Bill Clinton was blessed: just when he looked like being crushed by right-wing zealots, the Oklahoma bombing put them on their heels and gave him the chance to play wise, consoling father of moderate America. Keating never got that kind of break, and if it had come his way he might not have been the type to take advantage of it. Alexander Downer was his break, but in the end his sad example helped Howard more than Keating. We were not blessed, but on Australia Day as usual we said that the country was.

I thought the Pope's visit might have helped to weld the Prime Minister's old-fashioned Catholicism to a new-fashioned conservatism. I would have liked to persuade him that salvation was not a millimetre away. It was in him—in the Catholic who believed in core values in education, commonsense environmentalism, multiculturalism without the pieties, the virtues of community and family, a capacious safety net but plenty of standing on your own two feet. He could make the solution to the current account problem through government-inspired private sector investment in industry and technology—in 'tradeable goods'—sound like the last great Keating crusade. He could give some attention to the regions where old Australia was under siege. This was what the people wanted, according to the polls. To give it to them, Paul Keating did not have to reinvent himself, just rediscover the original buried under two decades of modern Labor orthodoxy and economics. John Howard would have to do the reinventing, and when he did, I thought, Keating could ambush him. Howard would say he loved trees and different cultures and other things he had not loved before but needed to neutralise. And Keating would emerge dressed in his natural garb—his father's garb—and say it was time to get back core values and personal responsibility.

Governments don't raise children, parents do. And Howard would be left without a stream to swim in.

With certain adjustments for local conditions, and without sacrificing too much of the social democratic agenda, Clinton's hardline State of the Union address could be mined for our messages. The chance was there at the beginning of 1995. It was there all year. But it drifted by. I'll never know quite how. He thought it was too late to quarrel with the people on whose support Labor had counted for so long. It might look like proof of terminal decline. It might start an avalanche.

CHAPTER 19

*Anyone who does not lose his reason over certain things has
no reason.*

G. E. LESSING

J UST BEFORE CHRISTMAS, when everyone was tired, I saw the
office fax jammed with protesting letters from environment
groups. I thought for a second that I should go round the
office and find out what was at the bottom of it. But it was not
my responsibility. I had a plane to catch. The faxes were the first
sign most people in the PMO saw of a fiasco that left the government wounded for the rest of its life.

We discovered it had been taking shape for months, that
relations between the offices of David Beddall, the Minister for
Resources, and John Faulkner, the Environment Minister, were
poisonous. Beddall's people had been threatening to increase the
woodchip quota, which meant more logging of old-growth
forests, and Faulkner's people had been threatening to tear the
place down if he did. It happened according to the threats. That
was the remarkable thing: no-one called the warring parties
together and demanded a political compromise. Despite
Faulkner's dire warnings, Beddall increased the woodchip quota
and made more forest coupes available for logging. The green
groups declared war on the government and the loggers.

Everyone seemed to know but us. The issue never went

to cabinet, mainly because the Prime Minister was not driven to consider it seriously. The result was a debacle, the beginning of the end in the government's relationship with the environment movement, a humiliation for the Prime Minister and an unimaginably splendid start for John Howard when in the New Year he became the leader of the Opposition.

Twenty-four hours after leaving Canberra for Christmas I was in the Melbourne office writing a press release on the Prime Minister's instructions. The aim was to win back the favour of the greens; yet it seemed a measure of how dull our instincts had become that one had to argue for the middle road. It was not instinctively assumed that we needed to say that on the one hand Australians wanted to see their unique environment preserved, but on the other did not want to see jobs lost and communities wither. When many coupes were removed from the schedule, the loggers declared war on the government and the greens. Thus the year began with logging trucks ringing the national parliament. The sight of them struck the Prime Minister as an affront to democracy. It struck the press as an affront to the Prime Minister. He walked to work through the trucks, the loggers and their families. They blew their horns and jeered him. Perhaps it was paranoia, but it felt as if the loggers represented all that section of the community which wanted to be rid of the Keating Government. It was an attack on the government's legitimacy and standing. But it felt like something more gratuitous and base, like mindless vandalism. With just enough seriousness to make it funny, he talked about getting a couple of Leopard tanks rolling down Commonwealth Avenue. 'They reckon they've got big trucks,' he said: 'Let them see what the Commonwealth's got.'

He had met the loggers' leaders and didn't like them. He was never going to like them so long as they attempted to intimidate him. He had met the environmentalists as well and he didn't like them either. The environmentalists were also standing over him. Meanwhile the Prime Minister and the cabinet became overnight experts in old and new-growth forests and the location and number of coupes around the country. No-one had ever heard the word before. Now we heard it everywhere. We peered out the windows of aeroplanes looking for coupes.

Despite the fact that his action had precipitated the loggers' siege, the green groups seemed unable to believe that, while he disliked them personally, the Prime Minister's sympathies were firmly on their side. This was partly from a lack of political imagination and partly from a misguided political strategy of aggression. This carping, pugnacious attitude doubtless found its justification in the 1990 election when green votes possibly decided the result. Thereafter, the Wilderness Society became a species of woodland Trotskyist; and then, with the departure of Phillip Toyne and the arrival of the abrasive Tricia Caswell, the ACF threw in their lot with them. Together, they always wanted more than any government could deliver.

The greens maintained that the hardwood forest industry was all but finished and further destruction was pointless. The government, they said, should ban logging of native hardwoods and invest in softwood plantations. The loggers maintained that their work was a scientific exercise in management and did the forests and the environment the world of good. Of course they also said it was good for the current account deficit. However, the emotional core of their argument, which was the one that counted in this debate, concerned the loss of their jobs, the shattering of families, the annihilation of communities and towns. Some in caucus and cabinet reached the conclusion that while the timber industry was not all reason and light, doing anything for the greens was futile, because it only gave them an excuse to say it wasn't enough. A few believed that the logging dispute would cost them their seats and talked about resigning.

In an effort to rescue us from the horns of this hideous dilemma, Richard Pratt, the Melbourne entrepreneur who had built an empire out of cardboard, offered to announce that he would be establishing a new environmentally pure pulp mill in the vicinity of Tumut south of Canberra. We were very grateful for the offer of a lifeline but the government side of the deal could not be done in time. There was no solution without political pain and damage. Every night and morning Australians saw images of a government under siege and heard how it was at war with itself. No-one in the Prime Minister's Office felt entirely guiltless. The Prime Minister had been determined to escape all but his inescapable duties in the last two weeks of the year. Reluctant to have an end-of-year fight with him, his advisers let the matter go. We knew that in part we brought the disaster on ourselves. We had let it become a public drama, which meant it had to be played out to its conclusion—or as long as it took to satisfy honour, ego and love of the limelight.

At the risk of losing all future credibility I suggested that as he walked through the demonstrators one morning the Prime Minister approach one or two of them—one of them at least a woman—and invite them in for a chat. I thought it might change the atmosphere of the thing, create a new direction in the drama—anything to stem the flow of strength and legitimacy from the Prime Minister. And truly it was like watching his strength drain away before our eyes. Strength was the one quality the public recognised in him. He also had charm. Perhaps he could use the charm to regain his strength. He thought not. And he was probably right. In the meantime, however, he had no hope of mounting a concerted strategy against his new opponent, John Winston Howard.

He went some way to galvanising a semi-mutinous caucus and, in our view, landed some heavy blows on the old enemy when they met for the first time as party leaders in the first Question Time for the year. They spoke behind the Speaker's chair before battle was joined: according to the Prime Minister, Howard said, 'We're not going to fight dirty,' and Keating said that he replied, 'Congratulations. But you know I'm going to crush you.' Ralph Willis said Howard's performance was 'content free', but the new Liberal leader was articulate and, cheered on by his troops, confident. And Willis's warning of tough times ahead gave him the inspiration for a line that resounded all year, even when the evidence confounded it. 'The people of Australia cannot understand why they should suffer the indignity, the denial and the disappointment of a bare five minutes of economic sunshine and then it is on again.'

One would have thought from the press next morning that nothing so devastating had ever been seen or heard in living memory. The Prime Minister was angry. He had already complained to Paul Kelly about an *Australian* leader that said Howard should not be judged on his past. Howard was inveterate, Keating insisted—he had been a bad treasurer and he had bad social attitudes. Kelly had not taken kindly to being told. All year long it riled Keating that the press refused to recognise that Howard's past spoke for his real beliefs. The press took the view that Howard's past would only mean something if present behaviour proved it. It was easy to understand the PM's frustration, and why he found the prospect of dealing with Howard exhausting. He had dealt with him before. He had buried him. And the media who had seen it happen and declared Howard politically dead were now pronouncing him resurrected and giving him the leniency they had never given Keating. They were granting him a clean slate, the absence of a past. He sat there now, grinning across the dispatch box: it was as if some stuffed animal had suddenly winked and stepped from the glass case into his living room.

The Prime Minister badly wanted to 'slice him up like a salami', but it was not useful to be seen constantly trying to do the deed. It needed subtlety, patience and sure-footedness. In deciding to announce the Treasury forecasts the office of the treasurer displayed none of these qualities. The forecasts painted a lowering picture of Australia's current account problem—much gloomier than the problem warranted as it turned out. That was the perfect gift for John Howard. Where at least for the last year the government had been able to claim credit for continuing economic growth, now Howard could say it was an illusion, that interest rates were bound to rise again and the spectre of recession hung over the land.

The Prime Minister thought the forecasts were wrong; that the current account would close; that the government had ambushed itself. The Prime Minister also favoured a savings plan for the country: he wanted to pay the second half of his promised tax cuts as superannuation which would yield a 15 per cent dividend to Australians on retirement, and massively increase national savings. Then on 1 February part of the plan turned up on the front page of the *Sydney Morning Herald* under the heading 'Threat of Levy on Wages'. 'Workers may be forced to sink 3 per cent of their pay into compulsory superannuation to help the federal government cut the massive current account deficit,' it began. For several days both the pros and cons were canvassed in the papers, but one had the feeling that the cons were in the ascendancy. Insofar as superannuation was understood at all, the consensus among voters seemed to be that it was a bad investment, that it meant workers lost control over their savings, that it was unwieldy and inflexible and that the lowest paid got the least out of it.

The decision to publicise the notion, and to foreshadow possible public asset sales and the abandonment of the second round of the tax cuts, had been made in Ralph Willis's office. When leaks followed, the Prime Minister was furious and wanted them investigated, although we had a fair idea who was responsible. John Howard made a great fuss about the propriety of Keating's threats to pursue the culprit, and Peter Costello said that sooling the police onto the public service was further evidence of the tendency in the Prime Minister towards forms of behaviour seen in Argentina and the Philippines. Ross Gittins in the *Financial Review* said that Howard was a rank hypocrite about the budget leaks, and the former Labor finance minister, Peter Walsh, made much the same point. It was some relief to hear criticism of the new Opposition leader.

The Prime Minister had another plan. He would wait until a week before the budget, then tell cabinet that the government was reimposing death duties. It would not win an election, but it was brave and proper and, if it could be made unequivocally a tax on unearned wealth and not on enterprise and effort, it might be possible to sell it. As a fundamental plank of any real Labor platform the left would love the idea, unless panic overtook their moral instincts. And it was something to extend perceptions of Keating—the broader and braver he seemed the harder for Howard to counter him.

But Howard had quickly established a substantial lead in the polls. Keating knew that it would be much harder to peg him back than Downer had been after his honeymoon. The economic forecasts, the budget leaks, the interest rate rises, the forests shemozzel, the resignation of Ros Kelly which out of friendship the Prime Minister had accepted and with it a by-election he needed like he needed a dagger in his ribs—Howard must have thought he was dreaming. News arrived that Peter Cook was thinking of leaving politics; that Michael Lavarch could make five times the income outside; Evans wanted to be Chief Justice; Faulkner was rattled by the forests experience and wanted to shift portfolios. Kelty still wanted Brereton out of industrial relations and Bob McMullan in his place; and like some others he wanted Brian Howe out of the regional development job he had been in since Griffiths' departure. The Speaker, Stephen Martin, like Leo McLeay, appeared to command no significant respect from either side. Like McLeay, he seemed unwilling to discipline the Opposition for fear of appearing biased, and when in frustration Keating drove him to it, biased was how he looked. Parliament was orchestrated chaos in which the Prime Minister was bound to look like an anarchist or a bully. Some of us had thought it would be a good idea to elevate the former attorney-general, the amusing black Irishman, Michael Duffy, to the Speaker's role but this went the way of countless good ideas.

Just for a moment the idea of leaving seemed to be the only one coming out of cabinet and caucus. And leaks were all that seemed to come out of the public service. No doubt the Prime Minister's somewhat unpredictable leadership style inspired less confidence than personal initiative often requires. Why take risks if Keating takes them for you? Why try to second-guess the completely unpredictable? We heard mutterings about people thinking that the government was too much driven by the Prime Minister and his office, yet we waited in vain for ideas from the public service, ministers' offices and for that matter from the national secretariat. Of course, a year later the muttering became a mighty roar. We spent the year in the political equivalent of that fog on the Mississippi: one would hear voices and noises but one was never certain where they were coming from, or whether in the gloom we had missed the turning we were meant to take to reach safety.

In the light of our experience it was hard to see why the suggestion that we take, if not an axe, a broom and scalpel to the public service met with such furious resistance. If they leaked budget documents, why were they not sacked? If they could not generate ideas or complete tasks in the time it would take a small business to complete them, or put out to expensive consultants projects they were paid to carry out themselves, why were they being paid? If they could not write plainly and coherently, was not reform imperative? No, according to most—but significantly not all—senior public servants. And no, according to the Prime Minister: because, he told me, there was no longer enough talent in the public service to reform. There was another reason, of course: namely, why stop at the public service? Why not the ministers' offices? But then again, why pick on your friends? And if by exercising so much zeal you created a quite perfect government, would the press think better of you? Would the press strive to reach the same heights of excellence? What would be gained by repairing just one among several faults in the machine?

The main reason democratic government and its institutions often fail to rise above the ordinary is not that they lack talent, though frequently they do. It is that they don't know necessity. They are not desperate. There is no competition to drive the separate elements, no threat of ruin which in private enterprise feels like grievous loss or even death. There is, as well, complicity in the ordinariness and the most thoroughgoing hedges against ruin.

One might want to sack them, or privatise the lot, but that was not the point. One wanted to *love* them, not turn them into poor relations or servants of the private sector. The point of the public service is that it runs on public spirit, which it uses in place of the private sector's desperation and fear, hunger and greed. In addition to spirit it needs intelligence, judgment, suppleness, freedom from cant. But it also needs drive, imagination, even an aesthetic. It is an indispensable source of the 'temperate' judgment that Jefferson thought indispensable to democracy. Because the public service can't pay salaries that even approach those paid in the private sector, there must be all kinds of compensations. Most of the public service chiefs during Paul Keating's prime minister-ship doubtless believed that their departments were models of modern efficiency, and one could not help thinking that all those compensations and career paths had some influence on this. If a public service is one of the measures of a country's capabilities, values, level of literacy and ability to solve problems, this country was truly second rate. But not always: the worst part was seeing sometimes just how good it could be.

They had seen the War Memorial no doubt and, like the rest of us, got to know the cafes of Manuka. On 3 February the loggers drove away. On the TV Laurie Oakes and Glenn Milne had lost interest in them and were talking about monetary policy and new taxes. So with a last toot of their horns they went back to their homes in the forest. Cabinet had decided on a compromise which preserved more trees than previously, but also preserved a number of coupes which it was hoped would satisfy the timber workers. While cabinet deliberated that night, in the Prime Minister's Office we drafted a press release that talked about the middle ground, the national interest, how the blockade served no useful purpose, how the government would never act under duress, and so on. We left a gap for the cabinet resolution. At 11 p.m. the Prime Minister came in tired but tolerably happy-looking, gave us a slip of paper with a couple of sentences scrawled on it and saun-tered off down the corridor. Mike Keating and a couple of his staff had followed the PM in with a draft of the resolution. We thought what they had written was beyond the reach of press and public comprehension and asked if they could take it somewhere and rewrite it. As the public servants left, Gareth Evans rolled in, as usual looking like he had spent the day in a henhouse or branding steers. He gave us his draft of the resolution, and asked where his leader was. I took him down the corridor and we found the Prime Minister sitting with a personal assistant, Cheryl Griffiths, in her cupboard-sized office. He had a large illustrated architecture book on the desk. 'I was just explaining to Cheryl,' he said to the Foreign Minister, who might have been expecting him to still have trees on his mind, or South-East Asia, or politics of some kind, 'about the way certain architectural styles have dropped out of one era into another . . .'

The Foreign Minister's resolution was a model of clarity so we inserted it after the words 'accordingly Cabinet has agreed' and before a conclusion that we had written some hours before. The Foreign Minister left. We reprinted the press release and boxed it in the gallery. Just as we were going home the public servants returned with their resolution. We had to tell them it was too late.

As the trucks went home honking the next morning the ACF rang up to say that it had been a terrible time for everyone. They just wanted to be part of the process, they said. In fact the ACF had appealed to the most primitive in its most primitive constituents, and their extremism had helped the loggers to justify their own thuggish behaviour. It felt better having told them this and Geoff Walsh said he had experienced the same pleasure after telling the Wilderness Society.

Soon afterwards Geoff Walsh left to become consul-general in Hong Kong. He was replaced by John Bowan, a former ambassador to Germany, an amiable and funny man who loved music and cricket. Sam Mostyn was at last persuaded to join the staff, arriving in her Saab convertible as a kind of proof that she was only on loan from private enterprise. And towards the middle of 1995 Mark O'Neill, an experienced political adviser with a degree in botany who had once spent a week in the wilderness watching Tasmanian devils feed at night, became the new adviser on the environment, Aboriginal affairs and sport. With broad and robust intelligence he spent most of the year trying to undo the damage of the coupes. If he did not get all the greens back in the government's cart he got more than might have been expected. He also kept the loggers off the lawns of the parliament and negotiated a path through a couple of near calamities with Aboriginal matters.

Bill Kelty wanted an economic round table to replace the Economic Planning Advisory Council (EPAC). Bruce Chapman wanted a wages council; Kelty said the idea had merit but we knew he wouldn't support it unless he got his round table. He wanted to establish a big sustainable development program, a big regional development program. So did I. But the Prime Minister said the problem was, mate, there is no money. Mate. Our thoughts therefore turned to superannuation, and the means by which the nation's savings could be channelled into national investment.

The government had delivered Native Title legislation and a Land Fund for Aborigines the legislation did not reach. The realities of Aboriginal life would be changed by these measures, but not quickly and not in ways that anyone would see immediately. What people saw when they saw Aborigines at all were degraded lives lived in squalid environments. They also saw statistics showing that among Aborigines, rates of alcohol and drug abuse, suicide, incarceration, disease, domestic violence and infant mortality were many times higher than for other Australians, and life expectancy was twenty-five years lower. Although they may have known nothing else about them, the great majority of Australians knew that Aborigines lived in Third World conditions. They also knew that a great deal of government money had been spent attempting to solve the problem. Yet the problem was worse. It was almost as if—and there must have been many Australians who believed this—the money was part of the problem. The money was largely distributed by ATSIC. No-one in Canberra was in much doubt that, under ATSIC, a lot of the money was not getting to the places it was needed.

Paul Keating did not want to leave office with Mabo and the Land Fund behind him but the realities of Aboriginal life unchanged. Some of those who opposed Mabo had taken to saying that Keating made high-sounding noises but had never seen what life was like, and wouldn't until he visited a remote Aboriginal community. To make the point John Hewson, Alexander Downer and the noisy new Liberal, Brendan Nelson, had all followed in Graham Richardson's footsteps out to these sad communities with an eager pack of media following.

For Keating, the political sting in the tail was obvious. He goes belatedly and it is claimed he goes only in response to political or media pressure. The media suddenly sprouts a conscience; every television channel and every newspaper shows him in the midst of squalor and demands that he does something. The public takes the spectacle to mean that Labor's policies have not worked, or Aborigines will not help themselves and do not deserve their sympathy or further help. The Prime Minister promises more money than the government can afford or more than the white community believes is deserved and is called a fool, a bleeding heart, a handmaiden of the politically correct. Or he says money is not the solution and the Aborigines, the churches and many on his own side charge him with callous neglect.

Money was certainly going to be part of the solution. Since Whitlam boosted funding massively in 1973–74, total per capita expenditure on Aboriginal and Torres Strait Islanders had more than doubled. But so had the number of people identifying as indigenous Australians and a significant proportion of the money now being counted as Aboriginal expenditure had previously been lumped into social welfare. So it turned out that expenditure per capita in 1992 was actually a couple of per cent lower than it had been in 1974. And with the number of indigenous Australians growing more rapidly than any other group, and a major backlog of basic services and facilities promised but still not provided, the situation could only get worse.

Eventually the Prime Minister visited the Aboriginal settlement at Hopevale near Cooktown on Cape York. He went out of duty. He also went because politically he did not have much choice. Rightly, he refused to go with a media circus. He wanted to go with no media at all, but a deal was cooked up with the

Hollows Foundation of which Channel 9's Ray Martin was chairman. Martin also qualified because he was a member of the Reconciliation Council. So, breaking just about every rule of media management, all journalists except Martin and the *Cairns Post* were told that the Prime Minister had 'no public engagements' on the appointed day and Martin was granted an 'exclusive'. We knew what would happen when the day came and, sure enough, Glenn Milne from the *Australian* and Channel 7 swore revenge. He told his audience that the Prime Minister was taking with him only Kerry Packer's channel. The *Cairns Post* headlined the visit, 'Keating Stunt'. More imaginatively, on their front page the Melbourne *Herald Sun* ran an attack on Keating by the war heroine Nancy Wake. We also knew we could not be sure that Martin's gratitude would overwhelm his media instincts. We told him in advance that if he wanted something useful for Aborigines to come out of the trip he ought to let the Prime Minister reach his own conclusions without inserting himself in the mix. He ought to report, not second-guess, or judge. That was the bargain we hoped he would keep. But Ray Martin was a media star and total self-abnegation was never really in prospect. We told him that we were not about to freely put our head in a trap, but we knew that this was precisely what we were doing.

Hopevale had been a Lutheran mission. Noel Pearson grew up there. In 1995 it was a relatively orderly, healthy and happy place. The housing was just adequate if not particularly appropriate to climate and lifestyle; the sewerage system was in need of an overhaul, but it was a wonder that there was a sewerage system at all. There was a school. There were signs of hope. And there was Noel Pearson. It had been Pearson's presence there which persuaded the Prime Minister to make the trip despite all the risks. And Pearson had told us what he thought the Prime Minister should say. Speak to them informally, he said; tell them that it's a 'partnership' and a lot of responsibility is theirs. He thought the Prime Minister should give them 'a kick in the pants'.

They both made speeches at the school. Along with other Cape York elders, they talked about what should be done to save

Aboriginal people from the cycle of misery, degradation and early death. Keating said that Mabo and the Land Fund had been essential steps, but it now remained to find practical solutions to the problems Aboriginal communities faced. He spoke gently and respectfully and could have left no-one doubting his goodwill. But did not deliver the kick in the pants that Pearson suggested. The Prime Minister and the elders spoke from the stage. Pearson stepped down among the children. He said the debate in recent years had been all about how the system oppressed Aboriginal people. We knew how bad it was and how bad their lives were. The debate had been critical, now it had to be creative. We had to put the pieces back together. As Pearson made his inspiring speech the uninvited press watched from the other side of a fence several hundred metres away and took photos with long lenses.

The incidence of diabetes on Cape York is many times greater than it is for any white community. Despite this and other chronic health and social problems of a kind familiar to the Third World, there are fewer doctors per head of population and less is spent on medical services. Before the Prime Minister arrived, the Channel 9 crew took the time to visit parts of Cape York where the evidence of this disaster was plainer than it was at Hopevale. Before they saw the Prime Minister viewers saw images of dreadful squalor. The most striking of them was of a child sitting on a floor eating sugar from a bag. No doubt Channel 9 hoped this scene would encourage Australians to demand that something be done. It seemed more likely to encourage the view that nothing could be. Even that nothing should be. The image did indicate a failure of policy; it also indicated a failure of personal responsibility.

After the meeting at the school and a tour of the community, the Prime Minister was interviewed by Ray Martin. It was clear from the first couple of minutes that he would be held responsible for the child eating the sugar. He survived the experience, but did not exactly prosper from it. Nor did the Aboriginal communities of Cape York gain much. Next day the PM talked enthusiastically about creating the taskforce on Aboriginal health.

John Dawkins, Fred Chaney, Janine Haines, Rick Farley, Llew Edwards and Noel Pearson were mentioned. He wanted a good engineer to solve the practical problems of housing, water and sewerage. He thought we should involve private companies and perhaps the army. All through 1995 he thought about it. The task-force was almost established half a dozen times, but then some new doubt would flood in, or some other necessity would overwhelm it. The fear was principally that the reward for the initiative would be to have a massive bill laid at the government's feet. It is possible that fear of failure also played a part.

In April, encouraged by Noel Pearson among others, it was decided to transfer responsibility for the distribution of health funding from ATSIC to the Department of Health. We expected a backlash from people who believed the move was a step backwards from self-determination. However, there were not many prepared to argue that the principles of self-determination must perforce mean declining health and reduced longevity—not to say institutionalised neglect and incompetence.

On 16 February the same Ray Martin conducted a much more accommodating interview with his boss, Kerry Packer. Packer told him that he wanted to control Fairfax but under the cross-media rules it wasn't legal. He also told Martin that he thought John Howard would make a good prime minister. He said he thought Howard was a 'decent man' and an 'honest man' and a 'man who has made mistakes' but wouldn't make them again. The Prime Minister heard about it in Perth and told the media that it meant Howard had given Packer 'the nod'—that a Howard government would change the cross-media rules enabling Packer ownership of both Channel 9 and Fairfax. He knew that Howard and Packer had recently met, so Packer's remarks merely confirmed his suspicion that a deal was being done. But it was no less shocking because he suspected it. To Keating it suggested war—or at least blackmail with the threat of annihilation. It was Keating's immediate instinct to alert such allies as he had to the import of events, and if possible deliver a pre-emptive strike. As a tactical response this had one major shortcoming: he had no proof of the deal. It would be assumed his information came from Barron and Richardson, but they were hardly going to confirm it for him publicly. Without corroboration, he could not talk as if the wickedness were real without looking cranky or paranoid. 'Rantings' John Howard called it, and most of the journalists took the same view.

The problem would be the same all year: how to fight back without looking spooked or appearing to be the aggressor. Howard was already showing signs of mastering what would become his best tactic, that of provoking Keating's wrath and then affecting innocence. Keating risked giving the impression of a man trying to throttle his enemy in the back seat while the car he was driving careered all over the road. He had to fight Howard, Packer, Fairfax—all his enemies—with one arm firmly round the national waist. Think of Errol Flynn, I said, sword in hand and fencing madly, but without letting go of the heroine. In the case of Packer at least, no evidence emerged to indicate the metaphor impressed him.

The Prime Minister gave Laurie Oakes one of his more remarkable interviews. It was not elegant or subtle and a lot of viewers would not admire him for it. But it did make the issues clearer, it did earn him his first good headlines for weeks and it might have done something to galvanise opinion in the party. A Keating Government, he said, would not change the rules: if Packer wanted more than 20 per cent of Fairfax he would have to give up Channel 9. And if Howard denied he was now the Packer candidate, don't believe him. He might as well have been addressing the owner of the channel. In fact at one point he called Oakes 'Kerry'. Kerry, he said, should be grateful for what he had already been given, but Kerry wanted more. He wanted a deal equivalent to Rupert's pay TV deal; he wanted half of what was Telstra's! Kerry was trying a 'scam' the size of the one alleged of Murray Farquhar on the Philippines National Bank! And when last October Keating denied him the deal, Packer had resolved to re-route his ambitions through the Liberal Party. And having said this, the Prime Minister, with all the grace of a piece of plaster falling from the ceiling, and as much apparent forethought, announced that he wanted a fourth network—a family network. Oakes looked for a moment as if he might giggle. Next morning, the influential educationist Patricia Edgar supported the Prime Minister—and the story ran all day in the news.

The Oakes interview was intended as a psychological depth charge, the Keating 'throw a bloody big rock in the pond' theory in practice. Some in the office were horrified by the apparent crudeness of it. But Keating was trying to reshape the environment in which the battle would be fought and, with this as their measure, others reckoned that even if the performance scored only 6 out of 10, they were points worth winning.

Hoping that he had captured a bit of the high ground on the Packer/Fairfax debate, we flew off to Germany for an international information technology exhibition, CEBIT, at which Australia was to be the star turn. It should have been a breeze, selling Australia as a front-runner in IT. We could use it to prove the great benefits of the reformed economy; that we were integrating with the global economy; that we were a significant player in Asia—and that, therefore, we were very useful to Europeans seeking fortunes there. Like all trips, this one had the disadvantage of leaving one's opponents free to make mischief at home. But it also had the advantage of offering a forum to sell the domestic message in an international context, that is to say, with nothing else on the screen save other international leaders nodding their heads in agreement. And he would stop off at Singapore for a meeting with Goh Chok Tong on the way, the real and symbolic point being that our engagement with Asia and our relationship with Europe were not exclusive of each other.

Along these propitious lines speeches were constructed as the usual large contingent of advisers and civil servants flew in the bowel of the Black Pig to Singapore, and thence to Bonn. These trips frequently seemed to throw up one arresting fact, from whence I never knew. Annual sales of Australian crayfish tails to

Japan exceed the value of all exports to Vietnam. The subsidy attaching to one French milking cow is greater than the annual earnings of a citizen of Chad. For Germany it was: in the middle of the information revolution half the world's population have never made a telephone call.

The Prime Minister did not need much instruction in the information revolution, or any concerning Germany and the European Union. He had made it his business to know Europe well since his days as treasurer and he had well-placed friends there. He would deliver the message about Australia that he knew off by heart—and he would also tell Chancellor Kohl, and later a meeting hosted by former chancellor Helmut Schmidt, that Germany needed to make some crucial decisions. Germany, he would tell them, must be as generous to Europe as Marshall and Truman had been after the war. It must surrender the Deutschmark to Europe. Otherwise, Keating said, Britain and France, who are already growing anxious about a reunified Germany, will hive off from the union and Europe will again divide. He also intended to tell Kohl, and spread the message wherever he went, that Germany had to abolish its subsidies and grow its economy much faster to soak up unemployment. He was sure of his ground and with APEC behind him felt he had a little virtue on his side. He had figures which showed that of all the OECD countries only three would at present meet the Maastricht 'convergence criteria' for entry into the European Union—Germany, Luxembourg and Australia. None of this would persuade some in the Australian press that he had a right to tell the Europeans their business. But they would not stop him, any more than their contempt for his interest in architecture would stop him stalking the streets of Berlin to look at Walter Schinkel's buildings.

Something bigger than all this was on his mind, however—something more urgent. When he went down the back to speak to the journalists between Canberra and Singapore, we thought it was to tell them about his views on Europe. In fact he talked to them about the deal that he knew Howard had done with Packer.

He told them that Packer could not run his business properly. Murdoch had left Packer for dead.

Then, while Goh Chok Tong stood next to him at a joint press conference in Singapore, the journalists asked him if the Opposition was right to say he was running a vendetta against Packer. He might have said, 'No. Next question.' Or, 'I have just had the most fruitful meeting with my friend Goh Chok Tong, and I would sooner talk about this than Mr Packer.' Instead he waded in. The Opposition were 'crawling to Kerry Packer', he said. When the plane stopped at Dubai to refuel, a press release from Packer was waiting for us. Keating was engaging in 'intimidation', Packer said. It seemed a reasonable assumption that Peter Barron had written it. So between Dubai and Germany we drafted a reply, calling the allegation of intimidation a 'bizarre pretence'. 'Bizarre' was the word. In Bonn we released it to the press. The press wanted to know what evidence he had to support his allegation of a Howard–Packer deal. Back in Australia Oakes asked the same question. They asked if the Prime Minister's behaviour meant that he could not live with the thought that Packer approved of someone other than himself? Was he not being paranoid and tyrannical? Was it not the case, after all, that Packer and Labor had been in bed for years; that Barron was Keating's chief unofficial adviser, the man who masterminded the debate with Hewson on Packer's channel that altered the course of the last election? Was this not the same Prime Minister who used to tell the press that he had made Packer his first billion? Whatever we said in reply to these questions, there remained one that defied explanation. With much justification he had often complained about journalists failing to cover the real story on his trips abroad, so why on this occasion did he lead them away from the real story before the plane had reached Darwin?

It had been deliberate. In Hanover, where the CEBIT conference was taking place, this became clear. We arrived to hear that Oakes had torn into the Prime Minister in the *Bulletin*. By then both Barron and Richardson, the two ex-Labor NSW right Packer employees, had assured Australians that they had not told

Keating of any deal between Howard and Packer. Privately, according to Keating, Barron had told him that the Liberals were 'in the bag' about changing the cross-media rules in Packer's favour, and Richardson had said, 'Don't drive us to Howard.' Keating was in no doubt about it, but he could not prove it. We told him that Barron and Richardson had dumped on him in the two minutes it took to walk from his meeting with Kohl to the press conference. It was agreed that when asked he must say that the hired hands could be expected to do whatever was necessary to back up their employer; that he knew this when he took Packer on. He told the press conference the meeting with Kohl had been a very good one—as by all other accounts, including Kohl's, it had been. He had told Kohl what he had intended to tell him about the currency and Kohl agreed. He also told Kohl he must do these things now, because when he and Mitterrand were gone their replacements were likely to be less passionate 'Europeans'. They had also talked about architecture and, encouraged by the Chancellor, the rebuilding of Berlin, a departure for which some journalists mocked him. He had 'lectured Kohl', they said. Kohl described it as a 'rare' meeting. It had gone over time to accommodate the breadth of their discussions. There seemed to have been a high degree of immediate mutual regard. And he had talked to the German chancellor about the prospect of an Australian republic. He offered him the view that the German model with a president elected by the parliament was a good one for Australia.

In due course he was asked a question about Packer and answered it on the lines agreed. But outside the hotel later the journalists were saying how clever he had been to throw them a 'big smelly republican bone' to divert them from the Packer fiasco. And they noted how they had all taken the bait! We nodded with knowing smiles, though no-one had given the republic a thought. Inevitably, back in Canberra, John Howard said that as soon as Keating had a problem he pulled out the republic.

Despite the republican bone, that night Greg Turnbull brawled with Laurie Oakes by phone, and the rest of us sat drinking with the journalists trying to persuade them that Barron and Richardson were not credible witnesses. We knew that Howard had a week ahead in which he need only repeatedly intone, 'put up or shut up'.

By now it was clear that we were in the middle of another public relations calamity abroad. It was also clear that because of the Packer story we had missed not only the benign news that might have flowed from the visit, but a big political opportunity. Back in Canberra the Opposition was in trouble for the first time since Howard took over the leadership. Ian McLachlan had received a parcel of letters relating to a proposed bridge from Goolwa to Hindmarsh Island in South Australia, which the government had blocked as a consequence of objections from some local Aboriginal women. A South Australian, McLachlan wanted the bridge built and saw no genuine argument against it. In this he agreed not only with the developer but with an anthropologist the developer employed, the Aboriginal Heritage branch of the South Australian Government and Aborigines with traditional associations to Goolwa and the island. It is possible that the letters were less bona fide than at the time seemed to be the case. But McLachlan's use of them was inept at best. The letters came in a parcel marked Strictly Confidential and though addressed to 'Sean McLaughlin' were marked 'Minister for Atsic' suite MF 17—Tickner's office. Though the error was obvious, McLachlan's office photocopied them, including two separate appendixes marked 'To be read by women only'. Three days later, the parcel was sent on to Tickner. Subsequently, the *Adelaide Advertiser* received copies of the letters bearing a Canberra postmark. South Australian politicians also received copies. In the House two months later, first McLachlan then the Opposition Aboriginal Affairs spokeswoman Chris Gallus asked Tickner if he had read the letters, if male eyes had seen them? No, said Tickner to both questions. And then McLachlan threw on the table a package that he said contained the letters and asked how come the Minister allowed these things to be 'sent around Australia like flotsam from a wreck'.

A week later, after Michael Lavarch, the Attorney-General, had thoroughly researched and comprehensively answered the question, McLachlan felt compelled to resign from the shadow ministry. In the *Sydney Morning Herald* Alan Ramsey made the point that John Howard must have been party to the parliamentary strategy and therefore must have known the status of the documents and what his colleague had done with them. It was odd that Ramsey noticed before we did. When he heard in Berlin that McLachlan had resigned, the Prime Minister cursed his luck for not being there to send Howard packing with him. That is the problem with going overseas; you can be sitting there at a turning point in world history talking about the future of Europe with the huge Herr Kohl, or standing ten metres from the bunker in which Hitler died, and all the time a great political opportunity is passing you by. It is an even bigger problem when you are fighting with a media proprietor and two former friends, colleagues and confidants.

In Hanover, before the McLachlan resignation, I got angry and asked the Prime Minister what he hoped to achieve by whipping up the Packer story. It had made a fiasco of the trip, I said. He went to a phone. Have a talk to Laurie, he said. Laurie will explain it. I had never spoken to Laurie Brereton in my life. Laurie told me not to worry, it was all going much better than it seemed. 'If you're going to pin the tail on the donkey, you've got to expect to get a bit of donkey shit on you,' he said. It seemed obvious that the cock-up had been carefully orchestrated. The PM and Brereton had agreed to try to nail Packer and Howard at whatever cost. I asked Brereton if in the next twenty-four hours he would make an effort to extract the Prime Minister from the melee and allow the good news we had been spreading in Germany to be heard in Australia. He said he would do that, mate. He said not to worry. It was messy now but it would be worth it in the end, he said. I sat down to eat lunch with Annita. What did he say? asked the Prime Minister. I told him about the donkey. He smiled as if to indicate that I should now be on his side.

We wanted the public to hear those things which the Prime Minister had come 10,000 miles to say—his own thoughts and the things his staff, who admired him even more than they were frustrated by him, had composed. His CEBIT speech, intended to be the showpiece of the trip, received little notice. In Berlin he addressed the luncheon meeting with Helmut Schmidt, former president von Weizsacker and twenty German businessmen. The press, it had been agreed with the Germans, would not be present. The press, of course, complained. We wrote three pages of notes describing what the Prime Minister would be telling the meeting in his extemporaneous address. We found we had produced something like a government manifesto, but the press did not show much interest, and when a few days later in The Hague they were invited to a similar meeting all but two of them preferred to go sightseeing in Amsterdam.

Keating's performance at the Berlin meeting was more impressive than the notes. More impressive than journalists ever saw him. He was relaxed, persuasive, even commanding. His hosts professed both admiration and agreement. Schmidt, overweight and smoking, spoke at length in reply. He said that world population growth and its impact on the environment was the great problem. Keating said this was an argument for economic growth, and that one of the growth areas would be environmental industries, employment and programs. Some things Schmidt said might have reminded Australians that perspectives are conditioned by culture and by generations. While other countries surrounded Germany and bore down upon the German consciousness, Schmidt told us, Australia had no neighbours except New Zealand for 'thousands and thousands of miles'. 'What about Indonesia?' whispered the German next to me. While Germany was attracting too many undistinguished immigrants, Australia was wisely choosing the cleverest races in Asia—the Chinese and the Vietnamese. And Germany had something else to deal with which Australia did not—Auschwitz would hang over Germany for another hundred years. Some of those present wondered if it would not be more than that.

Buoyant after the meeting, to what might have been my evident surprise, Keating introduced me to Schmidt as his 'alter ego'. Never had I felt less like his alter ego. But how could I not be touched? In the evening gloom we went hunting Schinkel buildings, stealing round corners to evade the press in streets still blackened and bullet-pocked from fifty years before. I told him that Europe smelt of death and always would, and that I preferred the Asian knock-it-down and whack-it-up again style. He took it well. With Annita and Allan Gyngell we dined at a bad restaurant in the Grand Maritim hotel in Friedrichstrasse where Honecker and his East German thugs used to dine. As if suddenly aware that he had been statesmanlike today and in the same instant frightened that we might expect him to maintain these standards, the PM did an imitation of James Dean at his most disturbed and delinquent. I said a lot of his aggression was counterproductive because the people took it to be self-serving rather than serving them. It was an old theme. He said, look at all the monuments to Konrad Adenauer, his name everywhere—what good does that do? Gyngell said it was important to be Adenauer if the situation required it and you were capable of being it. It seemed possible that the Prime Minister was employing some larrikin technique of fishing for compliments and reassurance. 'When you're dead, you're dead,' I said. Adenauer lent his name to German postwar liberalism; you could lend yours to Australian social democracy. It would be stupid to go out remembered for nothing much more than your ability to throw political punches. He sank lower in his chair and asked the waiter to turn the heating up. It was a good conversation, though not the first time we had had it, nor the last. Gyngell and I agreed later that it meant he wanted his ambition reinforced and his recent sins forgiven.

The mayor of Berlin walked with him through the Brandenburg gate and put on a dinner in his honour. At the dinner a young German beside me, who was engaged in some way with the rebuilding project, said Germans of his generation would never surrender the DM. The Prime Minister rose and, speaking extemporaneously before coming to his notes about the prospects for Australian involvement in the regeneration of his city, said

Germany must do precisely what the young German said could not happen. This, said our Prime Minister, was the path to 'German destiny'. The expression instantly produced under my arm a bead of sweat that made steady progress down my ribs as the Prime Minister continued to paint his word pictures. The walls of East Berlin were 'dripping tears'. The young German registered his surprise with a smile. It seemed likely that for once on such an occasion everyone would know what the guest of honour meant and remember what he said.

He went to Copenhagen and delivered a speech to a UN conference on social development. The department's draft was twice as long as the time allowed and it took until 4.30 on the morning he was to fly out to get the speech written. Then at 5.30 news came that McLachlan had resigned and we had to write a press release, and get the Attorney-General on the phone and try to organise Howard's nailing from the hotel room.

The PM rang in the afternoon, walking in the Tivoli Gardens to say the speech had gone down very well. It was an argument for Australian social democracy, the fusion of the market with intelligent government initiative, the head and the heart. It was an advertisement for the Job Compact, the progress we had made in raising the status of women, the multicultural success. He pitched the case for the twenty-two nations of the Pacific Forum. And he spoke about Aboriginal Australia.

It was very well reviewed, but on the basis of this one paragraph I had inserted at the end, the *Sydney Morning Herald* headlined its front page, 'Abs: Keating apologises to the world'. Nothing in the words he used could justify that conclusion. On the same day the paper failed to publish a letter the Prime Minister had faxed complaining about their treatment of his trip: they published instead an editorial which said his concentration on 'absurd allegations of a conspiracy' had caused him to miss the chance to damage John Howard. The Prime Minister's letter appeared the following day among sixteen anti-Keating letters. The trip began as a media calamity and never ceased to be one. It began with the admirable Jim Middleton, a few drinks in, standing in the aisle of the plane, poking his finger in the Prime Minister's chest and complaining about the Ray Martin 'exclusive' at Hopevale. It ended with Alan Ramsey saying the PM was 'unhinged' and Nikki Savva writing that the best measure of the failure was that the centrepiece of the trip—the CEBIT speech in Hanover—went largely unreported. Of course, she did not think, and it is doubtful if any of her colleagues did, that some measure of failure on her side was also indicated.

Soon after the German trip, as a fourth autumn descended on the Keating Government, I sat next to Kim Beazley on a Friday night plane to Melbourne. As I got off he had to fly on to Perth. He had been doing this for more than a decade. All week I had been thinking about resigning. Naturally I did not tell him this, even when he told me that he was on the verge of giving up. He wanted to go back to the university and write a book. People told him to wait, that Keating would soon go and the prime minister-ship would be his. But he did not want to wait. He had had enough. And there was more money in retirement than he would earn on the Opposition benches. Everyone was thinking about being in Opposition because Howard's honeymoon continued and Keating could not land a blow. We agreed that, apart from rest, the only imaginable pleasure to come from losing the election might be watching the demise of political correctness.

Between the political impulse and the political consequence lies a hall of mirrors. You throw an idea in—you may throw it in several times—but how it is seen and what reaction it provokes depends on forces largely beyond your control. It is a random business and all is vanity and vexation of the spirit, as the poet said. But he also said there is no wisdom in the grave so one might as well do it, whatever the risks to one's sanity and health. It was difficult to say how much donkey shit the Prime Minister was prepared to cop, but it was surely much less than the drayload he received. Worse, pursuit of the Packer donkey had probably been a factor in our failing to inflict the first serious damage on Howard. These are the body blows of politics.

Had the Prime Minister done better in the previous two weeks it is possible that he would not have been disposed to tell a student protester in Adelaide to 'Get a job. Do some work like the rest of us.' This was not his reading of it when I rang and asked him why, and said he should go on the radio and defuse it at once, that otherwise it would haunt us all the way to the polls. He said he'd seen the ALP's research and it showed we were playing too much to the left, too much Aboriginal stuff and too much republic. Out in white heterosexual Australia where Labor's traditional support was, folk were dropping off like flies, apparently—as if we hadn't known for years. He would not try to defuse the situation. He would let it go away by itself. When Jones and Laws on 2UE next morning said his words had been well chosen I supposed he felt vindicated. I supposed as well that the *Sydney Morning Herald* front page from the Copenhagen speech had had some effect upon his thinking. There was nothing to be gained from saying that one had been telling him for months that he was talking too much about Mabo and the republic and too little about employment, education, export growth, communities and hope. One said it anyway, and one also said that while his comment might have been directed at a few Young Liberals masquerading as impoverished students, it alienated youth generally and parents who were anxious about the children's prospects. It contradicted the spirit of Working Nation—though not the central premise that for every young Australian there was a job or training or both. It reinforced the view that he was out of touch and had no understanding of real lives. And so on. None of it produced any sense of vindication, least of all when in the last debate of the election he reflexively denied making the remark, and the Liberals made from his denial and a recording of the remark itself their most damaging advertisements.

That Labor research was indeed depressing, enervating. The people were sick of him. They didn't like the way he behaved when he was abroad. They didn't like the way he behaved in the parliament. They didn't like his arrogance. It was all as we had said in the Berlin restaurant: he was squandering his substance with his style. And his behaviour since returning had been all that he had said. Something in his psyche told him that he wouldn't be Paul Keating if he let me or Allan Gyngell or Greg Turnbull or Annita govern his behaviour. If we wanted him to stop swinging punches he would swing them all the harder. What had been the point of his life if at its pinnacle he had to submit to his staff? If he had to be someone who was not, essentially, the man he had always imagined being?

The same research also showed that speculation about interest rates and Howard's 'five minutes of sunshine' remark had caused serious damage. What hadn't damaged us? The research as usual showed what any fool knew—that the government was in a tailspin. As for Packer, the worst of it was not that Keating could not prove his case; or even that it distracted attention from the government's good works; rather that it looked like Paul Keating was pursuing Paul Keating's enemies at the expense of the people's interests. And then, when Labor was trounced first in the Canberra Assembly elections and then, in March, in the by-election for Ros Kelly's seat he brushed it off. 'So what?' he said after the first result, and after the 16.4 per cent swing against him in the Kelly seat he sounded scarcely more contrite. In his *Bulletin* column Graham Richardson said the result called for a mea culpa from the Prime Minister, which eradicated any chance of the Prime Minister reaching the same conclusion. Richardson, he said, had taken his 'thirty pieces of silver' and he no longer spoke for Labor's interests. The press also decided the Prime Minister should say sorry. They lashed themselves into a feeding frenzy. In Question Time the Opposition joined in, and the Prime Minister sounded and looked like a wounded animal fighting for its life.

We could only sit and wait for the swing of the pendulum. It was a long time coming, and as usual the tactic brought on that stage in the process when the press say—he's in the bunker, he's under siege, he's cut himself off. And then there comes the realisation among some of them that they are feeding on their own tails, and in the weekend columns they write very considered pieces about whether the Prime Minister has yet learned the lesson they have read him, and wonder if he can save himself.

The last weeks of March and the first in April 1995 might have been the worst of all. I was an alter ego in exile. When I heard that the Prime Minister had complained that Simon Balderstone and I were pushing him too often into Aboriginal and republican matters it became unpleasant, not least because I felt certain that this opinion was coming from a new set of political geniuses who knew nothing. In fact I was forever trying to pull him away from these subjects, and with Balderstone encourage him to go among ordinary folk who might yet be persuaded to vote for him. It was one of several moments that year when my feeling for the Prime Minister approached dislike. It rose like a boil, and subsided in the fullness of things, like the drop in the home loan rate the NAB announced around 10 April. Or he lanced it with some staggeringly good performance, or visited the regions or did some other surprising thing that against all reason I took as meaning he had turned the corner. Or he would give me some sign of his misery. Whatever it was, I would in an instant realise that it was neither my inclination nor my role to be hostile. What else, after all, can a political adviser do? The job demands a level of obsession. It is not always rational. You subvert your own better judgment about your own better interests. You refuse to be offended by refusal. But what is a bit of lost dignity if it is necessary to persuade the powerful? It is not power over him that you want, but seeing his power expanded. It is not making him submit, but seeing him flourish. This process, when it is boiled down, puts his dignity at greater risk than yours. And he cannot be powerful without dignity. His dignity is worth everything and yours is a trifle. And in any case you have to love the bastard. A lot of us used to say it, you couldn't work for him unless you did. Who else on either side of politics has such a capacity to inspire, or make you laugh as much? With who else but Keating could you develop the necessary obsession?

He had gone out west to Bourke where the windows are protected by iron bars against the depredations of the blacks. We stood on the motel's lawn behind a three-metre fence, the Prime Minister, Frank Lowy, Mark Ryan, Simon Balderstone and me. As the sun went down the Aborigines went home, arguing mainly; a man stopped and through the fence asked the Prime Minister of the Commonwealth and its second richest citizen for a light. The PM paid his respects at Fred Hollows' grave, started a foot race to Sydney that Lowy sponsored, appeared live on the *Today* show from the main street where Monty was doing the weather, inspected a new wharf on the Darling, and planted a tree in a new plantation.

He went up north to Winton for celebrations to mark the centenary of 'Waltzing Matilda'. When he got out of the car a woman sitting on a doorstep with a XXXX in her hand shouted, 'He looks uglier in the flesh than he does on TV.' One took it personally. A moment later a famous folksinger thrust a microphone in his hand and demanded he sing 'Waltzing Matilda', and next thing he was planting a coolabah tree. He sat on a Winton motel bed and talked to Wayne Goss about a COAG deal, and then in dinner suits the two of them and the Governor went down for dinner at the North Gregory Hotel. Outside, under the outback's vast canopy of stars we could hear them laughing at the jokes in the Prime Minister's speech and assumed it was going well, but a local switched the lights out just before the end and he couldn't see to finish. We escaped a striking miner from Mount Isa who had lectured us all afternoon about the injustice of a working man like him paying 47 cents in the dollar—deaf as he was to Bruce Chapman's advice that he was only paying 47 cents on dollars in excess of 50,000—and flew under that beautiful sky to Rockhampton and Yeppoon. Here he addressed a gathering of fifteen local businessmen and suffered an abusive front page from the local newspaper. He returned to Canberra sick of politics and with an irregular heartbeat. I was unsympathetic and said he ought to have a stress test. Then I felt guilty and phoned him at the Lodge to say I was sorry to sound unsympathetic.

People wanted him to act as if each day was his first in the job. As if he had not been in it most of his life, and did not know what would work in these towns and what was wishful thinking; as if he had never climbed a mountain, or built a bridge between two impossible places. As if his achievements were nothing, his public spirit unproved. It was not the insult or the lack of recognition, it was the way it ground you down, body and soul. He was like an actor in a long-running play, touring the country night after night, year after year. The difference was that he was on stage all day. And every day he got reviewed. They asked him to submit to the basic dramatic conceit that every performance was a new one staged just for that audience. Only bad politicians played to the audience. Good politicians saw it for the democratic fantasy it was. They only did it when necessary. But these days he was expected to do it every day. Well they could forget it. He wasn't going to do it any more. And if John Bowan and Bill Bowtell (and anybody else in the office) reckoned he was going to change his mind and start going to every Question Time again, they could pack their bags, or he would. 'If I have to exist to please the office,' he said to me, 'it's not worth hanging around.'

It was a bad month. It was often impossible to confront his personal torment with those things that are the inescapable business of governments and prime ministers—good governments and prime ministers at least, or those in trouble. I had the feeling he was punishing me for my discontent and lack of sympathy. The marriage grew steadily unhappier, I knew. And I knew he was seeking kindness, not responsibilities. Ideas oppressed him as much as public duties. He did not want to talk about the things an adviser needs to talk about—what he must do, what he might do, what is happening. He wanted to talk about his life. So one talked about it, and occasionally tried to insert a little bit of one's own—for balance. I read *Huckleberry Finn* and it did feel like the long night when Huck and Jim got separated on the river in the fog. The important thing was to keep talking—and holler every now and then.

Towards the end of the month he took a few days off at Port Douglas with Annita, telling me as he left that he was going to consider his future. When he came back he seemed much better. He was received with great enthusiasm at a United Nations Cultural Diversity Conference in Sydney. Agreement was reached with the ACTU on Accord Mark VIII. There would be publicly funded maternity allowance paid in lump sum to mothers in work and at home, safety-net increases of between $8 and $14 per week. The unions would commit to the generation of 600,000 new jobs by 1999 and an inflation rate of 2 to 3 per cent. The PM and Martin Ferguson, the ACTU president, said it provided a four-year framework for low inflation, high productivity, high growth and more employment. But employer groups and the Opposition leader attacked the Accord as devastating to business and workers alike and a proven failure. In fact the Accord had evolved from the centralised wage fixing model of 1983 to one under which workers negotiated wages rises through collective bargaining in individual enterprises, with no limit on the size of the rise. The centralised part remained the safety net for the low paid. To many people on the Labor side the Accord was like new marrow in their bones—it gave them strength, substance and defi-nition. Somehow Mark VIII, while as noble from this Labor point of view as any other, passed with less of a sense of satisfaction and achievement than the others, and less fanfare than it deserved.

There was the Accord, then he got the Hilmer reforms through COAG, which meant in future the States would be subject to the same rules of competition as business. It was good; it was more micro-economic reform. Then the NAB lowered its home loan rates. Then John Howard stumbled by failing to rule out a future GST. It gave us some relief and political bedding for the coming budget.

The budget energised him. He was like a painter who had just stretched a canvas. His mind was full of the picture he would paint. He got excited about the superannuation changes, excited about the politics of it. He loved budgets. He sent me down to the Treasury to work on the words. I asked them if we could have examples of what these changes might mean for ordinary folk— how much they would have on retirement if they started saving now. Examples that he could use to explain the budget and generate in the Prime Minister's constituents some of the enthusiasm he felt. I thought they looked at me as if I had asked for dirty pictures—the Treasury did feel like the headquarters of some nonconformist sect—but we got the examples. And then, incredibly, Newspoll had our Prime Minister ahead of Howard.

People talk about the 'political landscape', but it changes too quickly and unpredictably to be a landscape. It changed before our eyes and often for no apparent reason. Every time you looked it was different. One small cloud would change the colour. An event beyond the horizon, or too deep to comprehend, changed the mood from benign to belligerent in a flash. You would look back on a week or a month and wonder where the change began, but there was no saying. The experts would say they saw it coming, but they had to say it if they were to remain experts. The truth was no-one really knew. It was not a landscape so much as a seascape. That might also help explain why one minute politics seemed huge, like the source of all life itself; and a moment later a sad, puny, unarguable reminder of Nietzsche's observation that 'The living are only a species of the dead.' It might also be why Caligula rode his horse into the waves and commanded Neptune to obey him. Politics was like the sea, though it also looked very like one of those television weather charts that show fronts swirling across the continent at a million times their real speed.

I had become a de facto member of the same nameless party of the disaffected whose members choked the fax machine and sent more complaining letters and phone calls than the Prime Minister's Office could ever answer. If not quite one of them, a projection of their mindset. Knowing what anybody who was familiar with ordinary life would know, and now also what scope one has for rectifying things in government, how could anyone not be as frustrated as they were? When I looked at the Prime Minister I think I imagined that what I needed from him was precisely what they needed. This extraordinary conceit was only reinforced when, staring back, he told me his problems, how hard his life was, and how little appreciation one got for effort in this country. Like all the other disaffected, I wanted a prime minister who embodied hope and relief, not the same alienation and anxiety I felt myself.

It was a form of fanaticism, there is no denying it; imagining that I knew what the people wanted and that my convictions carried their moral force. It must have been ugly to observe. I wanted to rattle the gates of the public service, the multiculturalists, the femocrats, the economists' conclave and every other orthodoxy and smug petty establishment. I wanted to do this at least as much as I wanted to inflict damage on our opponents. I wanted to make them think, work and obey the people's wishes, for which read mine.

Not that it was ever going to get out of hand. Politics was politics and those who forgot were halfway to the meditation centre. There was always the top of the news to catch or some piece of beard-stroking commentary in the *Bulletin* to ponder. And when one had done that, one would toddle off to write a letter, or rewrite someone else's to the effect that the Prime Minister had noted the writer's concerns and appreciated his or her interest, and took a keen interest in the matter, and so on . . . and if the elector cared to read the policy document enclosed he or she would see that indeed the government was addressing the question—we hoped, with the passage of time, to the elector's satisfaction.

I wanted every front opened. Industry, information technology, innovation, infrastructure. I wanted what Bill Kelty wanted: 'Call it a referendum on ideas,' he told Keating; 'and then pour on the ideas.' A regional development policy built, in part, around deployment of the superannuation funds; a national policy for the environment that people understood, that connected to their interests through employment, communities and local industry, that made the quality of life inseparable from the quality of the environment. Like Kelty, I wanted an environment levy at least assayed. I wanted the HECs scheme extended to TAFE colleges as Bruce Chapman said it could be. I wanted a greatly enlarged food industry linked to the regional and environment policies, which Ric Simes now believed was possible. I wanted this nonpareil free-market economy linked to a nonpareil education system and civic culture. Much more than a republic I wanted these things.

With Bill Kelty I wanted to go through every region and work out with the residents what was wanted and what was feasible and worth doing; and when it got too late to do every region, then I wanted to do it in every marginal seat. Give the candidates the task of working out the four or five most wanted measures in their electorates, and have the Prime Minister say he would attempt to provide them. It would be called pork-barrelling, but then everything the government did in the next twelve months would be called pork-barrelling. If this was pork-barrelling it was also good policy. In five years' time politicians would count the electoral cost of not doing it. Of course, everyone said concerted regional policy would cost too much money. So let the people share in the responsibility. Let them decide what the priorities were. Tell them it would mean taxes or levies or the sale of public assets. Face the people up to it.

CHAPTER 20

Only he has the calling for politics who is sure that he will not crumble when the world from his point of view is too stupid or base for what he wants to offer.

MAX WEBER

F OR ALL ITS virtues, the new, dynamic, deregulated Australian economy did not efface the need for government interventions, real and emblematic. On the contrary, the need for a government presence in society grew in proportion to the degree of public sector retreat in the economy—unless the government was prepared to say that society did not exist and demonstrate the truth of that proposition by letting society rot or wither away. Because no Labor person could own to this proposition, no Labor government could for long act as if it did. When capital fled the regions, government could not escape the task of picking up the pieces. Conversely, where, through deregulation, capital was more easily raised, it was the more necessary to have government planning controls. Jobs lost through tariff cuts and 'productivity' improvements demanded government investments in, at the very least, welfare and education. The new economy required skills which governments in large part were required to provide. The nature of the economy had changed, but the nature of capital had not. Capital still went where there was a promise of profit, and not where there was social or national need. New it was, but in the national economy the victims of natural disasters like droughts were compensated through the same channels as the old—through governments. It provided for the victims of market failure and private enterprise restructuring in exactly the same way—through government. The same new economy required incentives and bonuses to create businesses which could succeed in the new economy. In time it would require bail-outs as well. And increasingly it required politicians to defend and people to accept a number of curious maxims—that, for example, international competitiveness in the new, dynamic economy demanded the highest possible salaries for senior executives and the lowest possible wages for workers.

Even more problematic for politicians was the culture of chronic complaint that the new, dynamic, deregulated economy bequeaths. The new world of private enterprise opportunity sat well only with those who succeeded in it. Those who tried and failed were left as bruised as those who lost jobs, or found themselves working longer hours for no commensurate reward, or saw themselves worse off in relative terms, or depending on direct government allowances. Tariffs had one great political advantage over the social wage: they were invisible to the majority of beneficiaries. In these and other ways deregulation of the economy brought the government into the lives of more people—through family allowances, child care, HECs, unemployment benefits. And an intrinsically cantankerous relationship it was. The more governments affected to evacuate the stage the more they were expected to perform, or perform and evacuate at the same time.

The very principle at the heart of the new economy—unrestrained pursuit of self-interest—nurtured the complaints. The marketplace is hard and fraught, and for every individual who reaps a satisfying material reward for personal risk and effort there are countless souls who don't. Governments can provide compensations for those who fall hardest or who never get off the ground. Much harder to satisfy are those who rise by their own efforts but never manage to fly. When they hear the same politician tell the talkback host that 'it doesn't get any better than this', the words infuriate and never stop ringing in their ears. Recognition for their pains is the very least they expect of governments, and the more help they see go to those who will not help themselves, the more recognition they require. The government must provide it. Who else?

The same new economy stretched the bonds between the people and body politic. Governments sold the public's interest in utilities and institutions symbolic of the nation's collective achievement, pulled away supports from industry and regulations on the private sector, talked for a decade and a half about the economy as if it were the same thing as a society or something of a higher order and promised to make themselves 'smaller'. Civic culture weakened with the institutions which used to be its pillars—the political parties, the trade unions, the extra-political and voluntary groups, the churches. Civic knowledge departed with the culture as education became vocational to meet the market's needs and dumbed down a generation in the process. Mature nationalism of the kind fostered by Paul Keating competed with globalisation, free-market ideology and the narcissistic individualism of the culture that went with it—and with a general sensation of continuous loss.

In the nineties, with hardly a sound, the tide reversed and everyone without the wit to change was swamped. In the words of the American economist Robert Heilbroner, the 1990s witnessed the emergence of an 'often uncomfortable awareness that the economic order of the system is more integrally connected with, and dependent on, the political order than used to be thought the case'. Had they not been in varying degrees still attached to the idea that good governments were in essence managers of the economy, politicians in the nineties should have needed no convincing. The people expected governments to serve them. Whatever the theory had been, successful adoption and management of the new economic order meant enlarged, not reduced, political responsibilities. It meant more political activity, including politics of the old-fashioned kind, not less. Pulling the economic levers would not be enough. It would be necessary to prime the parish pump, perhaps as never before, and compete with the talkback hosts and other species of celebrity for popular affection. Perhaps if Keating had Hawke's (or Nixon's) shameless knack of drawing the people to his own life story, even to his suffering or persecution, it might have helped to take the sting from the people's complaints. But Paul Keating could no more make his unhappiness known to the people than he could renounce the faith or become a professional wrestler. He was the last of the lever pullers. And, in truth, by 1995 no amount of solipsism or self-abasement would have diverted the public from their quarry.

But Keating loved policy, and the thought developed that if his character and style were the wrong sort to satisfy the people he must make policy the proof of his affection for them. We would enter into a dialogue of ideas. By 'ideas' one meant not values or ideology, but notions born of ordinary necessity—for better communities, easier lives, more rewards. For instance, an environment policy which engaged the whole country and melded with its economic potential; education which fed the civic culture and the quality of life as well as the market's needs; the great venture in Asia and with APEC explained as a crusade for the Australian people and their children. By our good works we would recognise the people, and by them they would recognise us. By good works they would see what they could not see in his actions or hear in his language—that he addressed their needs and not his own. And the money? Dialogue with them would help them understand the limits. Engage them—make it *their* money. There were the superannuation funds which were *their* money. And who could say that the people would not pay a levy to save *their* country's environment?

Of course it was fanatical. It fell just short of those poor obsessive people we knew as cranks, who phoned every second day and who we put on 'hands free' and got on with our work while they raved away. They were mad, but it was not hard to see how it had happened.

And it was not hard to see why a prime minister who had devoted such energy to the national project should be cranky when his efforts were belittled, misrepresented, dramatically discounted. The budget addressed the nation's savings problem and through that the current account. Three billion dollars came off expenditure and (the government claimed but not everyone agreed it was real) a surplus was restored. The second half of the promised tax cuts would be paid, but as superannuation. It gave the Prime Minister great satisfaction, and he jumped on the radio to tell Australians what it would mean to this couple now entering the workforce when they were fifty, or to that person who began work a decade ago when he was fifty-five—and more than that, what it would be to the nation's savings in ten years and fifteen years. It would be worth 'trillions'. 'That's a million million,' he would say again and again. 'Fifteen million million.' The budget's superannuation measures not only met the government's obligation to those awaiting the second half of their tax cuts, he said, it met the great challenge of our ageing population and the call they would soon be making on the nation's resources. Linked to Working Nation and the expanded safety net in the freshly designed Accord, the 1995 Budget gave the government the pillars of credible policy— compassionate and creative in meeting its obligations to the marginalised and young, to women and the low paid, and responsible yet also far-sighted in its approach to the economy. The Prime Minister got on the airwaves to add verve to Ralph Willis's decidedly temperate sales pitch. They did well in tandem, and in general the budget bedded down felicitously. But within a week one could tell that in the public mind it had gone like smoke.

So it would be with everything the government did in the last twelve months of its existence. Every initiative was judged an election 'bribe' or 'ploy' or 'gamble'. A $160 million Justice Statement two weeks after the budget adopted most of the recommendations of an Australian Law Reform Commission report that found bias, inefficiency and excessive complexity in the Australian justice system. The new policy established women's legal centres in every State and Territory in an effort to end systemic bias against women; spent $50 million on programs for preventing and mediating family breakdowns; introduced a wide variety of grassroots measures to help people resolve their disputes without recourse to lawyers and the courts. It was almost universally welcomed, even by the Opposition spokesman on consumer affairs. The Prime Minister presented it as a considered, conscientious policy for a more equitable and democratic society. The newspapers had no argument with this assessment, but the *Sydney Morning Herald* began their report, 'In what is seen as an opening shot in the coming federal election campaign . . .' The election was not due until March, but from May the year before nothing the government did was declared at its face value. We waded towards salvation thigh-deep in cynicism and disbelief.

And yet we picked up momentum in May and it was possible to imagine that Keating might yet have the measure of Howard's honeymoon. Our cause was not helped when the Prime Minister called Tim Fischer 'illiterate', and in a press photograph next morning he was standing with his eyelids down, looking like a mongoose after a kill. Tim Fischer was possibly the most popular politician in the country, especially those parts of it Labor needed to win. We were helped by the Liberals' patently calculated overreaction. Downer said the Prime Minister was like Goebbels. Someone else said he was like Goering. These were considerable advances on Bronwyn Bishop's judgment that he was like Ned Kelly—a comparison which was more credible than perhaps she knew, but not necessarily insulting. In his occasional self-destructive rages, his intemperate speech, his radical vision, his Irish loathing of the Establishment and his odd old-world honour, Paul Keating *was* like Ned Kelly. Like Ned he had the Irishman's 'fanatic heart'. I often used to think the psychopathology was alarmingly similar. And why would it be otherwise if he had had the same powerful mother and idealised father, and the older men who taught him the legends of the tribe. Somewhere I read that when he was captured at Glenrowan a doctor observed that the bushranger's body was remarkably clean and well cared for, and I thought at once how the Prime Minister in the same situation would be bound to have his trousers pressed and polish on his shoes. Bishop's comparison was the most astute thing any member of the Opposition ever said about Paul Keating. The insight was disquieting, and I resolved in future to dwell not on his likeness to Kelly, but to Simon Bolivar or an Albanian blood cultist.

The *Financial Review* reported that a Fairfax executive had received an abusive and threatening phone call from the Prime Minister and the national television audience saw him in a radio studio saying that he did not recall the event. Such things constituted an unnecessary nuisance; they burned his energy for assuredly no gain and almost certain detriment. It was impossible to measure how much these sallies cost him, but no doubt those who loathed him loathed him all the more, those who didn't trust him trusted him less, and those who wanted to like and believe in him were discouraged from doing so. In the monthly magazine, *Eureka Street*, Nugget Coombs praised Keating's apparent passion and vision and apparent integrity at least as far as Aboriginal matters were concerned. But Coombs said he was confounded by the Prime Minister's personal style. 'I wish he would still this awful vulgar blackguarding . . . it is so demeaning. I do not know where the balance lies in him.' Who did know just then? On hearing that Malcolm Turnbull planned to publicly accuse the government of squibbing on the republic, the same prime minister declined to phone him because, cooler and more astute than some of his advisers, he reasoned that Turnbull was not the type to plead with. It was true: there was no more reliable source of sober analysis than Paul Keating. For every furious assault and thrust there were a hundred times when he would recommend caution or choose to let a bait drift past.

Late in May on a visit to Tokyo he received an honorary doctorate from Keio University. His acceptance speech stressed the need for 'openness' and urged the Japanese to recognise the truth about the Pacific War in the interests of their leadership aspirations. In speeches of introduction the university leaders praised his statesmanship and expressed their regrets that Japan had no leaders of his substance. The citation specifically referred to his efforts to stage a referendum on a republic, a matter of some satisfaction to the Prime Minister, but an embassy official took it upon himself to tell the university and the press that it was a mistake. Neither this story, nor the content of the speech, nor the impressive official welcome interested the media as much as an Australian food promotion at a swank hotel. Ordered to treat all proceedings as part of an official visit, the Japanese police prevented Australian cameramen from entering the crowded room to report on the Prime Minister's encounter with a prominent chef. There was much pushing and grunting, a sound man achieved a very dramatic effect by banging his microphone on a camera, and next day the pictures ran all over the media in both countries.

The official welcome, however, was extraordinarily warm. Massed schoolchildren waved flags which rustled in the wind outside the Akasaka Palace, a band with white tubas played oompa-pa and Prime Minister Murayama put his arm round Prime Minister Keating's back. At the dinner at his residence Murayama said Japan should and would acknowledge its war crimes. The flamboyant prime minister in waiting, Hashimoto, who arrived late and glistening with hair gel, said Japan should only apologise if it was also acknowledged that her army had gone into those countries to liberate them. Keating spoke off the cuff, again about openness and leadership and the Minister for Construction (who was adamant that Japan must apologise) told me that no Japanese leader ever spoke so well. It was a noisy, warm-hearted, extraordinarily unrestrained and invigorating dinner. Perhaps the explanation lay in some arcane reaches of Japanese culture; it might have been all show, but a lay observer would have more likely concluded that Japan and Australia were each other's best friends in the world.

The Australian people would never reflect on this remarkable possibility, because like so many of Paul Keating's best moments, this had been a private one. In private he was carrying out his mission to persuade the Japanese to lead on the APEC agenda, to 'face them up' to the task and abandon any thoughts of compromising the free-trade goals with special treatment for agriculture. Instead the people read how Australian spies had been gathering intelligence throughout Asia. There was always something. And at the very end the war returned. Back at the Palace when the DFAT people had, as usual, retired by 11 p.m., I completed the revisions to the speech he was to give the next day in the Australian war cemetery in Yokohama. Stirred up, perhaps, by Murayama and the Minister for Construction, I wrote that we 'would never forget the evil that was done to Australians in those prison camps'. I was referring to the victims of Burma, Borneo and Ambon, as well as those whose last days were spent neglected, abused and despised in Japan. At that moment it seemed less than honourable to refer only to their 'suffering', even knowing that as they died, Tokyo was being razed in firestorms and the people of Hiroshima and Nagasaki would very soon suffer the most appalling violence and misery.

At eight the next morning the Prime Minister asked me to come round to his room which was decorated, he said, 'like a Yukon bordello'. He liked the speech but thought 'evil' too strong under the circumstances. Allan Gyngell thought it on the very edge of what was acceptable. I thought they were both right, but too late: the speech had been boxed and the journalists were on their way to the cemetery with copies in their hands. Immediately I imagined the bonhomie of the past four days turned into a horrible Mahathir-like incident. It produced stomach cramps. On his way to the cemetery with the press, Greg Turnbull reported that none of the journalists had mentioned the 'evil' line. And what was wrong with the word? he asked. Hadn't we said much the same before? But not on an official visit, apparently. Not on their soil, on the anniversary of the annihilation of their cities. As we travelled to the cemetery we decided that while the offending sentence could not be dropped, he could add the ameliorating words—'as indeed we will never forget the suffering that was experienced on all sides in that terrible war'. But while we could see the Prime Minister's car ahead of us on the freeway, we could not reach him. I phoned Ambassador Calvert whose balding head we could see in the car in front; saw him answer; saw, I swear, his head turn pink as I told him about 'evil'. It was unconscionable to Ashton. All seemed lost and then our Japanese driver spoke—in perfect English. The gravity of the situation was not lost on him. Somehow, he made contact with the police in the Prime Minister's car. We dictated the new words to the PM as he drove into the cemetery.

It was yet another moving ceremony; Australian eucalypts swayed among the Japanese trees, three sailors fainted in the dank humidity, the Prime Minister's words hung sweetly in the air. The journalists did not seem to think the addition to the text significant. Most of their reports quoted the 'evil'. The *Sydney Morning Herald* thought it justified the headline, 'Keating wants an apology'. And when Bruce Ruxton bellowed about the Japanese, it was simple enough for anyone to see what sort of domestic appetites we had to satisfy. If the Japanese thought it offensive to suggest the evil had all been on one side, even if the suffering was shared, they did not say so.

In the two months from the middle of May the government announced a budget (in surplus with a national savings plan and maternity allowance); a new Accord; the completion of a single-gauge rail link from Brisbane to Perth; a justice statement; a national program for civics education in schools; and, in the House of Representatives on 7 June, the blueprint for an Australian republic.

Inevitably, the preparation of the Prime Minister's speech on the republic came with a certain amount of discord: not over the detail of policy but over the politics of it. Between the Prime Minister, cabinet and the department it was agreed that the model should be the minimalist one: the head of state, to be called the president, should be elected by a two-thirds majority of both Houses in a joint sitting and subject to censure or removal by the same procedure; the president must be an Australian, but serving politicians and people who had served in parliaments within the previous five years should be excluded from nomination; the name Commonwealth of Australia should be retained; the president should perform the same duties and exercise all the constitutional powers currently vested in the governor-general and, like the governor-general, be required to act in accordance with ministerial advice; the reserve powers of the governor-general should continue with the president and they should not be 'codified'.

Understandably, the Prime Minister wanted to have a hand in the writing of the speech and some of it was the product of a conversation I taped at the Lodge. Through all the deliberations, codification of the reserve powers and the method of electing the president were the two major points of dispute. The Republic Advisory Committee recommended that the powers—to appoint the prime minister; to dismiss the prime minister and the government; and to refuse a prime minister's request to dissolve the Houses of Parliament—be spelt out. As late as 1 June, Malcolm Turnbull wrote on behalf of the Australian Republican Movement (ARM) urging him to the view that the Constitution should be amended so that the 'powers and functions of the Prime Minister and the Head of State are clearly defined'. The people would not accept a president with unspecified powers, he said. Turnbull was at pains to say the republic needed to be got out of the hands of elites, and the education of the public could not be achieved by erudite lectures on the Constitution—it needed to be taken to the people.

Remembering the events of 1975, plenty of others on the republican side were, to say the least, uncomfortable with the idea of a president who had powers to dismiss a democratically elected government and was governed only by convention. However, Keating and the department had already decided that it was not possible to codify the powers in a way that covered 'every possible contingency for the remainder of our history' and they would therefore be potentially justiciable; that this would 'alter the status of the High Court in relation to the Executive and the Parliament' and draw the court into arbitrating political disputes properly left to the electorate. Imperfect though the system was, it was best to transfer the reserve powers from the governor-general to the president unaltered and leave them governed by convention. A repetition of 1975 was best avoided by addressing separately the fundamental cause of it—the Senate's power to deny supply bills.

It followed from the decision not to delimit the reserve powers that the president's authority should not be such as to threaten the balances in the Westminster system. This was why the government took the unpopular view that the president should not be popularly elected—indeed, privately Keating said he preferred the existing monarchical system to a republic on the model of popular election. A president whose power derived from general election would nominally have much greater power than the prime minister and cabinet whose powers derive from indirect election. The parliaments, 'the repositories of the diffuse power of Australian democracy', would be threatened by a president in whom were vested both unprecedented powers and the embodiment of the nation. By contrast, election by a two-thirds majority of both Houses with the prospect of removal by the same process, would act as a brake on wilful or inappropriate behaviour by any president and as a counterweight to the powers vested in the position. In addition there was the considerable disincentive of public opprobrium of the kind that confronted Sir John Kerr and accompanied him to the grave after he dismissed the Whitlam Government.

But, however impeccable the reasoning, it was wrapped in a deep political problem. While the people did not want the head of state to be a politician or more than the largely symbolic figure that the governor-general is—and did not like the name 'president' for these reasons—the people also did not want to be left out of the process of election. Before Keating delivered his speech to the House the polls showed as many as eight out of ten Australians wanted to elect their head of state. After the speech, in which he carefully explained that popular election would greatly enlarge the head of state's power and proportionately diminish the parliament's, and guarantee that the head of state was a politician, the same number still wanted to elect the president. It was probably a reflection of benighted times in which politicians were not trusted and the political system not understood. Soon it would become fodder for populists, egomaniacs and opportunists whose combined exertions no amount of public education could ever overcome.

The speech, however, was about a model, and the model was for the moment at least to please commonsense and feasibility, not popular prejudice. So there was agreement. It was also agreed that the speech should say that the government proposed to put the question to a referendum in 1997 or 1998, in time for Australia to be a republic by the year of the centenary of Federation, 2001—and that the speech should remind the people that to pass at a referendum any proposal must win a majority of voters in a majority of the States and a majority of voters overall. The most thorough public debate on all issues would occur between the introduction of the Bill and the referendum vote, but in addition the government would undertake to issue materials and organise a program of public awareness well before the campaign got underway. And finally it was agreed that, despite his quite unshakeable belief in the correctness of the model, the Prime Minister should say in his speech that he was putting the government's preferred position, not suggesting it was the 'only position and not open to change'.

What was not so readily resolved was how the Opposition, in particular its stalwart monarchist leader, should be dealt with. The fundamental difference in point of view stemmed from the Prime Minister's belief that his political opponents had from the start done everything they could to sink the republic and so long as Howard led them their position would not change. Pro-republic Liberals would remain in hiding. Howard would play spoiler and every opinion he uttered or measure he proposed would be calculated to serve that end, yet he could escape responsibility to say where he stood. This view was supported by an account of a conversation Howard had with a Sydney journalist two years earlier. The journalist, Alex Mitchell, ran the story in the *Sun-Herald* on 25 June without actually naming Howard. Asked how he would deal with the republican issue, he had said, 'No worries. We can kick the whole thing into touch with a people's convention.' A convention would be a 'perfect talking shop' in which the Liberals could 'bury the issue for as long as we want'. This was the essence of it in Keating's view. An accommodation with Howard was impossible and none should be suggested.

On the other side, Greg Wood, the deputy secretary in the department with principal carriage of the issue, tended to the view that the government should seek as much common ground with the republic's opponents as it could, and offer at least provisional support to the constitutional convention that Howard had recently proposed. Wood, who not long before had been invited to consider becoming the Prime Minister's principal adviser, combined an astute mind with a certain loftiness that soon got under the Prime Minister's skin. That he should, by implication at least, try to instruct Paul Keating in politics was bound to create strife.

The speech was to be given in the evening at 7.30. ABC television would broadcast it live after the news. In mid-morning I was dictating revisions to Nina England, while Greg Wood watched from behind. The Lodge light blinked on the phone and Nina answered. Soon she began typing. Wood and I watched as the words appeared on the screen. By any standards they were inflammatory. They took Howard on directly. I took the phone and told him he couldn't do it; that overt party politics would undermine the prime ministerial authority he needed to carry it through. He was truly furious. He said no public servant would teach him politics, especially Greg Wood. He said other things about Wood. I said to politicise the issue would guarantee the republic was seen as Paul Keating's and that would guarantee the failure of the campaign. I said if he insisted on these words I would walk away now. An argument with Keating left me feeling as one does after a family argument—sick, as if some deadly long-buried toxins had been hawked up. It was the kind of argument that made you want to hit the next person you saw. When the Prime Minister at last relented, and new words were typed in, I wanted to hit Greg Wood.

We agreed, with useful contributions from Gareth Evans,

that he would say while a convention might be part of the consultative process it could not be used to advance decision-making. The constitutional conventions of the 1970s and 1980s had produced very little. Comparisons with the conventions of the 1890s were not valid for the simple reason that the Federation they foreshadowed established the national decision-making processes available to the republic and every other constitutional issue. Those conventions had been held to create a nation and a constitution. We *had* a nation and a constitution. Howard's name would not be mentioned. The tone would be respectful but resolute.

It was not a matter of disrespect for the British monarchy or any other British institution, or a matter of rejecting them. Rather, it was a matter of 'recognition'—that the Australian head of state should 'embody and represent Australia's values and traditions, Australia's experience and aspirations'. It was as much about commonsense as patriotism. Indeed the Australian republic was not 'accompanied by the beat of drums—or chests'. It asserted nothing more than our identity, expressed nothing more than our desire for a head of state who is 'truly one of us'. 'In this decade,' the Prime Minister said, 'we have a chance which few other countries have; in declaring ourselves for an Australian republic, we can give expression to both our best traditions and our current sensibilities and ambitions.' If Australians were drawing up their constitution now, the head of state would be an Australian. Nothing else could be imagined. It would go without saying.

For a party that had not always agreed about the wisdom of promoting a republic, members that night showed extraordinary enthusiasm. They gave the PM a standing ovation when he entered the chamber, and half an hour later rose as one and cheered. They queued to shake his hand and get his signature on copies of the speech. The ABC managed to miss both the entry and the ending, and with it much of the drama. It was a pity because the moment was rare and might have warmed many hearts. There was great elation in the office afterwards, and the press next morning congratulated him for his statesmanlike approach, his shrewdness, his courage, the 'brilliance' of the politics of it. Some wrote as if the game was almost won. With the mainstream media and nearly all the senior commentators behind the republic, Tom Burton said it seemed 'inevitable that community thinking will swing behind Keating'.

Howard's response was feeble and the press said so. It was remarkable that he seemed so unprepared. For several days his angst and confusion were plain. The Prime Minister found the spectacle irresistible and wanted to go on television to finish him off. But, we said, his misery has been created by the statesmanlike spell you cast in delivering the speech and in the universal praise you earned in the newspaper columns. We heard that Ian Sinclair had confessed to interjecting after ten minutes of the speech because he felt it was going down too well. Why give them another story when they are running such a good one now? And then Howard would say something even more inept and the Prime Minister would grab the phone and say he had to go on Lyneham to flush him out. But if you do that, we'd say, he'll ask you what you've got against a 'people's convention' which will only give the idea more publicity and what's more the public will see the politicians fighting and say that Keating has given us a brawl—a plague on him. So he said, okay. Then Beazley said that if the first referendum failed the government would put the question again, and seizing on this crumb, Howard said, see, they'll give it to you again and again and again. It was silly but the press thought it would do for the day. The Prime Minister reckoned he would not have made the same mistake. He got very shirty, and was heard in the office complaining that his staff wouldn't let him go on television. 'I'm the fucking Prime Minister and my fucking staff are telling me what to do!' He rang me in the laundromat saying that he could have knocked Howard over by now. I said the sooner he slid gently from the republic to the economy the better. Don't let them think that it's the most important thing to you because it's certainly not to them, I said.

Who knows what might have happened if this advice had not been followed? Nine months later, with two weeks to go in the election campaign, Hugh Mackay was telling us that victory would go to the side which could find some passion. We could not find any. Had Keating torn into Howard for lacking courage and vision, and Howard had not been able to respond, who can say that he would not have done him mortal damage—and so re-shaped the landscape we might have the republic now. For a moment after the speech in the House it seemed possible that we had a triumph on our hands. When Howard's response in the House was, in Laurie Oakes's words, 'almost entirely devoid of content' and he found himself, also in Oakes's words, 'on the ropes, in desperate political trouble', we might have thought his game was up. But within a week one could feel the cynicism seeping in like acid. Three days later when polls showed the public wanted to be more thoroughly consulted, Howard's lack of a credible response began to be depicted as an astute reading of the public mind. He came up with the promise of a people's convention that would consider a number of options and take the preferred one to a referendum. Oakes called it a 'cop-out'. Nonetheless, when this palpable tactic to defeat the republic was found to correspond with public feeling, it was declared smart politics, 'in-touch' politics, and Keating's protest that no referendum could pass without the support of the government of the day, like his example of leadership, faded on the wind. A 'senior Liberal' was reported to have said the morning after Keating's speech, 'He bet the bank and won.' Like many of his political opponents, the 'senior Liberal' had mistaken a standing ovation on opening night for a hit at the box office.

Our strategy of statesmanlike silence was impeccable in its logic, but achieved nothing. A ferocious assault was madness itself, but it might have headed off the public mood and made Howard's faint-heartedness the issue. Chances are he would have failed and people would now say that this was when Keating lost the republic debate—that he lost it by politicising it. But then he lost it anyway. Our opponents had a cunning, lower middle-class character from Balzac or Dickens; we had an escapee from a novel by Garcia Marquez, a character from Macondo. It was not necessarily in our interests to eliminate from the contest the advantage of surprise this gave us.

You could feel it—not sinking, but not sailing either. We launched the republic and immediately it was becalmed. We were not oblivious to the desire of the public to have a say, and knew that in the end the greatest obstacle would be their determination to elect their head of state (within days we also wished we had used some title other than president). In our defence we could say that Turnbull's committee had consulted with communities all over the continent, a more democratic process than any convention would be. And as for the vote, only education could persuade a majority to recognise that popular election was a threat to the democracy it seemed to assert, and certain to give the people the very result they sought to avoid which was a politician as their president.

In time we came to believe that the 7 June speech should have called for an indicative plebiscite to establish the desire for a republic, and in the process stimulate the enthusiasm and understanding needed to carry a referendum. When the monarchists saw they could not resist the movement, they could hardly side with the advocates of popular election. Howard, who understood the dangers better than most, certainly could not. If not now, while he was waiting to see what political windfall might come his way, later we thought, when the writing is on the wall, he might be driven to say that Australians who wanted a republic should choose the minimalist model. In the meantime we had to assume that the public knew what plebiscites and referendums were, and trust that a way could be found to change or overleap the attitude a Labor candidate found in a Melbourne suburban shopping mall a few days after the Prime Minister's rousing speech in the House: it was being 'rammed down their throats', they said. He was not talking to them about it, not giving them a chance to choose. He 'just wanted to be president'. Howard, the man who said he would 'die a monarchist', had picked up the vibe perfectly.

In May the French Government announced that it was about to test nuclear weapons on Mururoa Atoll, in the South Pacific. The

French said they needed to conduct the tests before signing the Comprehensive Nuclear Test Ban Treaty. It was an unhappy event, but Gareth Evans was not entirely wrong to say as he did in Tokyo soon after the announcement that it could have been worse. Not so wrong in substance—the French might have been intending to conduct the tests without signing the treaty—but a dreadful misreading of the public mood. Indeed it was a response with the same sleepiness about it as the government's reaction to Beddall's woodchip licences. Both sides got it wrong at first. This was because, at first, both sides made rational assessments. The tests were obnoxious (though not by the standards of the major powers in the past) and if they were as harmless as the French said they were, they ought to have conducted them in the Massif Central or some such place much closer to Paris. The decision directly contradicted President Mitterrand's pronouncements the year before. 'No other tests will take place after me because France will not want to offend the whole world,' he said. The volte-face gave every sign of being a bit of Gaullist hubris to shore up Jacques Chirac's political base.

The tests deserved the condemnation they received from countries throughout the Pacific, Latin America, Asia and Europe. For all that, Mururoa is 6000 kilometres from the east coast of Australia. The risks to this country and the nations of the Pacific were not quite as great as the protesters would have had people believe. France had conducted about 140 tests since 1975, and it was not easy to see why the eight announced in June 1995 warranted slashing the tyres on Peugeots and smashing windows in French bakeries and boycotting French restaurants to the point of closing them down, when the others had not provoked such violence. The tests did not constitute an act of war, or the violation of Australia's territorial integrity. And the French would sign the CTBT. It soon became obvious, however, that rational protest would not be enough and only hysteria would do. Alexander Downer noticed and joined in, charging the French with unspeakable acts and Evans and Keating with a loathsome quiescence.

Traipsing around in freezing sleet and mud in Launceston, looking at the railway yards which were to be the site of the town's Musée d'Orsay, as Lance Barnard told me stories about El Alamein and Borneo and the great first weeks of the Whitlam Government when they abolished conscription at a stroke, word came that Howard too had castigated the Prime Minister for failing to mount a sufficiently heroic response. The Prime Minister soon recalled Howard's opposition to the creation of the Pacific Nuclear Free Zone in the 1980s, his less than avid opposition to French testing in those days, and his somewhat accommodating response to the criminal destruction of the Greenpeace vessel *Rainbow Warrior* by the French secret service in 1985. Warm and smiling Launceston ladies served us cups of tea, orange cake and egg and bacon pie, and at the press conference which followed, the Prime Minister declared that John Howard was acting like an 'old tart'.

One had recommended that perhaps he say Downer, the chief sabre rattler, had battleships in his bath—and the Prime Minister did say this, and added that he knew what their names were; they were *Repulse*, *Prince of Wales* and *King George V*. But 'old tart' was all his own. It was hardly the worst insult ever delivered. Nevertheless, within the hour it was running in news bulletins all over the country, and the usual types among the press put on their expressions of disingenuous outrage and clicked their tongues, not because they thought 'tart' offensive, but as if to say, 'Fool! Can't he see that we must call it stupidity? And if he can't, we must punish him the more.' Downer declared that if the British were exploding bombs at Mururoa, Mr Keating would not be so soft on them.

It was true that we were a couple of days too late in getting very angry. It was also true that we could never be angry enough. There were reports of abuse of French residents, French businesses boycotted and vandalised, baguette sales down in Double Bay. Schoolchildren sent letters to the office urging the Prime Minister to stop the French from poisoning Queensland and blowing up the world. 'Recall the ambassador!' the Opposition shouted. The government obliged, but waited an extra week when he was due home on holiday anyway. On learning this the Opposition said it was a Clayton's recall—and it did rather take the sting out of it. Australian foot-stamping and arm-waving would do nothing for the South Pacific countries; giving them a credible voice in Paris might win them sympathy. A South Pacific Forum delegation went to Paris but failed to persuade anyone. I suggested that we put the Australian case in an article for *Le Monde* and on 28 June *Le Monde* ran the Prime Minister's article very prominently. Later some of the Australian (and Asian) papers picked it up.

The article stressed that Australia's protests were not against the French people or the French nation with whom we shared a great deal of history. Nor did they reflect in any way a desire on Australia's part to see the French remove themselves from the Pacific. On the contrary, their presence was greatly valued. It was all the more 'tragic' that after several years of rebuilding her repu-tation in the Pacific the French Government should now shatter it. Australia spoke for the fifteen members of the South Pacific Forum, all of them in 'a profound material and spiritual relation-ship with the Pacific Ocean' and all of them of the view that this was 'an assault upon the rights of small nations by a large one'. The tests were a threat to the Nuclear Non-Proliferation Treaty, and in violation of an undertaking by the nuclear states to practise 'utmost restraint' until the CTBT was signed. In the non-nuclear states the French action raised doubts about the good faith of the nuclear states. It gave comfort to proliferators. And above all, it failed to comprehend what it is to live in the South Pacific. On a map, Sydney or Auckland or Suva may seem a long way from Mururoa. 'But when you live in these places you know that, vast though it is, the South Pacific is one environment and it binds all those who share it.'

A month or so later, the right-wing French newspaper *Le Figaro* editorialised in an open letter to Keating, 'one is aghast at the fetish-like hatred of your government towards us'. But they could see his 'ulterior motives', namely, 'Oceania would be all yours . . . if France was not there to hinder you.' And what was more—indeed it was the substance of the editorial—Australia had committed atrocities against the Aborigines and had no right to lecture France upon colonialism.

Nothing would satisfy the loathing. Caucus seethed. In the House on 19 June Keating read a motion condemning the actions of the French Government. The Opposition supported the motion and then moved amendments. The Prime Minister said the Opposition had been shameless in the affair and raked up Howard's very different utterances in the past. The Opposition defended itself on the reasonable grounds that their position had been determined by the threat of Soviet influence in the Pacific. Still, we thought the Prime Minister must have hurt Howard.

In the end the French withdrew their ambassador and announced retaliatory sanctions, a gratifying sign that they had noticed. After much debate it was agreed that we should send a vessel into the area for the last of the tests. It would not be, as people on both sides had on occasion recommended, a naval vessel. The Prime Minister put it very simply: what happened if the French insisted on turning it around? The only question remaining was who should sail in it. It was not hard to think of names.

It was a curious footnote to the affair that John Major's government did not join with other European countries in condemning the French action. Indeed John Major expressed the view that it was a sovereign matter for the French and if they said they needed to test some weapons then the British Government would accept a decision taken on that advice. In November on a Melbourne radio station the Prime Minister took a swipe at the British position, particularly insofar as it reflected its attitude to Australia and other former colonies in the Pacific. The High Commissioner in London, Neal Blewett, cabled DFAT full of concern and indignation that the PM's comments were unjustified, inaccurate and could cause 'collateral damage' to the relationship. John Bowan took the cable to Keating and later wrote to Blewett that on reading it 'the Prime Minister inquired immediately what had happened to you. He said Stanley Melbourne

Bruce developed similar tendencies but after prolonged exposure to high British cant.' The letter went on to report Keating as saying that if Britain valued its relationship with Australia, or indeed with the other Commonwealth countries of the Pacific, Major would have known their feelings about the French tests, and at least 'cleared the words with us'. Instead he had treated these countries with 'undiluted contempt', and in arguing that France's sovereign status gave it the right to 'violate the territory, the ground, sea and air space of another community' he was putting a case not unlike Saddam Hussein's defence of his country's chemical weapons facilities. The Prime Minister had said he was relieved that Blewett thought the relationship would survive the 'collateral damage' of his remarks, and said he would do 'all that could be done within the bounds of polite diplomacy to express some aggravation at France's arrogant and unjustifiable decision and Britain's reprehensible connivance with it'.

Rarely had the government worked so hard. Perhaps never had the Prime Minister been so disciplined. And in the third week of June Newspoll recorded a 6 per cent fall in his popularity, and Morgan showed the government losing ground. The French tests had done much of the damage, no doubt. We had not expected much improvement and would have been happy to have held our ground. But this was cruel, and crueller still because it would be so much harder to justify and find the will to persist in the idea of conscientious policy-making and calm deliberative leadership.

Brian Howe stepped aside for Kim Beazley. The new Accord, which had been negotiated to a close in May, was announced. I sat with Bill Kelty in the PM's suite while Martin Ferguson and the Prime Minister spoke to the press in the court-yard. With Bruce Chapman I had written a kind of philosophical manifesto, nominating the Accord as a kind of core of the social contract, but the press showed little interest in philosophy and the PM and Ferguson opted for comparisons between the govern-ment's good works and the prospects for wage-earners under a Coalition government. At that moment I dreaded the election. As we watched the press conference on television, I asked Kelty if he still got satisfaction out of these things. 'Not really,' he said. He would rather do a big environment policy, he said. Nine months later, after the election, he believed we had made a big mistake with the Accord: we should have staged a stand-off, made agreement seem beyond the reach of any mortal, and then at the extreme of hopelessness the PM would pluck victory. Through the drama we might have reminded Australians that these Accords were hard-won and valuable, and that only Labor could deliver them. It could have been a little triumph for the Prime Minister. Instead, Accord Mark VIII passed the way of everything else achieved that year—it was just 'clearing the way for the election'.

In step with the government's descent, the economy slowed. The *Financial Review* talked of a recession. We waited anxiously for the next set of figures and went to Singleton's advertising agency. Singleton's had moved to Darling Harbour, on the eighteenth floor of the building which housed the *Sydney Morning Herald*. Labor Party officials could not visit its advertising people without half the *Herald* staff seeing them. Remarkably enough, Greg Turnbull and I did not know this until we found ourselves outside the building. Nor did we know that the former national secretary of the ALP, who was now a partner at Singleton's, would be at the meeting. As we sat at a long table eating designer sandwiches, Hoggy did not say much. Gary Gray said it would be a regional election. The government might pick up seats in Victoria, but Queensland was likely to be horrible and Western Australia no better. Singo said the Prime Minister was absolutely hopeless at pieces 'to camera' and recalled the dreadful day in February 1993 when he was locked in a room with the Union Jack. The people thought he was strong, he said, but did not like his aggression. The Opposition front bench was a weakness to be exploited, but we should not play the man. The forlorn recital of known facts went on for some time, but in the end it was agreed we were better placed than at the same stage last election. In Tasmania, where the reception had been very encouraging, the Prime Minister read about the Singleton's gathering on a plane between Hobart and

Launceston. He read about it because Greg Turnbull and I had been seen passing by the *Herald*'s offices on the way to see Singo. The article said our presence was more evidence that he was 'clearing the way for an early election'. He was seriously displeased, and when we told him that Hoggy had been there he was livid. Get Gary Gray to get him off the case, he fumed. We can't have Hoggy off the case if Singo's on the case, we said—he's a partner. Then get Singo off the case, he said. A likely story, we thought.

He didn't really mean that Singleton should be sacked. If he had, he would not have told Turnbull and me to do it. That was the telling part, not the contract with Singleton which after the 1993 success was bound to be maintained, but the absence of anyone in the office with the authority to negotiate such things. John Bowan, his principal adviser, had scant authority with the Prime Minister and therefore could bring little to the secretariat. The political adviser, Bill Bowtell, had little more influence with him than Bowan and was not trusted at the secretariat. The media adviser, Greg Turnbull, had the Prime Minister's respect, but like me did not carry much weight at the secretariat and none in the caucus. Turnbull was smart enough and probably tough enough to be a head honcho in other prime minister's offices, but to have real clout with Keating a person needed policy expertise as well as political nous. Turnbull did not venture into policy, and the media job gave him little hope of doing so. All manner of tricks and strategies we could manufacture. As often as not we could pull him from the fire; we could get a headline, make things happen. We could be emissary, salesperson, philosopher and assassin, but nine months from the election none of us had a fraction of the authority necessary to move the Australian Labor Party.

I was trudging through soft ground on my father's back hill when the Prime Minister phoned to say he had just had Sir William Deane to the Lodge and Sir William had agreed to leave the High Court and become Governor-General. Sir William had told him there was nothing in their politics or philosophy in which disagreement could be found, he said. He had had Deane in mind for months. He saw him as the 'intellectual leader' of the High Court, knew him to be republican in sympathy, the most ardent of the Mabo judges and a man of compassion and integrity. Keating knew that many people expected him to appoint a woman. Some newspapers had decided it was between Lois O'Donoghue, Justice Elizabeth Evatt and the National Gallery director, Betty Churcher. The Prime Minister knew that Lois O'Donoghue in particular would be disappointed. But he believed that with constitutional debates looming, Deane would be the best person for the job. Better if O'Donoghue were to be the first president of the republic.

Deane's credentials were such that the media was unlikely to press hard on behalf of any other candidate and, sure enough, the announcement made in mid-August met almost universal approval. His first public appearance confirmed the view that Keating had chosen a man of warmth and integrity. Some of the press noted that he would suit the Prime Minister's republican plans, but chose not to hold this against him. That he was a friend of the Prime Minister's brother-in-law, a practising Catholic and briefly in the 1950s a member of the DLP did not enter into the debate. It was nowhere proposed with any force that the appointment was made with a view to the composition of the High Court; that, while welcoming the Mabo judgment, the Prime Minister might have been concerned by some of the assumptions about the court's authority which underlay it.

Keating sent me down to meet Sir William the day before the appointment was announced, and soon after he sent Greg Turnbull to talk to him about the media. The man left an impression of grace. Good Catholics can have that effect on lapsed Protestants. It was also the contrast he provided to the prevailing style: Yarralumla's 'Cliveden-like arrangements', as the Prime Minister called them, the constant demand for travel and expenses, the gladioli and Grange Hermitage gracing planes after vice-regal use of them, the vice-regal letters to the palace that ended in the archaic way, 'I am, Ma'am, your most obedient and humble servant'. Deane said emphatically that his style would be very different. He was 'not interested in social life or cars'. He had no political axe to grind beyond his interests in reconciliation and 'looking after the disadvantaged'. It would be a little too much to say that a half-hour meeting with Deane tended to prove the truth of our rhetoric, and the Governor-General would indeed embody the best in the character and aspirations of the people. But the meeting did encourage the slightly less pious thought that while all governors-general are appointed in a political context and reflect a prime minister's political judgment and needs, some appointments are more political than others and the more political they are the deeper the betrayal of the people and the country.

The Deane phone call was the second one from the PM that day. The first came before Sir William arrived at the Lodge. It concerned the *Sydney Morning Herald*. The *Herald* had treated Keating's republic speech favourably, but in everything else marked itself as an implacable enemy. I was in my mother's kitchen as he described to me the carnage he envisaged for Fairfax. I was glad she couldn't hear. Blood and gore would spatter the country, arms and legs would go everywhere. We would get some on us, but there would be a lot more on them. With the *SMH* perpetually on his heels, Glenn Milne at Channel 7 nightly carrying out his threat of revenge, and Packer now our enemy, the government was not well placed with the media. We heard from a former adviser that he had it from Barron that Keating's time was up with Packer. It was not clear to us if he meant to destroy the government, or roll Keating for Beazley. Just a couple of months earlier we could have phoned Barron and asked him. Someone else told the Prime Minister that Packer had instructed his people at *60 Minutes* to produce a soft profile of Howard. Even if it was not true, it was depressing. In the last week of June the Prime Minister told me that he did not think we could win the election. They wanted a change of government and they would get one.

CHAPTER 21

Polina Andreyevna: Our time is passing
Arkadina: What can we do?

ANTON CHEKHOV, THE SEAGULL

THE CURRENT ACCOUNT blew out and Ralph Willis had to defend the fort. It was the drought. It was the dollar. We should wait for the budget to kick in. The Prime Minister told me that it had a good deal to do with our getting out of the savings habit in the seventies; then spivs wasting all the investment in the eighties, squandering the good conditions, selling out to overseas interests, lacking real export drive. I asked what the Foreign Investment Review Board was good for in these circumstances. He said that he might use it to save Goodman Fielder; that Doug Shears had told him they would buy Pacific Dunlop, but Nestlé and other overseas companies could pay a premium he couldn't match, and with the dollar where it was it didn't feel like a premium to them at all. So didn't that suggest deregulation required some means of protecting Australian business against foreign takeover? And that you couldn't talk seriously about national savings without productive investment of them in Australia? And you couldn't solve the current account problem without lifting the level of locally owned production for export? I did not know the questions, let alone the answers—but then in four years I never found anyone who did. The Coalition had recently nudged the issue of tariffs and the Prime Minister thought this might create an opportunity to beat them up for backsliding. At once I could hear him hectoring them about the Menzies days and industrial archaeology. I said I thought the recent figures could tempt them back to the GST, but he said the GST had nothing to do with the CAD. I had thought there was a relationship, or could be. Was it not alleged that a GST encouraged exports and made economies more efficient? I wondered if it mattered anyway. And a few weeks later, though apparently not for the reason which led me to predict it, they were tempted—which made my foresight all the more astounding, albeit no more likely to be remarked upon.

We had twenty-four hours' notice of the Liberals' little exercise in economic nationalism, because Tony Staley had lunched with an acquaintance of mine and told her that Keating was a clever man but he had failed to protect Australian manufacturing industry in the new deregulated environment. On a plane to Canberra that day I heard three businessmen saying what a dreadful thing the current account deficit was, and how weak Keating had been to send his treasurer out to defend the position. There were times when it was as if one were shadowing the devil and everyone the devil shadowed thought of himself as put upon as Job. The Liberals were spreading stories that the Prime Minister was engaged in a dubious business involving imported clocks. In fact the Prime Minister's interest went no further than clocks that had belonged to Louis XVI and Bonaparte when Emperor. There were not, he said, enough clocks for anyone to have a dubious interest in—not enough clocks and not enough kings, he said. We understood that the Liberals had people looking for dirt on him everywhere, including in Europe: and in the space of six months, three people I knew told me they had been fed the story that the Prime Minister was 'corrupt'. We had no doubt a campaign was running. Then the Liberal Party President went public, telling the West Australian conference that Keating was 'one of Australia's richest men', that he was worth between $5 million and $10 million, the richest Australian prime minister ever, and that alone among Australian prime ministers he had entered politics to make himself rich. But John Howard had 'something that Keating and all his millions will never buy—and that precious something is respect'.

The charges were ludicrous and fantastic and profoundly insulting. In time there would be little doubt remaining that it was a deliberate campaign to destroy his reputation and his prime ministership. Tom Mockridge advised Keating not to rise to Liberal Party bait. What could have been better for the Coalition than a public brawl, with or without a court case, about the Prime Minister's character? Mockridge was right. But it was easier for him to say it than it was for someone who had to work with the Prime Minister every day. He did not see the psychological damage done to Keating and to us when he had no outlet for his rage. At times for a few days following he *was* like Ned Kelly—a man driven mad by bad treatment. He cursed his enemies and all the Establishment and swore oaths of vengeance, mainly of a self-immolating kind. He rang journalists and demanded they go after Staley. He did not go public. His anger was kept within the office as best it could be. But we had seen before how these episodes somehow seeped into the public consciousness, as if the people knew instinctively the moods of their prime minister, and like a long-suffering spouse, were sick of them. In the office the storm would pass as quickly as it set in, but one sensed that in the public mind a little more damage had been done and, even if unconsciously, it was increasingly ruled by something unforgiving.

The media whipped up a frenzy about the deficit, and the Opposition whipped it harder still. The economic commentators, with one or two exceptions, reckoned it was a 'crisis week' for the economy. Would the dollar go through US70 cents? Working Nation was the culprit, some of them said, although some of them had also said that something ought to be done about long-term unemployment and the country's skills base. The fiscal tightening in the Willis budget had been too little too late, they said. US economic experts were reported as saying that the government would have to raise the full-year forecast for the CAD and, quite possibly, interest rates as well. Ross Gittins, on the other hand, pointed out that it was not the first time the CAD had reached 6 per cent of GDP, and while concern was appropriate there was no need for alarm. This was the very opposite of John Howard's intentions, of course—he said the 'economic sunshine' had now been blown away in interest rates and hardship. Ralph Willis said Howard's remark was 'an egregious piece of self-serving nonsense', but everyone believed it was an effective piece. The Prime Minister attacked the markets and the commentators, saying the deficit was a result of 6.5 per cent growth in the previous year, but the growth had 'yielded to policy' and levelled out, and the CAD would level out too. The markets and the commentators had wanted to kill the growth with a mini-budget and more interest rate rises on top of the 2.75 per cent the Reserve Bank had applied, but the government had ignored the hysteria and it would ignore it now. He did not mention those in his own office and department who had agreed with the commentators. There would be no 'voodoo and incantations'. Instead, there would be the existing policy framework: 'lift savings, underpin investment, grow the capital stock with exports and import replacements'. There would be low inflation, underpinned by Accord Mark VIII. 'We are going to govern,' he told them. Bernie Fraser attacked the 'hysteria' on the same grounds, and the Opposition attacked Fraser for what they said was a political intervention.

The economic 'hysteria' lasted a week, then employment rose dramatically, and exports soared and the markets took sudden heart; the dollar shot up to US73.4 cents, and not long after the CAD came down as the Prime Minister had predicted (although no-one remembered he had) and the dollar went beyond US75 cents; a record sixteenth quarter of economic growth was achieved with no sign of a downturn and the Prime Minister and his treasurer declared the boom–bust cycle over. But some of the press said the figures pointed to an early election, and others said they pointed to inflation, and others were reminded by them that unemployment was still 8 per cent or more and the foreign debt was of alarming proportions. And very few people, in the broader scheme of things, knew what to make of it all. Yet it was all part of what political experts call 'noise'. Noise is bad for governments because it prevents them getting their message across. The Keating Government was never without loud 'noise'. It has to be counted among the reasons why the Queensland by-election in mid-July went so badly for Labor. Half the commentators seemed to think it was not Keating and the federal 'noise' he generated, but Wayne Goss's own 'blundering' campaign that brought his government undone. However, when Keating said that he didn't think the result had federal implications he was rounded on for failing to listen and heed the lesson.

'Hysteria' about the economic sky falling ran on the heels of a diplomatic 'fiasco'. The Indonesian government appointed as the new ambassador to Australia General Herman Mantiri, a Christian from Sulawesi. The second-in-command of the Defence Forces, General John Baker, who had engaged in several defence cooperation exercises with Mantiri, was delighted and phoned to congratulate him. But it transpired that General Mantiri had once said that the actions of the Indonesian army in the Dili massacre had been 'proper', and although he also said that he regretted the massacre 'from the bottom of my heart' he would not withdraw his description of the army's action. Suharto was said to take the view that the relationship between the two countries should go further than a remark of General Mantiri's. The appointment of someone of Mantiri's stature was a measure of the importance Suharto now attached to the relationship with Canberra. And Suharto, after all, had dismissed the two most senior generals responsible for East Timor. The embarrassment was not Suharto's, but the Australian Government's, and it was because DFAT had again underestimated (and possibly undervalued) Australian public opinion. It would not have been difficult, surely, to advise Jakarta that Mantiri would cause embarrassment before Mantiri did cause embarrassment. On 6 July in an act which, as Patrick Walter said in the *Australian*, proved the strength of the relationship, Indonesia cancelled Mantiri's appointment.

As so often with challenging economic figures, the current

account deficit seemed to invigorate the Prime Minister. He lunched with the Reserve Bank board and returned in good spirits, even saying that he saw some promise in the recent polls because he thought Labor could pick up the Green and Democrat preferences. At a long meeting in the office he gave his blessing to the innovation statement, to an environment statement and to developing a food industry policy along environmentally sustainable lines. He was almost gung-ho about pulling in the private sector and the regional development authorities, and devising the instrument by which a portion of national savings could be invested in regional infrastructure, and building freight terminals and creating a great export food industry. Ric Simes had become an avid supporter of these plans and we were charged with unlikely hope. In Melbourne I met Steve Vizard who imagined developing Essendon airport as an international film studio. Bill Kelty was also keen on the idea. Kelty believed the Brisbane–Sydney highway should be made a major national project. With much justification he thought it essential to give Simon Crean the regional development portfolio: the two old ACTU campaigners could team up again across the country, and achieve great things in the marginal seats. He continued to push for the kind of environment statement that ordinary people could identify with their own interests and sentiments. This could only sound meaningless to someone who had not dealt with those who regularly spoke for the environment. An ABC *7.30 Report* in mid-July suggested that the national broadcaster had fallen under the spell: bypassing all debate about the position Australia had been taking or could reasonably take, or what the real dangers were, it featured instead Peter Garrett and 500 fans screaming 'Fuck the French!' Garrett was a kind of Trot, Kelty said, always trying to extract more than a fair bargain could contain. On this night, as on one or two others, the ABC seemed to fall into the same category.

Garrett came to a meeting in the Prime Minister's Office, with two people from Greenpeace and a man from the Wayside Chapel. They had an hour, and Garrett was given another forty-five minutes after that. 'World theatrics' was what the people from Greenpeace wanted. 'You must express the anger of the people,' the man from the Wayside Chapel said. The Prime Minister said he believed that it was his major responsibility to do the best thing by the country. All of them, but most particularly Garrett, spoke through their estimation of what public opinion was. The arrogance was blinding, but no other light was shed. Garrett gave every impression of being on the government's side, but there he was on the ABC urging demonstrators to 'Fuck the French' and tell Paul Keating to forget 'diplomatic niceties' and be 'strong' and be 'angry'. It was sick-making. As Sam Lipski pointed out, the French tests had been met with infinitely more outrage than genocide in Bosnia.

To overcome the problem of our initiatives being treated as election ploys of one kind or another and create firmer ground on which to operate, there was a case for announcing that the election would be held next March. The Prime Minister saw the point but did not want to lock himself in. At the same time, we contemplated rolling the innovation, industry, infrastructure, regional development and environment policies into an omnibus national investment policy. If it could be invested with a definitive dimension—something organic and indestructible; not the answer to the nation's problems, but the historic turning point—the Prime Minister might put his mind to it. And if he did that, we would be hard to stop. Nonetheless, we wondered if there was enough energy left in the government, and whether it would not meet too much resistance from those in cabinet and elsewhere, Kim Beazley among them, who had decided that, politically speaking, all these statements were a waste of time. There were some who would object on grounds of free-market purity. Don Russell was not among these, and the thought occurred to me that if we were to do it, we should ask him to come back and lead the project. The idea was not so strange; no stranger than one John Bowan told me a Victorian senator and faction leader had put to him at about the same time: namely, the Victorian left should be given the seat of Lalor in compensation for the loss of the seat of Batman, and the incumbent in Lalor, Barry Jones, should be compensated with the office of governor-general.

Of course it was true that everything the government did was calculated to improve its position for an election. Everything any government does is weighed against that interest—especially in Australia. Introducing Paul Keating at the lunch in Berlin, a German banker said the achievements of the Labor Government were the more remarkable because Australian governments have only three-year terms. No government was ever more conscious of this than Keating's in its last year. There were the things that had to be done, and the things the government wanted to do, and within both categories there were things that would likely do the government harm. It could not be said that the election was the reason for any of them, but nor did they exist independently of the political facts.

And then there were the matters that concerned nothing but the election. In aid of Tony Blair's election strategies, Keating spent a weekend with him on Hayman Island as Rupert Murdoch's guest. He told Murdoch 'firmly' that Labor wanted fair coverage in Brisbane and Adelaide. He also told him that the government could not approve any procedure by which Murdoch divested his media holdings to Ken Cowley and put himself in a position to buy Fairfax.

The Prime Minister was also worried about New South Wales. He did not believe he could win while John Alexander was at the *Sydney Morning Herald*: 'I know you think I'm obsessed,' he said, 'but we can't.' Glenn Milne at Channel 7 was at least as hostile as the *Herald* and the proprietor, Kerry Stokes, was said to have promised that he would do something about it. Stokes, we were told, had made his fortune in an environment created by Labor and he would not fail to help Labor in return. If he did make this promise, no-one noticed any evidence of his keeping it. Nor could anyone say whether John Alexander or Glenn Milne bore any responsibility for what ANOP researchers had discovered among Australian women. It was that little had changed in the past three years: for every one or two who liked Paul Keating three or four positively disliked him, and they disliked him in the same old terms. He was 'arrogant' and 'out of touch'. What was much more dispiriting, most of them believed that the government had broken all its promises. The only glimmer of hope lay in their belief that Howard stood for nothing, and that was small comfort because they also believed he was capable of leading the country.

It was a measure of life in the last year: up at Hayman Island for the Murdoch/Blair gathering, the Prime Minister swam in the sea with a school of minke whales. He described to us how wonderful it had been. Believing that it could only help to reveal his love of the natural world, we suggested he mention it in an interview some time. Just in time, perhaps, we learned that it is an offence to swim with whales and dolphins in the wild. He protested that the whales had joined him, not the other way around. But he never mentioned it in public, and for weeks we hoped that no spiteful green or Liberal had seen him or got wind of it.

He wanted to go to the Press Club and blast Howard who had given the second of his rather vacuous Headland speeches. It seemed wiser to choose environments where he might reveal himself as more in tune with popular feeling and at least give the impression that he was listening. He decided on an interview with Laws, which was never less than hazardous. He rang the night before in good spirits and ready for the fray. I suggested—it was a desperate idea—that he explain his 'get a job' remark by talking about the value of jobs; that, sure it was phrased a little intemperately, but it was also the best advice you could give someone. That was why the government was investing vast amounts, so that young people could get themselves trained and ready for jobs. The gist of it was: Don't boast, reflect. Get on their trajectory, speak as if on their behalf. He woke to find Geoff Kitney in the *Sydney Morning Herald* writing that he had cancelled a cabinet meeting and a tour of Australia to bunker down with colleagues and work out ways to recover from the Queensland by-election. In future, Kitney said, Beazley would be going to Queensland because Keating was so thoroughly on the nose up there. So Keating cancelled Laws because Laws would be all over Kitney's article. He reprimanded Greg Turnbull for speaking to Kitney, but as Turnbull said, the article would have been worse had he not. Kitney had intended to say the government was in a state of panic. The Prime Minister phoned Kitney, told him he worked for an anti-Labor newspaper, that his story was wrong (which it was) and that Australia had enjoyed the best year of governance it had ever had (which was arguable). Kitney replied that he was one of the Prime Minister's few remaining friends in the gallery. How come he was never offered an interview?

That day, while Bruce Chapman and I went to lunch with Sandy Hollway and his colleagues to talk about the industry statement, the Prime Minister lunched at the Ottoman with his friend from Abel's record shop, Ross Gengos. To show the press he would not have them dictate his behaviour, he instructed Turnbull to tell them precisely what he was doing.

The next day I told him what a good meeting it had been with Hollway and his colleagues, and what potential the statement had for reviving the government's standing. He expressed approval of the ideas, and did not even recoil at the suggestion of government assistance for selected new industries. It is possible he wasn't listening. He had a plan for Telstra: to vest it in the people never to be sold, and to charge it with creating a flagship Australian company in South-East Asia. As an additional advantage the scheme would deprive the Liberals of the $30 billion they hoped to take to the election. I said that industry policy based on superannuation funds ingeniously applied would complete the Keating story which otherwise unravels with the current account. He did not resist the argument or try to set me straight. I said I had been thinking we ought to ask Don Russell back to help us. He thought we should, for six months, like Jim Baker had for Bush. These policy things are fine, but they won't win an election, he said. We'll only win, he said, by knocking John Howard's lights out.

A few days later, John Howard knocked the Prime Minister's out for a moment by turning up as the special guest of the Collingwood Football Club. The event was widely publicised as an embarrassing slight on the Prime Minister. Whatever lay behind the invitation mattered less than the ingratitude. The incident hurt Keating. Then Howard almost knocked his own lights out when he told a group of schoolchildren that Liberal Party policy was not to export uranium to France (where, small minds might easily infer, it would be used by the evil French people to make bombs to kill people and poison the air). Two hours later Howard told the press that he had made a mistake—it *was* Liberal Party policy to export uranium to France. In the climate of the time we thought it likely that he won points for his frank admission. When the Prime Minister went, at last, to the postponed interview with Laws he intended to say that John Howard was programmed to say the things his audience wanted to hear.

It can be said with certainty that the Prime Minister was not programmed in this way. I woke to hear him on Laws taking talkback calls. Laws had promised a fifteen-minute interview with fifteen minutes of listeners' calls, but he went directly to talkback. Laws would say that the Prime Minister needed to know just how angry and alienated the voters were. Far from telling the voters what they wanted to hear, Keating was telling them the story of the economy. He was talking in that mixture of abstraction and hectoring which in recent times he had shown promise of abandoning. Far from getting on their trajectory, he was resolutely on his own; and far from reflecting, he was claiming and defending. It was a public relations disaster from the first five minutes. The current account seemed to have spooked the whole nation. And then a woman from the country told him how girls in her district were having children just to get the supporting parents' benefit from the government. Was the woman saying that all supporting parents should forgo assistance because a few were taking unfair advantage of it? Should the children be punished? His agitation spilled into his voice and he said, 'What are people going on about?'

Within an hour it was playing on the news. That night the televisions called it a disaster, and the *7.30 Report* followed up with a hard—we thought inaccurate and unfair—item on the current account. It hung around for days: the usual talk of caucus disaffection, a renewed push for Beazley, then it was reported that the member for Kalgoorlie, Graeme Campbell, had told a League of Rights meeting in May that the biggest contribution Paul Keating could make to Australian life would be his own state funeral. In August he said he would not apologise. Campbell's timing could not have been worse. The Prime Minister was about to clobber Howard for his failure to engage in the problems of the Liberal Party in Western Australia. Now journalists were writing that Keating should show the Liberals what discipline meant and disendorse the redneck from Kalgoorlie.

At no time through the winter of 1995 was it certain that Paul Keating would lead the government into the election. Late in July he came out of a cabinet meeting to tell us, as if to allay contrary indications, that he was on for the fight until March and for at least a year after that, six if he began to feel better. Yet we had many conversations in the same period when he talked of giving it away, and he had the same discussion with many others including Kelty, Ryan, Mockridge and Russell. They all had the same view: he should make up his mind to give it all he had, or resign from the job at once. This uncertainty did not have reality at its core. Never did we actually think he would resign or, for that matter, that he could not win—but there were times when one murmured that he should and couldn't. Talk of resignation and defeat was the currency of his emotional extremes: and of mine for that matter, and I dare say some others who had to live with them. Early in August I told Tom Mockridge that I thought I should go and the Prime Minister should employ Christine Wallace in my place. I felt half unhinged. I had his ear, his confidence and trust, but I could not make a difference to the political chaos which surrounded him. The idea of resigning seems better now than it did then. It might have changed the mix. He said after the election that he had always seen me as 'the spit in the crucible', and it was worth putting up with my hissing and expectorating for the creative spark that went with it. I think if he had offered this analysis six or nine months earlier I really might have gone—not because I objected to the metaphor but because it meant I had been categorised, which was halfway to being taken for granted. I was a firecracker. Not a rock for throwing in the pond, but one already thrown, part of the aquatic environment. It had all grown familiar and predictable. But the natural balance was wrong—he was getting from me what he thought he needed, not what I thought he needed.

We could not get into stride for even twenty-four hours, we tripped ourselves or were tripped by events, or by galling indecision. Should we take France to the International Court of Justice? The Attorney-General's Department and the DFAT people said we did not have a case. Gough Whitlam, whom I had never met, rang me and said tell Keating to take no notice of those bastards at A-G's. He also said tell him not to use Latinisms; if you haven't got Latin you should never use Latin; Snedden used Latin and it was laughable. Keating, if I recall rightly, had recently mispronounced vice versa. Keating was brighter than most people in my cabinet, Whitlam said, and probably saw a lot of us as intellectual snobs. I said that might have been why he took to economics so keenly; it was something you lot didn't have. Whitlam said that might be true. In subsequent conversations he began by saying that I was to tell him if he rambled on like an old bore. I should just hang up. I never did, of course. How could I? The things he said fed me for weeks. Bob Ellicott, of all people, had given him the opinion of an international lawyer who believed we did have a case against the French. I could not see that it mattered much whether we had a case or not. We had to take them to court, any court. And if we absolutely could not go to the Court of Justice, we had to let the public know why not. The departmental brief, concerning a matter about which their minds were firmly made up, took days to assemble. In the end we supported New Zealand's case. Why there was more than a minute's hesitation I do not know.

But then everything took longer than it needed to. A large private agency had been contracted by the department to devise advertising for the jewel in the government's crown and the key to its salvation—the new superannuation policy. The document the agency produced was to be distributed to every household in the country. It was all but unreadable. It was profoundly bad. We corrected and rewrote it in the office but it did not become what it should have been. Political carriage of the package had been given to a parliamentary secretary. When the advertising was prepared for release, incredibly, he was overseas.

The day after the Laws interview I phoned Don Russell and told him that the Prime Minister needed him. He said he had just two questions. Did the PM really want him back? And was his heart set on winning? I said the answer to both was 'yes', with predictable reservations attached to the second. The current account was killing us, ripping up the story of reform which was, after all, Don Russell's story too. The coming productivity state-ment, which was partly an attempt to put the story back together, would be better for his leadership. I said that from time to time the Prime Minister remarked that Don must be irked by our succeeding so well without him, but he felt a great need for him now. Dr Russell laughed the laugh of a man who knows he is indispensable. It was flattery I offered him, but flattery of a heart-felt kind. Within moments of his answering the phone, I knew he would come back, and not because he knew this offer came with another one in the shape of the Reserve Bank. Not everyone saw it my way, and for genuine and not so genuine reasons some people opposed the idea; but Russell not only had the best and most supple economic brain at the government's disposal, he also had, like no-one else, Paul Keating's trust. He would give him, I thought, a sense of security that none of the rest of us could. If only by reason of his own example of devotion he might inspire discipline. And it *was* an act of devotion. There was nobility in what Russell did.

To try to stem the flow against us and disprove the univer-sal belief that the Prime Minister was out of touch, he flew up to Roma to give a speech to the Queensland grain growers. He would not countenance the explicit reference to the Laws inter-view I had included, demanded one less acknowledgment of the perception that he was out of touch, and when he got to Roma he asked that public recognition of our political problem be diluted still more. But more remained than he had ever accepted before, and afterward Bob Collins, Michael Lee and a couple of others phoned to say it was a triumph. The Queensland media gave it extensive coverage. Jim Middleton also phoned to say it was a good speech, but what a pity there was no Canberra media crew there. I assured him it was not to spite them, but he might not have been convinced. The real reason was to enable him to fly unnoticed to a semi-secret meeting at Port Douglas with Do Muoi who the Liberals had, for fairly cheap political reasons, made a point of snubbing. It was a pity: had the press or any demonstrators gone there they would have seen a scion of the old Groupers and the most powerful communist leader in the world riding among the palm trees in a golf buggy.

I flew back to Melbourne on 4 August thinking, like everyone else who knew of the case, that in an hour or two Carmen Lawrence would offer her resignation to the Prime Minister. Urged to come to Canberra by Keating, Beazley and John Dawkins, when Lawrence made the move she brought the expectation of great things: she would be a formidable political partner for Keating in the pursuit of the women's vote, a more than credible cabinet minister, and in time a possible prime minister. It all went according to plan until in April 1995 one of her former cabinet colleagues, Keith Wilson, contradicted the account Lawrence, as Premier, had given State parliament about certain events in 1992. In November that year a petition in the name of Brian Easton had been filed in the Legislative Council by a Labor backbencher, John Halden. The petition claimed that Easton's ex-wife, Penny Easton, had perjured herself in the Family Court during their divorce settlement, and also that Penny Easton had been provided with confidential documents by the leader of the Opposition, Richard Court. Four days after the petition was filed Penny Easton killed herself. Lawrence had told the Western Australian parliament she knew nothing about the petition until it was tabled. Wilson claimed she knew of it long before, that it had been discussed at a cabinet meeting three days prior to its tabling, and that despite his and other members' warnings and disapproval, she had vigorously urged that the petition be filed—the aim being to embarrass Court and divert attention from her own recent embarrassment about a matter of expenses. By 1995 Court was Premier. When Wilson came forward with his new account of these events, Court established a royal commission to 'establish the facts' surrounding the tabling of the petition. The terms of reference given to Kenneth Marks QC called on him to determine whether an inappropriate or improper use of executive power had been exercised in the tabling of the petition, or whether the decision had been motivated by improper considerations.

That the commission was a witch hunt for the purpose of destroying Lawrence and causing major collateral damage to federal Labor was beyond doubt and widely accepted in the press. That it had the additional advantage of distracting attention from the ructions in the WA Liberal Party was equally certain. The Prime Minister would demonstrate this in the parliament, and Marks would concede that his findings would be open to doubt, and the press would say that the royal commission was 'in tatters'. The foundations of the commission were rotten from the start: after all, a parliamentary committee with a non-Labor majority had already found that Halden would have erred had he not tabled the petition, and Lawrence would have been in error had she prevented him from doing it. But the commission was established for the purpose of showing that Lawrence had lied and that is what it succeeded in doing—not only in its final judgment, but long before that, in the broad expanse of the public mind. We expected Carmen Lawrence to resign this night, not because we were convinced that she had lied, but because we thought that by resigning she would be spared a savaging in the coming session of parliament and her political future might be preserved. The government too would benefit from a chance to turn the public's mind from Lawrence's credibility to continuing improvement in the economy and the continuing absence of policy among the Liberals. For all that, it would not be easy. Kim Beazley, we heard, had urged her to stay, and there is little doubt that others had done the same. The defections would come three weeks later. Paul

Keating, we knew, would find it as galling to let her go as she would find it to be driven out in this way. We nevertheless expected Carmen Lawrence to offer and the Prime Minister to reluctantly accept. But Carmen Lawrence did not resign. She offered, but he refused.

I dreamed on a Sunday morning that I was jogging across a bridge on the Yarra River. On a parallel bridge traffic zoomed by. Suddenly my bridge stopped in mid-air. I looked down hundreds of feet to a valley below. And the bridge narrowed—it was no wider than my body. I fell on to my back and gripping the edges tried to pull myself backwards with my hands, pushing with my legs. I was less terrified of falling than of bites from spiders and scorpions each time I gripped the edges of the bridge. When finally I reached safety I found I had somehow picked up various weeds and grasses. A passer-by told me to throw some of them away and from the others make herbal remedies. The meaning seemed obvious.

I went to work with a five-page letter in my briefcase. In it I proposed my resignation. It was not because Nestlé had just bought Pacific Dunlop; though this did confirm—to my simple mind—that Australia was no less a branch office economy than it had always been. It made a farce of the government's posture and rhetoric, and every day on the airwaves this was precisely what people said. The gist of their complaints was less that Paul Keating was out of touch and arrogant; more, that he was hollow. Whatever strength or mystique he once had was gone. It was infuriating for him, of course: the economy continued to grow at a healthy rate without inflation, the government continued to take brave steps at home and abroad. Yet no-one seemed to recognise the dimensions of this achievement. It was infuriating for all of us. In this context, another foreign takeover—approved as always by the FIRB—would have been a poor reason for resigning. My letter was triggered by what I thought was an abysmal political reading of the takeover; a failure to see how it signified the futility of the economic revolution, the barrenness of his rhetoric. It would not show up much in the polls or the party's research, and certainly not among the mainstream commentators, most of whom were too well trained (and to no small extent by Keating) to be seen questioning even one dimension of the economic orthodoxy. But I was certain (and likely wrong) that among the people whose votes would count it was telling proof that the government had no answers any more and Keating had feet of clay. These people interpreted foreign takeovers as the country losing what they had lost themselves—self-sufficiency, respect, the ability to stand on their own two feet . . . All those things which Pauline Hanson would later inchoately recite into the vacuum left by Keating's departure. The fact is the vacuum had begun to form months— even years—before that.

Keating and the Australian people were in gridlock. The people wanted Keating to recognise them. Keating wanted the people to recognise him. They wanted to tell their story. He wanted to tell his. The difference was that the people had time on their side, and they held the gun. Keating might knock out John Howard's lights a dozen times, but it would make no difference if he did not give the people unmistakable evidence that he would make it possible for them to resume control of their lives. There was no promised land any more: if there was a single image we needed, it was of the Prime Minister with his head side by side with a couple of battlers looking down the same imaginary road towards the same imaginary future. It was less what that future might contain than the fact of his looking with them.

It was because he had not engaged with this simple, Lang-like political proposition that I carried a letter of resignation. Before a meeting with Peter Cook and Sandy Hollway, I pleaded. The productivity (innovation, industry—we didn't have a name) statement would be our last big throw of the dice. Better not to do one if all we did with it was draw the Opposition's fire. It had to have mass and effect, it had to signal a turning. It had to concern the super funds, to give the whole superannuation thing some concrete, recognisable, political meaning. And it had to address the matter of foreign takeovers. The Prime Minister agreed, but not passionately. Peter Cook, in that slightly formal manner which trade unionists sometimes have, pitched his case for the statement. There were plenty of ideas, including some about the funds and some about foreign ownership. The Prime Minister listened, but distractedly. He had a heavy cold. At one point he buzzed Guy and asked for his overcoat. 'I'd rather look ridiculous than get crooker than I already am,' he said. The Minister continued. When he had finished, I wondered if the Prime Minister had heard anything he said, but once he got started he was riveting. He had no quibble with anything in Cook's pitch. Some of the ideas had 'weight—real weight'. And we did have to start saving these companies from being picked off. But he thought the answer was probably not in any of Cook's proposals; rather it was deeper, most likely in the tax system. He would tee up a meeting with Willis and Beazley and a couple of Treasury and Finance heavies and they would find the solution. There was no point tinkering on the outside, we would go into the engine room and adjust the timing gear. He gave the Minister the chance to object on the grounds that it meant conceding territory, but the Minister, who always seemed among the most genuine in the cabinet, said he was delighted to have his statement expanded to whatever dimensions the problems required. It was a definitive display of gentlemanly Keating elan. It not only inspired and gratified, but actually moved his listeners—this one, anyway. The letter of resignation stayed in my briefcase for the next eight months, a reminder of the boorish depths to which the job had sunk me.

It was the year of Australia Remembers. Up and down the eastern seaboard, under all manner of trees and tents and awnings the Prime Minister made speeches about the war. On the fiftieth anniversary of VJ Day, as he waited to speak at the memorial in Brisbane with John Howard beside him and 'Digger' James speaking, word came through from Reuters that in Japan Prime Minister Murayama had delivered an apology of unprecedented candour for the 'tremendous damage and suffering' caused by

Japanese 'colonial rule and aggression'. 'In the hope that no such mistake be made in the future,' the statement read, 'I regard, in a spirit of humility, these irrefutable facts of history, and express here once again my feeling of deep remorse and my heartfelt apology.'

Murayama was not the Emperor of course, or the LPD or the Diet, but it was significant; and the significance might be considerably enlarged if the Prime Minister were to mention in the televised speech he was just moments from delivering. Suddenly the war with Japan was again a matter of urgency—and frustration. From the nearby hotel we tried to contact Greg Turnbull at the ceremony, but he had switched his phone off in case it rang during the minute's silence. The police had done the same. One day there would be vibrating phones and we would alter the course of history whenever the opportunity presented itself. We could see our prime minister on the television but could not reach him. The opportunity passed. Paul Keating was able to quote some of Murayama's words at a Brisbane Girls' Grammar school function later that afternoon, and again at an arts affair in the evening. He described it as a 'fairly comprehensive apology' and thought 'most opponents of Japan would be satisfied'. But we knew the chance was lost when he couldn't read it hot off the wire to the television audience and the assembled diggers. The arts people managed to put it all in perspective with their program: directly before the Prime Minister's address they had printed R.A. Simpson's poem, 'Unknown Soldier', which talks about the politicians' speeches being lies.

On that night in Brisbane I visited two friends I had not seen for years. They told me that they liked Keating, even thought that he was the best leader the country had, but they reckoned he had lost touch. They thought he underestimated how much bruising the recession had left and how much nervousness remained. They hated his saying that 'it doesn't get any better than this'. The sentiments of the Redfern speech they shared, but did not think their children should take a back seat to Aboriginal children at school. And with their accountant they had worked out that under the social security system they would not be substantially worse off if one of them stopped working. With three children, government benefits would add up to $533 a week, which was not a great deal less than they had at their disposal working two jobs. They shunned the word as thoroughly as they did the politician who used it, but they could easily understand why large sections of the population responded to Howard's term, 'battlers'. They were not poor, and congenitally disinclined to whinge; they believed, however, that the extra effort they made reaped fewer rewards and gave them no more security than those who did not try as hard. In their view there was now something fundamentally wrong with the society that Labor had created. They were republicans and Labor voters (and had neither time nor inclination to listen to talkback radio), but their perspective had shifted. It was as if the government had ceased to understand the consequences of its actions or the meaning of its words. With a bit of prompting from the media it was hard to see why they and people like them would vote Labor at the next election. Back in Canberra I asked the colleagues if my friends and their accountant were right, and our social wage had begun to reward effort and laziness equally. They accepted that the 'tapers' made it almost impossible to avoid the kind of overlap I had described. Some also said, and I wanted to agree, that given the choice, few people capable of working would choose to live on benefits. This proposition might have been debated all the way to the election, but just then it mattered less than the possibility that a very large number of people felt like my friends did.

A mid-July Newspoll had been encouraging, but not sufficiently so to ward off rumours that our leader's downfall was being plotted. Laurie Oakes's column tended to confirm that something was afoot; then Glenn Milne wrote that the caucus was disgruntled with the Prime Minister: his visit to Bundanon, the land on the Shoalhaven River granted to the Commonwealth by the artist Arthur Boyd, exemplified his failure to appreciate the discontent in the community and hardened the widespread belief that his interests were elitist. It was nonsense—Keating went there to present Boyd with his Australian of the Year Award—but it was in the nature of self-fulfilling prophecy. It would create discontent.

The government was a horse in need of a spell. Carmen Lawrence gave it colic. She had become a permanent national target, not only in the Marks Royal Commission but in the media and the parliament. Indeed the principal political drama in the last half of 1995 concerned the efforts of Carmen Lawrence to dodge the traps set for her, stare down the accusations and abuse and, in the midst of the psychological warfare, credibly maintain her innocence. She did it for the most part with steely calm and intensity. And the more she did this, and the more she returned the Opposition attack with controlled aggression, the more the Prime Minister felt she was a minister who deserved his support and the less caucus was likely to turn concertedly against her. It was a tense, agonising ordeal, not only for Lawrence but for her prime minister, her party and the government.

When she had offered her resignation at the Lodge in the first week of August, Keating had refused it. In the fortnight between then and parliament sitting again the pressure grew for the Prime Minister to sack her. The party secretary, many back-benchers and advisers including some in the PMO grew adamant. One night they gathered in my office, urging that he be urged to push her. When they left I went to see him and urged him not to. He needed no persuading. He would give her a chance to resign but he would not force her. He was not the only one to take this view. Bob McMullan, it was reported, counselled Lawrence to stay and fight. The argument against the commission was persuasive, even conclusive, but the outrage against it could not keep pace with the gathering weight of evidence that the Minister had lied. Each day another colleague came forward and testified that she knew of the petition, that she had urged it to be tabled. Her former deputy premier, Ian Taylor, testified on 21 August that they had argued about the petition in cabinet, that she wanted to use it to discredit Court but that Taylor threatened to resign if she did. More followed after Taylor. And that was the news, not the impropriety of the commission's terms of reference or the questions it raised about the powers of the executive. The columnists began to say, in line with many in Labor's ranks, that the commission was a sham but Lawrence was lying—and even if she was telling the truth she should step down for the sake of the government. After Taylor's testimony Michelle Grattan declared on the front page of the *Age*: 'If there is any honour in politics Carmen Lawrence must quit the cabinet.'

As he prepared for the last two sitting weeks of the budget session, the Prime Minister told Lawrence in a telephone conversation that, if she were so inclined, this was the time to step aside. She could save herself from the parliamentary blood-letting. It was the Neville Wran option: stand down citing the good of the government, and come back when you're cleared of wrongdoing with extra wind in your sails. Lawrence, he told me, sounded a 'bit surprised' at the suggestion. She did not ring him back that weekend, and Monday's headlines said she wouldn't be quitting. He rang me three times over that weekend, worried. He said she was a bit 'wilful'. But he would not push her. He did not want to disown the person he had urged to make the move to Canberra; or give the Coalition a prize scalp, and one they did not deserve; or create a vacancy in the cabinet which he might have to fill with an incompetent woman; and no-one could say for certain that Lawrence's exit would not be taken badly in the electorate, as weakness on his part or as abandoning a woman who had been scandalously treated. He prepared to defend her while hoping like everyone else that he would not have to. And if it had to be done he would do it properly: who knows, if he saved the Minister from the Opposition—if he beat them in the contest for her scalp— some good might flow the government's way or some ill the Opposition's. The Minister stayed. On the Canberra plane on the Monday of the new sitting week I sat behind Peter Reith snorting sachets of menthol for his sinuses, and Peter Costello as ever spouting noisily, like a couple of crows on their way to a carcass.

The Prime Minister spoke at the Press Club in what was essentially an effort to right the ship by reminding the gallery that, whatever the imperfections of its politics, this was a good government providing strong and conscientious leadership. He reprised some of the themes from Roma, stressed the virtues of policy and promised plenty of it, reminded the country that the changes had to keep coming—and did not mention John Howard once. It was a speech to build a platform for political recovery. It was also difficult to write, another sign that it might be beyond us to make people believe the answers to their problems lay with a government in its thirteenth year. There seemed to be no words they hadn't heard before; and, with Howard making himself such a small target, no means of creating that world of black and white which generates passion in politics. From this point on, we always felt an enervating lack of oxygen, as if the airlessness of that rabbit warren of an office was becoming a metaphor for political extinction. It was around this time that Gerard Henderson wrote about the way the media's passion for Keating had turned to poison. And many in the gallery, he claimed, now felt guilty about their past treatment of Howard and wanted to make amends. It rang decidedly true. Nothing in a political culture exists independently of anything else: if the media mark the government down to the point of writing off its chances, old supports become unstable, nothing is reliable and with each new sign of isolation the government is marked down further. It was not only Graeme Campbell: in August Bob Carr decided to break his six-month-old election promise to lift the tolls on Sydney's freeways. Keating thought this would hurt the federal government badly and there is no doubt it did. It would not be the only damage Carr did to Keating, and he would not be the only Labor figure to do it. And yet the more exhausting factor was the electorate's refusal to respond to the old economic stimuli—670,000 new jobs since the last election, far in excess of predictions; continuous growth with low inflation. But no votes. It was the voteless recovery.

The Prime Minister explained it to the *Financial Review*: house prices won't be rising at 10 per cent a year, or wages at 8 per cent, but the future will be more secure and living standards will improve. It felt better when you explained it. But you felt the stars were in some weird conjunction, that they had contrived to make it seem that Howard knew something when he said the times would suit him. Late in August the *Sydney Morning Herald* detailed his policy U-turns—from supporter of the GST to saying there would be no GST; he had reversed on Asian immigration, Medicare, the Native Title Act and Land Fund; dropped his higher education voucher system; agreed to a wages safety net and the right of workers to stay on awards; he agreed to hold a referendum on the republic, said he would not slash the public service, became an opponent of French nuclear testing. His Liberal colleague Nick Greiner attacked him for 'gutless policies' and the Prime Minister jumped in behind him saying he was trying to slide under the electoral wire—he was, and he could be seen; and he knew he was and he knew he could be seen! And still they said they'd vote for him. And still one could not help feeling that the media coverage contained the message that this was not gutless or duplicitous, but clever politics.

With a combined strategy of policy virtue and knocking Howard's lights out he went to the Press Club. That morning he had decided an effective defence of his Minister for Human Services and Health demanded that he turn the afternoon's Question Time into a censure motion on Howard. He arrived at the Press Club breathing fire because some colleagues were sceptical (not to say aghast) about the tactic. Advisers were instructed not to listen to them. He buried the rage while he delivered the speech and answered the gallery's questions. Then he returned to the House to slay the dragon of Carmen's accusers. His censure motion charged John Howard and the Liberal Party with being a party to the West Australian Government's politically inspired royal commission, a kangaroo court which aimed to destroy Lawrence by effectively blaming her for the suicide of Penny Easton. The Opposition claimed the commission was appointed to investigate the truth, including the truth or falsity of the Minister's remarks about her role in the affair. The Prime Minister said the terms of reference were 'narrow and corruptly defined' to exclude investigation of others who might be culpable. He cited the frustration of Roger Gyles, Lawrence's counsel, who had been told by the commissioner what he was not investigating but had been given no clear idea of what he was investigating. 'What Mr Gyles has sought is what the Commissioner is investigating, and the Commissioner has made it quite clear he does not know.' The Opposition objected violently that the matters were sub judice, to which the Prime Minister replied that the commissioner was not a judge but a deputy of the executive, and deserved no more respect than any other 'cat's paw' of the premier. These matters had been canvassed elsewhere: 'What is the Opposition arguing,' asked the Prime Minister, 'that the *Sydney Morning Herald* can comment but not the Parliament?' When pushed, the Speaker appeared to rule in the Prime Minister's favour. In the heat of it all the PM tossed a piece of paper in the direction of his opponent and the Opposition demanded that he be removed from the chamber as Peter Costello had been for an identical action a few days before. Hopelessly compromised, during a division on the matter the Speaker wrote a letter of resignation to the Governor-General. Only the calming intervention of the former Speaker, Leo McLeay, and something in the form of an apology from the Prime Minister saved the government from a Whitlamesque disaster.

The Prime Minister quoted remarks made publicly by three members opposite, Wilson Tuckey, Bronwyn Bishop and Michael Wooldridge, which admitted only one interpretation—namely that Carmen Lawrence was in some measure responsible for the suicide of Penny Easton. That it was a tactic of the Liberal Party seemed beyond doubt when the normally moderate Wooldridge added his opinion to that of the notoriously immoderate pair who preceded him in the charge. 'I don't think you could say Carmen Lawrence killed Penny Easton,' he told a doorstop interview, 'but I think you can say that if she had exercised proper judgment Penny Easton might still be alive today.' Tabling the petition might have been the 'trigger', he said. At the Press Club and later in the House the Prime Minister said that the Liberal Party had put 'Carmen Lawrence on trial for the suicide of Penny Easton'. But in the House the Liberal Party affected outrage and made a huge noise. Many points of order were taken. It was a very ugly afternoon and no-one knew who had won or lost.

Then on the following Monday Glenn Milne had an exclusive in the *Australian*. Milne revealed that Gary Gray and the secretary of the Western Australian branch of the ALP, Mark Nolan, had told Lawrence on the weekend that she should resign. She had refused. Later they watched her on television twice deny that Gray had asked her to resign. The effect of the article was to leave the Prime Minister looking isolated and weak, and the effect of that might have been to make him all the more determined to defend his minister. This he did most spectacularly on the last day of the session, the last day of winter. Determined to read into the parliamentary record a series of remarks that damned the commission, he laboured on in a chaotic chamber for nearly three hours. He said he would keep them there for as long as it took, until they all missed their planes if necessary. He went further than the commission: he referred to Michael Baume's pursuit of his private interests, Staley's scandal-mongering in every airport lounge across the country, Bishop clutching a psychiatry textbook and calling him insane.

The censure motion had been messy, but there was something heroic about Keating's performance on the last day. It was truly like a battlefield, but despite the lack of conviction in his troops, the Prime Minister waded through to what most in the office thought was victory—and a moving victory at that. Among the media, so did Paul Lyneham and Christine Wallace. No-one imagined that it did anything to make people change their minds about him, but it ought to have. And it should have opened the eyes of those who had never seen or imagined the real dimensions of politics. That night he said that he couldn't wait for the campaign to start. 'I am lusting to get after him,' he said. 'It is an absolute lust.'

If it was a victory in the parliament that day, it was not one that brought rewards or gratitude. The Prime Minister would carry a crippled minister for the last six months of the government. He would be politically hobbled by the certain knowledge that in nine out of every ten media appearances he would be asked about Carmen Lawrence. Many media appearances were not made for this reason. The issue of health on which the government should have enjoyed a clear advantage became principally the Lawrence issue. And for every day that Lawrence was the issue we could not make Howard the issue, or any of the uninspiring faces of his shadow cabinet, or any of the good works the government did. It was no surprise when after the election the Liberals said that Lawrence had been a great boost to their fortunes.

The Lawrence episode was a torture in the way a bad performance of *Hamlet* is. It was neither tragedy nor farce, despite the Prime Minister likening the royal commission to *Fawlty Towers*. It corroded the government dreadfully, and no doubt the people's respect for government. No-one can authoritatively say what might have happened had Lawrence stood aside, but while she was there it was not possible to draw focus on the government's achievements and Howard's lack of policy. It was impossible to apply pressure to Howard. Without Lawrence the government even might have built enough momentum to hold the election before Christmas. Yet the enduring interest of the Lawrence affair lies much less in these speculations than in what it suggests about the political culture. The *Australian*'s political editor, Michael Gordon, wrote perhaps the most telling article on 7 September: he pointed out that when the royal commission asked whether Lawrence had a duty 'not to elevate personal or party advantage' over her 'constitutional' obligation to act in the community interest, it set her an 'impossible test'. All politicians, he pointed out, would feel constrained to say that his or her 'constitutional' obligation was the greater. But then all politicians (successful ones at least) must in truth concede that they had in various ways and degrees frequently been less than truthful—that they had exaggerated, misrepresented, dissembled, made promises and failed to keep them, because the adversarial system of politics does not always permit the unvarnished truth. Politics might be an unpleasant world in this regard, but for politicians it is the real world, and for the executive to demand that they answer to the rules of another one is at once an invitation to the kind of folly which the Marks Commission was, and an exercise in the same abuse of executive power as Lawrence was accused of. The fraud at the heart of it was never clearer than when, amid the national joke about Lawrence's faulty memory, Court said he could not remember if he had spoken to John Howard about the commission's terms of reference. Then the commissioner said that his inquiry did not concern the issue of whether Lawrence lied to parliament, but listed instead a dozen other questions about the use of executive power which the law might find improper but which are grist to parliament and get resolved there. It canvassed, for instance, that Lawrence might have been improper in failing to report truthfully the extent of her knowledge outside the parliament, as if in future, politicians might be held to account for not telling the press everything they know.

Court's royal commission exposed the generic distortion of truth in politics, not with the intention of eliminating it but of exploiting it. When the skin was peeled back the whole thing smelt: but only Lawrence's lie to parliament, the one thing that Marks said was not relevant to his commission, was politically relevant. That was where the damage was done—to Lawrence, to Keating, to the government, to the standing of politicians and the parliament. And that was why the media carried so many stories which said in effect that the commission was corrupt but it did not matter because Lawrence had lied to the parliament, which is not so far from saying that drowning a witch is only bad if it turns out she wasn't one. This conclusion sat nicely alongside the one about Keating—that it was very fine of him to stand on a point of immutable principle, but very foolish politically. And why was it foolish politically? Because the media, despite the agonising and insights among its more conscientious members like Gordon, Wallace and Mike Seccombe, were bound to draw that conclusion. The media said: You fool, don't you know where your interests lie? They lie where we say they do. And while we admire your principle and courage, have you not noticed by now that it does not sell newspapers?

It would have been easier to blame the press if I had not felt in almost equal measure that Paul Keating was magnificent in this and that he should have framed his offer to Lawrence in terms that were much harder to refuse. As it happened, principle and his unstoppable instinct to win any fight in which he engaged drew Keating to the battle and kept him there. It was surely not part of his opponents' grand plan, but they must have been delighted to have made so much from so little. It was very faint, but something in Paul Keating's defence of Lawrence echoed Evatt and the Petrov Royal Commission.

Keating's performance on the afternoon of that last day was the more remarkable in view of the events which had occurred in the morning. Bill Kelty, whose mood had grown darker as the year progressed and the gulf between his thinking and the government's grew broader, was determined to prevent the sale of the Australian National Line to P&O. The Prime Minister understood the political reasons for Kelty's position but it was not a position the government could defend. On the morning of 31 August the Prime Minister, flanked by his deputy and Laurie Brereton and senior public servants, met the secretary of the ACTU flanked by his vice-presidents and representatives of the Maritime Union of Australia (MUA) including the national secretary, John Coombs. A stenographer sat behind the Prime Minister taking notes. After a bit of surly to-ing and fro-ing across the very broad table, the Prime Minister, almost imperceptibly at first, wound into a venomous assault on the MUA and, in particular, Coombs. In language that was ripe by any standards he said that whatever agreement was reached, the government knew and the ACTU and Kelty knew, that Coombs would not keep it. And he described Coombs in terms that on the wharves might have invited homicide. Through all this Kelty sat perfectly still with his head down. No-one interrupted or even snorted. The stenographer's pencil kept scratching away. Most remarkable of all was the unblinking Coombs, with the trace of a smile on his face but no sign of anger or embarrassment. When the Prime Minister had finished, and a few throats had been cleared, Kelty spoke. He said, in terms as vivid and visceral as Keating's, that Coombs was a good man, a man to be trusted, and the Prime Minister should not have made the remarks that he did, and he would regret them—the government would pay for them. Soon after we all got up and went to have a cup of tea in the PM's suite. I never found out what happened in the hour or so between the end of morning tea and the Prime Minister's departure to address a luncheon sponsored by the *Economist*. However, that afternoon, while on the television monitor in my office he fought his war with the Coalition over Carmen Lawrence, I helped Kelty and Coombs write out the terms of an agreement between the government and the unions. Coombs did not mention the meeting, but Kelty did. He said Keating shouldn't have said those things about Coombs, and one had the feeling that, whatever seemed to be the case, he wouldn't be forgetting.

An election seemed possible at the beginning of spring. Fearing wage inflation, the Reserve Bank was wobbly on interest rates. It was all Kelty could do to hold them out. The job market was soft. The polls were against us, but they had been worse, and nothing the government did was likely to make them better. And the Prime Minister was frisky and spoiling for a fight. He wanted Don Russell back if he was still prepared to come. I wondered if it was not the worst possible idea, and if I had not been mad to encourage it. He and the Prime Minister would form a united front against the ideas we had been working for in the productivity statement and the environment policy. They would take one look at each other and regress. Even thinking about it made me want to brain them. Just as I wanted to brain the Prime Minister when he refused to make a televised address to the nation on the night before France held the last of its nuclear tests. I could not think of another political leader, I said, who would not have gained from the French tests, but we had actually lost ground. We failed at every step to speak spontaneously for the general feeling and create a realistic and reassuring perspective for it. The more hysterical public opinion was, the more manipulated by Coalition opportunism and empty-headed grandstanding, the more obvious the government's failure to lead. The *Le Monde* article aside, as with so much else, we never seemed to anticipate or understand the public mood, but reacted to it, and no doubt it often seemed reluctantly—as if we would have liked to say, what do you expect us to do, stand on our heads?

But the Prime Minister said it did not feel right and he would not do it. He would risk all in the defence of Carmen Lawrence, but he would not risk speaking to the country about something on which the country was agreed. That night Jacques Chirac attacked the Australian Government for its unreasonable opposition to the tests. How much better then if Australians had been reminded by the Prime Minister of what the Australian Government really believed. Then the people might have shared their outrage with their leader.

And yet there he was a couple of days later sitting down with the tribal elders at the bowling club on Thursday Island and gently encouraging them to put aside ideas of self-government, and seeming perfectly at home with the evening feast of trepang, turtle and dugong. And while he had complained in between about the impossible program his staff were setting, and said he simply wouldn't do it, and had to be talked out of cancelling a visit to Orange—as if the election he fancied holding on 26 October could be won without visiting such places—one had to marvel at his skills, the instant rapport he generated and the empathy he seemed to have with people whose culture and perspective could not be further from his own. He stepped across cultural divides without nervousness or condescension, and gave the impression somehow that he would be as happy living on their side as his. In other countries or in his own, one always knew that the Prime Minister would look at ease and leave the people he met feeling better for knowing him. It was as true of his visits to old men's homes or leagues clubs or country towns as it was of his meetings with the highlanders of New Guinea. He was never fazed by circumstances which preserved an element of truth and spontaneity. It was boredom that he couldn't stand—or the prospect of it which nearly every domestic political expedition contained. That's why he didn't want to go to Orange. He'd genuinely enjoy the company when he got there, but the idea of it sapped his spirit. Boredom was the enemy: you could drop him on a raft in the Orinoco and he'd soon be sipping tea with the natives, but tell him he had to traipse around some shopping mall for the sake of the cameras and his good nature would be replaced by the bad. I think more than anything in life he dreaded the rictus grin. He didn't have one. It might have been because the politician's grin is rictus when politics devours him. Dead men have rictus grins.

Wherever the sentiment was genuine and the stakes substantial Keating was sure-footed and would generally shine. So he was good at counter-punching, reacting to danger. 'My long suit is reply,' he used to say. The adrenalin created the reality. Abroad, where he did not have to pretend that the familiar was new to him, or that trivial matters were substantial, he was at home. Whenever he was on a frontier in the presence of something different, something that really mattered or really could be changed, he felt at home and alive. Once he was in that context, be it Jakarta or the suburbs of Adelaide, so long as it felt genuine, his performance was assured. He was more likely to stumble, and much more likely to resist, when the reality was manufactured as it is in mall crawls, talkback radio, televised parliamentary proceedings, to-camera advertisements, addresses to the nation. When so much of modern politics, and therefore political leadership, depends on manufactured reality, it is true to say that by the time of his prime ministership Paul Keating was in some fundamental ways unsuited to political life.

CHAPTER 22

So the government is unhappy with the people: then let the
government elect a new people.

BERTOLT BRECHT

S UPPORTED BY FOUR upside-down palm trees and bamboo
scaffolding, the platform stood five or six metres above the
ground. He stood up there with the big sculpture on his
head like the monarch of the glen, the black rain clouds billowing behind him. All around the highlanders had gathered to confer
on our prime minister the title of Paramount Chief—that was the
meaning of the five-hornbill headdress—and witness the opening
of a new hospital and other facilities financed by the Australian
Government since the 1992 visit. An Australian resident of
Kokoda sidled up to tell me that this was the first time in ten years
there had been water in the tank next to the shed, and the first
time the WC had functioned. When we had gone it would not
function for another ten years, and the facilities we were now
bestowing on them would fall immediately into similar disrepair.
They were all high on betel, he said, and strolled away with a
desolate smile.

It was drawn to our attention early that hornbills are a
World Heritage endangered species and wearing them on one's
head violated an international covenant. We were therefore
relieved when a day or two before we left for Kokoda assurance

came that the birds in the headdress had died many years before they were declared endangered. We were aware that a great platform had been constructed, but had been led to believe—indeed, *assured*—that the Prime Minister would make his speech on the ground and without the hornbill headdress on his head. It was a cultural question. What signified pre-eminence in the New Guinea Highlands might invite derision in Australia. But there he was, aloft and wearing the headdress and they had given him the microphone. His speech, however, was on the ground. The cameras flashed in the gloomy light. He began to extemporise. A member of the media leant over and said—'I'll bet you're enjoying this.' I wasn't, but the Prime Minister seemed to be. He talked about the bonds forged between Australians and the PNG people during the war, and what the battles at Kokoda meant to Australia, and what the people of PNG meant to us. Margaret Mead could not have looked more at home. When finally he descended from the platform he was smiling happily, the mighty hornbill crown still balanced on his head.

He opened the new hospital, the bushwalkers' guest house, the museum and the airport—the things he had promised on his previous visit. He had come to believe that eco-tourism might be the means of creating an income for the people and conserving the forests of New Guinea. He saw the buildings as a beginning. He was in no hurry to leave, even when it began to rain. That had been another concern, if the rain came the Caribou might not get off the ground and we would have to spend the night there, or drive all the way to Popondetta. The Prime Minister remained unconcerned. At Popondetta, while the staff and press filed into the planes, he made another impromptu speech about not destroying the forests, and they beat their drums in appreciation. And as we flew down to Moresby he pointed out to his three daughters the great scars in the landscape where clearing was underway. I told him that it was possibly not all bad, that I grew up on a patch of cleared forest. He gave me one of his very blank looks.

Paul Keating had spent three days at the South Pacific Forum in Madang, where he felt he had persuaded the PNG and

Solomon Islands leaders to change their minds about logging and the conversion of rainforest to palm oil plantations. No green could have been more passionate about it. At the resort in Madang there were *live* hornbills in the garden outside the window, and each evening I watched the New Zealand Prime Minister, Jim Bolger, walk down the path to his unit carrying his briefcase, like a bank manager going home to his family. It wouldn't have surprised to see him out mowing the lawn in the front. With Annita in Europe, the Prime Minister brought his daughters on the trip and it added greatly to his happiness. They left him in Port Moresby to fly back to Canberra, and he flew on to Bali in search of the prize he had been after for two years.

On the way he said he wanted to tell Suharto that Indonesia should get out of Irian Jaya; that if anything started there it would be his Vietnam. Allan Gyngell said the Indonesians were not interested in PNG and wished they weren't in Irian Jaya. They wished they weren't in East Timor. But they believed they could not leave either place without triggering rebellion throughout the fringes of their population. They had softened the regime and it ended in the Dili massacre. They opened the borders and got riots against newcomers. When the Portuguese walked out of Goa the Indians walked in and hardly a dog barked. But Timor had always been fraught. Gyngell believed that Australia's hands were as tied as Suharto's were. It seemed to be a knot of the kind that afflicts families and neighbours; if it is ever undone it is only by the passage of generations.

The Bali press conference promised to be difficult. East Timor and the appointment of General Mantiri were bound to provoke questions. Whatever the questions and whatever answers the PM gave to them, he needed to speak to the country, not the journalists. Could he not say something like: I think Australians recognise that the national interest is served by a stable and productive relationship with Indonesia, and that is the principal goal in my dealings with President Suharto. I also think Australians care about human rights in Indonesia, so we pursue human rights as part of our agenda. Could he not try to co-opt Australians to his cause?

With Michael Thawley I sat through a meeting with Ali Alatas and other Indonesian officials that was required to run as long as it pleased Keating and Suharto to keep their meeting going in an adjoining room. For want of anyone else on board to make up the numbers, I had been plonked in a foreign pool. I did not know the issues or the protocols of speech. I could not think of a single thing to say and I cannot now recall a single thing that was said by anyone else. I tried to look knowledgeable, but not to the extent that might encourage someone to address me. While Ali Alatas smiled a lot, it became clear after half an hour or so that it was not always a real smile, and I wondered if by returning his smile I had not made myself a toady or a clown in his eyes.

The Prime Minister and Suharto emerged beaming, Gyngell following with his trademark tight-lipped grin. Back in Keating's hotel room he and Gyngell were gleeful—and so was Michael Thawley when Keating told us that at the end of their meeting Suharto had said Indonesia was ready to proceed with a draft security agreement. Negotiations led by General Peter Gration and Allan Gyngell on the Australian side and State Secretary Moerdiono on the Indonesian had been going well until late 1994, when the Indonesians suddenly seemed to lose interest. Now, just as suddenly, it was on again and it seemed possible that the agreement could be signed before the end of the year.

The Prime Minister said Suharto had been razor sharp and very warm. In addition to the treaty, they had at Keating's instigation discussed Indonesian policy on logging rainforests, East Timor and the creation of a 'triangle' comprising Australia, Indonesia and Vietnam as a counterweight to China. Keating told Suharto that East Timor was damaging to Indonesia for several reasons, not the least of them the fact that Indonesia was developing a bad reputation in the world when its general cultural tolerance entitled it to a better one. It was absurd that one of the world's worst colonial powers, the Portuguese who, after 300 years, left East Timor with a 5 per cent literacy rate, were strutting about the globe delivering moral lectures. Suharto as usual had said nothing in reply.

Michael Thawley, whose politics were conservative and who would become John Howard's foreign policy adviser and later ambassador in Washington, admired Keating's skills in foreign policy. Where others had failed, he believed that Keating succeeded with Suharto for the same reason that he was respected by other Asian leaders—because he acted with strength and dignity. No minister in his cabinet and no-one in DFAT could have done it, he said.

The defence pact would remain a secret until it was signed: public discussion, obviously, would mean the end of it, and quite possibly the end of the new relationship. Gyngell and I, and Don Russell when he returned, remained until the announcement the only members of the PMO to know about it.

When he went to the press conference I suggested he say that we had a built a web of relationships with Indonesia and Timor was a tear in it. We had to try to repair the tear, but in doing so we must not pull down the whole web. Just before he went to meet the journalists, he suggested 'fabric' instead of 'web'. I said stick with web—and from that moment until the next day when the newspapers appeared I lived in dread of cartoon images showing East Timor caught in Suharto and Keating's 'web'. When it was suggested on the way back that the Australian people might not see the significance of the agreement with Indonesia and might even resent it, the Prime Minister snarled at their ingratitude in a way which might have been taken to mean that this was a prospect he anticipated.

Perhaps he wanted to punish them. Soon after his return, without telling anyone, Keating went into the House following Question Time and in a personal explanation rebutted the Opposition's patently mischievous allegation that he had asked the Speaker to change the rules to prevent photographers taking pictures of his bald spot. He lashed out at the chief of ACOSS, Robert Fitzgerald, who was as if created to annoy him; and Fitzgerald's lash back made the front pages. It was probably an argument we couldn't win, but having embarked on it we had to try, so we wrote a letter to the newspapers replying to Fitzgerald.

But no doubt by then most of the public were more interested in the Woollahra house, St Kevin's, the PM had bought for about $2 million. Soon after the purchase, Channel 7 featured St Kevin's in a program called *The Extraordinary* which claimed the place was haunted. It was not a house to everyone's taste, nor would everyone have thought it suited Keating's. Why he wanted to live so much in the public view in the heart of Queen Street, Woollahra, was almost as mysterious as why he would create such a story six months or less from an election. But I knew why he did it. It wasn't all wilfulness and defiance. There was love and desperation underlying it as well.

We also knew how much of it was debt. But the public didn't know that—and if Tony Staley did he wasn't saying. With all this and Carmen Lawrence, a keynote address to an agribusiness conference at Orange on 20 September which we hoped would show that he was in touch with the people, wherever they lived, was never going to get much of a run in the media. And by now our efforts in the regions were competing with the Coalition's 'Debt Truck', political casuistry on wheels, travelling the continent to tell the people how much Australia (under Labor) owed the rest of the world.

Keating and Kelty had a meeting: Keating lean in his Zegna suit with the coat buttoned, his patent leather shoes gleaming like his smile because he was with his mate—though his mate told me that morning he hadn't forgotten his behaviour at the ANL meeting and the MUA never would. And Kelty in his fawn jumper stretched tight across his belly, dark fawn trousers on his short legs, one foot cocked on his knee and on it an elastic-sided boot. Kelty did most of the talking: urging the 'referendum on ideas', his regional/marginal seat strategy to commit to the four or five small most wanted projects in the electorates and to larger national projects; offering petrol price cuts in the regional areas; local call charges throughout Tasmania and in extended areas around the capital cities. It was his style to flood his listener's brain. It seemed to make his mate happy, until his mate let him in on the secret of the Indonesia treaty. Kelty said there was not a vote in it. Despite this hiccup it was a jollifying meeting and put the PM in good spirits, although not for a moment did I think he would do half of what Kelty suggested, and he'd need pushing to do any of it. Kelty had not won too many rounds in the three years of the Keating Government, but no-one had more ideas or better ones than he did, and events after the Labor Government fell suggested that no-one had a better grasp of the political reality. A few days later the Prime Minister addressed the ACTU congress. Kelty rang in advance to say that he was going to introduce him as 'Australia's most misunderstood man'. But listening to Kelty even when he was being generous, you could not help feeling that his patience was running out.

The truth was that somewhere in every mind in or around the government lurked either disillusionment or a sense of looming defeat. One could say the election was winnable, one could even believe it—but one could not help thinking about life when it was over. At the end of August we heard that the Liberals had no policies prepared; we could make the productivity statement the centrepiece of the government campaign and build more regional initiatives into it. We might catch Howard out, confirm the view of him as weak and opportunistic. We might sneak through. Keating talked about going on 11 November, Armistice Day, the day Ned Kelly was hanged and John Kerr sacked Gough Whitlam. If we were going to die it would be a great day for it. And then the day passed for calling it and he could not call it later without missing the APEC meeting in Osaka. That was something he would not do. So he resigned himself uneasily to March, which most if not all had long preferred, though now I wish we had encouraged him to follow his more radical instinct to risk six months of prime ministership and wrong-foot Howard in November. Long before the decision was made, the press began saying that the country was in the midst of a 'phoney election', which meant that even less of what the government and the Prime Minister said or did would be taken at face value. His motives creaking noisily, Tim Fischer said the Prime Minister should stop conducting this 'phoney election' and concentrate on APEC.

Yet Howard, whose honeymoon had lasted all year, showed signs of stumbling. His Headland speeches were unconvincing. In an Adelaide speech he said that cutting business costs was the most important issue facing Australia. It had just enough of the old Howard about it, a flavour of the 1980s new right and their zany think tank, the H.R. Nicholls Society, to add zest to the Prime Minister's speech on industrial relations policy to West Australian nurses given the following night. Labor believed West Australia's labour market legislation was a prototype of the federal Coalition's industrial relations policy, and was therefore an opening through which it could launch an attack at the heart of Coalition philosophy. Wages and conditions were the essential supports of families so, Paul Keating said to the nurses, 'next time the Coalition talks about families, ask them about wages'. And the next time they talk about 'battlers', ask them the same question. The West Australian Government was denying nurses access to the federal award, which included two $8 a week safety-net increases. The matter had gone to the IRC, where the federal government was supporting the nurses. Also at stake were overtime rates and penalty rates which formed a substantial part of nurses' incomes. The WA Government said—and Coalition policy echoed it—only those who want to leave the award *will* leave the award. But each year 1.7 million Australians, including 40,000 nurses, started work with a new employer. If the new employer said the job came without penalty and overtime rates, the worker had no choice. Bruce Chapman, who had no peer when it came to crossing the vast gap between data and social experience, provided numerous examples, both real and hypothetical. Keating told the nurses John Howard's speech the night before demonstrated his belief that industrial relations laws should be designed with the overriding purpose of cutting business costs, and that his mind had never got beyond the conceit of nineteenth-century capitalism that workers' wages and conditions were governed best, not by social legislation but by an ethic of responsibility among employers. He also accused him of putting around a myth that wages had fallen under Labor—in fact since 1983 they had risen by 7.2 per cent.

It was, he said, a lie compounded by hypocrisy because John Howard had opposed every wage increase bar one since 1978. To all this the nurses of Western Australia responded warmly.

This was the attack right through to the election—that industrial relations was the ground on which many other battles could be fought, including the crucial battle about Howard himself. Keating told the ACTU Congress that whatever image Howard contrived, he had not changed his fundamental spots. People were beginning to think that Howard was a less reactionary figure than Hewson, that Hewson was an aberration. But 'Hewson was not an aberration. He was a Liberal.' Just like John Howard. Howard had been 'every kind of Liberal it is possible to be—old Right and new Right, Fraserite and Hewsonite, wet and dry, hard and soft, honest by name and rank opportunist by nature. What kind of Liberal John Howard is depends on which way the Liberal Party thinks the wind is blowing.' But 'the man with the airbrushed past' would always be the most reactionary leader the Liberals had ever had. And he would always see the Accord as 'some profane cabal. Some horrid thing.'

And then Howard said that 'essentially' voters at the next election had to decide if it was time for a new team of people to lead Australia into the new century. It did make it easy for the Prime Minister to suggest that John Howard was something less than 'new'. It so happened that on the day when Howard rediscovered his new right rhetoric, the Pope criticised this brand of thinking for the social inequalities it created. On Perth radio the Prime Minister vigorously enlisted His Holiness against his opponent, and he might have done it more vigorously still had not the Protestant and female members of his travelling staff argued that a large majority of Australians were disinclined to acknowledge the Pope's authority.

There were other good reasons for not going early to the polls, but one of them was psychological. Doubts, resentments and fatigue had eroded everyone's conviction. The edge in Kelty's voice; Keating's swings from lethargy to crankiness (with bursts of murderous brilliance in between); even Beazley dragging himself back to Perth that Friday night groaning about the accumulation of political correctness—the signs were everywhere. The miracle sometimes seemed to be that these people maintained any resolve at all. The Opposition ground away at everything but policy. The press seemed intent on the same strategy. The *Australian* on 2 October had a three-month-old poll on the front page announcing that the government would lose; an article by Steketee saying that Keating's attack on Howard for vacillation and weakness was 'in the gutter'; another article by Tingle saying the government had failed to make any substantial policy reforms in the last year; and Milne being what he had been all year. The Opposition escaped judgment entirely, as they did when the owner of the *Australian*, Rupert Murdoch, told the press in Adelaide that the Australian economy was a 'disgrace' and that any economy with such a high level of youth unemployment had to be 'terrible'. The Prime Minister was privately mortified by Murdoch's outburst: this was the man who earlier in the year had described him as one of the world's very few strong leaders. Murdoch's CEO, Ken Cowley, rang him to explain that the remarks had been made at the end of a long day, his boss meant to say that all Western governments required some structural change if they continued to grow at a fraction of the rate of the Asian economies. Cowley assured the Prime Minister that Murdoch would continue to 'play it down the middle'. So the Prime Minister was placatory and put it to the press that 'reactionaries were whispering in [Murdoch's] ears'. Meanwhile, the poet Les Murray described the republic as a project of 'the ugly elite'; it was an assessment to match Murray's denunciations of the Australia Council from which he had received perhaps more government funding than any poet in the country's history. It was the week that O.J. Simpson was found not guilty of murdering his wife. There seemed to be no justice anywhere.

Preparation of the big statement continued, despite the many voices heard to say it was useless or worse. By now, however, its worst critics knew that it could not be abandoned without humiliation. The choice was between a statement of modest dimensions with only modest claims made for it, or creating something on a scale that might prove the government still had energy and ideas and leave Howard needing to bridge a bigger policy gap than he already had. At my regular Thursday night meal with Michael Gordon of the *Age* I thought I made it clear that while the government would continue to be driven by policy, no-one imagined the statement would be big enough to significantly change the political landscape. When Gordon wrote about the thing as if it was intended as a policy king hit, the Prime Minister was displeased and the media office derided my capacities as a spin doctor. There was nowhere to hide.

It was all hunting for advantage. In *Business Review Weekly* on 23 October it was reported that Peter Costello had been talking to conservative State leaders about means for ending what is known to experts as 'vertical fiscal imbalance' and everyone else as an over-reliance on Commonwealth grants. Costello said the aim would be 'to breathe new life into federalism'. Much of the work was being done in secret, the *BRW* reported, but the 'most likely scenario' was giving the States the income taxing powers they had relinquished to the Commonwealth during World War II. Seizing on it like a Rottweiler, the Prime Minister went into Question Time determined to demonstrate that the Coalition planned to 'hollow out the Commonwealth' and introduce a State-based GST. The Coalition, he said, had 'no sense of nation'. Indeed, taken with Howard's Adelaide speech, there were grounds for saying that Fightback had re-emerged. And, in a moment of inspiration, he produced from a drawer of the desk in the chamber the old copy Mark Ryan and I had marked ACME. But the pitch of the debate got too high and the news recorded it as not much more than the two sides hurling accusations at each other.

The Prime Minister got on the phone to Oakes to tell him that he had missed the substance of the story. And he had. Oakes was better the night following, and the Prime Minister invited Tom Burton in for a briefing on the subject. He told Burton that, if necessary, Labor would hold a referendum to 'embed the income tax power exclusively in the Commonwealth'. The existing arrangements allowed the Commonwealth to exert downward pressure on spending; change them as the Coalition proposed and the States would soon be 'tearing away at their own purpose spending' and the Commonwealth would lose control of the national economic policy. The story ran in the *Financial Review* and the PM put the same argument in an article he wrote for the *Daily Telegraph*. It was a promising issue, but we could never get such substance out there for more than a moment. He also told Burton that he had every right—'heaps of prerogatives'—to decide where the superannuation funds directed investment. Where did the right reside, he asked—with the 'founding treasurer' of award superannuation, or the trade unions 'which actually made the commitments', or with these fund managers who consistently failed to support small and medium-sized Australian companies? This was also a good issue. It arose in the course of a noisy argument about the Coles Myer board, in which Bill Kelty had come out in defence of Lindsay Fox's friend Solomon Lew, and the Prime Minister followed suit as a means of defending Kelty. In the course of the debate Keating attacked AMP for marking down the share price of Australian companies like Pacific Dunlop: Pacific Dunlop wanted to diversify, they wanted to create a great Australian food industry, but the funds refused to help them and Pacific Dunlop had to sell its interests out. The fund managers, Keating said, were 'donkeys'.

It would have been comic if it happened to somebody else. The Governor-General, Bill Hayden, addressed the United Nations and took such a leisurely approach that he failed to read the three key paragraphs about the French tests. The French had announced that there would be two fewer tests than they planned. On the Larry King show Chirac said Australia had been 'excessive' in its criticism. The Prime Minister said it showed the government's approach was working. In the International Court of Justice Australia would not only argue that the French tests were illegal but that nuclear weapons were illegal. The Governor-General's UN debacle was followed by attacks in the press on his excessive spending and travel. The PMO kept quiet though there was a good deal that might have been said—the more so when Hayden publicly attacked the Prime Minister's model for a republic.

And the Liberals were busy again with the story that the PM had had a conflict of interest which he had failed to declare to cabinet in 1988: namely, that he was a friend of the developer Warren Anderson, who had profited from a Loan Council decision to allow the Northern Territory to borrow for the purpose of developing the new parliament building with Anderson. Howard demanded a Senate inquiry. The PM was unconcerned about the charge, which had been around for years and had no more truth to it, he said, than the Liberals' other slanders. But he *was* concerned about the prospect of a Senate inquiry running all the way up to an election campaign. It took time to dig out the files with which to persuade the Democrats and anyone else who needed convincing that there was nothing for an inquiry to find. It took his concentration with it, particularly because the story had been resurrected through the *Sydney Morning Herald*—and we were quite certain it had been given directly to the *Herald* by the Liberal Party. In the end Howard did not get his Senate inquiry, but he did get his opponent several days of noisome publicity.

If Geoff Kitney was to be taken seriously, it was the Prime Minister's fault that the press would not run his way. Kitney was one of those who recognised the base motives in the establishment of the Marks Royal Commission but never stopped telling readers that Keating was wrong to defend its victim. On the first day of spring he told them how John Howard had the day before toured the press gallery without his minders, dropping in on journalists unannounced, and compared this with the Prime Minister's 'extraordinary "cut off my nose to spite my face" attitude to the gallery'. If only he would walk about the gallery and be nice to them—on such simple courtesies his political fortunes rested.

Then, presumably, he would get some decent coverage for taking the government through a record sixteen continuous quarters of growth and would not have to prevail on the party

With Annita Keating in
New Zealand, 1993.
Courtesy of Paul Keating

The Prime Minister chats
with Casino residents at the
airport. They told him to
'keep sticking it up them
bastards in Canberra'.
Courtesy of Warren Croser, The
Northern Star, *18 March 1994*

Min and Paul Keating at the commemoration of the Sandakan Monument,
Burwood NSW, 1994. *Courtesy of Paul Keating*

Opening the National Portrait Gallery Exhibition, Canberra, March 1994.
Courtesy of National Library of Australia

Left: The Prime Minister and the Premier, 1995. *Courtesy of Fairfax Photo Library*
Right: Bill Kelty. *Courtesy of Andrew Chapman*

The worker's friend tells them Labor will not go to zero tariffs.
Courtesy of Fairfax Photo Library

With Arthur Boyd, Australian of the Year, Bundanon NSW, 1995.
Courtesy of Kirk Gilmour, Illawarra Mercury

Australian War Memorial,
1995. *Courtesy of Paul Keating*

Welcoming Pope John
Paul II to Sydney, 1995.
*Courtesy of Michael Amendolia,
News Limited.*

Mobbed by schoolgirls, 1996 election. *Courtesy of Lyndon Mechielson, News Limited*

Campaigning, 1996. *Courtesy of Andrew Chapman*

Left: Mary Ann O'Loughlin, Don Russell, Greg Turnbull. *Courtesy of Andrew Chapman*

Below: Don Russell and Don Watson, Cairns, after the Black Hawk incident, 1996. *Courtesy of Andrew Chapman*

Paul Keating in his other natural environment. He made more appearances at the National Press Club than anyone else in the club's history. Clockwise from top left: National Press Club 1994, 1995, 1995 and the last address, 1996.

Courtesy of National Library of Australia

Pointy head observes bleeding heart, Fairbairn, last days of the 1996 campaign.
Courtesy of Andrew Chapman

The office on the day everyone left, 1996. *Courtesy of Paul Keating*

to place full-page advertisements in the newspapers. Then they would give Howard what he deserved for snubbing Do Muoi when he visited in September, and the Prime Minister some credit when Australia became one of the four countries to receive priority treatment in tendering for major projects in Vietnam. If only he would drop in for a cup of tea, they might mention the major mining project worth many billions he opened at McArthur River in the Northern Territory—a project held up for years and now made possible by government initiative, including passage of the Native Title Act. They were good pictures, after all; out there in the heat and dust, Aboriginal men dancing while smiling company executives watched on. And one would have thought it was right in the groove of the current account. If only he had dropped in unannounced on more journalists they might have taken him seriously when he discerned in the *Business Review Weekly* article or Howard's speeches certain unspoken intentions in the Coalition's thinking; and perhaps they may have listened when he said that any judgment of John Howard must rely as substantially as it does with everyone else on his record. They might have seen confirmation of this when, in one of his Headland speeches, John Howard stressed stronger ties between Australia and the US, and gave every indication of reviving old attitudes to Asia and scaling back the effort to engage. One or two might have mentioned it in passing, but the foreshadowed retreat was hardly news, much less reason for comment. If Paul Keating would not come round seeking the gallery's favours, the gallery would not do him any.

The drought broke, the dollar climbed back past US75 cents, growth continued at 3.5 per cent or better, inflation remained low, the Accord was intact. Early in October the *Sydney Morning Herald* reported on 'Keating's Economy—Running Like Clockwork'. Where substance could be found in the Opposition's policy position, the Prime Minister got his teeth into it. When they say they want 'flexibility' in the industrial relations system, he said, read 'pay cuts'. Only a Labor government guaranteed workers pay increases to compensate for conditions lost when they traded in awards. He went to Melbourne to celebrate Jenny George's appointment as the first woman president of the ACTU, and the photos next day recorded his genuine pleasure. He had the unions with him, at least; and he did well at the New South Wales State Conference of the ALP, contrasting his big picture with Howard's little one and declaring the next election a 'referendum on ideas'.

Yet it seemed all but impossible to get our wheels on the tracks and the Prime Minister's mind open to advice on matters that needed resolution. Or did they? Would it matter if the government lost office without delivering an industry or environment statement; without a national taskforce on Aboriginal health; if our initiative with the food industry came to nothing; if the Murray–Darling was left to our successors; and half a dozen other things were left undone? None of them would win an election for us. Nailing Howard would win an election, even if trying to nail him made fools of us sometimes. Phillip Adams wrote that in the end Keating's smiling personality would triumph over Howard's gloomy one.

The Prime Minister had begun talking about nuclear weapons. Ultimately, he said, it was not a matter of controls because ultimately no controls served as a guarantee against their use or proliferation. With the potential supply of fissile material greatly increased by the collapse of the Soviet Union and the technology readily available, other countries were bound to develop nuclear weapons—and actions like those taken by France were sure to encourage them. The Prime Minister said it was pointless to talk about non-proliferation without *de*-proliferation. It was decided that, in case the International Court of Justice decided that a judgment should be made on the legality of nuclear weapons, Gareth Evans should put the case that they were illegal. The main hope, however, was that the court would not make a judgment: declaring them legal was bound to encourage countries wanting nuclear capacity; declaring them illegal was just as likely to be ignored by the nuclear powers and the court's standing would be diminished. The legal nicety pointed to the endemic horror—the weapons themselves. Evans went off to The Hague to argue the case on 30 October, while in Canberra the Prime Minister announced that the government would establish an international commission—the Canberra Commission—to develop 'concrete and realistic steps for achieving a nuclear weapons-free world'. It had been done with chemical weapons, it could be done with the 50,000 nuclear warheads in the world. It was the logical and necessary dividend of the Cold War's conclusion. It was another opportunity for Australia to employ its skills in multilateral diplomacy, the kind that had helped produce the Cambodia peace agreement, APEC, the Chemical Weapons Convention and the Antarctic Wilderness Reserve. When the names of the people comprising the Canberra Commission were announced, the Prime Minister observed that they had not come down in the last shower. The former French prime minister, Michel Rocard; the former chief of US Strategic Forces, General Lee Butler; the former chief of the British Defence Staff; the Nobel Peace Prize winner Joseph Rotblatt; the former US secretary of state Robert McNamara; and the Australian strategic studies expert Robert O'Neill would meet for the first time in January 1996. None of them was likely to lend his time to a hopeless or worthless cause. But Alexander Downer called it a 'stunt'. As the Prime Minister announced it a woman protester was taken away screaming, and that strange Labor MP from south of Sydney, Peter Knott, grabbed most of the news by staging his own demonstration outside the French Embassy.

It was a measure of the uncertainty that well into October no-one knew how to describe the thing—the 'Innovation Statement', the 'Productivity Statement', 'Industry', 'Information'? I preferred to call it 'Community and Nation' and highlight investment in local and national infrastructure, but the word 'community' was still despised. Some of us still held high hopes for a food industry policy. Ric Simes organised a remarkable meeting of potential players. In Parliament House the entrepreneurial capitalists, Richard Pratt, Doug Shears, John David and Roger Fletcher; the CEOs of Kellogg's and TNT; deputies for Don Argus from the

NAB and Reg Clairs from Woolworths; Don Blackmore from the Murray–Darling Basin Commission; Don McGauchie from the NFF; Helen Alexander from Landcare; Bill Kelty; Collins, Cook, Brereton and the PM. The discussion was almost enough to make one believe that an approach to industry policy on this scale—combining transport infrastructure, environmental sustainability, marketing and major regional and rural readjustment programs—might be feasible. Strangely, the people present did not seem to think that in an era of deregulation and globalisation it was necessarily foolish to contemplate a country setting out to create sustainable new industries. They seemed to think that if it was within the limits of a nation's imagination it was probably within its capabilities. There were no signs they thought it a laughable Keynesian conceit, an efflorescence of bleeding heart economic nationalism. Instead they seemed to think it was something worth doing, especially in a country with scarcely a substantial business to call its own and a chronic current account deficit, and with a food market in East Asia set to reach $2000 billion.

Later at the Lodge, Kelty told the Prime Minister that he was trying to organise an Australian—Linfox/BHP—buy-out of the Australian National Line in preference to P&O. He also reminded him that he had behaved badly towards John Coombs at that morning meeting. When Kelty had gone, the Prime Minister played Klemperer conducting Tchaikovsky's Fifth. He was a very unhappy man, less because the politics was proving so gruelling than because he thought his marriage was drying up.

Don Russell changed his mind about returning, and had to be persuaded again. Upon announcing his departure from Washington he made a widely reported speech to his staff about the sense of duty that had guided him. He said he feared that a Coalition government would see some of the inequalities of America replicated in Australia, and some of the best things Labor had done would be undone. Michael Costello, the departmental secretary, reprimanded him for making political statements and the reprimand was leaked to the press, through McMullan's office we heard. This was not helpful and Russell let the culprits know how he felt. Yet it was in keeping with Russell's style: in Washington, the *Sydney Morning Herald* reported, he had ruffled feathers but generally impressed the cognoscenti with his mixture of high intelligence, eccentricity and alarming bluntness. In general, the press response to his return would not have done the government much good, but it was predictable and short-lived. Everyone, including Dr Russell, had doubts about the exercise. Some in the PMO were bound to be unimpressed; in other corners of the government and the party feelings doubtless went beyond that. Having urged the idea and done all I could to persuade him to return, I found myself telling the PM that I would not have him trampling on me or any other adviser. The Prime Minister reminded me that Russell's return also gave him a fair lump to publicly swallow.

Every signal seemed to contradict the others. In a Sydney hotel Eric Walsh told me that ordinary punters hated Keating and rightly so. They would vote him out in a landslide. Keating did an interview with Andrew Denton that the press declared was splendid for revealing the real and likeable side of the Prime Minister. They did not notice, or thought it less important than we feared, that he called the punters 'them' and spent much of the half hour with his arms folded—a terrible look for a politician, according to experts. We had talked about the need for him to convey the message that his actions were driven by his perception of the national interest, and what was good for the people, and that succeeding in this gave him his greatest satisfaction. It was not expressed quite as we hoped, but the public reaction clearly suggested it was a tack worth trying. On the night of recording, Denton told us—sadly—he was sure we would lose the election. Yet the Prime Minister was cheered to the rafters when he spoke to nurses and health workers (ordinary punters, surely) in Perth; and, less surprisingly, to arts people in Melbourne. Despite a dramatic one-night dip in the dollar, rumours of a snap election were still circulating in the first week of November. In the same week a Morgan poll showed a 3.5 per cent improvement for the government, a 3.5 per cent decline for the Opposition. The government trailed by only 3 per cent, yet rumours of the Prime Minister's intention to resign were almost as common as the rumours of a pre-Christmas election.

The Israeli Prime Minister, Yitzhak Rabin, was assassinated and the Prime Minister flew to Jerusalem for the funeral. Even on this most brief and solemn foray abroad, political trouble accompanied him. Howard had phoned before he left, requesting a seat on the plane. Keating had refused: he rang me, saying that he knew Howard would make capital out of his refusal. But refuse he must. He simply could not bear the prospect of a forty-eight hour journey with his rival; the boredom of it was unthinkable. So Allan Gyngell told Howard's office there was no room on the plane, and the press were told that the Prime Minister alone would represent Australia. As predicted, Howard made great play with the apparent pettiness and partisanship of it and the funeral of Yitzhak Rabin went badly for us.

From Jerusalem the PM reported that the city was wonderful. He had been around the different quarters and followed the Via Dolorosa. 'You know you can see where Christ walked on the way to the Crucifixion,' he said. I wished I had gone. 'But I think that little bastard's done us some damage,' he said. 'Ignore him,' I said, not wanting politics to spoil any miracles the Holy Land might work. 'I'm not going to ignore him,' he said. 'I'm going to drive an axe into his chest and lever his ribs apart,' he said.

Bill Kelty had new, bigger ideas. Like the rest of us he was worried that a statement of modest dimensions might signal exhaustion, and open the way for the Opposition to say that the government no longer had the will or the imagination to tackle difficult problems. Don Russell and I sat with Kelty and Jenny George in the little recently refurbished lounge of ACTU House with its window onto Swanston Street and the walls of RMIT. Sitting together on the ACTU's new couch, Kelty's corduroy covered legs barely touched the ground; Russell's knees, wrapped in charcoal

Boss trousers, almost touched his chin. Great friends they were, but they looked like creatures from two different planets. Kelty wanted to abolish the banks: put another way, he wanted to extend banking facilities to the super funds. It was the way things were going anyway, he said, but the government should be the first in the world to announce it. He also wanted to guarantee that no financial institution had more than 15 per cent of the market. His second big idea was a second board of the stock exchange for SMEs—small and medium-sized enterprises. His third idea was an environment policy built on a voluntary levy. His fourth was a national infrastructure bond at around 8.5 per cent. The government would say it could not stand back and watch Australians paying 17–18 per cent for their roads. Russell, who liked the last idea, said it would amount to the Commonwealth resuming responsibility for transport infrastructure which had been relinquished to the States in the 1980s. Politically, it allowed for the Commonwealth to ride to the rescue of the people of New South Wales and Victoria as they faced the prospect of punitive tolls. It would enable the government to occupy the increasingly fertile anti-privatisation ground. And it would demonstrate the value, not to say the meaning, of superannuation to the nation and the people. Russell agreed to follow up the idea and he did.

But doubt subverted our will. What if the people saw it as Keating up to something again? What if they resented his muscling in on a government they had elected and policies they had implicitly approved? Would they believe that a champion of privatisation now wanted roads built in the old-fashioned way? If Kennett or Carr staged a brawl, could we win it? Was it too radical? If the pollsters were right and the people were as tired of change as they were of Keating, was it wise to offer more of both? Wasn't it smarter to stand on the record, play the unsinkable ship of state—and take at least a sidelong glance into suggestions of corruption in the Kennett Government? The last seemed reasonable if only to balance the rumours that the Liberals were spreading about Keating. Peter Abeles had told Kelty the Liberals were running a dirty tricks campaign. A journalist had phoned him to ask if he paid for a Kelty family holiday in Switzerland. He hadn't. Which was safer in the circumstances—counter-attack or cool disdain, the gutter or the high moral ground? Abeles also told Kelty that he had seen Bob Hawke recently and had been shocked by his hatred of Keating. It was true we could never entirely relax with Hawke. He declared that in discussions about the war in Kuwait Keating had questioned the wisdom of joining in with the Americans, remarking, 'What have the Americans ever done for us?' And we had no peace until I had run to ground the happily retired John Button and begged and cajoled him, as one last contribution to the government, to confess the heresy had been his not Keating's.

People were always telling Paul Keating to take the moral high ground. Towards the end of 1995 he was on his way to Question Time when one of his advisers said, 'Keep to the moral high ground.' One could tell instantly it was bad timing. He said, 'Yes, but it's not the ground I prefer to be on. I like the moral low ground.' In the hope that it might help prevent a practical demonstration of his point, I said, 'The high ground suits you, actually. You look good on it.' It was so easy to tell him to keep the high ground, or to be 'prime ministerial', or 'statesmanlike'. He held a doorstop when he came back from Jerusalem, and instead of talking about peace in the Middle East and the tragedy of Rabin's death, he immediately raised the matter of Howard's 'sleights of hand' on industrial relations and superannuation while he had been away. As one journalist pointed out, he had given up the high ground for the low. But that is the turf on which politicians fight—and journalists as well, of course. Keating would talk sometimes about getting above the fight and adopting a more 'haughty' demeanour, but the idea was so foreign to his philosophy and his instincts he could never make it a reality for more than five minutes. The moral high ground had certain virtues but it was not a natural home, he thought, for any leader. It was a tactic for the weak-minded; the types who click their tongues when they hear their hosts click theirs. If politics is war, who is to be trusted—those who fight or those who posture? If he led on policy and in the parliament, and he led the politics of the government and the party—if he took the risks and wore the injuries—was that not being 'prime ministerial' and more useful than occupying the moral high ground?

In any event, these sorts of debates were only marginally relevant. For months he had insisted that the party buy newspaper space to advertise the fact that Labor had delivered the longest period of continuous economic growth since figures were kept. The executive was reluctant to spend the money, believing it would have at best a minimal impact on the government's standing. At worst the sight of the figures might turn voters who reckoned they had got no benefits from the growth more ardently against us. Keating was riled by Gary Gray's resistance to the idea and by the time the advertisements appeared on 1 September the national secretary had begun to take on a shape in the Prime Minister's mind not unlike his predecessor in 1993. In monster type the advertisements said: 'Australia's June quarter growth economic growth +1%. 3.7% for the year. 16 consecutive quarters of growth. Australia's best result in 24 years. Labor. The Way Forward.' If the people were impressed they did not shout about it; there was a fair chance that they thought it was more boasting, another sign that the government was out of touch.

The advertisements described the year just completed: in mid-November word came that Treasury reckoned that growth in the year we were in would be significantly lower than predicted—at 3.5 per cent, and the budget would be in deficit. They reckoned 3.5 per cent optimum if inflation was to be kept under 4 per cent, which in turn meant that the government could not pretend that its target of 5 per cent unemployment by the end of the century was within reach. On hearing this, the Prime Minister was ropable. Had he known a fortnight earlier, he said, he would have called a pre-Christmas election. But how could the figures slip so badly? He wanted an immediate interest cut, if only to signal there was reason for confidence. It would, of course, be meaningless if the forecasts leaked, which given recent experience we thought distinctly possible. The election backdrop was going to be good low inflation growth, falling unemployment and a budget surplus. In an instant that would be torn down, and with it all hope of winning.

This news came at the same time as the PM heard that President Clinton, in the face of his budget crisis in Congress, was planning to stay in Washington and send Al Gore to the APEC meeting in Osaka. With this another piece of Keating's edifice would fall. APEC would be diminished: without the US to help stare down the Chinese, Koreans and Japanese in Osaka, it might be permanently crippled. He resolved to ring the President and tell him that his failure to attend would not only weaken APEC but damage the US relationship with Japan and its strategy in the Pacific.

The new economic forecasts had immediate ramifications for the industry statement. Beazley wanted to abandon it—on the grounds, Don Russell reported, that the government was travelling moderately well and a statement only added risk and diversion. Unemployment benefits had blown out from $700 million in 1995–96 to $1.3 billion in 1996–97. That was one reason why the budget was headed for a deficit, and another reason for not adding a big statement to expenditure. The alternative was a statement with something a little grander in it. This the Prime Minister preferred, but not with anything as grand as Kelty's proposals. At a meeting at the Lodge, Don Russell argued Kelty's case for transport infrastructure. The Prime Minister said it would put too much pressure on the budget. He had begun by dismissing all Kelty's suggestions, but after listening to Russell he proposed a modified version: the Commonwealth would help the States put transport on the public account by enabling them to borrow at the Commonwealth rate, and perhaps with extra dollars kicked in. The Labor Government would present itself as the champion of publicly owned roads. If only we could persuade ourselves that the people would believe him. But this suggestion, and every other one, had been put in doubt by the forecasts. One hoped that on the way to Osaka for the APEC leaders' meeting it might be possible to practise some persuasion.

Two days before leaving for Osaka the ACTU declared war on CRA's operations at Weipa, including a national maritime strike. The timing could hardly have been worse. It was much too cute to say, as the union leaders seemed inclined to, that this was a taste of what Australia could expect under a conservative government. Three months before the election it destroyed Labor's advantage on industrial relations. Now the government could not credibly claim that the system worked, that the culture had changed. If the wharves were closed, for all political purposes, a successful Osaka APEC meeting would be meaningless. The event was already weakened by Clinton's absence. Calls were made to Washington, but the President and his advisers were adamant he would not be coming. Then, on the day before leaving for Japan, as the Prime Minister negotiated with Bill Kelty and the CRA chief executive, Leon Davis, the report of the Western Australian royal commission was released. As was to be expected after no less than eight former ministers in her government testified that they remembered the then premier discussing the Easton petition before she said it had been, Commissioner Marks found that Carmen Lawrence had repeatedly lied. The Prime Minister simply reminded Australians that the commission had been established for base political motives and the commissioner had admitted in advance that his findings were open to doubt.

The matters of Clinton and Lawrence, though important in themselves, were crucial in this instance mainly because they helped distract attention from the approaching industrial storm. In particular we failed to discern the mood, much less the motives, of Bill Kelty—not that Kelty was disposed to reveal the nature of either of them. The unions' dispute with CRA had begun weeks before when union members blocked the wharves at Weipa in protest at what they claimed was discrimination against their members relative to those on individual contracts. Essentially CRA was trying to drive unions and collective bargaining out of the operation. On 10 November, with permission from the Australian Industrial Relations Commission (AIRC), the company took common law action against the employees and the unions, and the unions responded by striking at CRA's coal mines. On 13 November the CRA unions met with the ACTU and determined to intensify the strike. Two days later they announced a five-day stoppage at Australian ports from midnight on the day following, and a seven-day strike in the nation's coal industry from the 21st. In Osaka the Prime Minister would extol the virtues of free trade while Australian ports and mines were closed by industrial action.

That these actions had Bill Kelty's support is beyond doubt. The company's attempts to 'buy off' workers from their collectively bargained agreements into individual contracts he saw as a profound threat to Australian trade unionism. He had lost patience with the AIRC. He saw a chance to turn the union tide—the one that had been retreating for a decade. That CRA was deliberately undermining the unions is equally beyond doubt. Workers on individual contracts were on much higher salaries than those doing the same task on awards. Nearly all new workers were on contracts. The company itself admitted that it had been discriminating and that there was a case to increase the pay of unionists. For Kelty, and the new ACTU president, Jenny George, there was much more at stake. Kelty had been the Labor Government's key partner in reform of the economy, including reform of the industrial relations system. Australian unionism was in decline, and plenty of those who remained in unions blamed Kelty for it. Plenty of them also believed that Kelty's partnership with the Labor Government had compromised union principles and kept wages down. Kelty loved and admired Keating but he had now drawn a line. In this defining struggle no interest beyond the unions' would be protected—not old mates and partners, not Accords, not Labor governments. Kelty wanted a victory at any cost. And Keating wanted him to have one. On Keating's side, mutual trust and goodwill were assumed. Two days before Japan I asked the PM if the rest of us should be feeling as relaxed about the CRA thing as he seemed to be. He seemed to think so.

The night before Keating left for Osaka, the unions' negotiator, Tim Pallas, was in the Prime Minister's Office. By midnight, telephone discussions with Comalco CEO, Terry Palmer, seemed to have produced an agreement. The Prime Minister had gone home, but not to bed, while the details were agreed. An in-principle agreement was drawn up: the company's litigation would 'never be actioned'; the company would not discriminate against unionists and agreed to 'the principle of equal pay for work of equal value'. The parties would meet the following morning to finalise the agreement and report to the AIRC by 2 p.m. Pallas signed the document for the unions. Palmer wrote on the bottom of it: 'There is a lot here I can agree with but a couple of points give me concern.' He said he would need to speak to 'a few people' in the morning. He noted that it was 'all one way', but said in conclusion, 'Why don't we let the PM go to bed and assure him that we will sort out the details tomorrow?' Pallas faxed the Prime Minister that 'the company have agreed to the wording over the phone'. With this assurance the Prime Minister went to bed, and he still had it when he drove to the airport the next morning.

Sometime shortly after midnight Pallas called at Bruce Chapman's home and showed him the agreement. Chapman asked why Palmer's signature was not on it. Pallas went back to Parliament House to send a fax to Palmer for his signature. He returned, Chapman said 'subdued', and without the signature. He told Chapman that he would finalise things at a meeting in Melbourne in the morning, and that he had told the Prime Minister that it should all be over by lunchtime. Knowing that the Prime Minister's plane was leaving at 8.30 in the morning and that he would be giving a doorstop before boarding, Chapman told Pallas to phone him not a minute later than 8.15. At 8.18 Pallas had not phoned. He phoned Pallas and Pallas told him that things did not look as hopeful now. Chapman began phoning mobiles 'to stop Paul saying anything remotely like it will be fixed by lunchtime'.

Apparently Bill Clinton tried to ring the Prime Minister that morning but for some reason contact was not made. Bruce Chapman had the same problem. As I waited to board the plane the Prime Minister phoned me from his car: he wanted to know if I thought it would be a good idea to say that Commissioner Marks was 'intellectually incontinent'. I said I thought that it was not; better to say that the commission had been a vicious stunt, that it was 'drowning in hypocrisy' and that Australians could recognise a hypocrite a mile away. By this time his car was approaching the airport. So long as this conversation continued, Chapman could not get through. Nor could he get through to Greg Turnbull, who switched off his phone when the PM arrived and began the doorstop. I watched through the window of the plane. Chapman got through at last to Don Russell and told him to grab the PM before he said anything. Too late, said Russell. The doorstop had been going for thirty seconds. The Prime Minister was telling journalists that Australians could recognise a hypocrite in fog from ten kilometres. 'Distract them! Grab Danny's gun and shoot somebody,' Chapman said to Russell. When they asked about the strike, the PM said that CRA had been trying to hurt the unions: they had taken a 'religious view' that contracts were good and awards were bad. But negotiations were now proceeding well and 'I think we might be able to tidy it up by midday or thereabouts'.

When the Prime Minister's plane reached Osaka he found that, far from being resolved, the dispute seemed to have intensified. The Opposition were mocking the declaration he made at the airport—'peace in our lunch time', we heard Peter Costello had called it. And Laurie Oakes reported that Paul Keating had 'egg all over his face'. From a Japanese restaurant Keating rang Kelty to say in a very friendly way that he had put him somewhat in a hole. Kelty, he said on hanging up, seemed to understand. For the time being he was more concerned about Clinton: he rang Charles Panetta and told him that the consequences of the President not coming were very serious, and sending the Vice-President only compounded them. It was a precedent that APEC did not need. He argued persuasively enough for Panetta to say that he would go back and put the case to the President. But Sandy Berger and George Stephanopolous both told Don Russell that nothing would change their minds. Clinton had called the Prime Minister to explain that morning, they said, but for some reason he could not get through.

As the Prime Minister flew to Osaka and through the next day, Chapman tried to get Davis and Kelty to agree to a basis of settlement. He told Davis what was at stake for the country, that it had taken twelve years to change international opinion about Australian industrial relations and with the Prime Minister in Osaka the strike would shatter the emerging perception of cooperation and accord. CRA's own interests might be damaged. Davis was sympathetic. Chapman phoned the PM and suggested he ring Davis and drive the point home. Between head to head meetings with APEC leaders the Prime Minister spoke to Davis, Kelty and Brereton. He spoke from his room and from a Japanese restaurant. Then he spoke to them again. Chapman rang Kelty to say that he might get a decent deal out of Davis. Kelty said he wanted an 8 per cent backdated pay increase. If he got this he would be '50 per cent in'. When Chapman told Davis of Kelty's demands, the CEO said he would have to consult his board. He did and got their agreement. He produced a redraft of the original document which in clear and precise language committed the company to the same concessions and included the 8 per cent increase backdated for twelve months. It was everything and more than the unions could hope to win at the IRC. Chapman told him to fax it to Kelty. When he rang to tell Kelty it was coming, Kelty's assistant told him that her boss would not take his call, that he did not want to talk to him. Davis sent the fax both to the ACTU and to Kelty's home. He got no response.

When the Prime Minister put down the phone after his last conversation with Kelty he told us that the maritime strike had been called off and the dispute would go before the full bench of the AIRC on the following Tuesday—which, as Bruce Chapman said, was where it could have gone the previous Tuesday, but Kelty had taken the view that the commission had messed them around too often and he wasn't buying any of it. We had hoped the headlines would say that Paul Keating had stepped in and created industrial peace, rather in the manner of Bob Hawke two decades earlier. Instead they said that the country stood on the verge of industrial chaos and that Paul Keating was 'severely embarrassed'. The signs were still confusing. What did Kelty see lurking in Davis's offer that we could not? But with the case now set down for hearing we thought our trials must soon be over.

While Leon Davis seemed to be a decent man who genuinely thought that CRA's approach to the unions had been misguided until now, in the PMO we had assumed that one way or another the company was doing Liberal Party business. As the days passed we wondered if that really had been the case. On the face of things Davis could not have been more conciliatory or more disposed to put the national interest first. It was hard to see how the AIRC could deliver more than he was offering. But Kelty's good faith, of course, we never doubted. He was passionate about this case and had a right to be. The Prime Minister knew that this was one his best mate had to win and in a way that made the case emphatically for the unions and unionism. He would do all he could to see that he won. He also knew that Kelty was aware of the government's vulnerability on the issue. He assumed that Kelty would do nothing to hurt him or harm his interests, including his interest in APEC which he recognised as one of Keating's greatest achievements.

Don Russell and I were sitting in the hotel coffee shop next morning when Greg Turnbull sat down with us, saying that a table full of press were watching for our reaction to what he was about to tell us. It was that Kelty and George had appointed Bob Hawke as the union advocate for the CRA hearing at the AIRC. It would not have been such a shock if a train had gone through the foyer. It was sickening. When Kelty told Bruce Chapman that 'there might be another way' was this what he meant? Had he never intended to settle the thing? Later we wondered if this was why he had asked for the 8 per cent loading: to push it out of reach for Davis and give him his excuse to conjure his indelible symbolic moment—the return of his predecessor, the man who played master to his apprentice, the legendary union advocate, Robert James Lee Hawke.

When the Prime Minister reached Kelty on the phone, he told him that what he had done was 'surreal'. For once the word seemed appropriate. Nothing could have been more surprising. No greater violence could have been done to the world as we understood it an hour before.

It took that long to get Kelty on the phone. Bruce Chapman tracked him down. He spoke first to Tim Pallas and asked him if this was *The Goon Show*. How could they do this? 'What's wrong with Hawkey?' Pallas asked. Chapman spoke in similar terms to Jenny George who said, 'Yes, we wondered if you might be a bit sensitive about that.' Then she told him that they were at that moment in Hawke's office. Chapman told her that one of them had to speak to Keating, but not from where she was. When Keating took Kelty's call half an hour later he did not know that Kelty was in Hawke's office. None of us knew. The conversation went for thirty minutes. Don Russell, Ashton Calvert and I stayed in the room. The Prime Minister told Kelty it was 'treachery' and that he could never trust him again. He told him that Hawke had tried to bring Keating down at the last election. He went through the history and the character of the man. And Kelty, he said, must have known what he was doing—that Keating's triumph at APEC would now be Keating's humiliation at the hands of Kelty and Hawke. All week he had told Kelty that he would deal with CRA, and on this as on everything in the past he would not let him down. He had never let him down. Not once—ever. It was like watching an earthquake or a divorce. Every now and then Keating would stop talking and we could hear Kelty's insistent, defiant voice with the characteristic rising inflection: maybe, he said, I trust people more than you do. He didn't think Labor could afford feuds like the one between Keating and Hawke. In any case, he had to do this to win the workers back to the union. CRA, he said, was going to destroy them. But we won't let them, Keating said.

Don Russell wrote on a piece of paper and handed it to me, 'BK no longer wants to be part of the ruling group.' It was never going to be CRA which destroyed you, Keating said. It was never going to be the Labor Government either. It was the failure of the union leaders to pick up all the new entrants to the labour market in the past decade—the service industries. It was the lunkheads around him at the ACTU, as he well knew. Keating scarcely raised his voice in the entire conversation. When it was over there seemed to be no other conclusion to draw than Russell's: the Accord was over, the government would need to go beyond the partnership and somehow make the psychological transition this involved. In truth, we did not know how to read Kelty's motives. Revenge, perhaps, for the slights he felt he had suffered: the way his regional development study had been derided and ignored; the appointment of Brereton as minister; the long silences in the government's mid-term—his suspicion that Keating was forgetting his old friends; the abuse of John Coombs in the Canberra meeting; that speech soon after the 1993 election which failed to confirm the principle of no-disadvantage for workers shifting from awards. 'What did you expect after that?' Grant Belchamber of the ACTU later said to Bruce Chapman. Judith Sloan, the conservative economist, told him the speech was a perfect statement of the Liberals' position.

Even before Keating finished the conversation with him there seemed no doubt that Kelty had never intended to settle the strike in the way he had let Keating believe. It also seemed that he underestimated the depth of the wound he would inflict. The injuries he felt had been inflicted on him might have made it possible for Kelty to do what he did, but it is doubtful that they motivated it. It is even possible that he did not see the way his action would be read. How else could such a close friend employ his most bitter enemy to humiliate the PM and deny him a moment he had worked so hard for, deserved and needed badly? In the climate of the times Keating was not likely to be bathed in glory by the Osaka meeting, but he stood a chance of being confirmed as a prime minister and leader of real standing.

It was true. Despite the absence of Clinton, Osaka was a magnificent achievement for Keating. Two years earlier he had persuaded the Americans. Then he had pulled Suharto into the campaign to a degree no-one would have thought possible. He had urged it throughout Asia. And then he had faced Japan up to the task. He had stared down their Liberal Democrats when they wanted to backslide on agriculture, telling the Japanese that by 2000, effective manufacturing tariffs in Australia would be 5 per cent, compared with 40 per cent in the 1970s, and that Japan had been among those to benefit. And while Australian farmers had suffered badly from the distortions in agricultural markets, and Australia had lost a quarter of its farms and a fifth of its farm labourers, Australia had not resorted to protection. He told the Japanese it was 'unthinkable' that the second biggest economy in the world should backslide on agreements made at a meeting which had been led by a developing country, and he passed on the message that Suharto had given him—that Osaka must make concrete the principles agreed at Bogor. Keating had not been short of assistance: Gareth Evans's energy and good name were critical, he had a good department led by Michael Costello, and very good advisers in Gyngell, Calvert, Thawley and Russell. Keating was not the only one with the vision for APEC. He was not the only architect of the APEC building, but no-one else but Keating could have sold it off the plan.

The Osaka meeting resolved to press on with a process to achieve the goals agreed at Bogor: free trade and investment in the Asia-Pacific by 2010 for the developed countries, and 2020 for the developing. It meant a $40 billion boost to the Australian economy by 2010. The Osaka meeting *was* more proof of APEC's growing stature, and Keating's standing among regional leaders. In the *Australian* Greg Sheridan said that Keating had 'transformed the political architecture of the Asia-Pacific. He deserves almost every accolade he will heap upon himself.'

Back in Canberra, on the Monday night we watched Hawke receive the credit for ending the strike, as Kelty and George watched, smiling. The strike ended on terms that were in no way an improvement on the agreement offered by Davis on the previous Friday. We wondered if Hawke felt restored as an

Australian folk hero; if Kelty and George really imagined that it would be a watershed and workers would now come flooding back to unions. If the $5–8 increase would trigger a stampede to awards. It all seemed very unlikely. It felt like betrayal, and (most unlikely of all) we heard that some of Keating's most bitter opponents in the labour movement felt that way too. When the polls that week revealed Howard's popularity declining, and the press showed signs of turning on him, we wondered what might have been.

Keating returned saying privately that the Accord was over. We did not see or hear from Kelty for several weeks. The PM declined an invitation to speak because it meant appearing with him. Kelty rang me one day to say he was in Canberra. He had driven up. I met him in the courtyard outside Aussie's coffee shop. He looked sick and depressed. I found it hard to think of anything to say, and in half an hour not a lot of any substance was said. He did say that he had hurt Keating badly. He had not realised how badly, he said—and I believed him, and still do. I think it might have stemmed from a sense of injury; under siege from his enemies and taken for granted by his friends he was momentarily possessed by longing for the simpler dimensions of the old class war or just the old times. Whatever it was, it took hold of him and drove him to renounce his present attachments and do something he would not have done in his normal frame of mind.

CHAPTER 23

*That splendid shield he gripped before his chest and shaking a
pair of spears went stalking out like a mountain lion starved for
meat too long and the lordly heart inside him fires him up to
raid some stormproof fold, to go at the sheep . . .*

HOMER, THE ILIAD, BOOK 12

IN THE SAME horrible fortnight of the CRA strike, the Labor
Party summoned the courage to disendorse Graeme
Campbell. For months the press—and Labor supporters—
had asked how long he could be tolerated. His remarks about the
Prime Minister and various other issues including race and immigration had not only at times breached the spirit if not the letter
of party policy, since his address three months earlier to the
League of Rights they broke his own undertakings to the party's
national secretariat. In November he addressed a group called
Australians Against Further Immigration. The left and right
factional leaders, Nick Bolkus and Robert Ray, had for some time
been agreed that Campbell should go. Late in November, while
the Prime Minister attended a business dinner, they met with
Gary Gray and Bill Bowtell and decided that the time was now.
How could the Prime Minister talk about APEC and Australia's
future in Asia when Campbell was opposing Asian immigration
and talking about the 'betrayal' inherent in 'Asianisation'? Or
preach the cause of reconciliation when Campbell preached
against Mabo. How could he lead with Campbell's rank disloyalty?
How could he speak for tolerance and multiculturalism, here and

abroad, when Campbell was reported declaring that no-one whose culture was 'incompatible with Western liberal democracy' should be allowed into Australia—and no-one 'who can't speak English'?

But there was no great sense of relief or triumph or virtue when Bowtell told us of the decision. Had not Lyndon Johnson been right to say that it was better to have your enemies inside the tent pissing out, than outside pissing in? And didn't Campbell speak for the old Australia that Labor had lost touch with? Was there no place for them in the Labor Party? Could Labor survive without them? When we told the Prime Minister on his return from dinner, he was far from pleased. The Member for Kalgoorlie might have obnoxious views on certain things, he might publicly wish his leader dead, but his leader thought him a basically decent bloke with a loose shingle or two. It was true he caused embarrassment from time to time, but as the Labor candidate some control could be kept on him; disendorsed he might be a much greater menace. In any event, amid all the humbug and bigotry, he did speak a language Keating liked. And Kim would be bloody furious—and Kim was, not least because Kim had not been consulted. The Prime Minister would not approve the decision immediately. He said he would sleep on it, and when at last he acceded it was without enthusiasm.

Campbell and the usual crew called it a triumph of political correctness—the 'marshmallow fascists of political correctness' according to the Melbourne pundit, Terry Lane—but it was hard to see Ray and Gray as fitting that description. It was also hard to see how Campbell was a victim. Political correctness was pervasive, but so was its opposite. The so-called politically correct pilloried Helen Garner's criticism of feminism in *The First Stone,* but the book sold exceptionally well and, far from being ostracised in the community at large, Garner was everywhere. It had been the same with Blainey in the 1980s. For all the protests about these 'marshmallow fascists' denying him a hearing, it was impossible to avoid the man. Gerard Henderson, who did not normally attract the term politically correct, applauded the decision to disendorse

Campbell. It was a very fraught affair that went to the core not only of Labor's dilemma, but of the country's.

Don Russell and I half-conceived the notion of bamboozling Howard with a couple of dramatic shifts of policy direction. Impressed by the success of Clinton's 'New Covenant' with emphasis on personal responsibility, Russell wanted to expand on the principle of mutual obligation which inhered in the Working Nation employment and training programs. Programs and benefits would be retained but subjected to greater scrutiny and tests of reciprocity. This would be perceived as a lurch to the right, and outflanking Howard on that side was in fact the political aim. But at the heart of it there lurked the principle that in return for government assistance more effort should be required of those capable of making it, that welfare had a capacity to be destructive and self-defeating, and that the political survival of good welfare programs depended on eliminating the bad ones. It is difficult to see why this should cause offence to the left, or any other devotee of 'social justice'. Ten minutes of talkback told anyone prepared to listen that Paul Keating would not lose votes by declaring that Labor's social wage was not designed to reward sloth equally with industry and ambition. Sadly, it seemed to me at least, neither the Prime Minister nor the party would ever be persuaded to consider a scheme of national civic service. But a form of 'work for the dole' should not have been beyond us. The minimum gesture was one that indicated recognition of the discontent the so-called 'battlers' felt. If their complaints derived more from unlovely envy than actual hardship, it was all the more urgent to recognise them. The political precondition of the social wage was public acceptance, and the public would only accept what seemed to be just. This was the government's imperative—to reinvest the social wage with a consensus view of justice. If 'social justice' was to be more than a cliché of Labor ideology and government departments, it needed to be vigorously extended to those who worked and earned and had ambition. The answer was not to send everyone in the town or street a cheque, but to assure them all that they were part of the equation and no-one was getting a cheque he did not deserve.

Working Nation had signalled the tendency, so a more dramatic shift late in 1995 need not be seen as too great a heresy. The lobbies thought they smelt it long ago and were hanging us for it anyway. Similarly, the government had already indicated its desire for a less ideologically driven species of multiculturalism and an environment policy with roots in Landcare, sustainable agriculture and brown as opposed to exclusively green issues. If to these were allied policies on Aboriginal health and education dedicated to practical results in preference to arguments about who should own the programs; an intelligent 'back to basics' education policy; and, in a further outflanking move, the redis- covery of a place for public ownership of infrastructure, it was possible that Paul Keating might in a single swoop revive and reinvent the image and ideology of the Labor Government. He might win back an election-winning segment of the old Australia.

Still, it might have been too late to change perceptions or win the public's trust. As Don Russell said, they might decide that Keating was trying to trick them again. And there was the risk of getting lost in transition: a fortnight after Keating had again stressed that multiculturalism must never be 'a repository of political correctness or something beyond criticism', a report commissioned from an American academic by the shadow immi- gration minister recommended that intending migrants be required to speak English and Keating was immediately obliged to quote the report derisively, to show how Labor's ready acceptance of multiculturalism differed from the Liberals who thought it was no more than 'heading for the nearest Chinese restaurant [and] chasing a meatball round a plate with a pair of chopsticks'. It was a good line and of course it left no sign that Graeme Campbell had recommended the same approach to migrants and the English language and been disendorsed just a few days before.

A makeover might squander routine political advantage. It was an entirely plausible makeover, nonetheless: Keating made- over as a less politically correct Labor leader might have been more credible than Howard made-over as a more politically correct Liberal one.

It was never done. The government went to the polls standing on what was on balance an admirable record, but it also went with a perception of staleness about it which defied the consistently impressive economic data and every strenuous policy effort of the past three years. There had not been time to signal such a radical change, of course: time for Labor's remaining rusted-on supporters to absorb the shock and get over the outrage, for cabinet and caucus to absorb it, for the media to put it through its mincer and decide. No-one was game. It was what made Russell hesitate before he came back; there was not enough time to turn things around, or start a new chapter to the story. It was truly a pity, not because it was a foolproof idea and bound to succeed, but because it was the only *political* idea. Little else was heard of, and nothing at all from those who grumbled loudest about Keating being out of touch or barmy, and offered as their most heartfelt contribution the observation that Labor would not win.

The media demanded policy from the government, for a government without policy was a tired government, a government without ideas and inspiration. Not wishing to be seen in this light, the government laboured through the days and nights and delivered policy, whereupon the media declared it an election sweetener or proof that the government had lost touch with reality because, politically speaking, these big policy statements had a political half-life of five minutes. The people were cynical about policy, the media said, as if the media were not cynical as well. That was why oppositions were smart to release no details of policy until very late in election campaigns—or even, as Jeff Kennett showed, after them. That way, as well, oppositions avoided the charge that there was no money to pay for the policy—a charge that one section of the media always made about government policy statements, while another spoke for the lobbies who said they were miserly.

When it was put to the Prime Minister that all these big policy statements achieved nothing for the government, he asked if people would prefer small policy statements. From the relatively generous response to the industry statement it might have been concluded that they did. The statement—eventually called Innovate Australia—was small. Treasury fears about the budget making it into surplus overwhelmed months of effort in the PMO and DIST. Late in the piece, Peter Cook found $200 million in his department, but Treasury would not countenance his claim that it was savings. There would be no venture capital fund, no super computer, no Essendon airport development, no significant new investment in IT-based industry. Hopes I shared with Sandy Hollway for public service reforms, including means by which the public could have some window on to its operation, and public servants in turn could see a little more of society and business at large, were drowned at birth. The proposals were warmly supported by the Public Service Commissioner, but when Hollway notified Mike Keating of the proposals, the PMC Secretary went past my door a grey blur. Don Russell wandered in to my office half an hour later to say that the secretary was beside himself with rage and there would be no public service reform. There would be, of course—six months later the new government was cutting it to pieces.

It was like Napoleon surrendering to his accountant. Treasury set rules and the Prime Minister felt he had no choice but to obey them. He had managed to get more than they were initially prepared to give, but Willis had been intransigent and Keating did not want to buy into a fight with him that would last into the election. He was downcast about it. His principal adviser was gloomy. So was Ric Simes. It was hardly the work of fiscal bandits. Sandy Hollway, as ever, was philosophical; his colleague, John Spasojevic, who had put in a huge amount of work, was furious and disappointed. The two of them had found the savings for their minister and conceived the programs to match them. How could the Prime Minister bow to his treasurer?

The statement aimed at generating more research and encouraging innovative businesses to manufacture and market new products. Banks were allowed to buy equity in companies and given tax breaks to invest in small and medium-sized enterprises. There were five new cooperative research centres and seven 'visionary science projects'. Forty million dollars in research and development grants was to be carried over until 1999, but the 150 per cent tax break for research and development was modified to cut out various abuses. The statement announced spending of less than $150 million but, through the cuts to tax and tariff concessions, saved more than twice that much. A 'smorgasbord of small, sensible measures', Tim Colebatch called it in the *Age*, but given that the statement was aimed at Australia's most urgent economic need—to speed the growth of manufactured exports and import replacements that was essential if Australia was to lower its trade deficit and succeed in the global economy—'inadequate' would have done as well as 'small'.

It is always hard to write a grand speech on a modest subject. It is doubly hard to write when one has rage and indignation burning in one's brain, but that also went with the job. We worked all night and in the end produced a speech that was better than the statement. And that is how it played. Sir Gustav Nossal gave the rhetoric 9 out of 10, and the statement 5. It was a little too kind to the rhetoric, but the point was well made.

A few days later, in Beenleigh in Queensland, the government delivered another statement—on housing—which Brian Howe called *Community and Nation*. About 500,000 people on low incomes in private rental housing received increased rent assistance; low income earners would be able to convert government rent assistance into deposits on houses; new public housing tenants had their rent capped at 25 per cent of their income; and the Better Cities program received $80 million in extra funds. Programs were underpinned by the radical and welcome decision to move all responsibility for government rental assistance to the Commonwealth and give the States control of public housing stock. The figures were modest—$93 million over four years—but again the reception from both the lobbies and the press was fundamentally positive. It was a good statement: it spoke for the government's sympathetic attention to the real world. The Prime

Minister put it in the category of things that should be done by a social democratic government, faithful to Australian traditions. It was a policy to attack disadvantage, and would stand as a memorial to the retiring Brian Howe, an 'outstanding member of this Labor government' who believed that it was 'Labor's mission and a government's duty' to give everyone a chance in life. The good press lasted one day.

Privately Paul Keating was being overwhelmed by waves of hurt and confusion. His perfect marriage had begun to fray. For Keating the blessings of his family had become something of a burden. Old certainties and supports had gone. It had to make him wonder about the point of political ambition if this was the ultimate reward. He drew his enthusiasm from those moments when the job took on dimensions that fired his imagination and pushed the sadness aside.

The Security Agreement with Indonesia, for example. On the morning of 14 December when he announced it, nothing and no-one could have quelled his enthusiasm, or penetrated his thinking with the obvious reminder that the people of Australia might not see the thing as necessarily good. To Keating the Agreement was 'so important' because it provided for Australia's security in the likely event that the United States retreated from our part of the world. The premise was regional security in the face of US isolationism. Australia had the choice between taking certain refuge under the US umbrella and finding its own security—'in Asia, not from Asia'. The Agreement was a keystone in the second strategy. Stripped of this—to some—disturbing doctrine, the measures themselves were hardly the cause for alarm. The two countries declared a common commitment to: regularly consult about matters affecting their common security and cooperate in the interests of their own security and the region's; consult in the event of adverse challenges to either party or to their common security interests and, if appropriate, consider measures which might be taken by them individually or jointly and in accordance with the processes of each government; and promote, in accordance with the policies and priorities of each, cooperative activities in the security field. Yet even properly understood, which was always unlikely, it would be difficult to persuade people.

As plainly as this seemed to speak for the country's benefit, the Prime Minister needed to assure people that the Agreement would make Australia more secure, not less; that it would not get us into unwanted wars; that it was not betrayal, either of the East Timorese or of some notion of our nationhood, that there was nothing to fear in stepping out on our own. Television used the massacre in Dili and the usual military images for its visual background to the announcement, and one wondered if the nation would offer the Prime Minister any thanks at all. His television interview that evening was not distinguished by a reassuring tone. He looked, if anything, rather menacing. No-one could say at day's end how it had gone down, but it was certain that no-one thought it would win the election for us. That it might help lose the election became a possibility when, a few days later, with Kim Beazley, Gareth Evans, Robert Ray and General Gration, the PM flew out to sign the treaty in Jakarta, and Alexander Downer asked why the people were not consulted. His point was to suggest that the whole thing might not be Paul Keating's 'greatest single foreign policy achievement', a stunning 'coup' or a triumph of 'leadership', but rather a 'secret' agreement, the product of a conspiracy of some kind.

Of course Downer knew, as should have any serious commentator, that the negotiation of international agreements is the province of the executive rather than the parliament, and that no agreement could have been reached in public view. It is almost as certain that, freed of its association with Keating, he knew the real value of it. But a few months from an election no-one on the Opposition side would resist the political opportunity to play on the electorate's unease.

Up at the Lodge the week before, while John Singleton and Bill Currie explained the 'leadership' strategy they had devised for the election, I read John Howard's Headland speech on Australian identity. Full of ire against Keating's republicanism, his criticism of Menzies, his so-called 'heist' on nationalism and the political correctness of his government, the speech mentioned him more than forty times and multiculturalism and reconciliation not once. I went back to the office and wrote a press release that said it 'will go down in history as one of the most vapid statements about Australia ever delivered by an Australian political leader'. Some murderous sentiment towards a rival may have been involved here, but the press generally agreed with the assessment. In the *Sydney Morning Herald* Eva Cox called it 'a footstep back in time'.

Encouraged, I wrote another slightly satirical press release on the Opposition leader's new pamphlet entitled The Things I Believe In. (One did wonder what possible benefit was imagined to accrue from these sorts of documents.) The press seemed to agree with this as well, branding it feeble and uninspired and freely quoting our observation that the leader of the Opposition seemed to believe in so many things it was a wonder he had left out Christmas. The Prime Minister asked, now that his opponent was all things to all people, if next we would hear him say he was a Fabian socialist. Just for a moment we had the faintest scent of success. With the press now turning on Howard for his failure to spell out serious policy, Newspoll revealed a big jump in the PM's approval rating and a slide in Howard's. The government remained behind, but not hopelessly by any means, and it felt just possible that Keating had timed his run perfectly. Hugh Mackay recommended we make 'Don't Let the Fire Go Out' a slogan. It was a sentiment that ought to have favoured us. Yet the dispiriting thing about John Howard's tactic, and its essential strength, was that it fitted the people's inclination to delay judgment. We must work until exhaustion just to stay within striking distance. Howard needed only to hold his nerve and make the most of our misfortunes.

We had never had a better office; not perfect, but it now seemed comprised of whole beings who were also very capable, devoted and alert. There was some youth in the mix, principally in the form of Michael Fullilove who at twenty-four had a disconcertingly mature grasp of politics and assisted with the

speeches and gave advice on young people. At the other end
Russell gave us ballast. In both Russell and Ric Simes the econo-
cratic disposition had evolved certain characteristics that were
almost indistinguishable from a bleeding heart's, and it is possible
that the bridge was more complete because now the bleeding
hearts were harder. Such old resentments and ideological differences as remained stayed out of sight and new ones were
subsumed beneath what is best described as a creative ethic. No
doubt the prospect of defeat was driving us, as if every shot we
fired might be the last one in the locker. But it was more than
that: there was a consensus about the shape of our ambitions and
indeed about more of the detail than we'd ever had before. There
was room for argument but it all concerned the same idea, that in
Australia we might in ways unique in the world weld the good
economy to the good society and have some influence abroad. It
had always been the guiding light of the Labor Government, but
I doubt if it ever seemed as clear or reachable as it did in the office
over the last six months.

There were days when, to me at least, it felt as if we had just
learned what the main game really was and what possibilities it
contained. Days when, if everything else including the never-
ending search for ways of knocking Howard's lights out had been
suddenly suspended, Ric Simes would still be working on IT or a
transport infrastructure for a national food industry; Mark O'Neill
on a deal between miners and Aboriginal communities in the
Gulf of Carpentaria; Bruce Chapman on a HECs scheme for
TAFE students and its equivalent for drought-afflicted farmers;
Don Russell on the republic, or roads or national superannuation;
Mary Ann O'Loughlin on a carers' pension or the implementation of the Job Compact; and Allan Gyngell would be bedding
down the resolutions of Osaka. No doubt it was also happening
in ministers' offices throughout the building, and down in the
departments, but this was Santa's *main* workshop, and it had never
been as busy or devoted as in those last days. It was slogging punctuated by occasional epiphanies. Of course you can never say with
such things, but it has since occurred to me that the sensation of

epiphany might indicate we had reached or come close to the light on the hill. It borders on the profane, of course: the deregulators and privatisers and Jakarta apologists taking Chifley's great vision unto themselves. I would say that Chifley's was less a great vision than a great line, and if a vision can be measured Keating's comes out much the greater of the two; but no doubt it will be said that every prime minister's office has delusions of this kind. It's in keeping with the way in politics we mistake good intentions for good deeds and effort for effect. We can't see ourselves as others see us. It wasn't the light *on* the hill, it was the light *in* the hill. If it had been on the hill people would have noticed, surely. And surely they wouldn't have turned off the mains.

Perhaps it was the unprecedented warmth of that environment and the landscape between Canberra and Melbourne, which was remarkably green for that time of the year, but it was possible to go home for Christmas thinking that in some ways we were in good shape. Newspoll showed that voters were angry and victory would go to the party Australians loathed least. It was plain enough when the Prime Minister did a talkback session with John Laws: you could feel the whinge factor. In fact you could feel it looking out the window of the plane, and you wondered if Australians were unique in thinking that they lived in the best country and were the best people in the world, and yet were governed by the worst people in the worst possible way. One expected this of Queenslanders; the party up there was always telling us what we should be doing, how blind to the general disenchantment we were; they thought the first principle of politics was to embody that disenchantment, surpass it if the strategy demanded. The second principle was to blame someone else, preferably someone with the name Keating. The message from Queensland scarcely ever changed: the people up here hate you and the national sails should be set accordingly. If Queensland was half as good as the advertising told us, why were they so bleak about everything? It was the land of tropical abundance yet they measured everything in fractions. Queensland always made me an avid Keatingite. All State governments did for that matter. They seemed to be, as it were, constitutionally disposed to boast and complain simultaneously. It was bred in their bone to blame someone. Talkback radio, with its capacity to make every individual at least *feel* sovereign, had created thousands of voters who reckoned their interests along the same lines as Wayne Goss and Jeff Kennett and saw no reason why they should not represent them in the same way. It was rare to meet them—no-one in those days actually knew someone who had been on talkback radio—but you knew they were real. Like the Sydney jeweller who phoned to blame the Prime Minister because his business was slow. It made you want to shout. Not because you thought that they didn't have a right, or their grievances weren't real—it was because they were the *only* opinions you ever heard and you knew they were conditioning others to have the same opinions, or to draw from them the opinion that, even if they were not suffering personally, there must be something wrong with the country. Still, the Prime Minister had to get his Christmas message out. It was all about the great things we Australians had done together in 1995, how much we all had to look forward to in 1996, how we all depend upon each other, how we should all 'celebrate the work we've done this year, and the future which is ours'.

Before the government could decide when the federal election would be the Queenslanders had to decide when to hold a by-election. Any by-election was bound to be unpleasant, but this one was particularly noxious because if Goss lost it he lost office. Keating did not want to go to an election before March. He was to visit Mahathir in Kuala Lumpur in January and deliver the Singapore Lecture on his way home. It would be useful to indicate that the dispute with Mahathir was behind him. Together with the lecture, the trip might help to persuade voters that a good relationship with Asia was the key to their security and that Paul Keating was the key to the relationship. He was determined to make the relationship with Asia a major theme in his campaign. Asia was Australia's great opportunity: it was growing at a rate unprecedented in history, much faster than Europe and North America had when they became industrial societies. It followed that if Australians were guided by only one consideration in the forthcoming election it should be this: who was more capable of building the harmonious and creative relationships with Asian leaders on which our future so heavily depended? Would this generation seize the opportunity with Keating or let it drift out of reach with Howard? This had the broad dimensions of a good strategy, but there were obvious problems even before the campaign started.

At Kirribilli House in mid-January, the Prime Minister recorded some brief statements for the free-to-air advertisements with which general elections begin. He drafted his own words and Don Russell and I made some suggestions. We did not think that 'ruefully' (as in 'looking ruefully back to the past') and 'mournfully' (as in 'mournfully towards great and powerful friends') were the right adverbs, or that he needed adverbs at all. I now think we might have been wrong. More substantially, I suggested he let a little soft democratic light into what were pretty uncompromising spiels on leadership. Instead of the Cold War tone—there is no choice, we must be strong—should we not give the people a chance to believe that they are in charge, that the decision is theirs? Empower them with your words instead of telling them what to think. Suggest something like 'we must find the answers in ourselves'. Could we not use pincers rather than a hammer? He was impatient with this approach and accepted only minimal amendments. He read it very persuasively: as persuasively as anyone who is not an actor or a practised fraud could read such a thing in the circumstances. Bill Currie from Singleton's agency applauded the performance, but he needed another thirty seconds, he said. I added a paragraph concerning Medicare, industrial relations, child care and the government's new maternity allowance. He did not like any of it and he particularly did not like the maternity allowance. He was talking about Asia—what did the maternity allowance have to do with 2 billion people in Asia? Half the people of Australia were doing the ironing and didn't think Asia had anything to do with them, I said across the uncrossable divide between the camera and its subject. Ninety per cent of the people don't have babies, he shouted back. What sort of a statistic is that, I asked. What are more Australian women interested in, babies or Asia? The crew watched as if they had seen it all before on *Water Rats*. He read it again from the top and got it all except the maternity allowance which he comprehensively blew. Drop the maternity allowance, we said. Yeah drop it, he said.

We flew to Malaysia in two stages, because soon after take-off the Black Pig's windscreen developed a crack and could not fly higher than 15,000 feet. The plane would have to be abandoned in Darwin. The RAAF, extraordinary as it seemed, had nothing else available. Prime Minister Mahathir could tell all the soldiers awaiting our inspection to go back to barracks, and the official party may as well go home because the Australian Prime Minister was going to be half a day late. Miraculously, Mr Nick Paspaley, the pearl merchant, was leaving Darwin for KL in one of his Falcon jets that very afternoon. The Prime Minister had met him on a couple of occasions and on the Black Pig's radio he asked him if a lift to the Malaysian capital was out of the question. Recognising at once his duty to save the government from ignominy, Mr Paspaley put off so many of his passengers as would allow the Prime Minister, his wife, two advisers, the protocol officer and a policeman to keep their appointment with history. With the remainder of the party, including the press, still waiting in a hangar in Darwin, the PM arrived at the official reception with minutes to spare. We asked Mr Paspaley if he would like to join us in the official party to make our tiny contingent look a little more respectable, but very properly he chose to simply observe. Thus only five of us lined up to meet the Malaysian Prime Minister and witness the military salutes and hear the national anthems. Perhaps Dr Mahathir, who had a very intelligent look about him and met one's eyes as if inquiring into one's character, thought it was an austerity measure. Nick Paspaley thought it was a farce. How could the Prime Minister of Australia fly around in an old and unreliable plane? It is the people's will, we told him. He still thought it was a farce.

Don Russell, Allan Gyngell and I worked well into the

morning on the Singapore speech. It was one of the more satisfying and creative encounters in the whole four years. Naturally enough it was not worth a political crumpet, but it made for a warm glow and a good speech—and all the better because the Prime Minister had been able to find the time to make a significant contribution. It began in the familiar way with those figures that told the recent story of Australia: the increase in the ratio of exports to GDP, the eightfold increase in direct investment from abroad, the sevenfold increase in Australian investment overseas. More graphically than he had done before with an Asian audience, he also told the story of Australian social and cultural change. He described the path to greater openness, diversity and tolerance. We had left behind the racism and xenophobia, but not, he thought, the traditional egalitarian and democratic values by which Australians largely define themselves. As a consequence, in Australia we would not 'let the market rip'. We were not Asian and did not seek to be. But then we were not European or American either. We could only *be* Australian. Yet many values often declared to be 'Asian' were also 'Australian': family, work, education, order and accountability, for example. And the word used to describe the core value of Australia, 'mateship', was 'an ethic of communitarianism and mutual obligation which in other contexts is called "Asian"'.

All contrary evidence notwithstanding, some in the press and some academic writers insisted that Paul Keating wanted to 'Asianise' Australia. The Singapore excursion into comparative values might have encouraged them, but he said nothing in support of the claim. Rather, his point was to demonstrate that the cultures were different but not incompatible, at least not in ways which need inhibit cooperation of the APEC or Indonesia Security Agreement kind. And on cooperation, he was keen to say, a great deal depended. The essentially bogus 'values' divide served as something of a metaphor for the so-called north–south divide, and the rigid and inadequate global structures it exemplified. Australia, living and trading in the south, was nevertheless supposed to be a 'north' country, categorised in the United Nations as 'Western European and other'. We therefore knew something about inappropriate global and regional frameworks in which nations could not properly pursue their interests.

Paul Keating never offered a more articulate or far-reaching summary of his view. It included the observation that if growth in the region was not environmentally sustainable it would be for nothing and betray the 'Asian' value of sacrificing personal gratification for the good of future generations. But the heart of his speech was, as always, an awareness of possibility—good and bad. There was a moment to be seized. If we did not lay down an effective institutional structure now, the price in the twenty-first century could prove as calamitous as it did in the twentieth. We were at the end of the Cold War and the end of the millennium, but we were not at the end of history.

'Leadership' was the agreed campaign slogan. The focus groups decided it. Whatever else people thought about our man, they thought he was a strong leader. It did not do to reflect on those times when he told us leadership was an overrated concept and actually recoiled from the idea. He now embraced the notion with a certain enthusiasm. Nevertheless in a restaurant in Kuala Lumpur he turned on a minor version of the performance he had staged in Berlin, dismissing the importance of the things he did best and most needed to do—as if, I wondered, it quiets the little terrors of his subconscious and appeases the vestiges of a Bankstown disposition to tear down all tall poppies, including yourself should you become one.

One never had the slightest doubt that if the democracy itself were under threat Paul Keating would hurl himself into the front line of its defenders. Where its safety could be assumed, however, he did not always make a great effort to sound obviously democratic. In many ways it was a comfort: he was more likely to make hard points and much less prone to what the Americans call 'bomfog'. Just the same, with the slogan 'Leadership' and theme of 'Strength', it was wise to keep a watch on the extemporised campaign rhetoric. At the very least he needed to give people reason to believe they were included in his plans. The Indonesian

Security Agreement was an extreme example of a wider syndrome: among the people who had been recently called the 'chattering classes' it went under the name of 'hubris'; in the broader society and a press determined to reflect its views, it was called being 'out of touch'.

Australia Day addresses were good vehicles for democratic sentiment. The PM gave two of them on the usual popular themes. But he could hardly *not* include the people on Australia Day. It was in the casual rhetoric, the stuff in interviews, press conferences and doorstops, that the people needed his embrace.

He launched a very good environment policy—and a very expensive one. The NFF were positive about it, the Greens were predictably and tiresomely cool. Nothing in it impressed Bob Brown, apparently: lean and pious in his suit, like one half of a pair of Mormons, I could never see him on the television without thinking someone almost identical but shorter should be standing alongside. The press reaction was not unfavourable—and lasted for a day or less. A great deal of work had gone into the environment statement, many very difficult decisions had been made; as with all policy commitments, other useful programs had been reduced, compromised or scrapped to make room for this one. But in the end the environment policy, which had occupied several excellent people for months, secured no more votes for the Labor Government and earned it no more credit than an Australia Day speech written in a couple of hours on the morning it was given.

The Prime Minister gave a dozen or so speeches in the space of a couple of weeks. In one of them, the unthinkable happened. The kind of thing that made you sweat all night. Worse than the most egregious error of fact: a joke which backfired, such as might happen to Alexander Downer or Ronald Reagan. He said that Howard was like General Custer at the Battle of Bull Run. It did no good to say that Custer had indeed fought at Bull Run, and on the losing side; everyone knew that he meant the last stand at Little Bighorn. Laurie Oakes picked it up and mocked him for it. I had written it late at night and no-one in the office picked it up. If the Prime Minister felt angry or humiliated he did not say so. He rarely did. It was the sort of slip which might even make the difference in a tight election. And it was exactly the little confidence-building fillip we did not want to give Howard. We wanted to give him doubt and fear and see it on his face.

Then, just a few days before the election was announced, Bob McMullan called in to say that three seats in Canberra, including the one he was attempting to win, would be lost unless Labor committed itself to building the national museum. The Liberals had said they would build it, and the lobby group, Friends of the National Museum, had decided to support them unless Labor matched the offer. It was the worst possible message to carry to Keating a few days from the campaign. Nothing had done more to wear out my welcome than persisting in the face of the PM's mysterious intransigence on this matter. Now, when I needed every ounce of credibility, I was forced to take the matter to him.

Within twenty-four hours of McMullan's ultimatum, Max Bourke rang to suggest that one part of the museum should go in Old Parliament House with the National Portrait Gallery, and another could be built out at Yarramundi. This convenient, low cost option I put to the Prime Minister the next day at the Lodge, prefacing it of course with the minister's warning of electoral annihilation in Canberra. Don Russell watched this with a sadistic smile. Even as I spoke I sensed what the Prime Minister was about to say. I knew he would confound me. He said he thought it would be better to build a good building on the Acton peninsula, where the old hospital is—in other words, the mausoleum by the lake he had always adamantly opposed. But, I said, the museum's collection is probably too small to justify a building on that scale and of that cost. In support I quoted the director, Bob Edwards, and others I had spoken to that afternoon. I reminded him of our earlier plan to digitalise the collection, make it a virtual museum, take it to the people. But he didn't like it so much; he liked the building. However, Edwards and his likely successor, Peter Spearritt, and everyone in Michael Lee's office liked the IT option. I imagined it included in the Australia Day address, the headlines announcing 'Keating's Australia Day gift to the nation'; 'PM launches People's Museum'. It was right in the groove.

But cabinet knocked over the proposal. I heard it was because McMullan had cruelled his pitch by cavilling about the dollars spent on the environment statement in what he judged to be a futile attempt to buy votes. In any case, the department had estimated the cost at $84 million and that was too much. Then, when everything lay in ruins once more, Jim Moore in Lee's office came up with a proposal for a $20 million museum. So it was announced on Australia Day in a press release approved by the Prime Minister as he went to present the Australian of the Year Awards with a speech that had the winner's name as Peter Yu when it should have been John. I ran all the way from the new Parliament House to Old Parliament House and fell over the steps and skinned my knee before I caught up with the Prime Minister as he strolled in with Phillip Adams and Lois O'Donoghue. 'It's not Peter Yu, it's John,' I panted. 'I know, mate,' he said.

The press release announced a museum of the IT kind we had long ago envisaged would be built by the next Keating Labor Government. Had it been announced three years earlier we might have been opening it—and not just in Canberra. In various electorates all over the country locals might have gathered to view the nation's heritage and even interact with it. Instead the National Museum, in any form a useful and harmless project, became another mausoleum by the lake in Canberra and in March 2001 it was opened by John Howard.

I walked back to the House feeling the sort of triumph one feels about succeeding in small but hard-earned things—like undoing an impossible knot. The election date had been set. In two days he would tell the country that voting day was 2 March. It created a sense of vast relief. I had dinner with Michael Gordon and told him that we might yet recall the parliament. Meanwhile, on the cusp of his last campaign, the Prime Minister took the Young Australian of the Year, the twelve-year-old violinist, Sally Cooper, to the Lodge to meet his children. He played some Heifetz. She played some Bach. The next morning he was over the moon about it.

CHAPTER 24

Next to man and their own species, the animal probably most responsible for premature mortality among lions is the inoffensive porcupine.

J. STEVENSON-HAMILTON
WILD LIFE IN SOUTH AFRICA

T HE SHADOW PRECEDED the substance. It hung over Paul Keating's government for three years. Very occasionally an unmitigated triumph for Keating or a disaster for his opponents would scatter it, but it lurked not far away and in a day or two it came back. You could see the shape of it at the Press Club when he spoke there on 24 August, seven months before the election. Read five years later, the speech and the questions and answers following say as much about the election campaign as anything said in the campaign itself—as much about the government, about Paul Keating, about the media, about the mood of the country.

He spoke eloquently for the government's achievements and philosophy, modestly about its failings and, in keeping with the prevailing attitudes, recognised the gap between economic data and comparisons and the reality of ordinary lives. To a degree he did it in defiance of the clamour about Carmen Lawrence. He would share with them instead 'some thoughts about where our country is going. What is good and what needs to be improved.' And he would answer the recent claim that Australian politicians were becoming 'risk averse'. It might be true of Howard who

686 | Recollections of a Bleeding Heart

made those bland, policy-free Headland speeches, but Paul Keating reminded listeners that he was more inclined to 'headlong' speeches.

Current account deficit notwithstanding (and the budget had put the solution in place), the Australian economy was out-performing almost all its OECD counterparts and the forecasts suggested the trend continuing. The government's approach to the social and economic equation had been 'largely vindicated'. But reform had to continue. 'You never entirely get out of the woods'. There was no last chapter with 'The End' emblazoned in the sky beyond the next hill. It was like farming, as he'd told them up in Roma: 'you fix the tractor and the generator goes on the blink. You get through a drought and you have to deal with a flood.' He wished there was no need for more change; but there was a need. It was a marathon that never ended and like a marathon runner, if once a country got up with the leading pack, it must not break stride—once you lose touch with the leaders you never make up the ground again. 'If they go faster we have to go faster,' he said.

By 'stride' he meant the model: economic liberalisation combined with social cohesion and egalitarian values. Working Nation was the model. One Nation, Creative Nation, the Accord were all the model. 'Breaking stride' meant abandoning the model. Cutting the Working Nation programs which were training the young, getting the long-term unemployed back in the workforce, making the country both fairer and more efficient. It meant scrapping the Accord. The Accord had given Australia industrial peace, low inflation, high employment growth and economic growth that outstripped the OECD. It had given industry enterprise agreements and superannuation which was laying the basis of a national savings program. And with the Accord, since 1983 household incomes had risen by nearly 20 per cent. 'You keep the monarchy and you ditch the Accord! It is an amazing perspective on contemporary Australia,' he said. Since Working Nation and Accord Mark VIII, 500,000 new jobs had been created; unemployment had dropped by a near-record 1.7 per cent; long-term unemployment had fallen 20 per cent;

young long-term unemployment by 23 per cent; 376,000 people had received case-managed assistance.

Breaking stride meant lowering wages and working conditions. It meant an army of working poor. It meant individual contracts. An American labour market model meant an American social model. Or was it the New Zealand model the Opposition wanted? Since 1991 when they introduced individual contracts, New Zealand had managed a productivity increase of 1 per cent per annum—in Australia the increase was over 2.5 per cent.

It was a 'why change horses?' speech, one of a kind that Labor had been making for a decade. A couple of the more reputable economic forecasters were predicting a 'long lasting upswing . . . through to at least 2000'. The newspapers were beginning to say that it might be the 'healthiest recovery the country has had'. Not every step had been the right one, he knew. Not every problem was behind us. And he knew that this recovery did not translate into 'ease and comfort for every household and community'. Not everyone was as confident as the share markets seemed to be. There was a lot of uncertainty around, and a lot of people preying on it. In the face of their dissatisfaction there were people saying in the newspapers that these big Labor policy statements were politically useless. That it was smarter to listen to the electorate and respond accordingly. And it was true—good governments did listen, but, as he also told them up in Roma, so did bad governments.

The Labor Government would listen but it would also continue with policy. Labor had been re-elected every time on policy. Voters expected policy and governments had a duty to produce it. And insofar as the country had prospered and had a future, it was because Labor had done more than listen—it had done policy. The prospect of a free-trading Asia–Pacific had not been achieved by listening. Similarly, the big policy statements. Those statements did more than meet the interests of those sectors of the economy and the population which they addressed; they had done more than kick-start the economy (One Nation); or create a stimulus for regional development (Working Nation); or a new deal for the creative arts (Creative Nation). Beyond the practical effects they 'pick up on forces within the country. I mean things as intangible as collective needs and ambitions, emerging ideas and perspectives—they give them a concrete force.' Policy was 'a process of national reinvigoration and reinvention. I see it as a process of national character building,' he said.

It was a good, coherent speech on national issues and the philosophy of the government, and a window half-opened on Keating's mind. When the speech was over the journalists asked questions. The first two questions concerned Carmen Lawrence and the royal commission. The next three concerned the bad polls, national savings and the possible need for a big policy statement. Then Glenn Milne brought it back to Carmen Lawrence. Nikki Savva asked another on Carmen Lawrence, and Randal Markey from the *West Australian* asked another. Half the questions asked by the journalists concerned Carmen Lawrence. Another one concerned his possible retirement. Yet their minds had seemed to be on the speech. They had laughed at the odd joke. Malcolm Farr asked if the low inflation recovery was not actually hurting home owners and buyers who were getting little capital gain on their properties without low interest rates to compensate. The Prime Minister had said reform was an endurance test: Farr asked the Prime Minister if he expected people to endure this and vote for him on election day. The Prime Minister found a way to answer Farr, but he never found an answer to the problem his question described. The low inflation recovery threw its shadow on everything, the harder to live with because it contained the curse of ingratitude.

Similarly, the Prime Minister found ways to answer the Carmen Lawrence questions—shortly he would go back to Question Time and nail them to Opposition skulls. But Carmen Lawrence threw a shadow too. It was there in the Press Club that day, and while they seemed to be listening to the substance, it was the shadow they were watching. That too was a pattern that continued to polling day. One day it was the shadow of longevity, and the next the shadow of impending destruction. It was both—

it was everything that stopped light shining on the government's ambition and achievements.

There is just a chance that the person who paid the closest attention to Paul Keating's speech was John Howard. It's possible that when he heard the Prime Minister liken reform to a marathon and talk about endless renewal and 'a culture of continuous initiative', and acknowledge that reform and recovery did not bring 'ease and comfort' to all, an idea took root in his mind. Perhaps the hope he later expressed for a 'relaxed and comfortable' Australia erupted independently from the Sandy Stone region of his consciousness. But I read Keating's speech now and it seems to contain the keys to Howard's success in positioning himself: it is as if on 24 August, like the journalists, as he watched Paul Keating project himself as proof of the government's virtue and the country's future he saw the shadow lurking and recognised it as the natural ally of his own conservative, timorous self. And he formed a coalition with the shadow, knowing his old prediction had come true, that the times suited him at last.

And if he was smart enough to know that, who can be sure he did not also sense that Keating was in a form of denial—that those calls for the endurance of a marathon runner were coming from an exhausted man. I knew they were, and wrote the words for the Press Club knowing it. Who in Australia had been more exhausted by change than Keating? He had been exhausted from the first day he took the job. From our first meeting, when he said we were very nearly out of the woods and there was not a great deal more to do. When Howard suggested that Australians wanted to be comfortable and relaxed he might have been using the Prime Minister as a measure.

Labor's late 1995 research revealed that its vote was shot to pieces. The government would go in a landslide, voted out by two dominant sentiments—that it was time to give the other side a chance, and that Paul Keating was out of touch with ordinary people. Contrary to certain elements of received wisdom then and later, no-one, including Paul Keating, believed that the situation was not critical: in private, nine days out of ten Paul Keating would have said the government was going to get it in the neck. He told Robert Ray exactly this on the way to Jakarta to sign the Agreement. And he was under no illusion that the blame would land anywhere else but on his head—the more so because they would remember him always saying, as leaders are required to, that he was going to win.

For all that, the situation had looked just as grim in January 1993, and we clung to the idea that two miracles could occur if one could. Strangely, a couple of days before the election was called we heard that the back bench—even the Queenslanders on it—were less gloomy than they had been in 1993. Someone said that the last weekend's party polling had been promising. The newspapers were disconcertingly restrained and civil: one reported the content of a speech on multiculturalism, as if suddenly deciding that a political leader's meaning was to be found in the words he used. The words in this case described a principle of multicultural mutual obligation: tolerance and supports in return for loyalty and allegiance to Australia and democracy. Further meaning was discerned in the absence of any reference in the speech to John Howard. We hoped they did not expect him to maintain the silence until polling day.

Then, into this halcyon fortnight or so, one night came a nameless Queensland caller saying on the phone that the Prime Minister had sold out the working class. And a gaggle of inimical voices seemed to follow from the next morning on, as if they were all of the same coven, all saying he was arrogant and out of touch. And others said, in the same kind of unison, people hate it when he hops into Howard—whatever you do, don't let him hop into Howard. It so happened that insofar as we had a strategy, not hopping into Howard was the core of it. Hopping into Howard was not consistent with the slogan 'Leadership', even if it was consistent with the leader's skills, nature, instinct and judgment. A leader embodied a vision for his country and fidelity to its interests. He was wise and strong. His enemies were the enemies of the people—unemployment, inflation, current account deficits, welfare cheating. He did not waste his virtue on the vices of a petty political opponent. He was not spiteful or crude. His aggression was sparing and controlled. If we had wanted to hamstring him we could not have done better than give Paul Keating the slogan—'Leadership'. Not that it failed to describe his best quality and the one which research showed most people recognised. 'You might not like him but you've got to respect him' was the subtext of 'Leadership'. It was logical to think that it was the only way to neutralise the anti-Keating factor. But if 'Leadership' was the watchword, how could he play to the other side of himself—the side that expressed itself in furious aggression towards his political enemies? This side of Keating gave him victory in 1993 and made him a formidable player in every election Labor had won in the eighties. 'Leadership' built the great Keating contradiction into the campaign. Even when circumstances demanded it, when it became obvious that going quietly meant going quietly to the political grave, he had to bend to the strategy. The constraints 'Leadership' put on him sometimes made it look as if the public were breaking Keating's will—a good look very often, but the ultimate objective in elections is, of course, the reverse. That might have been what happened in the last debate: it is possible the people read into Keating's unusual repose the idea that they had defeated him, and by this default Howard's transparently manufactured aggression swept him away. At the Press Club a few days later the press drew the same conclusion from what we thought was one of his finest performances.

'Leadership' had seemed a good idea. It was logical to play on his strength and screen the weakness from view—the strength being what the voters liked or were at least prepared to concede; the weakness, the arrogance and aggression that they perceived and loathed. As with so much else in our thinking, subtler or more radical imaginations never threatened the grip of the obvious. No-one saw what it meant. It was not a good idea: it was a dumb idea, a grievous error. How could he go into the campaign as the bearer of the political idea that caused him most unease? Leadership was the one thing in the world that produced signs of insecurity in Paul Keating. Worse, leadership suggested arrogance. And arrogance was the one thing in the world that produced signs of unconquerable rage in a large cohort of the people. Worse still, 'leadership' tied his hands. Many things beat him in the election, including some he inflicted on himself before and during the campaign, but he had always wrestled his way over the obstacles, just as he had overcome the contradictions in himself. Some people said he fought the campaign as if half asleep, that he seemed not to be able to raise any passion; not even to chase down the old enemy, the man who stood for everything he despised and from whose small, mean grasp he reckoned he had saved the country. He wasn't half asleep so much as half out of character. He was our Achilles and we had sent him out to fight like Paris. He needed war or chaos and was permitted neither. It was a telling irony of the campaign that Keating consistently told his audiences how he was the real thing and Howard was a cardboard cut-out. In truth Keating was also not entirely himself.

After thirteen years in government, to participate in an election is still a great adventure—like flying ten successive missions over Germany in a Lancaster bomber or piloting a Japanese midget submarine was a great adventure in World War II. Like walking the plank is an adventure. An election is a mass of possibility competing with a heightened sense of fate: one contrives to act as if the world belongs to the smiling and bold without ever escaping the (mainly nocturnal) sensation that one might be contriving in a tumbrel. An election draws politicians into more intense contact with voters and in doing so intensifies the difference between them. One can see a parallel in the difference between the journalist's record of an election and the participant's. It is like the difference between what the doctor sees and what the patient feels. At best it is like this; at worst it is convincing evidence that modern politics can be likened to a schizophrenic condition. On both sides, the electors and the would-be elected, they hear voices and say to themselves it's not me who's mad, it's them. And at the end of it all we are left with dozens of accounts, all of them revealing to those who were there things they did not know, not only about their opponents but also about their colleagues, even about themselves. These things we did not see or know ourselves have the ring of truth about them. What strikes us as untruth is the story of what we did know and see— even when the authors tell it in words we gave them. Did Gary Gray really say, as the Fairfax journalist Pamela Williams later reported, that everyone in the PMO supported Keating's every idea, no matter what? It's the opposite of every memory and the record that I kept. Did Robert Ray really believe that no-one from outside could ever get through the circle of Russell, Bowan, Watson and Bowtell? But I never received a phone call, a note or a word of information from Robert Ray in four years and three months. I never met the man. I would have loved advice. And after asking me to go on to the campaign committee instead of Bill Bowtell which, even if I had been prepared to insult Bowtell, I could not do and still write speeches, I hardly saw Gary Gray again. I don't know why. I liked him. I thought our thinking was alike. To me it felt as if the secretariat abandoned ship, but only at the end did it cross my mind that they might have done it to leave all blame with Keating. And I'm sure I did tell Pamela Williams when she was researching her book about the election that, by the end of the campaign, I would not have crossed the road to rescue a member of the press gallery from a rabid dog. I wish I hadn't: it's a rotten metaphor and demonstrably untrue. It's claptrap and since it's now part of the record, the record is that much closer to claptrap.

If the 1996 election mess reduces to one single dynamic, it is that Keating had a record of government behind him, and Howard had a record of opposition. Keating was the recent past. He stood for everything that had been done. He lived, breathed and felt it. It was his essence. His state of mind, his state of health and the state of his marriage were all proof of the effort he had put in—and so, always, in some sense the electorate's disgruntlement was to him proof of their ingratitude. Only rarely did it surface, and those incidents cost him dearly; but the ever-present unspoken antagonism might have been just as corrosive. It had got beyond Paul Keating to feel what he used to feel for the people—he felt for the country, for the great project and for the people who shared his vision with him. But about the others he had come to feel as they felt about him. Insofar as they doubted him or denied the scope of his achievement, he no longer had quite the will to pretend he liked or even respected them. The syndrome was not unknown to Menzies or Churchill or Disraeli, but the people saw the expression on their faces and heard the tone of their voices much less frequently. They did not do talkback radio. It was only a degree of his old passion that Keating lost, but it was enough. And for those around him it was not even necessary to read the papers, listen to the radio or read the research to know that the people sensed he was as disenchanted with them as they were with him.

For Howard there were ghosts and other menaces lurking: holding out should a modest siege be raised to demand his policies; remaking himself as a likeness of those he had always opposed; remembering his lines when they asked him those difficult questions. Why, if he had always opposed Medicare, did he now support it? (Or, why if he supported it, had he opposed it?) Why he would not now tear down the Native Title Act? What had brought about his conversion to environmentalism? Why did he no longer see a threat in Asian immigration? His answers were all versions of the generic, 'because I have heard the people', or 'I was wrong and I'm big enough to admit it'. But he never knew when the question might come in some unexpected form and he would stumble and deceit would show in his face. John Howard was the rarest of things, a man trying to win an election while on the run. He was like a character in a Graham Greene novel—a burnt-out case the Fates would not abandon to remote oblivion. He had been resurrected; hauled into service for one last mission and in a new disguise. Yet anyone could see that behind the mask was the old John Howard. Therefore it was likely that he feared actual discovery less than the circumstances of it. It was not that they would see *him* should the mask fall, it was that he would see them—and there was no saying how he would react. He might jump in the air, or his head might jerk sharply, he might sweat, he might look guilty. If ever it was true that a man had nothing to fear but fear itself it might have been true of John Howard. Because the rest was comparatively simple. Keating had to play to the electorate's long-term memory, Howard to the much less demanding short-term. Keating had to give them a vision for the future, Howard had only to expound on any little thing that presently irritated them. Keating was working on a twenty-year front, Howard on twenty minutes, or as long as it took to get a ten-second news grab.

On Saturday 27 January the Prime Minister announced that the election would be held on 2 March. He said the election would be about leadership. He sought a further mandate for a government that had given Australia a more creative role in the world, and a successful trading economy, and strong economic and employment growth. He challenged John Howard to two head-to-head television debates and called for other debates between the deputies, Beazley and Fischer; foreign ministers, Evans and Downer; and treasurers, Willis and Costello. John Howard said Australians had an opportunity to remove a Labor government that showed 'all the signs of atrophy and decay' and to remove a prime minister who made 'worthless, exaggerated political promises' and broke them. Labor trailed in the polls by upwards of 8 per cent.

The day after the poll was called, Kim Beazley and John Howard were interviewed by Laurie Oakes on the *Sunday* show. Beazley was excitable. Howard studiously pedestrian. Graham Richardson was also on the show. The pollster, Gary Morgan, said the economy was the big issue; the former Liberal Party president, John Valder, said it was unemployment. Everyone agreed it was about 'security'—principally job security, but other types of security were desired as well no doubt. It didn't take a genius to reach any of these conclusions, but that didn't make them any less true. As the gurus went about their business, over in the church outside my flat in Kingston, the Baptists were singing hymns. I thought of them as Methodists by then. We would have to work 'security' into the bigger picture—adequate education and training were the keys to secure jobs; a sophisticated manufacturing sector with export markets was just as crucial; what could do more for security than a massive boost to national savings and personal retirement funds through superannuation; APEC was about securing the nation's future; Medicare was about security; maintaining awards was the best thing you could do for job security; the Agreement with Jakarta—like the whole effort at engagement with Asia—was about security; voting for Labor was a vote for security, a vote for the others, whatever their leader might say, was a vote for the unknown. 'Security' might have been a better slogan than 'Leadership'. Not that I thought so at the time. I was happy enough with 'Leadership', though I would have preferred 'Community and Nation'; it suggested both strength and affection and directly addressed the sense of alienation in the provinces and the perception that our leader was 'out of touch'. It addressed those Baptists singing in the church across the road, for instance. In the classic sociological dichotomy, our banner should read *Gemeinschaft*—kinship and community: and theirs should have been *Gesellschaft*—isolation and individualism. In Australia at any time, but particularly in 1996, whoever laid claim to *Gemeinschaft* had the best chance of winning. It would of course be very important not to mention these words to anyone during the campaign. The Baptists filed out of the church and stood around chatting under the trees in Telopea Park. As a body of people they expressed the ideal of community perfectly, but not one of them looked remotely like a Keating voter.

When he announced the election Paul Keating looked almost alarmingly relaxed and thoroughly in the groove. Later when he spoke to his staff, he was thoroughly out of it. To say he was revved was understating it. His mind was on the conduct of press conferences and doorstops, and miles distant from what he should say at them. He admitted he was tense and put his arm around my shoulders and said it was him and me together. That night I dreamt that I was in a Solzhenitsyn-like cancer ward, being treated with LSD and awaiting the amputation of my arm which, like the rest of my body, I had given to science. The Prime Minister rang before the arm was removed. The dream left me inexplicably doleful—or more doleful than usual—for the first three or four days of the campaign, and not even other dreams in which I died eradicated the misery of this first one.

We blew the start badly. We had wanted at least one debate to be chaired by Kerry O'Brien on the ABC, but the Liberals would not have O'Brien. We attempted to stand firm but only managed to look weak. The ABC looked weaker still. Gray appeared to be comprehensively outfoxed by the Liberals' Andrew Robb and we ended up with both debates on Channel 9 with Ray Martin and lost the publicity war as well. Worse still, we not only failed to get the Coalition to agree to debates on policy with their shadow ministers, we failed to draw attention to the weakness of their cabinet relative to Labor's, which was the principal purpose of asking for the debates. We failed in this because the colleagues responsible for doing it apparently did not understand the argument we put to them. The argument was that good government depended on more than a prime minister, it depended on a team; Australians needed competent, credible ministers; ministers with policies; ministers who understood the issues. We thought that if we could get some legs into this demand we might expose the policy and talent deficit on the other side. A vote against Keating was also a vote against Beazley and Willis and McMullan, Evans, Ray, Crean and Cook; and a vote for Downer, Fischer, Bishop, Costello and Abbott—not to say people they had never heard of. It was part of the 'You might want to punish Keating, but don't punish yourselves' line. We wanted to begin the campaign by saying that this was not a presidential race, it was a contest between a good government and people who wished to prove that they would be a better one, so we were offering our leader and our ministers to debate the Opposition, jointly or severally. But we missed the opportunity in the first forty-eight hours and that was the end of the strategy. David Epstein confessed that he had not understood our intentions. Perhaps I explained them poorly. Perhaps it was a bad strategy anyway.

We lost the first week. The debate about the debates, a couple of scratchy interviews—in one of which he called the ABC's Fran Kelly an 'apologist' for his opponents—and a beat-up when Ralph Willis remarked that he could not guarantee unchanged tax scales over the next three years, left us scrambling for a foothold. More damaging because it sounded at once wrong, arrogant and desperate, in a friendly interview on a Melbourne radio station, the Prime Minister said that Asian leaders, including Suharto, would not deal with John Howard. Somewhat dumbfounded, the interviewer, Ross Stephenson, gave him the opportunity to qualify. But the Prime Minister did not qualify. On hearing this Howard told a doorstop that the Prime Minister was 'crazy', and because it looked spontaneous it looked genuine and was genuinely damaging. Later I asked the PM if he had planned the remark and didn't tell us so we couldn't tell him not to, or if it just slipped out. He gave no clear answer and one had to suspect that he had been acting on his belief in branding an opponent early. There was, as always, a significant element of truth in what at face value looked like lunacy. Asian leaders would not listen to Howard as they listened to Keating. They would not be persuaded as they had been persuaded. The momentum of engagement would be lost. There would be costs to the national interest. All that could be convincingly argued. But it wasn't argued, and it was not, in any event, an issue on which Howard was likely to unravel.

Meanwhile John Howard re-badged himself as a green and got away with it. He stood in the forest with the media and Downey from the ACF and Marr from the Wilderness Society, and had he announced that he was now a python or a green tree frog they would have believed him. The main plank of his policy was a $1 billion heritage fund to be financed out of the sale of Telstra. Watching the greens' leaders enthuse about this was nauseating enough. We presumed it was their tactic to use the Liberal bribe as ransom for an even bigger bounty from Labor. Over the next few weeks the greens would drift to the conclusion that, as

Bob Brown said, the sale of one public asset should not be the precondition for preserving another. Of course it was easier for Brown to say this than it was for Paul Keating: Brown had never sold a public asset and he was not widely believed to fancy selling Telstra. While we sought words to deride Howard's green credentials without leaving our prime minister with his own yawning credibility gap, we also pondered the other inescapable implication of that day's events—namely, that Howard's makeover was marketable. Everyone on the campaign agreed that Howard had only to look credible to win, but only some drew the inference that beating him depended on making him look fraudulent. Keating drew it, but the campaign team did not. Others could see the logic of it but thought it too risky: the research showed— everything showed—that people did not like to hear him belting Howard. Keating said to win the election risks had to be taken. People might not like it, but they would hear it and they would be forced to think about it. However, as in 1993, the secretariat was not thinking of winning—it was thinking of losing in the smallest possible landslide.

In the first week the secretariat made mistakes and did not admit them. The Prime Minister did the same: he created distractions everywhere, sounded sullen if not half dead, and generally contrived to give the lie to the leadership slogan. Gary Gray also sounded sullen; he sounded like Bob Hogg had sounded in the last campaign. Indeed in almost every regard it repeated the first week of the 1993 campaign. We therefore had hope.

We got Singleton's down to Canberra and asked them to turn the heat on Howard. If the research showed that people thought Keating was the better leader and the government had the better policies, why was so much of the advertising not affirming the idea? Why not demand to see their policies? Ask why it has taken so long to come clean. Cast doubt on the credibility of Howard's conversion to Medicare, the environment, awards, safety nets. Get out the old pictures and words. Cast doubt everywhere. Singleton's said they had already been thinking about it. But one had a feeling that so long as the secretariat were convinced an anti-Howard campaign would be counterproductive, thinking about it was all they would do. Working at odds with the secretariat was not new, but it made life harder. Keating campaigned with a deep sense of frustration and anger—frustration that he was being denied the best means to move opinion his way, anger that having done more than anyone else to bring Labor the million miles it had come he was being treated like a mug. And by the same people who got it wrong in 1993. In these circumstances, it was remarkable that he campaigned as well as he did.

In the second week we had the kind of accident for which there is no accounting—the one which produces in all honest observers feelings of gratitude, because they were not the people standing under the tree when the lightning struck. Labor's campaign headquarters routinely taped an Adelaide radio interview on the telephone with Howard and transcribed it. They saw what every campaign worker hopes for—a gaffe. They issued the transcript to the gallery and urged Carmen Lawrence to get on the radio and make merry with it. This she did. Howard rose in the morning to find that Labor had been crawling all over him—but for something he had not said. Labor campaign headquarters had misheard, or mistranscribed. Howard got onto the radio station with a copy of what he really said. The radio station played the master tape which proved that Howard was right. Howard said Carmen Lawrence—why did it have to be Carmen?—had committed a 'cold-blooded deception'. He demanded an apology. She must have been in shock because she said that if there had been a mistake Howard should take it up with the people who made it, but the mistake was made by her people at the campaign headquarters. Then, after she had spoken to headquarters and after the matter was out of control, she apologised for an honest mistake.

But Keating's attitude to the affair incited Alan Ramsey— fatally for their relationship, as it turned out. In his Saturday column he wrote that Keating had treated the whole matter with disdain, 'sneering down his nose at the question of an apology'. It was 'graceless and self-defeating as Keating usually is when it comes to admitting error'. The TV coverage was dreadful, he said, and was sure to confirm voters' feelings about his behaviour and personality. They were no longer listening to him. They were tired of him, 'irrespective of Labor's achievements and its energy of earlier years, they're tired of his formidable mouth'. A few in his party were clinging to the hope that he might pull off another last ditch victory, but not Ramsey. Three weeks out Ramsey was convinced the game was over. 'Paul Keating got his reprieve three years ago and squandered it.'

Keating phoned him and cited policy achievements by the score. Ramsey wasn't talking about policy. I'm sick of you—we're all sick of you, he said. We want to see you go. The Prime Minister seemed shocked when he hung up, Don Russell said. He rang Ramsey back, but there was nothing to be done. Through the eighties and all the way to the Lodge, Ramsey had been one of Keating's most eloquent supporters. For five and half years after this phone call in February 1995 Keating did not speak or correspond with him.

Sometime in the second week he seemed to get the lines down: the electorate is conscientious and Labor knows it must re-establish its credentials. So must John Howard prove his. Howard is a cardboard cut-out with words given him by Andrew Robb who is the real Opposition leader, the puppet master. Their environment statement is a 'sting' and, like everything else they have offered so far, less a product of conviction or vision than a cynical reading of the polls. They are phoney. We are genuine. It was not very deep but at least it was a groove and might keep us on the track and allow some respite.

Everyone Keating still listened to—Russell, Mockridge, Turnbull, Ryan, me (even Barron phoned)—told him to exercise restraint in the first debate. Bob Ellis sent notes—he sent them every day—suggesting that Keating ask Howard 'What countries does Thailand border on?' 'What is the name of the present Prime Minister of Japan? And the one before him?' We should have tried it, and hoped to God that Howard wasn't quick enough to ask the Prime Minister the price of a litre of milk and a kilo of mince. When dentistry was added to Medicare, Ellis gave us 'our policy has teeth'. I don't know what happened to render this campaign so bleak. I bumped into Barry Jones in a Melbourne street one morning when I hadn't been to bed: he put his face very close to mine as was always his habit, and squinted and said loudly through the corner of his mouth—in exactly the same way as he would tell you why Bach's 32nd Cantata was superior to his 33rd, or who was state secretary of the Queensland branch in 1911, or what Ludwig of Bavaria said on his deathbed—you've lost your sense of humour! And he walked on, leaving me even bleaker.

Restrained the Prime Minister was, and the 'worm' scored it 51 to 49 in his favour. Like most commentators, we also thought he won, but by a smaller margin than he might have. As Howard recited his research-driven answers, the impeccably calm Paul Keating could not get any pressure on him and did not land the decisive blow we hoped for. The media tended to make the same point, which meant that far from swinging the campaign Labor's way, the debate might have consolidated Howard's vote. And yet hope sprang: some of us thought, and Hugh Mackay agreed, that when people went to work the next morning they would remember that Howard looked twitchy and Keating looked calm and relaxed, and this might mean the victory was decisive after all.

By the beginning of the third week the campaign was on the rails, but the train did not seem to be going anywhere in particular. We sailed dreamlike through familiar country with the windows tightly closed, in perfect silence. Mark Ryan and Hugh Mackay continued to urge us to get some fire into the campaign, but it was as if we had run out of oxygen.

Up and down the country the Prime Minister told audiences the same story, with the somewhat arcane beginning about the opportunity for Australia in Asia, which was modernising many times faster than the US had a hundred years ago when the Mellons and Rockefellers and Carnegies had made their fortunes. The Mellons, Rockefellers and Carnegies had never received so much attention in an Australian election, but if it puzzled many people in the halls where they gathered to see him, they did not show it. They liked the story he told, seemed surprised and beguiled by his quiet charm. One would never have thought from merely travelling with Paul Keating that the electorate was about to crush him. If it was not exactly a royal progress, it had a certain melancholy grace about it—something otherworldly, like the Mellons perhaps.

At the end of the third week confidence crept strangely into the camp, or was it fatalism? It struck me that Paul Keating was acting like a man going to meet his maker, confident that he would not be spurned. But what would a blessing mean? That he could continue to lead his people or be set free from them? In some part of his mind I think Keating had worked out a compact with Providence: either he would be granted dispensation to continue in public life, or he would be welcomed into some heaven beyond its reach. Some power higher than the people, or one constituted by them but above them, would judge him and either way it would judge him kindly. Perhaps I was projecting, even hallucinating; since the Malaysian trip less than a month ago there had been many nights without any sleep at all. Words were harder than ever to find. Every speech or press release loomed as an insurmountable obstacle. Fear set in. Most days I felt like bawling or breaking things. The most insurmountable of all was upon us—the policy launch. From the room in the Ramada I watched the ferries come and go, the freighters slipping out towards the heads and tried not to think of life after politics. The first words were written in Sydney at four o'clock on Monday afternoon; the last with difficulty as Don Russell sat nearby and people hovered, waiting to take it to the printer, at 8.00 a.m. on Wednesday, three hours before he delivered it.

In Melbourne at midnight on Tuesday, the Prime Minister and half his staff had gathered in Treasury Place with copies of a draft looking as mournful as I felt. Some of it worked, some of it was sludge. And it had no end. I think they were sorry for me. The word 'mate' was used a lot. They suggested going to the main themes—health, industrial relations and other familiar things. I said to the Prime Minister: you never talk about the future, no-one knows what you think about it. If you want this speech to rise above the ordinary, go away and write me two pages about how you see the future of Australia.

I'm not sure that everyone in the room got the point. The first third of the speech went over the progress we had made, reminded folk that our promises had been kept, that Labor had been resourceful and conscientious in office. Another section contrasted the Labor team with the Coalition's and was intended as a cheer-up, light relief, a laugh. Thereafter I wanted the speech to suggest momentum, a feeling that the last three years were propelling us towards something that could be described. That's what I wanted Paul Keating to describe. He had done it in a hundred speeches but not in his own words. The paradox, occurring to me in desperation, was that the Prime Minister, who had been around longer than anyone else, might be the only one with something live to say.

It was the hardest speech to write because the government was too old. The big picture was fine if people listened, but he'd been doing it every day for years. If they hadn't liked it then, why would they like it now? If he gave up on ideas and philosophy and savaged his opponents they would say he had run out of ideas. He could stand on the record but it would take forever to recite, and they were sick of him doing it. It sounded like boasting. He could give them promises, but they didn't believe his promises, they believed he broke promises.

He returned from another room at about 2.30 with just what I had hoped for. No-one was ever better at describing what the game was about. He went back to the Windsor Hotel to bed. Don Russell and I fiddled with his words and got them working. Then we fiddled with the words Donald had written about the republic after the PM had reported an informal conversation he had held with Tony Mason of the High Court and Sir William Deane. The PM had already rewritten them and now we rewrote them again. The crucial point was the proposal to hold a non-binding plebiscite on the matter of whether Australians wanted a republic.

If the policy speech made no difference in the campaign it did commit to the record some of the ambitions and achievements of a generally good government. The speech was deliberately light on promises, but at 6.00 a.m. we added computers to every schoolroom. We now had a speech ending with a noble but uninspiring promise to increase the cut-off point on the Health Concession Card by 10 per cent. The sun came up. I said to Donald, let's say that old people will be a special concern of the next Keating Government, a special policy concern. We thought this a great idea, and because it was a general rather than a specific promise it sounded uncommonly genuine, almost moving.

A few more hours and the timing would have been better. Speeches need beats, rather like a television sit-com. It was hard for Keating to read life into it. Some of the press remarked superciliously on the flatness of his delivery, but the substance was generally acknowledged. Outside the media the speech received quite excellent reviews. I heard that a party heavy reckoned it was the most brilliantly strategic speech he had ever heard. And a few days later the Prime Minister himself said it had put the campaign on the rails. He had always been generous, but there was something unusually gratifying about this expression of approval, and something about his tone that touched me. It was pleasing to think that in the end I might have got the mood of the thing right. Just as satisfying was the fact that the speech was written collectively; his contribution got it over a hump, most of the office had kicked in— the memory of the moment when they gathered in Treasury Place that night has proved indelible. Later it felt as if this was how it always should have been. He had such talented, devoted staff, and now when it was almost over he had begun to use them. The Prime Minister had begun to talk like a prime minister. We knew that if he had talked like this—to the people, not at them, investing them with some power of their own, giving them a sense that it was a joint enterprise—his lead over Howard would have been unassailable. The politics had been terrible: Mabo needed twice as much explaining; Asia twice as much again. Not just the unemployed, but the employed needed reassurance. We never praised the people enough, never gave them recognisable signs that we shared their experience. We could persuade ourselves that we had done it: it was there in the words, but the gestures weren't there. Grotesque as it sounds, and would have been, we needed a Redfern speech for all the other Australians.

It was not arrogance, but a conception of the role that was misshapen and too narrow. Paul Keating's thinking had been formed in the fierce crucible of the fifties and nothing between then and his becoming prime minister persuaded him that the arts of popular politics were worth studying. On the contrary he saw much evidence that they were generally inimical to good government and the national interest. Much of the advice he received, but by no means all, tended to reinforce this view. That is not to say his shortcomings in the role were all a product of this philosophy: simple perversity or poor judgment played their parts, and more often than anything else circumstances beyond his control or chain reactions he may have started but could not stop. Politics is not a perfect science and the longer a government is in office the less perfect it gets. There was never a congenial climate for working or explaining: there was no honeymoon at the beginning and bitter divorce at the end. In the middle it was always estrangement of one kind or another. Nevertheless there was much we could have done on the political side, and much we could have done without—and midway through the last campaign it seemed to me Paul Keating knew it.

Howard delivered his policy launch at Ryde, in his seat of Bennelong. They sang their slogan 'For All of Us', which as Noel Pearson pointed out was code for 'Not for the marginalised and disadvantaged', and indulged in the now familiar US-style fresh-faced family hoopla. Howard pitched his speech right into the mainstream—tax cuts for families with children. And, he said, he would restore trust in politicians and the political system. At the end of the campaign Keating claimed he had won both debates and the policy launch. He was probably right, but only in a technical sense. The Howard launch was no media triumph, and if the electorate was as cynical as we thought, it seemed possible that their big promise might not wash. Keating said it was a 'confidence trick', that Howard knew he could not fund cuts of that size. Some pointed out that if the Democrats wouldn't pass the Bills he didn't have the money. Other critics said that the cuts were too generous to those on relatively high incomes. When John Laws questioned him about this, Howard made a horrible mistake: he said that the cuts did not apply to people on incomes of more than $70,000. A minute or two later, after a minder delivered a note to him, he interrupted the interview to announce his error—he *was* promising tax cuts to people on more than $70,000.

The Prime Minister didn't hear Howard make his mistake because he was on the phone to Laws's producer seeking an opportunity to tell the listeners that Howard had a funding gap he couldn't bridge. While a crew from Singleton's who had come to shoot the last TV commercials waited under the trees in the Lodge gardens, the Prime Minister paced between the brown room and his study still in his pyjamas, a telephone plug in his ear. Russell, Turnbull, Gray and I were there, and picked up the Howard blunder. Russell tried to explain it to Keating but, distracted by the phone and concentrating on his own lines, he had not grasped it when he began to speak to Laws, and still hadn't when their conversation was interrupted by 2UE's 10 a.m. news. The news led with the gaffe, although it did not report that Howard's correction came only with a minder's prompt. Keating missed the news because he was talking to Russell. For the rest of us it was a sniff of something rousingly reminiscent of the moment in 1993 when Hewson could not explain the centre-piece of Fightback—a sniff of salvation—and there was great agitation as the Prime Minister, plugged into Laws and his three million listeners, tried to make sense of what Russell was saying. By the time the news ended he had it, and told Laws in effect what his listeners had just been told on the news.

It was very messy media, and in this imitated life more than the media usually do. Gary Gray later depicted the scene as a terrible error, more evidence of Keating's 'wackiness' and the chaos of his office. The fact that he was in his pyjamas seemed to be material to his case. It was as well that Gray was not Churchill's secretary—he may have had to deal with him naked. In fact, while the response was not exactly a model of military precision, the point was made clear soon enough: Howard did not understand his own policy, and his tax cuts were not only for low income earners.

On the TV news that night it was there for all to see. Russell Barton's story on the ABC, in particular, carried graphic footage of Howard saying one thing, receiving the note, and awkwardly correcting the story. He looked feeble, vulnerable. The moment we saw it we thought it was gold. Keating had been asking Gray for harder negative advertisements in the last two weeks of the campaign. The film of Howard seemed to provide the perfect material. Gray, however, would not use it. He believed, it seemed, that negative advertising of this kind would hurt Keating more than Howard. He told us that, in any case, the footage could not be used in a way that made sense of Howard's mistake. No-one who had seen the footage—or who later saw an advertisement the Liberals made to embarrass Keating—could accept the second reason. Instead the Labor Party made advertisements in which actors, Bill Hunter and Jacki Weaver, told their compatriots that John Howard was pretending to be something that he was not. In retrospect it was perhaps surprising that the people who affected to dismiss, or even despise, Keating's association with the arts 'elites' should choose actors to make Labor's case.

The Prime Minister had a letter delivered to Gary Gray's desk. He told him that, whatever the focus groups and advertising agencies said, he could only win with hard-edged advertisements in the last weeks. 'Focus groups would have talked us into submission two weeks before the last election,' he wrote. Advertising agencies were useful and could 'even be incisive, but they will never, never be decisive'. Gray later took great exception to this. He said that he read into it indications that Keating was planning to dump the inevitable loss on him and the secretariat. This was at best an overreaction. Keating's letter was unexceptional in everything but its tone, which was more reasonable than it might have been. The only passage which could be read as overbearing said: 'I cannot have a position where my instincts as party leader run for three years but not the last week of the election campaign . . .' To understand his position Gray needed only to remember 1993, when the secretariat's free-to-air advertisements were a grizzly miscalculation and the focus groups were, like the advice we received from party headquarters, unrelentingly defeatist. Keating may have been wrong in his assessment this time, but he had good reasons and a perfect right to send Gary Gray a letter. Howard, who once described himself as the most conservative leader in the Liberal Party's history, had put on new ideological clothes. There was film of him saying he would destroy Medicare, footage of him stumbling over policy he had announced the previous day—he had a huge quantity of baggage.

There were arguments against a full-blooded negative campaign. There were also arguments for it: one of the arguments is that most elections everywhere are won with full-blooded negative campaigns. The election of 1993 had been won with such a campaign. With his opponents sustaining a relentless personal attack on him, it was hardly a wonder that Keating wanted to respond. He could have been forgiven rage and panic, the more so because he believed—knew—that Howard's mask would drop after the election and the country would be profoundly changed. What Labor had achieved would be lost. Yet while the whole edifice was undermined, they asked him to watch the sand sift through the hourglass. With everything at stake, minimising damage was not an option.

But Gray and his team believed that the Medicare film was too old and would only convey the physical change in Howard to match the change in attitudes he claimed. They said the focus groups liked him when they saw him saying he was the most conservative leader ever. But even if this was true and provable, Keating's case remained intact: after all, if advertising depended on the existence of an unarguable documentary record there would be very little advertising. This aside, for Gary Gray to say that Keating had no right to put his case was strange indeed; to suggest that he did it to shift the blame for impending defeat was stranger still, and pregnant with psychological possibility.

With the contents of the policy launch reduced to one page of dot points for easy speech-making, we set out on a bus tour of provincial electorates west of Sydney. It was Tom Mockridge's idea. The press had been complaining about a lack of good pictures. Everyone in the media complained about a lack of spontaneity in modern political campaigns. Bus pictures, meeting the people in streets and halls and pubs we thought useful, if unexceptional ways to add a little colour and spontaneity to the campaign. We would, within reason, give something a chance to happen. Not much did. We sailed along the roads breathing the bus's deodorised air, stopping to speak to quiet and respectful crowds, sailing on again. Meanwhile, in Drummoyne, Min Keating listened to the shock-jocks and the talkback, day and night, to see what people were saying about her son and his enemies.

Only when the election was over did we learn how thoroughly the bus trip was resented and mocked by Gray and Epstein. Who can say whether it did much good? Who can say what else would have? The good was done by Howard himself. Twice at one function he tripped and almost fell as if giving physical expression to his stumble with Laws and confirming the Freudian maxim that there are no accidents. Watching, we couldn't help thinking that if only we could get some pressure on him, he might begin to look unelectable.

Through these days, in private Paul Keating was sometimes refractory and sour. He watched Howard on television like a dog watches a rabbit in a cage, driven mad by the spectacle of its inadequacy and his inability to lay a paw on it. He wanted to sink his teeth into its neck and shake it. One couldn't blame him: people of half his competence gambling with what was substantially his achievement and almost entirely his vision, telling him how to behave, how to win. The press, meanwhile, watched the same rabbit and turned blind eyes. People who should have known better wrote him off, traduced him, wrote down his accomplishments. The ageing author, Morris West, wrote a vicious article in the *SMH*—a diatribe laced with loathing, contempt and ignorance of the kind that we reserve the right to inflict on political leaders. I did not mention it to him and hoped he did not see it, but doubtless he did. As we flew down to Melbourne for an arts launch we came upon David Williamson's opinion in the *Daily Telegraph* that there was little difference in arts policy between the two parties and most of the intelligentsia felt let down by Labor. For ten minutes on the plane he was determined to devote his speech to tearing strips off Williamson.

He needed an arts launch like a hole in the head, he told Don Russell as he walked in. I'm sure he was right. Jacki Weaver read a speech full of derision and loathing for Howard, and unqualified love for Keating. Next day the *Herald Sun* called it a love-in and said it would alienate still further the ordinary people who were not part of the elites. You do not know how much you are loved, Jacki Weaver said. And all the contumely for Howard was greeted with tumultuous applause. The smiling, gracious PM told them they had given him a lift last time and they were doing it again. The Arts Centre was packed and he talked to them for a long time. In the end it seemed to be a triumph and, whether it gave him a lift or a hole in the head, he could not help but enjoy the swell of their affection.

It was hard to say just where the votes were to be found. Did it cost us when in working-class Lithgow he stepped out of the bus in a blue reefer jacket with gold buttons, and with one hand greeted workers while the other rested elegantly in his coat's side pocket. I asked him to leave the jacket in the bus. I asked Annita to persuade him. He wouldn't hear of it. At least he had a beer in the pub—Annita had a Campari. I bought Laura Tingle a drink because I had a feeling she had overheard me telling him not to wear the jacket. In Byron Bay he was, as we expected, greeted warmly by the counterculture and kissed by a young woman as he stepped on to the street. But at the bar of the pub where he spoke, Craig McGregor, the semi-retired countercultural commentator who back in the seventies when he thrived had written the first substantial article on Keating, told me he would lose and Howard would make an acceptable prime minister. In nearby Lismore the PM's spirits were high; they played one of his favourite Tom Jones tracks and the cameras caught him singing along and dancing a few steps in the corridor. It was the kind of spontaneity the press had wanted and, one would have thought, it played better for us than Howard's spontaneous falls had played for them. Yet we thought it might go down badly: that it might semaphore his confidence and they would think, that smug bastard is going to go unpunished again. When a hundred schoolgirls spontaneously mobbed him in Parramatta we did not know what to think, except it was a pity they were too young to vote. He reckoned if he'd fallen off the fence they'd have torn him limb from limb.

Graeme Campbell's measure of the electorate was not to be scorned—or was it? We spent the campaign circling the issue of race, knowing that our opponents had engaged in a campaign of dog-whistling, although we did not know the term at that stage and without it could not describe with much assurance what was going on. It was the unspoken message which rafts of Australians, many of whom later became supporters of Pauline Hanson, recognised in Coalition advertising and the slogan 'For all of us'. Looked at one way, what they heard in the whistle was the *cri de coeur* of the old Australia; the one referred to by Keating in his first Australia Day address, which was being trampled in the rush to modernise and globalise and ignored by the politically correct 'elites' in favour of Aborigines, Asians and single mothers. Looked at another way, it was the disaffected responding to the ancient call of race and xenophobia—the ethnic idea of the nation which, though dormant for long periods, has coexisted with the political conception since the Australian Commonwealth was born. That was the difference between Hanson's One Nation and Keating's.

There were outbursts of old-fashioned prejudice from politicians in Queensland, the best of them a reference to citizenship ceremonies as 'dewoggings'. The politically correct who objected were called 'slanty eyed ideologues'. About such antipolitical correctness Howard was to say later everyone felt a sense of relief. But no-one could say that John Howard was condoning racism. He disowned such sentiments. And he withdrew Hanson's Liberal endorsement. And were we so stupid as to think that these people had no reason other than racism for their disenchantment—no economic reasons, for instance? No loathing of Keating? And many of them were Labor people, after all—people who felt Labor had lost touch and even betrayed them. Who was Paul Keating to call them racists and bigots? Looked at either way, dog-whistling was impossibly difficult to combat. After the election I heard Graeme Campbell say that the Redfern speech gave birth to One Nation, but that was not what John Howard said during the campaign. Keating badly wanted to pin Howard with what he was sure were his real feelings and the real intentions underlying his party's campaign, but the Liberals knew it was no less dangerous to accuse someone of playing the race card than it was to actually do it. In the end Labor could do little more than nod in the direction of the Coalition motives. The consequences would be seen later.

The Prime Minister had never liked the idea of redeveloping Essendon airport—it was handy having a place to land the Falcon, he used to say. His more substantial objections were never very clear. Don Russell was not enthusiastic, and Laurie Brereton did not like it either, apparently. I suspected a Sydney bias. Flying to Perth, I pleaded the case to Keating and Russell in pure political terms: that is to say, I said we needed every vote we could get, and every good news story. I promised I'd get them the story. They agreed. In Canberra Ric Simes, who had become a keen and imaginative designer of industry and infrastructure plans, quickly filled in some details for the grand plan we had sketched out months before. Essendon's light-aircraft traffic would be moved to Moorabbin and Avalon, and Avalon, with its 747-sized runway, would also become an international freight terminal for the food industry. At Essendon there would be film studios, a multimedia business enclave, a theme park and a public housing development. Small businesses presently operating at Essendon were to be relocated. In the space of twelve hours with Simes and his associates in the department working feverishly on the detail, I organised a spread with the Melbourne *Age*, phoned around and got several pledges of public support for the project from film producers. Don Russell helped. It was a masterpiece of pan-continental coordination, pulled together in the end with only minutes to spare.

The story filled the front page of the *Age*: there were pictures and break-outs and dot points and headlines. The radios ran it freely. It was easily our best day in the Melbourne media—the best anywhere. When the Prime Minister boarded the plane in Perth to fly back east, the *Age* was sitting among the other newspapers. I watched as he looked at the front page, glanced up and down, and without a word or a flicker of discernible interest moved on to the next newspaper. A couple of days later as we drove past Essendon—it couldn't handle the 707s that were used in elections—I said to Russell, 'Just imagine, Donald, in ten years a thriving film industry and theme park and housing for hundreds of families.' 'I will bet you a hundred dollars,' he said, 'that in ten years time grass will be pushing up through the tarmac and there won't be a new building in sight.'

Keating would snarl in private about the same old things. In a Chinese restaurant at Yamba in northern NSW I told him his vendettas bored me to death. He said in fact I loved them. I hate them, I said. Don Russell and I had been trying to persuade him about the benefits of his new democratic style. Recent days had demonstrated that if he presented his warm side to the people and showed even a minimum of interest in their lives they would repay it with interest. If he won the election a different style might give him a new lease of political life. In the Yamba restaurant as usual it did no good to chastise him. Inevitably he dug his heels in deeper. He never conceded the need to change, for the same reason, one presumed, that he never conceded a mistake. It was one of the more depressing nights of the campaign, for me at least, though I couldn't say that he did not have both good reasons and a right to think the way he did. By any of the accepted measures of policy and leadership he had not failed. Howard had not scored a single point of substance against him. Yet Howard enjoyed what seemed like huge favours from the press. How, for instance, could the same press that for years demanded leadership and discipline from the Labor Government let Howard say, in answer to inquiries about his vision for the nation, that he would like to see Australians 'comfortable and relaxed'? It did not go unnoticed, but it was treated as a minor heresy, whereas anything comparable from Keating would have been treason. There always came a moment when you had to ask if the wonder was that he coped so well with it.

As a perfect illustration, Howard's second last week of the campaign was gruesomely bad, ending with him hopelessly wrong-footed at a news conference when presented with a letter he had co-signed offering to cut the tax on savings. After he looked and sounded terrible on the Friday evening news we thought the morning's papers must hit him hard enough to open cracks. He was beginning to look unfit to lead. Just then we really thought there was a chance that we might repeat the last week surge of 1993. And Newspoll supported the view. The gap had closed to just 4 per cent. But the Saturday papers were not about Howard's horror week; they were about a court ruling in favour of the Australian Rugby League against Rupert Murdoch. Not just the papers whose proprietors had a financial interest, and not just the papers where the game was played—the ARL dominated the front page of the Melbourne *Age*! It was a body blow, a spear tackle.

Perhaps the editors thought the rugby a pleasant respite before the last week of the campaign. Perhaps they thought it balanced Howard's bad week with Bill Kelty's big mistake at a Melbourne union rally. Kelty had responded to Howard's 'comfortable and relaxed line' by calling him 'Captain Snooze'. The pity was he didn't leave it there. The Prime Minister was attending the meeting and the night before it Kelty phoned, and from what he said I gathered that he intended to make the line between the parties unmistakable. There was no doubt it would be an aggressive speech. He asked if we wanted to see it in advance. I said to send it if he liked, but I might have also said something like, but I'm sure we can trust your judgment.

But Kelty had assumed the public shared his awareness of Opposition industrial relations policy. To him it was a declaration of war on the unions, and so he declared the unions would give as good as they got—'the full symphony', he said, as if in recognition of Keating's tastes. So Howard wanted Australians to be comfortable and relaxed—a 10 per cent pay increase would help them. But with no award, why not 20 per cent? Why not 30 per cent? They wanted a return to the marketplace, well let them see what that meant.

Keating's strong, relatively temperate speech and the great enthusiasm he generated went unremarked. The media made a meal of Kelty's declaration of war on a Howard government. Worse, in the last week of the campaign Labor could not make ground in the area where it held a huge advantage: now if the Prime Minister spoke of a return to industrial chaos after the Accord, Howard and Peter Reith needed only to point to Kelty. It had been no more than a statement of aggressive self-defence, a rallying call to the beleaguered tribe, but it sounded too much like blackmail. He rang the next day, close to devastated by what had happened and wondering what he could do to rescue the situation.

If it was Kelty's fault it was also ours. At a time in the campaign when any slip was fatal it was stupid not to read his speech, especially when he himself had doubts and offered it for checking. It was a blunder which approximated a disaster because Labor had had an almost flawless week and the Liberals a woeful one. This helped to save them from themselves. At different times all of us had ventured lines for speeches that would have done us damage had someone else not recognised the danger in advance. One tried to control the doorstops and press conferences, but errors in those contexts were inevitable and usually forgivable. But this was not. This was easy to avoid. In earlier days surely a dozen people, including possibly the Minister, might have been apprised of what Bill Kelty had in mind. It was yet another symptom of an exhausted and depleted outfit: the sort of self-inflicted wound sustained when a company has lost order and discipline, and operates on instinct, and messages must travel on the one or two uncertain lines of trust remaining.

In the same week Labor also saw another advantage neutralised. We had been claiming with good effect that a privatised Telstra would mean higher prices and cuts to services in rural Australia. To counter this attack the Liberals released advertisements claiming that Labor was selling 'big chunks' of Telstra by default through a joint venture with Lend Lease and IBM. It was a long bow, but according to the research it worked for them, and Labor's effort to force withdrawal of the advertisements did not succeed.

The weekend headlines which did not concern the rugby concerned Labor's surge in the polls. It was 'neck and neck' one of the Sunday papers said. Everything conspired to give the impression that 1993 might be about to repeat itself. The Liberals opened the throttle on the Keating factor. Howard asked his audiences to imagine how smug Keating would be if he won again. They ran advertisements using a clip from the previous year of Keating saying that Labor was 'going to bolt in'. It was perfectly timed with the appearance given by the tabloids that a Labor victory was in prospect. The second debate went much the same way as the first, insofar as the commentators and the audience called it marginally Keating's way. But it was not decisive. To most of us in the Keating camp he was already winning, until Ray Martin asked them to answer questions about groceries and guns. We had gone half-prepared for the groceries at least, but our man looked marginally less comfortable and more demeaned than Howard when it came to answering. It was not that he didn't know the price of milk, but the ludicrous measure of social awareness inherent in the question. In one stroke Martin reduced his country's political leaders to puppets. It was the media flexing their indomitable muscle over the political system. Yet on balance it was a points victory, and to our eyes Howard looked foolish trying to sound tough as he did in the opening rounds. We thought our bloke showed admirable restraint when he said, 'You're not very nice tonight, John.' But this might not have been the way soft voters saw it. After the election the Liberals claimed Howard had shown people in that debate that he had the mettle to take on Keating, and his performance gave them their biggest boost of the campaign.

It would have needed divine intervention to see it, but he should have said: 'So it's all right to be aggressive is it, John? And here I've been keeping myself in check and going easy on you.' And then he should have turned the hoses on him. It might have changed the history of Australia. The day after we heard that one of the talkback jocks had told his listeners how one of the Prime Minister's advisers, Don Russell, had left behind at the Channel 9 studio notes on the prices of milk and bread.

There was one more cause for worry to emerge from the debate, and again it was a product of poor discipline and planning. When Howard recalled that the Prime Minister had once told a group of young Australians to 'get a job', the Prime Minister reflexively denied having said it. He should have been briefed in anticipation: he should have had a rehearsed reply: yes I did say that, and on the spur of the moment the words were not well chosen, but I'll tell you what I meant. And then he might have explained the government's philosophy and initiatives embodied in Working Nation; or talked about the future of work in the new economy—he might have become very philosophical, or passionate and rhetorical. There might have been something better still to say, but we did not give it any thought. Almost certainly it cost us dearly. All the last week the Liberals ran advertisements juxtaposing film of him making the remark with film of his denial. It was painful to watch. Four years later I met a man, a professor of history, who spent polling day at a booth in Adelaide and has believed ever since that the people's decision finally came down to who they trusted, and Keating's denial which the advertisement highlighted cost Labor the election.

There is no doubt that the mood changed over that weekend. Labor ceased to be the underdog. Who knows if, rather than any of the blunders, this was the fatal blow. After the election the pollster Gary Morgan showed Keating evidence that he was continuing to peak into the last week, and still might have won had the events of the Wednesday not occurred. Yet against that there was Newspoll on the Monday night showing the Coalition leading on the primary vote by 10 per cent. Michael Gordon forewarned Bruce Chapman and me in a restaurant across the lane from the Ramada. It was simply impossible to deny we were beaten. Nevertheless we did.

We went to Cairns to sign a regional land use agreement for Cape York constructed on the Native Title Act and negotiated by Noel Pearson with the traditional owners, the Cattlemen's Union, the ACF and the Wilderness Society. While there, to get those photographs the press had been lacking we sent the PM in an army Blackhawk helicopter out to a remote part of the Daintree Forest called Tully Mill stream, there to announce he would save it from a power station the Queensland Nationals planned to build. Mark O'Neill and I had urged the expedition, thinking at least we might get some green preferences out of it; and in response to the frequent cries of 'do something' both from our own side and the press who constantly charged that both sides' campaigns were too carefully orchestrated and sealed off from reality—and when misfortune struck leapt on it with glee and doubled up by saying that the victim's campaign lacked discipline. It was part of the plan—Tom Mockridge was the main proponent—to fill the PM's last week with travel and colour and movement. While Howard worked the radio studios we would get the good pictures. We would be 'real'.

Three Blackhawks took off from Cairns airport early in the morning, carrying press, police and the Prime Minister's party which included Jim Downey of the ACF. Don Russell had agreed to go, so I was surprised to find him at the hotel later in the morning. He had actually boarded the helicopter, but while sitting there with the blades spinning, had a premonition of disaster and got out. He came with me to meet them at the airport and go through notes I had written for Keating's press conference back at the Radison—the new hotel on the Cairns waterfront which the Prime Minister abominated. We waited for three-quarters of an hour behind a high wire fence, catching up with phone calls and watching the hills beyond the tarmac. Just when we began to worry seriously two black dots appeared. 'But there were three,' said Russell. Later an army report found that when the helicopter carrying the Prime Minister and his party clipped the tops of trees while trying to land in the forest only the skill of the pilot saved them from what the press called a 'near tragedy'. But the helicopters were not meant to land there, according to Federal Police who waited at a clearing for them with vehicles to take them further in. They watched the Blackhawks fly on past and thought it strange.

Only two helicopters came back because the one with the Prime Minister in it had been damaged and could not fly out. But the PM was alive and remarkably unconcerned. Mark O'Neill was less relaxed. We picked them up off the tarmac and headed for the Radison. They had no idea that we did not know what had happened: in politics it is assumed that everyone knows what happened immediately wherever they might be. We hit the trees, Keating said, taking from his coat pocket the notes I'd put under his door the night before and handing them to me. They were stained with blood. A leech, he said, and pulled up his trousers to reveal a bloody handkerchief wrapped round his leg. He dug deeper into his pockets and found chips of wood hacked out of the trees by the rotor blades. Don Russell marvelled at his own premonition. O'Neill was very pale. The Prime Minister was no more fazed than if he had had a puncture on his bicycle, and at his press conference brushed off the incident as the usual political 'thrills and spills'. He was often like this when some calamity struck, or someone made a horrible mess of things: instead of anger or neurosis it produced in him a kind of trance, and he would muse quietly in another world.

This touring the continent was like a convulsion before death. Or was it an attempt to prove that we could organise a great show, that we could still do it? Not knowing if the helicopter episode would play for us or against us, we left for the airport via the ABC radio studios where the Prime Minister recorded a five-minute talk about why Australians should vote for him. Pushing on to the airport we listened to an interview he had also recorded. It was a good interview but when we arrived he was in a rage. They had cut parts of it. He ordered Greg Turnbull to get the station manager on the phone, and now he tore into him. Then he swore revenge on the general manager, Brian Johns, and demanded that Greg Turnbull get him on the phone as well. It was pointless and stupid: Annita and I both said so, which may be why he was so determined to do it and sulked for half an hour when it was denied him. It was curious how often his staff acquiesced in these self-destructive outbursts. It was not cowardice, but that fealty which requires the servant to show courage only on behalf of his master and never against him.

The team flew down to Adelaide, over the Darling River and the ravaged plains. No-one expected to win, and everyone had felt the same thing on the Monday after the debate. The debate didn't do it, but the mood had changed. The head of steam we had going on the Friday was exhausted. The people had drifted back to the Coalition. Gray and Keating had spoken about it on the phone. In a long letter at the beginning of the last week, Gray told Keating that the election was winnable and suggested ways to improve our chances. Later he explained it as the only kind of letter that Keating would read, and he hoped that by reading it he might do better rather than worse in the last week and keep the loss to a rout rather than a debacle. It is difficult to believe that the letter was entirely deceitful, but then Gray also said later that he deceived Keating about the state of the advertising budget. Whatever reasoning and machinations underlay Gary Gray's position, or were imposed on him by the Schadenfreude of others, the Prime Minister and his office were essentially of the same mind—we would lose. But as in 1993, the office—and Paul Keating most of all—simply could not afford to concede it. This mental gymnastics which circumstance required should not have been so difficult to understand, however easy it was to lampoon afterwards. People in war or other kinds of peril have always done it. People in marriages do it. It is a mechanism for survival, and if in this election it presented as something like blind faith that was surely because in 1993 the faith had been justified.

So it was with minds set as if we were going to win that on landing in Adelaide the Prime Minister, Russell and Turnbull went off to a barbecue in Gordon Bilney's seat of Kingston, and I went to the hotel to prepare notes for various speeches. There, as I stepped into the room, Tom Mockridge rang. He was desperate to reach Keating to tell him to tell Willis he had to back off and apologise. Back off what? I asked. He explained, amazed I didn't know that Ralph Willis had told a press conference he had letters showing that a Howard government planned to cut grants to the States to pay for his election promises. One from Jeff Kennett, on Premier's Office letterhead, told John Howard that if the choice was between his election promises and maintaining State grants he had better cancel the promises. In another letter, Peter Costello's chief of staff assured Howard that he need not worry about Kennett's complaint because the grant-cutting plan would not become public until after both the federal and Victorian State elections.

By the time the letters reached Ric Simes at the PMO, Epstein, Gray and Willis's adviser, David Cox, had persuaded the Treasurer to hold a press conference. Cox, who had received the parcel of letters from an anonymous source, and checked the letterheads and signatures against others from the same source, and run checks on the figures, was convinced they were genuine. Everyone wanted to believe it was a miracle, the more so because that afternoon Willis had done a less than satisfactory press conference on the Coalition's funding gap, and Costello was replying at 4.00. The Willis conference was called for 3.50. If he could drop the story just before Costello, it might create mayhem—it might knock them over. Ric Simes thought the letters looked suspicious. John Bowan thought at once that they were forgeries. Why would anyone commit such thoughts to paper? he asked. He and Simes took off round the corridors to stop the conference. One pack in pursuit of another. They arrived too late.

By the time Tom Mockridge got through to Keating and his staff they had spoken to Simes, Bowan and Bowtell and had seen the letters. I asked them if it was remotely possible that they were genuine: Kennett had just been on television and looked distinctly foxy. No, he couldn't remember sending such a letter, he had said, as if he might be trying to draw Willis further in. Keating and Russell were in no doubt that the letters were fakes. They read like fakes, the letterhead on Kennett's correspondence had not been used for years; it was the one used when I was working for John Cain. Willis had no choice but to make a humiliating apology. No doubt it looked like deceit to some, and to others like incompetence. But perhaps what it looked most like was a government with no more cards to play.

No-one knew where they came from. Keating was trying to track Kennett down when Kennett phoned him. He swore to Keating that the letters did not come from him, but from Willis's office. Keating said he would take his word that he didn't do it, but Kennett would have to extend the same courtesy and accept that Labor had not played the hoax. That Kennett might have been right to say it was the Willis office was not a thought we could allow ourselves. Keating had taken the phone into an adjoining room to talk to Kennett. He emerged at the end of it wearing a wry grin. Kennett had said to him about the coming Saturday, 'I hope you do well.'

We ate in the Keatings' hotel room, in gloomy unreality, as if we knew there was someone dead under the table but no-one wanted to look and confirm it. Bill Currie from Singleton's agency rang in the midst of it to say how brilliant the Prime Minister had been at the press conference after the helicopter incident in Cairns; he had looked like a Vietnam vet; it had to be worth a lot of votes. Tell him 'congratulations', he said. Don Russell rang David Cox and told him in lethal tones what he thought of the advice he had given a good minister and servant of the Labor Party and what damage had been done to the government.

Later it was claimed that vitriol was heaped on Gray and Epstein by the Prime Minister's Office. If it was, I did not see or

hear it. None of us could say for certain that under the circumstances we would have recognised the letters as fakes, or that our
instincts would not have suggested the same action that suggested
itself to them. Everyone dreaded that kind of mistake, and
everyone from the Prime Minister down had made one. For this
reason it was impossible not to feel a degree of 'There but for the
grace of God' forgiveness. It was not incomprehensible that they
proceeded to a press conference without making absolutely sure
that the letters were genuine; or that they believed they were
genuine when Bowan and Simes, and Cheryl Kernot's office,
quickly saw that they were not; or that they did not wait for the
Prime Minister's plane to land and check with him before sending
Willis out to make a fool of himself. But it was incomprehensible
that they *all* made all these mistakes, in concert as it were. Had
they thought for half a second longer they might have come to
the same conclusion as John Bowan—that no-one in their right
mind would have committed these things to paper. Had they
consulted the Prime Minister's Office immediately the letters
were delivered, the whole horror would have been averted. What
defied comprehension was the collective folly, the sudden serial
abandonment of commonsense, as if governed by some primal
pack instinct. But they would not deal with Bowtell, and the
Prime Minister's Office was said to be an impenetrable fortress. It
seemed permissible to wonder privately whether their most
powerful subconscious desire was to insult and trample on
Keating's office? The ostensible prey, after all, not only survived
their attack but prospered hugely from it, whereas what little hope
that remained to Keating was wiped out at a stroke.

Next morning we flew out to Hobart with the headlines
we expected. I wondered if instead of sending the Treasurer of the
Commonwealth into the breach, they had loaded up a journalist
to ask a question about the letters at Costello's press conference
the disaster might have been less complete. It might even have
kept the mystery of the letters going long enough to get some
advantage in the next day's headlines. Better still, such a decision
not to throw the Minister into the flames would have allowed

time for Simes, Bowan and Bowtell to turn the pack, and there would have been no disaster. It was impossible not to ponder these things, but the last remaining thread of hope was a possible young culprit with Liberal Party history and affiliations. His girlfriend swore an affidavit that he told her he had done it. The police were investigating. Late at night on television, Gareth Evans, who would not give in, ferociously debated Costello. We came back from Hobart via Melbourne. We had called off the plan to meet with a few high profile film and multimedia enthusiasts at Essendon airport and say for the media cameras that this would be the place for a great studio and housing development, and marvelled at our good instincts when we saw that employees from the businesses located there had gathered to disrupt this now cancelled function. We flew back to Canberra on the Wednesday. The last diary entry for the campaign read: 'Flew out the next morning to Hobart, then Melb on the way through. Some hope of find [sic] a Coalition culprit emerged. Ross Campbell [Stephenson] of 3AW told me he thought we were still in front. Press Club, Sydney—hope bloomed for a moment. But it was all over.' But no-one confessed to abandoning hope, and late on the last day, when political advertising was no longer permitted, people were walking on the lawns of Kirribilli talking on mobile phones as if victory was still on the cards and strategies still worth considering.

The Prime Minister's address to the Press Club was as good a speech as he ever made. The reaction of many in the press was as lousy as it had ever been. Asked about Ralph Willis and the letters, he said that they were not the main issue; but Ralph Willis had acted in good faith; that if Ralph Willis wanted to be treasurer in the next Keating government the job was his; that he, Paul Keating, had accepted Jeff Kennett's assurance that the letters had not come from the Liberal side, and Kennett should accept his assurance that they had not come from Labor—yet Kennett was saying now that the handwriting in the forged signature looked suspiciously like something he had seen before from the treasurer's office.

He spent most of the rest of the hour he was on his feet attempting to wrest attention back to what was at stake in the election. The papers said he looked tired and defeated, that the speech was a valedictory. Fran Kelly asked him if it was a 'last supper'. They missed the point entirely, including the point of the Last Supper. Five years later the tape leaves no doubt about his intention. The PM looked and sounded tired, but his speech bore no resemblance to a concession. It was a last rallying cry, a plea to remember the great things that had been done and that still needed doing. It was, in the classical way, an embrace: the media had been partners in the great reforms, they had recognised the imperative for change and the need to keep the change going; the need for 'energy' and 'accountability' in government. This election would put it to the test. Would Australia maintain the energy or would it slip back? His appearance spoke for the energy expended, but what did John Howard speak for? When he talked of people being 'relaxed and comfortable' John Howard was playing off what the polls told both sides about people being tired of change. If Howard won this election he would not bring energy: he would bring a few paltry commitments, most of which had 'unravelled' in the course of the campaign. His tax cuts couldn't be funded. His environment policy was just a stunt to sell Telstra. Most of the rest had been 'photocopied' from Labor and we were asked to believe that after years of opposing the government's principal philosophical positions John Howard now supported them. Under Labor, Australia had not only undertaken the big economic reforms, it had welded to them social policies with few equals in the world. The government had been conscientious and hard-working. APEC, Mabo, the republic, the record growth, Working Nation, Creative Nation, the job growth, the transport infrastructure, the shift to manufactures, the treaty with Indonesia—'all that quality in there'. In the four years of his prime ministership he did not think they could have done another thing. He repeated his line that, despite Howard's attempts to blur the differences, when the government changes the country changes. It changed when Whitlam took over from McMahon; from

Whitlam to Fraser; from Fraser to Hawke. It was a more important point than it might have seemed to the younger members of the gallery. Who knows what they made of his remark that, for the country, a change to Howard would be a 'straight appalling loss'? One listened then—and listens now—with wonder at his grasp of the story, the meaning of every detail and how each related to the others, with 'all the calibrations'. He was the party historian par excellence. Michael Gordon asked him if in view of Howard's line—'If you think he's arrogant now, imagine what he would be like if he won the election'—he thought he should have addressed the perception of arrogance. The test of arrogance, Keating said, was how you treat the community. In the office and in the campaign he had treated the people conscientiously and with integrity. Howard had not released the policies by which the electorate might judge him. He had 'danced past the press gallery for a year'. That was arrogance.

Of course it was impossible not to wonder what a difference it might have made if throughout his prime ministership his focus could always have been so sober and intense. Could the gallery then have backed such a colourless reactionary advocating a national slowdown and refusing to release policies until deep into the campaign? A man whose record they knew well. Or would they have simply said much earlier that Paul Keating was tired and defeated? On that day at the National Press Club the journalists appeared to mistake their own feelings for Keating's. It was not his but *their* enthusiasm that had gone; they had lost the vision; they were reconciled to his defeat. They had also lost the capacity to recognise that people do fight to the end and hope against hope even when hope is gone. Keating's energy might have waned, but the philosophy and the passion were intact. In the press it had all but gone. Nothing in the four years and three months of the Keating Government hurt as much as the reporting of his last Press Club speech.

He spent the last day in Sydney hoping for a miracle—the most likely one being something along the lines of the police discovering that the Willis letters had been the work of that young man with Liberal connections, that he had been put up to it. In the evening at a Thai restaurant in The Rocks, with the entire office, drivers and police officers gathered, he made a funny and striking speech. He would not concede that he was beaten, but if the unthinkable happened and John Howard won, the country would change. Whatever Australians may have been persuaded into thinking, he repeated, you can't change the government without changing the country. And if they get a Howard government, 'welcome to the nerdorium', he said.

Twenty-four hours later, he stood before the same blue curtain in the Bankstown Sports Club and said, 'I wanted to deliver for all those who supported us but it wasn't to be.' He congratulated John Howard, wished him and his government well and said he had always believed that 'every last morsel' of power came from the public. The public had spoken. A few weeks later, the smiling, indefatigable Bill Bowtell sent me a paper he had written, in part based on an article by the economic journalist, Terry McCrann, which showed that the prosperous, pluralist, modern 'triangle' of Sydney, Melbourne and Canberra had in fact voted for Keating's vision. The new Australia, plugged into the international economy and information highway, comfortable in their diversity and relatively secure in their jobs, had endorsed the big picture. The old Australia comprehensively rejected it. Remote from the centres of power and influence, disgruntled and insecure, they bought the reactionary message on offer and demolished the Keating Government.

Rob Hunter of the Federal Police drove the former prime minister's driver and me back to Canberra in the former prime minister's car. Jimmy Warner was not well enough to drive. No-one could have asked for better company on the day after such a loss. We drove through housing developments in the south-west of Sydney which had been farmland when Rob was growing up there. We drove down the freeway with the toll that Bob Carr had promised to abolish and welched on and cost us votes. All the things that had cost us votes! That decision to kick the Governor out of Government House, for instance. But it seemed then, and it still might be the truest thought, that we may as well have called the election and gone to Tuscany for all the difference the campaign made. Very likely they had made up their minds a long way out—perhaps as long ago as the night he beat Hewson. As Keating said, we were asking not for three years, but sixteen.

It would have been *cheaper* to leave the country. I remembered that Gary Gray had rung a day or two before the poll to tell me that to save money he was pulling advertisements he had agreed to run in the Melbourne papers—advertisements about the Coalition's IR policy and how it resembled Kennett's and what Kennett's had done to workers. I did not demur one jot. I had rung Kelty and asked if the ACTU would pick up the bill for the ads. He said he would, because I had never asked for anything before. In the back seat of the former prime minister's car I remembered all this, thought of the cheque that would have to be written and felt sick. Yet there was one vote we got that Labor had never had before—my father said he had voted Labor for the first time in his life, because, he reckoned, he couldn't go out biting the hand that, through Medicare and the pharmaceutical benefits scheme, had fed him since his heart attack. It was not confirmation of man's evolution or progress; rather, it was evidence, comforting in the circumstances, that in politics nothing is immutable and history does not respond to invocations of any faith or conviction. We stopped in Goulburn for a steak and a beer at the cafe where Chifley used to stop on the way home to Bathurst. Jimmy Warner told us about the day he was arrested at the football in Queanbeyan and, needing him to drive, the Treasurer had to bail him out. Before he moved back to Sydney the same former treasurer and prime minister gave Jimmy his pristine thirty-year-old Mercedes Benz.

We arrived in Canberra mid-afternoon. Among many items urgent a few days ago but now of no consequence was a handwritten message from Graham Freudenberg which said: 'To all members of the PM's staff: I know and fully share your feelings at this time, having been through it all over the last 35 years. But you will be sustained, now and in the years ahead, by the knowledge that you have splendidly served a great government and a great Prime Minister, during some of the most important years in the country's history. Nothing can ever take that away from you.' It is possible that just then only this generous thought from one of Labor's more sublime spirits could have reminded me what the effort had been for and persuaded me that it had been worthwhile. It was a short speech at the graveside, a thread of meaning in the dark.

Paul Keating had used all sorts of terms to describe the enterprise, but they all came down to this—he wanted the country to grow. 'Increase' was the word. The department would have said 'enhance', but like nearly everyone else they had lost contact with real words. He wanted to double its capacity for economic growth, increase its stature and strength, fulfil its promise. When he said grow he meant flourish, multiply, bear fruit, wax bigger; increase in faith and esteem. He meant grow in the sense of the words he used a few years after the election when they named a park in Bankstown after him—he said it had all been to put 'a bloom on the country'. No-one, not even Graham Freudenberg, could have said it as well.

As well as Freudenberg's inspiriting note, there was also a package from Channel 9 that I did not open until several days later when I was back in Melbourne. It contained notes left behind after the debate—notes about the cost of items such as milk and bread. They were not Don Russell's notes; they were mine.

In those last weeks the Reserve Bank did not favour the government with a cut in interest rates. It would have been a useful—and surely deserved—tick of approval for the good inflation and productivity figures. Perhaps the board thought it would look political. The new government got the rate cut, and with the accretions of time under which many realities are buried, they also got the credit. Some credit flowed their way, some they looted: when Asia melted they would boast about the strength of the Australian economy as if it were of their making. Something similar would happen with superannuation. To be a good government and lose is doubly devastating; they take what they want and claim it as their own, and let what doesn't suit them go to waste. The figures Keating used to boast about—the increase in manufactured goods as a proportion of exports, the dramatic growth in exports of elaborately transformed manufactures, research and development spending, school retention rates—all stalled or fell away after 1996. The Working Nation programs were cut or compromised in the name of accounting, but as often we thought for ideological reasons. During the 1996 election the Australian dollar was worth more than it would be five years later; foreign debt was half what it would be five years later, but then it did not wash to say our capacity to service it was the only thing that mattered. In Keating's day the current account deficit was invariably front-page news and held up as the irrefragable measure of the government's economic failure, or at best the limits of success. When everything else was good the CAD was always bad. It was the depressing figure, particularly when John Howard used it to set a hare running about another recession. In Labor's day it set political and policy limits. Five years later, though the CAD was not much changed, the doctrine was altogether new. It turned out that in the past the press and policy advisers had 'thoroughly demonised' the thing, when in truth it was of 'essentially residual influence'. It was no less than the Secretary of the Treasury who laid out this new 'consensus' view; the Secretary who had once given advice to Treasurer Keating.

The press and the public servants abandon what have been the articles of faith for thirteen years and substitute such new ones as suit the times. New tunes replace the ones we danced to. His traducers, seemingly not content with victory, continue the campaign of personal slander. The most bizarre rumours circulate. The party also tries to plot a new course with what they now insist are the prevailing winds. They run up a new flag and will sail anywhere including the doldrums or over the horizon and out of sight to steer clear of the recent past. The new imperative is—do nothing that might remind the people of Keating. You know it must be like this and can't blame them. You decide that if the price of defeat is exile, for dignity's sake you must try to impose it on yourself.

Yet sporadically, for months after the loss we would act as if we still had it in our power to rectify things. I kept a file of Howard's broken promises; composed in my head speeches that Kim Beazley—or Paul Keating—might deliver; sent the odd note to Beazley's office; for nearly three months kept the political diary going. I talked a lot to Bill Kelty. He would say that there was no point going over it and recriminations were pointless, that we had better look to our strengths and regroup—and then we would go over it and, to be frank, there were recriminations. But Kelty was a marvel of resilience. Among other fragments of posthumous hope, a pollster came forth saying the vote was 50–50 on the Wednesday and his exit polls proved the shift was caused by the Willis letters. It was almost certainly not true: no other poll had Labor that close in the last week, and even had we been, it was as well to concede that when Saturday came the people would have found some other reason to vote us out of office. Paul Keating, while maintaining admirable dignity and despite his depression, felt each blow on his good name as it is said people continue to feel a limb after it has been amputated. I felt it too. Doubtless everyone in that office did. Political death is like the other kind— the body keeps twitching after the head is cut off.

ACKNOWLEDGMENTS

I T IS NOT POSSIBLE to acknowledge by name everyone who helped me with this book, but I thank all those who served in Paul Keating's office. The story told here, whatever they may think of it, is theirs as well as mine, and to write this book was to be reminded that the real privileges of office concern the exercise of the better human faculties in common cause. The whole project is collaborative. That's the pleasure of it, and the best part of the memory.

Some names must be mentioned. Much of the material for this book exists because of Nina England, and for her unfailing assistance I will always be grateful; as, for other reasons, I will be to Don Russell, Mark Ryan, Bruce Chapman, Anne Summers, Allan Gyngell, Ashton Calvert, Cheryl Griffiths, Mark O'Neill, Susan Grusovin, Bill Bowtell, Wendy Guest, Simon Balderstone, John Edwards, Jimmy Warner and many others; and for what they did in the hardest times, especially, Mary Ann O'Loughlin, Greg Turnbull, Ric Simes.

My family paid a large price and for their forbearance, I thank my daughter, Ellie, and stepson, James. Also Rupert, Heidi, Sophie, Peter, Charlotte and Cook for holding the fort. I thank

Annita Keating for taking the time to talk about some of the issues raised in this book. I am grateful to Min Keating and Anne Keating for interviews they gave me.

The book and its author have had no better friend than my agent, Rose Creswell, unless it is my publisher, Jane Palfreyman, whose faith was limitless. I am hardly less grateful to Jane Cameron for support and other forms of management. Carl Harrison Ford was a sensitive and encouraging editor. Nadine Davidoff for everything she brought to the final stages. Katia Zanutta for all her help.

Thanks to Iain MacCalman, the director of the Humanities Research Centre at the Australian National University for an invaluable two-month writing stint. Murray Bail nudged me in certain useful directions. Jan and Helen Senbergs were essential friends. Harold Bridger gave me wise and intriguing counsel.

Above all, my thanks go to Hilary McPhee, who urged me to take the job, put up with the consequences, and then helped me to shape (and believe in) this account of what happened: and to Paul Keating, not only for the raw material, but also for the inspiration and rare generosity.

PERMISSIONS

Permission to quote material from the following sources is gratefully acknowledged:

H. Gordon Bennett, *Why Singapore Fell*, Angus and Robertson, HarperCollins Pty Ltd.

Elias Canetti, *Crowds and Power*, trans. Carol Stewart, Penguin, Penguin Putnam Inc.

Anton Chekhov, *The Seagull,* in *Chekhov: The Major Plays*, Signet Classics, New American Library, trans. Anne Dunnigan, Penguin Putnam Inc.

Carl von Clausewitz, *On War*, trans. Col. J.J. Graham, Princeton University Press.

Norman Dixon, *On the Psychology of Military Incompetence*, Jonathan Cape, The Random House Group Limited.

Homer, *The Iliad*, Book 12, trans. Robert Fagles, Penguin, Penguin Putnam Inc.

Robert Heilbroner, *21st Century Capitalism*, W.W. Norton and Company.

James Joyce, *A Portrait of the Artist as a Young Man*, Penguin, Penguin Putnam Inc.

J.M. Keynes, *Collected Writings*, Pan Macmillan.

G.E. Lessing quoted in Viktor Klemperer, *I Shall Bear Witness*, trans. Martin Chalmers, Weidenfeld & Nicholson.

Robert Musil, *The Man Without Qualities*, trans. Eithne Wilkins and Ernst Kaiser, Pan Macmillan.

George Orwell, 'Politics and the English Language' from *Shooting an Elephant and Other Essays*. Copyright George Orwell 1946. Permission granted by Bill Hamilton as the Literary Executor of the Estate of the Late Sonia Brownell Orwell and Secker & Warburg Ltd.

Permission to reproduce Paul Keating cartoon on page ii kindly granted by Bruce Petty, courtesy the *Age*.

Gore Vidal, 'The Holy Family', *Collected Essays*, Heinemann.

W.B. Yeats, *Collected Poems*, Pan Macmillan.

INDEX

738 | *Recollections of a Bleeding Heart*

advertising: elections 318–20, 325–6,
595–6, 611–12, 678–9, 707, 708–9,
729; economic growth 653
Affirmative Action Act 145
Age 37, 191, 193, 200, 204, 222, 396,
442, 454, 642, 671, 714, 715
aged care 321
AIRC *see* Australian Industrial
Relations Commission (AIRC)
airlines 198–200, 220
airports 439
Alatas, Ali 173, 178, 635
Alexander, Helen 648
Alexander, John 527, 606
Ali, Muhammad 242
Alice-Darwin railway 321
Alice in Wonderland 186
ALP *see* Australian Labor Party (ALP)
ALRC *see* Australian Law Reform
Commission (ALRC)
Ambon 580
AME *see* Australian Multimedia
Enterprise (AME)
America *see* United States
AMP (company) 643
Amsterdam 559
Anderson, Warren 472, 644
ANL *see* Australian National Line
(ANL)
Annus, Susie 111
ANOP 606–7
ANTA *see* Australian National Training
Authority (ANTA)
Antarctic Wilderness Reserve 647
Anzac Day address180–1
Anzac legend 7, 181, 290, 374, 426
ANZUS 502
APEC *see* Asia-Pacific Economic
Cooperation forum (APEC)
Arafat, Yasser 411
arbitration 265, 366
Argentina 542
Argus, Don 647
ARM *see* Australian Republican
Movement (ARM)
armed forces *see* Australian Defence
Forces (ADF)
Armstrong, Mark 515
Arnotts (company) 284
Arrow, Kenneth 101–2

'arse-end of the earth' remark 500–1,
506, 507, 508, 521
Arts Advisory Council 333
arts and culture 93, 127–8, 210–11,
231–2, 341, 711: elitism 333, 518,
520; policy 333, 334–7; and speech
337; debate over portfolio 362–3;
cultural statement *see Creative Nation*
Arts for Labor 337, 351
ASEAN (Association of South-East
Asian Nations) 77, 174
Asia-Australia Institute 170, 172
Asia-Pacific region: engagement with
70–1, 77–8, 83, 93, 165, 170–5, 182,
214, 281, 285, 320–1, 334, 414, 446,
496, 529, 575, 645, 677–8; new
'complementarities' 70–1; 'Australia
and Asia: Knowing Who We Are'
170–2, 175 ; other speeches 320–1,
414, 678–9, 680–1
see also APEC; ASEAN; Asia-Australia
Institute; Asia Society; South Pacific
Forum; and individual Asian and
Pacific countries
Asia Society (New York) 414, 415
Asia–Pacific Economic Cooperation
forum (APEC) 77–8, 174, 175, 177,
213, 397, 438, 502, 503, 504, 524,
554, 575, 647, 665, 680, 696, 726:
'Australia and Asia: Knowing Who
We Are' 170–2, 175; Japan 373–4,
392, 508, 579, 663; South Korea
389–90; China 390–2; Clinton 395,
412–13, 446–7, 527–8, 535, 536,
654, 655, 657, 658–9, 662; Suharto
437, 528, 663; Seattle meeting 412,
445–8, 449, 528; 'Present at the
Creation' 446–7; United States 374,
445–8, 525–6, 654, 658–9; Bogor
meeting 508, 525, 527–9, 530;
Bogor Declaration 527–9, 530, 663;
Osaka meeting 638, 654–5, 656,
661, 662–3, 675
Atlantic Monthly 499
ATSIC *see* Aboriginal and Torres Strait
Islander Commission (ATSIC)
Attorney-General's Department 611
Auckland 384, 592
Ausmusic (company) 282
'Australia and Asia: Knowing Who We

current account deficit 280; wants to 'break the mould,' 283, 295; election campaign 284–6; Fightback Mark II 292–4, 295, 297; Telstra sale 296; PK's piggery interests 298, 305; book about 299, 304; tax minimisation 304; driven to the right 316, 317; 1993 election campaign 308, 314, 315, 318, 321, 323–4, 334, 338–40, 343–8, 354, 360; TV debates with PK 324–5, 327, 342, 344; republic 372, 377, 378, 429; response to Mabo 382, 398, 437, 444, 445; Native Title 446, 451, 452, 453; PK's 'recalcitrant' remark 449; Vietnam War 482; loses leadership to Downer 493; leadership contrasted with PK 494; post defeat 525, 526; Aboriginal communities 548; compared with Howard 640

see also Fightback; GST

Higgins, Chris 21, 22, 80, 333

High Court of Australia 204, 302, 380, 388, 408, 434, 435, 436, 443, 453, 512, 582, 596, 597, 704

Higher Education Contribution Scheme (HECS) 88, 505, 509, 570, 573

Hill, David 515, 516

Hilmer reforms 568

Hinch, Derryn 236

Hindenburg, the 156

Hindmarsh Island Bridge affair 557–8, 561

Hiroshima 580

Hirst, John 377

history 123, 385, 387, 405: as storytelling 84; interpreting 128, 374–5, 424–5; cathartic effect 485

Hitler (Adolf) 14, 15, 75, 169, 558

HIV/AIDS 505

Ho Chi Minh City 413, 481, 482, 483

Hobson, David 456, 518

Hogan, Paul 219, 230, 231–2

Hogg, Bob 37, 138, 207, 269–70, 307, 308: PMO 42; tariff cuts 195; speculates on Hewson 223; 'feminising Australia' 269; opposes calling an election 274; 'themes and

rhetoric' 295, 302, 306; meeting with Singleton 296–7; criticises PK's leadership 300–1; PK calls election 305–6; election slogan 317–18; 1993 election campaign 317–19, 330, 344–5, 346, 350, 699; True Believers Ball 365; partner with Singleton 595–6

Hollingworth (Archbishop) 293

Hollows, Fred 323, 566

Hollows, Gabi 323

Hollows Foundation 549

Hollway, Sandy, 616: PMO 41; republic 223; Mabo 380, 444; COAG meeting 388; Native Title 433, 434, 444; on elections 524; industry statement 608; public service reforms 670

Holst, (Gustav) 364

Home Child Care Allowance 409

homosexuals 266, 280, 510

Honeker, (Erich) 560

Hong Kong 546

Hope, Deborah 35

Hopevale 548–50

Horne, Donald 220

Horner, David 181, 183, 187, 220

horseracing industry 325

Horta, Jose Ramos 168

housing 257: *Community and Nation* 671–2

Howard, John 49, 120, 132, 253, 263, 270, 273, 274, 292, 326, 374, 465, 468, 472, 494, 523, 525, 577, 601, 617, 622, 626, 636, 638, 641, 642, 646, 684: 1987 tax proposals 25; 'five minutes of economic sunshine' 49, 531, 541, 564, 602; PK's reception of the Queen 116; PK's 'museum' jibe 120; 'Loans Affair' 271; republic 370–1, 429, 584–5, 587–8; PK launches book on Burma–Thailand railway 374; historic failings 465, 526, 541; policies 526; wins the leadership 534, 535, 538; relations with the press 541, 562, 598, 644–5, 674; budget leaks 542; polls 543, 569, 607, 650; Howard-Packer 'deal' 551–3, 554–7, 558, 562, 564; Hindmarsh Island Bridge affair

752 | Recollections of a Bleeding Heart

557–8; GST U-turn 568, 623;
response to republic 584–5, 587,
588, 674; French nuclear tests 591,
593; Collingwood Football Club
608–9; uranium 609; pursuit of
Lawrence 623–4, 627; policy U-
turns 623, 640, 652; industrial
relations policy 639–40; compared
with Hewson 640; NT parliament
house 644; denied trip to Rabin's
funeral 650; Headland speeches 607,
639, 645, 673–74, 686; *The Things I
Believe In* 674; author's Custer gaffe
682–3; PK's Press Club speech 689;
'relaxed and comfortable,' 689,
714–15, 716, 726; 1996 election
campaign 694–5, 698–9, 701,
706–8, 713, 715, 717–18, 722;
television debates with PK 695,
697, 698, 701–2, 717–18; goes
Green 698–9; Lawrence misquotes
700; 1996 election policy launch
706–7; income tax cuts gaffe 707;
Kelty declares war on 715–16;
forged letters affair 722; wins the
election 728
Howe, Brian 42, 104, 474, 543, 594:
Community and Nation 671–2
H.R. Nicholls Society 639
Huckleberry Finn 567
Hudson, W. J. 221
Hughes, Bill 317
Hughes, Billy 424
Hughes, Robert 472
human rights 391–2, 634–5
Humphreys, Ben 122
Humphries, Barry 259
Hunter, Bill 708
Hunter, Rob 728
Hunting Party (singing group) 518
Hurd, Douglas 417
Hussein, Saddam 68, 594
H.V. Evatt Memorial Lecture 376–7,
379, 392–3

I
IBM (company) 717
immigration 299, 437, 523–4, 623, 665,
694: Australians Against Further
Immigration 665

Independent 141
India 171, 479
Indigenous Peoples, International Year
of 288
Indonesia 173, 187, 559: recent history
165–7; Australia's relations with
165–70; PK's visits 176–80, 502,
634–6, 673; Clinton 413; republic
418; Security Agreement 478, 502,
503, 524, 528, 635–6, 637, 672–3,
680, 681–2, 690, 696; appointment
of General Mantiri 603
see also Dili massacre; East Timor;
Suharto (President); Sukarno
(President)
Indonesian Observer 176
Industrial Groups 11
industrial relations 241, 500: AIRC
264, 366–70, 655–7, 660, 678;
Kennett's legislation 264, 265,
269–70, 282–3, 326, 729; policies
282–3, 366–9; 639–40, 648, 655;
Edwards 369; PK's speeches
639–40, 366–70
see also enterprise bargaining; workplace
agreements
Industrial Relations Commission (IRC)
264, 282, 366, 368, 659
Industrial Relations Reform Act 490
Industry, Science and Technology,
Department of 517
Industry Commission 283, 440
industry policy 104, 220, 233–4, 240,
247–8, 378–9, 490, 605, 616–17,
654: industry statement *see Innovate
Australia; Working Nation*
inflation 40–1, 87, 108, 137, 206, 241–2,
257, 279, 323–4, 366, 466, 504, 568,
602, 653,
information revolution 68, 70, 378–9,
487, 503, 516, 517, 554
see also CEBIT exhibition; information
technology
information technology 93, 512–13,
515, 534: CEBIT exhibition 553–4,
555, 559
infrastructure 457–8, 605: regional 500,
529–30, 604, 605
Innisfail 237
Innovate Australia (statement) 457, 524,

708–9; polls 695, 717, 718–19; Gray
697, 699, 707–10, 721–4; Lawrence
misquotes Howard 700; policy
launch 703–5; bus tour 710; arts
launch 711; Kelty declares war on
Howard 715–16; forged letters affair
722–5, 727–8; election loss 728; exit
polls 732
Nissan (company) 160
NMLS *see* National Media Liaison
Service (NMLS)
Noakes, Bryan 282
Nolan, Mark 625
Non-Aligned Movement 177
North America 382
North American Free Trade Agreement
(NAFTA) 281, 412, 413, 446, 528
North West Shelf 12
Northern Territory parliament 644
Nossal, Sir Gustav 671
Notre Dame University (Perth) 471
NSW Department of School Education
492
Nuclear Non-Proliferation Treaty 592
nuclear weapons: French tests 589–94,
605, 609, 611, 623, 629–30, 643,
646; Comprehensive Test Ban Treaty
590, 592; Nuclear Non-Proliferation
Treaty 592; non-proliferation
646–7; Canberra Commission 647

O
Oakes, Laurie 131, 157, 164, 198, 262,
292, 299–300, 324, 408, 445, 448,
460, 466, 472, 485, 500, 510, 545,
552–3, 555, 619, 642, 658, 682, 695
Oath of Allegiance 221, 256, 276–7, 286
O'Brien, Kerry 299, 324, 499–500, 697
Obscure Man, An 471
O'Chee, Bill 429
O'Donoghue, Lois 377, 597, 684:
Native Title 434, 436
OECD 74, 188, 206, 245, 316, 554, 686
O'Faolain, Sean 416, 420
Office for the Status of Women (OSW)
142–3, 146, 147
Office of Regional Development 359
O'Hearn, Dinny 365, 388
Oklahoma bombing (US) 535
O'Loughlin, Mary Ann 155, 195–6,

203, 407, 408, 471: the 'main game'
675–6
Olsen, John 92
Olympic Games : Barcelona 236;
Sydney bid 197, 384, 424, 425–6,
427: China bid 390, 425;
Manchester bid 425
One Nation (Pauline Hanson's) 712,
713
One Nation (statement) 132, 140, 158,
159, 197, 203, 206, 255, 297, 299,
300, 316, 325, 457–8, 477, 686, 687:
gestation 104, 106–11; naming
116–17; National Press Club
119–20; polls 124; puritan ethic
129; women's program 145; tax cuts
188, 246, 397; 'Free Market Bastard
Son of One Nation' 203; forecasts
206, 220, 299; visibility 223; media
calls for apology 228–9; economist's
view of 233; vocational education
and training 235; investment
development allowance 301
O'Neill, Mark: 546–7, 675, 719–20
O'Neill, Robert 647
opinion polls *see* polls and surveys
Orange 630–31, 637
Orange County (California) 446, 447
Orwell, George 47–48
Osaka 654, 655, 656, 658–9, 662–3
OSW *see* Office for the Status of
Women (OSW)
overseas trips (PK's):Indonesia 176–80,
502, 634–6, 673; PNG 180–4, 630,
632–3; Japan 206, 211–14, 262, 508,
578–81, 655; Cyprus 378, 437; New
Zealand 383–5; South Korea
389–90; China 390–2; United States
408, 411–14; Britain 416–19, 496–8;
Ireland 411, 420–3, 445, 447; France
411, 423–4, 498; Monaco 411, 424,
425–6; Thailand 478–81, 484;
Singapore 553, 554, 555, 677,
679–81; Germany 553–4, 556,
558–61; Copenhagen 561; Jerusalem
650; Malasia 679
see also APEC; South Pacific Forum

P
Pacific Dunlop (company) 599, 615, 643